Fourth Edition

PRINCIPLES OF MICROECONOMICS

Economics and the Economy

Timothy Taylor

Journal of Economic Perspectives
Macalester College

▓ TEXTBOOK\MEDIA

The Quality Instructors Expect.
At Prices Students Can Afford.

Replacing Oligarch Textbooks since 2004

For instructors:
• PowerPoint® slides
• Computerized test disk

When ordering this title, use ISBN 978-0-9969963-2-7

To order the complete volume, use ISBN 978-0-9969963-1-0

To order the Macro version, use ISBN 978-0-9969963-3-4

Principles of Microeconomics: Economics and the Economy, 4th Edition

Copyright © 2017, 2014, 2011, 2008 Timothy Taylor. Published by Textbook Media Press.

ISBN-13: 978-0-9969963-2-7

Printed in the United States of America by Textbook Media Press.

Brief Contents

APPENDIX CHAPTERS

Contents

3 International Trade 35

PART II SUPPLY AND DEMAND

4 Demand and Supply 53

5 Labor and Financial Capital Markets

79

6 Globalization and Protectionism 93

PART III THE FUNDAMENTALS OF MICROECONOMIC THEORY

7 Elasticity 115

8 Household Decision Making
135

9 Cost and Industry Structure
153

10 Perfect Competition 169

11 Monopoly 189

15 Technology, Positive Externalities, and Public Goods 251

16 Poverty and Economic Inequality 265

17 Issues in Labor Markets: Unions, Discrimination, Immigration
283

18 Information, Risk, and Insurance
301

19 Financial Markets 315

20 Public Choice 335

APPENDIX CHAPTERS

Preface

When authors describe their reasons for writing an economics textbook, it seems customary to proclaim lofty goals, like teaching students "to think like economists" so that they can become more informed voters and citizens. Paul Samuelson, the author of the most famous introductory economics textbook for the second half of the twentieth century, famously said: "I don't care who writes a nation's laws—or crafts its advanced treaties—if I can write its economics textbooks." On my best days, I have sufficient time and energy to lift my eyes to the horizon, strike a statuesque pose, and proclaim exalted goals. But most of the time, I'm just a workaday teacher and my goals are more limited and concrete.

The pedagogical approach of this textbook is rooted in helping students master the tools that they need to solve problems for a course in introductory economics. Indeed, one of the great pleasures of writing the book is having the opportunity to share my teaching toolkit of step-by-step explanations, practical examples, and metaphors that stick in the mind. On quizzes and exams, I do not ask broad or open-ended questions about informed citizenship and thinking like an economist. At the most basic level, my goal for an economics class is that students should feel well-prepared for quizzes and exams.

The preparation that students need to perform well in an introductory economics class can be divided into three parts. First, an introductory economics class involves mastering a specialized vocabulary. I sometimes tell students that learning economics is akin to learning a foreign language—with the added difficulty that terms in economics like "demand" or "supply" or "money" sound like standard English, and thus learning economics often requires that students drop their preconceptions about what certain words mean.

Second, students need to acquire some basic analytical tools. There are four central analytical models in an introductory economics course: budget constraints, supply and demand, cost curves, and aggregate demand–aggregate supply. These four models are used for a very wide variety of applications; still, there are only four of them. There

are also a few key formulas and equations to learn with regard to topics like growth rates over time and elasticity.

Third, students must learn to recognize when these terms and tools apply and to practice using them. I often tell students not to bother memorizing particular questions and answers from the textbook or homework, because my quiz and exam questions will ask them to apply what they have learned in contexts they have not seen before. To provide a variety of contexts, this book describes many economic issues and events, drawn from recent times and past history, and also drawn both from U.S. and international experiences. When students see a concept or analytical skill applied in a number of ways, they learn to focus on the underlying and unifying idea. I've also found that students do take away knowledge of many economic events and episodes—although different students seem to focus on an unpredictable (to me) array of examples, which is perhaps as it should be in an introductory course.

As a workaday teacher, the goal of helping students master the material so that they can perform well on my quizzes and exams is lofty enough—and tough enough— for me. There's an old joke that economics is the science of taking what is obvious about human behavior and making it incomprehensible. Actually, in my experience, the process works in the other direction. Many students spend the opening weeks of an introductory economics course feeling as if the material is difficult, even impossible, but by the middle and the end of the class, what seemed so difficult early in the term has become obvious and straightforward. As a course in introductory economics focuses on one lesson after another and one chapter after another, it's easy to get tunnel vision. But when you raise your eyes at the end of class, it can be quite astonishing to look back and see how far you have come. As students apply the terms and models they have learned to a series of real and hypothetical examples, they often find to their surprise that they have also imbibed a considerable amount about economic thinking and the real-world economy. Learning always has an aspect of the miraculous.

As always, my family makes a significant contribution to the existence of this book. In the nine years since the first edition, the U.S. and world economy has been convulsed by a Great Recession and then by an ungainly process of sluggish recovery, replete with questions about what is likely to happen next. The task of updating figures and examples for this fourth edition is inevitably large, but thinking about how to build connections from the concepts in the text to the economic events of the last few years made it larger. During the process of preparing this revised edition, my wife has dealt lovingly with a distracted husband; my children, with a father who was sleep-deprived or "at the office." In a very real sense, then, this book is from my dear ones to the students and instructors who use it. I hope that it serves you well.

Timothy Taylor
St. Paul, Minnesota
December 1, 2016

About the Author

Timothy T. Taylor

Timothy T. Taylor has been the Managing Editor of the *Journal of Economic Perspectives*, published by the American Economic Association, since the first issue of the journal in 1987. All issues of the journal are freely available online at http://e-jep.org. Taylor holds a B.A degree in economics and political science from Haverford College. He holds an M.S. degree in economics from Stanford University, where he focused on public finance, industrial organization, and economic history.

Taylor has taught economics in a variety of contexts. In 2012, his book *The Instant Economist: Everything You Need to Know About How the Economy Works,* was published by Penguin Plume. It was named an "Outstanding Academic Title" by *Choice* magazine of the American Library Association. He has recorded a variety of lecture courses for The Teaching Company, based in Chantilly, Virginia, including *Economics* (3rd edition), *Unexpected Economics, America and the New Global Economy, Legacies of Great Economists*, and *History of the U.S. Economy in the 20th Century*. In 1992, he won the Outstanding Teacher Award from the Associated Students of Stanford University. In 1996, he was named a Distinguished Instructor for his courses in introductory economics at the University of Minnesota. In 1997, he was voted Teacher of the Year by students at the Humphrey Institute of Public Affairs at the University of Minnesota.

He has published articles on various topics in economics in publications such as *Finance & Development*, the *Milken Institute Review*, and the *Journal of Economic Perspectives*. He blogs regularly at http://conversable economist.blogspot.com.

CHAPTER

1

The Interconnected Economy

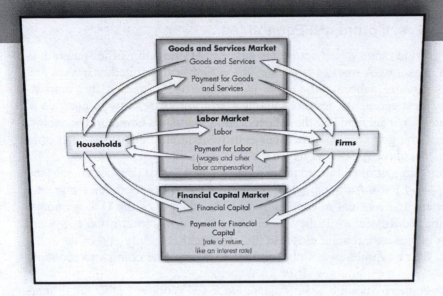

People don't produce most of what they consume. They don't grow most of their own food, make their own clothes, build their own houses, or provide their own health care and education. Instead, people mainly consume goods and services that others have produced, and in turn, what most people produce is mainly consumed by others. This pattern raises questions. What goods will be produced? What quantities of each good will be produced? How will the goods that are produced be allocated across the population? What role will be played by individuals making decisions about consuming, working, and saving? What role will be played by organizations like businesses? What role will be played by government?

Since a modern economy contains thousands upon thousands of different products that are produced, bought, and consumed, the study of economics must address an extraordinary array of topics. Are gasoline prices likely to rise? What causes a new restaurant to open or an existing restaurant to close? Will it pay off for a high school graduate to attend college? Can environmental protection go hand in hand with a rising level of consumption of goods and services? Why did the U.S. and world economies suffer such a sharp slowdown during the Great Recession from 2007–2009? What determines the number of people who want to work but cannot find jobs? When should the government cut taxes, and when should it raise them? Why do people in some countries have high incomes while those in other countries have low incomes? An introductory course in economics will help you develop the analytical tools and vocabulary for thinking and communicating about these issues.

questions to think about

This first chapter introduces some ways in which economies are interconnected. It discusses the range of alternatives from a market-oriented economy to a command economy. It describes how an economy divides up the tasks that are involved in production of goods and services, and how the total production of goods and services increases as a result. This chapter will also explain the difference between "microeconomics" and "macroeconomics" and preview how the chapters of this book are organized.

What Is an Economy?

An **economy** is the set of social arrangements that answers three fundamental questions: (1) What is produced? (2) How is it produced? (3) For whom is it produced? Thus, **economics** is the study of the production, distribution, and consumption of goods and services. In an economics textbook published in 1890, the famous English economist Alfred Marshall (1842–1924) wrote more poetically that economics involved the study of people "as they live and move and think in the ordinary business of life."

Market-Oriented vs. Command Economies

Countries display a wide range of economic institutions. At one end of the spectrum is a market-oriented economy. A **market** is an institution that brings together buyers and sellers of goods or services, who may be either individuals or businesses. In a **market-oriented economy**, most economic decisions about what to produce, how to produce it, and for whom to produce it are made by these buyers and sellers. In a **command economy**, at the other extreme, the government either makes most economic decisions itself or at least strongly influences how the decisions are made.

The U.S. economy is positioned toward the market-oriented end of the spectrum. Many countries in Europe and Latin America, while primarily market-oriented, have a greater degree of government involvement in economic decisions than does the U.S. economy. Countries like China and Russia, while they are closer to having a market-oriented system now than several decades ago, remain closer to the command economy end of the spectrum. In countries such as Zimbabwe, Cuba, and North Korea, the command economy predominates.

Markets and government rules are always entangled. Even economies that are primarily market-oriented have laws and regulations to support the operation of markets. At a minimum, these laws govern matters like safeguarding private property against theft, protecting people from violence, enforcing legal contracts, preventing fraud, and collecting taxes. Conversely, even the most command-oriented economies operate with substantial **black markets**, which are markets where the buyers and sellers make transactions without the government's approval. The question of how to organize economic institutions is typically not a black-or-white choice between all market or all government, but instead involves a balancing act over the appropriate combination of market freedom and government rules.

The Interconnectedness of an Economy

In a modern economy, the economic life of every individual is interrelated, at least to a small extent, with the economic lives of thousands or even millions of other individuals. Imagine that when an economic transaction occurs, it leaves behind a line that is visible for people who wear special economist glasses.

For example, if you buy a loaf of bread at the grocery store, a blue line stretches from the store to your kitchen. When you pump gas into your car, a red line runs from the gas station to your car. A green line connects you to your employer, a purple line to the bank where you keep your checking and savings accounts, and a yellow line to the shop where you get your hair cut. This network of lines would also capture the transactions through which goods are produced. A loaf of bread would have colorful lines running to the bakery, to the company that manufactured the plastic bag for packaging, to the farm where the wheat was grown, and to the mill where the wheat was ground into flour. In turn, because the wheat farm used tractors, and trucks transported the bread to the store, lines would also extend from the loaf of bread to tractor and truck manufacturers and to trucking companies. These lines representing economic transactions also extend to those concerned with the financial side of these businesses: the bankers who provide loans and checking and savings accounts to firms, the accountants who deal with payroll and taxes, and the managers who authorize sending out the checks.

economy: The social arrangements that determine what is produced, how it is produced, and for whom it is produced.

economics: The study of the production, distribution, and consumption of goods and services.

market: An institution that brings together buyers and sellers of goods or services.

market-oriented economy: An economy in which most economic decisions are made by buyers and sellers, who may be individuals or firms.

command economy: An economy in which the government either makes or strongly influences most economic decisions.

black markets: An illegal market that breaks government rules on prices or sales.

If you could put on special economist glasses to see all the economic lines of connection, a single loaf of bread would appear with a network of lines that eventually reached all over town, across the state and the country, and even around the world. In a modern economy, every person, every business, and every product is at the center of a starburst of economic interconnections.

The Division of Labor

The formal study of economics began when Adam Smith (1723–1790) published his famous book *The Wealth of Nations* in 1776. Many authors had written on economic subjects in the centuries before Smith, but he was the first to address the subject in a comprehensive way. In the first chapter of *The Wealth of Nations*, Smith introduces the idea of the **division of labor**, which refers to how the work required to produce a good or service is divided into a number of simpler tasks that are performed by different workers.

division of labor: Dividing the work required to produce a good or service into tasks performed by different workers.

To illustrate the division of labor, Adam Smith used the example of how the tasks of making a pin were divided in a pin factory. He counted the multiple tasks involved with making a pin, including the steps involved in drawing out a piece of wire, cutting it to the right length, straightening it, putting a head on one end and a point on the other, and packaging pins for sale. In observing pin factories, Smith counted 18 distinct tasks that were often done by different workers. Modern businesses divide tasks as well. Even a relatively simple business like a restaurant divides up the task of serving meals into a range of jobs including top chefs, less-skilled kitchen help, servers to wait on the tables, a host at the door, janitors to clean up, and a business manager to handle paychecks and bills—not to mention the economic connections a restaurant has with suppliers of food, furniture, kitchen equipment, and the building where it is located. A complex business like a large manufacturing factory or a hospital can have hundreds of job classifications.

Adam Smith was once walking with a friend, talking enthusiastically about the division of labor, and he got so excited with the subject that he tumbled into a pit where workers were tanning hides, a foul-smelling process. Smith was the prototypical never-married, absent-minded professor. He frequently went walking, started talking to himself, and would completely lose track of time and distance. But being one of the first to put on economist glasses and perceive the division of labor must have been a highly distracting experience.

Why the Division of Labor Increases Production

When the tasks involved with producing a good or service are divided and subdivided, workers and businesses can produce a greater quantity of output. In his observations of pin factories, Smith observed that one worker alone might make 20 pins in a day, but that a small business of 10 workers (some of whom would need to do two or three of the 18 tasks involved with pin-making), could make 48,000 pins in a day. How can a group of workers, each focused on certain tasks, produce so much more than the same number of workers who try to produce the entire good or service by themselves? Smith offered three reasons.

specialization: When workers or firms focus on particular tasks in the overall production process for which they are well-suited.

First, specialization in a particular small job allows workers to focus on the types of production where they have an advantage. People have different skills, talents, and interests, so they will be better at some jobs than others. The particular advantages of specific workers may be based on educational choices, which are in turn shaped by interests and talents: for example, only those with medical degrees qualify to become doctors. For some goods, specialization will be affected by geography: for example, it's easier to be a wheat farmer in North Dakota than in Florida, but easier to run a tourist hotel in Florida than in North Dakota. If you live in or near a big city, it's easier to attract enough customers to operate a successful dry cleaning business or movie theater than if you live in a sparsely populated rural area.

Second, workers who specialize in certain tasks often learn to produce more quickly and with higher quality. This pattern holds true for many workers, including assembly line laborers who build cars, stylists who cut hair, and doctors who perform heart surgery. In fact, specialized workers often know their jobs well enough to suggest innovative ways to do their work faster and better. A similar pattern often operates across businesses. In many cases, a business that focuses on one or a few products (sometimes called its "core competency") is more successful than firms that attempt to make a wide range of products.

economies of scale: When the average cost of producing each individual unit declines as total output increases.

Third, specialization allows economic agents, or actors, to take advantage of economies of scale, which refers to the common pattern for many goods and services that as the level of production increases, the average cost of producing each individual unit declines. For example, if a factory produces only 100 cars per year, each car will be quite expensive to make on average. However, if a factory produces 10,000 or 50,000 cars each year, then it can set up an assembly line with huge machines and workers performing specialized tasks, and the average cost of production per car will be lower. The ultimate result

CLEARING IT UP

Firm, Business, Company, Corporation

What's the difference between a "business," a "firm," a "company," and a "corporation"? The short answer for practical purposes is "not much." A *business* is an organization that produces and sells, regardless of whether the customers are individuals or other businesses. A *company* is one term for the group of people who form a business. One definition of a *firm* is a "business company." A *corporation* refers to a specific legal status, where the business is treated as a separate legal entity that can sign contracts, own property, and borrow money, apart from those who manage or own the business. In this book, "business" and "firm" will typically be used to refer to all kinds of companies, whether they are officially corporations or not.

of workers who can focus on their preferences and talents, learn to do their specialized jobs better, and work in larger organizations is that society as a whole can produce and consume far more than if each person tried to produce individually all of the goods and services that the person wishes to consume.

Trade and Markets

The division of labor helps to explain why most workers do not consume most of what they produce. Instead, workers within an economy use the pay that they receive for doing their jobs to purchase the other goods and services that they desire.

As a result, you don't have to know anything about electronics or software to use a touch screen on your smartphone—you just buy the phone and start tapping away. You don't have to know anything about artificial fibers or the construction of sewing machines if you need a jacket—you just buy the jacket and wear it. You don't need to know anything about internal combustion engines to operate a car—you just climb in and drive. Instead of trying to acquire all the knowledge and skills involved in producing all of the goods and services that you wish to consume, the market allows you to learn a specialized set of skills and then use the pay you receive to buy goods and services. The economy is a social mechanism that coordinates this division of labor, specialization, and markets.

The Rise of Globalization

Recent decades have seen a trend toward **globalization**, which means that buying and selling in markets have crossed national borders to an increasing extent. As a result, firms and workers from different countries are increasingly interconnected. Globalization has occurred for a number of reasons. Improvements in shipping and air cargo have driven down transportation costs. Innovations in information and communications technology have made it easier and cheaper to manage long-distance economic connections of production and sales. Many valuable products and services in the modern economy can take the form of information—for example, computer software; financial advice; travel planning; music, books and movies; and blueprints for designing a building. These products and many others can be transported across national borders, using telephone and computer networks, at ever-lower costs. Finally, international agreements and treaties between countries have encouraged greater trade.

Exhibit 1-1 presents one measure of globalization. It shows the percentage of domestic economic production that was exported for a selection of countries from 1970 to 2014. **Exports** are the goods and services that are produced domestically and sold in another country; conversely, **imports** are the goods and services that are produced abroad and then sold domestically. The size of total production in an economy is measured by the gross domestic product, often abbreviated as GDP. Thus, the ratio of exports divided by GDP measures what share of a country's total economic production is sold in other countries.

In recent decades, the ratio of exports/GDP has generally risen, both worldwide and for the U.S. economy. Interestingly, the share of U.S. exports in proportion to the U.S. economy is well below the global average, in part because large economies like the United States can contain more of the division of labor inside their national borders. However, smaller economies like those of South Korea and Canada need to trade across their borders with other countries to take full advantage of division of labor, specialization, and economies of scale. In this sense, the enormous U.S. economy is less affected by globalization than most other countries. Exhibit 1-1 also shows that many medium- and low-income countries around the world, like Mexico and China, have also experienced a surge of globalization in recent decades. If an astronaut in orbit around planet Earth could put on special economist glasses that make all economic transactions visible as brightly colored lines, globalization means that the astronaut would see more connections stretching around the world.

globalization: The trend in which buying and selling in markets have increasingly crossed national borders.

exports: Goods and services that are produced domestically and sold in another country.

imports: Goods and services produced abroad and sold domestically.

EXHIBIT 1-1 The Extent of Globalization (Exports/GDP)

One way to measure globalization is to look at the exports/GDP ratio. For the world economy and for most individual countries, the exports/GDP ratio has risen in recent decades.

Country	1970	1980	1990	2000	2010	2014
Some High-Income Countries						
United States	6%	10%	10%	11%	13%	14%
Canada	22%	28%	26%	46%	29%	32%
France	16%	21%	21%	29%	26%	29%
Japan	11%	13%	10%	11%	15%	16%
South Korea	14%	32%	28%	39%	52%	51%
Sweden	24%	30%	30%	47%	49%	45%
Some Upper-Middle-Income Countries						
Brazil	7%	9%	8%	10%	11%	12%
China	3%	11%	16%	23%	31%	23%
Mexico	8%	11%	19%	31%	30%	32%
Some Lower-Middle-Income Countries						
India	4%	6%	7%	13%	23%	23%
Nigeria	8%	29%	43%	54%	35%	18%
Some Low-Income Countries						
Bangladesh	8%	5%	6%	14%	18%	19%
Chad	16%	17%	13%	17%	39%	34%
Nepal	5%	12%	11%	23%	10%	12%

Microeconomics and Macroeconomics

microeconomics: The branch of economics that focuses on actions of particular actors within the economy, like households, workers, and business firms.

macroeconomics: The branch of economics that focuses on the economy as a whole, including issues like growth, unemployment, inflation, and the balance of trade.

Microeconomics focuses on the actions of particular actors within the economy, like households, workers, and businesses. In contrast, **macroeconomics** looks at the economy as a whole, focusing on issues like the growth rate of production of goods and services, unemployment, price inflation, and levels of exports and imports. Microeconomics and macroeconomics are not separate subjects, but rather complementary perspectives on the overall subject of the economy.

To understand why microeconomic and macroeconomic perspectives are both useful, consider the problem of studying a biological ecosystem like a lake. One person who sets out to study the lake might focus on specific topics: certain kinds of algae or plant life, the characteristics of particular fish or snails, or the trees surrounding the lake. Another person might take an overall view and instead consider the entire ecosystem of the lake from top to bottom: what eats what, how the system stays in a rough balance, and what environmental stresses affect this balance. Both approaches are useful, and both examine the same lake, but the viewpoints are different. In a similar way, both microeconomics and macroeconomics study the same economy, but each has a different viewpoint.

Whether you are looking at lakes or economics, the micro and the macro insights should blend with each other. In studying a lake, the micro insights about particular plants and animals help to understand the overall food chain, while the macro insights about the overall food chain help to explain the environment in which individual plants and animals live. In economics, the micro decisions of individual households and businesses are influenced by whether the macroeconomy is healthy; for example, firms will be more likely to hire workers if the overall economy is growing. In turn, the performance of the macroeconomy ultimately depends on the microeconomic decisions made by households and businesses.

In this book, Chapters 1–6 introduce some basic tools of economics. This first chapter lays out the basic meaning of the economy and economics. Chapter 2 explains how economic decision-making works. Chapter 3 shows how trade can be mutually beneficial, using the example of trade between nations in the global economy. Chapters 4 and 5 discuss how forces of supply and demand determine prices—and what happens when government attempts to set prices directly. Chapter 6 discusses the debate over globalization and protectionism. With this foundation established, Chapters 7–20 focus on microeconomics. Regardless of whether you are looking through the microeconomics microscope or the macroeconomics telescope, the fundamental subject material of the interconnected economy doesn't change.

Microeconomics: The Circular Flow Diagram

The **circular flow diagram** in Exhibit 1-2 pictures the economy as consisting of two groups—households and firms—that interact in three markets: a *goods and services market*, a *labor market*, and a *financial capital market*.

In the **goods and services market**, firms are sellers and households are buyers, so the arrow for goods and services leads from firms to households. Payments for these goods and services flow back in the other direction, from households to firms, so the arrow for payments flows back in the opposite direction.

In the **labor market**, households sell their labor to firms. Conversely, firms buy labor when they hire workers. Thus, the flow of labor runs from households to firms, but the flow of payments for labor—in the form of wages, salaries, bonuses, and benefits—flows from firms to households.

In the **financial capital market**, individuals or firms who save money and make financial investments are suppliers of financial capital. Those who borrow money or receive financial investments are the recipients of financial capital. For example, someone who deposits money in a savings account at a bank is supplying financial capital, and someone who receives a loan from the bank is demanding financial capital. Individual households and firms can be either suppliers or demanders of capital, depending on whether they are

circular flow diagram: A diagram that illustrates the economy as consisting of households and firms interacting in a goods and services market, a labor market, and a financial capital market.

goods and services market: A market in which firms are sellers of what they produce and households are buyers.

labor market: The market in which households sell their labor as workers to businesses or other employers.

financial capital market: The market in which those who save money provide financial capital and receive a rate of return from those who wish to raise money and pay a rate of return.

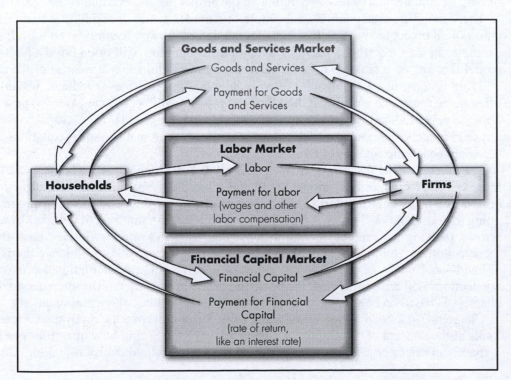

EXHIBIT 1-2 The Circular Flow Diagram

The circular flow diagram shows how households and firms interact in the goods and services market, the labor market, and the financial capital market. The direction of the arrows shows that in the goods and services market, households receive goods and services and pay firms for them. In the labor market, households work and receive payment from firms. In the financial capital market, households provide financial capital—that is, savings and financial investment—while firms pay them for that capital by providing a rate of return—for example, an interest payment.

Real and Financial Capital and Investment

The concept of a financial capital market can be confusing because the words "capital" and "investment" can have two different meanings. Financial capital or financial investment refers to flows of money from those people or firms who save and make a financial investment to those who borrow or receive the financial investment. Real capital or real investment usually refers to physical items like buildings or equipment, although the terms are sometimes also applied to intangible business investments, like the spending on research and development that seeks to produce new inventions. In short, you can stub your toe on real capital investment, but not on financial capital investment. Financial capital and real capital are often interrelated. Those who receive financial capital often invest those funds in real physical capital. Discussions of capital and investment throughout the book will specify whether the discussion is about real or financial capital and investment. But be warned: outside the pages of this book, and in casual conversation, the terms "capital" and "investment" can take on either meaning.

rate of return: The payment in addition to the original investment from those who have received financial capital to those who provided it.

principal: The amount of an original financial investment, before any rate of return is paid.

interest rate: A payment calculated as a percentage of the original amount saved or borrowed, and paid by the borrower to the saver.

model: A simplified representation of an object or situation that includes enough of the key features to be useful.

saving or borrowing. However, in the circular flow diagram, the convention is to draw the most common direction of the financial capital flow as running from households to firms—that is, households taken as a group are saving and making financial investments.

Payment for financial capital is called the **rate of return**. Suppliers of financial capital expect that they will eventually receive back both the amount of their original financial investment, called the **principal**, plus an additional amount called the rate of return. Conversely, demanders of financial capital expect to pay back the original principal they received, plus a rate of return, in exchange for receiving the financial investment. One common example of a rate of return is an **interest rate** charged for borrowing financial capital. If one person loans $10,000 to another person for one year at an 8% annual interest rate, then the lender—the supplier of financial capital—expects to be repaid $10,000 of principal plus $800 of interest as a rate of return. Meanwhile the borrower—the demander of financial capital—expects to pay back the $10,000 of principal plus $800 in interest. However, the rate of return is not always an interest rate. For example, a person might pay $10,000 for a half-ownership of a small business, with an agreement that the rate of return will be half of any future profits earned by the business. In this case, the actual rate of return could be high or low, depending on the profits that are eventually earned, if any.

The circular flow diagram is an example of a **model**, which is a simplified representation of an object or situation that includes enough of the key features to be useful. For example, an architect who is planning a major office building will often build a physical model that sits on a tabletop to show how the entire city block will look after the new building is constructed. Companies often build models of their new products, which are often more rough and unfinished than the final product will be, but can still demonstrate how the new product will work. Economic models like the circular flow diagram are not physical models, but instead are diagrams or graphs or even mathematical equations that represent economic patterns or theories.

The circular flow diagram shown in Exhibit 1-2 is a deliberately simple model. A more complex circular flow model could add a box for "government," and then show arrows for taxes paid flowing to the government and government spending programs going to households and firms. A box could also be added for the "rest of the world," with arrows showing the exports flowing to those countries and imports flowing back from those countries. But models should be only as complex as needed to illustrate the issue at hand—and not more so. Although issues of government and international economic connections will arise throughout the book, the structure and order of the microeconomics chapters is based on how households and firms interact in these three main markets.

Chapters 7–12 build a theoretical framework for microeconomic analysis. Chapter 7 looks at the concept of "elasticity," which is a way of measuring how quantities react to a change in prices or incomes. Chapter 8 focuses on household decision-making. Chapters 9–12 discuss how firms make decisions about production, ranging from firms that face many competitors to monopoly firms that face no competitors at all. Chapters 13–20 build on that theoretical framework to discuss some policy issues that arise in microeconomic markets. Chapters 13–15 focus on policies that involve markets for goods: assuring competition between firms, protecting the environment, and encouraging beneficial new technology. Chapters 16–17 then discuss issues that arise in labor markets: poverty, inequality, unions, discrimination, and immigration. Chapters 18–19 discuss issues that arise in financial capital markets involving insurance and financial investments like stocks and bonds. Finally, Chapter 20 discusses how economists analyze some of the political issues involved in setting microeconomic policy.

Macroeconomics: Goals, Frameworks, and Tools

When nations desire a healthy macroeconomy, they typically focus on four goals: growth in the standard of living, a low level of unemployment, low inflation, and a sustainable balance of trade between countries.

Macroeconomics involves thinking about how these four goals relate to each other, and in particular how pursuing any one of these goals might necessitate trade-offs with other goals. Such analysis requires an understanding of how the macroeconomy works, both in the short-run (ranging from months to a couple of years) and in the long-run (ranging from several years to a decade and more).

With macroeconomic goals in mind and the frameworks for analyzing how these goals relate to each other in place, the final step is to think about how macroeconomic policy pursues these goals. The two main tools of macroeconomic policy include **monetary policy**, which involves policies that affect bank lending, interest rates and financial capital markets, and **fiscal policy**, which involves government spending and taxation.

monetary policy: Policy that involves altering the quantity of money and thus affecting the level of interest rates and the extent of borrowing.

fiscal policy: Economic policies that involve government spending and taxation.

Studying Economics Doesn't Mean Worshiping the Economy

Many newcomers to the study of economics either fear or hope that the subject will mainly discuss why businesses and markets are always right. Such expectations are inaccurate. Economics overlaps with the study of business decisions, but it reaches much farther to encompass all aspects of production, distribution, and consumption. Economics is concerned with the well-being of *all* people, including those with jobs and those without jobs, and those with high incomes and low incomes. Economics acknowledges that production of useful goods and services can create problems of environmental pollution. It explores the question of how investing in education helps to develop workers' skills. It probes questions like how to tell when big businesses or big labor unions are operating in a way that benefits society as a whole, and when they are operating in a way that benefits their owners or members at the expense of others. It discusses how government spending, taxes, and regulations affect decisions about production and consumption. Economics is a structured methodology for investigating these kinds of issues and many others. John Maynard Keynes (1883–1946), one of the greatest economists of the twentieth century, addressed this theme when he wrote: "[Economics] is a method rather than a doctrine, an apparatus of the mind, a technique of thinking, which helps its possessor to draw correct conclusions."

While the study of economics requires paying attention to the problems that can be generated in society's process of production, distribution, and consumption, economics is based on the belief that a higher standard of living is a goal worth pursuing. In 1900, the population of the United States had the highest average income level of any country in the world. However, from a modern perspective, people had a very low standard of living. In the United States of 1900, only one-third of all homes had running water; in rural areas, almost nobody did. Just 3 percent of homes were lit by electricity; most used coal, oil, or kerosene. About 10 percent of those aged 14–17 attended high school; about

6 percent of students graduated from high school; and about 2 percent graduated from college. Life expectancy at birth was just 47 years, and out of every 1,000 babies born, 140 died before they were a year old. (Now life expectancy is above 75 years, and out of every 1,000 babies born, fewer than 10 die in the first year.) The typical workweek for a man was 60 hours, spread over six days. While relatively few women worked in the paid labor force, the typical woman spent about 40 hours a week on meals and meal clean-up, another seven hours per week on laundry, another seven hours on cleaning the home, and an untold number of hours on child care, gardening, making and repairing clothes, fetching water, and filling the stove with wood or coal. The average woman had 10 pregnancies, so even with a high level of infant mortality, she spent about 15 years of her life either pregnant or looking after an infant. Child labor was widespread; the 1900 U.S. Census reports that one-fourth of boys aged 10–15 held a job.

Today, we look back at the people who lived 100 years ago and wonder how they managed. But remember that in 1900, the United States had the highest average income of any country in the world. It had an average standard of living slightly above that of the United Kingdom; almost double that of France or Germany; almost triple that of the richer nations of Latin America at that time, including Argentina and Chile; and quadruple the standard of living of Japan or Mexico (which had about the same standard of living at that time).

Few of us today would wish to return to the standard of living in 1900 because most of us believe that it is better to be educated than illiterate, to live longer and to have fewer babies die, to work fewer hours at less physically demanding tasks, and to have all the life-saving, labor-saving inventions that have been developed over time. This pattern of dramatic advances in the standard of living continues today. For example, consider the extraordinary advances in recent years in information and communications technology, in medicine and health, in biological sciences and genetics, and in new materials.

The economic challenge for society is to chart a course that encourages the beneficial aspects of economic growth while finding ways to curb undesirable and unwanted side effects like pollution, unemployment, and poverty. The introductory course in economics should make you more discerning about these issues. When you read newspaper or magazine articles about economic issues, you will begin to recognize terminology and arguments. When you hear classmates, co-workers, or political candidates talking about economics, you will improve your ability to distinguish common sense from nonsense. You will find new ways of thinking about current events and about personal and business decisions, as well as current events and politics. The study of economics does not dictate the answers, but it can illuminate the different choices.

Key Concepts and Summary

1. The **economy** is the way in which a society organizes the production, distribution, and consumption of goods and services. It is the set of social institutions that answers three questions: what is produced, how is it produced, and for whom is it produced.

2. In a **market-oriented economy**, individuals and businesses make most economic decisions, with government playing a background role. In a **command economy**, the government makes most economic decisions; individual and business decisions play only a background role. Most economies lie somewhere between these two extremes and have a substantial role for both the market and the government, although the emphasis varies in different countries.

3. A modern economy is amazingly interconnected. Every person and every good is linked by economic transactions—sometimes directly, often indirectly—to a vast array of other goods, people, and businesses.

4. A modern economy displays a **division of labor**, in which people earn income by specializing in what they produce and then use that income to purchase the products they desire.

5. The division of labor allows individuals and firms to specialize and to produce more for several reasons: (a) it allows the agents to focus on areas of advantage due to natural factors and skill levels; (b) it encourages the agents to learn and invent; (c) it allows agents to take advantage of **economies of scale**.

6. The last few decades have seen **globalization** evolve as a result of growth in commercial and financial networks that cross national borders, making businesses and workers from different economies increasingly interdependent.
7. **Microeconomics** and **macroeconomics** are two different perspectives on the economy. The microeconomic perspective focuses on parts of the economy: individuals, firms, and industries. The macroeconomic perspective looks at the economy as a whole, focusing on overall issues like growth in the standard of living, unemployment, inflation, and levels of foreign trade.
8. The **circular flow diagram** shows how households and firms interact in the **goods and services market**, the **labor market**, and the **financial capital market**.
9. Macroeconomics has four main goals: growth in the standard of living, low unemployment, low inflation, and a sustainable balance of trade. It has two types of policies for pursuing these goals: **monetary policy** and **fiscal policy**.

Review Questions

1. What are the three basic questions that every economy must address?
2. What is the key difference between a market-oriented economy and a command economy?
3. What does the phrase "division of labor" mean?
4. What three reasons explain why the division of labor increases an economy's level of production?
5. What is globalization? How do you think it might have affected the economy over the past decade?
6. What is the difference between microeconomics and macroeconomics?
7. Are households primarily buyers or sellers in the goods and services market? The labor market? The financial capital market? Are firms primarily buyers or sellers in each of these three markets?
8. What are the four primary goals of macroeconomics?

Choice in a World of Scarcity

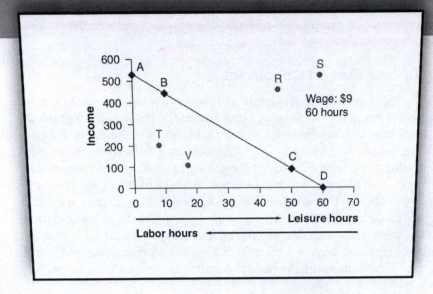

In November 1968, the Rolling Stones recorded a song called: "You Can't Always Get What You Want." But economists had already been singing a similar tune for many years. For example, an English economist named Lionel Robbins (1898–1984) wrote *An Essay on the Nature and Significance of Economic Science* in 1932, in which he described the problem of not always getting what you want in this way:

> The time at our disposal is limited. There are only twenty-four hours in the day. We have to choose between the different uses to which they may be put. The services which others put at our disposal are limited. The material means of achieving ends are limited. We have been turned out of Paradise. We have neither eternal life nor unlimited means of gratification. Everywhere we turn, if we choose one thing we must relinquish others which, in different circumstances, we would wish not to have relinquished. Scarcity of means to satisfy given ends is an almost ubiquitous condition of human nature. Here then, is the unity of subject of Economic Science, the forms assumed by human behavior in disposing of scarce means.

Economics studies how every person, every firm, and every society must make choices, because none of them can have everything that they desire.

This chapter begins with a discussion of three broad categories of choices made by individuals and households: choices about which goods to consume, how many hours to work, and how much to borrow or save. Not coincidentally, these three categories of choices match the three main markets of microeconomics discussed in the circular flow diagram in Chapter 1: the markets for goods, labor, and financial capital. The discussion then introduces a framework for thinking about society's choices. Finally, the chapter discusses some concerns over whether the economic approach to facing scarcity and making choices describes accurately either how choices *are* actually made or how choices *should* be made.

Choosing What to Consume

People live in a world of scarcity: that is, they can't have all the time, money, possessions, and experiences they wish. Since people must choose, they inevitably face trade-offs, in which they have to give up things that they desire to get other things that they desire more. When economists analyze how individuals make these choices, they divide the decision process into two steps. The first step is to consider what choices are possible for individuals. The second step is to think about which choices individuals actually make, based on their individual preferences. The model that economists use for illustrating the process of individual choice in a situation of scarcity is the **budget constraint**, sometimes also called the **opportunity set**, a diagram that shows the possible choices.

budget constraint: A diagram that shows the possible choices.

opportunity set: Another name for the budget constraint.

A Consumption Choice Budget Constraint

To illustrate how the budget constraint model applies to choices about how much of each good to consume, consider the case of Alphonso, illustrated in Exhibit 2-1. Each graph in Exhibit 2-1 shows a different combination of Alphonso's income and the prices for two goods, burgers and bus tickets. In Exhibit 2-1a, Alphonso has $10 in spending money each week that he can allocate between bus tickets for getting to work and the burgers that he eats for lunch. Burgers cost $2 each, and bus tickets in Alphonso's town are 50 cents. Different combinations of choices that are possible for Alphonso are shown in the table and also depicted graphically in the accompanying budget constraint. Each combination of burgers and bus tickets shown in the table and the budget constraint adds up to exactly $10. As one example, if Alphonso buys 1 burger for $2, he has $8 remaining and could purchase 16 bus tickets. The points along the budget constraint represent what consumption opportunities are possible for Alphonso.

How Changes in Income and Prices Affect the Budget Constraint

Changes in income will alter the budget constraint. For example, say that Alphonso's spending money increases to $12 per week. Exhibit 2-1b shows both his original budget constraint and his new budget constraint. In the new budget constraint, each combination of burgers and bus tickets at the given prices now adds up to $12. A higher income level means that the budget constraint will shift to the right of the original budget constraint; conversely, a lower income level means that the budget constraint will lie to the left of the original budget constraint.

Now suppose Alphonso's income remains the same, but the price of one of the goods increases. Changes in the price of goods will affect Alphonso's budget constraint. In other words, his income level stays at $10 per week, but the price of bus tickets rises to $1 each, while the price of burgers remains at $2. Exhibit 2-1c shows how this change in price alters the budget constraint. A higher price for one good causes the budget constraint to move inward; more specifically, the budget constraint swings inward as if on a hinge attached to the vertical axis or the horizontal axis—depending on which good's price has

---

CLEARING IT UP

Sketching Budget Constraints

As an economics student, you will need to know how to sketch budget constraints quickly and accurately. When graphing a choice between two goods, it does not matter which good is on the horizontal or the vertical axis. Start by calculating, based on income and the prices of the two goods, what quantity of each good each person could buy if that person were not buying any of the other good. These calculations will determine the points on the two axes of the budget constraint. The other points then form a straight line between these endpoints.

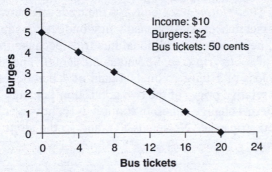

Quantity of Burgers (at $2)	Quantity of Bus Tickets (at 50 cents)
0	20
1	16
2	12
3	8
4	4
5	0

(a) First set of choices: Total income $10.

Each point on the opportunity set represents a combination of burgers and bus tickets whose total cost adds up to Alphonso's income of $10. The slope of the budget constraint line is determined by the relative price of burgers and bus tickets. All along the budget constraint, giving up a burger means gaining four bus tickets.

Quantity of Burgers (at $2)	Quantity of Bus Tickets (at 50 cents)
0	24
1	20
2	16
3	12
4	8
5	4
6	0

(b) Second set of choices: Total income $12.

If Alphonso's income increases from $10 to $12, his opportunity set shifts to the right of the original budget set. The lower line is the original budget constraint, and the upper line is the new budget constraint. On the new budget constraint, each combination of burgers and bus tickets now adds up to a total cost of $12. However, because the trade-off of burgers for bus tickets is unchanged—still one burger for every four bus tickets—the slope of the budget constraint line is unchanged.

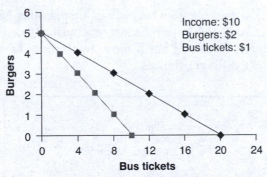

Quantity of Burgers (at $2)	Quantity of Bus Tickets (at $1)
0	10
1	8
2	6
3	4
4	2
5	0

(c) Third set of choices: Total income $10.

Alphonso's income remains at $10, as in (a), but the cost of bus tickets rises from 50 cents to $1. This change causes the opportunity set to swing inward, as if on a hinge at the upper left. If Alphonso wishes to purchase only burgers, the change in price of bus tickets doesn't alter how many he can buy. However, giving up a burger now adds only two bus tickets, not four. The budget constraint line slopes more steeply as a result.

EXHIBIT 2-1 Alphonso's Consumption Choice Opportunity Set

risen. Conversely, a lower price for one good would lead to an outward movement of the budget constraint.

A change in income causes the budget constraint to shift so that the new budget constraint is parallel to the original. However, a change in prices causes the slope of the budget constraint to change so that the budget constraint is steeper or flatter. Why are the effects different? The slope of the budget constraint is determined by the relative price of the two goods, which is calculated by taking the price of one good and dividing it by the price of the other good. The *relative* price conveys the trade-off between the two goods, in this case burgers and bus tickets. In Alphonso's first budget constraint in Exhibit 2-1*a*, if he gives up 1 burger, he can take 4 additional bus trips because the price of a burger is four times the price of a bus trip (i.e., $2 versus 50 cents). The slope of this budget constraint shows that a loss of 1 burger equals a gain of 4 bus tickets. In Exhibit 2-1*b*, income changes but the relative prices of the two goods don't change, and so the slope of the budget constraint doesn't change either. In Exhibit 2-1*c*, however, giving up 1 burger means gaining only 2 bus trips (i.e., $2 versus $1), and so the slope of the budget constraint changes accordingly.

Personal Preferences Determine Specific Choices

utility: The level of satisfaction or pleasure that people receive from their choices.

What choice will Alphonso make along his budget constraint? The answer is simple: Alphonso will choose what he personally prefers. In economics, **utility** refers to the level of satisfaction or pleasure that people receive from their choices. Thus, when people make the choices that provide the highest level of satisfaction, economists say that they are "maximizing utility." In Alphonso's case, if he prefers to sit at home and eat, he buys a lot of burgers and chooses some point like *A* or *B* on the budget constraint in Exhibit 2-2. If he prefers to travel around town, he buys lots of bus tickets and chooses some point like *D* or *E* on the budget constraint. It's Alphonso's choice.

However, the logic of the budget constraint dictates that Alphonso's choice will be a point on the actual budget constraint itself—not a choice that is above the budget set or below it. Alphonso might desire a point like *H* in Exhibit 2-2 with five burgers and 16 bus tickets, offering more of both goods than choice *B*. However, choice *H* is outside the budget constraint, which means that Alphonso can't afford it. Conversely, Alphonso won't choose a point like *J* with 2 burgers and 4 bus tickets, which is inside the boundary of the budget constraint, because he could instead select a choice on the budget set itself like *B* that would have at least as much of one good and more of the other—or a choice that would offer even more of both goods. In this simple model, Alphonso doesn't have any other goods on which to spend his money, and so if he doesn't spend his money, it is wasted.

The budget constraint diagram shows what choices are possible, but it does not specify which choice is made. If two people have the same income and face the same prices, then they have identical budget constraints, but if those two people have different personal preferences, they will make different choices.

EXHIBIT 2-2 Personal Preferences Determine the Actual Choice

If Alphonso likes burgers a lot, he will probably make a choice like *A* or *B*. If he likes bus tickets a lot, he will probably make a choice like *D* or *E*. Points *H* and *G* beyond the opportunity set are unattainable for Alphonso, given his level of income, no matter how much he might like them. Points *J* and *K* would be wasteful. For example, rather than choosing point *J*, he could have both more burgers and the same number of bus tickets at point *B*. Similarly, instead of choosing point *K*, he could have the same number of burgers but many more bus tickets at point *D*.

From a Model with Two Goods to the Real World of Many Goods

The budget constraint diagram containing just two goods may seem too simple. In a modern economy, people choose from thousands of goods, not just two.

However, thinking about a model with many goods is straightforward. Instead of drawing just one budget constraint, showing the trade-off between two goods, you can draw multiple budget constraints, showing the possible trade-offs between many different pairs of goods. Or in more advanced classes in economics, you would use mathematical equations that include many possible goods and services that can be purchased, together with their quantities and prices, and show how the total spending on all of the goods adds up to the overall amount of money available. However, the graph with two goods clearly illustrates three basic concepts: (1) the budget constraint is determined by income and prices; (2) changes in income or relative prices cause a budget constraint to move; and (3) the personal preferences of an individual are represented by the point that is chosen on the budget constraint.

Choosing between Labor and Leisure

People also make choices about how to allocate their time; in particular, they choose how to divide their available hours between work and leisure. The concept of the budget constraint applies to the labor-leisure choice just as it does to the decision of what quantity of goods to consume. Again, the first step is to use the budget constraint to show what is possible, given the wage that can be earned and the number of hours in a day, while the second step is for individuals to make their personally preferred choice that maximizes utility.

An Example of a Labor-Leisure Budget Constraint

Beulah has a job as an assistant manager of a fast-food restaurant. She can work as many as 60 hours per week if she chooses. Of course, most people don't have jobs that let them choose exactly how many hours to work each week, but most people have at least some flexibility about whether to look for a part-time or a full-time job or whether to work overtime or take on a second job. Thus, it isn't unreasonable to imagine people making choices about the number of hours they work. Exhibit 2-3 shows two of Beulah's labor-leisure budget constraints.

In Exhibit 2-3a, Beulah's wage is $9 per hour. The table and the budget constraint show the trade-off that she faces between income and leisure. Because Beulah receives an hourly wage, the more hours she works, the more her income rises and her leisure

Hours Worked	Leisure Time	Income
0	60	$0
10	50	$90
20	40	$180
30	30	$270
40	20	$360
50	10	$450
60	0	$540

(a) First set of choices: Wage $9 per hour.

The points on the opportunity set show what combinations of leisure and income that Beulah can have with her 60 hours of time, given that she can earn a wage of $9 per hour. The trade-off between leisure and income, which is the wage $9 per hour, determines the slope of the line.

Hours Worked	Leisure Time	Income
0	60	$0
10	50	$110
20	40	$220
30	30	$330
40	20	$440
50	10	$550
60	0	$660

(b) Second set of choices: Wage $11 per hour.

If Beulah's wage increases from $9 per hour to $11 per hour, her 60 hours of time has not changed, but the trade-off that she faces between leisure and income has changed. With the higher wage, giving up a certain number of hours of leisure brings a higher income, so the budget set rotates upward.

EXHIBIT 2-3 Beulah's Labor-Leisure Opportunity Set

diminishes. The horizontal axis of the graph measures *both* labor hours and leisure hours, but in opposite directions. The quantity of hours of leisure is measured from left to right, while the quantity of hours of labor is measured from right to left. Since Beulah has a total of 60 hours available that she could work, the horizontal axis shows how she divides up this time between leisure and work.

How a Change in Wages Affects the Labor-Leisure Budget Constraint

A change in the wage will rotate Beulah's budget constraint. If her wage rises to $11 per hour, perhaps because she has gained more experience or training, then the trade-offs that she faces change as well. Both her original budget constraint and her new set of trade-offs are shown in Exhibit 2-3b. A new wage changes the slope of the budget constraint because a new wage means a different trade-off between hours of leisure and income.

Making a Choice along the Labor-Leisure Budget Constraint

Living in a world of scarcity—no one has more than 24 hours in a day—requires that people must make choices about how to spend their time, but the fact of scarcity doesn't dictate what choices they make. In deciding how many hours to work, Beulah will make a choice that maximizes her utility; that is, she will choose according to her preferences for leisure time and income. If she chooses to work 60 hours per week, she will have more income to spend on food, rent, clothing, cars, vacations, or other goods and services.

Measuring Labor and Leisure on the Same Axis

The labor-leisure budget constraint involves illustrating three factors—hours of labor, hours of leisure, and dollars of income—on only two axes. This illustration only works because the hours of both labor and leisure appear on the horizontal axis. After all, all leisure means no labor, and all labor means no leisure. On the horizontal axis, hours of leisure are measured from left to right, but hours of labor are measured from right to left. The fundamental trade-off here is between the two goods of leisure and income. In this model, labor is not a "good" in itself, but instead a mechanism for earning income.

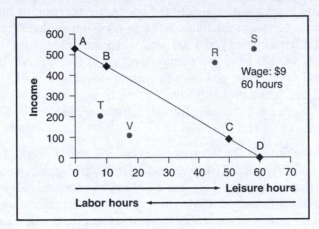

EXHIBIT 2-4 Beulah's Personal Choice on a Labor-Leisure Opportunity Set

If Beulah strongly prefers income, she will work a lot of hours and choose a point like *A* or *B*. If she strongly prefers leisure, she will work few hours and make a choice like *C* or *D*. Given that she has 60 hours of time and a wage of $9 per hour, she cannot choose points like *R* or *S* that are outside her budget set. Points like *T* or *V* inside her budget set would be wasteful; they would be like working extra hours but not being paid.

However, if she prefers leisure time, she may choose to work fewer hours so that she has more time for family, friends, and low-cost hobbies such as reading or yoga. Exhibit 2-4 illustrates both possibilities. If Beulah prefers a relatively high level of income, then she will choose a point close to *A*, with $540 of income, 60 hours of work, and no leisure. If she prefers instead a relatively high level of leisure, she might choose a point like *C* with 50 hours of leisure, 10 hours of work, and $90 in income.

Beulah might desire a combination of income and leisure that is outside her budget constraint; for example, she would probably like to have both 60 hours of leisure and $540 of income, which is the choice shown at point *S*. However, the budget constraint shows what choices are possible, given the wage and hours available, and choices beyond the budget constraint are not possible. Moreover, Beulah will not choose a point inside the budget constraint like *T*, which is 50 hours of labor, 10 hours of leisure, and $200 of income. In effect, a choice like *T* would mean that Beulah was working for only $4 per hour (i.e., $200 of income divided by 50 hours of work), when she can actually earn a wage of $9 per hour. Thus, the labor-leisure budget constraint illustrates: (1) the opportunity set of possible choices for leisure and income is determined by the wage rate and the total quantity of hours that can be worked; (2) changes in the wage rate cause the budget constraint to move; and (3) the personal preferences of an individual choosing between leisure and income are represented by the point that is selected on the budget constraint.

Choosing between Present and Future Consumption

An intertemporal choice reaches across time. Borrowing money is an intertemporal choice, because it involves borrowing money to spend in the present but promising to repay in the future. Saving money is also an intertemporal choice, because it involves less consumption in the present, but the ability to consume more in the future. The intertemporal choice budget constraint shows the trade-off between present and future consumption.

Interest Rates: The Price of Intertemporal Choice

In the consumption choice budget constraint presented earlier, the trade-off between goods is determined by the relative prices of the two goods. In the labor-leisure budget constraint, the trade-off between leisure and income is based on the wage. In the intertemporal choice budget constraint, the trade-off between present consumption and future consumption is based on the interest rate or the rate of return. The price of borrowing money is the interest that you pay on the loan. The reward for saving money is the interest that you receive. The key to understanding the economic function of interest rates is to recognize that receiving $100 in the future has less economic value than receiving $100 today. Imagine that a friend owes you $100, and when the time comes to pay, the friend says: "Hey, no problem, I'll have the money for you in five years." You protest, and your supposed friend says, "Hey, you are still getting repaid your full $100, so what are you complaining about?" You probably aren't going to persuade this loser, your former friend, to repay you sooner, but you can offer three arguments as to why $100 in the future doesn't have the same value as $100 today:

1. *Risk of not being repaid.* The future is uncertain. Your friend could get hit by a bus. You could get hit by a bus. (The way this friendship is going, you could run over your former friend with a bus.) Having $100 in your pocket is a sure thing. Having a promise of $100 is uncertain. Anytime someone borrows money, whether the lender is a friend or a bank, the lender must be concerned about the risk of not being repaid. Part of the interest rate is a **risk premium**, that is, a payment to make up for the risk of not being repaid in full.

2. *Inflation.* In most years, there is a rise in the overall level of prices called **inflation**. In recent U.S. history, this increase has typically been 1–3% per year, but in other times and places, the rate of inflation has been much higher. If the overall level of prices rises by 3%, then on average a dollar will buy 3% less in terms of goods and services at the end of the year. As a result of the higher overall level of prices, being repaid $100 in the future will provide less buying power than receiving the money immediately. A lender demands an interest rate in part to compensate for any expected inflation, so that the money that is repaid in the future will have at least as much buying power as the money that was originally loaned. (The concept of inflation, along with its underlying causes and policy solutions, is discussed at length in the macroeconomics section of the book.)

3. *Time value of money.* Even if you knew with complete certainty that the $100 will be repaid in the future, and even if the rate of inflation is zero, it is still annoying to wait several years for repayment. If you have the money now, you can spend it on something now if you wish to do so and receive benefits from that spending. Being forced to wait is an intangible cost, but still a cost. This cost of having to wait is referred to as the **time value of money**.

Thus, when explaining to your friend why you should receive interest payments if you need to wait five years for your money, you can point out that an interest rate has three components:

Interest rate = Risk premium + Expected rate of inflation + Time value of money.

In effect, interest payments are a compensation for the risk of not being repaid, the fact that inflation tends to reduce the buying power of money over time, and the unpleasantness of having to wait to have money available.

Thinking about these three components of interest rates helps to explain why interest rates differ across times and places. At times and places when inflation is high, interest

risk premium: A payment to make up for the risk of not being repaid in full.

inflation: Rise in the overall level of prices.

time value of money: The cost of having to wait for repayment.

rates will also be high. Differences in interest rates at a point in time can usually be traced to the different risk premiums involved. For example, when the U.S. government borrows money, the interest rate is quite low, perhaps an annual rate of 2–4%, because the chance that the federal government will not repay what it has borrowed is quite low. A large corporation might pay an annual interest rate of 6–7% because, although the large firm is likely to pay back the loan, the risk is greater than with the federal government. A medium-size or small firm would pay an even higher interest rate because it has a greater risk of not repaying the loan. Individuals pay a relatively low interest rate when they borrow money from a bank to purchase a home because the bank (the lender) does a credit check before lending any money in the first place. The credit check is supposed to ensure that a home buyer has the financial means to cover the cost; if the buyer is unable to meet the payments, the bank can take the house and sell it. However, individuals pay a higher interest rate on credit card borrowing, in part because there is a greater risk that such loans will not be repaid.

The Power of Compound Interest

Interest rates are usually expressed in annual terms. For example, an annual interest rate of 7% means that if you borrow $100 you will need to repay $107 a year from now, or if you save $100 you will receive $7 in interest payments a year from now. But what if you are planning to save money for a period of many years, allowing the interest to accumulate over time? The formula for starting with a certain amount of money in the present, and a certain interest rate or rate of return, and figuring how much it would be worth at a date in the future is:

$$\text{Future amount} = (\text{Present amount}) \times (1 + \text{interest rate})^{\text{number of years}}$$

For example, Christopher is planning to make a financial investment of $500. He will put this money in an investment that pays an interest rate of 6% annually and leave it there for some years as the interest accumulates.

Exhibit 2-5 applies this formula for Christopher and shows what his financial investment would be worth at various dates in the future. Notice that if he leaves the financial investment alone for 20 years, the original $500 will more than triple in value to $1,603; if he leaves the financial investment alone for 40 years, it will increase more than 10-fold to $5,143. How can a seemingly moderate interest rate like 6% per year produce such large increases? The answer lies in the power of **compound interest**, when interest payments are allowed to accumulate so that in later time periods, the interest rate is paid not only on the original amount, but also on the interest that has accumulated in previous years. In the equation for how a financial investment increases in value over time, the number of years is an exponent. When quantities are raised to high exponential powers, they will eventually expand very quickly. The exponent represents the power of compound interest—as time goes by, Christopher is not just earning interest on his original $500, but also on the earlier interest he earned. If interest rates are relatively low, compound interest doesn't make much of a practical difference over a short time period of a few years. But over several decades, even a relatively low interest rate will compound in a way that yields significant returns on the initial financial investment.

compound interest: When interest payments in earlier periods are reinvested, so that in later time periods, the interest rate is paid on the total amount accumulated during previous years.

EXHIBIT 2-5 Christopher's Potential Savings

Starting with $500, Interest Rate of 6%			
After 1 year	$500 (1 + .06)^1 = $530	After 10 years	$500 (1 + .06)^{10} = $895
After 2 years	$500 (1 + .06)^2 = $562	After 20 years	$500 (1 + .06)^{20} = $1,603
After 5 years	$500 (1 + .06)^5 = $669	After 40 years	$500 (1 + .06)^{40} = $5,143

An Example of Intertemporal Choice

Consider the case of Desdemona, who is lucky enough to receive a gift of $10,000 from a wealthy aunt. She faces a choice: how much money should she consume now, and how much should she save for future consumption? Again, the first step is to use the budget constraint to show the range of possible choices, and then the second step is to illustrate the individually preferred choice that maximizes her utility.

In the intertemporal choice budget constraint, the two axes represent consumption in the present and consumption in the future. Let's assume that if Desdemona saves some of the money, she can earn an annual interest rate of 9% for the next 10 years. Exhibit 2-6 shows Desdemona's choices in both a table and a budget constraint. The levels of future consumption that are available to her 10 years from now are calculated by using the formula for compound interest. At one extreme, she can consume all of the $10,000 in the present and have nothing left in the future. At the other extreme, she can save the entire $10,000, consume none of it in the present, and have $23,673 to spend 10 years from now.

In Exhibit 2-6, both present consumption and present savings are shown on the horizontal axis. Consumption is measured from left to right; saving is measured from right to left. In effect, the horizontal axis shows how the income that is available in the present is divided into either consumption or savings. (This approach applies the same logic as the way in which hours of labor and leisure were both shown on the horizontal axis in the labor-leisure budget constraint.) If the interest rate rises, then the budget constraint has a steeper slope; a lower interest rate causes the budget constraint to rotate downward to a flatter slope.

Desdemona will seek to maximize her utility and choose the option that brings her the greatest degree of satisfaction. Inevitably, this choice will be one of the points on the budget constraint such as A, B, C, D, E, or F. Even if Desdemona wants to choose a point like Q, with $8,000 of consumption in the present, $2,000 of savings, and $20,000 of future consumption, she can't have it because choice Q is outside her budget constraint. Moreover, Desdemona will not choose a point inside the budget constraint like R, with $2,000 in present consumption and $10,000 in future consumption because such a choice would be like throwing away money. Instead of choosing R, Desdemona would certainly prefer a choice like C with more consumption in both the present and the future.

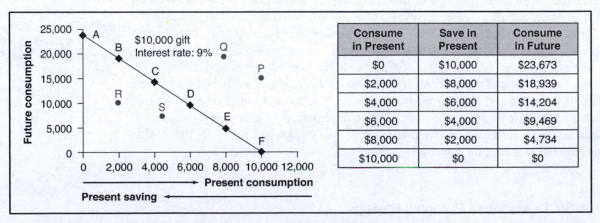

Consume in Present	Save in Present	Consume in Future
$0	$10,000	$23,673
$2,000	$8,000	$18,939
$4,000	$6,000	$14,204
$6,000	$4,000	$9,469
$8,000	$2,000	$4,734
$10,000	$0	$0

EXHIBIT 2-6 Desdemona's Intertemporal Budget Constraint

The points along the budget set represent the combinations of present and future consumption that are available to Desdemona, based on her inheritance of $10,000, an interest rate of 9% per year, and a time period of 10 years The trade-off between present consumption and future consumption—and thus the slope of the budget line—is determined by the interest rate. Choices like Q or P are unavailable to Desdemona, even if she would like them. She will not make choices like R or S because they give up present consumption without taking future consumption, which would be wasteful. Thus, she will choose among points like A through F, based on her personal preferences.

Opportunity Cost in the Airport

After the terrorist plane hijackings on September 11, 2001, many steps were proposed to improve air travel safety. For example, the federal government could provide armed "sky marshals" who would travel inconspicuously with the rest of the passengers. The cost of having a sky marshal on every flight would be roughly $3 billion per year. Retrofitting all U.S. planes with reinforced cockpit doors to make it harder for terrorists to take over the plane would have a price tag of $450 million. Buying more sophisticated security equipment for airports, like three-dimensional baggage scanners and cameras linked to face recognition software, could cost another $2 billion.

But the single biggest cost of greater airline security doesn't involve spending money. It's the opportunity cost of additional waiting time at the airport. About 750 million passengers took plane trips in the United States in 2016. Since the 9/11 hijackings, security screening has become more intensive, and consequently, the procedure takes longer than in the past. Say that, on average, each air passenger spends one extra hour in the airport per trip. Economists commonly place a value on time to convert an opportunity cost in time into a monetary figure. Let's say that the average price of time for air travelers is $25 per hour. By these estimates, the opportunity cost of delay in airports is 750 million hours × 25 dollars/hour, or $18.75 billion per year. Clearly, the opportunity costs of waiting time can be just as important as costs that involve direct spending.

In the real world, the trade-off between present and future consumption is considerably more complex than the basic intertemporal budget constraint shown here. Instead of making one decision in the present about whether to consume now or save for 10 years from now, people receive income in many different years and make decisions about how much to save over different periods of time. Moreover, financial investments often don't pay a guaranteed rate of return, so people need to take into account the risk and uncertainty of investments. Later chapters will take up the details of financial investing in greater detail. But the basic intertemporal budget constraint here illustrates three themes: (1) the budget constraint of possible choices for present and future consumption are determined by the quantity of income in the present and the interest rate; (2) changes in the interest rate will cause the intertemporal budget constraint to rotate; and (3) the personal preferences of an individual for present and future consumption are represented by the point that is chosen on the intertemporal budget constraint.

Three Implications of Budget Constraints: Opportunity Cost, Marginal Decision-Making, and Sunk Costs

The budget constraint framework has some possibly unexpected implications for how a sensible utility-maximizing individual will make decisions. Let's now draw out three of those implications, involving *opportunity cost*, *marginal decision making*, and *sunk costs*.

Opportunity Cost

When most people want to know the cost of an item or a service, they look for a price tag. When economists want to determine cost, they go one step further. They use the idea of **opportunity cost**, which is whatever must be given up to obtain something that is desired. In the examples discussed earlier, if Alphonso wants more burgers, the opportunity cost is measured in bus tickets; if he wants more bus tickets, the opportunity cost is measured in burgers. In Beulah's labor-leisure choice, if she wants more income, the opportunity cost is hours of leisure; if she wants more leisure time, the opportunity cost is dollars of income. In Desdemona's intertemporal choice, the opportunity cost of greater consumption in the present is less consumption in the future and vice versa. The idea of opportunity cost, as its name implies, is that the cost of one item is the lost opportunity to do or consume something else.

In many cases, it is reasonable to refer to the opportunity cost as the price. If your cousin buys a new bicycle for $300, then $300 measures the amount of "other consumption"

opportunity cost: Whatever must be given up to obtain something that is desired.

that would have been possible. For practical purposes, there may be no special need to identify the specific alternative product or products that could have been bought with that $300, but sometimes the price as measured in dollars may not accurately capture the true opportunity cost. This problem can arise when costs of time are involved. For example, consider a boss who decides that all employees will attend a two-day retreat to "build team spirit." The out-of-pocket monetary cost of the event may involve hiring an outside consulting firm to run the retreat. But an opportunity cost exists as well: during the two days of the retreat, none of the employees are doing their regular work. Attending college is another case where the opportunity cost exceeds the monetary cost. The out-of-pocket costs of attending college include tuition, books, room and board, and other expenses. But in addition, during the hours that you are attending class and studying, it is impossible to work at a paying job. Thus, college imposes both an out-of-pocket cost and an opportunity cost of lost earnings—and both costs should be taken into account.

In some cases, making the opportunity cost explicit can alter behavior. Imagine, for example, that you are an employee who goes out to lunch every day and spends $8 at a local restaurant. You may know perfectly well that bringing a lunch from home would only cost $3 a day, but somehow referring to the opportunity cost of buying lunch at the restaurant as $5 each day (i.e., the $8 it costs minus the $3 your lunch from home would cost) doesn't seem to matter much. However, if you work 250 days a year, that $5 per day adds up to $1,250 for a year—which is the cost of a decent vacation. If the opportunity cost is described as "a nice vacation" instead of "$5 a day," you might make different choices.

Marginal Decision-Making and Diminishing Marginal Utility

The budget constraint framework helps to emphasize that most choices in the real world aren't about getting all of one thing or all of another; that is, they aren't about choosing either the point at one end of the budget constraint or else the point all the way at the other end. Instead, most choices involve **marginal analysis**, which compares the benefits and costs of choosing a little more or a little less of a good.

marginal analysis:
Comparing the benefits and costs of choosing a little more or a little less of a good.

The utility that a person receives from consuming the first unit of a good is typically more than the utility received from consuming the fifth or the tenth unit of that same good. When Alphonso makes his choice between burgers and bus tickets, for example, the first few bus rides that he chooses might provide him with a great deal of utility— perhaps they help him get to a job interview or a doctor's appointment. But later bus rides might provide much less utility—they may only serve to kill time on a rainy day. Similarly, the first burger that Alphonso chooses to buy may be on a day when he missed breakfast and is ravenously hungry. However, if Alphonso has a burger every single day, the last few burgers may be less appealing. Similarly, if Beulah is working 60 hours per week and thinking about whether to take a few hours of leisure, that break may provide her with a great deal of utility. But if she is working only 10 hours a week, with 50 hours of leisure already, then taking a few more hours of leisure would probably provide much less utility.

The general pattern that consumption of the first few units of any good tends to bring a higher level of utility to a person than consumption of later units is a common pattern. Economists refer to this pattern as the **law of diminishing marginal utility**, which means that as a person receives more of a good, the additional or marginal utility from each additional unit of the good declines.

law of diminishing marginal utility: As a person receives more of a good, the marginal utility from each additional unit of the good is smaller than from the previous unit.

The law of diminishing marginal utility explains why people and societies rarely make all-or-nothing choices. You wouldn't say, "My favorite food is ice cream, so I will eat nothing but ice cream from now on." Even if you get a very high level of utility from your favorite food, if you ate it exclusively, the additional or marginal utility from those last few servings would not be very high. Similarly, most workers don't say: "I enjoy leisure, so I'll never work." Instead, workers recognize that even though some leisure is very nice, a combination of all leisure and no income isn't so attractive. Thus, the budget constraint framework suggests that when people make choices in a world of scarcity, they will use marginal analysis and think about whether they would prefer a little more or a little less.

Sunk Costs

In the budget constraint framework, all decisions involve what will happen next: that is, what quantities of goods will be consumed, how many hours will be worked, or how much will be saved. These decisions do not look back to past choices. Thus, the budget constraint framework assumes that **sunk costs**, which are costs that were incurred in the past and cannot be recovered, should not affect the current decision.

sunk cost: Costs that were incurred in the past and cannot be recovered, and thus should not affect current decisions.

Consider the case of Edgar, who pays $8 to see a movie, but after watching the film for 30 minutes, he knows that it's truly terrible. Should he stay and watch the rest of the movie because he paid $8, or should he leave? The money he spent is a sunk cost and unless the theater manager is feeling kindly, Edgar won't get a refund. But staying in the movie still means paying an opportunity cost in time. Thus, Edgar's choice is whether to spend the next 90 minutes suffering through a cinematic disaster or to do something—anything—else. The lesson of sunk costs is to forget about the money that's irretrievably gone and instead to focus on the marginal costs and benefits of future options.

For people and firms alike, dealing with sunk costs can be frustrating. It often means admitting an earlier error in judgment. Many firms, for example, find it hard to give up on a new product that is selling poorly because they spent so much money in creating and launching the product. But the lesson of sunk costs is to ignore them and make decisions based on what will happen in the future.

The budget constraint or opportunity set provides a framework for thinking about how individuals make economic decisions like what to consume, how much to work, and how much to save. The purpose of this model is not to tell utility-maximizing individuals what they *should* do, but only to convey the range of available choices for what individuals *could* do, and to provide a way of showing what choices people actually make.

The Production Possibilities Frontier and Social Choices

In a world of scarcity, individuals cannot have everything they want and must instead make a choice along a budget constraint. Firms cannot have all the profits they want and must come up with new and ongoing ways of pleasing customers. Society as a whole cannot have everything it might want, either. A **production possibilities frontier** is an opportunity set for the economy as a whole. It is typically displayed as a diagram that shows the combinations of output that are possible for an economy to produce.

production possibilities frontier: A diagram that shows the combinations of output that are possible for an economy to produce.

An example of a production possibilities frontier faced by every economy is the macroeconomic choice between consumption and real investment. Consumption refers to goods

EXHIBIT 2-7 The Consumption and Investment Trade-off

A production possibilities frontier shows the possible combinations of output that a society can produce. Points A, B, C, and D illustrate some possible choices along PPF₁, moving from all consumption at A to greater investment at B, C, and D. PPF₂ and PPF₃ show an outward shift of the frontier, which would happen as an economy grows and can afford more of both consumption and investment.

and services that are used up this year. Real investment (as opposed to financial investment) refers to expenditures on equipment (like machinery) that can be used to produce goods or services for some years into the future. Thus, expenditures on consumption often serve a more immediate need or desire, but expenditures on investment typically help to increase the economy's level of output in the future.

A production possibilities frontier for the choice between consumption and investment is shown in Exhibit 2-7 by the line labeled PPF₁. At point A, the economy is devoting all of its resources to producing goods for current consumption and nothing to investment. At points B, C, and D, the economy is gradually shifting toward lower levels of consumption and higher levels of investment. At point E, at the other end of the production possibilities frontier, the economy is devoting all of its resources to producing goods for real investment and no resources to current consumption. In a market-oriented economy, the choice between consumption and real investment is not made by the government or by any single organization, but rather is the result of many decisions made by households and firms. However, the government can use taxes, regulations, and other policies to influence the choices of individuals as to how much they should consume or save, and also to influence the eagerness of firms to make real investments. Just as people will make choices along a budget constraint, according to their personal preferences, societies will make choices about how much to consume and to invest.

Over time, societies that invest a greater share of GDP will tend to expand their ability to produce output. Therefore, a society that chooses a high level of consumption and low level of investment, like point B, will find that in the future its production possibilities frontier shifts outward only a bit, perhaps from PPF₁ to PPF₂. However, a society that consumes relatively less in the present and invests more, like point D, will find that in the future its production possibilities frontier has shifted outward more dramatically, perhaps from PPF₁ to PPF₃. Thus, a consumption-investment production possibilities frontier shows the range of choices available to society, illustrates which choice actually happens, and even has implications for how the PPF will shift in the future.

The Shape of the Production Possibilities Frontier and Diminishing Marginal Returns

The budget constraints presented earlier in this chapter, showing individual choices about what quantities of goods to consume, how much to work, and how much to save, were all

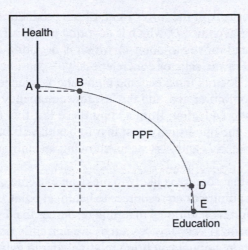

EXHIBIT 2-8 A Health vs. Education Production Possibilities Frontier

This production possibilities frontier shows a trade-off between devoting social resources to health and devoting them to education. At choices like *A* and *B*, most social resources go to health. At choices like *D* and *E*, most go to education. The curvature of the PPF shows that when a large share of resources is already devoted to health (as at point *B*), devoting still more resources to health and moving to point *A* produces only a small gain in health but a substantial loss in education. Thus, the curvature of the PPF demonstrates the law of diminishing marginal returns.

straight lines. The reason for these straight lines is that the slope of the budget constraint is determined by relative prices of the two goods in the consumption budget constraint, by the wage in the labor-leisure budget constraint, and by the interest rate in the intertemporal budget constraint. However, the production possibilities frontier for consumption and investment is often drawn as a curved line. Why does the PPF have a different shape?

Consider another example of a production possibilities frontier that arises when government decision makers must decide how much money to spend on competing government priorities, like education and health. Exhibit 2-8 shows a production possibilities frontier for this trade-off. In this diagram there are no specific numbers on the axes because there is no single way to measure levels of education and health. However, when you think of improvements in education, you can think of accomplishments like more years of school completed, fewer high-school dropouts, and higher scores on standardized tests. When you think of improvements in health, you can think of longer life expectancies, lower levels of infant mortality, and fewer outbreaks of disease. At choice *A*, the government is committing all of its resources to producing health and none to education; at choice *E*, the government is committing all resources to education and none to health. As the economy grows over time, this production possibilities frontier will shift to the right, making it possible for society to have more of both education and health. But in the immediate present, choosing more of one means choosing less of the other.

To understand why the PPF is curved, start by considering point *A* at the top left-hand side of the PPF. At point *A*, all of the available resources are being devoted to health and none to education. This situation would be extreme and even ridiculous. For example, children are seeing a doctor every day, whether they are sick or not, but not attending school. People are having cosmetic surgery on every part of their bodies, but no high school or college education exists. Now imagine that some of these resources are diverted from health to education, so that the economy is at point *B* instead of point *A*. Diverting some marginal resources away from *A* to *B* causes relatively little reduction in health because the last few marginal dollars going into health care services aren't producing much additional gain in health. However, putting those marginal dollars into education, which is completely without resources at point *A*, can produce relatively large gains. For this reason, the shape of the PPF from *A* to *B* is relatively flat, representing a relatively small drop-off in health and a relatively large gain in education.

Now consider the other end, at the lower right, of the production possibilities frontier. Imagine that society starts at choice D, which is devoting nearly all resources to education and very few to health, and moves to point E, which is devoting all spending to education and none to health. For the sake of concreteness, you can imagine in the movement from D to E, the last few doctors must become high school science teachers, the last few nurses must become school librarians, and the last few emergency rooms are turned into kindergartens. The gains to education from adding these last few resources to education are very small. However, the opportunity cost loss to health will be fairly large, and thus the slope of the PPF between D and E is steep, showing a small gain in education and a large drop in health.

The lesson here is not that society is likely to make an extreme choice like devoting no resources to education at point A or no resources to health at point E. Instead, the lesson is that the gains from committing additional marginal resources to education depend on how much is already being spent. If very few resources are currently committed to education, then an increase of a certain amount can bring relatively large gains; on the other side, if a large number of resources are already being committed to education, then an increase of a certain amount will bring relatively smaller gains. This pattern is common enough that it has been given a name: the **law of diminishing returns**, which holds that as additional increments of resources are added to a certain purpose, the marginal benefit from those additional increments will decline. This pattern arises in many contexts. When government spends a certain amount more on reducing crime, for example, the original gains in reducing crime could be relatively large. But additional increases typically cause relatively smaller reductions in crime, and paying for enough police and security to reduce crime to nothing at all would be tremendously expensive.

The curvature of the production possibilities frontier shows that as additional resources are added to providing education, moving from left to right along the horizontal axis, the original gains are fairly large, but gradually diminish. Similarly, as additional resources are added to improving health, moving from bottom to top on the vertical axis, the original gains are fairly large, but again gradually diminish. In this way, the law of diminishing returns produces the outward-bending shape of the production possibilities frontier.

Productive Efficiency and Allocative Efficiency

The study of economics does not presume to tell a society what choice it should make along its production possibilities frontier. In a market-oriented economy with a democratic government, the choice will involve a mixture of decisions by individuals, firms, and government. However, economics can point out that some choices are unambiguously better than others. In everyday usage, the concept of efficiency refers to lack of waste. An inefficient machine operates at high cost, while an efficient machine produces without wasting energy or materials. An inefficient organization operates with long delays and high costs, while an efficient organization meets schedules, is focused, and performs within budget.

To an economist, **efficiency** refers to the situation in which it is impossible to get more of one thing without experiencing a trade-off of less of something else. The production possibilities frontier can illustrate two kinds of efficiency: *productive efficiency* and *allocative efficiency*. Exhibit 2-9 illustrates these ideas using a production possibilities frontier between consumption and investment.

Productive efficiency means that, given the available inputs and technology, it is impossible to produce more of one good without decreasing the quantity that is produced of another good. Thus, all choices on the PPF in Exhibit 2-9, including A, B, C, D, and E, display productive efficiency. As a firm moves from any one of these choices to any other, either consumption increases and investment declines or vice versa. However, any choice inside the production possibilities frontier is productively inefficient and wasteful because it is possible to produce more of one good, the other good, or some combination of both goods. For example, point R is productively inefficient because it is possible at choice C to have more of both goods: investment on the horizontal axis is higher at point

law of diminishing returns: As additional increments of resources are added to producing a good or service, the marginal benefit from those additional increments will decline.

efficiency: When it is impossible to get more of something without experiencing a trade-off of less of something else.

productive efficiency: When it is impossible to produce more of one good without decreasing the quantity produced of another good.

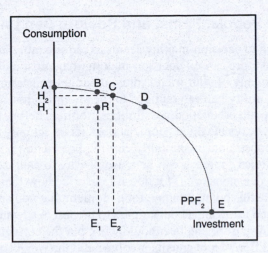

EXHIBIT 2-9 Productive and Allocative Efficiency

Productive efficiency means it is impossible to produce more of one good without decreasing the quantity that is produced of another good. Thus, all choices along a given PPF like A, B, C, D, and E display productive efficiency, but R does not. Allocative efficiency means that the particular mix of goods being produced—that is, the specific choice along the production possibilities frontier—represents the allocation that society most desires.

C than point R (E_2 is greater than E_1) and consumption on the vertical axis is also higher at point C than point R (H_2 is great than H_1).

Allocative efficiency means that the particular mix of goods being produced—that is, the specific choice along the production possibilities frontier—represents the allocation that society most desires. How to determine what a society desires can be a controversial question, and it will be addressed in political science, sociology, and philosophy classes as well as in economics. Only one of the productively efficient choices will be the allocatively efficient choice for society as a whole.

allocative efficiency: When the mix of goods being produced represents the allocation that society most desires.

Why Society Must Choose

Every economy should consider two situations in which it may be able to expand consumption of all goods. In the first case, a society may discover that it has been using its resources inefficiently, in which case by improving efficiency and moving to the production possibilities frontier, it can have more of some or all goods. In the second case, as an economy grows over a period of years, the production possibilities frontier for a society will tend to shift outward, and society will be able to afford more of all goods. But improvements in productive efficiency take time to discover and implement, and economic growth happens only gradually. Thus, a society must face scarcity and choose between trade-offs in the present. For government, this process often involves trying to identify where additional spending could do the most good and where reductions in spending would do the least harm. At the individual and firm level, the market economy coordinates a process in which firms seek to produce goods and services in the quantity, quality, and price that people want. But for both the government and the market economy in the short term, increases in production of one good typically mean offsetting decreases somewhere else in the economy.

Confronting Objections to the Economic Approach

It's one thing to understand the economic approach to decision-making and another thing to feel comfortable applying it. The sources of discomfort typically fall into two categories: that people don't act in the way that fits the economics model, and that even if people did act that way, they should try not to. Let's consider these arguments in turn.

A First Objection: People, Firms, and Society Don't Act Like This

The economic approach to decision-making seems to require more information than most individuals possess and more careful decision-making than most individuals actually display. After all, do you or any of your friends draw a budget constraint and mutter to yourself about maximizing utility before you head to the shopping mall? Do members of the U.S. Congress contemplate production possibilities frontiers before they vote on the federal budget? The messy ways in which people and societies actually decide doesn't much resemble neat budget constraints or smoothly curving production possibilities frontiers.

However, the economics approach can be a useful way to analyze and understand the trade-offs of economic decisions even if it doesn't describe how those decisions are actually made. To appreciate this point, imagine for a moment that you are playing basketball, dribbling to the right, and throwing a bounce-pass to the left to a teammate who is running toward the basket. A physicist or engineer could work out the correct speed and trajectory for the pass, given the different movements involved and the weight and bounciness of the ball. But when you're playing basketball, you don't perform any of these calculations. You just pass the ball, and if you're a good player, you will do so with high accuracy. Someone might argue: "The scientist's formula of the bounce-pass requires a far greater knowledge of physics and far more specific information about speeds of movement and weights than the basketball player actually has, so it must be an unrealistic description of how basketball passes are actually made." This reaction would be wrongheaded. The fact that a good player can throw the ball accurately because of practice and skill, without making a physics calculation, doesn't mean that the physics calculation is meaningless or incorrect.

Similarly, from an economic point of view, someone who goes shopping for groceries every week has a great deal of practice with how to purchase the combination of goods that will provide that person with utility, even if the shopper doesn't phrase decisions in terms of a budget constraint. Government institutions may work imperfectly and slowly, but in general, a democratic form of government feels pressure from voters and social institutions to make the choices that are widely preferred by people in that society. Thus, when thinking about the economic actions of groups of people, firms, and society, it is reasonable as a first approximation to analyze them with the tools of economic analysis.

A Second Objection: People, Firms, and Society Shouldn't Do This

The economics approach portrays people as self-interested. For some critics of this approach, even if self-interest is an accurate description of how people behave, these behaviors are not moral. Instead, the critics argue that people should be taught to care more deeply about others. Economists offer several answers to this concern.

First, economics is not a form of moral instruction. Rather, it seeks to describe economic behavior as it actually exists. Philosophers draw a distinction between **positive statements**, which describe the world as it is, and **normative statements**, which describe how the world should be. In the study of economics, positive and normative arguments often blend into each other: for example, if an economist analyzes a proposal for building a subway system in a certain city and finds that the benefits are higher than the costs, then is this study a positive analysis that merely states what *will* happen or a normative analysis that describes what *should* happen? But even if the line between positive and normative statements isn't always crystal clear, economic analysis does try to remain rooted in the study of the actual people who inhabit the actual economy. Yes, if the world were populated by saints, the economy would look different. But it isn't.

Second, self-interested behavior and profit-seeking can be labeled with other names, such as "personal choice" and "freedom." The ability to make personal choices about buying, working, and saving is an important personal freedom. Some people may choose high-pressure, high-paying jobs so that they can earn and spend a lot of money. Others may earn a lot of money and give it to charity or spend it on their friends and family. Others may devote themselves to a career that can require a great deal of time, energy,

positive statements:
Statements that describe the world as it is.

normative statements:
Statements that describe how the world should be.

The Budget Constraint and the Production Possibilities Frontier

When you study economics, you may feel buried under an avalanche of diagrams: diagrams in the text, diagrams in the lectures, diagrams in the problems, diagrams on exams. Your goal should be to recognize the common underlying logic and pattern of the diagrams, not to memorize each of the individual diagrams.

This chapter uses only one basic diagram, although it is presented with different sets of labels. The consumption choice budget constraint, the labor-leisure budget constraint, and the intertemporal choice budget constraint for individuals, along with the production possibilities frontier for society as a whole, are all the same basic diagram. The exhibit shows an individual budget constraint and a production possibilities frontier for two goods, Good 1 and Good 2. This kind of diagram always illustrates three basic themes: scarcity, trade-offs, and economic efficiency.

The first theme is scarcity. It is not feasible to have unlimited amounts of both goods. Budget constraints can shift, either as a result of movements of income or of prices. Production possibilities frontiers can shift, too, either as a national economy expands or as the trade-offs between the two goods shift. But even if the budget constraint or a PPF shifts, scarcity remains—just at a different level.

The second theme is trade-offs. As depicted in the budget constraint or the production possibilities frontier, it is necessary to give up some of one good to gain more of the other good. The details of this trade-off vary. In a budget constraint, the trade-off is determined by the relative prices of the goods: that is, the relative price of two goods in the consumption choice budget constraint; the relative price of labor and leisure (the wage) in the labor-leisure budget constraint; and the

relative price of present and future consumption (the principal saved plus the interest rate or rate of return) in the intertemporal choice budget constraint. These trade-offs appear as a straight line. However, the trade-offs in many production possibilities frontiers are represented by a curved line because the law of diminishing returns holds that as resources are added to an area, the marginal gains tend to diminish. But regardless of the specific shape, trade-offs remain.

The third theme is economic efficiency or getting the most benefit from scarce resources. All choices on the production possibilities frontier show productive efficiency because in such cases, there is no way to increase the quantity of one good without decreasing the quantity of the other. Similarly, when an individual makes a choice along a budget constraint, there is no way to increase the quantity of one good without decreasing the quantity of the other. The choice on a production possibilities set that is socially preferred, or the choice on an individual's budget constraint that is personally preferred, will display allocative efficiency.

The basic budget constraint/production possibilities frontier diagram will recur throughout this book. Some examples include using these trade-off diagrams to analyze one source of the gains from international trade and to examine the trade-offs between environmental protection and economic output, between equality of incomes and economic output, and the macroeconomic trade-off between consumption and investment. Don't be confused by the different labels. The budget constraint/production possibilities frontier diagram is always just a tool for thinking carefully about scarcity, trade-offs, and efficiency in a particular situation.

THE TRADE-OFF DIAGRAM

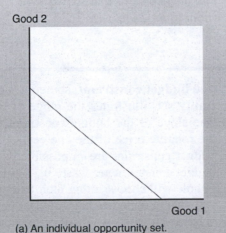

(a) An individual opportunity set.

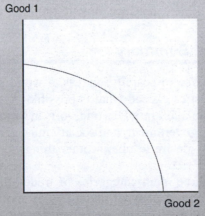

(b) A social production possibilities frontier.

and expertise but does not offer high financial rewards, like being an elementary school teacher or a social worker. Still others may choose a job that does not take lots of their time or provide a high level of income, but still leaves time for family, friends, and contemplation. Some people may prefer to work for a large company; others might want to start their own business. People's freedom to make their own economic choices has a moral value worth respecting.

Third, self-interested behavior can lead to positive social results. For example, when people work hard to make a living, they create economic output. Consumers who are looking for the best deals will encourage businesses to offer goods and services that meet their needs. Adam Smith, writing in the *Wealth of Nations*, christened this property the "invisible hand." In describing how consumers and producers interact in a market economy, Smith wrote:

> Every individual . . . generally neither intends to promote the public interest, nor knows how much he is promoting it. He intends only his own security, only his own gain. And he is in this led by an invisible hand to promote an end which was no part of his intention. By pursuing his own interest he frequently promotes that of society more effectually than when he really intends to promote it.

The metaphor of the invisible hand suggests the remarkable possibility that broader social good can emerge from selfish individual actions.

Fourth, even people who focus on their own self-interest in the economic part of their life often set aside their own narrow self-interest in other parts of life. For example, you might focus on your own self-interest when asking your employer for a raise or negotiating to buy a car. But then you might turn around and focus on other people when you volunteer to read stories at the local library, help a friend move to a new apartment, or donate money to a charity. Thus, self-interest is a reasonable starting point for analyzing many economic decisions, without needing to imply that people never do anything that is not in their own immediate self-interest.

Facing Scarcity and Making Trade-offs

The study of economics is rooted in a fundamental insight about the human condition. The world we live in is a place of scarcity, whether measured in terms of time, money, natural resources, or material goods. As a result, people must face trade-offs and make choices. The main economic trade-offs for individuals are their decisions about what to consume, how much to work, and how much to save. For society as a whole and for government decision-makers, the task is to use scarce resources as efficiently as possible to meet people's needs. Economics delves into the questions of how individuals, firms, and government will interact, and thus into the decisions that society will make about what to produce, how to produce, and for whom to produce.

Key Concepts and Summary

1. The real world is one of scarcity: that is, a world in which people's desires exceed what is possible. As a result, economic behavior involves trade-offs in which individuals, firms, government, and society must give up things that they desire to obtain other things that they desire more.

2. Individuals face three main categories of trade-offs: the consumption choice of what quantities of goods to consume, the labor-leisure choice of what quantity of hours to work, and the intertemporal choices that involve costs in the present and benefits in the future, or benefits in the present and costs in the future.

3. The **budget constraint**, sometimes called the **opportunity set**, illustrates the range of choices available. The slope of the budget constraint is determined by the relative price of the choices. Choices beyond the budget constraint are impossible. Choices inside the budget constraint are wasteful.

4. People will choose along their budget constraints in a way that maximizes their satisfaction or **utility**, which is based on their own distinctive personal preferences.

5. An interest rate has three components: the **risk premium** to cover the risk of not being repaid, the rate of expected **inflation**, and the **time value of money**, as

compensation for waiting to spend. The formula for how **compound interest** accumulates over time is:

Future amount = (Present amount)
$$\times \ (1 + \text{Interest rate})^{\text{number of years}}$$

6. **Opportunity cost** measures cost by what is given up in exchange. Sometimes opportunity cost can be measured in money, but it is often useful to consider whether time should be included as well, or to measure it in terms of the actual resources that must be given up.

7. Most economic decisions and trade-offs are not all-or-nothing. Instead, they involve **marginal analysis**, which means they are about decisions on the margin, involving a little more or a little less.

8. The **law of diminishing marginal utility** points out that as a person receives more of something—whether it is a specific good or another resource—the additional marginal gains tend to become smaller.

9. Because **sunk costs** occurred in the past and cannot be recovered, they should be disregarded in making current decisions.

10. A **production possibilities frontier** defines a set of choices faced by society as a whole. The shape of the PPF is typically curved outward, rather than straight. Choices outside the PPF are unattainable, and choices inside the PPF are wasteful. Over time, a growing economy will tend to shift the PPF outwards.

11. The **law of diminishing returns** holds that as increments of additional resources are devoted to producing something, the marginal increase in output will become smaller and smaller.

12. All choices along a production possibilities frontier display **productive efficiency**; that is, it is impossible to use society's resources to produce more of one good without decreasing production of the other good. The specific choice along a production possibilities frontier that reflects the mix of goods that society prefers is the choice with **allocative efficiency**.

13. **Positive statements** describe the world as it is, while **normative statements** describe how the world should be. Even when economics analyzes the gains and losses from various events or policies, and thus draws normative conclusions about how the world should be, the analysis of economics is rooted in a positive analysis of how people, firms, and government actually behave, not how they should behave.

Review Questions

1. Explain why scarcity leads to trade-offs.
2. Name the three main categories of economic trade-offs that individuals face.
3. What determines the slope of the consumption choice budget constraint? The labor-leisure budget constraint? The intertemporal budget constraint?
4. Explain why individuals make choices that are directly on the budget constraint, rather than inside the budget constraint or outside it.
5. Does the economic approach specify what choices people should make? Why or why not?
6. What does it mean to "maximize utility"?
7. What are the three components of the interest rate?
8. What is the formula for how compound interest accumulates over time?
9. What is opportunity cost?
10. What is the law of diminishing marginal utility?
11. What are sunk costs?
12. What does a production possibilities frontier illustrate?
13. Why is a production possibilities frontier typically drawn as a curve, rather than a straight line?
14. Explain why societies cannot make a choice above their production possibilities frontier and should not make a choice below it.
15. What are diminishing marginal returns?
16. What is productive efficiency? Allocative efficiency?
17. What's the difference between a positive and a normative statement?
18. Is the economic model of decision-making intended as a literal description of how individuals, firms, and the government actually make decisions?

International Trade

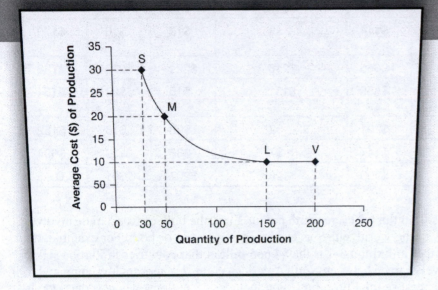

National economies are becoming more intimately interconnected in the process known as globalization. From 1970 to 2015, the size of the world economy as measured by production of goods and services almost quadrupled, and world exports—that is, goods produced in one country but sold in another country—rose by a multiple of more than 10. Similarly, the size of the U.S. economy more than tripled from 1970 to 2015, and U.S. exports rose by a multiple of more than 11. When trade as measured by exports is growing faster than the economy as a whole, international economic forces will have a greater effect on national economies. Reminders of international trade are all around. As a consumer, the food on your table might include fresh fruit from Chile, cheese from France, or bottled water from Scotland. Your phone might have been made in Sweden or Finland. The clothes you wear might be designed in Italy and manufactured in China. The toy you give to a child might have come from India. The car you drive might be from Japan, Germany, or Korea. The gasoline in the tank might be from Saudi Arabia, Mexico, or Nigeria. As a worker, if your job involves farming, machinery, airplanes, cars, scientific instruments, or many other technology-related industries, the odds are good that a hearty proportion of the sales of your employer—and hence the money that pays your salary—comes from export sales.

Exhibit 3-1 shows the volume of international merchandise trade (i.e., trade in goods) between countries in different regions of the world. The columns of the table show the region of the country where trade started; the rows show the region of the country where the exports ended up. Thus, the first entry in the top column shows that $1,251 billion in exports originated in one country in North America and went to another country in North America. The first entry in the second column shows that $214 billion in exports traveled from countries in North America to countries in South and Central America. Most of the region names should be self-explanatory, but one that may be unclear is the Commonwealth of Independent States, which includes Russia, Ukraine, and other countries that before 1991 were republics of the Soviet Union.

EXHIBIT 3-1 The Network of World Trade in Merchandise, 2014 (in billions of U.S. dollars)

The rows of the table show where trade is originating; the columns show the destination of trade. For example, the second entry in the first row shows that $214 billion in merchandise was originated in North America and was sold in South and Central America.

Origin	Destination						
	North America	South and Central America	Europe	Commonwealth of Independent States	Africa	Middle East	Asia
North America	$1,251	$214	$379	$17	$43	$79	$504
South and Central America	$172	$179	$114	$9	$18	$16	$170
Europe	$540	$119	$4,665	$218	$221	$229	$738
Commonwealth of Independent States	$28	$7	$385	$131	$15	$22	$134
Africa	$39	$28	$201	$2	$98	$18	$152
Middle East	$99	$11	$147	$7	$36	$113	$694
Asia	$1,064	$185	$900	$126	$207	$301	$3,093

Several patterns from this table are worth noting. First, the bulk of world trade involves high-income areas of the world, either as exporters, importers, or both. For example, the single biggest number in Exhibit 3-1 is the $4,665 billion that countries in Europe sell to each other. The level of trade between North American countries appears low compared to Europe, but this is because the European Union includes 28 nations, whereas the trade in the North American region is between the United States, Canada, and Mexico. Remember, exports from Germany to Sweden count as international trade, but sales from California to New York would not be counted in this table, since they occur within the U.S. economy.

Second, trade between high-income regions and low-income regions is fairly extensive. Perhaps the most vivid example of this point is trade of $3,093 billion between the nations of Asia, which is the second-highest number in Exhibit 3-1. The region of Asia includes the high-income economies like Japan and Korea, upper-middle-income countries like China and Thailand, lower-middle-income countries like Indonesia and Vietnam, and low-income countries like Cambodia. More generally, high-income regions of the world are important as markets for other regions. The countries of Africa, for example, export roughly twice as much to the European Union as they do to other countries of Africa. The countries of South and Central America sell as much to North America as they sell to one another.

Finally, trade between some regions is very low, for example, between Africa and South and Central America, or between the Middle East and the Commonwealth of Independent States. Indeed, some regions appear to have relatively few connections to other regions of the global economy.

The American statesman Benjamin Franklin (1706–1790) once wrote: "No nation was ever ruined by trade." Many economists would phrase their attitudes toward international trade in an even more positive manner. The circumstantial evidence that international trade confers overall benefits on the economy is strong. Trade has accompanied economic growth in the United States and around the world. Many of the national economies that have shown the most rapid growth in the last few decades—for example, Japan, South Korea, China, and India—have also dramatically expanded their international trade. There is no modern example of a country that has shut itself off from world trade and still become prosperous.

This chapter will explore the reasons that international trade provides economic gains. The discussion will draw on themes and analytic tools developed in earlier chapters. For example, Chapter 1 suggested three reasons why the division of labor and specialization, followed by trade, can increase output among individuals: specialization allows the parties to produce according to their advantages; it encourages learning and innovation; and it allows taking advantage of economies of scale. This chapter will spell out in detail how these three reasons create benefits in international trade. The production possibility frontier (PPF), introduced in Chapter 2, will be used to analyze how all countries can benefit from trade.

But although international trade provides economic gains, it is also a powerful and disruptive force. World exports of goods and services totaled over $23 trillion dollars in 2015. Domestic producers of goods often feel threatened by competition from those trillions of dollars of imports flowing into their country. Workers fear that their jobs may be at risk when foreign producers sell within their country. These fears create an awkward situation for politicians, who both want to embrace the benefits of international trade and also to block international trade from causing disruption for the firms and workers in their country. Chapter 6 will discuss public policy with regard to international trade, which often consists of a contradictory mix of international treaties to encourage trade and national actions to limit trade.

Absolute Advantage

Perhaps the most obvious case where international trade can benefit the countries that participate is the situation in which each country has a particular product that it can produce relatively cheaply compared to other countries. For example, finding oil in Saudi Arabia is pretty much just a matter of drilling a hole, but producing oil in other countries can require considerable exploration and costly technologies for drilling and extraction—if indeed other countries have any oil at all. The United States has some of the richest farmland in the world, which makes it relatively easier to grow corn and wheat here than in many other countries—like the deserts of Saudi Arabia, for example. Brazil and Colombia have climates especially suited for growing coffee. Chile and Zambia have some of the world's richest copper mines. When each country has a product that it can produce relatively cheaply, then all countries can benefit from producing that product and trading with each other.

A Numerical Example of Absolute Advantage and Trade

To illustrate the potential benefits of trade between two countries that each have a product that they produce more cheaply than the other, consider a hypothetical world with two countries, Saudi Arabia and the United States, and two products, oil and corn. Saudi Arabia can produce oil more cheaply, while the United States can produce corn more cheaply. Exhibit 3-2 illustrates the advantages of the two countries, expressed in terms of how much a worker can produce in each country. A worker in Saudi Arabia can produce six barrels of oil, while a worker in the United States can produce only two barrels of oil. However, a worker in the United States can produce eight bushels of corn, while a worker in Saudi Arabia can produce only one bushel of corn.

When one nation can produce a product at lower cost relative to another nation, it is said to have an **absolute advantage** in producing that product. In this example, Saudi Arabia has an absolute advantage in the production of oil, and the United States has an absolute advantage in the production of corn. Two nations that each have an absolute advantage in certain products can both benefit if each nation specializes (at least to some extent) in the area of its absolute advantage and then the nations trade with each other.

absolute advantage: When one nation can produce a product at lower cost relative to another nation.

EXHIBIT 3-2 Absolute Advantage: How Much Can One Worker Produce?

A worker in Saudi Arabia can produce more oil, by a margin of 6 barrels to 2 barrels. However, a worker in the United States can produce more corn, by a margin of 8 bushels to 1 bushel.

	Saudi Arabia	United States
One worker can produce	6 barrels of oil	2 barrels of oil
One worker can produce	1 bushel of corn	8 bushels of corn

EXHIBIT 3-3
Production Possibilities Frontiers and Absolute Advantage

The tables show several points along the production possibilities frontiers for each country, based on the numbers for what workers produce in Exhibit 3-2 and assuming 40 Saudi workers and 80 U.S. workers. Our assumption here is that point A in the two figures is the choice that each country would most prefer, given its production possibilities in the absence of trade. Each country would prefer a point like B in the two figures, with more of both goods, but in a world without trade, a choice like B is impossible. Through specialization and trade, however, a point like B becomes possible for both countries.

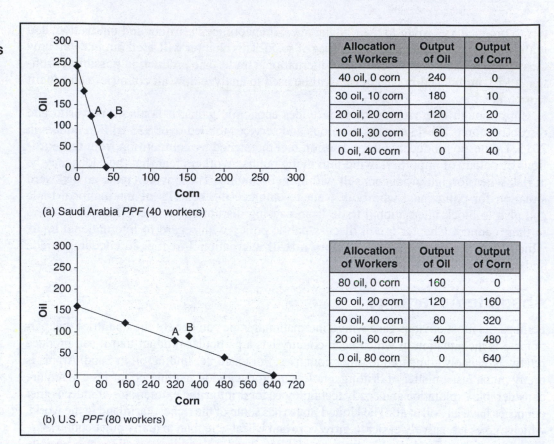

(a) Saudi Arabia *PPF* (40 workers)

Allocation of Workers	Output of Oil	Output of Corn
40 oil, 0 corn	240	0
30 oil, 10 corn	180	10
20 oil, 20 corn	120	20
10 oil, 30 corn	60	30
0 oil, 40 corn	0	40

(b) U.S. *PPF* (80 workers)

Allocation of Workers	Output of Oil	Output of Corn
80 oil, 0 corn	160	0
60 oil, 20 corn	120	160
40 oil, 40 corn	80	320
20 oil, 60 corn	40	480
0 oil, 80 corn	0	640

The production possibilities frontier provides an analytical tool for illustrating this point. Exhibit 3-3 presents two production possibility frontiers for the possible levels of production in a world without trade, one for Saudi Arabia and one for the United States, based on the assumption that the economy of Saudi Arabia has 40 workers and the U.S. economy has 80 workers. If all 40 workers in the Saudi economy produced oil, that country could produce 240 barrels (i.e., 40 × 6 = 240); if all the Saudi workers focused on corn, that economy could produce 40 bushels (40 × 1 = 40). The table next to the figure shows some of the in-between choices, and the points from the table are graphed on the production possibilities frontier. Meanwhile, if the U.S. economy devoted all 80 workers to oil, it could produce 160 barrels (i.e., 80 × 2 = 160), but if it devoted all 80 workers to corn, it could produce 640 bushels (80 × 8 = 640).

The slope of the production possibility frontier is determined by the opportunity cost of expanding production of one good, measured by how much of the other good would be lost. The information in Exhibit 3-2 can be interpreted in terms of opportunity costs. For example, in the U.S. economy the opportunity cost of producing 2 barrels of oil, which requires one worker, is the loss of the 8 bushels of corn that the worker could have produced otherwise. Thus, in the U.S. production possibility frontier in Exhibit 3-3, every increase in oil production of 1 barrel reflects a decrease of 4 bushels of corn. In the economy of Saudi Arabia, the opportunity cost of producing 1 bushel of corn, which requires one more worker, is the loss of the 6 barrels of oil that workers could otherwise have produced. The slope of the Saudi production possibility frontier shows that every rise of 1 bushel of corn leads to a fall of 6 barrels of oil.

For the sake of the argument, let's say that before trade occurs, the most desired point for each nation—as determined by the preferences of its citizens—is the point halfway down each production possibility frontier, shown as point A on each production possibility frontier. Thus, in the world before trade, the economy of Saudi Arabia will devote 20 workers to each product, and produce 120 barrels of oil and 20 bushels of corn, while the U.S. economy devotes 40 workers to each product and produces 80 barrels of oil and 320 bushels of corn. Of course, each nation would prefer a choice like point B, which

EXHIBIT 3-4 How Specialization by Absolute Advantage Expands Output

The first two columns show the quantity of oil and corn that would be produced in each country, at its preferred point *A* as shown in Exhibit 3-3 before trade occurs. The last two columns show output after specialization has occurred, so that each country is producing only one good. The bottom "TOTAL" row shows the combined production of each good. The total quantity produced of each good is greater than in the situation before specialization, which is what allows both countries, after trade, to consume more of both goods. As a result, both countries can be better off.

	Quantity Produced before Trade		Quantity Produced after Specialization	
	Oil	*Corn*	*Oil*	*Corn*
Saudi Arabia	120	20	240	0
United States	80	320	0	640
TOTAL	200	340	240	640

offers more of both goods, but since choice B is above the production possibility frontier, that choice isn't possible for either country.

However, if each of the two nations specializes in its area of absolute advantage and then trades, it becomes possible to expand global production of both goods. Exhibit 3-4 provides the calculations. The table shows output of oil and corn in the two countries before trade, and by adding up the output in the countries, it shows global output of the two goods. Now assume that Saudi Arabia decides to specialize in its absolute advantage and produce only oil, thus producing 240 barrels of oil, and the United States specializes in its absolute advantage in farming, producing 640 bushels of corn. When each nation specializes in this way, Exhibit 3-4 shows that the total global output of both products rises. It becomes possible, with trade, to consume at higher levels than would have been possible without trade.

Consider the trading positions of the United States and Saudi Arabia after they have specialized in their areas of absolute advantage, so that the United States is producing 640 bushels of corn and zero oil, while Saudi Arabia is producing 240 barrels of oil and zero corn. If the United States can trade an amount of corn *less than* 320 bushels and receive in exchange an amount of oil *greater than* 80 barrels, it will have more of both goods than it did in the situation with no trade at all. Similarly, if Saudi Arabia can trade an amount of oil less than 120 barrels and receive in exchange an amount of corn greater than 20 bushels, it will have more of both goods than it did before specialization and trade. Exhibit 3-5 illustrates the range of trades that would benefit both sides. Any trade where the United States exports more than 20 bushels of corn but less than 320 bushels of corn, and receives in exchange imports from Saudi Arabia of at least 80 barrels of oil but no more than 120 barrels of oil, will benefit both sides. As a specific example, a trade where the United States exports 200 bushels of corn to Saudi Arabia and Saudi Arabia exports 100 barrels of oil to the United States would allow both countries to consume more of both goods than they could before specialized production and trade occurred.

EXHIBIT 3-5 The Range of Trades That Benefit Both the United States and Saudi Arabia

The U.S. Economy, after Specialization, Will Benefit If It:	The Saudi Arabian Economy, after Specialization, Will Benefit If It:
Exports no more than 320 bushels of corn in exchange for	Imports at least 20 bushels of corn in exchange for
Imports of at least 80 barrels of oil	Exports of less than 120 barrels of oil

Trade and Opportunity Cost

The underlying reason why trade can benefit both sides is rooted in the concept of opportunity cost. If the United States wants to expand domestic production of oil in a world without trade, its opportunity cost (based on the numbers in Exhibit 3-2) is that it must give up 4 bushels of corn for every 1 additional barrel of oil. If the United States could find a way to give up *less than* 4 bushels of corn to receive 1 barrel of oil, it would be better off. Thus, any trade where the United States gives up less than 320 bushels of corn to receive at least 80 barrels of oil—notice the 4:1 ratio—makes the United States better off. By specializing in corn production and then trading with Saudi Arabia for oil, the U.S. economy can possess more corn and oil at a cheaper opportunity cost than its own domestic production allows.

The same insight holds for Saudi Arabia. If Saudi Arabia wishes to expand domestic production of corn in a world without trade, then based on its opportunity costs (as shown in Exhibit 3-2), it must give up 6 barrels of oil for every 1 additional bushel of corn. If Saudi Arabia could find a way to give up less than 6 barrels of oil for an additional bushel of corn (or equivalently, to receive more than 1 bushel of corn for 6 units of oil), it would be better off. Thus, any trade where Saudi Arabia can export no more than 120 barrels of oil in exchange for at least 20 units of corn—notice again that the ratio of 120:20 is the country's domestic opportunity cost of 6:1—will make the country better off.

Cost is measured as opportunity cost. In this example, the opportunity cost of 1 bushel of corn is only 1/4 barrel of oil in the United States, but the opportunity cost of 1 bushel of corn is 6 barrels of oil in Saudi Arabia. Similarly, the opportunity cost of 1 barrel of oil in the United States is 4 bushels of corn, but the opportunity cost of 1 barrel of oil in Saudi Arabia is 1/6 bushel of corn. In effect, trade lets each country take advantage of the lower opportunity cost of production in the other country. This example would reach the same general conclusion showing benefits from specialization and trade if the number of workers in the two economies was altered, or if the original starting point was not assumed to be point *A* in Exhibit 3-3, but instead involved dividing up the labor in some way other than having half the workers producing each good.

Limitations of the Numerical Example

This demonstration of how both nations can benefit from specializing in their absolute advantage and trading has some limitations.

First, the example does not explain how the extra output of oil and corn will be divided up. It describes a range of trades that can benefit both sides, but it doesn't say who will receive what share of the total benefit. Perhaps the two countries will split the extra output equally. Perhaps the U.S. economy will get most of the extra output, and the Saudi economy only a little bit. Perhaps the reverse will be true. In the real economy, the price at which corn exchanges for oil will be determined by demand and supply (discussed in

Different Ways of Presenting Absolute Advantage

There are several different ways of presenting information that shows absolute advantage in producing at lower costs. Exhibit 3-2 showed the different quantities that a single worker could produce. Exhibit 3-6 shows the different number of workers needed to produce a fixed quantity of output. Other alternatives would be to measure work with hours, instead of workers, and to say how many hours it takes to produce a unit of a good or how many units could be produced in an hour. Don't be confused by the different labels in these kinds of tables. Focus on the underlying economic meaning: which nation can produce a certain good more cheaply, which means producing either the same amount with a lower level of inputs or producing more with the same level of inputs If in a certain nation a single worker produces more of a product, relative to the other country, or if it takes fewer workers to produce a fixed amount of a product, relative to the other country, then that nation has an absolute advantage in producing that product.

Chapter 4), which will lead to a specific price and quantity for each good. This example shows only that both countries *can* be better off with specialization and trade, not *how much* each country is better off.

Second, this example has only two hypothetical countries and two goods, while the real world has over 200 countries and tens of thousands of goods. However, the example remains useful as a model that illustrates a key underlying principle: Differences in opportunity costs can allow trade to benefit all participants.

Third, this example assumes that the opportunity costs of trading oil for corn production, or vice versa, are always constant in both countries. This premise simplifies the calculations. In the real world, countries will typically find that they have a variety of resources that are better-suited or worse-suited to producing different products. For example, Saudi Arabia has some relatively fertile land and some land where drilling for oil is more costly. Conversely, the United States has some areas of poor farmland, as well as areas where oil is more accessible. In numerical examples with constant opportunity costs, it often makes sense to specialize in the production of just one product. But in the real world, it will make sense to give up only on the more costly ways of producing certain products, and the specialization in one product won't be so extreme.

A skeptic about the gains from international trade might start asking other questions at this point. What if one nation becomes dependent on the other for oil or food, and then the exporter cuts off the supply? What if oil workers in the United States lose jobs when oil is imported from Saudi Arabia and farmers in Saudi Arabia lose jobs when corn is imported from the United States? These questions are good ones, and they will be taken up, along with many other questions, in the discussion of public policies about international trade in Chapter 6. But first, let's continue painting the picture of how international trade can provide economic benefits.

Comparative Advantage

The concept of absolute advantage is based on the assumption that each nation has a cost advantage in producing a certain product. But what happens to the possibilities for trade if one country, typically a high-income country with well-educated workers, technologically advanced equipment, and the most up-to-date production processes, can produce all products more cheaply than a low-income country? If the high-income country has a cost advantage in all products, then it may seem as if the low-income country would have nothing to trade. However, one of the most powerful insights in economic analysis, developed by the famous English economist David Ricardo (1772–1823) early in the nineteenth century, points out that even when one country has an absolute advantage in all products, trade can still benefit both sides.

The First Wave of Globalization

A second wave of globalization began in the second half of the twentieth century. But the first wave of globalization started in the nineteenth century and lasted up to the beginning of World War I. Over that time, global exports as a share of global GDP rose from less than 1% of GDP in 1820 to 9% of GDP in 1913. As the Nobel Prize-winning economist Paul Krugman of Princeton University wrote in 1995:

> It is a late-twentieth-century conceit that we invented the global economy just yesterday. In fact, world markets achieved an impressive degree of integration during the second half of the nineteenth century. Indeed, if one wants a specific date for the beginning of a truly global economy, one might well choose 1869, the year in which both the Suez Canal and the Union Pacific railroad were completed. By the eve of the First World War, steamships and railroads had created markets for standardized commodities, like wheat and wool, that were fully global in their reach. Even the global flow of information was better than modern observers, focused on electronic technology, tend to realize: the first submarine telegraph cable was laid under the Atlantic in 1858, and by 1900 all of the world's major economic regions could effectively communicate instantaneously.

This first wave of globalization crashed to a halt in the first half of the twentieth century. World War I severed many economic connections. During the Great Depression of the 1930s, many nations misguidedly tried to fix their own economies by reducing foreign trade with others. World War II further hindered international trade. Global flows of goods and financial capital rebuilt themselves only slowly after World War II. It was not until the early 1980s that global economic forces again became as important, relative to the size of the world economy, as they were before World War I.

Identifying Comparative Advantage

Consider the situation described in Exhibit 3-6 of costs of production in the United States and Mexico. In this example, it takes 4 U.S. workers to produce 1,000 pairs of shoes, but it takes 5 Mexican workers to do so. It takes 1 U.S. worker to produce 1,000 refrigerators, but it takes 4 Mexican workers to do so. In this example, the United States has an absolute advantage in productivity with regard to both shoes and refrigerators; that is, it takes fewer workers in the United States than in Mexico to produce both a given number of shoes and a given number of refrigerators. However, even in this case, Ricardo showed that both sides could benefit from trade.

Ricardo's insight was that even though the United States has an absolute advantage at producing both products with less labor, the United States does not produce both products more cheaply from an opportunity cost point of view. In Mexico, the opportunity cost of producing 1,000 extra pairs of shoes, and using the labor of 5 workers, means taking those 5 workers away from the production of refrigerators, where they would have produced 1,250 refrigerators. (Exhibit 3-6 shows that in Mexico it takes 4 workers to produce 1,000 refrigerators, so 5 workers would produce 1,250 refrigerators; that is, $5/4 \times 1,000$.)

EXHIBIT 3-6 Identifying Comparative Advantage

It takes fewer workers in the United States (4) to produce 1,000 pairs of shoes than it does in Mexico (5). It also takes fewer workers in the United States (1) to produce 1,000 refrigerators than it does in Mexico (4). Thus, the United States has an absolute advantage in the production of both goods. However, the comparative advantage of the United States—where its absolute advantage is relatively greatest—lies in refrigerators. The comparative advantage of Mexico—where its absolute disadvantage is relatively least—lies in shoes.

	United States	Mexico
Production	*Amount of Labor*	*Amount of Labor*
1,000 pairs of shoes	4 workers	5 workers
1,000 refrigerators	1 worker	4 workers

In the United States, the opportunity cost of producing an extra 1,000 pairs of shoes involves the labor of four workers, and moving those four workers away from refrigerator production has an opportunity cost of 4,000 refrigerators (i.e., one worker can produce 1,000 refrigerators in the United States, so 4 workers could produce 4,000). Measured in opportunity cost terms, it is cheaper to produce shoes in Mexico, where the opportunity cost is 1,250 refrigerators for every 1,000 shoes, and more expensive to produce shoes in the United States, where the opportunity cost of 1,000 pairs of shoes is 4,000 refrigerators.

Next consider the opportunity cost of producing refrigerators. Producing an extra 1,000 refrigerators in Mexico requires 4 workers. If those four workers are moved out of shoe production, the opportunity cost is 800 pairs of shoes (if it takes 5 Mexican workers to produce 1,000 pairs of shoes, than 4 workers can produce 800 shoes—4/5 × 1,000). Producing an extra 1,000 refrigerators in the United States, using one worker, would have an opportunity cost of only 250 pairs of shoes (i.e., if it takes 4 U.S. workers to make 1,000 pairs of shoes, then one worker can make 250 pairs). Measured in opportunity cost terms, producing 1,000 refrigerators is more expensive in Mexico, where it costs 800 pairs of shoes, and less expensive in the United States, where the opportunity cost is only 250 pairs of shoes.

A nation that can produce at a lower cost *when measured in terms of opportunity cost* is said to have a **comparative advantage**. Even though the United States has an absolute advantage in needing fewer workers to produce a given quantity of either shoes or refrigerators, Mexico has a comparative advantage in the production of shoes, and the United States has a comparative advantage in the production of refrigerators. Comparative advantage identifies the area where a producer's absolute advantage is greatest, or *where the producer's absolute disadvantage in productivity is least*. The United States can produce 1,000 shoes with four-fifths as many workers as Mexico (4 versus 5), but can produce 1,000 refrigerators with only one-quarter as many workers (1 versus 4). Thus, the comparative advantage of the United States, where its absolute productivity advantage is relatively greatest, lies with refrigerators, and Mexico's comparative advantage, where its absolute productivity disadvantage is least, is in the production of shoes.

comparative advantage: The goods in which a nation has its greatest productivity advantage or its smallest productivity disadvantage; also, the goods that a nation can produce at a lower cost when measured in terms of opportunity cost.

Mutually Beneficial Trade with Comparative Advantage

When nations increase production in their area of comparative advantage and trade with each other, both sides can benefit. Again, the production possibility frontier offers a useful tool. Consider a situation where the United States and Mexico each has 40 workers. The tables in Exhibit 3-7 show the level of output for different divisions of labor, using the figures for the productivity of labor given in Exhibit 3-6. For example, if the United States divides its labor so that 40 workers are making shoes, then since it takes 4 workers in the United States to make 1,000 shoes, a total of 10,000 shoes will be produced (if 4 workers can make 1,000 shoes, then 40 workers will make 10,000 shoes). If the 40 workers in the United States are making refrigerators, and each worker can produce 1,000 refrigerators, then a total of 40,000 refrigerators will be produced. The choices from the tables are graphed on the production possibility frontiers in Exhibit 3-7. As always, the slope of the production possibility frontier for each country is determined by the opportunity costs as labor is transferred from production of shoes to production of refrigerators, or vice versa.

Let's assume that in the situation before trade, each nation prefers to allocate half of its labor to production of each good, as shown at point A. Exhibit 3-8 shows the output of each good for each country and the total output for the two countries. Of course, both countries would prefer a choice like point B with more of both goods, but a choice like B that is above the production possibility frontier is impossible in a world without trade. (Choosing the halfway point is only to make a convenient example. The argument for how trade according to comparative advantage can benefit both parties works just the same if the nation's original choice is a point one-third of the way, or one-quarter of the way, or any choice between the endpoints of the production possibility frontier.)

Now, have each country transfer some amount of labor toward its area of comparative advantage. For example, the United States transfers 6 workers away from shoes

(a) U.S. *PPF* (40 workers)

How Many Workers Producing Each Good?	Output of Shoes	Output of Refrigerators
40 to shoes, 0 to refrigerators	10,000 pairs	0 refrigerators
30 to shoes, 10 to refrigerators	7,500 pairs	10,000 refrigerators
20 to shoes, 20 to refrigerators	5,000 pairs	20,000 refrigerators
10 to shoes, 30 to refrigerators	2,500 pairs	30,000 refrigerators
0 to shoes, 40 to refrigerators	0 pairs	40,000 refrigerators

(b) Mexico *PPF* (40 workers)

How Many Workers Producing Each Good?	Output of Shoes	Output of Refrigerators
40 to shoes, 0 to refrigerators	8,000 pairs	0 refrigerators
30 to shoes, 10 to refrigerators	6,000 pairs	2,500 refrigerators
20 to shoes, 20 to refrigerators	4,000 pairs	5,000 refrigerators
10 to shoes, 30 to refrigerators	2,000 pairs	7,500 refrigerators
0 to shoes, 40 to refrigerators	0 pairs	10,000 refrigerators

EXHIBIT 3-7 Comparative Advantage with Production Possibility Frontiers

The tables show several points along the production possibilities frontiers for each country, based on the numbers for what workers produce in Exhibit 3-6 and assuming 40 workers for each country. In the absence of trade, let's assume that each country would most prefer point A, given its production possibilities. While a point like B provides more of both goods, in a world without trade, a choice like B is impossible. Through specialization and trade, a point like B becomes possible for both countries, showing that both countries can benefit from trade.

EXHIBIT 3-8 Calculating Gains from Trade with Comparative Advantage

This table shows the total production of shoes and refrigerators before trade. It also shows total production after the United States transfers 6 workers from shoes to refrigerators and Mexico transfers 10 workers from refrigerators to shoes through specialization.

	Production before Trade		Production after Specialization	
	Shoes	Refrigerators	Shoes	Refrigerators
United States	5,000	20,000	5,000 – 1,500	20,000 + 6,000
Mexico	4,000	5,000	4,000 + 2,000	5,000 – 2,500
Total	9,000	25,000	9,500	28,500

Choosing Numbers So Comparative Advantage Examples Work

In the example in the text, why have the United States move 6 workers from shoes to refrigerators, and why have Mexico move 10 workers from refrigerators and shoes? Why 6? Why 10?

To show that specializing according to comparative advantage can benefit all parties, the shift in production must allow total combined production of both goods to increase. But here's a potential problem: If the United States shifts an equal amount of labor away from shoes that Mexico shifts toward shoes, then overall combined production of shoes will decline—because the U.S. economy has an absolute advantage in shoe production. Thus, Mexico must shift more labor toward shoes than the United States shifts away from shoes to make up for its absolute productivity advantage in shoes, so that overall combined production of shoes will increase. Having Mexico shift 10 workers toward shoes when the United States shifts 6 workers away from shoes will work for this purpose. So will any combination of numbers where the ratio of Mexican labor toward shoes to U.S. labor away from shoes is at least 5/4 to make up for the fact that it takes 5 workers in Mexico to produce the same number of shoes that takes 4 U.S. workers.

and toward producing refrigerators. As a result, U.S. production of shoes decreases by 1,500 units ($6/4 \times 1,000$), while its production of refrigerators increases by 6,000 (i.e., $6/1 \times 1,000$). Mexico also moves production toward its area of comparative advantage, transferring 10 workers away from refrigerators and toward production of shoes. As a result, production of refrigerators in Mexico falls by 2,500 ($10/4 \times 1,000$), but production of shoes increases by 2,000 pairs ($10/5 \times 1,000$). Notice that when both countries shift toward their comparative advantage, their combined production of both goods rises, as shown in Exhibit 3-8. The reduction of shoe production by 1,500 pairs in the United States is more than offset by the gain of 2,000 pairs of shoes in Mexico, while the reduction of 2,500 refrigerators in Mexico is more than offset by the additional 6,000 refrigerators produced in the United States.

This numerical example illustrates the remarkable insight of comparative advantage: Even when one country has an absolute advantage in all goods and another country has an absolute disadvantage in all goods, both countries can still benefit from trade. Even though the United States has an absolute advantage in producing both refrigerators and shoes, it makes economic sense for the United States to specialize more in refrigerators, where it has a comparative advantage, and to import some shoes instead. Conversely, even though Mexico has an absolute disadvantage in both refrigerators and shoes, it can still play an active and productive role in world trade by focusing on its comparative advantage in shoes.

How Opportunity Cost Sets the Boundaries of Trade

This example shows that both parties can benefit from specializing in their comparative advantage and trading. By using the opportunity costs in this example, it is possible to identify the range of possible trades that would benefit each side.

Mexico started out before specialization and trade by producing 4,000 pairs of shoes and 5,000 refrigerators. Then in the numerical example given, Mexico shifted production toward its comparative advantage and produced 6,000 shoes but only 2,500 refrigerators. Thus, if Mexico can export no more than 2,000 pairs of shoes in exchange for imports of at least 2,500 refrigerators, then it will be able to consume more of both goods than before trade and it will be unambiguously better off. Conversely, the United States started off before specialization and trade producing 5,000 pairs of shoes and 20,000 refrigerators. In the numerical example given, it then shifted toward comparative advantage, producing only 3,500 shoes but 26,000 refrigerators. If the United States can export no more than 6,000 refrigerators in exchange for imports of at least 1,500 pairs of shoes, then it will be able to consume more of both goods and will be unambiguously better off. The range of trades that can benefit both nations is shown in Exhibit 3-9. For example, a trade where

EXHIBIT 3-9 The Range of Trades That Will Benefit Both the United States and Mexico

The U.S. Economy, after Specialization, Will Benefit If It:	The Mexican Economy, after Specialization, Will Benefit If It:
Exports Fewer than 6,000 refrigerators in exchange for	*Imports* at least 2,500 refrigerators in exchange for
Imports of at least 1,500 pairs of shoes	*Exports* of no more than 2,000 pairs of shoes

the U.S. exports 4,000 refrigerators to Mexico in exchange for 1,800 pairs of shoes would benefit both sides, in the sense that both countries would be able to consume more of both goods than in a world without trade.

Trade allows each country to take advantage of lower opportunity costs in the other country. If Mexico wants to produce more refrigerators without trade, it must face its domestic opportunity costs and reduce shoe production. But if Mexico instead produces more shoes and then trades for refrigerators produced in the United States, where the opportunity cost of producing refrigerators is lower, Mexico can in effect take advantage of the lower opportunity cost in the United States for producing refrigerators. Conversely, when the United States specializes in its comparative advantage of refrigerator production and trades for shoes produced in Mexico, international trade allows the United States to take advantage of the lower opportunity cost of shoe production in Mexico.

The theory of comparative advantage shows that the gains from international trade do not just result from the absolute advantage of producing at lower cost, but also from pursuing comparative advantage and producing at a lower opportunity cost.

Comparative Advantage Goes Camping

To build a greater intuitive understanding of how comparative advantage can benefit all parties, set aside examples that involve national economies for a moment and consider the situation of a group of friends who decide to go camping together. The friends have a wide range of skills and experiences, but one person in particular, Jethro, has done lots of camping before and is a great athlete, too. Jethro has an absolute advantage in all aspects of camping: carrying more weight in a backpack, gathering firewood, paddling a canoe, setting up tents, making a meal, and washing up. So here's the question: Because Jethro has an absolute productivity advantage in everything, should he do all the work?

Of course not. Even if Jethro is willing to work like a mule while everyone else sits around, he still has only 24 hours in a day. If everyone sits around and waits for Jethro to do everything, not only will Jethro be an unhappy camper, but there won't be much output for his group of six friends to consume. The theory of comparative advantage suggests that everyone will benefit if they figure out their areas of comparative advantage; that is, the area of camping where their productivity disadvantage is least, compared to Jethro. For example, perhaps Jethro is 80% faster at building fires and cooking meals than anyone else, but only 20% faster at gathering firewood and 10% faster at setting up tents. In that case, Jethro should focus on building fires and making meals, and others should attend to the other tasks, each according to where their productivity disadvantage is smallest. If the campers coordinate their efforts according to comparative advantage, they can all gain.

The Power of the Comparative Advantage Example

The two-country, two-good numerical illustration of comparative advantage, like the example of absolute advantage, has its limitations. While the example shows that both sides can benefit from specialization according to comparative advantage and trade, it doesn't explain exactly how much extra production will occur, or how the gains from trade will be divided up. It is (again) an example with two goods and two countries. It assumes production possibility frontiers that are straight lines representing constant trade-offs, rather than outward-bending curves with varying trade-offs.

These limitations can all be summarized in one basic point: this example is a model, not a literal description of the U.S. or the Mexican economy. The power of a model is to reveal the key features of how something works. The model of comparative advantage shows that even the most productive country in the world and the least productive country can both gain from trading with each other, if they each focus on the products where they possess a comparative advantage. Even the most productive country will have some product where its absolute advantage is greatest. A country can have an absolute advantage in all goods, but it is logically impossible to have a comparative advantage in all goods. Even the country with an absolute productivity disadvantage in every single product will have an area where its absolute disadvantage is smallest. Comparative advantage ranks among the most sophisticated insights in all of economics; indeed, an understanding of comparative advantage is one way of distinguishing economists from non-economists.

Intra-industry Trade between Similar Economies

Absolute and comparative advantage explain a great deal about patterns of global trade. For example, they help to explain the patterns noted at the start of this chapter, like why you may be eating fresh fruit from Chile or Mexico, or why lower productivity regions like Africa and Latin America are able to sell a substantial proportion of their exports to higher productivity regions like the European Union and North America. But absolute and comparative advantage, at least at first glance, do not seem especially well-suited to explain other common patterns of international trade.

The Prevalence of Intra-industry Trade between Similar Economies

The theory of comparative advantage suggests that trade should happen between economies with large differences in their opportunity costs of production. However, roughly half of all world trade involves shipping goods between the fairly similar high-income economies of the United States, Canada, the European Union, Japan, Australia, and New Zealand. Nearly half of U.S. trade is with the other high-income economies of the world, like Canada, Europe, and Japan, as shown in Exhibit 3-10, rather than with the much more different economies of Latin America or Africa.

Moreover, the theories of absolute and comparative advantage suggest that each economy should specialize to a degree in certain products, and then exchange those products. But a high proportion of trade is **intra-industry trade**—that is, trade of goods within the same industry. Exhibit 3-11 shows some of the largest categories of U.S. exports and imports. In all of these categories, the United States is both a substantial exporter and a substantial importer of goods from the same industry. For example, in 2015 the United States

intra-industry trade: International trade of goods within the same industry.

EXHIBIT 3-10 Where U.S. Exports Go and U.S. Imports Originate (2014)

About half of U.S. trade is with similar high-income nations of the world, like Canada, the countries of the European Union, and Japan.

	U.S. Exports Go to...	U.S. Imports Come from...
Canada	19.2%	14.9%
European Union	17.1%	17.8%
Mexico	14.7%	12.7%
China	7.6%	19.7%
Japan	4.2%	5.7%

EXHIBIT 3-11 Some Intra-Industry U.S. Exports and Imports in 2015

Many of the leading U.S. exports, as measured by these broad categories, are also leading U.S. imports. This pattern illustrates the importance of intra-industry trade for the U.S. economy.

Some Traded Products	Quantity of U.S. Exports (billions of dollars)	Quantity of U.S. Imports (billions of dollars)
Agricultural, forestry, and fishery products	$70	$56
Food	$62	$58
Manufactures	$1,112	$1,944
Paper products	$23	$20
Chemicals	$184	$217
Transportation equipment	$251	$374
Machinery (except electrical)	$123	$156
Petroleum and coal products	$80	$69
Computers and electronic products	$120	$371

exported $251 billion of transportation equipment, but imported $374 billion of transportation equipment. About 60% of U.S. trade and 60% of European trade is intra-industry trade.

Why do similar economies engage in intra-industry trade? What can be the economic benefit of having workers with fairly similar skills making cars, computers, machinery, and other products, which are then shipped in directions across the oceans to and from the United States, the European Union, and Japan? There are two reasons: how the division of labor leads to learning, innovation, and unique skills; and economies of scale.

Gains from Specialization and Learning

Consider the category of "machinery," where the U.S. economy has considerable intra-industry trade. Machinery comes in many varieties, so the U.S. may be exporting machinery for manufacturing with wood, but importing machinery for photographic processing. The underlying reason why a country like the United States, Japan, or Germany produces one kind of machinery rather than another is usually not related to U.S., German, or Japanese firms and workers having generally higher or lower skills—but just that in working on very specific and particular products, firms in certain countries have developed unique and different skills.

Specialization in the world economy can be very finely split. In fact, recent years have seen a trend in international trade called **splitting up the value chain**. The "value chain" describes how a good is produced in stages: for example, the value chain for making a toaster oven would include making metal and plastic parts, elements that provide the heat, and electrical cords; designing how the parts will fit together; assembly of the toaster ovens; packaging and shipping; and selling in a retail store. Thanks in part to improvements in technologies for communication, sharing of information, and transportation, it has become easier to split up the value chain so that instead of being done in a single large factory, these steps can be split up among different firms operating in different places and even different countries. Because of splitting up the value chain, international trade often doesn't involve whole finished products like automobiles or refrigerators being traded between nations. Instead, it can involve shipping more specialized goods like, say, automobile dashboards or the shelving that fits inside refrigerators. Intra-industry trade between similar countries produces economic gains because it allows workers and firms to learn and innovate by focusing on very particular parts of the value chain.

splitting up the value chain: When many of the different stages of producing a good happen in different geographic locations.

Economies of Scale, Competition, Variety

A second broad reason that intra-industry trade between similar nations produces economic gains involves economies of scale. The concept of economies of scale, as introduced in Chapter 1, means that as the scale of output goes up, average costs of production decline—at least up to a point. Exhibit 3-12 illustrates economies of scale for a hypothetical set of plants that produce toaster ovens. The horizontal axis of the figure shows the quantity of production by a certain firm or at a certain manufacturing plant. The vertical axis measures the average cost of production. Thus, Production Plant S, which produces a small level of output 30, has an average cost of production of $30 per toaster oven. Production Plant M, which produces at a medium level of output 50, has an average cost of production of $20 per toaster oven. Production Plant L, which produces at a large level of output 150, has an average cost of production of only $10 per toaster oven. However, Production Plant V, which produces at the very high level of output of 200, still has an average cost of production of $10 per toaster oven. In this example, a small or medium plant, like S or M, will not be able to compete in the market with a large or a very large plant like L or V, because the firm that operates L or V will be able to produce and sell at a lower cost. In this example, economies of scale operate up to point L, but beyond point L to V, additional scale of production does not continue to reduce average costs of production. (The reasons behind economies of scale, the different forms that economies of scale can take, and their implications for the size of companies will be analyzed in greater detail in Chapter 9.) Economies of scale are a common feature in many industries.

The concept of economies of scale becomes especially relevant to international trade when one or two large producers could supply the entire country. For example, a single large automobile factory could probably supply all the cars purchased in a smaller economy like the United Kingdom or Belgium in a given year. However, if a country has only one or two large factories producing cars, and no international trade, then consumers in that country would have relatively little choice between kinds of cars (other than the

EXHIBIT 3-12 Economies of Scale

Production Plant S, which produces a small level of output 30, has an average cost of production of $30 per toaster oven. Production Plant M, which produces at a medium level of output 50, has an average cost of production of $20 per toaster oven. Production Plant L, which produces at a large level of output 150, has an average cost of production of only $10 per toaster oven. Production Plant V, which produces at the very high level of output of 200, would still have an average cost of production of $10 per toaster oven. Thus, production plant M can produce toaster ovens more cheaply than plant S because of economies of scale, and plants L or V can produce more cheaply than S or M because of economies of scale. However, the economies of scale end at an output level of 150. Plant V, despite being larger, cannot produce more cheaply on average than plant L.

color of the paint and other nonessential options), and little or no competition would exist between different car manufacturers.

International trade provides a way to combine the lower average production costs of economies of scale and still have competition and variety for consumers. Large automobile factories in different countries can make and sell their products around the world. If the U.S. automobile market was made up of only General Motors, Ford, and Chrysler, the level of competition and consumer choice would be a lot less than when the U.S. carmakers must face competition from Toyota, Honda, Suzuki, Fiat, Mazda, Mitsubishi, Nissan, Volkswagen, Kia, Hyundai, BMW, Subaru, and others. Greater competition brings with it innovation and responsiveness to what consumers want. America's car producers make far better cars now than they did several decades ago, and much of the reason is competitive pressure, especially from East Asian and European carmakers.

Dynamic Comparative Advantage

The sources of gains from intra-industry trade between similar economies—namely, the learning that comes from a high degree of specialization and splitting up the value chain and from economies of scale—do not contradict the earlier theory of comparative advantage. Instead, they help to broaden the concept of comparative advantage.

In intra-industry trade, the level of worker productivity isn't determined by climate or mineral deposits. It isn't even determined by the general level of education or skill. Instead, the level of worker productivity is determined by how firms engage in specific learning about specialized products, including taking advantage of economies of scale to the extent possible. In this vision, comparative advantage can be dynamic—that is, it can evolve and change over time as new specific skills are developed and as the value chain is split up in new ways. This line of thinking also suggests that countries are not destined to have the same comparative advantage forever, but must instead react flexibly in response to ongoing changes in comparative advantage.

Intra-industry trade between similar trading partners allows for gains from learning and innovation that arise when firms and workers specialize in the production of a certain product (and with the trend toward splitting up the value chain, this learning can become very specialized, indeed). It also allows the gains from using economies of scale for large-scale production, while avoiding the problem of having only one large supplier in a market, and instead allowing fierce competition between different producers to offer the combination of variety, price, and quantity that will satisfy their customers.

The Size of Benefits from International Trade

It's hard to measure the economic gains from international trade with precision. After all, measuring the gains from trade would require comparing the world economy with international trade to a world economy that did not have international trade—which means figuring out what the world economy would look like if international trade did not exist at all. Such calculations are bound to be controversial.

However, estimating the gains from expanding trade from existing levels is more practical. For example, the nations of the world meet together through the World Trade Organization (WTO) to negotiate ways in which they can reduce government taxes or regulations that have the effect of limiting trade. Negotiations in the WTO happen in "rounds," where all countries negotiate one agreement to encourage trade, then take a year or two off, and then start negotiating a new agreement. It often takes 7–10 years from beginning to end of a round of WTO negotiations. The current round of negotiations is called the "Doha round" because it was officially launched in Doha, the capital city in the country of Qatar, in November 2001. In a recent study, economists from the World Bank summarized recent research and found that the Doha round of negotiations would increase the size of the world economy by $160 billion per year, depending on the precise deal that ended up being negotiated. In the context of a global economy that currently produces more than $70 trillion or so of goods and services each year, this amount is not huge: it's less than 1% or less of the global economy. But before dismissing the gains from trade too quickly, it's worth remembering four points.

First, a gain of a few hundred billion dollars is enough money to deserve attention! Moreover, remember that this increase is not a one-time event; it would persist each year into the future.

Second, this estimate of $160 billion measures only the expected gains from the most recent round of trade negotiations. In other words, it measures only the economic gains from expanding international trade somewhat from the levels it had already reached a decade or so into the 21st century, before the Doha round of trade negotiations was finalized. Measuring the gains from all existing international trade would be a multiple of this number.

Third, this estimate of gains may be on the low side because some of the gains from trade are not measured especially well in economic statistics. For example, while it is possible to estimate the economic gains from taking advantage of comparative advantage or economies of scale, it is difficult to measure the potential advantages to consumers of having a variety of products available and a greater degree of competition among producers. Perhaps the most important unmeasured factor is that trade between countries, especially when firms are splitting up the value chain of production, often involves a transfer of knowledge that can involve skills in production, technology, management, finance, and law. These transfers of knowledge may be especially important in helping low-income countries improve their standard of living.

Fourth, the gains from expanding trade are probably most important for the low-income economies in the world. In some ways, the giant U.S. economy has less need for international trade, because it can already take advantage of internal trade within its economy. The United States has a variety of different climates, natural resources, and geographic areas where workers are more skilled or less skilled. It is a large enough economy that firms can become extremely specialized and focused on producing small slices of the value chain. In the huge U.S. economy, large firms can take advantage of economies of scale and still compete against each other within the U.S. economy. However, many smaller national economies around the world, in regions like Latin America, Africa, the Middle East, and Asia, have much more limited possibilities for trade inside their countries or their immediate regions. Their possibilities for gains from purely internal trade are smaller. Without international trade, they may have little ability to benefit from comparative advantage, slicing up the value chain, or economies of scale. Moreover, smaller economies often have fewer competitive firms making goods within their economy, and thus firms have less pressure from other firms to provide the goods and prices that consumers want.

The economic gains from expanding international trade are measured in hundreds of billions of dollars, and the gains from international trade as a whole probably reach well into the trillions of dollars. The potential for gains from trade may be especially high among the smaller and lower-income countries of the world.

From Interpersonal to International Trade

Most people find it easy to believe that they personally would not be better off if they tried to grow and process all of their own food, to make all of their own clothes, to build their own car and house from scratch, and so on. Instead, we all benefit from living in economies where people and firms can specialize and trade with each other.

This same argument applies at the level of the community. Most of us, whether we live in small towns or suburbs or large cities, would find it difficult if our town or city tried to be self-sufficient—for example, to produce all of its own food within the city limits, along with clothing, health care, housing, and all inputs and machinery that are used in producing these goods. There are clear economic gains when people and firms from one community trade with people and firms from other communities.

This same argument continues to apply at the level of states or provinces. The people of Vermont or New Mexico, for example, would find that their standard of living suffered considerably if they attempted to consume only what was produced inside the boundaries of their state, without trading with California, Texas, New York, and all the other states.

The benefits of trade do not stop at national boundaries, either. Chapter 1 explained that the division of labor could increase output for three reasons: workers with different characteristics can specialize in the types of production where they have an advantage (which this chapter has spelled out as comparative and absolute advantage); firms and workers who specialize in a certain product become more productive with learning and practice; and economies of scale. These three reasons apply from the individual and community level right up to the international level. If it makes sense to you that interpersonal, inter-community trade and inter-state trade offer economic gains, it should make sense that international trade offers gains, too.

International trade currently involves over tens of trillions of dollars' worth of goods and services thundering around the globe. Any economic force of that size, even if it confers overall benefits, is certain to cause disruption and controversy. This chapter has only made the case that trade brings economic benefits. Later chapters, especially Chapter 6, will discuss in detail the public policy arguments over whether to restrict international trade.

Key Concepts and Summary

1. A country has an **absolute advantage** in those products in which it has a productivity edge over other countries.
2. Two countries that each have an absolute advantage in different products can gain from specializing (at least to some extent) in the product where they have an absolute advantage and then trading.
3. A country has a **comparative advantage** where its cost of production, measured in opportunity cost terms, is lowest. Equivalently, a country has a comparative advantage in whatever product where either its absolute advantage is relatively greatest or where its absolute disadvantage is relatively least.
4. Two countries can benefit from specializing (at least to some extent) in the product where each has a comparative advantage and then trading with each other.

This statement holds true even if one of the countries has an absolute advantage in both products.
5. A large share of global trade happens between high-income economies that are quite similar in having well-educated workers and advanced technology. These countries practice **intra-industry trade**, in which they import and export the same products at the same time, like cars, machinery, and computers.
6. In the case of intra-industry trade between similar economies, the gains from trade come from specialized learning in very particular tasks and from economies of scale.
7. The gains of international trade are very large, especially for smaller countries, but can be difficult to measure with precision.

Review Questions

1. What is absolute advantage?
2. In what situations does absolute advantage provide a reason for gains from trade?
3. What is comparative advantage? Explain in two ways, first using the idea of opportunity cost and second using the idea of relatively large or small absolute advantages and absolute disadvantages.
4. Is it possible to have an absolute advantage in the production of a certain good but not to have a comparative advantage in the production of that good? Explain.
5. Is it possible to have a comparative advantage in the production of a good but not to have an absolute advantage? Explain.
6. In what situations does comparative advantage provide a reason for gains from trade?
7. What is intra-industry trade?
8. What are the two main sources of economic gains from intra-industry trade?
9. What is splitting up the value chain?
10. Why might intra-industry trade seem surprising from the point of view of comparative advantage? How does intra-industry trade fit with the idea of comparative advantage?
11. Are the gains from international trade more likely to be relatively more important to larger or smaller countries?

Demand and Supply

Whenpeople talk about prices, the discussion often takes a judgmental tone. A bidder in an auction pays thousands of dollars for a dress once worn by Diana, Princess of Wales. A collector spends thousands of dollars for some drawings by John Lennon of the Beatles. Mouths gape. Surely such purchases are a waste of money? But when economists talk about prices, they are less interested in making judgments than in gaining a practical understanding of what determines prices and why prices change. In 1933, the great British economist Joan Robinson (1903–1983) explained how economists perceive price:

> The point may be put like this: You see two men, one of whom is giving a banana to the other, and is taking a penny from him. You ask, How is it that a banana costs a penny rather than any other sum? The most obvious line of attack on this question is to break it up into two fresh questions: How does it happen that the one man will take a penny for a banana? and: How does it happen that the other man will give a penny for a banana? In short, the natural thing is to divide up the problem under two heads: Supply and Demand.

As a contemporary example, consider a price often listed on large signs beside well-traveled roads: the price of a gallon of gasoline. Why was the average price of gasoline in the United States $2.80 per gallon in June 2015? Why did the price for gasoline fall to $1.77 per gallon seven months later by February 2016? To explain why prices are at a certain level and why that level changes over time, economic analysis focuses on the determinants of what gasoline buyers are willing to pay and what gasoline sellers are willing to accept. For example, the price of a gallon of gasoline in June of a given year is nearly always higher than the price in January of that year; over recent decades, gasoline prices in midsummer have averaged about 10 cents per gallon more than their midwinter low. The likely reason is that people want to drive more in the summer, and thus they are willing to pay more for gas at that time. However, from June 2015 to February 2016, gasoline prices fell by much more than the average summer-to-winter fall, which suggests that other factors related to those who buy gasoline and firms that sell it changed during those six months, too.

This chapter introduces the economic model of demand and supply. The discussion begins by examining how demand and supply determine the price and the quantity sold in markets for goods and services, and how changes in demand and supply lead to changes in prices and quantities. In Chapter 5, the same demand and supply model is applied to markets for labor and financial capital. In Chapter 6, the same supply and demand model is applied to international trade. In situation after situation, in different places around the world, across different cultures, even reaching back into history, the demand and supply model offers a useful framework for thinking about what determines the prices and quantities of what is bought and sold.

Demand, Supply, and Equilibrium in Markets for Goods and Services

Markets for goods and services include everything from accounting services, air travel, and apples to zinc, zinfandel wine, and zucchini. Let's first focus on what economists mean by demand, what they mean by supply, and then how demand and supply interact in an economic model of the market.

Demand for Goods and Services

Economists use the term **demand** to refer to a relationship between price and the quantity demanded. Price is what a buyer pays (or the seller receives) for a unit of the specific good or service. **Quantity demanded** refers to the total number of units that are purchased at a given price. A rise in price of a good or service almost always decreases the quantity demanded of that good or service; conversely, a fall in price will increase the quantity demanded. When the price of a gallon of gasoline goes up, for example, people look for ways to reduce their purchases of gasoline by combining several errands, commuting by carpool or public transportation, or taking weekend or vacation trips by car close to home. Economists refer to the relationship that a higher price leads to a lower quantity demanded as the **law of demand**.

Exhibit 4-1 gives a hypothetical example in the market for gasoline. The table that shows the quantity demanded at each price is called a **demand schedule**. Price in this

demand: A relationship between price and the quantity demanded of a certain good or service.

quantity demanded: The total number of units of a good or service purchased at a certain price.

law of demand: The common relationship that a higher price leads to a lower quantity demanded of a certain good or service.

demand schedule: A table that shows a range of prices for a certain good or service and the quantity demanded at each price.

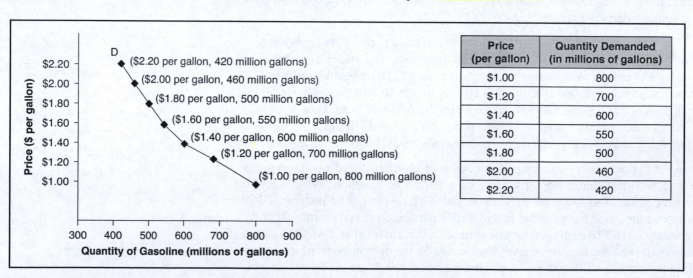

Price (per gallon)	Quantity Demanded (in millions of gallons)
$1.00	800
$1.20	700
$1.40	600
$1.60	550
$1.80	500
$2.00	460
$2.20	420

EXHIBIT 4-1 A Demand Curve for Gasoline

The table that shows quantity demanded of gasoline at each price is called a demand schedule. The demand schedule shows that as price rises, quantity demanded decreases. These points are then graphed on the figure, and the line connecting them is the demand curve D. The downward slope of the demand curve again illustrates the pattern that as price rises, quantity demanded decreases. This pattern is called the law of demand.

case is measured per gallon of gasoline. The quantity demanded is measured in millions of gallons. A **demand curve** shows the relationship between price and quantity demanded on a graph, with quantity on the horizontal axis and the price per gallon on the vertical axis. The demand schedule shown by the table and the demand curve shown on the graph are two ways of describing the same relationship between price and quantity demanded.

Each individual good or service needs to be graphed on its own demand curve, because it wouldn't make sense to graph the quantity of apples and the quantity of airplanes on the same diagram. Demand curves will appear somewhat different for each product; for example, they may appear relatively steep or flat, or they may be straight or curved. But nearly all demand curves share the fundamental similarity that they slope down from left to right. In this way, demand curves embody the law of demand; as the price increases, the quantity demanded decreases, and conversely, as the price decreases, the quantity demanded increases.

Supply of Goods and Services

When economists talk about **supply**, they are referring to a relationship between price received for each unit sold and the **quantity supplied**, which is the total number of units sold in the market at a certain price. A rise in price of a good or service almost always leads to an increase in the quantity supplied of that good or service, while a fall in price will decrease the quantity supplied. When the price of gasoline rises, for example, profit-seeking firms are encouraged to expand exploration for oil reserves; to carry out additional drilling for oil; to make new investments in pipelines and oil tankers to bring the oil to plants where it can be refined into gasoline; to build new oil refineries; to purchase additional pipelines and trucks to ship the gasoline to gas stations; and to open more gas stations or to keep existing gas stations open longer hours. The pattern that a higher price is associated with a greater quantity supplied is so common that economists have named it the **law of supply**.

Exhibit 4-2 illustrates the law of supply, again using the market for gasoline as an example. A **supply schedule** is a table that shows the quantity supplied at a range of different prices. Again, price is measured per gallon of gasoline and quantity supplied is measured in millions of gallons. A **supply curve** is a graphical illustration of the relationship between price, shown on the vertical axis, and quantity, shown on the horizontal axis. The supply schedule and the supply curve are just two different ways of showing the same

demand curve: A line that shows the relationship between price and quantity demanded of a certain good or service on a graph, with quantity on the horizontal axis and the price on the vertical axis.

supply: A relationship between price and the quantity supplied of a certain good or service.

quantity supplied: The total number of units of a good or service sold at a certain price.

law of supply: The common relationship that a higher price is associated with a greater quantity supplied.

supply schedule: A table that shows a range of prices for a good or service and the quantity supplied at each price.

supply curve: A line that shows the relationship between price and quantity supplied on a graph, with quantity supplied on the horizontal axis and price on the vertical axis.

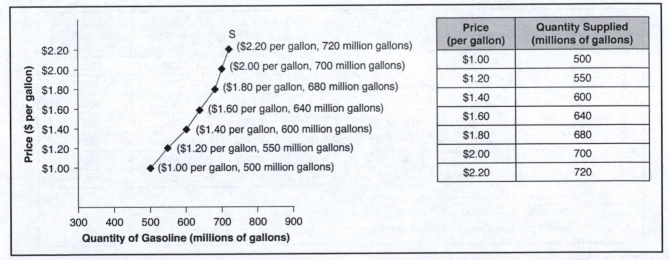

Price (per gallon)	Quantity Supplied (millions of gallons)
$1.00	500
$1.20	550
$1.40	600
$1.60	640
$1.80	680
$2.00	700
$2.20	720

EXHIBIT 4-2 A Supply Curve for Gasoline

The supply schedule is the table that shows quantity supplied of gasoline at each price. As price rises, quantity supplied also increases. The supply curve S is created by graphing the points from the supply schedule and then connecting them. The upward slope of the supply curve illustrates the pattern that a higher price leads to a higher quantity supplied—a pattern that is common enough to be called the law of supply.

Supply Is Not the Same as Quantity Supplied

In economic terminology, supply is not the same as quantity supplied. When economists refer to supply, they mean the relationship between a range of prices and the quantities supplied at those prices, a relationship that can be illustrated with a supply curve or a supply schedule. When economists refer to quantity supplied, they often mean only a certain point on the supply curve, or sometimes, they are referring to the horizontal axis of the supply curve or one column of the supply schedule.

information. Notice that the horizontal and vertical axes on the graph for the supply curve are the same as for the demand curve.

Just as each product has its own demand curve, each product has its own supply curve. The shape of supply curves will vary somewhat according to the product: steeper, flatter, straighter, or curved. But nearly all supply curves share a basic similarity: they slope up from left to right. In that way, the supply curve illustrates the law of supply: as the price rises, the quantity supplied increases, and conversely, as the price falls, the quantity supplied decreases.

Equilibrium—Where Demand and Supply Cross

Because the graphs for demand and supply curves both have price on the vertical axis and quantity on the horizontal axis, the demand curve and supply curve for a particular good or service can appear on the same graph. Together, demand and supply determine the price and the quantity that will be bought and sold in a market.

Exhibit 4-3 illustrates the interaction of demand and supply in the market for gasoline. The demand curve D is identical to Exhibit 4-1. The supply curve S is identical to Exhibit 4-2. When one curve slopes down, like demand, and another curve slopes up, like supply, the curves intersect at some point.

In every economics course you will ever take, when two lines on a diagram cross, this intersection means something! The point where the supply curve S and the demand curve D cross, designated by point E in Exhibit 4-3, is called the equilibrium. The **equilibrium price** is defined as the price where quantity demanded is equal to quantity supplied. The

equilibrium price: The price where quantity demanded is equal to quantity supplied.

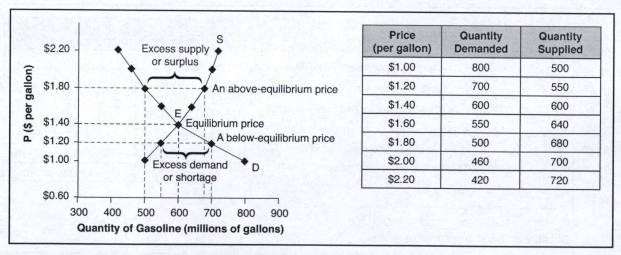

Price (per gallon)	Quantity Demanded	Quantity Supplied
$1.00	800	500
$1.20	700	550
$1.40	600	600
$1.60	550	640
$1.80	500	680
$2.00	460	700
$2.20	420	720

EXHIBIT 4-3 Demand and Supply for Gasoline

The demand curve D and the supply curve S intersect at the equilibrium point E, with a price of $1.40 and a quantity of 600. The equilibrium is the only price where quantity demanded is equal to quantity supplied. At a price above equilibrium like $1.80, quantity supplied of 680 exceeds the quantity demanded of 500, so there is excess supply or a surplus. At a price below equilibrium such as $1.20, quantity demanded of 700 exceeds quantity supplied of 550, so there is excess demand or a shortage.

equilibrium quantity is the quantity where quantity demanded and quantity supplied are equal at a certain price. In Exhibit 4-3, the equilibrium price is $1.40 per gallon of gasoline and the equilibrium quantity is 600 million gallons. If you had only the demand and supply schedules, and not the graph, it would be easy to find the equilibrium by looking for the price level on the tables where the quantity demanded and the quantity supplied are equal.

The word **equilibrium** means "balance." If a market is balanced at its **equilibrium** price and quantity, then it has no reason to move away from that point. However, if a market is not balanced at equilibrium, then economic pressures arise to move toward the equilibrium price and the equilibrium quantity.

Imagine, for example, that the price of a gallon of gasoline is above the equilibrium price and is priced at $1.80 per gallon. This above-equilibrium price is illustrated by the dashed horizontal line at the price of $1.80 in Exhibit 4-3. At this higher price of $1.80, the quantity demanded drops from the equilibrium quantity of 600 to 500 million gallons. This decline in quantity reflects how people and businesses react to the higher price by seeking out ways to use less gasoline, like sharing rides to work, taking public transportation, and avoiding faraway vacation destinations. Moreover, at this higher price of $1.80, the quantity supplied of gasoline rises from the 600 to 680 million gallons, as the higher price provides incentives for gasoline producers to expand their output. At this above-equilibrium price, there is **excess supply**, or a **surplus**; that is, the quantity supplied exceeds the quantity demanded at the given price. With a surplus, gasoline accumulates at gas stations, in tanker trucks, in pipelines, and at oil refineries. This accumulation puts pressure on gasoline sellers. If a surplus of gasoline remains unsold, those firms involved in making and selling gasoline are not receiving enough cash to pay their workers and to cover their expenses. In this situation, at least some gasoline producers and sellers will be tempted to cut prices, because it's better to sell at a lower price than not to sell at all. Once some sellers start cutting gasoline prices, others will follow so that they won't lose sales to the earlier price-cutters. These price reductions in turn will stimulate a higher quantity demanded. In this way, if the price is above the equilibrium level, incentives built into the structure of demand and supply will create pressures for the price to fall toward the equilibrium.

Now suppose that the price is below its equilibrium level at $1.20 per gallon, as shown by the dashed horizontal line at this price in Exhibit 4-3. At this lower price, the quantity demanded increases from 600 to 700 million gallons as drivers take longer trips, spend more minutes warming up their car in the driveway in wintertime, stop sharing rides to work, and purchase cars that get fewer miles to the gallon. However, the below-equilibrium price reduces gasoline producers' incentives to produce and sell gasoline, and the quantity supplied of gasoline falls from 600 to 550 million gallons. When the price is below equilibrium, there is **excess demand**, or a **shortage**; that is, at the given price the quantity demanded, which has been stimulated by the lower price, now exceeds the quantity supplied, which had been depressed by the lower price. In this situation, eager gasoline buyers mob the gas stations, only to find many stations running short of fuel. Oil companies and gas stations recognize that they have an opportunity to make higher profits by selling what gasoline they have at a higher price. As a result, the price rises toward the equilibrium level.

Shifts in Demand and Supply for Goods and Services

A demand curve shows how quantity demanded changes as the price rises or falls. A supply curve shows how quantity supplied changes as the price rises or falls. But what happens when factors other than price influence quantity demanded and quantity supplied? For example, what if demand for, say, vegetarian food becomes popular with more consumers? Or what if the supply of, say, diamonds rises not because of any change in price, but because companies discover several new diamond mines? A change in price leads to a different point on a specific demand curve or a supply curve, but a shift in some economic factor other than price can cause the entire demand curve or supply curve to shift.

equilibrium quantity: The quantity at which quantity demanded and quantity supplied are equal at a certain price.

equilibrium: The combination of price and quantity where there is no economic pressure from surpluses or shortages that would cause price or quantity to shift.

excess supply: When at the existing price, quantity supplied exceeds the quantity demanded; also called a "surplus."

surplus: When at the existing price, quantity supplied exceeds the quantity demanded; also called "excess supply."

excess demand: At the existing price, the quantity demanded exceeds the quantity supplied, also called "shortage."

shortage: At the existing price, the quantity demanded exceeds the quantity supplied, also called "excess demand."

The *Ceteris Paribus* Assumption

A demand curve or a supply curve is a relationship between two and only two variables: quantity on the horizontal axis and price on the vertical axis. Thus, the implicit assumption behind a demand curve or a supply curve is that no other relevant economic factors are changing. Economists refer to this assumption as **ceteris paribus**, a Latin phrase meaning "other things being equal." Any given demand or supply curve is based on the *ceteris paribus* assumption that all else is held equal. If all else is not held equal, then the demand or supply curve itself can shift.

ceteris paribus: Other things being equal.

An Example of a Shifting Demand Curve

The original demand curve D_0 in Exhibit 4-4 shows at point Q that at a price of $20,000 per car, the quantity of cars demanded would be 18 million. The original demand curve also shows how the quantity of cars demanded would change as a result of a higher or lower price; for example, if the price of a car rose to $22,000, the quantity demanded would decrease to 17 million, as at point R.

The original demand curve D_0, like every demand curve, is based on the *ceteris paribus* assumption that no other economically relevant factors change. But now imagine that the economy expands in a way that raises the incomes of many people. As a result of the higher income levels, a **shift in demand** occurs, which means that compared to the original demand curve D_0, a different quantity of cars will now be demanded at every price. On the original demand curve, a price of $20,000 means a quantity demanded of 18 million, but

shift in demand: When a change in some economic factor related to demand causes a different quantity to be demanded at every price.

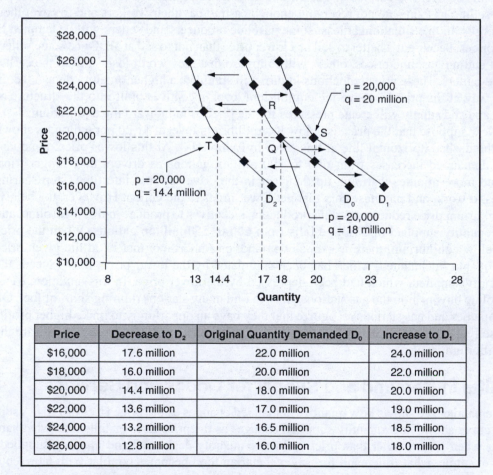

Price	Decrease to D_2	Original Quantity Demanded D_0	Increase to D_1
$16,000	17.6 million	22.0 million	24.0 million
$18,000	16.0 million	20.0 million	22.0 million
$20,000	14.4 million	18.0 million	20.0 million
$22,000	13.6 million	17.0 million	19.0 million
$24,000	13.2 million	16.5 million	18.5 million
$26,000	12.8 million	16.0 million	18.0 million

EXHIBIT 4-4 Shifts in Demand: A Car Example

Increased demand means that at every given price, the quantity demanded is higher, so that the demand curve shifts to the right from D_0 to D_1. Decreased demand means that at every given price, the quantity demand is lower, so that the demand curve shifts to the left from D_0 to D_2.

after higher incomes cause an increase in demand, a price of $20,000 leads to a quantity demanded of 20 million, at point S. Exhibit 4-4 illustrates the shift in demand as a result of higher income levels with the shift of the original demand curve D_0 to the right to the new demand curve D_1.

This logic works in reverse, too. Imagine that the economy slows down so that many people lose their jobs or work fewer hours and thus suffer reductions in income. In this case, the shift in demand would lead to a lower quantity of cars demanded at every given price, and the original demand curve D_0 would shift left to D_2. The shift from D_0 to D_2 represents a decrease in demand; that is, at any given price level, the quantity demanded is now lower. In this example, a price of $20,000 means 18 million are cars sold along the original demand curve, but only 14.4 million cars are sold after demand has decreased, at point T in Exhibit 4-4.

When a demand curve shifts, it does not mean that the quantity demanded by every individual buyer changes by the same amount. In this example, not everyone would have higher or lower income, and not everyone would buy or not buy an additional car. Instead, a shift in a demand captures an overall pattern for the market as a whole.

Factors That Shift Demand Curves

A change in any one of the underlying factors that determine what quantity people are willing to buy at a given price will cause a shift in demand. Graphically, the new demand curve lies either to the right or to the left of the original demand curve. Various factors may cause a demand curve to shift: changes in income, changes in population, changes in taste, changes in expectations, and changes in the prices of closely related goods. Let's consider these factors in turn.

A *change in income* will often shift demand curves. A household with a higher income level will tend to demand a greater quantity of goods at every price than a household with a lower income level. For some luxury goods and services, such as expensive cars, exotic spa vacations, and fine jewelry, the effect of a rise in income can be especially pronounced. However, a few exceptions to this pattern do exist. As incomes rise, many people will buy fewer bus tickets and more airplane tickets, less chicken and more steak; they will be less likely to rent an apartment and more likely to own a home; and so on. **Normal goods** are defined as those where the quantity demanded rises as income rises, which is the most common case; **inferior goods** are defined as those where the quantity demanded falls as income rises.

Changes in the composition of the population can also shift demand curves for certain goods and services. The proportion of elderly citizens in the U.S. population is rising, from 9% in 1960, to 13% in 2010, and to a projected (by the U.S. Census Bureau) 20% of the population by 2030. A society with relatively more children, like the United States in the 1960s, will have greater demand for goods and services like tricycles and day care facilities. A society with relatively more elderly persons, as the United States is projected to have by 2030, has a higher demand for nursing homes and hearing aids.

Changing tastes can also shift demand curves. In the demand for music, for example, 50% of sound recordings sold in 1990 were in the rock or pop music categories. By 2014, rock and pop had fallen to 44% of the total, while sales of rap/hip-hop, religious, and country categories had increased. Tastes in food and drink have changed, too. From 1970 to 2014, the per person consumption of chicken by Americans rose from 40 pounds per year to 84 pounds per year, and consumption of cheese rose from 11 pounds per year to 34 pounds per year. Changes like these are largely due to movements in taste, which change the quantity of a good demanded at every price: that is, they shift the demand curve for that good.

Changes in expectations about future conditions and prices can also shift the demand curve for a good or service. For example, if people hear that a hurricane is coming, they may rush to the store to buy flashlight batteries and bottled water. If people learn that the price of a good like coffee is likely to rise in the future, they may head for the store to stock up on coffee now.

normal goods: Goods where the quantity demanded rises as income rises.

inferior goods: Goods where the quantity demanded falls as income rises.

substitutes: Goods that can replace each other to some extent, so that a rise in the price of one good leads to a greater quantity consumed of another good, and vice versa.

complements: Goods that are often used together, so that a rise in the price of one good tends to decrease the quantity consumed of the other good, and vice versa.

The demand curve for one good or service can be affected by *changes in the prices of related goods*. Some goods and services are **substitutes** for others, which means that they can replace the other good to some extent. For example, if the price of cotton rises, driving up the price of clothing, sheets, and other items made from cotton, then some people will shift to comparable goods made from fabrics like wool, silk, linen, and polyester. A higher price for a substitute good shifts the demand curve to the right; for example, a higher price for tea encourages buying more coffee. Conversely, a lower price for a substitute good has the reverse effect.

Other goods are **complements** for each other, meaning that the goods are often used together, so that consumption of one good tends to increase consumption of the other. Examples include breakfast cereal and milk; golf balls and golf clubs; gasoline and sports utility vehicles; and the five-way combination of bacon, lettuce, tomato, mayonnaise, and bread. If the price of golf clubs rises, demand for a complement good like golf balls decreases. A higher price for skis would shift the demand curve for a complement good like ski resort trips to the left, while a lower price for a complement has the reverse effect.

Summing Up Factors That Change Demand

Six factors that can shift demand curves are summarized in Exhibit 4-5. The direction of the arrows indicates whether the demand curve shifts represent an increase in demand or a decrease in demand based on the six factors we just considered. Notice that a change in the price of the good or service itself is not listed among the factors that can shift a demand curve. A change in the price of a good or service causes a movement along a specific demand curve, and it typically leads to some change in the quantity demanded, but it doesn't shift the demand curve. Notice also that in these diagrams, the demand curves are drawn without numerical quantities and prices on the horizontal and vertical axes. The demand and supply model can often be a useful conceptual tool even without attaching specific numbers.

When a demand curve shifts, it will then intersect with a given supply curve at a different equilibrium price and quantity. But we are getting ahead of our story. Before discussing how changes in demand can affect equilibrium price and quantity, we first need to discuss shifts in supply curves.

EXHIBIT 4-5 Some Factors That Shift Demand Curves

The left-hand panel *(a)* offers a list of factors that can cause an increase in demand from D_0 to D_1. The right-hand panel *(b)* shows how the same factors, if their direction is reversed, can cause a decrease in demand from D_0 to D_1. For example, greater popularity of a good or service increases demand, causing a shift in the demand curve to the right, while lesser popularity of a good or service reduces demand, causing a shift of the demand curve to the left.

An Example of a Shift in a Supply Curve

A supply curve shows how quantity supplied will change as the price rises and falls, based on the *ceteris paribus* assumption that no other economically relevant factors are changing. But if other factors relevant to supply do change, then the entire supply curve can shift. Just as a shift in demand is represented by a change in the quantity demanded at every price, a **shift in supply** means a change in the quantity supplied at every price. In thinking about the factors that affect supply, remember the basic motivation of firms: to earn profits. If a firm faces lower costs of production, while the prices for the output the firm produces remain unchanged, a firm's profits will increase. Thus, when costs of production fall, a firm will supply a higher quantity at any given price for its output, and the supply curve will shift to the right. Conversely, if a firm faces an increased cost of production, then it will earn lower profits at any given selling price for its products. As a result, a higher cost of production typically causes a firm to supply a smaller quantity at any given price. In this case, the supply curve shifts to the left.

shift in supply: When a change in some economic factor related to supply causes a different quantity to be supplied at every price.

As an example, imagine that supply in the market for cars is represented by S_0 in Exhibit 4-6. The original supply curve, S_0, includes a point with a price of $20,000 and a quantity supplied of 18 million cars, labeled as point J. If the price rises to $22,000 per car, *ceteris paribus*, the quantity supplied will rise to 20 million cars, as shown by point K on the S_0 curve.

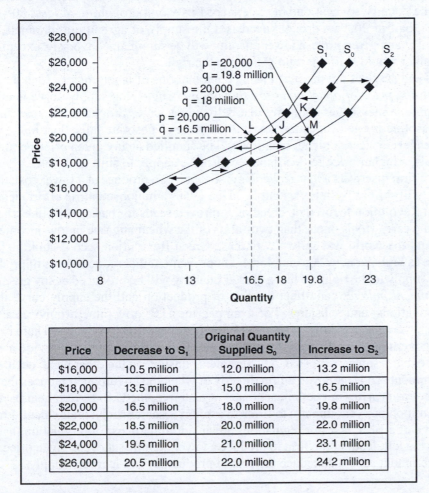

Price	Decrease to S_1	Original Quantity Supplied S_0	Increase to S_2
$16,000	10.5 million	12.0 million	13.2 million
$18,000	13.5 million	15.0 million	16.5 million
$20,000	16.5 million	18.0 million	19.8 million
$22,000	18.5 million	20.0 million	22.0 million
$24,000	19.5 million	21.0 million	23.1 million
$26,000	20.5 million	22.0 million	24.2 million

EXHIBIT 4-6 Shifts in Supply: A Car Example

Increased supply means that at every given price, the quantity supplied is higher, so that the supply curve shifts to the right from S_0 to S_2. Decreased supply means that at every given price, quantity supplied of cars is lower, so that the supply curve shifts to the left from S_0 to S_1.

Now imagine that the price of steel, an important material input in manufacturing cars, rises, so that producing a car has now become more expensive. At any given price for selling cars, car manufacturers will react by supplying a lower quantity. The shift of supply from S_0 to S_1 shows that at any given price, the quantity supplied decreases. In this example, at a price of \$20,000, the quantity supplied decreases from 18 million on the original supply curve S_0 to 16.5 million on the supply curve S_1, which is labeled as point L.

Conversely, imagine that the price of steel decreases, so that producing a car becomes less expensive. At any given price for selling cars, car manufacturers can now expect to earn higher profits and so will supply a higher quantity. The shift of supply to the right from S_0 to S_2 means that at all prices, the quantity supplied has increased. In this example, at a price of \$20,000, the quantity supplied increases from 18 million on the original supply curve S_0 to 19.8 million on the supply curve S_2, which is labeled M.

Factors That Shift Supply Curves

A change in any factor that determines what quantity firms are willing to sell at a given price will cause a change in supply. Some factors that can cause a supply curve to shift include: changes in natural conditions, altered prices for inputs to production, new technologies for production, and government policies that affect production costs.

The cost of production for many agricultural products will be affected by *changes in natural conditions*. For example, the area of northern China that typically grows about 60% of the country's wheat output experienced its worst drought in at least 50 years in the second half of 2009. A drought decreases the supply of agricultural products, which means that at any given price, a lower quantity will be supplied; conversely, exceptionally good weather would shift the supply curve to the right.

Goods and services are produced using combinations of labor, materials, and machinery. When *the price of a key input to production changes*, the supply curve is affected. For example, a messenger company that delivers packages around a city may find that buying gasoline is one of its main costs. If the price of gasoline falls, then in the market for messenger services, a higher quantity will be supplied at any given price per delivery. Conversely, a higher price for key inputs will cause supply to shift to the left.

When a firm discovers a *new technology*, so that it can produce at a lower cost, the supply curve will shift as well. For example, in the 1960s a major scientific effort nicknamed the Green Revolution focused on breeding improved seeds for basic crops like wheat and rice. By the early 1990s, more than two-thirds of the wheat and rice in low-income countries around the world was grown with these Green Revolution seeds—and the harvest was twice as high per acre. A technological improvement that reduces costs of production will shift supply to the right, so that a greater quantity will be produced at any given price.

Government policies can affect the cost of production and the supply curve through taxes, regulations, and subsidies. For example, the U.S. government imposes a tax on alcoholic beverages that collects about \$9 billion per year from producers. There is a wide array of government regulations that require firms to spend money to provide a cleaner environment or a safer workplace. A government subsidy, on the other hand, occurs when the government sends money to a firm directly or when the government reduces the firm's taxes if the firm carries out certain actions. For example, the U.S. government pays more than \$20 billion per year directly to firms to support research and development. From the perspective of a firm, taxes or regulations are an additional cost of production that shifts supply to the left, leading the firm to produce a lower quantity at every given price. However, government subsidies reduce the cost of production and increase supply.

Summing Up Factors That Change Supply

Weather patterns, changes in the cost of inputs, new technologies, and the impact of government decisions all affect the cost of production for firms. In turn, these factors affect firms' willingness to supply at a given price. Exhibit 4-7 summarizes factors that change the supply of goods and services. Notice that a change in the price of the product itself is

(a) Factors that increase supply

Favorable natural conditions for production

A fall in input prices

Improved technology

Lower product taxes/less costly regulations

(b) Factors that decrease supply

Poor natural conditions for production

A rise in input prices

A decline in technology (not common)

Higher product taxes/more costly regulations

EXHIBIT 4-7 Some Factors That Shift Supply Curves

The left-hand panel (a) offers a list of factors that can cause an increase in supply from S_0 to S_1. The right-hand panel (b) shows that the same factors, if their direction is reversed, can cause a decrease in supply from S_0 to S_1.

not among the factors that shift the supply curve. Although a change in price of a good or service typically causes a change in quantity supplied along the supply curve for that specific good or service, it does not cause the supply curve itself to shift.

Shifts in Equilibrium Price and Quantity: The Four-Step Process

Because demand and supply curves appear on a two-dimensional diagram with only price and quantity on the axes, an unwary visitor to the land of economics might be fooled into believing that economics is only about four topics: demand, supply, price, and quantity. However, demand and supply are really "umbrella" concepts: demand covers all of the factors that affect demand, and supply covers all of the factors that affect supply. The factors other than price that affect demand and supply are included by using shifts in the demand or the supply curve. In this way, the two-dimensional demand and supply model becomes a powerful tool for analyzing a wide range of economic circumstances.

To understand how this works, let's begin with a single economic event. It might be an event that affects demand, like a change in income, population, tastes, prices of substitutes or complements, or expectations about future prices. It might be an event that affects supply, like a change in natural conditions, input prices, or technology, or government policies that affect production. How does this economic event affect equilibrium price and quantity? We can analyze this question using a four-step process.

Step 1: Think about what the demand and supply curves in this market looked like before the economic change occurred. Sketch the curves.

Step 2: Decide whether the economic change being analyzed affects demand or supply.

Step 3: Decide whether the effect on demand or supply causes the curve to shift to the right or to the left, and sketch the new demand or supply curve on the diagram.

Step 4: Compare the original equilibrium price and quantity to the new equilibrium price and quantity.

To make this process concrete, let's consider one example that involves a shift in supply and one that involves a shift in demand.

Good Weather for Salmon Fishing

About 90% of the shrimp consumed in the United States is imported. In 2013, Thailand, Vietnam, and China—three main global shrimp producers—experienced an outbreak of disease that affected their shrimp supplies. How did the shrimp disease affect the

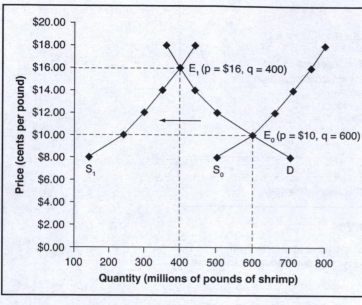

Price per Pound	Quantity Supplied in 2008	Quantity Supplied in 2013	Quantity Demanded
$8	500	140	700
$10	600	240	600
$12	660	300	500
$14	710	350	440
$16	760	400	400
$18	800	440	360

EXHIBIT 4-8 Sick Shrimp: The Four-Step Process

Step 1: Draw a demand and supply diagram to show what the market for shrimp looked like before the shrimp disease. The original equilibrium E_0 was $10 per pound, and the original equilibrium quantity was 600 million pounds of shrimp.
Step 2: Did the economic event affect supply or demand? A disease is a natural condition that affects supply.
Step 3: Was the effect on supply an increase or a decrease? Disease reduces the quantity that will be supplied at any given price. The supply curve shifts to the left from S_0 to S_1.
Step 4: Compare the new equilibrium price and quantity to the original equilibrium. At the new equilibrium, E_1, the equilibrium price rose from $10 per pound to $16 per pound, but the equilibrium quantity decreased from 600 million pounds to 400 million pounds. Notice that the equilibrium quantity demanded decreased, even though the demand curve did not move.

equilibrium quantity and price of shrimp in the United States? Exhibit 4-8 uses the four-step approach to work through this problem.

1. Draw a demand and supply diagram to show what the market for shrimp looked like before the shrimp disease. The original equilibrium E_0 was $10 per pound, and the original equilibrium quantity was 600 million pounds of shrimp.
2. Did the economic event affect supply or demand? A disease is a natural condition that affects supply.
3. Was the effect on supply an increase or a decrease? Disease reduces the quantity that will be supplied at any given price. The supply curve shifts to the left from S_0 to S_1.
4. Compare the new equilibrium price and quantity to the original equilibrium. At the new equilibrium, E_1, the equilibrium price rose from $10 per pound to $16 per pound, but the equilibrium quantity decreased from 600 million pounds to 400 million pounds. Notice that the equilibrium quantity demanded decreased, even though the demand curve did not move.

In short, the outbreak of shrimp disease decreased the supply of imported shrimp in the United States. The result was a lower equilibrium quantity of shrimp bought and sold in the market at a higher price.

Sand and Hydraulic Fracturing

The U.S. economy used about 46 million tons of sand and gravel in 2012, which is nearly twice as much as a decade earlier. In addition, the price of sand and gravel rose from $18.30/ton in 2003 to $52.80/ton in 2012. What happened? Sand is an input in products such as concrete and asphalt pavement, and it is also present in paint, paper, plastics, and glass. However, sand is also used in hydraulic fracturing, a method of extracting oil and natural gas, and use of this method expanded substantially in recent years. In some recent

EXHIBIT 4-9 The Market for Sand: A Four-Step Analysis

Step 1: Draw a demand and supply diagram to illustrate what the market for sand looked like before the fracking boom. The demand curve D_0 and the supply curve S_0 show the original relationships.

Step 2: Will the change described affect supply or demand? The more widespread use of hydraulic fracturing technology will affect the demand for sand, which is used in that process.

Step 3: Will the effect on demand be positive or negative? The growth of fracking will tend to mean a higher quantity demanded of the product, sand, at every given price, causing the demand curve for sand to shift to the right from D_0 to D_1.

Step 4: Compare the new equilibrium price and quantity to the original equilibrium price. The new equilibrium E_1 occurs at a higher quantity and a higher price than the original equilibrium E_0.

years, when oil and gas prices were high, "fracking" accounted for more than 60% of U.S. sand consumption. How could increases in fracking affect the demand for sand? Exhibit 4-9 illustrates the four-step analysis.

1. Draw a demand and supply diagram to illustrate what the market for sand looked like in the year before the fracking boom. In Exhibit 4-9, the demand curve D_0 and the supply curve S_0 show the original relationships. In this case, the analysis is performed without specific numbers on the price and quantity axes.

2. Did the change described affect supply or demand? The widespread use of hydraulic fracturing technology, encouraged by a large rise in the price of oil and natural gas during the first decade of the 2000s, will affect demand for sand.

3. Was the effect on demand an increase or a decrease? The changes meant a higher quantity demanded of the product, sand, at every given price, causing the demand curve for sand to shift right to the new demand curve D_1.

4. Compare the new equilibrium price and quantity at E_1 to the original equilibrium price and quantity at E_0. The new equilibrium E_1 occurs at a higher quantity and a higher price than the original equilibrium E_0.

The Interconnections and Speed of Adjustment in Real Markets

In the real world, many factors that affect demand and supply can change all at once. For example, the demand for cars might increase because of rising incomes and population, and it might decrease because of rising gasoline prices (a complementary good). Likewise, the supply of cars might increase because of innovative new technologies that reduce the cost of car production, and it might decrease as a result of new government regulations requiring the installation of costly pollution-control technology. Moreover, rising incomes and population or changes in gasoline prices will affect many markets, not just cars. How can an economist sort out all of these interconnected events? The answer lies in the *ceteris paribus* assumption. Look at how each economic event affects each market, one event at a time, holding all else constant.

In the four-step analysis of how economic events affect equilibrium price and quantity, the movement from the old to the new equilibrium seems immediate. But as a practical matter, prices and quantities often do not zoom straight to equilibrium. More realistically, when an economic event causes demand or supply to shift, prices and quantities set off in the general direction of equilibrium. Indeed, even as they are moving toward one new equilibrium, prices are often then pushed by another change in demand or supply toward another equilibrium.

Price Ceilings and Price Floors in Markets for Goods and Services

Controversy often surrounds the prices and quantities that are established by demand and supply. After all, every time you buy a gallon of gasoline, pay the rent for your apartment, or pay the interest charges on your credit card, it's natural to wish that the price had been at least a little lower. Every time a restaurant sells a meal, a department store sells a sweater, or a farmer sells a bushel of wheat, it's natural for the profit-seeking seller to wish that the price had been higher. In some cases, discontent over prices turns into public pressure on politicians, who may then pass legislation to prevent a certain price

---

CLEARING IT UP

Shifts of Demand or Supply versus Movements along a Demand or Supply Curve

One common mistake in applying the demand and supply framework is to confuse the shift of a demand or a supply curve with the movement along a demand or supply curve. As an example, consider a problem that asks whether a drought will increase or decrease the equilibrium quantity and equilibrium price of wheat. Lee, a student in an introductory economics class, might reason:

"Well, it's clear that a drought reduces supply, so I'll shift back the supply curve, as in the shift from the original supply curve S_0 to S_1 shown on the diagram (call this Shift 1). So the equilibrium moves from E_0 to E_1, the equilibrium quantity is lower and the equilibrium price is higher. Then, a higher price makes farmers more likely to supply the good, so the supply curve shifts right, as shown by the shift from S_1 to S_2 on the diagram (shown as Shift 2), so that the equilibrium now moves from E_1 to E_2. But the higher price also reduces demand and so causes demand to shift back, like the shift from the original demand curve D_0 to D_1 on the diagram (labeled Shift 3), and the equilibrium moves from E_2 to E_3."

At about this point, Lee suspects that this answer is headed down the wrong path. Think about what might be wrong with Lee's logic, and then read the answer that follows.

Answer: Lee's first step is correct: that is, a drought shifts back the supply curve of wheat and leads to a prediction of a lower equilibrium quantity and a higher

equilibrium price. The rest of Lee's argument is wrong because it mixes up shifts in supply with quantity supplied, and shifts in demand with quantity demanded. A higher or lower price never shifts the supply curve, as suggested by the shift in supply from S_1 to S_2. Instead, a price change leads to a movement along a given supply curve. Similarly, a higher or lower price never shifts a demand curve, as suggested in the shift from D_0 to D_1. Instead, a price change leads to a movement along a given demand curve. Remember, a change in the price of a good never causes the demand or supply curve for that good to shift.

---

from climbing "too high" or falling "too low." The demand and supply model shows how people and firms will react to the incentives provided by these laws to control prices, in ways that will often lead to undesirable costs and consequences. Alternative policy tools can often achieve the desired goals of price control laws, while avoiding at least some of the costs and trade-offs of such laws.

Price Ceilings

<mark>Price controls</mark> are laws that the government enacts to regulate prices. Price controls come in two flavors. <mark>A **price ceiling** keeps a price from rising above a certain level, while a **price floor** keeps a price from falling below a certain level.</mark> This section uses the demand and supply framework to analyze price ceilings; the next section turns to price floors.

In many markets for goods and services, demanders outnumber suppliers. There are more people who buy bread than companies that make bread; more people who rent apartments than landlords; more people who purchase prescription drugs than companies that manufacture such drugs; more people who buy gasoline than companies that refine and sell gasoline. Consumers, who are also potential voters, sometimes flex enough political strength to push for a law to hold down the level of a certain price. In some cities, for example, renters have pressed political leaders to pass rent control laws, a form of price ceiling that might require that rents can only be raised by a certain maximum percentage each year.

Rent control can become a politically hot topic when rents begin to rise rapidly. Rents might rise for many reasons. Perhaps a change in tastes makes a certain suburb or town a more popular place to live. Perhaps locally based businesses expand, bringing higher incomes and more people into the area. Changes of this sort can cause a change in the demand for rental housing, as illustrated in Exhibit 4-10. The original equilibrium E_0 lies at the intersection of supply curve S_0 and demand curve D_0, corresponding to an equilibrium price of $500 and an equilibrium quantity of 15,000 units of rental housing. The effect of greater income or a change in tastes is to shift the demand curve for rental housing to the right, as shown by the data in the table and the shift from D_0 to D_1 on the graph. In this market, at the new equilibrium E_1, the price of a rental unit would rise to $600 and the equilibrium quantity would increase to 17,000 units.

Long-time apartment dwellers will dislike these price increases. They may argue, "Why should *our* rents rise because a lot of newcomers want to move in?" The current apartment-dwellers are also voters, and they may elect local politicians who pass a price ceiling law that limits how much rents can rise.

price controls: Government laws to regulate prices.

price ceiling: A law that prevents a price from rising above a certain level.

price floor: A law that prevents a price from falling below a certain level.

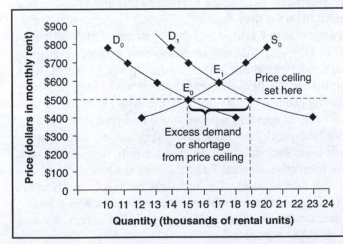

Price	Original Quantity Supplied	Original Quantity Demanded	New Quantity Demanded
$400	12,000	18,000	23,000
$500	15,000	15,000	19,000
$600	17,000	13,000	17,000
$700	19,000	11,000	15,000
$800	20,000	10,000	14,000

EXHIBIT 4-10 A Price Ceiling Example—Rent Control

The original intersection of demand and supply occurs at E_0. Demand shifts from D_0 to D_1. The new equilibrium would be at E_1—except that a price ceiling prevents the price from rising. Because the price doesn't change, the quantity supplied remains at 15,000. However, after the change in demand, the quantity demanded rises to 19,000. There is excess demand, also called a shortage.

What's a Price Bubble? A Story of Housing Prices

The average price of a U.S. single-family home rose about 1–3% per year in the first half of the 1990s; 3–5% per year in the second half of the 1990s; 7–8% per year in the early 2000s; and more than 10% per year from late 2004 to early 2006.

Although no one seriously expected price increases of 10% per year to continue for long, what happened next was still a shock. Certain metropolitan areas or states had seen declines in housing prices from time to time, but there had not been a nationwide decline in housing prices since the Great Depression of the 1930s. However, housing prices started falling in 2006, and through much of 2008 and 2009, housing prices were falling at a rate of 4–5% per year. Of course, these national averages understate the experience of certain parts of the country where both the boom and the bust were much larger.

Economists refer to this chain of events as a price "bubble." Remember that one possible reason for demand to shift is expectations about the future. If many people expect that housing prices are going to rise in the future, demand for housing will shift to the right—thus helping the prediction of higher prices come true. For a time, a cycle of expecting higher prices, in-creases in demand, and resulting higher prices can be self-reinforcing. But this process cannot last forever. At some unpredictable time, potential buyers recognize that the expectations of ever-higher future prices are unrealistic, at which point the expectation that future prices will stop rising or start falling causes demand to shift back in the other direction, and the price bubble deflates. Price bubbles are not just observed in housing: for example, they are also seen in markets for collectible items and in stock markets.

The bursting of the price bubble in housing—which happened in many countries around the world, not just the United States—has caused great economic difficulties. Those who owned homes watched the value of this asset decline. Some of those who borrowed money to buy a house near the peak of the bubble found a few years later, after the bubble had burst, that what they owed to the bank was much more than the house was worth. When many people began to default on their mortgage loans, banks and other financial institutions then faced huge losses. The bursting of the price bubble in housing helped to trigger the global economic slowdown that started in late 2007 and continued until 2009.

For simplicity, let's assume that a rent control law is passed to keep the price at the original equilibrium of $500 for a typical apartment. In Exhibit 4-10, the horizontal line at the price of $500 shows the legally fixed maximum price set by the rent control law. However, the underlying forces that shifted the demand curve to the right have not vanished. At that price ceiling, the quantity demanded exceeds the quantity supplied: that is, at a price of $500 the quantity supplied remains at the same 15,000 rental units, but the quantity demanded is 19,000 rental units. Thus, people who would like to rent in this area are knocking on the doors of landlords, searching for apartments. A situation of excess demand, also called a shortage, results when people are willing to pay the market price but cannot purchase (or in this case rent) what they desire.

Rent control has been especially popular in wartime and during times of high inflation. New York City, the most prominent U.S. city that has imposed rent control laws for a long period, put rent control in place as a "temporary" measure during World War II. Rent control was also especially popular during the 1970s, when all prices in the U.S. economy were rising rapidly as part of an overall process of inflation. By the mid-1980s, more than 200 American cities, with about 20% of the nation's population, had rent control laws. But in the last two decades, the political pendulum began swinging against rent control. More than 30 states adopted laws or constitutional amendments banning rent control outright. In many cities that kept some form of rent control, the focus of the law shifted from trying to hold rents below the equilibrium price to offering ways for resolving disputes between tenants and landlords, like disagreements about maintenance, pets, and noise.

Although the effect of rent control laws in the United States has faded in recent years, price ceilings are often proposed for other products. For example, price ceilings to limit what producers can charge have been proposed in recent years for prescription drugs, on doctor and hospital fees, the charges made by some automatic teller bank machines, and auto insurance rates. Many low-income countries around the world have also imposed price ceilings on basic items like bread or energy products. In the early 2000s, the gov-

Price Ceilings and Floors Do Not Change Demand or Supply

Neither price ceilings nor price floors cause demand or supply to change. Remember, changes in price don't cause demand or supply to change. Price ceilings and price floors can cause a different choice of quantity demanded along a demand curve, but they don't move the demand curve. Price controls can cause a different choice of quantity supplied along a supply curve, but they don't shift the supply curve.

ernment of the African country of Zimbabwe tried to help its ordinary citizens by placing ceilings on the prices of ordinary household items like bread, wheat, and cooking oil. But many producers of these items, faced with the low prices, went out of business. More recently, Venezuela tried a similar policy with similar results. The goal of the price ceiling had been to keep necessities affordable to all, but the result was that the quantity of the products declined and shortages occurred.

Price ceilings are enacted in an attempt to keep prices low for those who demand the product. But when the market price is not allowed to rise to the equilibrium level, quantity demanded exceeds quantity supplied, and thus a shortage occurs. Those who manage to purchase the product at the lower price given by the price ceiling will benefit, but sellers of the product will suffer, along with those who are not able to purchase the product at all.

Price Floors

Price floors are enacted when discontented sellers, feeling that prices are too low, appeal to legislators to keep prices from falling. A price floor is the lowest legal price that can be paid in markets for goods and services, labor, and financial capital. Price floors are sometimes called "price supports" because they prevent a price from falling below a certain level.

Around the world, many countries have passed laws to keep farm prices higher than they otherwise would be. In the annual budget of the European Union, roughly 40% of all spending late in 2014—more than $60 billion per year—was used to keep prices high for Europe's farmers. Thanks to this policy, the prices received by European farmers for such agricultural staples as wheat, barley, rice, milk, and beef have held substantially above the price prevailing in the world market for decades.

Exhibit 4-11 illustrates the effects of a government program that assures a price above the equilibrium by focusing on the market for wheat in Europe. In the absence of government

EXHIBIT 4-11 The European Wheat Prices: A Price Floor Example

The intersection of demand D and supply S would be at the equilibrium point E_0. However, a price floor set at p_f holds the price above E_0 and prevents it from falling. The result of the price floor is that the quantity supplied Q_s exceeds the quantity demanded Q_d. There is excess supply, also called a surplus.

When Floors Are Higher Than Ceilings

In economics, (price) ceilings often appear graphically lower than (price) floors. The reason is that binding price ceilings are below the equilibrium level, stopping the price from rising, and binding price floors are above the equilibrium level, stopping the price from falling. Thus, above-equilibrium price floors are higher than below-equilibrium price ceilings.

intervention, the price would adjust so that the quantity supplied would equal the quantity demanded at the equilibrium point E_0, with price p_0 and quantity Q_0. However, policies to keep prices high for farmers keeps the price above what would have been the market equilibrium level—the price p_f shown by the dashed horizontal line in the diagram. The result is a quantity supplied of Q_S in excess of the quantity demanded Q_d. When quantity supply exceeds quantity demanded, then a situation of excess supply exists, also called a surplus. The high-income countries of the world, including the United States, Europe, and Japan, spend roughly $1 billion per day in supporting their farmers. If the government is willing to purchase the excess supply (or to provide payments for others to purchase it), then farmers will benefit from the price floor, but taxpayers and consumers of food will pay the costs. Numerous proposals have been offered for reducing farm subsidies. But in many countries, political support for subsidies for farmers—and indirectly, for what is viewed as the traditional rural way of life—remains strong.

Responses to Price Controls: Many Margins for Action

Although a government can set price floors or price ceilings, such rules often have unintended consequences. The focus of the discussion so far has been on reactions that take the form of changes in quantity demanded or quantity supplied, and thus on understanding why price ceilings commonly lead to shortages and price floors lead to surpluses. However, buyers and sellers in real-world markets have many other ways in which they can react to price controls. The ability of households and firms to react in a variety of ways to government rules is called the problem of "many margins for action."

black market: An illegal market that breaks government rules on prices or sales.

One alternative reaction occurs when buyers and seller decide to break the government rules on prices or sales, which is referred to as a **black market**. Consider a landlord who

Price Controls of 1776

During the American Revolution, a number of states imposed price ceilings on many goods. After Rhode Island passed price control laws in 1776, the city of Providence reported on the effects to the state legislature in 1777:

> [The effect] is so intricate, variable, and complicated, that it cannot remain any time equitable. . . . It was made to cheapen the articles of life, but it has in fact raised their prices, by producing an artificial and in some respects a real scarcity. It was made to unite us in good agreement respecting prices; but hath produced animosity, and ill will between town and country, and between buyers and sellers in general. It was made to bring us up to some equitable standard of honesty . . . but hath produced a sharping set of mushroom peddlers, who adulterate their commodities, and take every advantage to evade the . . . act, by quibbles and lies.

Price control laws are often popular in the short run, because they look like an easy fix, but they become less popular over time as shortages occur, social tensions arise, and efforts to evade the laws gain force. The problems noted by the citizens of Providence, Rhode Island, in 1777 apply today as they did more than 200 years ago.

owns rent-controlled property. Suppose that although the law dictates the cap on the rent that the landlord can charge, a potential tenant is willing to pay more than the rent control law allows to live in the apartment. If this "extra rent" is paid in cash, then who will know?

A second margin for action is "side payments," which are additional payments that are made along with the actual price paid. In New York City, with its long history of rent control, landlords sometimes devise innovative charges like a "nonrefundable cleaning deposit" and a "nonrefundable key deposit," or they may require several months' rent in advance. These charges can have the effect of making the tenant pay more than the actual rent.

A third margin for action involves quality adjustment. In the case of rent control, a landlord may keep the rent low but put off needed maintenance or the installation of new appliances. The result is a lower-priced apartment—but also a lower-quality apartment.

A fourth margin for action involves shifting who is involved in the transaction. In cities with rent control, it isn't unusual for a tenant living in a rent-controlled apartment not to move out officially; instead, the tenant sublets the apartment to someone else. In this case, the original tenant pays the rent-controlled rate but charges the market rate to the new renter and pockets the difference.

Those who favor price floors and price ceilings are often quite aware of the actions that can circumvent the underlying purpose of price controls. Thus, supporters of price controls also favor rules that will include penalties for black markets, make side payments illegal, require certain quality levels, and prohibit shifts in who is involved in the transaction. However, establishing rules or laws that will limit all of the alternative margins for action is like trying to block a flowing stream with your fingers. Shutting down the many margins for action by which citizens and firms respond to price controls is much easier said than done.

Policy Alternatives to Price Ceilings and Price Floors

The economic analysis of how price ceilings can create shortages and price floors create surpluses can be disheartening. If you want to pursue a policy goal of assuring that people have a sufficient quantity of affordable housing, but rent controls are just price ceilings that cause housing shortages, what alternative policy can you advocate? If you want to pursue a policy goal of supporting farmers, but farm price supports lead to storehouses of surplus grain rotting at high cost to taxpayers and consumers, then what alternative policy can you advocate? The same demand and supply model that shows that price ceilings and price floors often have unintended, undesirable consequences of creating surpluses and shortages can also suggest alternate public policies that do not have these same trade-offs.

Let's return to the issue of rent control. If the goal is to have an expanded supply of affordable housing, then a rightward shift in a demand curve, a supply curve, or both as shown in Exhibit 4-12, can accomplish this goal. A shift to the right in the supply of affordable housing from S_0 to S_1, for example, might be achieved if a government grants subsidies to builders who construct apartment buildings that have relatively smaller rental units, which will have a more affordable price in the market. This step taken alone would cause a shift to the right from the original equilibrium E_0, to the new equilibrium, E_1, and would increase the quantity of housing from q_0 to q_1. A shift to the right in the demand curve from D_0 to D_1 might be achieved by giving a subsidy to low-income renters, perhaps in the form of cash or a voucher that the renters could use to pay some of the rent, so that low-income renters could then have more to spend on housing. This step taken alone would cause a shift to the right from the original equilibrium, E_0, to the new equilibrium, E_2, and would increase the quantity of affordable housing from q_0 to q_2. Instituting *both* sets of policies would shift supply from S_0 to S_1, demand from D_0 to D_1, the equilibrium from the original E_0 to E_3, and the quantity of affordable housing from q_0 to q_3.

Any combination of these policies is likely to be more useful in expanding affordable housing than rent control because these policies tend to increase the quantity of affordable

EXHIBIT 4-12 Policies for Affordable Housing: Alternatives to Rent Control

The original equilibrium is the intersection of demand D_0 and supply S_0 at the equilibrium E_0. Providing subsidies to low-income buyers of housing will shift the demand curve from D_0 to D_1, leading to a new equilibrium at E_2. Alternatively, a policy of providing subsidies to builders of affordable housing would shift the supply curve from S_0 to S_1, leading to a new equilibrium at E_1. Undertaking both demand-side and supply-side policies would move the market to equilibrium E_3, at the intersection of the new demand curve D_1 and the new supply curve S_1. As drawn here, both of these policies will increase the equilibrium quantity of affordable housing. An increase in demand will also raise the price of affordable housing, but as long as the subsidy received by buyers is larger than the higher price, buyers will not be adversely affected by the higher price that occurs from an increase in demand.

housing, whereas rent control tends to decrease it. Moreover, these alternative policies side-step many of the problems that arise when suppliers and demanders react to price controls.

Similarly, there are a number of alternative policies to support farmers or rural areas that do not involve setting price floors for crops. For example, the government could provide income directly to farmers, especially to small-scale farmers with lower incomes. The government might also assist rural economies in many other ways: establishing new branches of state colleges and universities in agricultural areas, creating parks or nature preserves that might attract tourists, supporting research into new methods of producing and using local crops to help the local farmers stay ahead, helping to build transportation links to rural areas, and subsidizing high-speed Internet cable connections across rural areas or wireless phone service. All of these alternative policies would help rural communities while avoiding the problem of price floors, because these alternative policies don't encourage farmers to produce an excess supply of surplus food.

With alternative policies readily available, why do governments enact price floors and price ceilings? One reason is that in public policy debates over price controls, people often don't take into account the unintended but predictable trade-offs. Another reason is that government sometimes views laws about price floors and ceilings as having zero cost, while giving subsidies to demanders or suppliers requires a government to collect taxes and spend money. The point here is not to endorse every proposal for using targeted subsidies or tax breaks to change demand and supply. Each policy proposal must be evaluated according to its own costs and benefits. But before reaching for the seemingly easy policy tool of price controls, with their predictable and undesired consequences and trade-offs, it is wise to consider alternative policies to shift demand and supply so as to achieve the desired new market equilibrium.

Supply, Demand, and Efficiency

In the market equilibrium, where the quantity demanded equals quantity supplied, nothing is wasted. No excess supply sits unsold, gathering dust in warehouses. No shortages exist that cause people to stand in long lines or rely on political connections to acquire goods—alternatives that waste time and energy. All those who wish to purchase or sell goods at the equilibrium market price are able to purchase or sell the quantity that they desire, as movements of the equilibrium price bring quantity demanded and supplied into balance.

The familiar demand and supply diagram holds within it the concept of economic efficiency, which was introduced in Chapter 2. To economists, an efficient outcome is one where it is impossible to improve the situation of one party without imposing a cost on someone else. Conversely, if a situation is inefficient, it becomes possible to benefit at least one party without imposing costs on others. Thus, the definition of productive efficiency in Chapter 2 was that the economy was producing without waste and getting all it could out of its scarce resources, in the sense that it was impossible to get more of good A without a reduction in good B. Efficiency in the demand and supply model has the same basic meaning: the economy is getting as much benefit as possible from its scarce resources, and all the possible gains from trade have been achieved.

Consumer Surplus, Producer Surplus, Social Surplus

Consider the example of a market for portable music devices shown in Exhibit 4-13. The equilibrium price is $80, and the equilibrium quantity is 28 million. To see the benefits received by consumers, look at the segment of the demand curve above the equilibrium point and to the left. This portion of the demand curve shows that at least some demanders

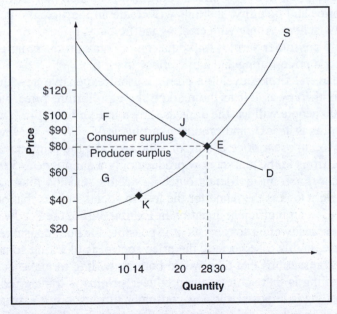

EXHIBIT 4-13 Consumer and Producer Surplus

The triangular area labeled by F shows the area of consumer surplus, which shows that the equilibrium price in the market was less than what many of the consumers were willing to pay. For example, point J on the demand curve shows that even at the price of $90, consumers would have been willing to purchase a quantity of 20 million. But those consumers only needed to pay the equilibrium price of $80. The triangular area labeled by G shows the area of producer surplus, which shows that the equilibrium price received in the market was more than what many of the producers were willing to accept for their products. For example, point K on the supply curve shows that at a price of $40, firms would have been willing to supply a quantity of 14 million. However, in this market those firms could receive a price of $80 for their production. The sum of consumer surplus and producer surplus—that is, F + G—is called social surplus.

would have been willing to pay more than $80 for a portable music player. For example, point J shows that if the price was $90, the quantity demanded of the portable music player would have been 20 million. Those consumers who would have been willing to pay $90 for a portable music player based on the utility they expect to receive from it, but who were able to pay the equilibrium price of $80, clearly received a benefit. Remember, the demand curve traces out the willingness to pay for different quantities. The amount that individuals would have been willing to pay minus the amount that they actually paid is called **consumer surplus**. Consumer surplus is the area labeled F—that is, the area between the market price and the segment of the demand curve above equilibrium.

The equilibrium price also benefits producers. The supply curve shows the quantity that firms are willing to supply at each price. For example, point K on Exhibit 4-13 illustrates that at a price of $40, firms would still have been willing to supply a quantity of 14 million. Those producers who would have been willing to supply the portable music players at a price of $40, but who were instead able to charge the equilibrium price of $80, clearly received a benefit. **Producer surplus** is the amount that a seller is paid for a good minus the seller's actual cost. In Exhibit 4-13, producer surplus is the area labeled G—that is, the area between the market price and the segment of the supply curve below the equilibrium.

Social surplus is the sum of consumer surplus and producer surplus. In Exhibit 4-13, social surplus would thus be shown as the area F + G. Social surplus is larger at equilibrium quantity and price than it would be at any other quantity. At the efficient level of output, it is impossible to increase consumer surplus without reducing producer surplus, and it is impossible to increase producer surplus without reducing consumer surplus.

Inefficiency of Price Floors and Price Ceilings

The imposition of a price floor or a price ceiling will prevent a market from adjusting to its equilibrium price and quantity, and thus will create an inefficient outcome. But there is an additional twist here. Along with creating inefficiency, price floors and ceilings will also transfer some consumer surplus to producers, or some producer surplus to consumers. Let's consider a price ceiling and a price floor in turn.

Imagine that several firms develop a promising but expensive new drug for treating back pain. If this therapy is left to the market, the equilibrium price will be $600 per month, and 20,000 people will use the drug, as shown in Exhibit 4-14a. The original level of consumer surplus is T + U, and producer surplus is V + W + X. However, the government decides to impose a price ceiling of $400 to make the drug more affordable. At this price ceiling, firms in the market now produce only a quantity of 15,000. As a result, two changes occur. First, an inefficient outcome occurs, and the total social surplus is reduced. **Deadweight loss** is the name for the loss in social surplus that occurs when the economy produces at an inefficient quantity. In Exhibit 4-14a, the deadweight loss is the area U + W. When deadweight loss exists, it is possible for both consumer and producer surplus to increase, in this case because the price control is blocking some suppliers and demanders from transactions that they would both be willing to make. A second change from the price ceiling is that some of the producer surplus is transferred to consumers. After the price ceiling is imposed, the new consumer surplus is T + V, while the new producer surplus is X. In other words, the price ceiling transfers the area of surplus V from producers to consumers.

For the case of a price floor shown in Exhibit 4-14b, envision a situation where a city has several movie theaters that are all losing money. The current equilibrium is a price of $8 per movie, with 1,800 people attending movies. The original consumer surplus is G + H + J, and producer surplus is I + K. The city government is worried that movie theaters will go out of business, thus reducing the entertainment options available to citizens, so it decides to impose a price floor of $12 per ticket. As a result, the quantity demanded of movie tickets falls to 1,400. The new consumer surplus is G, and the new producer surplus is H + I. In effect, the price floor causes the area H to be transferred from consumer to producer surplus, but also causes a deadweight loss of J + K.

consumer surplus: The benefit consumers receive from buying a good or service, measured by what the individuals would have been willing to pay minus the amount that they actually paid.

producer surplus: The benefit producers receive from selling a good or service, measured by the price the producer actually received minus the price the producer would have been willing to accept.

social surplus: The sum of consumer surplus and producer surplus.

deadweight loss: The loss in social surplus that occurs when a market produces an inefficient quantity.

FIGURE 4-14
Efficiency and Price Floors and Ceilings

(a) Reduced social surplus from a price ceiling

The original equilibrium price is $600 with a quantity of 20,000. Consumer surplus is T + U, and producer surplus is V + W + X. A price ceiling is imposed at $400, so firms in the market now produce only a quantity of 15,000. As a result, the new consumer surplus is T + V, while the new producer surplus is X. In effect, the price ceiling transfers the surplus V from producers to consumers, but also causes deadweight loss in social surplus of U + W.

(b) Reduced social surplus from a price floor

The original equilibrium is $8 at a quantity of 1,800. Consumer surplus is G + H + J, and producer surplus is I + K. A price floor is imposed at $12, which means that quantity demanded falls to 1,400. As a result, the new consumer surplus is G, and the new producer surplus is H + I. In effect, the price floor causes the area H to be transferred from consumer to producer surplus, but also causes a deadweight loss in social surplus of J + K.

This analysis shows that a price ceiling, like a law establishing rent controls, will transfer some producer surplus to consumers—which helps to explain why consumers often favor them. Conversely, a price floor like a guarantee that farmers will receive a certain price for their crops will transfer some consumer surplus to producers, which explains why producers often favor them. However, both price floors and price ceilings block some transactions that buyers and sellers would have been willing to make and create deadweight loss. Removing such barriers so that prices and quantities can adjust to their equilibrium level will increase the economy's social surplus.

Demand and Supply as a Social Adjustment Mechanism

The demand and supply model emphasizes that prices are not set only by demand or only by supply, but by the interaction between the two. In 1890, the famous economist Alfred Marshall wrote that asking whether supply or demand determined a price was like arguing "whether it is the upper or the under blade of a pair of scissors that cuts a piece of paper." The answer is that both blades of the demand and supply scissors are always involved.

The adjustments of equilibrium price and quantity in a market-oriented economy often occur without much government direction or oversight. If the coffee crop in Brazil suffers a terrible frost, then the supply curve of coffee shifts to the left, and the price of coffee rises. Some people—call them the coffee addicts—continue to drink coffee and pay the higher price. Others switch to tea or soft drinks. No government commission is needed to figure out how to adjust coffee prices, or which companies will be allowed to process the remaining supply, or which supermarkets in which cities will receive a certain quantity of coffee to sell, or which consumers will ultimately be allowed to drink the brew. Such adjustments in response to price changes happen all the time in a market economy, often so smoothly and rapidly that we barely notice them. Think for a moment of all the seasonal foods that are available and inexpensive at certain times of the year, like fresh corn in midsummer, but more expensive at other times of the year. People alter their diets and restaurants alter their menus in response to these fluctuations in prices without fuss or fanfare. For both the U.S. economy and the world economy as a whole, demand and supply is the primary social mechanism for answering the basic questions about what is produced, how it is produced, and for whom it is produced.

Key Concepts and Summary

1. A **demand schedule** is a table that shows the **quantity demanded** at different prices in the market. A **demand curve** shows the relationship between quantity demanded and price in a given market on a graph. The **law of demand** points out that a higher price typically leads to a lower quantity demanded.

2. A **supply schedule** is a table that shows the **quantity supplied** at different prices in the market. A **supply curve** shows the relationship between quantity supplied and price on a graph. The **law of supply** points out that a higher price typically leads to a higher quantity supplied.

3. The **equilibrium price** and **equilibrium quantity** occur where the supply and demand curves cross. The **equilibrium** occurs where the quantity demanded is equal to the quantity supplied.

4. If the price is below the equilibrium level, then the quantity demanded will exceed the quantity supplied. **Excess demand** or a **shortage** will exist. If the price is above the equilibrium level, then the quantity supplied will exceed the quantity demanded. **Excess supply** or a **surplus** will exist. In either case, economic pressures will push the price toward the equilibrium level.

5. Economists often use the *ceteris paribus* or "other things being equal" assumption, that while examining the economic impact of one event, all other factors remain unchanged for the purpose of the analysis.

6. Factors that can shift the demand curve for goods and services, causing a different quantity to be demanded at any given price, include changes in tastes, population, income, prices of **substitute** or **complement** goods, and expectations about future conditions and prices.

7. Factors that can shift the supply curve for goods and services, causing a different quantity to be supplied at any given price, include natural conditions, input prices, changes in technology, and government taxes, regulations, or subsidies.

8. When using the supply and demand framework to think about how an event will affect the equilib-rium price and quantity, proceed through four steps: (a) sketch a supply and demand diagram to think about what the market looked like before the event; (b) decide whether the event will affect supply or demand; (c) decide whether the effect on supply or demand is negative or positive, and draw the appropriate shifted supply or demand curve; (d) compare the new equilibrium price and quantity to the original ones.

9. **Price ceilings** prevent a price from rising above a certain level. When a price ceiling is set below the equilibrium price, quantity demanded will exceed quantity supplied, and excess demand or shortages will result. **Price floors** prevent a price from falling below a certain level. When a price floor is set above the equilibrium price, quantity supplied will exceed quantity demanded, and excess supply or surpluses will result.

10. Price floors and price ceilings often lead to unintended consequences because buyers and sellers have many margins for action. These margins include **black markets**, side payments, quality adjustments, and shifts in who is involved in the transaction.

11. Policies that shift supply and demand explicitly, through targeted subsidies or taxes, are often preferable to policies that attempt to set prices because they avoid the shortages, surpluses, and other unintended consequences that price ceilings and floors typically produce.

12. **Consumer surplus** is the gap between the price that consumers are willing to pay, based on their preferences, and the market equilibrium price. **Producer surplus** is the gap between the price for which producers are willing to sell a product, based on their costs, and the market equilibrium price. **Social surplus** is the sum of consumer surplus and producer surplus. Total surplus is larger at the equilibrium quantity and price than it will be at any other quantity and price. **Deadweight loss** is the loss in total surplus that occurs when the economy produces at an inefficient quantity.

Review Questions

1. In the economic view, what determines the level of prices?

2. What does a downward-sloping demand curve mean about how buyers in a market will react to a higher price?

3. Will demand curves have the same exact shape in all markets?

4. What does an upward-sloping supply curve mean about how sellers in a market will react to a higher price?

5. Will supply curves have the same shape in all markets?
6. What is the relationship between quantity demanded and quantity supplied at equilibrium?
7. How can you locate the equilibrium point on a demand and supply graph?
8. When analyzing a market, how do economists deal with the problem that many factors that affect the market are changing at the same time?
9. If the price is above the equilibrium level, would you predict excess supply or excess demand? If the price is below the equilibrium level, would you predict a shortage or a surplus?
10. Explain why a price that is above the equilibrium level will tend to fall toward equilibrium. Explain why a price that is below the equilibrium level will tend to rise toward the equilibrium.
11. Name some factors that can cause a shift in the demand curve in markets for goods and services.
12. Does a price ceiling attempt to make a price higher or lower?
13. How does a price ceiling set below the equilibrium level affect quantity demanded and quantity supplied?
14. Does a price floor attempt to make a price higher or lower?

15. How does a price floor set above the equilibrium level affect quantity demanded and quantity supplied?
16. Make a list of ways that buyers and sellers may respond to price ceilings and price floors, other than changes in quantity.
17. Why might economists commonly prefer public policies that shift demand and/or supply rather than imposing price ceilings or price floors?
18. What's the difference between demand and quantity demanded?
19. Name some factors that can cause a shift in the supply curve in markets for goods and services.
20. Is supply the same thing as quantity supplied? Explain.
21. What is consumer surplus? How is it illustrated on a demand and supply diagram?
22. What is producer surplus? How is it illustrated on a demand and supply diagram?
23. What is total surplus? How is it illustrated on a demand and supply diagram?
24. What is the relationship between total surplus and economic efficiency?
25. What is deadweight loss?

Labor and Financial Capital Markets

Chapter Outline

Demand and Supply at Work in Labor Markets

Demand and Supply in Financial Capital Markets

Don't Kill the Price Messengers

Thinking about demand and supply curves in markets for labor and markets for financial capital requires a shift in perspective about the identity of demanders and suppliers. In markets for goods and services, individuals act as consumers on the demand side of the market, while firms act as sellers on the supply side. But in labor markets, individuals are the suppliers of labor, while firms and other employers who hire labor are on the demand side. In markets for financial capital, both individuals and firms can play roles as savers who supply financial capital and also as borrowers who demand it.

Most college students play an active role in both labor and financial capital markets. Employment is a fact of life for most college students: 40% of full-time college students ages 16–24—and 76% of part-time students—were employed in 2013. Most college students are also heavily involved in financial markets, primarily as borrowers. Among full-time college students, over half take out a loan to help finance their education each year, and those loans average about $7,000 per year. Many college students also borrow using credit cards and car loans. As this chapter will illustrate, labor markets and financial capital markets can be analyzed with the same tools of demand and supply as markets for goods and services.

Demand and Supply at Work in Labor Markets

Markets for labor have demand and supply curves, just like markets for goods and services. The law of demand applies in labor markets just as it does in goods and services markets. Specifically, a higher salary or wage—that is, a higher price in the labor market—leads to a decrease in quantity of labor demanded by employers, while a lower salary or wage leads to an increase in the quantity of labor demanded. The law of supply functions in labor markets, too; that is, a higher price for labor leads to a higher quantity of labor supplied.

Equilibrium in the Labor Market

Consider the market for nurses in the Minneapolis–St. Paul, Minnesota, metropolitan area. They work for a variety of employers: hospitals, doctors' offices, schools, health clinics, and nursing homes. Exhibit 5-1 illustrates how demand and supply determine equilibrium in this labor market. Let's walk through the elements of the figure one step at a time.

The horizontal axis shows the quantity of nurses hired. In this example, labor is measured by number of workers, but another common way to measure the quantity of labor is by the number of hours worked. The vertical axis shows the price for nurses' labor—that is, how much they are paid. In this example, the price of labor is measured by salary on an annual basis, although in other cases the price of labor could be measured by monthly or weekly pay, or even the wage paid per hour. The demand and supply schedules accompanying the exhibit list the quantity supplied and quantity demanded of nurses at different salaries.

As the salary for nurses rises, the quantity demanded will fall. Some hospitals and nursing homes may cut back on the number of nurses they hire, or they may lay off some of their existing nurses. Employers who face higher nurses' salaries may also try to look after patients by investing in physical equipment, like computer monitoring and diagnostic systems, or by using lower-paid health care aides to reduce the number of nurses they need to hire.

As salaries for nurses rise, the quantity supplied will rise. If nurses' salaries in Minneapolis–St. Paul are higher than in other cities, more people will be willing to train as nurses; more nurses will move to Minneapolis–St. Paul to find jobs; and those currently trained as nurses will be more likely to pursue nursing as a full-time job, rather than trying other jobs.

At equilibrium, the quantity supplied and the quantity demanded are equal. Thus, every employer who wants to hire a nurse at this equilibrium wage can find a willing worker, and every nurse who wants to work at this equilibrium salary can find a job. In Exhibit 5-1, the supply curve S and demand curve D intersect at the equilibrium point E. The equilibrium quantity of nurses in this example is 35,000, and the average annual salary is $70,000. This example simplifies the nursing market by focusing on the "average" nurse. In reality, of course, the market for nurses is actually made up of many smaller

Annual Salary	Quantity Demanded	Quantity Supplied
$55,000	45,000	20,000
$60,000	40,000	27,000
$65,000	37,000	31,000
$70,000	35,000	35,000
$75,000	33,000	38,000
$80,000	32,000	41,000

EXHIBIT 5-1 A Labor Market Example: Demand and Supply for Nurses in Minneapolis–St. Paul

The demand curve D of those employers who want to hire nurses intersects with the supply curve S of those who are qualified and willing to work as nurses at the equilibrium point E. In this example, the equilibrium salary is $70,000 and the equilibrium quantity is 35,000 nurses. At an above-equilibrium salary of $75,000, quantity supplied increases to 38,000, but the quantity of nurses demanded at the higher pay declines to 33,000. At this above-equilibrium salary, an excess supply or surplus of nurses would exist. At a below-equilibrium salary of $60,000, quantity supplied declines to 27,000, while the quantity demanded at the lower wage increases to 40,000 nurses. At this below-equilibrium salary, excess demand or a shortage exists.

markets, like markets for nurses with varying degrees of experience and credentials. But many markets contain closely related products that differ in quality; for instance, even a simple product like gasoline comes in regular, premium, and super-premium, each with a different price. Even in such cases, discussing the average price of gasoline or the average salary for nurses can be useful.

When the price of labor is not at the equilibrium, economic incentives tend to move salaries toward the equilibrium. For example, if salaries for nurses in Minneapolis–St. Paul were above the equilibrium at $75,000 per year, then 38,000 people want to work as nurses, but employers want to hire only 33,000 nurses. At the above-equilibrium salary, excess supply or a surplus results. In a situation of excess supply in the labor market, with many applicants for every job opening, employers who hire nurses will have an incentive to offer lower wages than they otherwise would have. The salary will move down toward equilibrium.

In contrast, if the salary is below the equilibrium at, say, $60,000 per year, then a situation of excess demand or a shortage arises. In this case, employers encouraged by the relatively lower wage want to hire 40,000 nurses, but only 27,000 individuals want to work as nurses in Minneapolis–St. Paul. In response to such a shortage, some employers in this metropolitan area will offer higher pay in order to attract the nurses. Other employers will have to match the higher pay to keep their own employees. The higher salaries will encourage more nurses to train or work in Minneapolis–St. Paul. Again, price and quantity in the labor market will move toward equilibrium.

Shifts in Labor Demand

The demand curve for labor shows what quantity of labor employers wish to hire at any salary or wage, under the *ceteris paribus* assumption that all other relevant economic factors are held constant. At least three types of economic events can cause a shift in the demand for labor, so that a higher or lower quantity of labor is hired at every salary or wage: changes in the quantity of output produced with that kind of labor, changes in how that output is produced, and government regulations affecting firms that demand labor.

A change in the quantity of the product being produced with a certain kind of that labor will alter the demand for that kind of labor. Expenditures on health care increased from about 9% of the U.S. economy in 1980 to 17% of the economy by 2014. When people spend more dollars on health care services, the demand for nurses increases at every given wage level, too. Demand for nurses may expand even more rapidly in the future because the proportion of Americans over the age of 65 will increase in the opening decades of the twenty-first century, and the elderly tend to consume more health care. Conversely, when demand for a certain product decreases, then demand for workers who make that product decreases, too.

Demand for labor may also shift because of changes in how output is produced. Firms that want to earn high profits look for a combination of inputs—workers, materials, and equipment—to keep costs low. Hospitals have sometimes tried to hold down costs by hiring health care aides rather than better-trained and higher-paid nurses.

Government regulations can also affect the quantity of workers that firms wish to hire at any given wage. For example, government rules may require nurses, rather than less-trained health care workers, to carry out certain medical procedures, while prohibiting nurses from carrying out other procedures. Changes in government rules can increase or decrease the quantity demanded of nurses at any given price.

Shifts in Labor Supply

On the supply side of the labor market, two main factors will affect how many people want to work at a certain job at a given salary level. One issue is how the job is perceived by workers relative to other choices. For example, there seems to have been a shift in the tastes of workers such that nursing looks relatively less attractive compared to other alternative jobs. One reason for that shift is that the job options open to women in health care, law, and business have expanded in recent decades.

Government policies can also affect the supply of labor for jobs. On one side, the government may support rules that set high qualifications for certain jobs: academic training, certificates or licenses, or experience. When these qualifications are made tougher, the supply of workers in that job will decrease at any given wage. On the other hand, the government may also reduce the required level of qualifications or else subsidize training; for example, the government might offer subsidies for nursing schools or nursing students. Such provisions would shift the supply curve of nurses to the right.

A change in salary will lead to a movement along labor demand or labor supply curves, but it will not shift those curves. However, events like those sketched here will cause either the demand or the supply of labor to shift, and thus will move the labor market to a new equilibrium salary and quantity.

Technology and Wage Inequality: The Four-Step Process

Economic events can change equilibrium salary (or wage) and quantity of labor. Consider how the wave of new information technologies might affect low-skill and high-skill workers in the U.S. economy. From the perspective of employers who demand labor, these new technologies are often a substitute for low-skill laborers like file clerks who used to organize the paper records of transactions. However, these new technologies are a complement to high-skill managers, who benefit from the technological advances by being able to monitor more information, communicate more easily, and juggle a wider array of responsibilities. How would these specific effects of the new technologies affect the wages of high-skill and low-skill workers? For this question, the four-step process for analyzing how shifts in supply or demand affect a market (introduced in Chapter 4) works in this way.

1. What did the markets for low-skill labor and high-skill labor look like before the arrival of the new technologies? In Exhibits 5-2a and 5-2b, S_0 is the original supply curve for labor and D_0 is the original demand curve for labor. In each graph, the original point of equilibrium, E_0, occurs at the price w_0 and the quantity q_0. The equilibrium pay for high-skill labor in Exhibit 5-2b exceeds the equilibrium pay for low-skill labor.
2. Does the new technology affect the supply of labor from households or the demand for labor from firms? The technology change described here affects demand for labor by firms that hire workers.
3. Will the new technology increase or decrease demand? Based on the description earlier, as the technology substitute for low-skill labor becomes available, demand for low-skill labor will decrease and shift to the left from D_0 to D_1. As the technology complement for high-skill labor becomes cheaper, demand for high-skill labor will increase and shift to the right from D_0 to D_1.
4. The new equilibrium for low-skill labor, shown as point E_1 with price w_1 and quantity q_1, has a lower wage and quantity hired than the original equilibrium, E_0. The new equilibrium for high-skill labor, shown as point E_1 with price w_1 and quantity q_1, has a higher wage and quantity hired than the original equilibrium E_0.

Thus, the demand and supply model predicts that the new computer and communications technologies will raise the pay of high-skill workers but reduce the pay of low-skill workers. Indeed, from the 1970s through the first decade of the 2000s, the wage gap widened between high-skill and low-skill labor. In 1980, for example, a college graduate earned about 30% more than a high school graduate with comparable job experience, but by 2010, a college graduate earned about 60% more than an otherwise comparable high school graduate. Many economists believe that direct and indirect effects of the new information technologies were among the main causes behind the trend toward greater wage inequality in the United States during this period.

(a) Technological change and low-skill labor   (b) Technological change and high-skill labor

EXHIBIT 5-2 Technology and Wages: Applying Demand and Supply

Step 1: What did the market look like before the change? In this case there are two markets: low-skill labor and high-skill labor. In each market, the original demand curve for labor is D_0, the original supply curve for labor is S_0, and the original equilibrium is E_0, where the equilibrium wage is w_0 and the equilibrium quantity is q_0.

Step 2: Does the new technology affect the supply of labor or the demand for labor? The new technology affects demand for labor.

Step 3: How will the new technology alter demand for the two types of labor? As the technology substitute for low-skill labor becomes cheaper, demand for low-skill labor will shift to the left, as shown by the shift from D_0 to D_1 in the market for low-skill labor. As the technology complement for high-skill labor becomes cheaper, demand for high-skill labor will shift to the right, as shown by the shift from D_0 to D_1 in the market for high-skill labor.

Step 4: Compare the new equilibrium to the original equilibrium. The new equilibrium for low-skill labor at E_1 has a lower wage and quantity than the original equilibrium E_0 in the market for low-skill labor. The new equilibrium for high-skill labor at E_1 has a higher wage and quantity than the original equilibrium.

Price Floors in the Labor Market: Living Wages and Minimum Wages

In contrast to goods and services markets, price ceilings are rare in labor markets because rules that prevent people from earning income are not politically popular. There is one exception: sometimes limits are proposed on the high incomes of top business executives.

The labor market, however, presents some prominent examples of price floors, which are often used as an attempt to increase the wages of low-paid workers. The U.S. government sets a **minimum wage, a price floor that makes it illegal for an employer to pay employees less than a certain hourly rate.** In mid-2009, the U.S. minimum wage was raised to $7.25 per hour. Local political movements in a number of U.S. cities have pushed for a higher minimum wage, which they call a *living wage*. Promoters of living wage laws maintain that the minimum wage is too low to ensure a reasonable standard of living. They base this conclusion on the calculation that, if you work 40 hours a week at a minimum wage of $7.25 per hour for 50 weeks a year, your annual income is $14,500, which is less than the official U.S. government definition of what it means for a family with one parent and children to be in poverty.

Supporters of the living wage argue that full-time workers should be assured a high enough wage so that they can afford the essentials of life: shelter, food, clothing, and health care. Since Baltimore passed the first living wage law in 1994, several dozen other cities have enacted similar laws. The living wage ordinances do not apply to all employers, but they have typically specified that all employees of the city or employees of firms that are hired by the city be paid at least a certain wage that is usually a few dollars per hour above the U.S. minimum wage.

Exhibit 5-3 illustrates the situation of a city considering a living wage law. The wage appears on the vertical axis because the wage is the price in the labor market. Before the passage of the living wage law, the equilibrium wage is $10 per hour and the city hires

minimum wage: A price floor that makes it illegal for an employer to pay employees less than a certain hourly rate.

Wage	Quantity Labor Demanded	Quantity Labor Supplied
$8/hr	1,900	500
$9/hr	1,500	900
$10/hr	1,200	1,200
$11/hr	900	1,400
$12/hr	700	1,600
$13/hr	500	1,800
$14/hr	400	1,900

EXHIBIT 5-3 A Living Wage: Example of a Price Floor

The original equilibrium in this labor market is a wage of $10/hour and a quantity of 1,200 workers, shown at point E. Imposing a wage floor at $12/hour leads to an excess supply of labor. At that wage, the quantity of labor supplied is 1,600, and the quantity of labor demanded is only 700.

1,200 workers at this wage. However, a group of concerned citizens persuades the city council to enact a living wage law requiring employers to pay no less than $12 per hour. In response to the higher wage (the horizontal dashed line in the graph), 1,600 workers look for jobs with the city. At this higher wage, the city, as an employer, is willing to hire only 700 workers. At the price floor, the quantity supplied exceeds the quantity demanded, and a surplus of labor exists in this market.

The Minimum Wage as an Example of a Price Floor

The U.S. minimum wage is a price floor that is typically set very close to the equilibrium wage for low-skill labor. About 2% of American workers are actually paid the minimum wage. In other words, the vast majority of the U.S. labor force has its wages determined in the labor market, not as a result of the government price floor. In many cities, the federal minimum wage is apparently below the market price for unskilled labor because employers offer more than the minimum wage to checkout clerks and other low-skill workers without any government prodding.

Economists have attempted to estimate how much the minimum wage reduces the quantity demanded of low-skill labor. A typical result of such studies is that a 10% increase in the minimum wage would decrease the hiring of unskilled workers by 1–2%, which seems a relatively small reduction. In fact, some studies have even found no effect of a higher minimum wage on employment at certain times and places.

Let's suppose that the minimum wage set lies just slightly *below* the equilibrium wage level. Wages could fluctuate according to market forces above this price floor, but they would not be allowed to move beneath the floor. In this situation, the price floor minimum wage is said to be *nonbinding*—that is, the price floor is not determining the market outcome. Even if the minimum wage moves just a little higher, it will still have no effect on the quantity of employment in the economy, as long as it remains below the equilibrium wage. Even if the minimum wage is increased by enough so that it rises slightly above the equilibrium wage and becomes binding, only a small excess supply gap will result between the quantity demanded and quantity supplied of low-skill labor.

These insights help to explain why U.S. minimum wage laws have historically had only a small impact on employment. Because the minimum wage has typically been set close to the equilibrium wage for low-skill workers and at some times and places even below it, it hasn't had a large effect in creating an excess supply of labor. However, if the minimum wage were increased dramatically—say, if it were doubled—then its impact on reducing the quantity demanded of employment would be much larger.

Demand and Supply in Financial Capital Markets

In the U.S. economy, $3.2 trillion was saved in 2014. Some of the savings ended up in banks, which in turn loaned the money to individuals or businesses that wanted to borrow money. Some was invested in private companies or loaned to government agencies that wanted to borrow money to raise funds for purposes like building roads or public transportation. Some firms took their savings and reinvested the money in their own business.

At this point, we'll avoid becoming entangled in all the different kinds of financial investments—like bank accounts, stocks, and bonds. Chapter 19 examines these specific financial investments in more detail. The task at hand is to determine how the demand and supply model links those who wish to supply financial capital with those who demand financial investments. Those who save money and make financial investments, whether individuals or businesses, are on the supply side of the financial capital market. Those who borrow money or firms who receive financial investments are on the demand side of the financial capital market.

Who Demands and Who Supplies in Financial Capital Markets

In any market, the price is what suppliers receive and what demanders pay. In financial capital markets, those who supply financial capital through saving expect to receive a rate of return, while those who demand financial capital by receiving funds expect to pay a rate of return. This rate of return can come in a variety of forms, depending on the type of financial investment. A straightforward example of a rate of return, often used for simplicity, is the interest rate. For example, when you supply money into a savings account at a bank, you receive a certain interest rate. If you demand a loan to buy a car or a computer, you will need to pay interest on the money you borrow.

Let's consider the market for borrowing money with credit cards. The United States has about 160 million credit card holders, who hold a total of 1 billion cards (an average

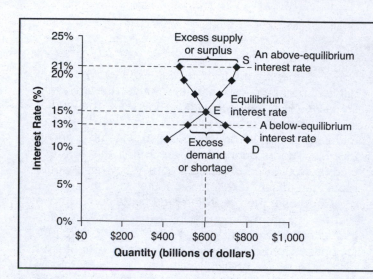

Interest Rate	Quantity of Financial Capital Demanded (borrowing)	Quantity of Financial Capital Supplied (lending)
11%	$800 billion	$420 billion
13%	$700 billion	$510 billion
15%	$600 billion	$600 billion
17%	$550 billion	$660 billion
19%	$500 billion	$720 billion
21%	$480 billion	$750 billion

EXHIBIT 5-4 Demand and Supply for Borrowing Money with Credit Cards

In this market for credit card borrowing, the demand curve D for borrowing financial capital intersects the supply curve S for lending financial capital at equilibrium E. At the equilibrium, the interest rate (the "price" in this market) is 15% and the quantity of financial capital being loaned and borrowed is $600 billion. The equilibrium is the price where the quantity demanded and the quantity supplied are equal. At an above-equilibrium interest rate like 21%, the quantity of financial capital supplied would increase to $750 billion, but the quantity demanded would decrease to $480 billion. A situation of excess supply or surplus would exist. At a below-equilibrium interest rate like 13%, the quantity of financial capital demanded would increase to $700 billion, but the quantity of financial capital supplied would decrease to $510 billion. A situation of excess demand or shortage would exist.

of about six cards per person). If you use a credit card to make a purchase, but do not pay the bill by the deadline, you have borrowed money from the credit card company and will need to pay interest. A typical credit card interest rate ranges from 12% to 18% per year. In 2015, Americans had about $900 billion outstanding in credit card debts not paid on time. About two-thirds of U.S. families with credit cards report that they almost always pay the full balance on time, but one-fifth of U.S. families with credit cards say that they "hardly ever" pay off the card in full. While credit card companies have different annual payments, different penalties for late payment, and different interest rates, let's say that on average the annual interest rate for credit card borrowing is 15% per year. Thus, Americans pay tens of billions of dollars every year in interest on their credit cards—a total that doesn't include fees, like basic fees for the credit card or fees for late payments.

Exhibit 5-4 illustrates demand and supply in the financial capital market for credit cards. The horizontal axis of the financial capital market shows the quantity that is loaned or borrowed in this market. The vertical or price axis of the financial capital market shows the rate of return, which in the case of credit card borrowing can be measured with an interest rate. The demand and supply schedule accompanying the figure shows the quantity of financial capital that consumers demand at various interest rates and the quantity that credit card firms (often banks) are willing to supply.

The laws of demand and supply continue to apply in the financial capital markets. According to the law of demand, a higher rate of return (that is, a higher price) will decrease the quantity demanded. As the interest rate rises, consumers will reduce the quantity that they borrow. According to the law of supply, a higher price increases the quantity supplied. Consequently, as the interest rate paid on credit card borrowing rises, more firms will be eager to issue credit cards and to encourage customers to use them. Conversely, if the interest rate on credit cards falls, the quantity of financial capital supplied in the credit card market will decrease.

Equilibrium in Financial Capital Markets

In the financial capital market for credit cards shown in Exhibit 5-4, the supply curve S and the demand curve D cross at the equilibrium point E. The equilibrium occurs at an interest rate of 15%, where the quantity of financial capital demanded and the quantity supplied are equal at an equilibrium quantity of $600 billion.

If the interest rate (remember, this measures the "price" in the financial capital market) is above the equilibrium level, then an excess supply, or a surplus, of financial capital will arise in this market. For example, at an interest rate of 21%, the quantity of financial capital supplied increases to $750 billion, while the quantity demanded decreases to $480 billion. At this above-equilibrium interest rate, firms are eager to supply loans to credit card borrowers, but relatively few people or businesses wish to borrow. As a result, some credit card firms will lower the interest rates (or other fees) they charge to attract more business. This strategy will push the interest rate down toward the equilibrium level.

If the interest rate is below the equilibrium, then excess demand or a shortage of financial capital occurs in this market. At an interest rate of 13%, the quantity of financial capital that credit card borrowers demand increases to $700 billion; but the quantity that credit card firms are willing to supply is only $510 billion. In this situation, credit card firms will perceive that they are overloaded with eager borrowers and conclude that they have an opportunity to raise interest rates or fees. Thus, the interest rate will face economic pressures to creep up toward the equilibrium level.

Shifts in Demand and Supply in Financial Capital Markets

The demand and supply of financial capital involves an intertemporal trade-off—that is, making a decision in the present with an eye on the future. Thus, an economic factor can shift demand or supply of financial capital if it alters the balance that people wish to strike between present and future.

Those who supply financial capital face two broad decisions: how much to save, and how to divide up their savings among different forms of financial investments. In thinking about how much to save, people must decide what they will need in the future to address expected or unexpected events. For example, the Social Security program, in which the government sends checks to workers and their families after retirement, tends to reduce the quantity of financial capital that workers save. In deciding between different forms of financial investments, suppliers of financial capital will have to consider the rates of return and the risks involved with different choices. If Investment A becomes more risky, or the return diminishes, then savers will shift some of their funds to Investment B—and the supply curve of financial capital for Investment A will shift back to the left while the supply curve of capital for Investment B shifts to the right.

Those who demand financial capital want the money now and are willing to repay in the future. For example, individuals might borrow money to purchase a long-term possession such as a condominium, a house, or a car. A business might seek financial investment so that it has the funds to build a factory or invest in a research and development project that won't pay off for five years, ten years, or more. Thus, when consumers and businesses have greater confidence that they will be able to repay in the future, the quantity demanded of financial capital at any given interest rate will shift to the right. For example, in the late 1990s many businesses became extremely confident that investments in new technology would have a high rate of return, and their demand for financial capital shifted to the right. Conversely, during the economic doldrums of 2008 and 2009, their demand for financial capital at any given interest rate shifted to the left.

Falling Global Interest Rates: The Four-Step Process

Interest rates in the global economy have declined since the late 1990s. For example, when the governments of countries with large and well-developed economies like the United States, Germany, and the United Kingdom wanted to borrow money in the late 1990s and early 2000s, they often paid an interest rate of 5–6%. By around 2015, they were typically paying an interest rate of around 2%. This pattern of falling interest rates started well before the Great Recession that rocked the global economy in 2008–2009. Economic studies have highlighted a number of factors that can affect the global interest

EXHIBIT 5-5 Falling Global Interest Rates: The Four-Step Process

Step 1: Draw a diagram showing demand and supply for financial capital that represents the original scenario. The demand curve D_0 intersects the supply curve S_0 of financial capital in global markets at the equilibrium E_0.

Step 2: Categorize the factors into those affecting supply and those affecting demand. An aging population, greater inequality of incomes, and the decisions of some governments around the world to hold larger financial reserves affect supply. Rapidly dropping prices of information technology and a drop in public spending on infrastructure affect demand.

Step 3: Which way will demand and supply shift? The supply-oriented factors tend to shift supply out to the right, from S_0 to S_1. The demand-oriented factors tend to shift demand back to the left, from D_0 to D_1.

Step 4: Compare the new equilibrium to the original. The new equilibrium E_1 occurs at the lower interest rate r_1, compared to r_0. In this example, the shifts in supply and demand result in the quantity of demand q_0 being the same at both equilibria.

rate: an aging population, greater inequality of incomes, the decision of some governments around the world to hold larger financial reserves against the risk of another economic and financial shock, the rapidly dropping prices of information technology, and a drop in public spending on infrastructure Using the four-step process for analyzing how changes in supply and demand affect equilibrium outcomes, how can these changing factors explain the fall in global interest rates?

Step 1: Draw a diagram showing demand and supply for financial capital that represents the original scenario in which foreign investors are pouring money into the U.S. economy. Exhibit 5-5 shows a demand curve, D_0, and a supply curve, S_0, for financial capital in global markets. The original equilibrium E_0 occurs at interest rate r_0 and quantity of financial investment q_0.

Step 2: The multiple factors affecting international capital markets can be categorized into those affecting supply and those affecting demand. In particular, three factors tend to affect the supply of capital: an aging population and rising inequality in incomes both affect people's desire to save, and when a government decides to hold larger financial reserves, it is demanding higher savings on its own behalf. Two factors tend to affect demand for capital: the rapidly dropping prices of information technology and a drop in public spending on infrastructure.

Step 3: Which way will demand and supply shift? The supply-oriented factors tend to shift supply out to the right, from S_0 to S_1. In particular, an aging population means a greater need for people to save for retirement; when incomes become more unequal, those with high incomes tend to save more; and when governments decide to hold larger financial reserves, they are desiring to save more. The demand-oriented factors tend to shift demand back to the left, from D_0 to D_1. Two factors tend to diminish demand for capital: the rapidly dropping prices of information technology, which reduce the amount firms need to spend for some of the main physical capital investments they wish to make, and a drop in public spending on infrastructure.

Step 4: Compare the new equilibrium E_1 to the original E_0. The new equilibrium E_1 occurs at the lower interest rate r_1, compared to r_0. In this specific figure, the quantity of demand q_0 is the same at both equilibria, which reflects the overall pattern that the total global saving rate doesn't seem to have moved much in the last two decades. To put it another way, the shifts in supply tended to push up the quantity supplied, but the shifts in demand tended to hold down the quantity supplied—and in this particular example, those two forces counterbalanced each other. However, you should be able to imagine a situation where the effect of shifts in supply and demand on quantity don't perfectly balance, and the quantity could end up being higher or lower at the new equilibrium.

The lower global interest rate has dramatic implications for those thinking about saving, including both households and organizations such as pension funds and life insurance companies, as well as for those thinking about borrowing, including households thinking about borrowing to buy a home and firms thinking about borrowing to purchase new plant and equipment. In a modern economy, financial capital often moves invisibly through electronic transfers between one bank account and another. Yet these flows of funds can be analyzed with the same tools of demand and supply as markets for goods or labor.

Price Ceilings in Financial Capital Markets: Usury Laws

As discussed earlier, more than 160 million Americans own credit cards, and their interest payments and fees total tens of billions of dollars each year. It's little wonder that political pressures sometimes arise for setting limits on the interest rates or fees that credit cards companies can charge. The firms that issue credit cards, including banks, oil companies, phone companies, and retail stores, respond that the higher interest rates are necessary to cover the losses created by those who borrow on their credit cards and who do not repay on time or at all. These companies also point out that credit card holders can avoid paying interest if they pay their bills on time.

Consider the credit card market as illustrated in Exhibit 5-6. In this financial capital market, the vertical axis shows the interest rate (which is the price in the financial capital market). Demanders in the credit card market are households; suppliers are the companies

EXHIBIT 5-6 Credit Card Interest Rates: Another Price Ceiling Example

The original intersection of demand D and supply S occurs at equilibrium E_0. However, a price ceiling is set at the interest rate r_c, below the equilibrium interest rate r_0 and so the interest rate cannot adjust upward to the equilibrium. At the price ceiling, the quantity demanded, Q_D exceeds the quantity supplied, Q_S. There is excess demand, also called a shortage.

Payday Advances: Valuable Service or Predatory Lending?

A "payday advance" works this way. When you receive a payday advance, you then write a personal check to the business that is providing the advance. For example, say that the check you write is for $200. The payday advance firm gives you $180 cash on the spot. It then agrees not to cash your check for a certain period of time—usually ranging from a week to a month—until you receive your next paycheck. In this example, when the payday advance firm cashes the check, it effectively collects a charge of $20 for lending $180 for a few weeks or a month.

Consumer protection groups have asserted that this charge, which is not officially an "interest rate" but a "fee," is outrageously high, and want a price ceiling to limit what they view as excessive interest rates. After all, a 10% interest charge per month, if compounded over 12 months, works out to an interest rate of $(1 + .10)^{12} = 314\%$ per year.

Companies that offer the payday advances point out that they provide cash on the spot, without credit checks or other fees. They point out that the cash advance may offer the recipient a way to pay for unexpected expenses like an emergency car repair. They argue that many of their customers have no other options for ready cash. They admit that some customers may borrow unwisely, but observe that customers can borrow unwisely in many ways; for example, customers can end up paying fees when they don't make minimum credit card payments or when they overdraw a checking account.

About 5% of the U.S. population—call it 15 million people—have taken out a payday loan. Roughly $40 billion in payday loans are made each year. Is a price ceiling law needed in the area of payday advances, to protect consumers who may be unsophisticated, low-income, or lacking access to regular banks? Or is a payday advance just another service that people should be free to buy or not buy, as they choose, without government rules?

---

that issue credit cards. This exhibit does not use specific numbers, which would be hypothetical in any case, but instead focuses on the underlying economic relationships. Imagine that a law imposes a price ceiling that holds the interest rate charged on credit cards at the interest rate r_c, which lies below the interest rate r_0 that would otherwise have prevailed in the market. The price ceiling is shown by the horizontal dashed line in Exhibit 5-6. The demand and supply model predicts that at the lower price ceiling interest rate, the quantity demanded of credit card debt will increase from its original level of Q_0 to Q_D; however, the quantity supplied of credit card debt will decrease from the original Q_0 to Q_S. At the price ceiling r_c, quantity demanded will exceed quantity supplied. Consequently, a number of people who want to have credit cards and are willing to pay the prevailing interest rate will find that companies are unwilling to issue cards to them. The result will be a credit card shortage.

usury laws: Laws that impose an upper limit on the interest rate that lenders can charge.

Many states have **usury laws**, which impose an upper limit on the interest rate that lenders can charge. However, in many cases these upper limits are so high that they are well above the market interest rate. For example, if the interest rate is not allowed to rise above 30% per year, it can still fluctuate below that level according to market forces. A price ceiling that is set at a relatively high level is non-binding, and it will have no practical effect unless the equilibrium price zooms high enough to exceed the price ceiling.

Don't Kill the Price Messengers

Prices exist in markets for goods and services, for labor, and for financial capital. In all of these markets, prices serve as a social mechanism for collecting, combining, and transmitting information that is relevant to the market—namely, the relationship between demand and supply—and then serving as messengers to convey that information to buyers and sellers. In a market-oriented economy, no government agency or guiding intelligence oversees the set of responses and interconnections that result from a change in price. Instead, each consumer reacts according to that person's preferences and budget set, and each profit-seeking producer reacts to the effect on its expected profits.

Demand and Supply Curves

Just as it would be foolish to try to learn the arithmetic of long division by memorizing every possible combination of numbers that can be divided, it would be foolish to try to memorize every specific example of demand and supply in this chapter, this textbook, or this course. Demand and supply is not a list of examples; it's a model to analyze prices and quantities. Even though demand and supply diagrams have many labels, they are fundamentally the same in their logic. Your goal should be to understand the underlying model. The demand and supply analysis is the second fundamental diagram for this course. (The opportunity set model introduced in Chapter 2 was the first.)

The exhibit displays a general demand and supply curve. The horizontal axis shows the different measures of quantity: a quantity of a good or service, or a quantity of labor for a given job, or a quantity of financial capital. The vertical axis shows a measure of price: the price of a good or service, the wage in the labor market, or the rate of return (like the interest rate) in the financial capital market.

The demand and supply model can explain the existing levels of prices, wages, and rates of return. To carry out such an analysis, think about the quantity that will be demanded at each price and the quantity that will be supplied at each price—that is, think about the shape of the demand and supply curves—and

how these forces will combine to produce equilibrium. Demand and supply can also be used to explain how economic events will cause changes in prices, wages, and rates of return. There are only four possibilities: the economic event may cause the demand curve to shift right or to shift left, or it may cause the supply curve to shift right or to shift left. The key to analyzing the effect of an economic event on equilibrium prices and quantities is to choose among these possibilities.

Demand and Supply Curves

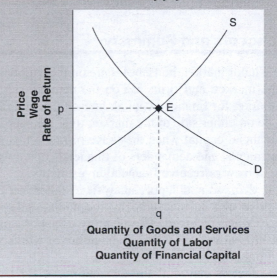

Quantity of Goods and Services
Quantity of Labor
Quantity of Financial Capital

For example, if you are thinking about taking a plane trip to Hawaii, but the ticket turns out to be expensive during the week you intend to go, you merely look at the price and decide, based on the price, whether to fly. The price could be high because the cost of an input like jet fuel increased or because demand surged during that week. Or maybe the airline has raised the price temporarily to see how many people are willing to pay it. Perhaps all of these factors are present at the same time. But you don't need to analyze the market and break down the price change into its underlying factors. You just look at the price of a ticket and decide whether to fly.

Producers also commonly react to price changes without much caring why they occur. Imagine the situation of a farmer who grows oats and learns that the price of oats has risen. The higher price could be due to an increase in demand caused by a new scientific study proclaiming that eating oats is especially healthy. Or perhaps the price of a substitute grain, like corn, has risen, and people have responded by buying more oats. But the oat farmer does not need to know the details. The farmer only needs to know that the price of oats has increased and that it will be profitable to expand production as a result.

The actions of individual consumers and producers overlap and interlock as they react to prices in markets for goods, labor, and financial capital. A change in any single market is transmitted through these multiple interconnections to other markets. The role of flexible prices helping markets to reach equilibrium and linking different markets together helps to explain why price controls can be so counterproductive. There is an old proverb: "Don't kill the messenger." This saying dates back to ancient times, when messengers carried information between distant cities and kingdoms. When a messenger arrived bearing bad news, there was an emotional impulse to kill the messenger. But killing the messenger didn't eliminate the bad news. Moreover, killing the messenger had an undesirable side effect: Other messengers would refuse to bring news to that city or kingdom, depriving the citizens of future information. A custom developed that messengers should not be held personally responsible for the news that they brought.

Those who seek price controls are trying to kill the messenger—or at least to stifle an unwelcome message that prices are bringing about the equilibrium level of price and quantity. But price controls do nothing to affect the underlying forces of demand and supply. Changes in demand and supply will continue to reveal themselves through consumers' and producers' reactions with respect to quantity demanded and quantity supplied. Moreover, immobilizing the price messenger through price controls will deprive the economy of critical information. Without this information, it becomes difficult for everyone—buyers and sellers alike—to react in a flexible and appropriate manner as changes occur throughout the economy.

Key Concepts and Summary

1. In the labor market, households are on the supply side of the market, and firms are on the demand side. In the market for financial capital, households and firms can be on either side of the market: they are suppliers of financial capital when they save or make financial investments, and demanders of financial capital when they borrow or receive financial investments.

2. In the demand and supply analysis of labor markets, the price can be measured by the annual salary or hourly wage received. The quantity of labor can be measured in various ways, like number of workers or the number of hours worked.

3. Three factors can shift the demand curve for labor: a change in the quantity of the product that the labor produces, a change in the production process that uses more or less labor, and a change in government policy that affects the quantity of labor that firms wish to hire at a given wage. Two factors can shift the supply curve for labor: how desirable a job appears to workers relative to the alternatives for reasons other than pay, and how government policy either restricts or encourages the quantity of workers trained for the job.

4. In the demand and supply analysis of financial capital markets, the "price" is the rate of return or the interest rate received. The quantity is measured by the money that flows from those who supply financial capital to those who demand it.

5. Two factors can shift the supply of financial capital to a certain investment: anything that makes people want to alter their existing levels of present and future consumption; and when the riskiness or return on one investment changes relative to other investments. Factors that can shift demand for capital include business confidence and consumer confidence in the future—since financial investments received in the present are typically repaid in the future.

Review Questions

1. What is the "price" commonly called in the labor market? What is the "price" commonly called in the financial capital market?

2. Are households demanders or suppliers in the goods market? Are firms demanders or suppliers in the goods market? What about the labor market and the financial capital market?

3. Name some factors that can cause a shift in the demand curve in labor markets.

4. Name some factors that can cause a shift in the supply curve in labor markets.

5. Name some factors that can cause a shift in the demand curve in financial capital markets.

6. Name some factors that can cause a shift in the supply curve in financial capital markets.

Globalization and Protectionism

protectionism: Government policies to reduce or block imports.

tariffs: Taxes imposed on imported products.

import quotas: Numerical limitations on the quantity of products that can be imported.

nontariff barriers: All the ways a nation can draw up rules, regulations, inspections, and paperwork to make it more costly or difficult to import products.

Imports of goods and services stir up worries everywhere. Some firms and workers in high-income countries like the United States, Japan, or the nations of the European Union fear that they will suffer if they must compete against firms in low-income countries of Latin America, Asia, or Africa that can pay lower wages. Conversely, some firms and workers in lower-wage countries like Mexico, India, or South Africa fear that they will suffer if they must compete against the very productive workers and advanced technology in high-income countries. Some environmentalists worry that multinational firms may evade environmental protection laws by moving their production to countries with loose or nonexistent pollution standards. Some politicians worry that their nation may become overly dependent on key imported products, like oil. All of these fears tend to reach the same basic policy recommendation: Imports of foreign products should be reduced or even cut off. Government policies to reduce or block international trade are called **protectionism** because they have the effect of protecting domestic producers from foreign competition.

Protectionism takes three main forms. **Tariffs** are taxes imposed on imported products. They discourage imports by making imported products more expensive to consumers. **Import quotas** are numerical limitations on the quantity of products that can be imported. Finally, **nontariff barriers** are all the other ways that a nation can draw up rules, regulations, inspections, and paperwork to make it more costly or difficult to import products. A rule that every imported product must be opened by hand and inspected with a magnifying glass by one of just three government inspectors available at any given time can limit imports just as effectively as high tariffs or low import quotas.

As one example, the United States has imposed barriers to imports of textiles for decades. From the mid-1970s up to 2004, for example, the international Multi-Fibre Arrangement specified exactly the quota of textile imports that each high-income country would accept from each low-income country. By 2009, the United States had phased out its import quotas on textiles. However,

U.S. tariffs on textile and apparel imports were among the highest for any industry, averaging 10% overall, but ranging as high as 32% on man-made fiber sweaters and 28% on certain men's pants and artificial fiber coats. There are also nontariff barriers in the form of "rules-of-origin" regulations, in which certain textiles are made in the United States, shipped to other countries, combined in making apparel with textiles made in those other countries—and then re-exported back to the United States at a lower tariff rate.

Despite these interlocking import quotas, tariffs, and nontariff barriers, the share of apparel sold in the United States that is imported rose from about half in 1999 to about three-quarters today. The number of U.S. jobs in textiles and apparel fell from 541,000 in 2007 to 383,000 in 2012, and the U.S. Bureau of Labor Statistics predicts that it will decline to 245,000 by 2022. The U.S. International Trade Commission (ITC) has estimated that removing the remaining tariff and nontariff barriers would cause the number of jobs in this industry to fall by 50,000 more. However, the U.S. textile industry jobs that are saved by import quotas come at a cost. Because textile and apparel protectionism adds to the costs of imports, consumers end up paying billions of dollars more for clothing each year. The ITC also points out that when the United States eliminates trade barriers in one area, then consumers spend the money they save on that product elsewhere in the economy—so that there is no overall loss of jobs for the economy as a whole. Of course, workers in some of the poorest countries of the world who would otherwise have jobs producing textiles, but find their opportunities blocked by tariff and nontariff barriers, would gain considerably if the United States reduced its barrier to trade in textiles.

This chapter begins with an economic analysis of who benefits from protectionism and who pays the costs of protectionism, using demand and supply analysis. The chapter then considers a list of concerns raised about global trade and in particular about imports. For example, how do imports affect the number of jobs, the level of wages, and work conditions? How might imports affect promising but immature domestic industries? What about the trade and environmental issues? The primary international body through which nations negotiate over their trade rules—including rules about tariffs, quotas, and nontariff barriers—is the World Trade Organization (WTO). The membership of the WTO includes over 160 nations. The chapter closes with a discussion of the history and direction of the WTO, as well as various regional trade treaties.

Protectionism: An Indirect Subsidy from Consumers to Producers

To the noneconomist, restricting imports may appear to be nothing more than taking sales from foreign producers and allowing domestic producers to achieve greater sales. But a demand and supply analysis of protectionism shows that protectionism is not just a matter of domestic gains and foreign losses, but a policy that imposes meaningful domestic costs as well.

Demand and Supply Analysis of Protectionism

Consider international trade in sugar between two countries called Tartar and Plaque, illustrated in Exhibit 6-1. In the original supply and demand equilibrium without trade, the equilibrium price of sugar in Tartar is 12 cents per pound, with an equilibrium output of 30 tons. In Plaque, the equilibrium price of sugar in a world without trade is 24 cents per pound, with an equilibrium quantity of 80 tons. These equilibrium points are labeled with the point E.

If international trade between Tartar and Plaque now becomes possible, profit-seeking firms will spot an opportunity: buy sugar cheaply in Tartar, and sell it at a higher price in Plaque. As sugar is shipped from Tartar to Plaque, the quantity of sugar produced in Tartar will be greater than the quantity consumed in that country (with the extra production being exported) and the amount produced in Plaque will be less than the amount consumed in that country (with the extra consumption being imported). The quantity of trade

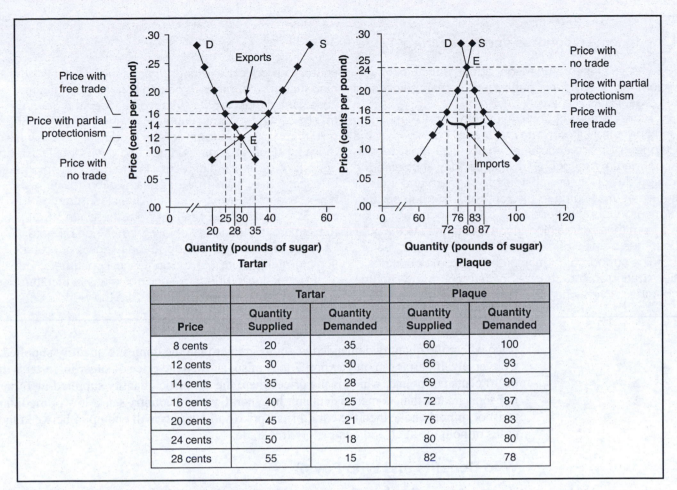

EXHIBIT 6-1 The Sugar Trade between Tartar and Plaque

Before trade, sugar sells in Tartar for 12 cents a pound and in Plaque for 24 cents per pound. When trade is allowed, businesses will buy sugar cheaply in Tartar and sell it in Plaque. The result with free trade will be that Tartar exports 15 pounds of sugar, Plaque imports 15 pounds of sugar, and the price is the same in the two countries at 16 cents per pound. If trade is only partly open between the countries, it will lead to an outcome between the free-trade and no-trade possibilities.

will be determined when price of sugar is the same in two countries—and thus there is no incentive to trade further. As shown in Exhibit 6-1, the equilibrium with trade occurs at a price of 16 cents per pound. At that price, the sugar farmers of Tartar supply a quantity of 40 tons, while the consumers of Tartar buy only 25 tons. The extra 15 tons of sugar production, shown by the horizontal gap between the demand curve and the supply curve in Tartar, is exported to Plaque. In Plaque, at a price of 16 cents, the farmers produce a quantity of 72 tons and consumers demand a quantity of 87 tons. The excess demand of 15 tons by the consumers of Plaque, shown by the horizontal gap between demand and domestic supply at the price of 16 cents, is supplied by imported sugar from Tartar.

The sugar farmers of Plaque are likely to argue that, if only they could be protected from sugar imported from Tartar, the country of Plaque would have higher domestic sugar production and more jobs in the sugar production industry, and Plaque's sugar farmers would receive a higher price. If the country of Plaque sets a high tariff on imported sugar, or sets an import quota at zero, then the result will be that the quantity of sugar traded between countries could be reduced to zero, and the prices in each country will return to their levels before trade was allowed.

Blocking only a portion of trade is also possible. For example, say that Plaque passed a sugar import quota of 7 tons; that is, Plaque will import no more than 7 tons of sugar, which means that Tartar can export no more than 7 tons of sugar. As can be seen in the table in Exhibit 6-1, the price of sugar in Plaque would then be 20 cents, which is the

Low-Income Countries and Agricultural Trade

Here is a stark comparison about social priorities, which has been widely publicized by the international aid organization Oxfam.

High-income countries of the world—meaning primarily the United States, Canada, countries of the European Union, and Japan—subsidize their domestic farmers by roughly $1 billion per day, including the value both of direct subsidies to farmers and indirect subsidies that come in the form of limiting imports of farm products. However, the total amount of foreign aid from these same high-income countries to the poor countries of the world is about $130 billion per year.

The support of farmers in high income countries is devastating to the chances of farmers in low-income countries. Even when their climate and land are well-suited to products like cotton, rice, sugar, or milk, the high-income countries block their exports. In some cases, the situation gets even worse when the governments of high-income countries, having bought and paid for an excess supply of farm products, gives away those products in poor countries and drives local farmers out of business altogether. In the past, shipments of excess milk from the European Union to Jamaica have caused great hardship for Jamaican dairy farmers. Shipments of excess rice from the United States to Haiti drove thousands of low-income rice farmers in Haiti out of business. The opportunity costs of protectionism aren't paid just by domestic consumers, but also by foreign producers—and for many agricultural products, those foreign producers are the world's poor.

---

price where the quantity demanded is 7 tons greater than the domestic quantity supplied. Conversely, if Tartar can only export 7 tons of sugar, then the price of sugar in Tartar will be 14 cents per pound, which is the price where the domestic quantity supplied in Tartar is 7 tons greater than domestic demand. In general, when a country sets a low or medium tariff or import quota, then the equilibrium price and quantity will end up in between the cases of no trade at all and completely free trade.

Who Benefits and Who Pays?

Using the demand and supply model, consider the impact of protectionism on producers and consumers in each of the two countries. For producers of the protected good, the sugar farmers of Plaque, restricting imports is clearly positive. Without a need to face imported products, these producers are able to sell more, at a higher price. For consumers in the country with the protected good, the sugar consumers of Plaque, restricting imports is clearly negative. They end up buying a lower quantity of the good and paying a higher price for what they do buy, compared to the equilibrium quantity and price with free trade.

The fact that protectionism pushes up prices for consumers in the country enacting such protectionism is not always acknowledged in public policy arguments, but it's not controversial. After all, if protectionism didn't benefit domestic producers, there wouldn't be much point in enacting such policies in the first place. Protectionism is simply a method of requiring consumers to subsidize producers. The subsidy is indirect, since it is paid by consumers through higher prices, rather than a direct subsidy paid by the government with money collected from taxpayers. But protectionism works like a subsidy nonetheless. The American humorist Ambrose Bierce defined "tariff" this way in his satirical 1911 book, *The Devil's Dictionary*: "Tariff, n. A scale of taxes on imports, designed to protect the domestic producer against the greed of his consumer."

How would Plaque's protectionism affect producers and consumers in their potential trading partner, Tartar? The sugar producers of Tartar will be unable to export to Plaque, and so they will experience lower prices. When Plaque uses import quotas to impose partial protectionism, the sugar producers of Tartar receive a lower price for the sugar they sell in Tartar—but a higher price for the sugar they are allowed to export to Plaque. Consumers of sugar in Tartar would seem to benefit from protectionism in Plaque because it reduces the price of sugar that they pay. On the other hand, remember that at least some of these consumers of sugar in Tartar also work as sugar farmers, so their incomes and jobs are reduced by protectionism. Moreover, if trade in all goods between the countries is shut down, consumers of Tartar would miss out on better prices for the goods that Tar-

Life Savers, the hard candy with the hole in the middle, were invented in 1912 by Clarence Crane in Cleveland, Ohio. Starting in the late 1960s and for 35 years afterward 46 billion Life Savers a year, in 200 million rolls, were produced by a plant in Holland, Michigan. But in 2002, the Kraft Company announced that Michigan plant would be closed and Life Saver production moved across the border to Montreal, Canada.

One reason is that Canadian workers are paid slightly less, especially since the Canadian government finances health care costs. But a main reason is that the U.S. government keeps the price of sugar high for the benefits of sugar farmers, with a combination of a government price floor program and strict quotas on imported sugar. In 2012, the U.S. price for refined sugar was 70 cents a pound; the price in the rest of the world was 27 cents a pound. Life Saver production uses over 100 tons of sugar each day because the candies are 95% sugar.

A number of other candy companies have reduced U.S. production and expanded foreign production, as well. But while the candy industry is especially affected by the cost of sugar, the costs are spread more broadly. U.S. consumers pay roughly $1 billion per year in higher food prices because of elevated sugar costs. Meanwhile, sugar producers in low-income countries are driven out of business because they cannot sell their output in the U.S. market.

tar is importing—a benefit that does not appear in our single-market example of sugar protectionism.

But the central focus here is not on how protectionism affects other countries, but how it affects one's own country. Protectionism is a policy where the domestic consumers of a product (consumers may include either households or other firms) are required to pay higher prices to benefit domestic producers of that product. In addition, when a country enacts protectionism, it loses the economic gains it would have been able to achieve through the combination of comparative advantage, learning, and economies of scale that were discussed Chapter 3. With these costs and benefits in mind, let us now consider, one by one, a number of arguments that have been made for restricting imports.

International Trade and Its Effects on Jobs, Wages, and Working Conditions

In theory, at least, imports might injure workers in several different ways: fewer jobs, lower wages, or poor working conditions. Let's consider these in turn.

Fewer Jobs?

In the early 1990s, the United States was negotiating the North American Free Trade Agreement (NAFTA) with Mexico, an agreement that would reduce tariffs, import quotas, and nontariff barriers to trade between the United States, Mexico, and Canada. H. Ross Perot ran for U.S. President in 1992 as a third-party candidate, and one of his prominent campaign arguments was that if the United States expanded trade with Mexico, there would be a "giant sucking sound" as U.S. employers relocated to Mexico so that they could pay lower wages. After all, average wages in Mexico were at that time about one-eighth the U.S. level. Well, NAFTA passed Congress, President Bill Clinton signed it into law, and it took effect in 1995. For the next six years, the U.S. economy had some of the most rapid job growth and lowest unemployment in its history. Those who feared that open trade with Mexico would lead to a dramatic decrease in jobs were proven 100% wrong.

This result was no surprise to economists. After all, the trend toward globalization has been going on for decades. U.S. imports were equal to 5.4% of the U.S. economy in 1970, but to about 15% in 2015. If trade did reduce the number of available jobs, then the United States should have been seeing a steady loss of jobs for decades. While the U.S. economy does experience rises and falls in unemployment rates—like the rising unemployment rate that started in spring 2008 and reached 10% by late 2009—the number of jobs is not falling over extended periods of time. The number of U.S. jobs rose from 78 million in 1970 to 143 million in 2015.

Protectionism certainly saves jobs *in the specific industry being protected*, but for two reasons, it costs jobs in other unprotected industries. First, if consumers are paying higher prices to the protected industry, they inevitably have less money to spend on goods from other industries, and so jobs are lost in those other industries. Second, if the protected product is sold to other firms, like sugar or steel, so that other firms must now pay a higher price for a key input, then those firms will have a hard time competing against foreign producers who don't need to pay the higher price. The hidden opportunity cost of using protectionism to save jobs in one industry sacrifices the jobs that are not created in other industries. This is why the U.S. International Trade Commission, in its study of barriers to trade mentioned near the start of this chapter, predicts that reducing trade barriers would not lead to an overall loss of jobs. Protectionism reshuffles jobs from industries that are not protected from imports to industries that are protected, but it does not create more jobs.

Moreover, the costs of saving jobs through protectionism can be very high. Exhibit 6-2 shows some estimates drawn from a variety of studies of the consumer costs in higher prices of "saving jobs" through protectionism. Saving a job through protectionism typically costs much more than the actual worker's salary. For example, a study published in 2011 compiled evidence that using protectionism to save an average job in the tire industry would cost $900,000 per job saved.

Why does it cost so much to save jobs through protectionism? The basic reason is that not all of the extra money paid by consumers because of protectionism goes to save the jobs of workers. For example, if tariffs are imposed on steel imports so that buyers of steel pay a higher price, U.S. steel companies earn greater profits, buy more equipment, pay bigger bonuses to managers, give pay raises to existing employees—and also avoid firing some additional workers. Only part of the higher price of protected steel goes toward saving jobs. Also, when an industry is protected, the economy as a whole loses the benefits of playing to its comparative advantage. Thus, part of the higher price that consumers pay for protected goods is wasted by this lost economic efficiency.

There's a bumper sticker that speaks to the threat some U.S. workers feel over imported products: "Buy American—Save U.S. Jobs." A more accurate, if less catchy, bumper

EXHIBIT 6-2 Cost to U.S. Consumers of Saving a Job through Protectionism

A number of different studies have attempted to estimate the cost to consumers in higher prices per job saved through protectionism. Here is a sample of results, compiled by economists at the Federal Reserve Bank of Dallas.

Industry Protected with Import Tariffs or Quotas	Annual Cost per Job Saved
Sugar	$826,000
Polyethylene resins	$812,000
Dairy products	$685,000
Frozen concentrated orange juice	$635,000
Ball bearings	$603,000
Machine tools	$479,000
Women's handbags	$263,000
Glassware	$247,000
Apparel and textiles	$199,000
Rubber footwear	$168,000
Women's nonathletic footwear	$139,000

sticker might say: "Block Imports—Save Jobs for Some Americans, Lose a Roughly Equal Number of Jobs for Other Americans, and Also Have Consumers Pay Higher Prices."

Trade and Wages

Even if trade does not reduce the number of jobs, it could affect the wages of workers. Here, it is important to separate issues about the average level of wages from issues about whether the wages of certain workers may be helped or hurt by trade.

Because trade raises the amount that an economy can produce by letting firms and workers play to their comparative advantage, trade will also cause the average level of wages in an economy to increase. Workers who can produce more will be more desirable to employers, which will shift the demand for their labor out to the right and increase wages in the labor market.

However, even if trade increases the overall wage level, it will still benefit some workers and hurt others. Workers in industries that are confronted by competition from imported products may find that demand for their labor decreases and shifts back to the left, so that their wages decline with a rise in international trade. Conversely, workers in industries that benefit from selling in global markets may find that demand for their labor shifts out to the right, so that trade raises their wages.

One concern is that while globalization may be benefiting high-skilled, high-wage workers, it may also impose costs on low-skilled, low-wage workers. After all, high-skilled U.S. workers presumably benefit from increased sales of sophisticated products like computers, machinery, and pharmaceuticals in world markets. Meanwhile, low-skilled U.S. workers must now compete against low-wage workers worldwide for making simpler products like toys and clothing. Chapter 16 will discuss the inequality of wages in the U.S. economy in detail. But there are a number of reasons to believe that while globalization has helped some U.S. industries and hurt others, there are a number of situations in which trade does not seem likely to disproportionately injure low-skilled Americans—and indeed, it will often benefit them.

First, it seems unlikely that intra-industry trade, where the United States trades similar goods like machinery, computers, and cars with other high-wage economies like Canada, Japan, Germany, and the United Kingdom, has a heavier impact on the wages of low-skill, low-wage Americans. After all, most U.S. workers in these industries have above-average skills and wages—and many of them are doing quite well in the world of globalization. Remember, intra-industry trade makes up about half of all U.S. trade.

Second, many low-skilled U.S. workers hold service jobs that cannot be replaced by imports from low-wage countries. For example, lawn care services or moving and hauling services or hotel maids cannot be imported from countries of long distances like China or Bangladesh. Competition from imported products is not the primary determinant of their wages.

Finally, while the focus of the discussion here is on wages, it's worth pointing out that low-wage U.S. workers suffer from protectionism *in all the industries that they don't work in* because protectionism forces them to pay higher prices for basic necessities like clothing and food.

The benefits and costs of increased trade in terms of its effect on wages are not distributed evenly across the economy, and may contribute to inequality of wages. However, the growth of international trade has helped to raise the productivity of U.S. workers as a whole—and thus has helped to raise the average level of wages.

Labor Standards

Workers in many low-income countries around the world labor under conditions that would be illegal for a worker in the United States. Workers in countries like China, Thailand, Brazil, South Africa, and Poland are often paid less than the U.S. minimum wage. For example, in the United States the minimum wage is $7.25 per hour; the wage in many low-income countries might be more like $7.25 *per day*, or even less. Moreover,

The International Labor Organization

The International Labor Organization (ILO), founded in 1919, is the international body for establishing and monitoring labor standards. The ILO has passed rules, or "conventions," affecting more than 180 areas of employment, but member nations have a choice of which to ratify. For example, the first convention, passed in 1919, calls for an eight-hour workday and a 48-hour work week. An example of a more recent convention, adopted in 2010, calls for improved working conditions for those who do domestic work.

If a nation has ratified a convention, the ILO has the power to investigate complaints about violations. Complaints can come from workers, employers, or other countries. The ILO does not have power to impose financial penalties or limitations on trade. Instead, it depends on building consensus and publicity to encourage nations to sign conventions and to comply with conventions they have signed.

As of 2015, the United States has ratified just 14 of the 189 ILO conventions. This isn't necessarily unreasonable. Many countries sign off on ILO conventions, but then do little to comply. For example, 172 countries have ratified a convention against discrimination in employment and occupation that was passed in 1958. The United States has not ratified this convention. But it seems clear from a glance around the world that employment discrimination by race, gender, and religion is lower in the United States than in many of the countries that have ratified the convention. The United States is quite cautious about ratifying ILO conventions because it views workplace issues as fundamentally a domestic issue, and not the business of other countries. Of course, this makes it hard for the United States to preach to other nations about their workplace issues, too.

Country	Number of ILO Conventions Ratified, 2015
High-Income Economies	
United States	14
Canada	34
France	127
Germany	85
Japan	49
Korea, Republic of	29
United Kingdom	87
Upper-Middle-Income Countries	
Brazil	96
China	26
Mexico	79
Russian Federation	73
Lower-Middle-Income Countries	
India	45
Indonesia	19
Chana	51
Nigeria	40
Low-Income Countries	
Bangladesh	35
Cambodia	13
Chad	28

working conditions in low-income countries may be highly unpleasant, or even unsafe. In the worst cases, production may involve the labor of small children or even workers who are treated nearly like slaves. These concerns over standards of foreign labor don't affect the majority of U.S. trade, which is intra-industry and carried out with other high-income countries that have labor standards similar to the United States, but it is nonetheless morally and economically important.

In thinking about labor standards in other countries, it's important to draw some distinctions between what is truly unacceptable and what is merely painful to think about. Most people, economists included, have little difficulty with the idea that production by six-year-olds confined in factories or by slave labor is morally unacceptable, and they would support aggressive efforts to eliminate such practices—including shutting out imported products made with such labor. But many cases are less clear-cut. An article in the *New York Times* several years ago described the case of Ahmed Zia, a 14-year-old boy from Pakistan. He earned $2 per day working in a carpet factory. He dropped out of school in second grade. Should the United States and other countries refuse to purchase rugs made by Ahmed and his co-workers? If the carpet factories were to close, the likely alternative job for Ahmed is farm work, and as Ahmed says of his carpet-weaving job: "This makes much more money and is more comfortable." Other workers may have even less attractive alternative jobs, perhaps scavenging garbage or prostitution. The real problem for Ahmed and many others in low-income countries isn't that globalization has made their lives worse, but rather that they have so few better life alternatives.

Similar issues apply to adult workers in low-income counties that produce goods for export to the United States and other high-income economies like the European Union and Japan. Many of these workers receive wages that would be illegally low in the United States and other high-income countries. They are unprotected by U.S. rules that seek to assure holidays, safe workplaces, and prohibitions against discrimination and sexual harassment. Nonetheless, the jobs they have making carpets or toys or shoes often pay much better than their alternative jobs. Low wages and poor working conditions are not a clever ploy by people in low-income countries to sell more in world markets. For them, jobs with wages and working conditions that Americans wouldn't touch with a 10-foot pole can still look like a great step forward.

There is some irony when the U.S. government or U.S. citizens take issue with labor standards in low-income countries, because the United States is not a world leader in government laws to protect employees. In western European countries and Canada, all citizens are guaranteed health insurance by the government; the United States does not offer such a guarantee. Many European workers receive six weeks or more of vacation per year; in the United States, vacations are often two or three weeks per year. If European countries accused the United States of using unfair labor standards to make U.S. products cheaply, and announced that they would shut out all U.S. imports until the United States adopted government-run national health insurance, added more national holidays, and doubled vacation time, Americans would be outraged. Yet when U.S. protectionists start talking about restricting imports from poor countries because of low wage levels and poor working conditions, they are making a very similar argument.

The Infant Industry Argument

Imagine a country that wants to start its own computer industry, but at present, the country has no computer firms that can produce at a low enough price and high enough quality to compete in world markets. However, the politicians, business leaders, and workers of this country hope that if the local industry only had a chance to get established before it needed to face international competition, then a domestic company or group of companies could develop the skills, management, technology, and economies of scale that it needs to become a successful profit-earning domestic industry. The **infant industry argument** for protectionism is to block imports for a limited time, to give an infant industry time to mature, before eventually it starts competing on equal terms in the global economy.

infant industry argument: An argument to block imports for a short time, to give the infant industry time to mature, before eventually it starts competing on equal terms in the global economy.

The infant industry argument is certainly theoretically possible: give an industry a short-term indirect subsidy through protection, and then reap the long-term economic benefits of having a vibrant healthy industry. But practical implementation is tricky. In many countries, infant industries have gone from babyhood to senility and obsolescence without ever maturing. Meanwhile, infant industry protectionism that is supposed to be short-term often takes a long time to be repealed. As one example, Brazil treated its computer industry as an infant industry from the late 1970s until about 1990. Thus, in an attempt to establish its computer industry in the global economy, Brazil largely barred imports of computer products for several decades. This policy guaranteed increased sales for the Brazilian computer industry. But by the mid1980s, Brazil had a backward and out-of-date computer industry, typically lagging behind the world standards for price and performance by 3–5 years—a long time in this fast-moving industry. After more than a decade, during which Brazilian consumers and industries that would have benefited from up-to-date computers paid the costs and Brazil's computer industry never competed effectively on world markets, Brazil phased out its infant industry policy for computers.

Protectionism for infant industries imposes costs on domestic users of the product and typically has provided little benefit in the form of stronger competitive industries.

Several countries in East Asia offer an exception where infant industry protection has been used with some success. Japan, Korea, Thailand, and other countries in this region have sometimes provided a package of indirect and direct subsidies targeted at certain industries, including protection from foreign competition and government loans at interest rates below the market equilibrium. In Japan and Korea, for example, subsidies helped get their domestic steel and auto industries up and running.

Why did the infant industry policy of protectionism and other subsidies work better in East Asia than in many other regions? A study by the World Bank in the early 1990s offered some guidelines to countries thinking about infant industry protection: (1) Don't hand out protectionism and other subsidies to all industries, but focus on a few industries where your country has a realistic chance to be a world-class producer. (2) Be very hesitant about using protectionism in areas like computers, where many other industries rely on having the most advanced products available, because it's not useful to help one industry by imposing high costs on many other industries. (3) Have clear guidelines for when the infant industry policy will end. In Korea in the 1970s and 1980s, a common practice was to link protectionism and subsidies to export sales in global markets. If export sales rose, then the infant industry had succeeded and the protectionism could be phased out. If export sales didn't rise, then the infant industry policy had failed and the protectionism could be phased out. Either way, the infant industry protectionism would be temporary.

Following these rules is easier said than done. Politics often intrudes, both in choosing which industries will receive the benefits of being treated as "infants" and in choosing when to phase out import restrictions and other subsidies.

Also, if the government of a country wishes to impose costs on its citizens so that it can provide subsidies to a few key industries, it has many tools for doing so: direct government payments, loans, targeted tax reductions, government support of research and development to develop new technologies, and so on. The point here is not necessarily to advocate such subsidies, but merely to point out that when industrial subsidies are desired, it is not necessary to provide them through protectionism.

The Dumping Argument

dumping: Selling internationally traded goods below their cost of production.

anti-dumping laws: Laws that block imports sold below the cost of production and impose tariffs that would increase the price of these imports to reflect their cost of production.

Dumping means selling goods below their cost of production. **Anti-dumping laws** seek to block imports that are sold below the cost of production and to impose tariffs that would increase the price of these imports to reflect their cost of production.

The Growth of Anti-Dumping Cases

Since dumping is not allowed under the rules of the World Trade Organization, nations that believe they are on the receiving end of dumped goods can file a complaint with the WTO. Anti-dumping complaints have risen in recent years, from about 100 cases per year in the late 1980s to about 200 new cases each year in the last decade or so. Individual countries also frequently started their own anti-dumping investigations. The U.S. government has dozens of anti-dumping orders in place from past investigations. In 2016, for example, some U.S. imports that were under anti-dumping orders included wooden bedroom furniture and wax candles from China, pistachios from Iran, fresh warm-water shrimp from Brazil, wire rods from Japan and Spain, and plastic tape from Italy.

Why Might Dumping Occur?

Why would foreign firms export a product at less than its cost of production—which presumably means taking a loss? This question has two possible answers, one innocent and one more sinister.

The innocent explanation is that market prices are set by demand and supply, not by the cost of production. Perhaps demand for a product shifts back to the left or supply shifts out to the right, which drives the market price to low levels—even below the cost of production. When a local store has a going-out-of-business sale, for example, it may sell goods at below the cost of production. If international companies find that there is an excess supply of steel or computer chips or machine tools that is driving the market price down below their cost of production—well, this may be the market in action.

The sinister explanation is that dumping is part of a long-term strategy in which foreign firms would sell at below the cost of production in the short-term for a time, and when they have driven out the domestic U.S. competition, they would then raise prices. This scenario is sometimes called "predatory pricing."

Should Anti-Dumping Cases Be Limited?

Anti-dumping cases pose two questions. How much sense do they make in economic theory? How much sense do they make as practical policy?

In terms of economic theory, the case for anti-dumping laws is weak. In a market governed by demand and supply, the government doesn't guarantee that firms will be able to make a profit. After all, low prices are difficult for producers, but benefit consumers. Moreover, although there are plenty of cases in which foreign producers have taken sales from domestic U.S. firms, there are zero documented cases in which the foreign producers then jacked up prices. Instead, the foreign producers typically continue competing hard against each other and providing low prices to consumers.

But even if one could make a case that the government should sometimes enact anti-dumping rules in the short term, and then allow free trade to resume shortly thereafter, there is an additional concern that anti-dumping investigations often involve more politics than careful analysis. Calculating the appropriate "cost of production" under law can be as much an art as a science; for example, if a company built a new factory two years ago, should part of the cost of factory be counted in this year's cost of production? When a domestic industry complains loudly enough, government regulators seem very likely to find that unfair dumping has occurred. Indeed, a common pattern has arisen where a domestic industry files an anti-dumping complaint, the governments meet and negotiate a reduction in imports, and then the domestic producers drop the anti-dumping suit. In such cases, anti-dumping cases often appear to be little more than a cover story for imposing tariffs or import quotas.

In the 1980s, almost all of the anti-dumping cases were initiated by the United States, Canada, the European Union, Australia, and New Zealand. But by the 2000s, countries like Argentina, Brazil, South Korea, South Africa, Mexico, and India were filing the majority of the anti-dumping cases before the WTO. As the number of anti-dumping cases has increased, and as countries like the United States and the European Union feel targeted by anti-dumping actions of others, the World Trade Organization may well propose some additional guidelines to limit the reach of anti-dumping laws.

The Environmental Protection Argument

The potential for global trade to affect the environment has become controversial. A president of the Sierra Club, an environmental lobbying organization, once wrote: "The consequences of globalization for the environment are not good. . . . Globalization, if we are lucky, will raise average incomes enough to pay for cleaning up some of the mess that we have made. But before we get there, globalization could also destroy enough of the planet's basic biological and physical systems that prospects for life itself will be radically compromised." If free trade means the destruction of life itself, then even economists would convert to protectionism! But while globalization—and economic activity of all kinds—can pose environmental dangers, it seems quite possible that with appropriate safeguards in place, the environmental impacts of trade can be minimal. In some cases, trade may even bring environmental benefits.

In general, high-income countries like the United States, Canada, Japan, and the nations of the European Union have relatively strict environmental standards. In contrast, middle- and low-income countries of the world like Brazil, China, India, and Nigeria have lower environmental standards. The general view of the governments of such countries is that as soon as their people have enough to eat, decent health care, and longer life expectancies, then they will spend more money on sewage treatment plants, scrubbers to reduce air pollution from factory smokestacks, national parks to protect wildlife, and so on. This gap in environmental standards between high-income and low-income countries raises two worrisome possibilities in a world of increasing global trade: the "race to the bottom" scenario and the question of how quickly environmental standards will improve in low-income countries. Let us consider these two issues in turn.

The Race to the Bottom Scenario

race to the bottom: When production locates in countries with the lowest environmental (or other) standards, putting pressure on all countries to reduce their environmental standards.

The **race to the bottom** scenario of global environmental degradation runs like this. Profit-seeking multinational companies shift their production from countries with strong environmental standards to countries with weak standards, thus reducing their costs and increasing their profits. Faced with such behavior, countries reduce their environmental standards to attract multinational firms, which after all provide jobs and economic clout. As a result, global production becomes concentrated in countries where it can pollute the most, and environmental laws everywhere race to the bottom.

Although the race-to-the-bottom scenario sounds plausible, it does not appear to describe reality. In fact, the financial incentive for firms to shift production to low-income countries to take advantage of their weaker environmental rules does not seem especially powerful. When firms decide where to locate a new factory, they consider many different factors: the costs of labor and financial capital; whether the location is close to reliable suppliers of the inputs that they need; whether the location is close to customers; the quality of transportation, communications, and electrical power networks; the level of taxes; and the competence and honesty of the local government. The cost of environmental regulations is a factor, too, but typically, environmental costs are no more than 1–2% of the costs faced by a large industrial plant. The other factors that determine choice of location are much more important than trying to skimp on environmental protection costs.

When an international company does choose to build a plant in a low-income country with lax environmental laws, it typically builds a plant similar to those that it operates in high-income countries with stricter environmental standards. Part of the reason for this decision is that designing an industrial plant is a complex and costly task, and so if a plant works well in a high-income country, companies prefer to use a similar design everywhere. Also, companies realize that if they create an environmental disaster in a low-income country, it is likely to cost them a substantial amount of money in paying for damages, lost trust, and reduced sales—and by building up-to-date plants everywhere, they minimize such risks. As a result of these factors, foreign-owned plants in low-income countries often have a better record of compliance with environmental laws than do locally-owned plants.

Perhaps the hardest task for those who predict a race to the bottom scenario is explaining why it hasn't already happened. After all, globalization has been expanding for decades—and at the same time, environmental standards have been growing stronger both in high-income and in low-income countries of the world. For low-income countries, globalization has often meant importing some of the environmental values of high-income countries—and also having higher income levels to afford greater environmental protection. Apparently, the competitive pressures from mobile multinational firms that might encourage governments to reduce their environmental standards are not nearly as strong as the counterbalancing pressures to increase environmental standards.

Pressuring Low-Income Countries for Higher Environmental Standards

In some cases, the issue is not so much whether globalization will pressure low-income countries to reduce their environmental standards, but instead whether the threat of blocking international trade can be used to pressure these countries into adopting stronger environmental standards. For example, restrictions on ivory imports in high-income countries, along with stronger government efforts to catch elephant poachers, have been credited with helping to reduce the illegal poaching of elephants in certain African countries.

However, it would be highly undemocratic for the well-fed citizens of high-income countries to attempt to dictate to the ill-fed citizens of low-income countries what domestic policies and priorities they must adopt, and how they should balance environmental goals against other priorities for their citizens. Also, if high-income countries want stronger environmental standards in low-income countries, they have many other options than the threat of protectionism. For example, high-income countries could pay for anti-pollution equipment in low-income countries or could help to pay for national parks. High-income countries could help pay for and carry out the scientific and economic studies that would help environmentalists in low-income countries to make a more persuasive case for the economic benefits of protecting the environment: after all, environmental protection is very important to two industries of key importance in many low-income countries—agriculture and tourism. Environmental advocates can set up standards for labeling products, like "this tuna caught in a net that kept dolphins safe" or "this product made only with wood not taken from rain forests," so that consumer pressure can reinforce environmentalist values. The United Nations sponsors treaties to address issues such as climate change and global warming, the preservation of biodiversity, the spread of deserts, and the environmental health of the seabed, as well as other issues. Countries that share a national border or are within a region often sign environmental agreements concerning air and water rights, too. The World Trade Organization is also becoming more aware of environmental issues and more careful about assuring that increases in trade don't inflict environmental damage. Along with these other policy tools, high-income countries could refuse to import a limited number of specific products where the product is very closely linked to the environmental danger—like not importing the ivory from elephant tusks.

These concerns about the race to the bottom or pressuring low-income countries for more strict environmental standards do not apply very well to the roughly half of all U.S. trade that occurs with other high-income countries of the world. Indeed, many European countries have stricter environmental standards in certain industries than the United States.

The Unsafe Consumer Products Argument

One argument for shutting out certain imported products is that they are unsafe for consumers. This fear seems exaggerated. The World Trade Organization explains its rules in this way: "It allows countries to set their own standards. But it also says regulations must be based on science. . . . And they should not arbitrarily or unjustifiably discriminate between countries where identical or similar conditions prevail." Thus, under WTO rules, it is perfectly legitimate for the United States to pass laws requiring that all, say, food products or cars sold in the United States meet certain safety standards approved by the U.S. government, whether or not other countries choose to pass similar standards. However, such standards must have some scientific basis, and it would be unfair to impose, say, one set of health and safety standards for domestically produced goods but a different set of standards for imports, or one set of standards for imports from Europe and a different set of standards for imports from Latin America.

The National Interest Argument

It is sometimes argued that a nation should not depend too heavily on other countries for supplies of certain key products. This argument has been made for commodities that are important to the U.S. economy as a whole, like oil, and for special materials or technologies that might have weapons applications. But upon closer consideration, this argument for protectionism proves rather weak.

The issue is not whether certain products, like oil, are highly important to the U.S. economy both for personal use in transportation and heating and for a wide array of

Public Attitudes about Global Trade

How do people around the world feel about expanding trade between nations? In summer 2014, the Pew Research Center surveyed approximately 48,600 people in 44 countries. One of the questions asked about opinions on trade ties between countries. The accompanying table shows the percentages for selected countries of those who believe that growing trade ties between countries are "good."

For those who think of the United States as the world's leading supporter of expanding trade, the survey results may be perplexing. Americans actually have a less favorable view of globalization than do individuals in many other countries, whereas Vietnam, Tunisia, and Israel rank at the top. In fact, among the 44 countries surveyed, the United States was tied at fourth-lowest, higher than only Turkey, Italy, and Thailand.

Growing Trade Ties between Countries Are Good: Some Examples	
Vietnam	95%
Tunisia	95%
Spain	91%
Uganda	90%
China	89%
Brazil	80%
Mexico	71%
United States	69%
Thailand	68%
Italy	59%
Turkey	57%

industrial uses. Oil provides about 35% of all the energy in the United States, and about one-quarter of the oil used in the U.S. economy in recent years is imported. Several times in the last few decades, when the global price of oil has risen sharply, the adverse effects have been felt across the U.S. economy.

But none of this makes a very convincing argument for restricting imports of oil. If the United States needs to be protected from a possible cutoff of foreign oil, then a more reasonable strategy would be to import 100% of the United States' petroleum supply now and save the U.S. domestic oil resources for when or if the foreign supply is cut off! It might also be useful to import extra oil and put it into a stockpile for use in an emergency, as the U.S. government did by starting a Strategic Petroleum Reserve in 1977. Moreover, it may be necessary to discourage people from using oil and to start a high-powered program to seek out alternatives to oil. A straightforward way to do this would be to raise taxes on oil. (Such a tax increase on oil could be offset with cuts in other taxes, so that the total tax burden need not rise.) But it makes no sense to argue that because oil is highly important to the U.S. economy, then the United States should shut out oil imports and use up its domestic supplies of oil more quickly.

Whether to limit imports of key technologies or materials that might be important to weapons systems is a slightly different issue. If weapons builders are not confident that they can continue to obtain a key product in wartime, they might decide to avoid designing weapons that use this key product, or they can go ahead and design the weapons and stockpile enough of the key high-tech components or materials to last through an armed conflict. Indeed, a U.S. Defense National Stockpile Center has built up reserves of many materials—from aluminum oxides, antimony, and bauxite to tungsten, vegetable tannin extracts, and zinc (although many of these stockpiles have been reduced and sold in recent years). But why shut out a high technology product, like a specialized type of computer chip or screen, for all the potential civilian-sector users—including businesses that may need the technology so that their products can be competitive in world markets—just because makers of weapons are hesitant to rely on it? If the concern is to build up top-level technological capabilities for domestic producers, it is usually better to have domestic firms competing hard in world markets—perhaps with some direct government subsidies for research and development in key areas—rather than sheltering domestic producers from foreign competition.

National Security and Scissors and Shears

What follows is actual testimony before Congress in 1962 from a lobbyist arguing that the national interest demands a higher tariff on imported scissors and shears.

[M]y name is B.C. Dueschle. I am vice president of the Acme Shear Co., located in Bridgeport, Conn. I appear before this committee as president of the Shears, Scissors & Manicure Implement Manufacturers Association, the only national trade association of domestic manufacturers of scissors and shears. The scissors and shears industry is a distinct industry and should not be confused with the larger industry and the flatware industries. . . .

We have never requested or suggested that a complete embargo be placed on the import of scissors and shears. All that we have asked for and desire is a fair competitive opportunity, not an advantage. . . .

We realize that the domestic scissor and shear industry with its 1,000-plus employees accounts for only a fraction of 1% of the gross national product, but we see this as no justification for letting the industry be completely destroyed by imports produced with low-cost labor.

The workers in the domestic scissor and shear industry do not want to become wards of the State; they want to use their skills, which have taken many years to develop. These workers are not interested in retraining; over many years they have developed a skill they are proud of and want to continue the work they are happy doing. . . .

Under the provisions of this bill, scissors and shears would be buried in a category with many other items and the duty cut 50%. This would mean a reduction of at least 20 cents per pair at the retail level for scissors and shears now being retailed at $1 to 1.29 per pair. . . .

These few remaining manufacturers would be forced to close their doors and discharge their employees. The United States would then become wholly dependent on imported scissors and shears.

We cannot understand how it would be in the national interest to permit such a loss. We would lose the skills of the employees and management of the industry as well as the capital investment in production equipment. In the event of a national emergency and imports cutoff, the United States would be without a source of scissors and shears, basic tools for many industries and trades essential to our defense.

The scissors and shear industry is one of the oldest in the world. The skill was brought to the United States from Germany at a time when the United States needed new industry and a scissors and shear industry in particular.

Scissors and shears of all sizes and types are used in every school, retail establishment, office, factory, hospital, and home in the United States. Scissors cannot be classified as a luxury, gimmick, or novelty.

Scissors are used to separate us from our mothers at birth; to cut our toenails; to trim the leather in our shoes; to cut and trim the materials used in every piece of clothing that we wear.

They are used to cut our fingernails, to trim our mustaches, the hair in our ears and nose, and to cut the hair on our heads—even down to the end of the road when our best suit or dress is cut down the back so that the undertaker can dress us for the last ride. Scissors are truly used from birth to death. They are essential to our health, education, and general welfare.

I ask you gentlemen, is this industry one that should be permitted to become extinct in this country?

One final reason why economists often treat the national security argument skeptically is that almost any product can be touted by lobbyists and politicians as vital to national security. In 1954 the United States became worried that it was importing half of the wool required for military uniforms, so it declared wool and mohair to be "strategic materials" and began to give subsidies to wool and mohair farmers. Although wool was removed from the official list of "strategic" materials in 1960, the subsidies for mohair continued for almost 40 years until they were repealed in 1993, and then reinstated in 2002. All too often, the national interest argument has become an excuse for handing out the indirect subsidy of protectionism to certain industries or companies. After all, decisions about what constitutes a key strategic material are made by politicians, not nonpartisan analysts.

How Trade Policy Is Enacted:
Global, Regional, and National

These public policy arguments about how nations should react to globalization and trade are fought out at several levels: at the global level through the World Trade Organization and through regional trade agreements between pairs or groups of countries.

The World Trade Organization

The World Trade Organization was officially born in 1995, but its history is somewhat longer. In the years after the Great Depression and World War II, there was a worldwide push to build institutions that would bind the nations of the world together. For example, the United Nations officially came into existence in 1945. The World Bank, with a focus on assisting the poorest people in the world, and the International Monetary Fund, with a focus on addressing issues raised by international financial transactions, were both created in 1946. The General Agreement on Tariffs and Trade (GATT), which provided a forum in which nations could come together to negotiate over reductions in tariffs and other barriers to trade, started in 1947. In 1995, the GATT transformed itself into the World Trade Organization.

The GATT process was to negotiate an agreement to reduce barriers to trade, sign that agreement, pause for breath, and then start negotiating the next agreement. The rounds of talks in the GATT, and now the WTO, are shown in Exhibit 6-3. Notice that the early rounds of GATT talks took a relatively short time, included a relatively small number of countries, and focused almost entirely on reducing tariffs. Since the 1970s, however, rounds of trade talks have taken years, included a large number of countries, and included an ever-broadening range of issues.

The sluggish pace of GATT negotiations led to an old joke that GATT really stood for Gentleman's Agreement to Talk and Talk. But the slow pace of international trade talks is understandable, even sensible. Having dozens of nations agree to any treaty is a lengthy process. The GATT often set up separate trading rules for certain industries, like agriculture, and separate trading rules for certain countries, like the low-income countries

EXHIBIT 6-3 Negotiating Rounds of the GATT and the World Trade Organization

Year	Place or Name of Round	Main Subjects	Number of Countries Involved
1947	Geneva	Tariff reduction	23
1949	Annecy	Tariff reduction	13
1951	Torquay	Tariff reduction	38
1956	Geneva	Tariff reduction	26
1960–61	Dillon round	Tariff reduction	26
1964–67	Kennedy round	Tariffs and anti-dumping measures	62
1973–79	Tokyo round	Tariffs, nontariff barriers	102
1986–94	Uruguay round	Tariffs, nontariff barriers, services, intellectual property, dispute settlement, textiles, agriculture, creation of WTO	123
2001–	Doha round	Agriculture, services, intellectual property, competition, investment, environment, dispute settlement	162

in the world. There were rules, exceptions to rules, opportunities to opt out of rules, and precise wording to be fought over in every case. Like the GATT before it, the WTO is not a world government, with power to impose its decisions on others. The total staff of the WTO in 2015 was about 630 people, and its annual budget was $200 million, which made it smaller in size than many medium-sized universities.

Regional Trading Agreements

Many nations belong both to the World Trade Organization and to regional trading agreements. The best-known of these regional trading agreements is the European Union. In the years after World War II, leaders of the nations of Europe reasoned that if they could tie their economies together more closely, they might be more likely to avoid another devastating war. Their efforts evolved into what is now known as the European Union. The EU, as it is often called, has a number of goals. For example, in the early 2000s it introduced a common currency for Europe—the euro—and phased out the old national forms of money like the German mark and the French franc. Another key element of the union is to eliminate barriers to the mobility of goods, labor, and capital across Europe.

For the United States, perhaps the best-known regional trading agreement is the North American Free Trade Agreement (NAFTA), which reduced barriers to trade between the United States, Mexico, and Canada. NAFTA was signed into law by President Bill Clinton in November 1993 and took effect in 1995. However, the U.S. also participates in some less-known regional trading agreements, like the Caribbean Basin Initiative, which offers reduced tariffs for imports from these countries, and a free trade agreement with Israel.

The world has seen a flood of regional trading agreements in recent years. Over 100 such agreements are now in place; a few of the more prominent ones are listed in Exhibit 6-4. Some are just agreements to talk and talk; others set specific goals for reducing tariffs, import quotas, and nontariff barriers. The current trade treaties have been described as a

EXHIBIT 6-4 Some Regional Trade Agreements

Trade Agreements	Participating Countries
Asia Pacific Economic Cooperation (APEC)	Australia, Brunei, Canada, Chile, People's Republic of China, Hong Kong, Indonesia, Japan, Republic of Korea, Malaysia, Mexico, New Zealand, Papua New Guinea, Peru, Philippines, Russia, Singapore, Chinese Taipei, Thailand, United States, Vietnam
European Union (EU)	Austria, Belgium, Bulgaria, Croatia, Cyprus, Czech Republic, Denmark, Estonia, Finland, France, Germany, Greece, Hungary, Ireland, Italy, Latvia, Lithuania, Luxembourg, Malta, Netherlands, Poland, Portugal, Romania, Slovakia, Slovenia, Spain, Sweden, United Kingdom
North America Free Trade Agreement (NAFTA)	Canada, Mexico, United States
Latin American Integration Association (LAIA)	Argentina, Bolivia, Brazil, Chile, Columbia, Cuba, Ecuador, Mexico, Panama, Paraguay, Peru, Uruguay, Venezuela
Association of Southeast Asian Nations (ASEAN)	Brunei, Cambodia, Indonesia, Laos, Malaysia, Myanmar, Philippines, Singapore, Thailand, Vietnam
Southern African Development Community (SADC)	Angola, Botswana, Democratic Republic of the Congo, Lesotho, Madagascar, Malawi, Mauritius, Mozambique, Namibia, Seychelles, South Africa, Swaziland, Tanzania, Zambia, Zimbabwe
Asia-Pacific Trade Agreement (APTA)	Bangladesh, China, India, Republic of Korea, Laos, Mongolia, Sri Lanka

"spaghetti bowl," which is what a map with lines connecting all the countries with trade treaties looks like. There is some concern among economists who favor free trade that some of these regional agreements may promise free trade, but actually act as a way for the countries within the regional agreement to try to limit trade from anywhere else. However, the more common pattern appears to be that although trade talks through the World Trade Organization have stalled, agreements to facilitate trade flows are happening through regional agreements instead.

Trade Policy at the National Level

In the arena of trade policy, there often seems to be a battle between national laws that increase protectionism and international agreements that try to reduce protectionism, like the World Trade Organization. Why would a country pass national-level laws or negotiate bilateral agreements to shut out certain foreign products, like sugar or textiles, while simultaneously negotiating at the regional and global levels to reduce trade barriers in general?

One plausible answer is that international trade agreements offer a method for countries to restrain their own special interests. A member of Congress can say to an industry lobbying for tariffs or quotas on imports: "Sure would like to help you, but that pesky WTO agreement just won't let me." In this way, international trade agreements are like hiring a personal trainer; they pressure you to follow through on the healthy behavior that you should be doing anyway.

Long-Term Trends Concerning Barriers to Trade

In the newspaper headlines, trade policy appears rife with disputes and acrimony. Countries are almost constantly threatening to challenge "unfair" trading practices of other nations. Cases are brought before the dispute settlement procedures of the WTO, the European Union, NAFTA, and other regional trading agreements. Politicians in national legislatures, goaded on by lobbyists, often threaten to pass bills that will "establish a fair playing field" or "prevent unfair trade"—although most such bills seek to accomplish these high-sounding goals by placing more restrictions on trade. Protesters in the streets may object to specific trade rules or to the entire practice of international trade.

But through all the controversy, the general trend in the last 60 years is clearly toward lower barriers to trade. The average level of tariffs on imported products charged by industrialized countries was 40% in 1946. By 1990, after decades of GATT negotiations, it was down to less than 5%. Indeed, one of the reasons that GATT negotiations shifted from focusing on tariff reduction in the early rounds to a broader agenda was that tariffs had been reduced so dramatically that there wasn't much more to do in that area. U.S. tar-

CLEARING IT UP

Trade Is Not War

People often think of international trade agreements as similar to arms control treaties. In arms control treaties, the two sides negotiate to reduce their weapons; in a trade agreement, they negotiate to reduce their trade barriers. From this point of view, nations enact trade barriers the way they build missiles, to build their strength and show their toughness, and they are willing to give up those trade barriers, like their missiles, only if other nations are also willing to disarm.

But this analogy, while it may appear reasonable on the surface, is terribly off the mark. Trade is not a form of warfare. War is fundamentally a lose-lose situation; both sides suffer losses until one side gives up. Trade is fundamentally a win-win situation, where both sides make voluntary exchanges and make mutual gains. One writer said: "As to trade as war, it is hard to think of two things more antithetical. When free to do so, buyers and sellers make deals to their mutual advantage, each walking away happy. This is some form of war? If it is, let's substitute it for all the other forms."

iffs have followed this general pattern; after rising sharply during the Great Depression, they dropped off to about 2% by the end of the century. Although measures of import quotas and nontariff barriers are less exact than those for tariffs, they generally appear to be at lower levels, too.

Thus, the last half-century has seen both a dramatic reduction in government-created barriers to trade, like tariffs, import quotas, and nontariff barriers, and also technological developments that have made international trade easier, like advances in transportation, communication, and information management. The result has been the powerful surge of international trade called globalization.

The Trade-offs of Trade Policy

Economists readily acknowledge that international trade is not all sunshine and roses and happy endings. On average and over time, the average person gains from international trade, both as a worker who has greater productivity and higher wages because of the benefits of specialization and comparative advantage, and as a consumer who can benefit from shopping all over the world for a greater variety of quality products at attractive prices. But the average person is hypothetical, not real, representing a mix of those who have done very well, those who have done all right, and those who have done poorly. It is a legitimate concern of public policy not just to focus on the average or on the success stories, but also on those who have not been so blessed. Workers in other countries, the environment, and prospects for new industries and materials that might be of key importance to the national economy are also all legitimate issues. The common belief among economists is that it is better to embrace the gains from trade, and then to deal with the costs and trade-offs with other policy tools, rather than cutting off trade to avoid the costs and trade-offs—but also losing the benefits of international trade.

To gain a better intuitive understanding for this argument, consider a hypothetical American company called Technotron. Technotron invents a new scientific technology that allows the firm to increase the output and quality of its goods with a smaller number of workers at a lower cost. As a result of this technology, other U.S. firms in this industry will lose money and will also have to lay off workers—and some of the competing firms will even go bankrupt. Should the U.S. government protect the existing firms and their employees by making it illegal for Technotron to use its new technology?

Most people who live in market-oriented economies would oppose trying to block new technology. Certainly, there is a case that society should provide temporary support and assistance for those who find themselves without work. Many would argue for government support of programs that encourage retraining and acquiring additional skills. Government might also support research and development efforts, so that other firms may find ways of outdoing Technotron. But blocking the new technology altogether seems like a mistake. After all, few people would advocate giving up electricity because it caused so much disruption to the kerosene and candle business. Few would suggest holding back on improvements in medical technology because they might cause companies selling older and less effective medical care to lose money. In short, most people view disruptions due to technological change as a necessary cost that is worth bearing.

Now, imagine that Technotron's new "technology" is as simple as this: the company imports what it sells from another country. In other words, think of foreign trade as a type of innovative technology. The objective situation is now exactly the same as before. Because of Technotron's new technology—which in this case is importing goods from another county—other firms in this industry will lose money and lay off workers. But just as it would have been inappropriate and ultimately foolish to respond to the disruptions of new scientific technology by trying to shut it down, it would be inappropriate and ultimately foolish to respond to the disruptions of international trade by trying to restrict trade.

Some workers and firms will suffer because of international trade. But in a living, breathing, market-oriented economy, some workers and firms will always be experiencing disruptions, for a wide variety of reasons. Corporate management can be better or worse. Workers for a certain firm can be more productive or less. Tough domestic competitors can create just as much disruption as tough foreign competitors. Sometimes a new product is a hit with consumers; sometimes it's a flop. Sometimes a company is blessed by a run of good luck or stricken with a run of bad luck. For some firms, international trade will offer great opportunities for expanding productivity and jobs; for other firms, trade will impose stress and pain. The disruption caused by international trade is not fundamentally different from all the other disruptions caused by the other workings of a market economy. Trying to prevent the disruptions of a market-oriented economy from happening has an opportunity cost: it means blocking the economic gains from trade.

In other words, the economic analysis of free trade doesn't rely on a belief that foreign trade is not disruptive or does not pose trade-offs; indeed, the story of Technotron begins with a particular disruptive market change—a new technology—that causes real trade-offs. But in thinking about the disruptiveness of foreign trade, or any of the other possible costs and trade-offs of foreign trade discussed in this chapter, the best public policy solutions typically don't involve protectionism, but instead involve finding ways for public policy to address the particular issues while still allowing the benefits of international trade to occur.

Key Concepts and Summary

1. There are three tools for restricting the flow of trade: **tariffs**, **import quotas**, and **nontariff barriers**. When a country places limitations on imports from abroad, regardless of whether it uses tariffs, quotas, or nontariff barriers, it is said to be practicing **protectionism**.

2. Protectionism will raise the price of the protected good in the domestic market, which causes domestic consumers to pay more but benefits producers.

3. As international trade increases, it contributes to a shift in jobs away from industries where that economy does not have a comparative advantage and toward industries where it does have a comparative advantage. Overall, however, the increase in trade does not have much effect on the number of jobs.

4. Global trade should raise the average level of wages by increasing productivity. However, this increase in average wages may include both gains to workers in certain jobs and industries and losses to others.

5. In thinking about labor practices in low-income countries, it's useful to draw a line between what is unpleasant to think about and what is morally objectionable. For example, low wages and long working hours in poor countries are unpleasant to think about, but for people in low-income parts of the world, it may well be the best option open to them. Practices like child labor and forced labor are morally objectionable, and the rules of the WTO allow any country to refuse to import products made using these practices.

6. The **infant industry argument** for protectionism is that small domestic industries need to be temporarily nurtured and protected from foreign competition for a time so that they can grow into strong competitors. In some cases, notably in East Asia, this approach has worked. But often, the infant industries never grow up.

7. **Dumping** occurs when prices are set at below the cost of production. The strategy is to set prices at a level below production costs, absorb losses until competitors are driven out of the market, and then, when competition has been eliminated or greatly reduced, to raise prices substantially and earn high profits. While there are some historical examples where this strategy has worked, it does not appear to arise very often, if at all, in global trade. More often, anti-dumping complaints seem to be a convenient excuse for imposing protectionism.

8. Low-income countries typically have lower environmental standards than high-income countries because they are more worried about immediate basics such as food, education, and health care. There are a variety of ways for high-income countries to encourage stronger environmental standards in low-income countries, including some movement to make sure that new opportunities opened up by free trade don't injure the environment. Except for a small number of extreme cases, shutting off trade seems unlikely to be an effective method of pursuing a cleaner environment.

9. Under the rules of the World Trade Organization, countries are allowed to set whatever standards for product safety they wish, but the standards must be the same for domestic products as for imported products. If there is a dispute over whether a health and safety standard is being imposed without a scientific basis, it can be appealed to the WTO.

10. The **national interest argument** for protectionism holds that it is unwise to import certain key products because if the nation becomes dependent on key imported supplies, it could be vulnerable to a cutoff. However, it is often wiser to stockpile resources and

to use foreign supplies when available, rather than preemptively restricting foreign supplies so as not to become dependent on them.

11. Trade policy is determined at many different levels: administrative agencies within government, laws passed by the legislature, regional negotiations between a small group of nations (sometimes just two), and global negotiations through the World Trade Organization.

12. During the second half of the twentieth century, trade barriers have in general declined quite substantially both in the U.S. economy and in the global economy.

13. One reason why countries sign international trade agreements to commit themselves to free trade is to give themselves protection against their own special interests. When an industry lobbies for protection from foreign producers, politicians can point out that because of the trade treaty, their hands are tied.

14. International trade certainly disrupts what would otherwise have been the pattern of an economy. This is hardly surprising, since all sorts of competitive market forces are disruptive, whether domestic or international, often causing companies and industries to rise and fall. Government has a role to play in cushioning workers against the disruptions of the market. But just as it would be unwise in the long term to clamp down on new technology and other causes of disruption in domestic markets, it would be unwise to clamp down on foreign trade. In both cases, the disruption brings with it economic benefits.

Review Questions

1. Who does protectionism protect? What does it protect them from?

2. Name and define three policy tools for enacting protectionism.

3. How does protectionism affect the price of the protected good in the domestic market?

4. Does international trade, taken as a whole, increase the total number of jobs, decrease the total number of jobs, or leave the total number of jobs about the same?

5. Is international trade likely to have roughly the same effect on the number of jobs in each individual industry?

6. How is international trade, taken as a whole, likely to affect the average level of wages?

7. Is international trade likely to have about the same effect on everyone's wages?

8. Do the jobs for workers in low-income countries that involve making products for export to high-income countries typically pay these workers more or less than their next-best alternative?

9. What's an infant industry? Why does protecting it often work better in theory than in practice?

10. What is dumping? Why does prohibiting it often work better in theory than in practice?

11. What is the race to the bottom scenario?

12. Which group of countries typically has more strict environmental standards: countries with higher incomes or lower incomes?

13. Do the rules of international trade require that all nations impose the same consumer safety standards?

14. What is the national interest argument for protectionism with regard to certain products?

15. Name several of the international treaties where countries negotiate with each other over trade policy.

16. What is the general trend of trade barriers over recent decades: higher, lower, or about the same?

17. If opening up to free trade would benefit a nation, then why don't nations just eliminate their trade barriers, and not bother with international trade negotiations?

CHAPTER

7

Elasticity

(a) Shifting Demand, Inelastic Supply

(b) Shifting Demand, Elastic Supply

Chapter Outline

Price Elasticity of Demand

Price Elasticity of Supply

Elastic, Inelastic, and Unitary Elasticity

Applications of Elasticity

Elasticity as a General Concept

A demand curve shows that a higher price will lead to a lower quantity demanded. But how much lower? A supply curve shows that a higher price will lead to a higher quantity supplied. But how much higher? Whether a change in price will affect quantity demanded or quantity supplied by a relatively large or small amount often has real practical significance. For example, the average tax per pack on cigarettes was $2.54 in 2015, including both federal and state-level taxes. Taxes on cigarettes serve two purposes: to raise tax revenue for government and to discourage consumption of cigarettes. But if a higher cigarette tax discourages cigarette consumption by quite a lot, then because a greatly reduced quantity of cigarettes is sold, the cigarette tax on each pack won't raise much revenue for the government. Alternatively, a higher cigarette tax that doesn't discourage cigarette consumption by much will actually raise more tax revenue for the government. Thus, when a government agency tries to calculate the effects of altering its cigarette tax, it must analyze how much the tax affects the quantity of cigarettes consumed.

This issue reaches beyond governments and taxes; every firm faces a similar issue. Every time a firm considers raising the price that it charges, it must consider how much a price increase will reduce the quantity demanded of what it sells. Conversely, when a firm reduces its price, it must expect (or hope) that the lower price will lead to a higher quantity demanded of its product.

This chapter introduces the concept of **elasticity**, which measures how much a percentage change in price leads to a percentage change in quantity demanded or quantity supplied. The chapter begins with the price elasticity of demand, which looks at the responsiveness of quantity demanded to a change in price, and then examines the price elasticity of supply, which looks at the responsiveness of quantity supplied to a change in price. The concept of elasticity is then applied to a number of real-world situations, including ticket prices at concerts, cigarette taxes, airline ticket prices, changes in world oil prices, and others.

elasticity: How much a percentage change in quantity demanded or quantity supplied is affected by a percentage change in price.

Price Elasticity of Demand

When investigating how sensitive the quantity demanded is to a change in price, looking at the demand curve might seem like an obvious starting point. But the visual appearance of demand curves can be misleading. Exhibit 7-1 illustrates the problem. The data on price and quantity demanded of cheese for Exhibit 7-1a and 7-1b are identical. But in Exhibit 7-1a, the demand curve for cheese is graphed with a tall vertical axis and narrow horizontal axis, so that the demand curve appears to slope down steeply. In Exhibit 7-1b, the identical data is graphed with a short vertical axis and a wide horizontal axis, so that the demand curve appears to slope down in a relatively flat way. Remember, the data behind these two demand curves is exactly the same! In both Exhibit 7-1a and 7-1b, the demand curve slopes down, but should the shape of the demand curve for cheese be described as "steep" or "flat"? Answering this question with "it depends on how you draw it" is not very useful.

The vocabulary of elasticity offers a method of discussing how quantity demanded responds to changes in price that doesn't depend on whether the axes are drawn relatively longer or shorter. It doesn't even depend on what units are used to measure price and quantity. Instead of trying to discuss the steepness or flatness of supply and demand curves based on their visual appearance, which can be misleading, elasticity discusses the shape of demand and supply curves with numerical calculations of percentage changes.

Calculating the Elasticity of Demand

elasticity of demand: The percentage change in quantity demanded divided by the percentage change in price.

The numerical example of a demand curve D for small television sets presented in Exhibit 7-2 can help to illustrate the issues. In this case, this demand curve for small televisions is a straight line. Let's calculate the elasticity between points A and B and between points G and H. The **elasticity of demand** is defined as the percentage change in quantity demanded divided by the percentage change in price. The percentage change between two

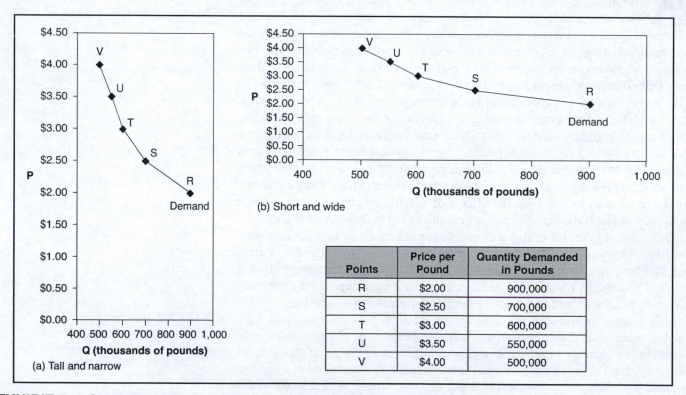

Points	Price per Pound	Quantity Demanded in Pounds
R	$2.00	900,000
S	$2.50	700,000
T	$3.00	600,000
U	$3.50	550,000
V	$4.00	500,000

(a) Tall and narrow

(b) Short and wide

EXHIBIT 7-1 Same Data for Demand Curve, Different Appearance

These two demand curves present exactly the same data on price and quantity. The only difference is that (a) is drawn with a longer vertical axis, while (b) is drawn with a longer horizontal axis. Both demand curves still slope down, but whether the slope appears steep or flat is determined by how the curve is drawn, not by the data.

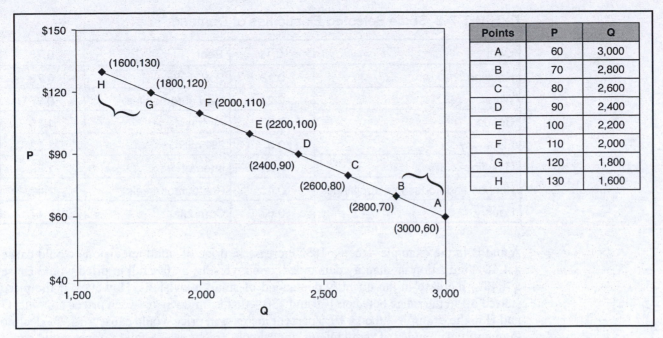

Points	P	Q
A	60	3,000
B	70	2,800
C	80	2,600
D	90	2,400
E	100	2,200
F	110	2,000
G	120	1,800
H	130	1,600

EXHIBIT 7-2 Calculating the Price Elasticity of Demand

The price elasticity of demand is calculated as the percentage change in quantity divided by the percentage change in price. Between two points like A and B, or between G and H, the formula is:

$$\text{Elasticity} = \frac{(\text{change in quantity})/[(\text{sum of the two quantities}/2)]}{(\text{change in price})/[(\text{sum of prices}/2)]}$$

quantities is calculated by taking the difference between the two quantities and dividing by the average of the two quantities—which will be the point halfway between the two quantities. Similarly, the percentage change between two prices is calculated by taking the difference between the two prices and dividing by the average of the two prices—which will be the point halfway between the two prices. Thus, the formula for elasticity of demand is:

$$\text{Elasticity of demand} = \frac{\%\ \text{change in quantity demanded}}{\%\ \text{change in price}}$$

$$= \frac{(\text{difference in quantity / average of original quantities})}{(\text{difference in price / average of original prices})}$$

First, apply this formula to the elasticity between A to B:

$$\frac{[3,000 - 2,800] / [(3,000 + 2,800) / 2]}{[60 - 70] / [(60 + 70) / 2]} = \frac{200/2,900}{-10/65} = \frac{0.069}{-0.154} = -0.448$$

Therefore, the elasticity of demand between these two points is = −0.069/0.154 = −0.448.

As a second example, apply the same formula to calculating the elasticity of demand from G to H.

$$\frac{[1,600 - 1,800] / [(1,600 + 1,800) / 2]}{[130 - 120] / [(130 + 120) / 2]} = \frac{-200/1700}{10/125} = \frac{-0.1176}{0.08} = -1.47$$

Therefore, the elasticity of demand from G to H is = −0.1176/0.08 = −1.47.

An elasticity number is not followed by any units. Elasticity is a ratio of one percentage change to another percentage change—nothing more.

Calculations of elasticity are all arithmetic, so what is the intuitive meaning of the number that emerges from the calculation? Hark back to the original meaning of elasticity: that is, the percentage change in quantity demanded that results from a percentage change in price. Thus, if the price started off at 65—midway between the price at points

EXHIBIT 7-3 Some Selected Elasticities of Demand

Coal	0.11	Beef	0.75
Housing	0.18	Soft drinks	0.79
Wine	0.24	New automobiles	0.87
Coffee	0.3	Air travel	1.15
Electricity	0.3	2% milk	1.22
Gasoline	0.31	Internet	1.29
Kitchen and household appliances	0.4	Restaurant meals	1.42
Poultry	0.68	Computer	2.17

A and B in the example—then a 10% increase in price of small televisions would cause a 4.48% reduction in quantity demanded, or conversely, a 10% fall in price would cause a 4.48% increase in the quantity demanded of small televisions. However, if the price started off in the range between 120 and 130—that is, midway between prices at points G and H in the example—then a 10% percent increase in price would cause a 14.7% decline in quantity demanded of small televisions, or conversely, a 10% fall in price would cause a 14.7% rise in the quantity demanded.

The word "elasticity," in its everyday use, refers to stretchiness: more elastic stretches more, while less elastic stretches less. The elasticity of demand has the same general meaning, except that in this case the stretchiness refers to how much the quantity demanded stretches or contracts in response to a change in price. Exhibit 7-3 shows a selection of demand elasticities for different goods and services drawn from a variety of different research studies by economists. A typical practice in these studies is to calculate the elasticity of demand using the current market equilibrium as the starting point.

A Possible Confusion, a Clarification, and a Warning

The most common confusion about elasticity is to think that it measures the slope of the demand curve. Elasticity is not the slope of the demand curve! The examples above have shown that whether a demand curve appears to have a steep or a flat slope depends on

Elasticity in the Vending Machine

America has 1.5 million vending machines that sell snacks and candy. Tens of millions of Americans are overweight. Could vending machines be used to nudge people toward a healthier diet? A group of researchers in the School of Public Health at the University of Minnesota have been carrying out studies to see how price and availability of snacks in vending machines affect people's purchases.

For example, one of their studies focused on vending machines at 12 worksites and 12 schools. They offered a range of price cuts for low-fat snacks. On some of the machines, they also posted signs identifying the low-fat snacks and encouraging people to buy them. The signs encouraging people to eat low-fat foods had little effect. But the study found that elasticity of demand for low-fat snacks is about 2. That is, a 10% cut in the price of low-fat snacks led to an increase of 20%

in the quantity of such snacks consumed, and a 50% cut in the price of such snacks led to an increase of 100% in sales of low-fat snacks. As it turned out, the price cuts for low-fat snacks didn't even cause the average profits per vending machine to decline because an increase in the volume sold was enough to compensate for the lower prices.

Another one of their studies looked at vending machines in four metropolitan bus garages. In this study, they cut prices for healthy snack options by an average of 30% and also made sure that healthier snacks represented half of the choices in these vending machines. In this study, the elasticity of demand for health snacks was about 1: that is, the 30% fall in prices for healthy snacks led to a rise of about 30% in the quantity consumed of these snacks.

Elasticity Is Not Slope

Although the elasticity of a supply or demand curve is obviously related to the shape of the curve, it isn't the same as what the mathematicians call "slope." Not even close. Slope, you may remember from a high school mathematics class (or from the Appendix to Chapter 1), is "rise over run"; that is, the change on the vertical axis (the rise) divided by the change on the horizontal axis (the run). This calculation differs from elasticity in two ways. First, elasticity involves the change in what is on the horizontal axis (quantity) divided by the change in what is on the vertical axis (price). Thus, elasticity involves run/rise, not rise/run. Second, elasticity is the *percentage* change, which is a different calculation from slope. A straight line has only one slope, but as the example in the chapter shows, a straight-line demand curve has a different elasticity at every point.

how it is drawn. Even when the demand curve is a straight line, with the same mathematical slope at all points, the elasticity will differ quite substantially in different parts of that line. The calculation of elasticity is based on percentage change, which is not the same as the calculation for slope.

Many students who are confronted with the elasticity formula wonder why, in the numerator and denominator, the formula divides by the average value of either the two quantities (in the numerator) or the two prices (in the denominator). The reason is to avoid a situation where in calculating the elasticity between points A and B, one person divides the change in quantity by the quantity level at A while another divides it by the quantity level at B—thus leading to two different answers for the same question. By using the average quantity and average price between A and B, this possible confusion is eliminated. At a more advanced level of economics, using the tools of calculus, elasticity can be calculated at a specific point—in which case the need to divide by the average quantity and price at two different points doesn't arise.

Finally, here's a warning: Because demand curves slope down, the percentage change in quantity demanded in response to a percentage change in price will be a negative number—that is, either a higher price leads to a lower quantity demanded, or a lower price leads to a higher quantity demanded. However, economists have often dropped the negative sign on the elasticity of demand for decades now. After all, economists know that demand curves generally slope downward, so they don't need the reminder of the negative sign. So when you are reading or listening to something about economics and run across an elasticity of demand that has no negative sign, don't be surprised.

Price Elasticity of Supply

Just as the price elasticity of demand reveals how a percentage change in price will lead to a percentage change in quantity demanded, the price elasticity of supply measures how a percentage change in price will lead to a percentage change in quantity supplied. Again, the elasticity cannot be easily inferred from glancing at the appearance of a supply curve. Instead, elasticity requires a numerical calculation.

Calculating the Elasticity of Supply

Assume that you are renting an apartment in the Philadelphia metropolitan area, where the cost of housing for renters is about $650 per month. Say that your neighborhood has 10,000 rental units. This situation is illustrated in both Exhibit 7-4a and Exhibit 7-4b, where the original equilibrium in both graphs is at a price of $650 and a quantity of 10,000 rental apartments. Now imagine that your neighborhood suddenly becomes a more popular and fashionable place to live—that is, demand for rental housing in your neighborhood shifts to the right. Both Exhibit 7-4a and Exhibit 7-4b show an identical shift of a demand curve for rental housing out to the right from D_0 to D_1. However, the shape of the supply curve for rental housing differs in the two graphs. As a result, in

(a) Shifting Demand, Inelastic Supply

(b) Shifting Demand, Elastic Supply

EXHIBIT 7-4 How a Shift in Demand Can Affect Price or Quantity More

The intersection E_0 between supply curve S and demand curve D_0 is the same in both (a) and (b). The increase in demand from D_0 to D_1 is the same in both (a) and (b). The new equilibrium E_1 has a higher price and quantity than the original equilibrium E_0 in both (a) and (b). However, the shape of supply differs in (a) and (b). As a result, in (a), the new equilibrium E_1 happens at a much higher price but only a small increase in quantity, while in (b), the new equilibrium happens at only a small increase in price but a relatively large increase in quantity.

Exhibit 7-4a, the new equilibrium E_1 in your neighborhood occurs at a higher rental price of $900 per month and a slightly higher equilibrium quantity of 11,000 rental units, while in Exhibit 7-4b, the new equilibrium E_1 results in a slightly higher rental price of $700 per month and a substantially higher equilibrium quantity of 13,000 rental units in your neighborhood. The elasticity of supply is a useful tool for explaining the different outcomes in these two situations.

elasticity of supply: The percentage change in quantity supplied divided by the percentage change in price.

Let's begin with the calculations. The **elasticity of supply** is defined as the percentage change in quantity supplied divided by the percentage change in price. Again, the percentage change between two quantities is calculated by taking the difference between the two quantities and dividing by the average of the two quantities. Similarly, the percentage change between two prices is calculated by taking the difference between the two prices and dividing by the average of the two prices. Thus, the formula for elasticity of supply is:

$$\text{Elasticity of supply} = \frac{\text{\% change in quantity supplied}}{\text{\% change in price}}$$

$$= \frac{(\text{change in quantity / average of original quantities})}{(\text{change in price / average of original prices})}$$

First, apply this formula to the elasticity of supply between E_0 and E_1 in Exhibit 7-4a.

$$\frac{[11{,}000 - 10{,}000] / [(11{,}000 + 10{,}000) / 2]}{[900 - 650] / [(900 + 650) / 2]} = \frac{1{,}000/10{,}500}{250/775} = \frac{.095}{.322} = .295$$

The elasticity of supply in this example is .095/.322 = .295.

Now apply the same formula for elasticity of supply to the change between E_0 and E_1 in Exhibit 7-4b.

$$\frac{[13{,}000 - 10{,}000] / [(13{,}000 + 10{,}000) / 2]}{[700 - 650] / [(700 + 650) / 2]} = \frac{3{,}000/11{,}500}{50/675} = \frac{.261}{.074} = 3.52$$

The elasticity of supply in this case is .261/.074 = 3.52.

Again, as with the elasticity of demand, the elasticity of supply is not followed by any units. Elasticity is a ratio of one percentage change to another percentage change—nothing more.

What is the intuitive meaning of these calculations? The elasticity of supply in Exhibit 7-4a is relatively small. A 10% rise in price causes only a 2.9% rise in the quantity supplied in Exhibit 7-4a. The elasticity of supply in Exhibit 7-4b is relatively large. In this case, a 10% rise in price would bring an increase in supply of 35%. The much greater elasticity of supply in Exhibit 7-4b means that quantity supplied will react much more to a certain percentage change in price.

In situations like this one, the supply curve in Exhibit 7-4a often reflects the situation in the short-term, when the quantity supplied of rental housing cannot increase much in a year or two. As a result, the elasticity of supply is fairly low, and the increase in demand is primarily reflected in higher prices. However, the supply curve in Exhibit 7-4b makes more sense from the longer run perspective of several years, when the quantity supplied of housing has time to rise more substantially because of new building activity or converting existing properties into rental units. As a result, in the long run the very same rise in demand is reflected more in a rise in the quantity of housing and less in a rise in price.

Elastic, Inelastic, and Unitary Elasticity

Numerical measures of elasticity can be usefully divided into three broad categories: elastic, inelastic, and unitary elasticity. The categories are summarized in Exhibit 7-5.

When quantity demanded or supplied is highly sensitive to changes in price, it is said to be **elastic.** Specifically, an elastic demand refers to a situation in which a certain percentage change in price leads to a larger percentage change in quantity demanded or quantity supplied. For example, a 1% rise in the price would cause a decline of more than 1%—perhaps 2%—in the quantity demanded of a good. Since elasticity refers to the percentage change in quantity divided by the percentage change in price, saying that a demand curve or supply curve is elastic means that the elasticity calculated from the formula is greater than 1.

elastic: The elasticity calculated from the appropriate formula has an absolute value greater than 1.

Demand will be elastic when consumers find it easy to shift back and forth between goods and services. For example, if the price of lamb rises, many consumers will shift to other meats and foods. Supply will be elastic when it is relatively easy to expand or contract production. For example, at a time when most of the factories in an industry are running at only about half of their full production level, it will be relatively easy to ramp up production higher.

Infinite elasticity refers to the extremely elastic situation where quantity changes by an infinite amount in response to any change in price at all. A demand curve with infinite elasticity appears in Exhibit 7-6a, and a supply curve with infinite elasticity appears in Exhibit 7-6b. Infinite elasticity creates horizontal demand and supply curves.

infinite elasticity: The extremely elastic situation where quantity changes by an infinite amount in response to even a tiny change in price.

EXHIBIT 7-5 Elastic, Unitary, and Inelastic: Three Cases of Elasticity

If . . .	Then . . .	And It's Called . . .
% change in quantity > % change in price	$\dfrac{\% \text{ change in quantity}}{\% \text{ change in price}} > 1$	Elastic
% change in quantity = % change in price	$\dfrac{\% \text{ change in quantity}}{\% \text{ change in price}} = 1$	Unitary elasticity
% change in quantity < % change in price	$\dfrac{\% \text{ change in quantity}}{\% \text{ change in price}} < 1$	Inelastic

EXHIBIT 7-6 Infinite Elasticity

The horizontal lines in (a) and (b) show that an infinite quantity will be demanded (a) or supplied (b) at a specific price. This illustrates the cases of a perfectly elastic or infinitely elastic demand and supply curve.

inelastic: The elasticity calculated from the appropriate formula has an absolute value less than 1.

At the other extreme from elastic is **inelastic**—the situation where a certain percentage change in the price will cause a smaller percentage change in the quantity demanded or supplied. For example, when demand is inelastic, a 1% rise in the price would cause a decline of less than 1%—say, only 0.3%—in the quantity demanded of a good. Since elasticity is calculated as the percentage change in quantity divided by the percentage change in price, inelastic means that the level of elasticity will be less than 1.

Demand will be inelastic when consumers find it difficult to shift back and forth between goods and services. For example, if you have an illness that requires a certain drug to reduce your pain or to keep you alive, and the price of that drug rises, you may not cut back very much, if at all, on consumption of that drug, but instead you will seek ways to save money elsewhere in your budget. Supply is often inelastic in the short run because over a time period of a few months or even a year or two, businesses often have a limited ability to expand their quantity supplied in a dramatic way, given that they have only so many factories and workers on hand.

zero elasticity: The highly inelastic case in which a percentage change in price, no matter how large, results in zero change in the quantity demanded or supplied.

Zero elasticity refers to the highly inelastic case in which a percentage change in price, no matter how large, results in zero change in quantity. A demand curve with zero elasticity appears in Exhibit 7-7a; a supply curve with zero elasticity appears in Exhibit 7-7b. Zero elasticity refers to demand and supply curves that are vertical.

EXHIBIT 7-7 Zero Elasticity

The (a) vertical demand and (b) vertical supply curves show that there will be zero percentage change in quantity demanded or supplied, regardless of the price. This illustrates the case of zero or perfect inelasticity.

On the borderline between elastic and inelastic, the percentage change in quantity demanded is equal to the percentage change in quantity supplied, which is the case of unitary elasticity. In this case, a rise of, say, 10% in price would lead to a decline of 10% in the quantity demanded, or a fall of, say, 5% in price would lead to a fall of 5% in the quantity supplied.

When economists are sketching examples of demand and supply, it is common to sketch a demand or supply curve that is close to vertical, and then to refer to that curve as "inelastic." It is also common to sketch a demand or supply curve that is close to horizontal, and then to refer to that demand or supply curve as "elastic." Such statements must be handled with care. Remember, a close-to-horizontal or close-to-vertical demand or supply curve may appear that way because of how the axes are drawn, not because of some inherent characteristic of the underlying data. Moreover, elasticity will usually vary along a demand or supply curve, so that one zone of a demand or supply curve can be elastic while another zone is inelastic. Nonetheless, for purposes of sketching diagrams and illustrating economic intuition, it is often convenient to treat inelastic as close to vertical and elastic as close to horizontal. As long as one remembers that such statements are only approximations for the purposes of illustration, no harm is done.

Applications of Elasticity

Elasticities are useful in a wide range of circumstances. Even knowing only that a demand or supply curve is elastic or inelastic can lead to interesting insights.

Does Raising Price Bring in More Revenue?

Imagine that a band on tour is playing in an indoor arena with 15,000 seats. To keep this example simple, assume that the band keeps all the money from ticket sales. (For example, you can imagine that the owners of the arena make their money by charging for parking and concessions.) Assume further that the band pays the costs for its appearance, but that these costs like travel, setting up the stage, and so on, are the same regardless of how many people gather in the audience. Finally, assume that all the tickets have the same price. (The same insights apply if ticket prices are more expensive for some seats than for others, but the calculations become more complicated.) The band knows that it faces a downward-sloping demand curve; that is, if the band raises the price of tickets, it will sell fewer tickets. How should the band set the price for tickets to bring in the most total revenue, which in this example, because costs are fixed, will also mean the highest profits for the band? Should the band sell more tickets at a higher price or fewer tickets at a lower price?

The key concept in thinking about collecting the most revenue is the elasticity of demand. Total revenue is price times the quantity of tickets sold. Imagine that the band starts off thinking about a certain price, which will result in the sale of a certain quantity of tickets. The three possibilities are laid out in Exhibit 7-8. If demand is elastic at that price level, then the band should cut the price because the percentage drop in price will result in an even larger percentage increase in the quantity sold—thus raising total revenue.

EXHIBIT 7-8 Will the Band Earn More Revenue by Changing Ticket Prices?

If Demand Is . . .	Then . . .	Therefore . . .
Elastic	% change in Q > % change in P	A given % rise in P will be more than offset by a larger % fall in Q, so that total revenue P × Q falls
Unitary	% change in Q = % change in P	A given % rise in P will be exactly offset by an equal % fall in Q, so that total revenue P × Q is unchanged
Inelastic	% change in Q < % change in P	A given % rise in P will cause a smaller % fall in Q, so that total revenue P × Q rises

What Does a Unitary Elasticity of Demand or Supply Look Like?

A demand curve with unitary elasticity at all points is a curved line, but a supply curve with unitary price elasticity at all points is a straight line running through the origin.

To gain some intuition about why this is true, first consider the demand curve with a unitary price elasticity of demand at all points. As you move down the demand curve from A to B, the price falls by 33% and quantity demanded rises by 33%; as you move from B to C, the price falls by 25% and the quantity demanded rises by 25% (although the numbers are chosen here so that a bit of rounding off is needed); as you move from C to D, the price falls by 20% and the quantity rises by 20%. Notice that in absolute value, the declines in price as you step down the demand curve are not identical. Instead, price falls by $2.80 from A to B, by a smaller amount of $1.50 from B to C, and by a still smaller amount of $1.00 from C to D. As a result, a demand curve with constant unitary elasticity moves from a steeper slope on the left to a flatter slope on the right—and a curved shape overall.

In moving up the unitary elasticity supply curve from left to right, each increase in quantity of 20, from 50 to 70 to 90 to 110, is equal in absolute value. However, in percentage value, the steps are decreasing, from 33.3% to 25% to 20%, because the original average quantity in each percentage calculation is getting larger and larger, which expands the denominator in the elasticity calculation. Next consider the price changes moving up the supply curve. From points D to E to F and G on the supply curve, each step of $2.00 is the same in absolute value. However, if the price changes are measured in percentage change terms, they are also decreasing, from 33.3% to 25% to 20%, because the original price points in each percentage calculation are getting larger and larger in value. Along the constant unitary elasticity supply curve, the percentage quantity increases on the horizontal axis exactly match the percentage price increases on the vertical axis—so this linear supply curve has a constant unitary elasticity at all points.

A Constant Unitary Elasticity Demand Curve

A demand curve with constant unitary elasticity will be a curved line. Notice how each step down, the demand curve has an identical percentage change in quantity demanded and in price using the elasticity formula.

A Constant Unitary Elasticity Supply Curve

A constant unitary elasticity supply curve is a straight line reaching up from the origin. Between each point, an application of the elasticity formula shows that the percentage increase in quantity demanded is the same as the percentage increase in price.

However, if demand is inelastic at that original quantity level, then the band should raise the price of tickets because a certain percentage increase in price will result in a smaller percentage decrease in the quantity sold—and total revenue will rise. If demand has a unitary elasticity at that quantity, then a moderate percentage change in the price will be offset by an equal percentage change in quantity—so the band will earn the same revenue whether it (moderately) increases or decreases the price of tickets.

What if the band keeps cutting price, because demand is elastic, until it reaches a level where all 15,000 seats in the available arena are sold? If demand remains elastic at that quantity, the band might try to move to a bigger arena, so that it could cut ticket prices further and see a larger percentage increase in the quantity of tickets sold. Of course, if the 15,000-seat arena is all that is available or if a larger arena would add substantially to costs, then this option may not work.

Conversely, a few bands are so famous, or have such fanatical followings, that demand for tickets may be inelastic right up to the point where the arena is full. These bands can, if they wish, keep raising the price of tickets. Ironically, some bands that are extremely popular among a smaller group could make more revenue by setting prices so high that the arena is not filled—but those who buy the tickets would have to pay very high prices. However, bands sometimes choose to sell tickets for less than the absolute maximum they might be able to charge, often in the hope that fans will feel happier about attending the concert and spend more on recordings, T-shirts, and other paraphernalia.

Passing on Costs to Consumers?

Most businesses face a day-to-day struggle to figure out ways to produce at a lower cost, as one pathway to their goal of earning higher profits. However, in some cases, the price of a key input over which the firm has no control may rise. For example, many chemical companies use petroleum as a key input, but they have no control over the world market price for crude oil. Coffee shops use coffee as a key input, but they have no control over the world market price of coffee. If the cost of a key input rises, can the firm pass those higher costs along to consumers in the form of higher prices? Conversely, if new and less expensive ways of producing are invented, can the firm keep the benefits in the form of higher profits, or will the market pressure them to pass the gains along to consumers in the form of lower prices? The elasticity of demand plays a key role in answering these questions.

Imagine that as a consumer of legal pharmaceutical products, you read a newspaper story that a technological breakthrough in the production of aspirin has occurred, so that every aspirin factory can now make aspirin more cheaply than it did before. What does this discovery mean to you? Exhibit 7-9 illustrates two possibilities. In Exhibit 7-9a, the demand curve is drawn as highly inelastic. In this case, a technological breakthrough that shifts supply to the right from S_0 to S_1, so that the equilibrium shifts from E_0 to E_1, creates a substantially lower price for the product with relatively little impact on the quantity sold. In Exhibit 7-9b, the demand curve is drawn as highly elastic. In this case, the technological breakthrough leads to a much greater quantity being sold in the market at very close to the original price. If you already consume large amounts of aspirin, then you tend to benefit more from a lower price than a greater quantity sold in the market; if you are not yet an aspirin consumer, but a small decrease in price makes you willing to purchase it, you benefit more from the expanded quantity sold in the market.

Producers of aspirin may find themselves in a nasty bind here. The situation shown in Exhibit 7-9a, with extremely inelastic demand, means that a new invention may cause the price to drop dramatically while quantity changes little. As a result, the new production technology can lead to a drop in the revenue that firms earn from sales of aspirin! However, if strong competition exists between producers of aspirin, each producer may have little choice but to search for and implement any breakthrough that allows it to reduce production costs. After all, if one firm decides not to implement such a cost-saving technology, it can be driven out of business by other firms that do. Since demand for food is generally inelastic, farmers may often face the situation in Exhibit 7-9a. That is, a surge

(a) Cost-saving with inelastic demand   (b) Cost-saving with elastic demand

EXHIBIT 7-9 Passing along Cost Savings to Consumers

Cost-saving gains cause supply to shift out to the right from S_0 to S_1; that is, at any given price, firms will be willing to supply a greater quantity. If demand is inelastic, as in (a), the result of this cost-saving technological improvement will be substantially lower prices. If demand is elastic, as in (b), the result will be only slightly lower prices. Consumers benefit in either case from a greater quantity at a lower price. But the benefit takes different forms, depending on the elasticity of demand.

in production leads to a severe drop in price that can actually decrease the total revenue received by farmers. Conversely, poor weather or other conditions that cause a lousy year for farm production can sharply raise prices so that the total revenue received by farmers rises—at least for those farmers who have something to sell.

Elasticity also reveals whether firms can pass on higher costs that they incur to consumers. In this case, some of the most vivid applications involve addictive substances. For example, the demand for cigarettes is relatively inelastic among regular smokers who are somewhat addicted; economic research suggests that increasing the price of cigarettes by 10% leads to about a 4% reduction in the quantity of cigarettes smoked by adults, so

Fluctuating Coffee Prices

Coffee is an international crop. The top five coffee-exporting nations are Brazil, Vietnam, Colombia, Indonesia, and Honduras. In these nations and others, 20 million families depend on selling coffee beans as their main source of income. These families are exposed to enormous risk because the world price of coffee bounces up and down. For example, in 1993 the world price of coffee was about 50 cents per pound; in 1995 it was four times as high, at $2.00 per pound. By 1997 it had fallen by half to $1.00 per pound. In 1998 it leaped back up to $2.00 per pound. By 2002 it had fallen back to 50 cents a pound; by the end of 2005 it went back up to about $1.00 per pound. By 2009 the price had fallen back to about 65 cents per pound, before spiking up to $3.00 per pound in 2011, and then falling back to $1.60 per pound in 2015.

The reason for these price bounces lies in a combination of inelastic demand and shifts in supply. The elasticity of coffee demand is only about 0.3; that is, a 10% rise in the price of coffee leads to a decline of about 3% in the quantity of coffee consumed. When a major frost hit the Brazilian coffee crop in 1994, coffee supply shifted to the left with an inelastic demand curve, leading to much higher prices. Conversely, when Vietnam entered the world coffee market as a major producer in the late 1990s, the supply curve shifted out to the right, and coffee prices fell dramatically. When heavy rains wreaked havoc on Columbia's coffee crop in 2011, the supply curve shifted back to the left, and coffee prices spiked up.

EXHIBIT 7-10 Passing along Higher Costs to Consumers

Higher costs, like a higher tax on cigarette companies for the example given in the text, lead supply to shift back to the left. This shift is identical in *(a)* and *(b)*. However, in *(a)*, demand is inelastic, and so the cost increase can largely be passed along to consumers in the form of higher prices, without much of a decline in equilibrium quantity. In *(b)*, demand is elastic, so the shift in supply results primarily in a lower equilibrium quantity. Consumers suffer in either case, but in *(a)*, they suffer from paying a higher price for the same quantity, while in *(b)*, they suffer from buying a lower quantity (and presumably shifting their consumption elsewhere).

the elasticity of demand for cigarettes is 0.4. If society increases taxes on companies that make cigarettes, the result, as shown in Exhibit 7-10*a*, is that the supply curve shifts from S_0 to S_1. However, as the equilibrium moves from E_0 to E_1, these taxes are mainly passed along to consumers in the form of higher prices. These higher taxes on cigarettes will raise tax revenue for the government, but they won't much affect the quantity of smoking. If the goal is to reduce the quantity of cigarettes demanded, this must be achieved by shifting this inelastic demand back to the left, perhaps with public programs to discourage the use of cigarettes or to help people to quit. For example, anti-smoking advertising campaigns have shown some ability to reduce smoking. However, if demand for cigarettes was more elastic, as in Exhibit 7-10*b*, then an increase in taxes that shifts supply from S_0 to S_1 and equilibrium from E_0 to E_1 would reduce the quantity of cigarettes smoked substantially. Youth smoking seems to be more elastic than adult smoking—that is, the quantity of youth smoking will fall by a greater percentage than the quantity of adult smoking in response to a given percentage increase in price.

The enforcement of laws against the production or sale of illegal drugs offers another application of this scenario. Laws against illegal drugs can be viewed as shifting the supply curve back to the left; that is, as a result of making certain drugs illegal, the quantity available for sale at any given price is lower than it was before. If demand for these drugs is inelastic, then producers of illegal drugs can essentially pass along the higher price from law enforcement, and these laws will not reduce the quantity consumed by much. However, if demand for these illegal drugs is quite elastic, shifting supply back to the right will reduce the quantity consumed dramatically. Many of the arguments over legalization of drugs ("Strict enforcement will cut drug use!" "No, it will only put more money in the pockets of drug dealers!") are really assertions about whether enforcement will have a greater impact on quantity or on price, and thus are really claims about the elasticities of demand and supply. But the truth is that we lack evidence on elasticities of supply and demand for illegal drugs. In 2001, the prestigious National Research Council published a report by a Committee on Data and Research for Policy on Illegal Drugs. The committee, which included several economists, concluded: "Viewing the unending public debate about drug policy, the committee became painfully aware that what we don't know keeps hurting us."

Long-Run vs. Short-Run Impact

Elasticities are often lower in the short run than in the long run. On the demand side of the market, it can sometimes be difficult to change quantity demanded in the short run, but easier in the long run. Consumption of energy is a vivid example. In the short run, it's not easy for a person to make substantial changes in energy consumption. Maybe you can carpool to work sometimes or adjust your home thermostat by a few degrees if the cost of energy rises, but that's about it. However, in the long run, you can purchase a car that gets more miles to the gallon, or choose a job that is closer to where you live, or buy more energy-efficient home appliances, or install more insulation in your home. As a result, the elasticity of demand for energy is somewhat inelastic in the short run, but much more elastic in the long run.

Exhibit 7-11 is an example, based roughly on historical experience, for the responsiveness of quantity demanded to price changes. In 1973, the price of crude oil was $12 per barrel and total consumption in the U.S. economy was 17 million barrels per day. That year, the nations who were members of the Organization of Petroleum Exporting Countries cut off oil exports to the United States for six months and did not bring exports back to their earlier levels until 1975—a policy that can be interpreted as a shift of the supply curve to the left in the U.S. petroleum market. Exhibit 7-11a and Exhibit 7-11b show the same original equilibrium point and the same identical shift of a supply curve to the left from S_0 to S_1.

However, Exhibit 7-11a and Exhibit 7-11b show two different possible shapes for the demand curve for oil. Exhibit 7-11a shows inelastic demand for oil in the short run, while Exhibit 7-11b shows more elastic demand for oil in the long run. In Exhibit 7-11a, the new equilibrium E_1 occurs at a price of $25 per barrel and an equilibrium quantity of 16 million barrels per day. In Exhibit 7-11b, the new equilibrium E_1 results in a smaller price increase to $14 per barrel and a larger reduction in equilibrium quantity to 13 million barrels per day. In 1983, for example, U.S. petroleum consumption was 15.3 million barrels a day, which was lower than in 1973 or 1975. U.S. petroleum consumption was down even though the U.S. economy was about one-fourth larger in 1983 than it had been in 1973. The primary reason for the lower quantity was that higher energy prices spurred conservation efforts, and after a decade of home insulation, lower mileage cars, more efficient appliances and machinery, and other fuel-conserving choices, the demand curve for energy had become more elastic.

On the supply side of markets, producers of goods and services typically find it easier to expand production in the long term of several years, rather than in the short run of a few months. After all, in the short run it can be costly or difficult to build a new factory, hire many new workers, or open new stores. But over a few years, all of these are possible. Earlier in this chapter, the example of rental housing in Philadelphia explained how a shift in demand for rental housing is likely to increase price relatively more than quantity in the

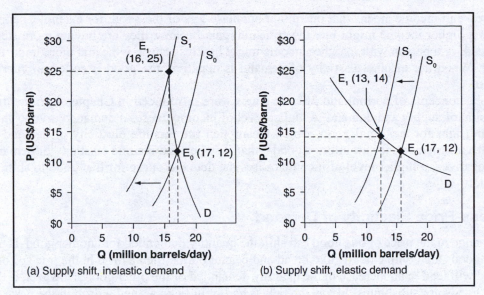

(a) Supply shift, inelastic demand   (b) Supply shift, elastic demand

EXHIBIT 7-11 How a Shift in Supply Can Affect Price or Quantity More

The intersection E_0 between demand curve D and supply curve S_0 is the same in both (a) and (b). The shift of supply to the left from S_0 to S_1 is identical in both (a) and (b). The new equilibrium E_1 has a higher price and a lower quantity than the original equilibrium E_0 in both (a) and (b). However, the shape of the demand curve D is different in (a) and (b). As a result, the shift in supply can result either in a new equilibrium with a much higher price and an only slightly smaller quantity, as in (a), or in a new equilibrium with only a small increase in price and a relatively larger reduction in quantity, as in (b).

short run because it's difficult for the quantity of rental housing to adjust dramatically in the short run. However, in the long run that same shift in demand will be reflected more in a rise in equilibrium quantity than a rise in equilibrium price.

Indeed, in most markets for goods and services, prices bounce up and down more than quantities in the short run, but quantities often move more than prices in the long run. The underlying reason for this pattern is that supply and demand are often inelastic in the short run; therefore, shifts in either demand or supply can cause a relatively greater change in prices. But since supply and demand are more elastic in the long run, the long-run movements in prices are more muted, while quantity adjusts more easily in the long run.

Elasticity as a General Concept

The basic idea of elasticity—how a percentage change in one variable causes a percentage change in another variable—doesn't just apply to supply and demand curves in the markets for goods and services, but can also apply to many economic relationships. In these ways, the idea of elasticity can be used to clarify and re-explain some concepts introduced earlier in this book, like normal and inferior goods, substitute and complement goods, and others. Indeed, the concept of elasticity can also be applied to factors other than price that affect quantity.

Income Elasticity of Demand

The income elasticity of demand is the percentage change in quantity demanded divided by the percentage change in income.

$$\text{Income elasticity of demand} = \frac{\%\text{ change in quantity demanded}}{\%\text{ change in income}}$$

For most products, most of the time, the income elasticity of demand is positive: that is, a rise in income will cause an increase in the quantity demanded. This pattern is common enough that these goods are referred to as **normal goods**. However, for a few goods, an

normal good: A good for which the quantity demanded rises when income rises.

increase in income means that one might purchase less of the good; for example, people with a higher income might buy fewer hamburgers because they are buying more steak instead, or a person with a higher income might buy less cheap wine and more imported beer. When the income elasticity of demand is negative, the good is called an **inferior good**.

inferior good: A good for which the quantity demanded declines as income increases.

The concepts of normal and inferior goods were introduced in Chapter 4, in the discussion of supply and demand. A higher level of income causes a demand curve to shift to the right for a normal good, which means that the income elasticity of demand is positive. However, for an inferior good—that is, when the income elasticity of demand is negative—a higher level of income causes the demand curve for that good to shift to the left.

Cross-Price Elasticity of Demand

A change in the price of one good can shift the quantity demanded for another good. If the two goods are complements, like bread and peanut butter, then a drop in the price of one good will lead to an increase in the quantity demanded of the other good. However, if the two goods are substitutes, like plane tickets and train tickets, then a drop in the price of one good will cause people to substitute toward that good and to reduce consumption of the other good. Cheaper plane tickets lead to fewer train tickets, and vice versa.

cross-price elasticity of demand: The percentage change in the quantity of good A that is demanded as a result of a percentage change in the price of good B.

The **cross-price elasticity of demand** puts some meat on the bones of these ideas. The term "cross-price" refers to the idea that the price of one good is affecting the quantity demanded of a different good. Specifically, the cross-price elasticity of demand is the percentage change in the quantity of good A that is demanded as a result of a percentage change in the price of good B.

$$\text{Cross-price elasticity of demand} = \frac{\text{\% change in quantity demanded of good A}}{\text{\% change in price of good B}}$$

If good A is a substitute for good B, like coffee and tea, then a higher price for B will mean a greater quantity consumed of good A, and so the cross-price elasticity of demand will be positive. But if good A is a complement for good B, like coffee and sugar, then a higher price for good B will mean a lower quantity consumed of good A, and the cross-price elasticity of demand will be negative.

Elasticity in Labor and Financial Capital Markets

The concept of elasticity also applies in labor markets and financial capital markets. In the labor market, for example, the **elasticity of labor supply**—that is, the percentage change in hours worked divided by the percentage change in wages—will determine the shape of the labor supply curve. Specifically:

elasticity of labor supply: The percentage change in hours worked divided by the percentage change in wages.

$$\text{Elasticity of labor supply} = \frac{\text{\% change in quantity of labor supplied}}{\text{\% change in wage}}$$

The wage elasticity of labor supply for teenage workers is generally thought to be fairly elastic: that is, a certain percentage change in wages will lead to a larger percentage change in the quantity of hours worked. Conversely, the wage elasticity of labor supply for adult workers in their 30s and 40s is thought to be fairly inelastic. When wages move up or down by a certain percentage amount, the quantity of hours that adults in their prime earning years are willing to supply changes but by a lesser percentage amount.

elasticity of savings: The percentage change in the quantity of savings divided by the percentage change in interest rates.

In markets for financial capital, the **elasticity of savings**—that is, the percentage change in the quantity of savings divided by the percentage change in interest rates—will describe the shape of the supply curve for financial capital. That is:

$$\text{Elasticity of savings} = \frac{\text{\% change in quantity of financial savings}}{\text{\% change in interest rate}}$$

Sometimes, laws are proposed that seek to increase the quantity of savings by offering tax breaks so that the return on savings is higher. Such a policy will increase the quantity if the supply curve for financial capital is elastic because then a given percentage increase in the return to savings will cause a higher percentage increase in the quantity of savings. However, if the supply curve for financial capital is highly inelastic, then a percentage increase in the return to savings will cause only a small increase in the quantity of savings. The evidence on the supply curve of financial capital is controversial, but at least in the short run, the elasticity of savings with respect to the interest rate appears fairly inelastic.

Stretching the Concept of Elasticity

The elasticity concept doesn't even need to relate to a typical supply or demand curve at all. For example, imagine that you are studying whether the Internal Revenue Service should spend more money on auditing tax returns. The question can be framed in terms of the elasticity of tax collections with respect to spending on tax enforcement; that is, what is the percentage change in tax revenue collected resulting from a percentage change in spending on tax enforcement? Or imagine that you are interested in a policy that trims back on Social Security payments in a way that might encourage some elderly people to continue working for a few more years rather than retire. The question can be framed in terms of the elasticity of hours of work with respect to Social Security payments; that is, what is the percentage change in work hours that will result from a certain percentage change in Social Security payments?

With all of the elasticity concepts that have just been described, some of which are listed in Exhibit 7-12, the possibility of confusion arises. When you hear the phrases "elasticity of demand" or "elasticity of supply," the terms refer to the elasticity with respect to price. Sometimes, either to be extremely clear or because a wide variety of elasticities are being discussed, the elasticity of demand or the demand elasticity will be called the **price elasticity of demand** or the "elasticity of demand with respect to price." Similarly, elasticity of supply or the supply elasticity is sometimes called, to avoid any possibility of confusion, the **price elasticity of supply** or "the elasticity of supply with respect to price." But in whatever context elasticity is invoked, the idea always refers to percentage change in one variable (almost always a price or money variable) and how it causes a percentage change in another variable (typically, a quantity variable of some kind).

price elasticity of demand:
Same as elasticity of demand.

price elasticity of supply:
Same as elasticity of supply.

$$\text{Income elasticity of demand} = \frac{\%\ \text{change in quantity demanded}}{\%\ \text{change in income}}$$

$$\text{Cross-price elasticity of demand} = \frac{\%\ \text{change in quantity demanded of good A}}{\%\ \text{change in price of good B}}$$

$$\text{Wage elasticity of labor supply} = \frac{\%\ \text{change in quantity of labor supplied}}{\%\ \text{change in wage}}$$

$$\text{Wage elasticity of labor demand} = \frac{\%\ \text{change in quantity labor demanded}}{\%\ \text{change in wage}}$$

$$\text{Interest rate elasticity of savings} = \frac{\%\ \text{change in quantity of savings}}{\%\ \text{change in interest rate}}$$

$$\text{Interest rate elasticity of borrowing} = \frac{\%\ \text{change in quantity of borrowing}}{\%\ \text{change in interest rate}}$$

EXHIBIT 7-12 Some Applications of the Elasticity Concept

Conclusion

Framing a question in terms of elasticity is often a very useful step. When summarizing or comparing the results of a number of different studies, which are often done using different data sources, time periods, or statistical methods, it is a great help if the studies are trying to estimate a single common concept. The concept of elasticity takes the shape of demand and supply curves out of the realm of guesswork based on appearance, depending on how the curves happen to be drawn. In this way, the concept of elasticity nails down the idea of how quantity changes in response to changes in price in a way that provides a shorthand for discussion and an engine for analysis.

Key Concepts and Summary

1. **Elasticity** is a tool for measuring how much a percentage change in price causes a percentage change in quantity demanded, quantity supplied, or other economic variables.

2. The **elasticity of demand** is the percentage change in quantity demanded divided by the percentage change in price. The **elasticity of supply** is the percentage change in quantity supplied divided by the percentage change in price.

3. An **elastic** demand or supply curve is one for which a given percentage change in price leads to a larger percentage change in quantity demanded or supplied, so that the percentage change in quantity divided by the percentage change in price will be greater than 1. An **inelastic** demand or supply curve is one where a given percentage change in price will cause a smaller percentage change in quantity demanded or supplied, so that the percentage change in quantity divided by the percentage change in price will be less than one. A **unitary elasticity** means that a given percentage change in price leads to an equal percentage change in quantity demanded or supplied, so that the percentage change in quantity divided by the percentage change in price will be equal to one.

4. A demand or supply curve with **zero elasticity**, also referred to as perfectly inelastic, would be extremely inelastic, or vertical in appearance. A demand or supply curve with **infinite elasticity**, also called perfectly elastic, would be extremely elastic, or horizontal in appearance.

5. The elasticity of supply and demand determines whether a shift in supply or demand will have a larger effect on quantity or price. If demand is elastic, then shifts in supply will have a larger effect on quantity than on price. If demand is inelastic, then shifts in supply will have a larger effect on price than on quantity. If supply is elastic, then shifts in demand will have a larger effect on quantity than on price. If supply is inelastic, then shifts in demand will have a larger effect on price than on quantity.

6. In the market for goods and services, quantity supplied and quantity demanded are often relatively slow to react to changes in price in the short run but react more substantially in the long run. As a result, demand and supply often (but not always) tend to be relatively inelastic in the short run and relatively elastic in the long run.

7. *Elasticity* is a general term, referring to percentage change divided by percentage change that can be applied to many economic connections. For instance, the **income elasticity of demand** is the percentage change in quantity demanded divided by the percentage change in income. The **cross-price elasticity of demand** is the percentage change in the quantity demanded of a good divided by the percentage change in the price of another good.

8. Elasticity applies in labor markets and financial capital markets just as it applied in markets for goods and services. The wage elasticity of labor supply is the percentage change in the quantity of hours supplied divided by the percentage change in the wage. The elasticity of savings with respect to interest rates is the percentage change in the quantity of savings divided by the percentage change in interest rates.

Review Questions

1. If you wanted to make a demand or supply curve appear relatively steep, would you stretch out the horizontal or the vertical axis? What about if you wanted to make it appear relatively flat?

2. What is the formula for calculating the elasticity of demand?

3. What is the formula for calculating the elasticity of supply?

4. If demand or supply is elastic, is the response of quantity to changes in price relatively large or small?

5. If demand or supply is elastic, what is the range of the possible numerical values it can have?

6. If demand or supply is inelastic, is the response of quantity to changes in price relatively large or small?

7. If demand or supply is inelastic, what is the range of the possible numerical values it can have?

8. What is the numerical value of a unitary elasticity?

9. What units of measurement, if any, are used with elasticity?

10. Describe the general appearance of a demand or supply curve with zero elasticity.

11. Describe the general appearance of a demand or supply curve with infinite elasticity.

12. If demand is elastic, will shifts in supply have a larger effect on equilibrium quantity or on price?

13. If demand is inelastic, will shifts in supply have a larger effect on equilibrium quantity or on price?

14. If supply is elastic, will shifts in demand have a larger effect on equilibrium quantity or on price?

15. If supply is inelastic, will shifts in demand have a larger effect on equilibrium quantity or on price?

16. Would you usually expect elasticity of demand or supply to be higher in the short run or in the long run? Why?

17. What is the formula for the income elasticity of demand?

18. What is the formula for the cross-price elasticity of demand?

19. What is the formula for the wage elasticity of labor supply?

20. What is the formula for elasticity of savings with respect to interest rates?

Household Decision Making

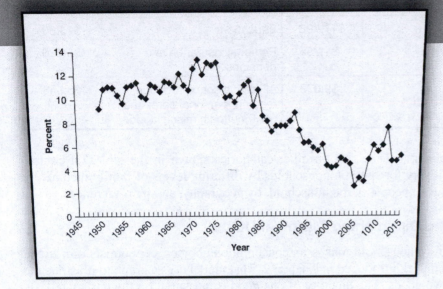

Everyone has their own personal tastes and preferences. The French say: "Chacun à son goût," or "Each to his own taste." An old Latin saying states, "De gustibus non est disputandum," or "There's no disputing about taste." But if people's decisions are based on their own tastes and personal preferences, then how can economists hope to analyze such decisions?

An economic explanation for why people make different choices begins with accepting the proverbial wisdom that tastes are a matter of personal preference. But economists also believe that the choices people make are influenced by their incomes, by the prices of goods, and by factors like climate or natural setting. This chapter will introduce the economic theory of how households make choices about what to buy, how much to work, and how much to save. The analysis in this chapter will build upon the three budget constraints introduced in Chapter 2: the consumption choice budget constraint, the labor-leisure budget constraint, and the intertemporal budget constraint. This chapter will also illustrate how economic theory offers a systematic way of thinking about the full range of possible events and responses, which can prevent jumping to possibly misguided conclusions about how households will respond to changes in prices or incomes.

Consumption Choices

Information on the consumption choices of Americans is available from the Consumer Expenditure Survey that is carried out by the U.S. Bureau of Labor Statistics. Exhibit 8-1 shows spending patterns for the average U.S. household. The first row shows income, and after taxes and personal savings are subtracted, it shows that the average U.S. household spent $53,495 on consumption. The table then breaks down consumption into various categories. The average U.S. household spent roughly one-third of its consumption on shelter and other housing expenses, another one-third of its income on food

EXHIBIT 8-1 U.S. Consumption Choices in 2014

| Average income before taxes | $66,877 |
| Average annual expenditure | $53,495 |

Major Categories of Spending			
Food at home	$3,971	Healthcare	$4,290
Food away from home	$2,787	Entertainment	$2.728
Housing	$17,798	Education	$1,236
Apparel and services	$1,786	Personal insurance and pensions	$5,726
Transportation	$9,073	All else: alcohol, tobacco, reading, personal care, cash contributions, miscellaneous	$3,548

and vehicle expenses, and the rest on other categories shown in the table. Of course, these patterns will vary for specific households by differing levels of family income, by the number and age of people in the household, by geography, and by preferences.

Total Utility and Diminishing Marginal Utility

To understand how a household makes its consumption choices, economists turn to the budget constraint model introduced in Chapter 2. That model uses a graph to illustrate the choice between two goods. The quantity of one good is measured on the horizontal axis and the quantity of the other good is measured on the vertical axis. The budget constraint line shows the various combinations of goods that it is possible to buy, given a certain level of income. For example, consider the situation of Jose, shown in Exhibit 8-2. Jose likes to collect T-shirts and watch movies. In the figure at the top of Exhibit 8-2, the quantity of T-shirts that Jose purchases is shown on the horizontal axis, while the quantity of movies that he attends is shown on the vertical axis. If Jose had unlimited income or goods were free, then he could consume without limit. But Jose must face a consumption choice budget constraint. Jose has a total of $56 to spend. The price of T-shirts is $14 and the price of movies is $7. Five specific choices along the budget constraint, combinations of T-shirts and movies, are shown on the graph and listed in the tables beneath the graph.

Jose wishes to choose the point that will provide him with the greatest **utility**, which is the term that economists use to describe a person's level of satisfaction or happiness. Let's begin with an assumption, which will be discussed in more detail later, that Jose can measure his own utility with a measurement called "utils." The first table in Exhibit 8-2 shows how Jose's utility is connected with his consumption of T-shirts or movies. The first column of the table shows the quantity of T-shirts consumed. The second column shows the total utility, or total amount of satisfaction, that Jose receives from consuming that number of T-shirts. The most common pattern of total utility, as shown here, is that consuming additional goods leads to greater total utility. The third column shows **marginal utility**, which is the additional utility provided by one additional unit of consumption. The most common pattern for marginal utility is **diminishing marginal utility**, which means that each marginal unit of a good consumed provides less of an addition to utility than the previous unit. For example, the first T-shirt Jose picks is his favorite. The fourth T-shirt is just to something to wear when all his other clothes are in the wash.

The first table in Exhibit 8-2 also shows the quantity of movies that Jose could attend, his total utility from consuming each quantity of movies, and his marginal utility from attending each additional movie. Total utility follows the expected pattern: it increases as the quantity of movies rises. Marginal utility also follows the expected pattern: each additional movie brings a smaller gain in utility than the previous one. The first movie

utility: The level of satisfaction or pleasure that people receive from their choices.

marginal utility: The additional utility provided by one additional unit of consumption.

diminishing marginal utility: The common pattern that each marginal unit of a good consumed provides less of an addition to utility than the previous unit.

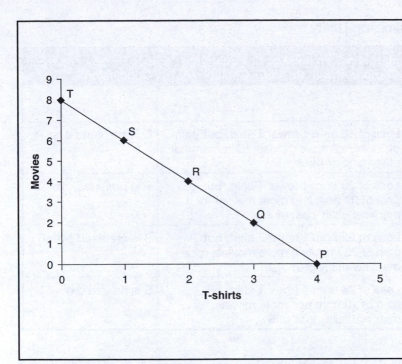

A Consumption Choice Budget Constraint

T-Shirts (Quantity)	Total Utility	Marginal Utility	Movies (Quantity)
1	24	24	1
2	46	22	2
3	66	20	3
4	84	18	4
5	100	16	5
6	114	14	6

Total and Marginal Utility

Point	T-Shirts	Movies	Total Utility
P	4	0	84 + 0 = 84
Q	3	2	66 + 31 = 97
R	2	4	46 + 58 = 104
S	1	6	24 + 81 = 105
T	0	8	0 + 100 = 100

EXHIBIT 8-2 A Choice between Consumption Goods

Jose has income of $56. Movies cost $7 and T-shirts cost $14. The points on the budget constraint show his possible choices. The first table shows total utility and marginal utility from consumption of T-shirts and movies. The typical pattern, illustrated here, is that total utility rises as the quantity consumed rises, but marginal utility falls as the quantity consumed rises. The second table shows total utility at each point along Jose's consumption choice budget set. The maximum level of utility occurs at choice S.

Jose attends is the one he wanted to see the most and thus provides him with the highest level of utility or satisfaction. The fifth movie he attends just to kill time.

Once Jose has defined in his own mind how much utility he will receive from consuming different quantities of T-shirts and movies, he is ready to make the choice that will give him the maximum amount of utility. The second table in Exhibit 8-2 looks at each point on the budget constraint , adds up Jose's total utility numbers for consuming T-shirts and movies, and calculates the total utility for each of Jose's possible choices. For Jose, the highest total utility for the possible combinations of goods occurs at point S, with a total utility of 105 from consuming 1 T-shirt and 6 movies.

Choosing with Marginal Utility

People are unlikely to carry around in their heads a mental picture of their total utility for every quantity consumed of every good. Instead, most people probably approach their utility-maximizing combination of choices in a step-by-step way. This step-by-step approach is based on looking at the trade-offs, measured in terms of marginal utility, of consuming less of one good and more of another.

For example, say that Jose starts off thinking about spending all his money on T-shirts and choosing point P in Exhibit 8-2. Jose chooses this starting point randomly; he has to start somewhere. Then Jose considers giving up the final T-shirt, the one that provides him the least marginal utility, and using the money he saves to buy two movies instead. Exhibit 8-3 tracks the step-by-step series of decisions Jose needs to make. The drop in marginal utility from giving up the fourth T-shirt is 18, but the gain in marginal utility from buying the first two movies is 31. So Jose clearly prefers point Q to point P. Now repeat this step-by-step process of decision-making with marginal utilities. Jose thinks about giving up the third T-shirt and thus surrendering marginal utility of 20, in exchange for purchasing two more movies that promise a combined marginal utility of 27. Jose

EXHIBIT 8-3 A Step-by-Step Approach to Maximizing Utility

Try	Which Has	Total Utility	Marginal Gain and Loss of Utility, Compared with Previous Choice	Conclusion
Choice 1: P	4 T-shirts and 0 movies	84 from 4 T-shirts + 0 from 0 movies = 84	—	—
Choice 2: Q	3 T-shirts and 2 movies	66 from 3 T-shirts + 31 from 2 movies = 97	Loss of 18 from 1 fewer T-shirt, but gain of 31 from 2 more movies, for a marginal utility gain of 14	Q is preferred over P
Choice 3: R	2 T-shirts and 4 movies	46 from 2 T-shirts + 58 from 4 movies = 104	Loss of 20 from 1 fewer T-shirt, but gain of 27 from two more movies for a marginal utility gain of 7	R is preferred over Q
Choice 4: S	1 T-shirt and 6 movies	24 from 1 T-shirt + 81 from 6 movies = 105	Loss of 22 from 1 fewer T-shirt, but gain of 23 from two more movies, for a marginal utility gain of 1	S is preferred over R
Choice 5: T	0 T-shirts and 8 movies	0 from 0 T-shirts + 100 from 8 movies = 100	Loss of 24 from 1 fewer T-shirt, but gain of 19 from two more movies, for a marginal utility loss of 5	S is preferred over T

prefers point R to point Q. What if Jose thinks about going beyond R to point S? Giving up the second T-shirt means a marginal utility loss of 22, and the marginal utility gain from the fifth and sixth movies would combine to make a marginal utility gain of 23, so Jose prefers point S to R.

However, if Jose seeks to go beyond point S to point T, he finds that the loss of marginal utility from giving up the first T-shirt is 24, while the marginal utility gain from the last two movies is only a total of 19. Through these stages of thinking about marginal trade-offs, Jose again concludes that S, with 1 T-shirt and 6 movies, is the choice that will provide him with the highest level of total utility. This step-by-step approach will reach the same conclusion regardless of Jose's original starting point.

A Rule for Maximizing Utility

This process of decision making suggests a rule to follow when maximizing utility. Because the price of T-shirts is twice as high in this example, the marginal T-shirt needs to provide twice the marginal utility of a marginal movie. If the marginal T-shirt provides less than twice the marginal utility of the marginal movie, then the marginal T-shirt isn't providing enough utility to justify its relative price and Jose should attend more movies. If the marginal T-shirt provides more than twice the marginal utility of the marginal movie, then Jose should buy more T-shirts. Notice that at Jose's optimal choice of point S, the marginal utility from the second T-shirt, of 22, is exactly twice the marginal utility of the sixth movie, which is 11. At this choice, the marginal utility per dollar is the same for both goods, which is the tell-tale signal that Jose has found the point with highest total utility.

This argument can be written as a general rule: the utility-maximizing choice between consumption goods occurs where the ratio of the prices of the two goods is equal to the ratio of the marginal utilities. When the price of good 1 is divided by the price of good 2, at the utility-maximizing point this will equal the marginal utility of good 1 divided by the marginal utility of good 2. This rule can be written in algebraic form:

$$\frac{P_1}{P_2} = \frac{MU_1}{MU_2}$$

Along the budget constraint, the prices of the two goods remain the same, so the ratio of the prices doesn't change. However, the marginal utility of the two goods changes with the quantities consumed. At the optimal choice of 1 T-shirt and 6 movies, point S, the price ratio of 2:1 matches the marginal utility trade-off of 22:11. A sensible economizer will only pay twice as much for something if, in the marginal comparison, the item confers twice as much utility.

Measuring Utility with Numbers

This discussion of utility started off with an assumption that it is possible to place numerical values on utility, an assumption that may smell questionable. You can buy a thermometer for measuring temperature at a hardware store, but what store sells a "utilimometer" for measuring utility? However, while measuring utility with numbers is a convenient assumption to clarify the explanation, the key assumption is not that utility can be measured by an outside party, but only that individuals can decide what they prefer.

To understand this point, think back to the step-by-step process of finding the choice with highest total utility by comparing the marginal utility that is gained and lost from different choices along the budget constraint. As Jose compares each choice along his budget constraint to the previous choice, what matters is not the specific numbers that he places on his utility—or whether he uses any numbers at all—but only that he personally can identify which choices he prefers. In this way, the step-by-step process of choosing the highest level of utility resembles rather closely how many people make consumption decisions. We think about what will make us the happiest; we think about what things cost; we think about buying a little more of one item and giving up a little of something else; we choose what provides us with the greatest level of satisfaction. The vocabulary of comparing the points along a budget constraint and total and marginal utility is just a set of tools for discussing this everyday process in a clear and specific manner. It's welcome news that specific utility numbers aren't central to the argument, because a good utilimometer is hard to find.

How Changes in Income and Prices Affect Consumption Choices

Just as utility and marginal utility can be used to discuss making consumer choices along a budget constraint, these ideas can also be used to think about how consumer choices change when the budget constraint shifts in response to changes in income or price. Indeed, because the budget constraint framework can be used to analyze how quantities demanded change because of price movements, the budget constraint model can illustrate the underlying logic behind demand curves.

How Changes in Income Affect Consumer Choices

Let's begin with a concrete example illustrating how changes in income level affect consumer choices. Exhibit 8-4 shows a budget constraint that represents Kimberly's choice between concert tickets at $50 each and getting away overnight to a bed-and-breakfast for $200 per night. Kimberly has $1,000 per year to spend between these two choices. After thinking about her personal utility and marginal utility and applying the decision rule that the ratio of the prices should be equal to the ratio of marginal utilities, Kimberly chooses point M, with 8 concerts and 3 overnight getaways as her utility-maximizing choice.

Now assume that the income that Kimberly has to spend on these two items rises to $2,000 per year, causing her budget constraint to shift to the right. How does this rise in income alter Kimberly's utility-maximizing choice? Kimberly will again consider the utility and marginal utility that she receives from concert tickets and overnight getaways and seek her utility-maximizing choice on the new budget line. But how will her new choice relate to her original choice?

The possible choices along the new budget constraint can be divided into three groups, which are divided up by the dashed horizontal and vertical lines that pass through the original choice M in the figure. All choices on the upper left of the new budget constraint that are to the left of the vertical dashed line, like choice P with 2 overnight stays and 32 concerts, involve less of the good on the horizontal axis but much more of the good on

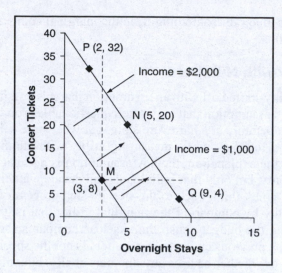

EXHIBIT 8-4 How a Change in Income Affects Consumption Choices

The utility-maximizing choice on the original budget constraint is M. The dashed horizontal and vertical lines extending through point M allow you to see at a glance whether the quantity consumed of goods on the new budget constraint is higher or lower than on the original budget constraint. On the new budget constraint, a choice like N will be made if both goods are normal goods. If overnight stays are an inferior good, a choice like P will be made. If concert tickets are an inferior good, a choice like Q will be made.

the vertical axis. All choices to the right of the vertical dashed line and above the horizontal dashed line—like choice N with 5 overnight getaways and 20 concert tickets—have more consumption of both goods. Finally, all choices that are to the right of the vertical dashed line but below the horizontal dashed line, like choice Q with 4 concert tickets and 9 overnight getaways, involve less of the good on the vertical axis but much more of the good on the horizontal axis.

All of these possibilities are theoretically possible, depending on Kimberly's personal preferences as expressed through the total and marginal utility she would receive from consuming these two goods. When income rises, the most common reaction is to purchase more of both goods like choice N, which is to the upper right relative to Kimberly's original choice M, although exactly how much more of each good will vary according to personal taste. Conversely, when income falls, the most typical reaction is to purchase less of both goods. As defined earlier in Chapter 4 and again in Chapter 7, goods and services are called "normal goods" when a rise in income leads to a rise in the quantity consumed of that good and a fall in income leads to a fall in quantity consumed.

However, depending on Kimberly's preferences, a rise in income could cause consumption of one good to increase while consumption of the other good declines. For example, a choice like P means that a rise in income caused her quantity consumed of overnight stays to decline, while a choice like Q would mean that a rise in income caused her quantity of concerts to decline. Goods where the quantity demanded declines as income rises (or conversely, where the quantity demanded rises as income falls) are called "inferior goods." An inferior good occurs when people trim back on a good as income rises because they can now afford the more expensive choices that they prefer. For example, a higher-income household might eat less hamburger or be less likely to buy a used car, and instead eat more steak and buy a new car.

How Price Changes Affect Consumer Choices

For analyzing the possible effect of a change in price on consumption, let's again use a concrete example. Exhibit 8-5 represents the consumer choice of Ichiro, who chooses between purchasing baseball bats and cameras. A price increase for baseball bats, the good on the horizontal axis, causes the budget constraint to rotate inward, as if on a hinge

EXHIBIT 8-5 How a Change in Price Affects Consumption Choices

The original utility-maximizing choice is M. When the price rises, the budget constraint shifts to the left. The dashed lines make it possible to see at a glance whether the new consumption choice involves less of both goods, or less of one good and more of the other. The new possible choices would be fewer baseball bats and more cameras, like point H, or less of both goods, as at point J. Choice K would mean that the higher price of bats led to exactly the same quantity of bats being consumed, but fewer cameras. Choices like L are theoretically possible but often ruled out as highly unlikely in the real world because they would mean that a higher price for baseball bats means a greater quantity consumed of baseball bats.

from the vertical axis. As in the previous section, the point labeled M represents the originally preferred point on the original budget constraint, which Ichiro has chosen after contemplating his personal utility and marginal utility and the trade-offs involved along the budget constraint. In this example, the units along the horizontal and vertical axis are not numbered, so the discussion will focus on whether more or less of certain goods will be consumed, not on numerical amounts.

After the price increase, Ichiro will make a choice along the new budget constraint. Again, his choices along the new budget constraint can be divided into three segments by the dashed vertical and horizontal lines. In the upper left portion of the new budget constraint, at a choice like H, Ichiro consumes more cameras and fewer bats; in the central portion of the new budget constraint, at a choice like J, he consumes less of both goods; at the right-hand end, at a choice like L, he consumes more bats but fewer cameras.

The typical response to higher prices is that a person chooses to consume less of the product with the higher price. This effect occurs for two reasons, which occur simultaneously. The **substitution effect** is that when a price changes, consumers have an incentive to consume less of the good with a relatively higher price and more of the good with a relatively lower price. The **income effect** refers not to a change in actual income, but to a price change that affects the buying power of existing income. In this example, a higher price means that the buying power of income has been reduced (even though actual income has not changed), which lead to buying less of the good. Thus, the higher price for baseball bats would cause Ichiro to consume a lower quantity of bats because the substitution effect will encourage him to substitute consumption away from the relatively higher-priced bats and the income effect of a higher price reduces his buying power and also encourages reduced consumption of bats.

How much will a higher price for bats cause Ichiro's consumption of bats to fall? Exhibit 8-5 suggests a range of possibilities. Ichiro might react to a higher price for baseball bats by purchasing the same quantity of bats, but cutting his consumption of cameras. This choice is the point K on the new budget constraint straight below the original choice M. Alternatively, Ichiro might react by dramatically reducing his purchases of bats, and instead buying more cameras, at a choice that represents buying fewer of both goods. The key conclusion here is that it would be imprudent to assume that a change in

substitution effect: When a price changes, consumers have an incentive to consume less of the good with a relatively higher price and more of the good with a relatively lower price; always happens simultaneously with an income effect.

income effect: A change in price affects the buying power of income, with a higher price meaning that the buying power of income has been reduced, so that there is usually (with normal goods) an incentive to buy less of both goods, and a lower price meaning that the buying power of income has been increased, so that there is usually an incentive to buy more of both goods; always happens simultaneously with a substitution effect.

the price of baseball bats will only or primarily affect the good whose price is changed, while the quantity consumed of other goods remains the same. A change in the price of one good can also have a range of effects, either positive or negative, on the quantity consumed of other goods.

What about a choice like point L in the lower right of the new budget constraint? In this case, Ichiro responds to a higher price for baseball bats by purchasing more bats. A good where a higher price leads to a higher quantity demanded for a good (or a lower price leads to a lower quantity demanded for a good) is a theoretical possibility, discovered more than a century ago, called a **Giffen good**. The demand curve for a Giffen good would slope up, rather than down! However, Giffen goods should be considered a theoretical possibility that is extremely rare in actual markets, rather than a likely event. A famous economist named Francis Ysidro Edgeworth (1845–1926) summed up the situation regarding Giffen goods in this way in 1914: "Only a very clever man would discover that exceptional case; only a very foolish man would take it as the basis of a rule for general practice."

Giffen good: The theoretical but unrealistic possibility that a higher price for a good could lead to a higher quantity demanded (or a lower price leads to a lesser quantity demanded).

The Logical Foundations of Demand Curves

Changes in the price of a good lead the budget constraint to shift. A shift in the budget constraint means that when individuals are seeking their highest utility, the quantity that is demanded of that good will change. In this way, the logical foundations of demand curves—which show a connection between prices and quantity demanded—are based on the underlying idea of individuals seeking utility. Exhibit 8-6a shows a budget constraint with a choice between housing and "everything else." (Putting "everything else" on the vertical axis can be a useful approach in some cases, especially when the focus of the analysis is on one particular good.) The preferred choice on the original budget constraint that provides the highest possible utility is labeled M_0. The other three budget constraints represent successively higher prices for housing of P_1, P_2, and P_3. As the budget constraint shifts in, and in, and in again, the utility-maximizing choices are labeled M_1, M_2, and M_3, and the quantity demanded of housing falls from Q_0 to Q_1 to Q_2 to Q_3.

Thus, as the price of housing rises, the budget constraint shifts to the left, and the quantity consumed of housing falls. This relationship—the price of housing rising from P_0 to P_1 to P_2 to P_3, while the quantity of housing demanded falls from Q_0 to Q_1 to Q_2 to Q_3—is graphed on the demand curve in Exhibit 8-6b. Indeed, the vertical dashed lines stretching between the top and bottom of Exhibit 8-6 show that the quantity of housing demanded at each point is the same in both (a) and (b). Thus, the shape of a demand curve is ultimately determined by the underlying choices about maximizing utility subject to a budget constraint.

Applications in Business and Government

The budget constraint framework for making utility-maximizing choices offers a reminder that people can react to a change in price or income in a range of different ways. For example, in the winter months of 2014, costs for heating homes skyrocketed in many parts of the country. Many people reacted by reducing the quantity demanded of energy; for example, by turning down the thermostats in their homes by a few degrees and wearing a heavier sweater inside. Even so, many home heating bills rose as much as $200 dollars per month or even more, so people adjusted their consumption in other ways, too. Each household cut back on what it valued least on the margin; for some it might have been some dinners out, or a vacation, or postponing buying a new refrigerator or a new car. Indeed, sharply higher energy prices can have effects beyond the energy market, leading to a widespread reduction in purchasing throughout the rest of the economy.

A similar issue arises when the government imposes taxes on certain products, like it does on gasoline, cigarettes, and alcohol. Say that a tax on alcohol leads to a higher price at the liquor store, the higher price of alcohol causes the budget constraint to pivot left, and consumption of alcoholic beverages is likely to decrease. However, people may also

EXHIBIT 8-6 The Foundations of a Demand Curve: An Example of Housing

(a) A budget constraint diagram

Original housing price P_0

Housing price rises for the first time to P_1

Housing price rises for the second time to P_2

Housing price rises for the third time to P_3

As the price increases from P_0 to P_1 to P_2 to P_3, the budget constraint rotates to the left. The utility-maximizing choice changes from M_0 to M_1 to M_2 to M_3. As a result, the quantity demanded of housing decreases from Q_0 to Q_1 to Q_2 to Q_3.

(b) Deriving a demand curve

The demand curve graphs each combination of the price of housing and the quantity of housing demanded. Indeed, the quantities of housing are the same at the points on both (a) and (b). Thus, the original price of housing P_0 and the original quantity of housing Q_0 appear on the demand curve as point E_0. The higher price of housing P_1 and the corresponding lower quantity demanded of housing Q_1 appear on the demand curve as point E_1.

react to the higher price of alcoholic beverages by cutting back on other purchases; for example, they might cut back on snacks like chicken wings and nachos at restaurants. It would be unwise to assume that the alcoholic beverage industry is the only industry affected by the tax on alcoholic beverages.

As a final example of the range of possible reactions, consider a proposal that came up in the aftermath of the terrorist airplane hijackings on September 11, 2001. Congress believed that it was necessary to provide some financial assistance to airlines. One possible method of providing that assistance was in the form of coupons for airline tickets that would be distributed to all Americans, thus providing assistance to ordinary Americans as well as to the airline companies. But what if most Americans spent their coupons on airplane trips they would have taken anyway, and then use the money they saved to purchase something else? Since airline coupons free up income to spend in other ways, they are very similar to receiving additional income in the form of cash. The result could have been that air travel coupons would not provide any special assistance to the airline industry—at least no more assistance than a distribution of government checks to individuals would have provided. Of course, this argument doesn't prove that the $15 billion package of government assistance to airlines passed in October 2001 was a sensible policy. But at least handing the money directly to the airlines made sure that the airlines actually received the money, rather than opening up the possibility that the main effect of an attempt to assist the airlines would be felt in other markets.

The budget constraint framework serves as a constant reminder to think about the full range of effects that can arise from changes in income or price, not just effects on the one product that might seem most immediately affected.

Labor-Leisure Choices

The decision-making process of a utility-maximizing household applies to decisions about what quantity of hours to work in much the same way that it applies to purchases of goods and services. Choices made along the labor-leisure budget constraint, as wages shift, provide the logical underpinning for the labor supply curve. The discussion also offers some insights about the range of possible reactions when people receive higher wages, and specifically about the claim that if people are paid higher wages, they will work a greater quantity of hours.

U.S. workers averaged 38.5 hours per week on the job in 2012. This average includes part-timers; for full-time workers only, the average was 42.5 hours per week. Exhibit 8-7 shows that more than half of all workers are on the job 35–48 hours per week of work, but significant proportions work less or more than this amount. Exhibit 8-8 breaks down the average compensation received by private industry workers, including wages and benefits. Wages and salaries are about three-quarters of total compensation received by workers; the rest is in the form of health insurance, vacation pay, and other benefits. The compensation received by workers differs for many reasons, including experience, education, skill, talent, membership in a labor union, and the presence of discrimination against certain groups in the labor market. Issues surrounding the inequality of incomes in a market-oriented economy are explored in Chapters 16 and 17.

EXHIBIT 8-7 Persons at Work, by Average Hours Worked per Week in 2015

Hours Worked per Week	Number of Workers	Percentage of Workforce
1–14 hours	6.6 million	4.6%
15–34 hours	29.5 million	20.5%
35–40 hours	71.6 million	49.8%
41–48 hours	12.5 million	8.7%
49–59 hours	14.1 million	9.8%
60+ hours	9.4 million	6.6%

Total compensation per hour	$38.11
Wages and salaries	25.65
Vacation and holiday pay	2.27
Sick leave and other leave	0.56
Bonuses and premium pay	1.84
Employee insurance (mainly health)	3.20
Company retirement plans	1.62
Employer payments to Social Security	1.65
Unemployment and worker's compensation insurance	0.86
Other benefits (Medicare)	0.44

The Labor-Leisure Budget Constraint

How do workers make their decisions about the quantity of hours to work? Again, let's
proceed with a concrete example. The economic logic is precisely the same as in the case
of a consumption choice budget constraint, but the labels are different on a labor-leisure
budget constraint.

Vivian has 70 hours per week that she could devote either to working or leisure, and
her wage is $10/hour. The lower budget constraint in Exhibit 8-9 shows Vivian's possible
choices at this wage level. As discussed in Chapter 2, the horizontal axis of this diagram
measures both leisure and labor, by showing how Vivian's time is divided between leisure
and labor. Hours of leisure are measured from left to right on the horizontal axis, while
hours of labor are measured from right to left. Vivian will compare choices along this budget constraint, ranging from 70 hours of leisure and no income at point S to zero hours of
leisure and $700 of income at point L. She will choose the point that provides her with the

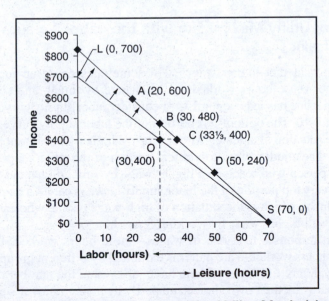

EXHIBIT 8-9 How a Rise in Wages Alters the Utility-Maximizing Choice

Vivian's original choice is point O on the lower opportunity set. A rise in her wage causes her
opportunity set to swing upward. In response to the increase in wages, Vivian can make a range
of different choices: a choice like D, which involves less work; and a choice like B, which involves
the same amount of work but more income; or a choice like A, which involves more work and
considerably more income. Vivian's personal preferences will determine which choice she makes.

highest total utility. For this example, let's assume that Vivian's utility-maximizing choice occurs at O, with 30 hours of leisure, 40 hours of work, and $400 in weekly income.

For Vivian to discover the labor-leisure choice that will maximize her utility, she doesn't have to place numerical values on the total and marginal utility that she would receive from every level of income and leisure. All that really matters is that Vivian can compare, in her own mind, whether she would prefer more leisure or more income, given the trade-offs she faces. If Vivian can say to herself: "You know, I'd really rather work a little less and have more leisure, even if it means less income," or "You know, I'd be willing to work more hours to make some extra income," then as she gradually moves in the direction of her preferences, she will seek out the utility-maximizing choice on her labor-leisure budget constraint.

Now imagine that Vivian's wage level increases to $12/hour. A higher wage will mean a new budget constraint that tilts up more steeply; conversely, a lower wage would have led to a new budget constraint that was flatter. How will a change in the wage and the corresponding shift in the budget constraint affect Vivian's decisions about how many hours to work? Vivian's choices of quantity of hours to work and income along her new budget constraint can be divided into several categories, using the dashed horizontal and vertical lines in Exhibit 8-9 that go through her original choice O. One set of choices in the upper-left portion of the new budget constraint involve more hours of work (i.e., less leisure) and more income, at a point like A with 20 hours of leisure, 50 hours of work, and $600 of income (i.e., 50 hours of work multiplied by the new wage of $12 per hour). A second choice would be to work exactly the same 40 hours and to take the benefits of the higher wage in the form of income that would now be $480, at choice B. A third choice would involve more leisure and the same income at point C (i.e., 33-1/3 hours of work multiplied by the new wage of $12 per hour equals $400 of total income). A fourth choice would involve less income and much more leisure at a point like D, with a choice like 50 hours of leisure, 20 hours of work, and $240 in income.

In effect, Vivian can choose whether to receive the benefits of her wage increase in the form of more income, or more leisure, or some mixture of these two. With this range of possibilities, it would be unwise to assume that Vivian (or anyone else) will necessarily react to a wage increase by working substantially more hours. Maybe they will; maybe they won't.

Applications of Utility Maximizing with the Labor-Leisure Budget Constraint

The theoretical insight that higher wages will sometimes cause an increase in hours worked, sometimes cause hours worked not to change by much, and sometimes cause hours worked to decline has led economists to consider labor supply curves that look like the one in Exhibit 8-10. The bottom-left portion of the labor supply curve slopes upward, which reflects the situation of a person who reacts to a higher wage by supplying a greater quantity of labor. The middle, close-to-vertical portion of the labor supply curve reflects the situation of a person who reacts to a higher wage by supplying about the same quantity of labor. The very top portion of the labor supply curve is called a **backward-bending supply curve** for labor, which is the situation of high-wage people who earn so much that they respond to a still-higher wage by working fewer hours.

backward-bending supply curve for labor: The situation when high-wage people can earn so much that they respond to a still-higher wage by working fewer hours.

These different responses to a rise in wages—more hours worked, the same hours worked, or fewer hours worked—are patterns exhibited by different groups of workers in the U.S. economy. Many full-time workers have jobs where the number of hours is held relatively fixed, partly by their own choice and partly by their employer's practices. These workers don't change their hours worked by much as wages rise or fall, so their supply curve of labor is inelastic. However, part-time workers and younger workers tend to be more flexible in their hours and more ready to increase hours worked when wages are high or cut back when wages fall.

EXHIBIT 8-10 A Backward-Bending Supply Curve of Labor

The bottom upward-sloping portion of the labor supply curve shows that as wages increase over this range, the quantity of hours worked also increases. The middle, nearly vertical portion of the labor supply curve shows that as wages increase over this range, the quantity of hours worked changes very little. The backward-bending portion of the labor supply curve at the top shows that as wages increase over this range, the quantity of hours worked actually decreases. All three of these possibilities can be derived from how a change in wages causes movement in the labor-leisure budget constraint, and thus different choices by individuals.

The backward-bending supply curve for labor, when workers react to higher wages by working fewer hours and having more income, is not observed often in the short run. However, some well-paid professionals, like dentists or accountants, may react to higher wages by choosing to limit the number of hours, perhaps by taking especially long vacations or taking every other Friday off. Over a long-term perspective, the backward-bending supply curve for labor is common. Over the last century, Americans have reacted to gradually rising wages by working fewer hours; for example, the length of the average workweek has fallen from about 60 hours per week back in 1900 to the present average of less than 40 hours per week.

Is America a Nation of Workaholics?

Americans work a lot. The table shows average hours worked per year in the United States, Canada, Japan, and several European countries, with most of the data from 2014. To gain some perspective on these numbers, someone who works 40 hours per week for 50 weeks per year, with 2 weeks off, would work 2,000 hours per year. The gap in hours worked is a little astonishing; the 250- to 300-hour gap between how much Americans work and how much, say, the French work amounts to roughly 7–8 weeks less of work per year! Economists who study these international patterns debate the extent to which average Americans and Japanese have a preference for working more than, say, French or German workers, or whether French and German workers and employers face particular kinds of taxes and regulations that lead to fewer hours worked.

Average Annual Hours Worked per Employed Person	
United States	1789
Japan	1729
Canada	1704
Spain	1689
Sweden	1609
United Kingdom	1677
France	1473
Germany	1371

Recognizing that workers have a range of possible reactions to a change in wages casts some fresh insight on a perennial political debate: the claim that a reduction in income taxes—which would, in effect, allow people to earn more per hour—will encourage people to work more. The leisure-income budget set points out that this connection will not hold true for all workers. Some people, especially part-timers, probably will react to higher wages by working more. Many will work the same number of hours. Some people, especially those whose incomes are already high, may react to the tax cut by working fewer hours. Of course, cutting income taxes may be a good or a bad idea for a variety of reasons, not just because of its impact on work incentives, but the specific claim that tax cuts will lead people to work more hours is only likely to hold for specific groups of workers and will depend on how and for whom taxes are cut.

Intertemporal Choices in Financial Capital Markets

Rates of saving in America have never been especially high, but they seem to have dipped even lower in recent years, with some especially low levels during the Great Recession years from 2007–2009, as shown in Exhibit 8-11. A decision about how much to save can be represented on the intertemporal budget constraint that was introduced in Chapter 2. Household decisions about the quantity of financial savings show the same underlying pattern of logic as the consumption choice decision and the labor-leisure decision.

The discussion of financial savings here will not focus on the specific financial investment choices, like bank accounts, stocks, bonds, mutual funds, or owning a house or gold coins. The characteristics of these specific financial investments, along with the risks and trade-offs they pose, will be detailed in Chapter 19. Here, the focus is on how a household determines how much to consume in the present and how much to save in the present and spend in the future, given the expected rate of return (or interest rate), and how the quantity of savings alters when the rate of return changes.

Using Marginal Utility to Make Intertemporal Choices

Savings behavior varies considerably across households. One factor is that households with higher incomes tend to save a larger percentage of their income. This pattern makes intuitive sense; a well-to-do family has the flexibility in its budget to save 20–25% of income, while a poor family struggling to keep food on the table will find it harder to put money aside.

EXHIBIT 8-11 Personal Savings as a Percentage of Personal Income

Personal savings were about 7–11% of personal income for most of the years from the late 1950s up to the early 1990s. Since then, the rate of personal savings has fallen substantially.

A second key factor is linked to age. The **life-cycle theory of savings** points out a common pattern that many people save little or borrow heavily early in life, so that they can pay for a college education and buy a first home; save more in the middle of life, to pay off college and home loans and to prepare for retirement; and then draw upon their accumulated savings later in life during retirement.

life-cycle theory of savings: The common pattern that many people save little or borrow heavily early in life, save more in the middle of life, and then draw upon their accumulated savings later in life.

A third factor that causes personal savings to vary is personal preference. Some people may prefer to consume more now and let the future look after itself. Others may wish to enjoy a lavish retirement, complete with expensive vacations, or to pile up money that they can pass along to their grandchildren. There are savers and spendthrifts among the young, middle-aged, and old, and among those with high, middle, and low income levels.

Yelberton is a young man starting off at his first job. He thinks of the "present" as his working life and the "future" as after retirement. Yelberton's plan is to save money during the time period ages 30–55, retire at age 60, and then live off his retirement money during the time period from ages 60–85. On average, therefore, he will be saving for 30 years. If the rate of return that he can receive is 6% per year, then $1 saved in the present would build up to $5.74 after 30 years (using the formula for compound interest, $1(1+.06)^{30} = 5.74). Say that Yelberton will earn $1,000,000 over the 25 years from age 30 to age 55 (this amount is an annual salary of $40,000 multiplied by 25 years). Thus, the question for Yelberton is what share of those lifetime earnings to consume during his working life and how much to put aside until retirement. This example is obviously built on simplifying assumptions, but it does convey the basic life-cycle choice of saving during working life for future consumption after retirement.

Exhibit 8-12 shows Yelberton's intertemporal budget constraint. Yelberton's choice involves comparing the utility of present consumption during his working life and future consumption after he retires. The rate of return that determines the slope of the intertemporal budget line between present consumption and future consumption in this example is the annual interest rate compounded over 30 years, not just one year. Thus, in the lower budget constraint line on the exhibit, future consumption in this table grows by increments of $574,000 because each time $100,000 is saved in the present, it compounds to $574,000 after 30 years at a 6% interest rate. If some of the numbers on the future consumption axis look bizarrely large, remember that this occurs because of the power of compound interest over substantial periods of time and because the figure is grouping together all of Yelberton's savings for retirement over his lifetime.

Yelberton will compare the different choices along the budget constraint and choose the one that provides him with the highest utility. For example, he will compare the utility he would receive from a choice like point A, with consumption of $1 million in the present, zero savings, and zero future consumption; point B, with present consumption of $800,000, savings of $200,000, and future consumption of $1,148,000; point C, with present consumption of $600,000, savings of $400,000, and future consumption of $2,296,000; or even choice D, with present consumption of zero, savings of $1,000,000, and future consumption of $5,740,000. Yelberton will also ask himself questions like: "Would I prefer to consume a little less in the present, save more, and have more future consumption?" or "Would I prefer to consume a little more in the present, save less, and have less future consumption?" In this way, by considering marginal changes toward more or less consumption, he can seek out the choice that will provide him with the highest level of utility. Let's say that Yelberton's preferred choice is B.

Imagine that Yelberton's annual rate of return rises from 6% to 9%. In this case, each time he saves $100,000 in the present, it will be worth $1,327,000 30 years from now (using the formula for compound interest that $100,000 (1 + .09)30 = $1,327,000$). A change in the rate of return alters the slope of the intertemporal budget constraint: a higher rate of return or interest rate will cause the budget line to pivot upwards, while a lower rate of return will cause it to swing downwards. If Yelberton were to consume nothing in the present and save all $1,000,000, with a 9% rate of return, his future consumption would be $13,270,000, as shown on Exhibit 8-12.

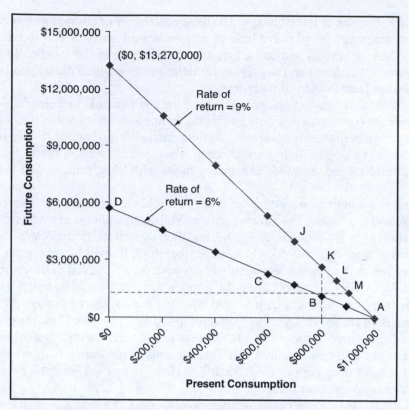

EXHIBIT 8-12 Yelberton's Choice: The Intertemporal Budget Set

Yelberton will make a choice between present and future consumption. With an annual rate of return of 6%, he decides that his utility will be highest at point B, which represents a choice of $800,000 in present consumption and $1,148,000 in future consumption. When the annual rate of return rises to 9%, the intertemporal budget constraint pivots up. Yelberton could choose to take the gains from this higher rate of return in several forms: more present saving and much higher future consumption (J), the same present saving and higher future consumption (K), more present consumption and more future consumption (L), or more present consumption and the same future consumption (M).

As the rate of return rises, Yelberton considers a range of choices on the new intertemporal budget constraint. The dashed vertical and horizontal lines running through the original choice B help to illustrate his range of options. One choice is to reduce present consumption (i.e., to save more) and to have considerably higher future consumption at a point like J above and to the left of his original choice B. A second choice would be to keep the level of present consumption and savings the same and to receive the benefits of the higher rate of return entirely in the form of higher future consumption, which would be choice K. A third choice would be that Yelberton could have both more present consumption—that is, less savings—but still have higher future consumption because of the higher interest rate, which would be a choice like L, above and to the right of his original choice B. Thus, the higher rate of return might cause Yelberton to save more, or less, or the same amount, depending on his own preferences. A fourth choice would be that Yelberton could react to the higher rate of return by increasing his current consumption and leaving his future consumption unchanged, as at point M directly to the right of his original choice B. The actual choice of what quantity to save and how saving will respond to changes in the rate of return will vary from person to person, according to the choice that will maximize each person's utility.

Applications of the Model of Intertemporal Choice

The theoretical model of the intertemporal budget constraint suggests that when the rate of return rises, the quantity of savings may rise, fall, or remain the same, depending on the preferences of individuals. For the U.S. economy as a whole, the most common pattern seems to be that the quantity of savings doesn't adjust much to changes in the rate of return. As a practical matter, many households either save at a fairly steady pace, by putting regular contributions into a retirement account or by making regular payments as they buy a house, or they don't save much at all. Of course, some people will have preferences that cause them to react to a higher rate of return by increasing their quantity of savings; others will react to a higher rate of return by noticing that with a higher rate of return, they can save less in the present and still have higher future consumption. One prominent example in which a higher rate of return leads to a lower savings rate occurs when firms save money because they have promised to pay workers a certain fixed level of pension benefits after retirement. When rates of return rise, those companies can save less money in the present in their pension fund and still have enough to pay the promised retirement benefits in the future.

This insight suggests some skepticism about political proposals to encourage higher savings by providing savers with a higher rate of return. For example, Individual Retirement Accounts (IRAs) and 401(k) accounts are special savings accounts where the money going into the account is not taxed until it is taken out many years later, after retirement. (The main difference between these accounts is that an IRA is usually set up by an individual while a 401(k) needs to be set up through an employer.) By not taxing savings in the present, the effect of an IRA or a 401(k) is to increase the return to savings in these accounts. IRA and 401(k) accounts have attracted a large quantity of savings since they became common in the late 1980s and early 1990s. For example, the amount in IRAs rose from $239 billion in 1992 to $7,200 billion by 2015. However, overall U.S. personal savings, as discussed earlier, actually dropped from low to lower in the late 1990s and has stayed relatively low since 2000. Evidently, the larger amounts in these retirement accounts are being offset in the economy as a whole either by less savings in other kinds of accounts, or by a larger amount of borrowing (i.e., negative savings).

A rise in interest rates makes it easier for people to enjoy higher future consumption. But it also allows them to enjoy higher present consumption, if that is what individuals desire. Again, a change in prices—in this case, in interest rates—leads to a range of possible outcomes.

The Unifying Power of the Utility-Maximizing Budget Set Framework

The choices of households are determined by an interaction between prices, budget constraints, and personal preferences. The flexible and powerful terminology of utility-maximizing gives economists a vocabulary for bringing these elements together.

Not even economists believe that people walk around mumbling about their marginal utilities before they walk into a shopping mall, accept a job, or make a deposit in a savings account. However, economists do believe that individuals seek their own satisfaction or utility and that people often decide to try a little less of one thing and a little more of another. If these gentle assumptions are accepted, then the idea of utility-maximizing households facing budget constraints becomes highly plausible, too.

Key Concepts and Summary

1. Economic analysis of household behavior is based on the assumption that people seek the highest level of **utility** or satisfaction. Individuals are the only judge of their own utility.

2. In general, greater consumption of a good brings higher total utility. However, the additional utility received from each unit of greater consumption tends to decline in a pattern of **diminishing marginal utility**.

3. The utility-maximizing choice on a consumption budget constraint can be found in several ways. You can add up total utility of each choice on the budget-line and choose the highest total. You can choose a starting point at random and compare the marginal utility gains and losses of moving to neighboring points—and thus eventually seek out the preferred choice. Alternatively, you can compare the ratio of the prices of goods 1 and 2 to the ratio of the marginal utilities of goods 1 and 2 and apply the rule that at the optimal choice, the ratio of prices must equal the ratio of marginal utilities: $P1/P2 = MU1/MU2$.

4. The budget constraint framework suggests that when income or price changes, a range of responses are possible. When income rises, households will demand a higher quantity of normal goods, but a lower quantity of inferior goods. When the price of a good rises, households will typically demand less of that good—but whether they will demand a much lower quantity or only a slightly lower quantity will depend on personal preferences. Also, a higher price for one good can lead to more or less of the other good being demanded.

5. When making a choice along the labor-leisure budget constraint, a household will choose the combination of labor, leisure, and income that provides the most utility. The result of a change in wage levels can be higher work effort, the same work effort, or lower work effort.

6. When making a choice along the intertemporal budget constraint, a household will choose the combination of present consumption, savings, and future consumption that provides the most utility. The result of a higher rate of return (or higher interest rates) can be a higher quantity of savings, the same quantity of savings, or a lower quantity of savings, depending on preferences about present and future consumption.

Review Questions

1. Who makes the decision about how much utility an individual will receive from consuming a good?

2. Would you expect total utility to rise or fall with additional consumption of a good? Why?

3. Would you expect marginal utility to rise or fall with additional consumption of a good? Why?

4. Is it possible for total utility to increase while marginal utility diminishes? Explain.

5. If people do not have a complete mental picture of their total utility for every level of consumption, how can they find their utility-maximizing consumption choice?

6. What is the rule relating the ratio of prices of two goods and the ratio of marginal utilities of those goods at the optimal choice? Explain why, if this rule does not hold, the choice cannot be utility-maximizing.

7. As a general rule, is it safe to assume that a change in the price of a good will always have its most significant impact on the quantity demanded of that good, rather than on the quantity demanded of other goods? Explain.

8. How will a utility-maximizer find the choice of leisure and income that provides the greatest utility?

9. As a general rule, is it safe to assume that a higher wage will encourage significantly more hours worked for all individuals? Explain.

10. How will a utility-maximizer find the choice of present and future consumption that provides the greatest utility?

11. As a general rule, is it safe to assume that a lower interest rate will encourage significantly lower financial savings for all individuals? Explain.

Cost and Industry Structure

A business or firm is a kind of social machine. It incurs costs as it combines the labor of workers, machinery or other tools, and supplies purchased from other businesses. The firm transforms these inputs into outputs of goods and services, and collects revenue from its sales.

When people think of firms, often giants like Walmart, General Electric, or IBM—which each has over 300,000 employees—come to mind. But firms come in all sizes, as shown in Exhibit 9-1. The U.S. Census Bureau counted 6 million firms with employees in the U.S. economy. About half of all the workers in private firms are at the 17,000 large firms with more than 500 workers. But another third of workers in the U.S. economy are at firms with fewer than 100 workers. These smaller-scale businesses include everything from dentists and lawyers to businesses that mow lawns or clean houses. Indeed, Exhibit 9-1 doesn't include a separate category of millions of small

EXHIBIT 9-1 U.S. Firms by Number of Employees in 2013

U.S. firms display a wide variety of sizes. Large firms with more than 500 employees hire about one-half of the labor force. Firms with fewer than 100 employees hire about one-third of the labor force.

	Firms (% of total firms)	Number of Paid Employees (% of total employment)
Total	**5,774,000 (100%)**	**118.1 million (100%)**
0–9 employees	4,567,000 (79.1%)	12.4 million (10.5%)
10–19 employees	600,000 (10.4%)	8.0 million (6.8%)
20–99 employees	503,000 (8.7%)	19.7 million (16.7%)
100–499 employees	85,000 (1.5%)	16.6 million (14.1%)
500 or more employees	19,000 (0.3%)	61.4 million (52.0%)

Many firms	Many firms	Few firms	One firm
Identical products	Similar but not identical products	Identical or similar products	No similar product
Perfect Competition	**Monopolistic Competition**	**Oligopoly**	**Monopoly**

EXHIBIT 9-2 The Spectrum of Competition

Firms face different competitive situations. At one extreme—perfect competition—many firms are all trying to sell identical products. At the other extreme—monopoly—only one firm is selling a product, and this firm faces no competition. Monopolistic competition and oligopoly fall between the extremes of perfect competition and monopoly. Monopolistic competition is a situation with many firms selling similar, but not identical, products. Oligopoly is a situation with few firms that sell identical or similar products.

"nonemployer" businesses where a single owner or a few partners are not officially paid wages or a salary, but simply receive whatever they can earn. Each of these businesses, regardless of size or complexity, tries to earn a profit, where:

$$\text{Profit} = \text{Total Revenue} - \text{Total Cost}.$$

Total revenue is calculated by taking the quantity of everything that is sold and multiplying it by the sale price. Total costs include all spending on labor, machinery, tools, and supplies purchased from other firms.

The total revenue for a profit-seeking firm is determined by the price that a firm can charge and the quantity that it can sell, which in turn will be related to demand for its products and on the number of other firms that are selling similar or identical products. Exhibit 9-2 illustrates the range of different competitive conditions, which will be explored in the next three chapters. Chapter 10 examines **perfect competition**, in which each firm faces many competitors that sell identical products. Chapter 11 examines the opposite of perfect competition, which is the **monopoly** firm that faces no competitors. Chapter 12 examines two situations between perfect competition and monopoly: the case of **monopolistic competition**, where many firms sell similar but different products, and the case of **oligopoly**, where a small number of firms sell a similar product but face no other competition.

Regardless of what type of competition exists in a market, the definition of profit implies that a profit-maximizing firm will always attempt to produce its desired level of output at the lowest possible cost. After all, if any firm—from a giant like Bank of America or Boeing down to the corner gas station—can produce its desired level of production at a lower total cost, it will earn higher profits. This chapter begins by examining the costs of firms from a short-term perspective. In the short run, some costs can be adjusted quickly, like hiring or firing workers, but other costs cannot be immediately changed, like building a large factory. The discussion then takes a long-run perspective on costs, when all costs can be adjusted. Firms can use this breakdown of their cost structure into what is adjustable in the short term and what is adjustable in the long term both to understand the situation that they face in trying to earn profits and also to recognize the likely patterns of competition in their market.

The Structure of Costs in the Short Run

A list of the costs involved in producing cars will look very different from the costs involved in producing computer software or haircuts or fast-food meals. However, the cost structure of all firms can be broken down into some common underlying patterns.

perfect competition: Each firm faces many competitors that sell identical products.

monopoly: A firm that faces no competitors.

monopolistic competition: Many firms competing to sell similar but differentiated products.

oligopoly: When a few firms have all or nearly all of the sales in an industry.

When a firm looks at its total costs of production in the short run, a useful starting point is to divide total costs into two categories: fixed costs that can't be changed in the short run and variable costs that can be.

Fixed and Variable Costs

Fixed costs are expenditures that must be made before production starts and that do not change regardless of the level of production, at least not in the short run of weeks and months. Fixed costs can take many forms: for example, machinery or equipment, physical space for a retail or manufacturing business, research and development costs to develop new technology, even an expense like advertising to popularize a brand name. The level of fixed costs varies according to the specific line of business: for instance, manufacturing computer chips requires an expensive factory, but a local moving and hauling business can get by with almost no fixed costs at all if it rents trucks by the day when needed.

fixed costs: Expenditures that must be made before production starts and that do not change regardless of the level of production.

Variable costs, on the other hand, are incurred in the act of producing and will increase with the quantity produced. Labor is treated as a variable cost, since producing a greater quantity of a good or service typically requires more workers. But for many firms, variable costs also include physical inputs, like the metal and plastic involved in manufacturing a car or the cloth for making shirts and trousers.

variable costs: Costs of production that increase with the quantity produced.

As a concrete example of fixed and variable costs, consider the barber shop called The Clip Joint shown in Exhibit 9-3. Fixed costs of operating the barber shop, like the space and equipment, are $160 per day. The fixed costs are represented in the exhibit as the point where the total cost curve touches the vertical axis; that is, they are the costs incurred even if output is zero.

Variable costs are the costs of hiring barbers, which is $80 per day. The first two columns of Exhibit 9-3 show the quantity of haircuts that the barbershop can produce as it hires additional barbers. The third column shows the fixed costs, which do not change regardless of the level of production. The fourth column shows the variable costs at each level of output; these are calculated by taking the amount of labor hired and multiplying by the wage. Adding together the fixed costs in the third column and the variable costs in the fourth column produces the total costs in the fifth column.

Once production starts, total costs and variable costs rise. Variable costs often show a pattern of **diminishing marginal returns**, which occurs when the marginal gain in output diminishes as each additional unit of input is added. In the figure, diminishing marginal returns is illustrated by the ever-steeper slope of the total cost curve—that is, the cost of

diminishing marginal returns: When the marginal gain in output diminishes as each additional unit of input is added.

Labor	Quantity	Fixed Cost	Variable Cost	Total Cost
1	16	$160	$80	$240
2	40	$160	$160	$320
3	60	$160	$240	$400
4	72	$160	$320	$480
5	80	$160	$400	$560
6	84	$160	$480	$640

EXHIBIT 9-3 How Output Affects Total Costs

The first column shows the number of barbers hired. The second column shows the quantity of haircuts produced. The fixed costs of setting up the shop are $160, and these fixed costs do not change with the quantity of production. Fixed costs are shown by where the total cost line intersects the horizontal axis. The variable costs of hiring barbers are $80. Total costs are calculated by adding up the fixed and variable costs. Variable costs rise with production.

What's the Difference between Business and Economics?

A certain tension exists between business and economics. Businesspeople sometimes tend to view economists as smart but theoretical and naive, with no idea of what it actually takes to run a business. One economist recalled his childhood this way: "Economists always talked a lot about business but, to my father, economists bore about the same relationship to business and the general economy as stamp collecting did to the delivery of the mail." Economists, for their part, sometimes seem to think that businesspeople are so wrapped up in day-to-day details of ordering paper clips and raking in executive bonuses that they have only a fuzzy perception of how the economic system as a whole works, or of their firm's place within that system.

Although both economists and businesspeople think about business issues, they do so from different perspectives. One useful metaphor is that economists are to businesspeople as mechanics are to chauffeurs. Both jobs involve cars. But the mechanic's view of how things are working under the hood is different from the driver's view of how to get to the destination. Economists often have a better perspective on the market-oriented system as a whole and how it fits together. But businesspeople have a wealth of detailed knowledge about specific products, human relations, management, accounting, new product launches, marketing, production, strategies of specific firms, and other issues that most economists cannot match.

producing each additional unit of output is rising. As the number of barbers increases from 0 to 1, the marginal gain in output is 16; as the number rises from 1 to 2, the output gain is 24—an increasing marginal output. From that point on, the marginal gain in output diminishes as each additional barber is added. To gain some intuition for the reason behind this pattern, consider that a one-person barber shop is a very busy operation. The single barber needs to do everything: say hello to people entering, answer the phone, cut hair, sweep up, and run the cash register. A second barber reduces the level of disruption from jumping back and forth between these tasks, and allows a greater division of labor and specialization. The result can be greater increasing marginal returns. However, as other barbers are added, at some point the additional barbers will begin bumping elbows and start to produce diminishing marginal returns. As a result, the total costs of production will begin to rise more rapidly as output increases.

This pattern of diminishing marginal returns is common in many industries. As another example, consider the problem of irrigating a crop on a farmer's field. The plot of land is the fixed factor of production, while the water that can be added to the land is the key variable cost. As the farmer adds water to the land, output increases. But adding equal amounts of additional water brings smaller and smaller increases in output, until at some point the water floods the field and actually reduces output. Diminishing marginal returns arise because, given a certain level of fixed costs, marginal increases in output eventually require an ever-increasing number of inputs, and thus come at a higher cost.

Average Costs, Average Variable Costs, Marginal Costs

The breakdown of total costs into fixed and variable costs can provide a basis for other insights as well. The first five columns of Exhibit 9-4 duplicate the previous exhibit, but the last three columns offer additional calculations, where the costs are now analyzed not as a total, but on a per-unit basis. These additional calculations are also plotted on a graph.

average cost: Total cost divided by the quantity of output.

Average cost is calculated by dividing the total cost by the quantity of output. Thus, because the total cost of producing 40 haircuts is $320, the average cost for producing each of 40 haircuts is $320/40 = $8. A similar calculation is performed for each entry in the average cost column.

The average cost curve is U-shaped, as shown in Exhibit 9-4. It starts off relatively high because at the far left end, average cost is calculated including all of the fixed costs and relatively little output, so the denominator in the average cost calculation is close to zero. Average costs then decline, as the fixed costs are spread over an increasing quantity

EXHIBIT 9-4 Cost
Curves at the Clip Joint

The information on total
costs, fixed cost, and
variable cost can also be
presented on a per-unit
basis. Average cost (AC) is
calculated by dividing total
cost by the total quantity
produced. The average cost
curve is typically U-shaped.
Average variable cost (AVC)
is calculated by dividing
variable cost by the quantity
produced. The average
variable cost curve lies below
the average cost curve and
is typically U-shaped or
upward-sloping. Marginal
cost (MC) is calculated by
taking the change in total
cost between two levels
of output and dividing by
the change in output. The
marginal cost curve is
upward-sloping.

Labor	Quantity	Fixed Cost	Variable Cost	Total Cost	Marginal Cost	Average Cost	Average Variable Cost
1	16	160	80	240	5	15	5
2	40	160	160	320	03.3	8	4
3	60	160	240	400	4	6.6	4
4	72	160	320	480	6.6	6.6	4.4
5	80	160	400	560	10	7	5
6	84	160	480	640	20	7.6	5.7

of output. In the average cost calculation, the rise in the numerator of total costs is relatively small compared to the rise in the denominator of quantity produced. But as output expands still further, the average cost begins to rise. At the right side of the average cost curve, total costs begin rising more rapidly as diminishing returns kick in.

Average variable cost is calculated by dividing the variable cost by the quantity of output. For example, the variable cost of producing 80 haircuts is $400, so the average variable cost is $400/80 = $5. The average variable cost curve will always lie below the curve for average cost, as shown in Exhibit 9-4, because average cost includes fixed costs in the numerator of the calculation and variable cost doesn't. However, as output becomes larger, fixed costs become relatively less important (because they don't rise with output), and so average variable cost sneaks closer to average cost.

average variable cost:
Variable cost divided by the quantity of output.

Marginal cost is the additional cost of producing one more unit. Marginal cost can be calculated by taking the change in total cost (or the change in variable cost because that will be the same amount) and dividing it by the change in quantity. For example, as quantity produced increases from 40 to 60, total costs rise by 80. Thus, the marginal cost for each of those marginal 20 units will be 80/20 = 4. A similar calculation is performed for each entry in the marginal cost column. The marginal cost curve is generally upward-sloping because diminishing marginal returns implies that additional units are more costly to produce. A small zone of increasing marginal returns can be seen in the figure as a dip in the marginal cost curve before it starts rising.

marginal cost: The
additional cost of producing
one more unit.

The marginal cost line intersects the average cost line exactly at the bottom of the average cost curve—which occurs at a quantity of 72 and costs of $6.60 in Exhibit 9-4. The reason why the intersection occurs at this point is built into the economic meaning of marginal and average costs. If the marginal cost of production is below the average cost for producing previous units, as it is for the points to the left of where MC crosses AC, then producing one more additional unit will reduce average costs overall—and the AC curve will be downward-sloping in this zone. Conversely, if the marginal cost of production for producing an additional unit is above the average cost for producing the earlier units, as it is for points to the right of where *MC* crosses *AC*, then producing a marginal unit will increase average costs overall—and the *AC* curve must be upward-sloping in this zone. The point of transition, between where *MC* is pulling *AC* down and where it is pulling it up, must occur at the minimum point of the *AC* curve.

This idea of the marginal cost "pulling down" the average cost or "pulling up" the average cost may sound abstract, but think about it in terms of your own grades. If the score on the most recent quiz you take is lower than your average score on previous quizzes, then the marginal quiz pulls down your average. If your score on the most recent quiz is higher than the average on previous quizzes, the marginal quiz pulls up your average. In this same way, low marginal costs of production first pull down average costs, and then higher marginal costs pull them up.

The numerical calculations behind average cost, average variable cost, and marginal cost change from firm to firm. However, the general patterns of these curves, and the relationships and economic intuition behind them, do not change.

Lessons Taught by Alternative Measures of Costs

Breaking down total costs into fixed cost, marginal cost, average cost, and average variable cost is useful because each statistic offers its own insights for the firm.

Whatever the firm's quantity of production, total revenue must exceed total costs if it is to earn a profit. Fixed costs are important because at least in the short run, the firm cannot alter them. Fixed costs are sunk costs, to use a term introduced in Chapter 2. In thinking about what to do next, sunk costs should typically be ignored, since this spending has already been made and cannot be changed. However, variable costs can be changed, so they convey information about the firm's ability to cut costs in the present and the extent to which costs will increase if production rises.

Average cost tells a firm whether it can earn profits, given the price in the market. But you can rewrite the equation for profit to spell out that total revenues are the quantity produced multiplied by the price, and that total costs are the quantity produced multiplied by the average cost:

> Profit = total revenue – total cost
> = (price) (quantity produced) – (average cost) (quantity produced).

This formula implies that if the market price exceeds average cost, profits will be positive; if price is below average cost, then profits will be negative.

The lesson to be learned from average variable cost is more subtle, but if a comparison between average cost and price reveals whether a firm is earning profits, then a comparison between average variable cost and price reveals whether the firm is earning profit *if fixed costs are left out of the calculation.* In certain circumstances, discussed in more detail in the next chapter, this information may prove useful.

The marginal cost of producing an additional unit can be compared with the amount of revenue gained by selling that additional unit to reveal whether the marginal unit is adding to total profit—or not. Thus, marginal cost helps in understanding how profits would be affected by increasing or reducing production.

CLEARING IT UP

Why Total Cost and Average Cost Are Not on the Same Graph

Total cost, fixed cost, and variable cost are all measured in dollars. In contrast, marginal cost, average cost, and average variable cost are all measured in dollars per unit produced. Thus, the vertical axes of the graphs are measured in fundamentally different units, and it wouldn't make practical sense to put these curves on the same graph.

A Variety of Cost Patterns

The pattern of costs varies among industries and even among firms in the same industry. Some businesses have high fixed costs, but low marginal costs. Consider, for example, an Internet company that provides medical advice to customers. Such a company might be paid by health care consumers directly, or perhaps hospitals or health care practices might subscribe on behalf of their patients. Setting up the website, collecting the information, writing the content, and buying or leasing the computer space to handle the web traffic are all fixed costs that must be undertaken before the site can work. However, when the website is up and running, it can provide a high quantity of service with relatively low variable costs, like the cost of monitoring the system and updating the information. In this case, the total cost curve might start at a high level because of the high fixed costs, but then might not rise much as the quantity of services provided rises, reflecting the low variable costs of operation. However, if the website is popular, a large rise in the number of visitors will overwhelm the website, and increasing output further would require an additional investment.

For other firms, fixed costs may be relatively low. For example, consider firms that rake leaves in the fall or shovel snow off sidewalks and driveways in the winter. For fixed costs, such firms may need little more than a car to transport workers to homes of customers and some rakes and shovels. Still other firms may find that diminishing marginal returns set in quite sharply. If a manufacturing plant tried to run 24 hours a day, seven days a week, then little time remains for routine maintenance of the equipment, and marginal costs can increase dramatically as the firm struggles to repair and replace overworked equipment.

Every firm can gain insight into its task of earning profits by dividing its total costs into fixed and variable costs, and then using these calculations as a basis for average cost, average variable cost, and marginal cost. However, making a final decision about the profit-maximizing quantity to produce and price to charge requires combining these perspectives on cost with an analysis of sales and revenue, which in turn requires looking at the competitive setting in which the firm finds itself. Before turning to the analysis of these competitive settings like perfect competition, monopolistic competition, and monopoly in the next three chapters, let's analyze the firm's cost structure from a long-run perspective.

The Structure of Costs in the Long Run

No costs are fixed in the long run. All costs are potentially variable over time. A firm can build new factories and purchase new machinery, or it can close existing facilities. In planning for the long run, the firm will compare alternative **production technologies,** where the term "technology" doesn't refer to a specific new invention like the laser beam or the assembly line, but refers to any alternative methods of combining inputs to produce output. The firm will search for the production technology that allows producing the desired level of output at lowest cost. After all, lower costs lead to higher profits—at least if total revenues remain unchanged. Moreover, each firm must fear that if it does not seek out the low-cost methods of production, then it may lose sales to competitor firms that find a way to produce and sell for less.

production technologies: Alternative methods of combining inputs to produce output.

Choice of Production Technology

Many tasks can be performed with a range of combinations of labor and physical capital. For example, a firm can have human beings answering phones and taking messages, or it can invest in an automated voicemail system. A firm can hire file clerks and secretaries to manage a system of paper folders and file cabinets, or it can invest in a computerized record-keeping system that will require fewer employees. A firm can hire workers to push supplies around a factory on rolling carts, or it can invest in motorized vehicles, or it can invest in robots that carry materials without a driver. Firms often face a choice between buying a number of small machines, which need a worker to run each one, or buying one larger and more expensive machine, which only requires one or two workers to run it. In short, physical capital and labor can often substitute for each other.

Consider the example of a private firm that is hired by local governments to clean up public parks. Three different combinations of labor and physical capital for cleaning up a single average-sized park appear in Exhibit 9-5. The first production technology is heavy on workers and light on machines, while the next two technologies substitute machines for workers. Since all three of these production methods produce the same thing—one cleaned-up park—a profit-seeking firm will choose the production technology that is least expensive, given the prices of labor and machines.

In Exhibit 9-5, example A shows the firm's cost calculation when wages are $40 and machines cost $80. In this case, technology #1 is the low-cost production technology. In example B, wages rise to $70, while the cost of machines does not change, in which case technologies #2 and #3 are tied for being the low-cost production technology. If wages keep rising up to $90, while the cost of machines remains unchanged, then technology #3 clearly becomes the low-cost form of production, as shown in example C.

This example illustrates that as an input becomes more expensive (in this case, the labor input), firms will attempt to conserve on using that input and will instead shift to other inputs that are now relatively less expensive. This pattern helps to explain why the demand curve for labor (or any input) slopes down; that is, as labor becomes relatively more expensive, profit-seeking firms will seek to substitute the use of other inputs. When

EXHIBIT 9-5 Three Ways to Clean a Park

Three Production Technologies			
Production technology 1	10 workers	2 machines	
Production technology 2	7 workers	4 machines	
Production technology 3	3 workers	7 machines	

All three technologies accomplish the same task; in this case, cleaning up one park. Production technology #1 uses the most labor and least machinery, while #3 uses the least labor and the most machinery. As the cost of labor rises from example A to B to C, the firm will choose to substitute away from labor and use more machinery.

Example A: Workers Cost $40, Machines Cost $80

	Labor Cost	Machine Cost	Total Cost
Cost of technology #1	10 × $40 = $400	2 × $80 = $160	$560
Cost of technology #2	7 × $40 = $280	4 × $80 = $320	$600
Cost of technology #3	3 × $40 = $120	7 × $80 = $560	$680

Example B: Workers Cost $60, Machines Cost $80

	Labor Cost	Machine Cost	Total Cost
Cost of technology #1	10 × $60 = $600	2 × $80 = $160	$760
Cost of technology #2	7 × $60 = $420	4 × $80 = $320	$740
Cost of technology #3	3 × $60 = $180	7 × $80 = $560	$740

Example C: Workers Cost $90, Machines Cost $80

	Labor Cost	Machine Cost	Total Cost
Cost of technology #1	10 × $90 = $900	2 × $80 = $160	$1,060
Cost of technology #2	7 × $90 = $630	4 × $80 = $320	$950
Cost of technology #3	3 × $90 = $270	7 × $80 = $560	$830

a multinational employer like Coca-Cola or McDonald's sets up a bottling plant or a restaurant in a high-wage economy like the United States, Canada, Japan, or western Europe, it is likely to use production technologies that conserve on the number of workers and focuses more on machines. However, that same employer is likely to use production technologies with more workers and less machinery when producing in a lower-wage country like Mexico, China, or South Africa.

Economies of Scale

The term **"economies of scale"** refers to the situation where as the quantity of output—the "scale" of production—goes up, average cost of production falls. When economies of scale exist, doubling of all inputs will result in more than doubling output (or equivalently, doubling all inputs will result in producing at a lower average cost). In everyday language, a larger factory can produce at a lower average cost than a smaller factory. Exhibit 9-6 illustrates the idea of economies of scale (which was originally introduced in Chapter 1), showing the average cost of producing an alarm clock falling as the quantity of output rises. For a small-sized factory like *S*, with an output level of 1,000, the average cost of production is $12 per alarm clock. For a medium-sized factory like *M*, with an output level of 2,000, the average cost of production falls to $8 per alarm clock. For a large factory like *L*, with an output of 5,000, the average cost of production declines still further to $4 per alarm clock.

The average cost curve in this economies-of-scale diagram may appear similar to the average cost curves presented earlier in this chapter, although it is downward sloping rather than U-shaped. But there is one major difference. The economies-of-scale curve is a long-run average cost curve because it allows all factors of production to change. The short-run average cost curves presented earlier in this chapter assumed the existence of fixed costs, and only variable costs were allowed to change.

One prominent example of economies of scale occurs in the chemical industry. Chemical plants have a lot of pipes. The cost of the materials for producing a pipe is related to the circumference of the pipe and its length. However, the volume of gooky chemical stuff that can flow through a pipe is determined by the cross-section area of the pipe. The calculations in Exhibit 9-7 show that a pipe that requires twice as much material to make (as shown by the circumference of the pipe doubling) can actually carry four times the volume of chemicals (because the cross-section area of the pipe rises by a factor of four). Of course, economies of scale in a chemical plant are more complex than this simple calculation suggests. But the chemical engineers who design these plants have long used what they call the "six-tenths rule," a rule of thumb that holds that increasing the quantity produced in a chemical plant by a certain percentage will increase total cost by only six-tenths as much.

economies of scale: When the average cost of producing each individual unit declines as total output increases.

EXHIBIT 9-6
Economies of Scale

A small factory like *S* produces 1,000 alarm clocks at an average cost of $12 per clock. A medium factory like *M* produces 2,000 alarm clocks at a cost of $8 per clock. A large factory like *L* produces 5,000 alarm clocks at a cost of $4 per clock. Economies of scale exist because the larger scale of production leads to lower average costs.

EXHIBIT 9-7 Comparing Pipes: Economies of Scale in the Chemical Industry

	Circumference (π2r)	Area (πr²)
4-inch pipe	12.5 inches	12.5 square inches
8-inch pipe	25.1 inches	50.2 square inches
16-inch pipe	50.2 inches	201.1 square inches

A circular pipe that is 4 inches in diameter will have a circumference of 12.5 inches. A circular pipe that is 8 inches in diameter will have a circumference of 25.1 inches—so it will take twice as much material to make that pipe. However, although the pipe that is 8 inches in diameter will take twice as much material to make, and thus cost roughly twice as much, it will carry four times as much, as can be seen in the area. The area of the cross-section of an 8-inch pipe is 4 times as great as the corresponding area of a 4-inch pipe. Thus, a doubling of the cost of producing the pipe allows the chemical firm to process four times as much material. This pattern is a major reason why economies of scale occur in chemical production, which uses a large quantity of pipes.

Shapes of Long-Run Average Cost Curves

The long-run average cost curve, where all costs are allowed to vary, is actually based on a group of different short-run average cost curves, each of which represents one specific level of fixed costs. Exhibit 9-8 shows how the long-run average cost curve is built up out of a group of short-run average cost curves. Five short-run average cost or *SRAC* curves appear on the diagram. Each *SRAC* curve represents a different level of fixed costs. For example, you can imagine $SRAC_1$ as a small factory, $SRAC_2$ as a medium factory, $SRAC_3$ as a large factory, and $SRAC_4$ and $SRAC_5$ as very large and ultra-large. Although this diagram shows only five *SRAC* curves, presumably there are an infinite number of other *SRAC* curves between the ones that are shown. This family of short-run average cost curves can be thought of as representing different choices for a firm, which is planning its level of investment in fixed costs such as physical capital—knowing that different

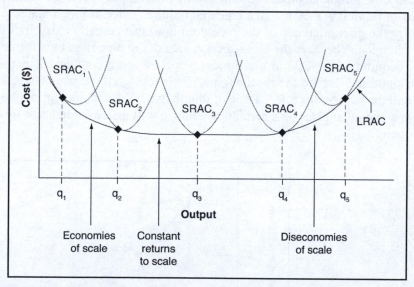

EXHIBIT 9-8 From Short-Run Average Cost Curves to Long-Run Average Cost Curves

The five different short-run average cost (*SRAC*) curves each represents a different level of fixed costs, from the low level of fixed costs at $SRAC_1$ to the high level of fixed costs at $SRAC_5$. Other *SRAC* curves, not shown in the diagram, lie between the ones that are shown here. The long-run average cost (*LRAC*) curve shows the lowest cost for producing each quantity of output when fixed costs can vary, and so it is formed by the bottom edge of the family of *SRAC* curves. If a firm wished to produce quantity q_3, it would choose the fixed costs associated with $SRAC_3$.

choices about capital investment in the present will cause it to end up with different short-run average cost curves in the future.

The long-run average cost curve shows the cost of producing each quantity in the long run, when the firm can choose its level of fixed costs and thus choose which short-run average costs it desires. Thus, if the firm plans to produce in the long run at an output of q_3, it should make the set of investments that will lead it to locate on $SRAC_3$, which allows producing q_3 at the lowest cost. A firm that intends to produce q_3 would be foolish to choose the level of fixed costs at $SRAC_2$ or $SRAC_4$. At $SRAC_2$ the level of fixed costs is too low for producing q_3 at lowest possible cost, and producing q_3 would require adding a very high level of variable costs and make the average cost very high. At $SRAC_4$, the level of fixed costs is too high for producing q_3 at lowest possible cost, and again average costs would be very high as a result.

The shape of the long-run cost curve as drawn in Exhibit 9-8 is fairly common for many industries. The left-hand portion of the long-run average cost curve, where it is downward sloping from output levels q_1 to q_2 to q_3 illustrates the case of economies of scale, which is sometimes also referred to as **increasing returns to scale**. In this portion of the long-run average cost curve, larger scale leads to lower average costs. This pattern was illustrated earlier in Exhibit 9-6.

In the middle portion of the long-run average cost curve ($LRAC$), in the flat portion of the curve around q_3, economies of scale have halted. In this situation, allowing all inputs to expand does not much change the average cost of production, and this situation is called **constant returns to scale**. In this range of the $LRAC$ curve, the average cost of production does not change much as scale rises or falls.

Finally, the right-hand portion of the long-run average cost curve, running from output level q_4 to q_5, shows a situation where as the level of output and the scale rises, average costs rise as well. This situation is called **diseconomies of scale** or **decreasing returns to scale**. A firm or a factory can become so large that it becomes very difficult to manage, resulting in unnecessarily high costs as many layers of management try to communicate with workers and with each other, and as failures to communicate lead to disruptions in the flow of work and materials. Not many overly large factories are observed in the real world because, with their very high production costs, they are unable to compete for long against plants with lower average costs of production, and so they go out of business. However, in some planned economies, like the economy of the old Soviet Union, plants that were so large as to be grossly inefficient were able to continue operating for a long time because the government economic planners protected them from competition and assured that they would not experience losses.

Although economies of scale may be easiest to visualize in terms of the size of manufacturing plants, the concept has many applications. In some cases, economies of scale may arise because doubling advertising or promotional expenses may expand sales more than proportionately, or because a larger retail space can expand sales more than proportionately, or because spreading the fixed costs of administration and record-keeping over

increasing returns to scale: When a larger-scale firm can produce at a lower cost than a smaller-scale firm, also called economies of scale.

constant returns to scale: When expanding all inputs does not change the average cost of production.

diseconomies of scale: Another term for decreasing returns to scale.

decreasing returns to scale: A situation in which as the quantity of output rises, the average cost of production rises.

CLEARING IT UP

Economies of Scale vs. Diminishing Marginal Returns?

The concept of economies of scale, where average costs decline as production expands, might seem to conflict with the idea of diminishing marginal returns, where marginal costs rise as production expands. But diminishing marginal returns refers only to the short-run average cost curve, where one variable input (like labor) is increasing, but other inputs (like capital) are fixed. Economies of scale refers to the long-run average cost curve, where all inputs are being allowed to increase together. Thus, it is quite possible and common to have an industry that has both diminishing marginal returns when only one input is allowed to change, and at the same time has increasing or constant returns to scale when all inputs change together to produce a larger-scale operation.

more customers (as in the banking or insurance industries, for example) can hold down average costs. In any industry where small firms have a difficult time competing because their average costs are too high, the notion that small firms often lack economies of scale offers one plausible explanation.

The Size and Number of Firms in an Industry

The shape of the long-run average cost curve has implications for how many firms will compete in an industry and whether the firms in an industry have many different sizes or tend to be the same size. For example, say that 1 million dishwashers are sold every year at a price of $500 each and the long-run average cost curve for dishwashers is shown in Exhibit 9-9a. In Exhibit 9-9a, the lowest point of the *LRAC* curve occurs at a quantity of 10,000 produced. Thus, the market for dishwashers will consist of 100 different manufacturing plants of this same size. If some firm built a plant that produced 5,000 dishwashers per year or 20,000 dishwashers per year, the average costs of production at such plants would be well above $500, and such firms would not be able to compete.

A more common case is illustrated in Exhibit 9-9b, where the *LRAC* curve has a flat-bottomed area of constant returns to scale. In this situation, any firm with a level of output between 5,000 and 20,000 will be able to produce at about the same level of average cost. Given that the market will demand 1 million dishwashers per year at a price of $500, this market might have as many as 200 producers (i.e., 1 million dishwashers divided by firms making 5,000 each) or as few as 50 producers (1 million dishwashers divided by firms making 20,000 each). The producers in this market will range in size from firms that make 5,000 units to firms that make 20,000 units. But firms that produce below 5,000 units or more than 20,000 will be unable to compete because their average costs will be too high. Thus, if one observes an industry where almost all of the plants are the same size, it is likely that the long-run average cost curve has a unique bottom point like in Exhibit 9-9a. However, if the long-run average cost curve has a wide flat bottom like Exhibit 9-9b, then firms of a variety of different sizes will be able to compete with each other.

The flat section of the long-run average cost curve in Exhibit 9-9b can be interpreted in two different ways. One interpretation is that a single manufacturing plant producing a quantity of 5,000 has the same average costs as a single manufacturing plant with four

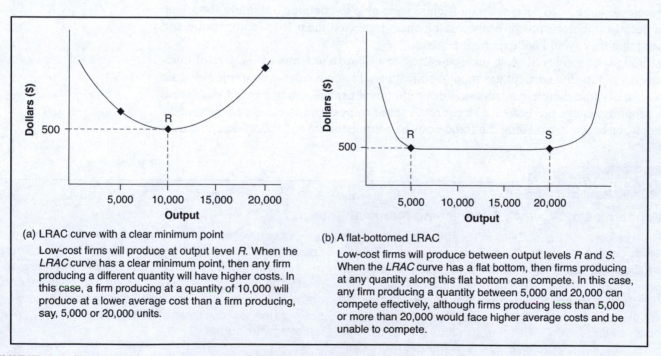

(a) LRAC curve with a clear minimum point

Low-cost firms will produce at output level *R*. When the *LRAC* curve has a clear minimum point, then any firm producing a different quantity will have higher costs. In this case, a firm producing at a quantity of 10,000 will produce at a lower average cost than a firm producing, say, 5,000 or 20,000 units.

(b) A flat-bottomed LRAC

Low-cost firms will produce between output levels *R* and *S*. When the *LRAC* curve has a flat bottom, then firms producing at any quantity along this flat bottom can compete. In this case, any firm producing a quantity between 5,000 and 20,000 can compete effectively, although firms producing less than 5,000 or more than 20,000 would face higher average costs and be unable to compete.

EXHIBIT 9-9 The *LRAC* Curve and the Size and Number of Firms times as much capacity that produces a quantity of 20,000. The other interpretation is that one firm owns a single manufacturing plant that produces a quantity of 5,000, while another firm owns four separate manufacturing plants, which each produce a quantity of 5,000. This second explanation, based on the insight that a single firm may own a number of different manufacturing plants, is especially useful in explaining why the long-run average cost curve often has a large flat segment—and thus why a seemingly smaller firm may be able to compete quite well with a larger firm. At some point, however, the task of coordinating and managing many different plants raises the cost of production sharply, and the long-run average cost curve slopes up as a result.

In the examples to this point, the quantity demanded in the market is quite large (1 million) compared with the quantity produced at the bottom of the long-run average cost curve (5,000, 10,000, or 20,000). In such a situation, the market is set for competition between many firms. But what if the bottom of the long-run average cost curve is at a quantity of 10,000 and the total market demand at that price is only slightly higher than that quantity—or even somewhat lower?

Return to Exhibit 9-9a, where the bottom of the long-run average cost curve is at 10,000, but now imagine that the total quantity of dishwashers demanded in the market at that price of $500 is only 30,000. In this situation, the total number of firms in the market would only be three. A small number of firms in a market is called an "oligopoly," and Chapter 12 will discuss the range of competitive strategies that can occur when oligopolies compete.

Alternatively, consider a situation, again in the setting of Exhibit 9-9a, where the bottom of the long-run average cost curve occurs at a quantity of 10,000, but total demand for the product is only 5,000. (For simplicity, imagine that this demand is highly inelastic, so that it does not vary according to price.) In this situation, the market may well end up with a single firm—a monopoly—producing all 5,000 units. If any firm tried to challenge

Cities as Economies of Scale

Why are people and economic activity concentrated in cities, rather than distributed evenly across a country? The fundamental reason must be related to the idea of economies of scale—in many cases, grouping economic activity together is more productive than spreading it out. For example, cities provide a large group of nearby customers, so that businesses can produce at an efficient economy of scale. They also provide a large group of workers and suppliers, so that business can hire easily and purchase whatever specialized inputs they need. Many of the attractions of cities, like sports stadiums and museums, can only operate if they draw on a large nearby population base. Cities are big enough to offer a wide variety of products, which is what many shoppers are looking for.

These factors are not exactly economies of scale in the narrow sense of applying to the production function of a single firm, but they are related to growth in the overall size of population and market in an area. They are sometimes called "agglomeration economies."

These agglomeration factors help to explain why every economy, as it develops, has an increasing proportion of its population living in urban areas. In the United States, about 80% of the population now lives in metropolitan areas (which include the suburbs around cities), compared to just 40% in 1900. However, in poor nations of the world, including India and much of Africa, the proportion of the population in urban areas is only about 30%. One of the great challenges for these countries as their economies grow will be to manage the growth of the great cities that will arise.

If cities offer economic advantages that are a form of economies of scale, then why don't all or most people live in one giant city? At some population size, agglomeration economies turn into diseconomies. For example, traffic congestion may reach a point where the gains from being geographically nearby are counterbalanced by how long it takes to travel. High densities of people, cars, and factories can mean more garbage and air and water pollution. Facilities like parks or museums may become overcrowded. There may be economies of scale for negative activities like crime because high densities of people and businesses, combined with the greater impersonality of cities, make it easier for illegal activities as well as legal ones. The future of cities, both in the United States and in other countries around the world, will be determined by their ability to benefit from the economies of agglomeration and to minimize or counterbalance the corresponding diseconomies.

this monopoly while producing a quantity lower than 5,000 units, the prospective competitor firm would have a higher average cost, and so it wouldn't be able to compete in the longer term without losing money. A firm producing 10,000 units could produce at a lower average cost—but it could only sell 5,000 units, and so it would lose money as well. Chapter 11 discusses the situation of a monopoly firm in this situation.

Thus, the shape of the long-run average cost curve reveals whether competitors in the market will be different sizes. If the LRAC has a single point at the bottom, then the firms in the market will be about the same size, but if the LRAC has a flat-bottomed segment of constant returns to scale, then firms in the market may be a variety of different sizes.

The relationship between the quantity at the minimum of the long-run average cost curve and the quantity demanded in the market at that price will foretell how much competition is likely to exist in the market. If the quantity demanded in the market far exceeds the quantity at the minimum of the LRAC, then many firms will compete. If the quantity demanded in the market is only slightly higher than the quantity at the minimum of the LRAC, a few firms will compete. If the quantity demanded in the market is less than the quantity at the minimum of the LRAC, a single-producer monopoly is a likely outcome.

Shifting Patterns of Long-Run Average Cost

New developments in production technology can shift the long-run average cost curve in ways that can alter the size distribution of firms in an industry.

For much of the twentieth century, the most common change has been to see alterations in technology, like the assembly line or the large department store, where large-scale producers seemed to gain an advantage over smaller ones. In the long-run average cost curve, the downward-sloping economies of scale portion of the curve seemed to extend over a larger quantity of output.

However, new production technologies do not inevitably lead to a greater average size for firms. For example, in recent years some new technologies for generating electricity at a smaller scale have risen to prominence. The traditional coal-burning electricity plants needed to produce 300–600 megawatts of power to exploit economies of scale fully. However, high-efficiency turbines to produce electricity from burning natural gas can produce electricity at a competitive price while producing the smaller quantity of 100 megawatts of electricity or less. These new technologies create the possibility for smaller companies or plants to generate electricity as efficiently as large ones. Another example of a technology-driven shift to smaller production runs is three-dimensional printing, in which solid objects are created by putting down thin layers of material on top of each other.

Controversy has simmered in recent years over whether the new information and communications technologies will lead to a larger or smaller size for firms. On one side, the new technology may make it easier for small firms to reach out beyond their local geographic area and find customers across a state, or the nation, or even across international boundaries. This factor might seem to predict a future with a larger number of small competitors. On the other side, perhaps the new information and communications technology will create "winner-take-all" markets in which one large company will tend to command a large share of total sales, as Google has done in the market for Internet search requests or Amazon has done in online bookselling. Moreover, improved information and communication technologies might make it easier to manage many different plants and operations across the country or around the world, and thus encourage larger firms. This ongoing battle between the forces of smallness and largeness will be of great interest to economists, businesspeople, and policymakers.

Conclusion

The cost structure of a firm reveals many useful lessons. From a short-run perspective, each firm should be thinking about what costs are fixed and what costs are variable, and comparing the market price to its average costs and marginal costs. In the long run, each firm should have an idea of the extent of economies of scale in its industry, what the range of sizes is to produce at the lowest possible average cost in its industry, and how technological conditions may be shifting the long-run average cost curve over time.

While a careful examination of costs is vital, it is only half the story of the decision-making for any firm. Decisions about the profit-maximizing level of output must always include total revenues as well as total costs. Thus, the next three chapters consider the different market situations of perfect competition, monopoly, monopolistic competition, and oligopoly. In each of these setting, firms must combine their insights about total revenues and total costs, and thus reach a decision about the profit-maximizing price to charge and quantity of output to produce.

Key Concepts and Summary

1. Since profits are equal to total revenues minus total costs, every firm must consider its costs with care. Indeed, a profit-maximizing firm will always seek to produce its chosen level of output at the lowest possible cost.

2. At one end of the spectrum of competition is **perfect competition**, with many firms selling extremely similar products. At the other end is monopoly, where only one firm sells a particular product. In the middle are the cases of **monopolistic competition**, where many firms sell similar but clearly different products, and the case of **oligopoly**, where only a few firms sell a particular product.

3. In a short-run perspective, a firm's total costs can be divided into **fixed costs**, which a firm must incur before producing any output, and **variable costs**, which the firm incurs in the act of producing.

4. **Fixed costs** are sunk costs; that is, because they are in the past and cannot be altered, they should play no role in economic decisions about future production or pricing.

5. **Variable costs** typically show **diminishing marginal returns**, so that the marginal cost of producing higher levels of output rises.

6. **Marginal cost** is calculated by taking the change in total cost (or the change in variable cost, which will be the same thing) and dividing it by the change in output, for each possible change in output. Marginal costs are typically rising. A firm can compare marginal cost to the additional revenue it gains from selling another unit to find out whether its marginal unit is adding to profit.

7. **Average cost** is calculated by taking total cost and dividing by total output at each different level of output. Average costs are typically U-shaped on a graph. If a firm's average cost of production is lower than the market price, a firm will be earning profits.

8. **Average variable cost** is calculated by taking variable cost and dividing by the total output at each level of output. Average variable costs are typically U-shaped. If a firm's average variable cost of production is lower than the market price, then the firm would be earning profits if fixed costs are left out of the picture.

9. A **production technology** refers to a specific combination of labor, physical capital, and technology that makes up a particular method of production.

10. In the long run, firms can choose their production technology, and so all costs become variable costs. In making this choice, firms will try to substitute relatively inexpensive inputs for relatively expensive inputs where possible so as to produce at the lowest possible long-run average cost.

11. **Economies of scale** refers to a situation where as all inputs increase at a certain rate, the quantity of output rises at a faster rate. For example, doubling all inputs might result in more than doubling output. **Constant returns to scale** refers to a situation where as all inputs increase at a certain rate, the quantity of output rises at the same rate. **Diseconomies of scale** refers to a situation where as all inputs increase at a certain rate, the quantity of output rises at a slower rate.

12. The long-run average cost curve shows the lowest possible average cost of production, allowing all the inputs to production to vary so that the firm is choosing its production technology. A downward-sloping *LRAC* shows economies of scale; a flat *LRAC* shows constant returns to scale; an upward-sloping *LRAC* shows diseconomies of scale.

13. If the long-run average cost curve has only one quantity produced that results in the lowest possible average cost, then all of the firms competing in an industry should be the same size. However, if the *LRAC* has a flat segment at the bottom, so that a range of different quantities can produce at lowest average cost, then the firms competing in the industry will display a range of sizes.

14. If the quantity demanded in the market of a certain product is much greater than the quantity found at the bottom of the long-run average cost curve, where the cost of production is lowest, the market will have many firms competing. If the quantity demanded in the market is only slightly greater than the quantity at the bottom of the *LRAC*, the market is likely to be an oligopoly. If the quantity demanded in the market is less than the quantity at the bottom of the *LRAC*, the result is likely to be a monopoly.

Review Questions

1. How are total costs related to profits?
2. What is the difference between perfect competition, monopolistic competition, oligopoly, and monopoly?
3. What is the difference between fixed costs and variable costs?
4. Are there fixed costs in the long run? What about in the short run? Explain briefly.
5. Are fixed costs also sunk costs? Explain.
6. What are diminishing marginal returns?
7. Which costs are measured on a per-unit basis: fixed costs, average cost, average variable cost, variable costs, and marginal cost?
8. How are each of the following calculated: marginal cost, average cost, average variable cost?
9. What shape would you generally expect each of the following to have on a cost-curve diagram: fixed costs, variable costs, marginal costs, average costs, and average variable costs?
10. What is a production technology?
11. In choosing a production technology, how will firms react if one input becomes relatively more expensive?
12. What is the difference between economies of scale, constant returns to scale, and diseconomies of scale?
13. What is a long-run average cost curve?
14. What shape of a long-run average cost curve illustrates economies of scale, constant returns to scale, and diseconomies of scale?
15. Why will firms in most markets be located at or close to the bottom of the long-run average cost curve?

Perfect Competition

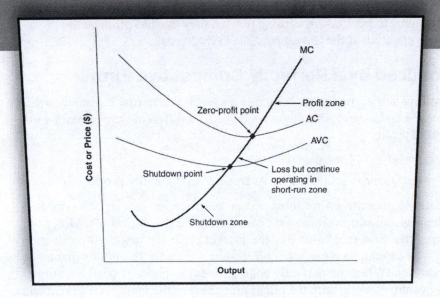

perfect competition: Each firm faces many competitors that sell identical products.

Any firm must recognize two stark realities: no consumer is required to buy the goods that it produces, and even consumers who might want its goods may choose to buy from other firms instead. Firms in a situation of **perfect competition** sell their product in a market with other firms who produce identical or extremely similar products. As a result, if a firm in a perfectly competitive market raises the price of its product by so much as a penny, it will lose all of its sales to competitors. Perfectly competitive firms are sometimes known as **price takers** because the pressure of other competing firms forces them to accept the prevailing price in the market as given. A related underlying assumption is that a perfectly competitive firm must be a relatively small player in the overall market, so that a perfectly competitive firm can increase or decrease its output without noticeably affecting the overall quantity supplied in the market.

price takers: A firm in a perfectly competitive market that must take the prevailing market price as given.

A perfectly competitive industry is a hypothetical extreme; after all, "perfect" is an extreme word. However, producers in a number of industries do face many competitor firms selling highly similar goods, in which case they must often act as price takers. For example, many farmers grow any given crop, and crops grown by different farmers are largely interchangeable. In 2015, U.S. corn farmers were receiving about $3.70 per bushel, and coffee (of the mild arabica variety) was selling for $1.60 per pound on world markets. A corn farmer who attempted to sell corn for $4.00 per bushel, or a coffee grower who attempted to sell for $2.00 a pound, would not have found any buyers. Similarly, gold was selling for $1,160 per ounce, which meant that sellers could not negotiate to receive $1,200 per ounce. Some manufactured products are similar enough that producers must sell at the price prevailing in the market. In the market for mid-sized color televisions, the quality differences are mostly not perceptible to the untrained eye, so price plays a major role in the decisions of purchasers. Gasoline is very similar between different gas stations. Blank flash drives are extremely similar, regardless of the manufacturer.

This chapter examines how profit-seeking firms make decisions about how much to produce in perfectly competitive industries. Such firms will analyze their costs as discussed in the previous chapter, using the concepts of total cost, fixed cost, variable cost, average cost, marginal cost, and average variable cost. In the short run, the perfectly competitive firm will seek out the quantity of output where profits are highest, or if profits are not possible, where losses are smallest. In the long run, the perfectly competitive firms will react to profits by increasing production further and to losses by reducing production or shutting down. Firms will tailor their decisions about the quantity of inputs like labor and physical capital to purchase according to what they need to produce the profit-maximizing quantity of output at the lowest possible average cost.

Quantity Produced by a Perfectly Competitive Firm

A perfectly competitive setting really has only one major choice to make: namely, what quantity to produce. To understand why this is so, consider a different way of writing out the basic definition of profit:

$$\text{Profit} = \text{Total revenue} - \text{Total cost}$$
$$= (\text{Price})(\text{Quantity produced}) - (\text{Average cost})(\text{Quantity produced})$$

Because a perfectly competitive firm must accept the price for its output as dictated by the forces of demand and supply, it cannot choose the price that it charges. Moreover, the perfectly competitive firm must also pay the market price for inputs to production like labor and physical capital, so it cannot control what it pays for the inputs that make up its costs of production. When the perfectly competitive firm chooses what quantity to produce, then this quantity—along with the prices prevailing in the market for output and inputs—will determine the firm's total revenue, total costs, and profits.

Comparing Total Revenue and Total Cost

As an example of how a perfectly competitive firm decides what quantity to produce, consider the case of the Overdrive Production Shoppe, which makes flash drives. Exhibit 10-1 shows total revenue and total costs for the firm. The horizontal axis of the figure shows the quantity of drives produced; the vertical axis shows both total revenue and total costs, measured in dollars.

A perfectly competitive firm can sell as large a quantity as it wishes, as long as it accepts the prevailing market price. Thus, the total revenue line slopes up at an angle, with the slope of the line determined by the price. In this example, a flash drive costs $3.50. Sales of one flash drive will bring in $3.50, two units will be $7, three units will be $10.50, and so on.

The total costs for the Overdrive Production Shoppe, broken down into fixed and variable costs, are shown in the table that also appears in Exhibit 10-1. The total cost curve intersects with the vertical axis at a value that shows the level of fixed costs, and then slopes upward. (If it bothers you that these numbers don't seem more realistic, you may wish to imagine that these total cost and quantity figures represent thousands: that is, fixed costs of the plant are $62,000, and the total cost of producing 10,000 flash drives is $90,000. The shape of the total revenue and total cost picture does not change if both quantity and cost are expressed with extra zeros.)

Based on its total revenue and total cost curves, a perfectly competitive firm like the Overdrive Production Shoppe can calculate the quantity of output that will provide the highest level of profit. At any given quantity, total revenue minus total cost will equal profit. On the figure, the vertical gap between total revenue and total cost represents either profit (if total revenues are greater than total costs at a certain quantity) or losses (if total costs are greater than total revenues at a certain quantity). In this example, total costs will exceed total revenues at output levels from 0 to 40, and so over this range of output, the firm will be making losses. At output levels from 50 to 80, total revenues exceed total costs, so the firm is earning profits. But then at an output of 90 or 100, total costs again

Quantity	Total Cost	Fixed Cost	Variable Cost	Total Revenue	Profit
0	$62	$62	—	0	−62
10	$90	$62	$28	$35	−55
20	$110	$62	$48	$70	−40
30	$126	$62	$64	$105	−21
40	$144	$62	$82	$140	−4
50	$166	$62	$104	$175	+9
60	$192	$62	$130	$210	+18
70	$224	$62	$162	$245	+21
80	$264	$62	$202	$280	+16
90	$324	$62	$262	$315	−9
100	$404	$62	$342	$350	−54

Total revenue for a perfectly competitive firm is a straight line sloping up. The slope is determined by the price of the good. Total cost also slopes up, but with some curvature. Total cost intersects the vertical axis at the level determined by fixed costs. At higher levels of output, total cost begins to slope upward more steeply because of diminishing marginal returns. At levels of output where total cost is higher than total revenue, like 10 or 20, the firm would suffer a loss. At levels of output where total revenue is higher than total costs, like 60 or 70, the firm would earn profits. The maximum profit will occur at the quantity where the gap of total revenue over total cost is largest.

exceed total revenues and the firm is making losses. Total profits appear in the final column of the table. The highest total profits in the table occur at an output of 70, when profits will be $21.

A higher price would mean a steeper slope for the total revenue curve, so that total revenue was higher for every quantity sold; a lower price would mean a flatter slope, so that total revenue was lower for every quantity sold. What happens if the price drops low enough that the total revenue line is completely below the total cost curve—that is, at every level of output, total costs are higher than total revenues? Then the best that the firm can do is to suffer losses, but a profit-maximizing firm will still prefer the quantity of output where total revenues come closest to total costs and thus where its losses are smallest.

Comparing Marginal Revenue and Marginal Costs

Firms often do not have the necessary data they would need to draw a complete total cost curve for all different levels of production. They can't be sure of what total costs would look like if they, say, doubled production or cut production in half because they haven't tried it. Instead, firms experiment; that is, they produce a slightly greater or lower quantity and observe how profits are affected. In economic terms, this practical approach to maximizing profits means looking at how changes in production affect marginal revenue and marginal cost.

Exhibit 10-2 presents the marginal revenue and marginal cost curves based on the total revenue and total cost curves in Exhibit 10-1. The **marginal revenue** curve shows the additional revenue gained from selling one more unit. For a perfectly competitive firm, the marginal revenue curve is drawn as a flat line equal to the price level, which in this

marginal revenue: The additional revenue gained from selling one more unit.

Quantity	Total Cost	Fixed Cost	Variable Cost	Marginal Cost	Total Revenue	Marginal Revenue
0	$62	$62		—	—	—
10	$90	$62	$28	$2.80	$35	$3.50
20	$110	$62	$48	$2.00	$70	$3.50
30	$126	$62	$64	$1.60	$105	$3.50
40	$144	$62	$82	$1.80	$140	$3.50
50	$166	$62	$104	$2.20	$175	$3.50
60	$192	$62	$130	$2.60	$210	$3.50
70	$224	$62	$162	$3.20	$245	$3.50
80	$264	$62	$202	$4.00	$280	$3.50
90	$324	$62	$262	$6.00	$315	$3.50
100	$404	$62	$342	$8.00	$350	$3.50

EXHIBIT 10-2 Marginal Revenues and Marginal Costs at the Overdrive Production Shoppe

For a perfectly competitive firm, the marginal revenue (MR) curve is a horizontal straight line because it is equal to the price of the good. Marginal cost (MC) is sometimes first downward-sloping, if there is a region of increasing marginal returns at low levels of output, but is eventually upward-sloping at higher levels of output as diminishing marginal returns kick in. If the firm is producing at a quantity where MR > MC, like 40 or 50, then it can increase profit by increasing output because the marginal revenue is exceeding the marginal cost. If the firm is producing at a quantity where MC > MR, like 90 or 100, then it can increase profit by reducing output because the reductions in marginal cost will exceed the reductions in marginal revenue. The firm's profit-maximizing choice of output will occur where MR = MC (or at a choice close to that point).

example is $3.50 per flash drive. The marginal revenue gained from selling one additional flash drive is just the price of that unit. Because a perfectly competitive firm is a price taker, it can sell whatever quantity it wishes at the market-determined price. Marginal cost, the cost per additional unit sold, is calculated by dividing the change in total cost by the change in quantity. In this example, marginal cost at first declines as production increases from 10 to 20, which represents the area of increasing marginal returns that is not uncommon at low levels of production. But then marginal costs start to increase, displaying the typical pattern of diminishing marginal returns.

In this example, the marginal revenue and marginal cost curves cross at a price of $3.50 and a quantity between 70 and 80 produced. If the firm started out producing at a level of 60, and then experimented with increasing production to 70, marginal revenues from the increase in production would exceed marginal costs—and so profits would rise. However, if the firm then experimented further with increasing production from 70 to 80, it would find that marginal costs from the increase in production are greater than marginal revenues, and so profits would decline.

The profit-maximizing choice for a perfectly competitive firm will occur at the point where marginal revenue is equal to marginal cost—that is, where MR = MC. A profit-seeking firm should keep expanding production as long as MR > MC because when revenue is rising faster that costs, profits increase, too. But at the level of output where MR = MC, the firm should recognize that it has achieved the highest possible level of profits and that expanding production into the zone where MR < MC will only reduce profits. Because the marginal revenue received by a perfectly competitive firm is equal to the price P, so that P = MR, the profit-maximizing rule for a perfectly competitive firm can also be written as a recommendation to produce at the quantity where P = MC. (If the firm's choices for quantity of output don't include a choice where MR is exactly equal to MC, then the highest output level where MR > MC will be the profit-maximizing choice.)

Marginal Cost and the Firm's Supply Curve

For a perfectly competitive firm, the marginal cost curve is identical to the firm's supply curve. To understand why this perhaps surprising insight holds true, first think about what the supply curve means. A firm checks the market price and then looks at its supply curve to decide what quantity to produce. Now think about what it means to say that a firm will maximize its profits by producing at the quantity where P = MC. This rule means that the firm checks the market price and then looks at its marginal cost curve to determine the quantity to produce. In other words, the marginal cost curve and the firm's supply curve contain the same information—that is, they both tell the firm what quantity to produce, given the market price.

As discussed back in Chapter 4, many of the reasons that supply curves shift relate to underlying changes in costs. For example, a lower price of key inputs or new technologies that reduce production costs cause supply to shift to the right; in contrast, lousy weather or added government regulations can add to costs of certain goods in a way that causes supply to shift to the left. These shifts in the firm's supply curve can also be interpreted as shifts of the marginal cost curve. A shift in costs of production that increases marginal costs at all levels of output—and shifts MC to the left—will cause a perfectly competitive firm to produce less at any given market price. Conversely, a shift in costs of production that decreases marginal costs at all levels of output will shift MC to the right, and as a result, a competitive firm will choose to expand its level of output at any given price.

Profits and Losses with the Average Cost Curve

If the price that a firm charges is higher than its average cost of production for that quantity produced, then the firm will earn profits. Conversely, if the price that a firm charges is lower than its average cost of production, the firm will suffer losses. Exhibit 10-3 illustrates three situations: (a) where price intersects marginal cost at a level above the average cost curve, (b) where price intersects marginal cost at a level equal to the average cost curve, and (c) where price intersects marginal cost at a level below the average cost curve.

First consider a situation where the price is equal to $4 for a flash drive. The rule for a profit-maximizing perfectly competitive firm is to produce the level of output where P = MR = MC, so the Overdrive Production Shoppe will produce a quantity of 80, which is labeled as q in Exhibit 10-3a. The firm's total revenue at this price will be shown by the large shaded rectangle, which represents a price of $4 per flash drive and a quantity of 80. Total costs will be the quantity of 80 times the average cost of $3.30, which is shown by the lightly shaded rectangle. Thus, profits will be the darker shaded rectangle that represents the large rectangle of total revenues minus the rectangle of total costs. It would be calculated as:

$$\text{Profit} = \text{Total revenue} - \text{Total cost}$$
$$\$56 = (80)(\$4.00) - (80)(\$3.30)$$

(a) Price intersects marginal cost above the average cost curve.

At a price of $4, price is at a level where producing at the quantity where P = MC leads to a price that is above average cost. In this case, the firm is earning a profit. Total revenue is the quantity of 80 times the price of $4, or $320, shown by the overall shaded box. Total cost is the quantity of 80 times an average cost of $3.30, or $264, shown by the bottom shaded box. The leftover rectangle where total revenue exceeds total cost is the profit earned.

(b) Price intersects marginal cost on the average cost curve.

At a price of $3.20, the price is now at a level where producing at the quantity where P = MC leads to a price that is equal to the average cost. Total revenue is now a quantity of 70 times a price of $3.20. Total cost is the same: a quantity of 70 times an average cost of $3.20. Zero profit is being earned in this situation.

(c) Price intersects marginal cost below the average cost curve.

At a price of $2.20, when the firm produces at a quantity where P = MC, the price is below average cost. Here, the firm is suffering losses. Total costs are the large rectangle with a quantity of 50 and a price of $3.32, for total costs of $166. Total revenues are a quantity of 50 and a price of $2.20, or $110, shown by the smaller shaded box. The leftover rectangle on top thus shows the losses; that is, the amount that total cost exceeds total revenue.

Quantity	Total Cost	Fixed Cost	Variable Cost	Marginal Cost	Average Cost
0	$62	$62	—	—	—
10	$90	$62	$28	$2.80	$9.00
20	$110	$62	$48	$2.00	$5.50
30	$126	$62	$64	$1.60	$4.20
40	$144	$62	$82	$1.80	$3.60
50	$166	$62	$104	$2.20	$3.32
60	$192	$62	$130	$2.60	$3.20
70	$224	$62	$162	$3.20	$3.20
80	$264	$62	$202	$4.00	$3.30
90	$324	$62	$262	$6.00	$3.60
100	$404	$62	$342	$8.00	$4.04

EXHIBIT 10-3 Price and Average Cost at the Overdrive Production Shoppe

Now consider Exhibit 10-3b, where the price has fallen to $3.20 for a flash drive. Again, the perfectly competitive firm will choose the level of output where P = MR = MC, but in this case, the quantity will be 70. At this price and output level, where the marginal cost curve is crossing the average cost curve, the price received by the firm is exactly equal to its average cost of production. Thus, the total revenue of the firm is exactly equal to the total costs of the firm, so that the firm is making zero profit.

In Exhibit 10-3c, the market price has fallen still further to $2.20 for a flash drive. Again, the perfectly competitive firm will choose the level of output where P = MR = MC, and in this case the firm will choose to produce a quantity of 50. At this price and output level, the price level received by the firm is below the average cost of production. The total costs for the firm will be $166 (i.e., the average cost of $3.32 multiplied by a quantity of 50), which appear as the large rectangle. Total revenue will be $110 (price of $2.20 multiplied by a quantity of 50), which is the smaller shaded rectangle. The firm's losses of $56 are shown by the darker rectangle created by subtracting the total revenue rectangle from the total cost rectangle.

If the market price received by a perfectly competitive firm leads it to produce at a quantity where the price is greater than average cost, the firm will earn profits. If the price received by the firm causes it to produce at a quantity where price equals marginal cost, at the point where the MC curve crosses the AC curve, then the firm earns zero profits. Finally, if the price received by the firm leads it to produce at a quantity where the price is less than average cost, the firm will make losses.

The Shutdown Point

The possibility that a firm may suffer losses raises a question: Why can't the firm avoid losses by shutting down and not producing at all? The answer is that shutting down can reduce variable costs to zero, but in the short run, shutting down does not reduce fixed costs. As a result, if the firm produces a quantity of zero, it would still make losses because it would still need to pay its fixed costs. Thus, when a firm is facing the possibility of losses, it must face a question: will its losses increase or decrease if it shuts down?

As an example of this decision, consider the situation of the Yoga Center, which has signed a contract to rent space that costs $10,000 per month. If the firm continues to operate, its marginal costs for hiring yoga teachers is $15,000 for the month. If the firm shuts down, it must still pay the rent, but it would not need to hire labor. Exhibit 10-4 shows three possible scenarios. In the first scenario, the Yoga Center shuts down, in which case it faces losses of $10,000. In the second scenario, the Yoga Center remains open, earns revenues of $10,000 for the month, and experiences losses of $15,000. In the third scenario, the Yoga Center remains open and earns revenues of $20,000 for the month and experiences losses of $5,000. In all three cases, the Yoga Center loses money. In all three cases, when the rental contract expires in the long run, the store should exit this business. But in the short run, in scenario 2, the store's losses increase because it remains open, so the store should shut down immediately. In contrast, in scenario 3, the revenue that the firm can earn is high enough that the store's losses diminish when it remains open, so the store should remain open in the short run.

EXHIBIT 10-4 Should the Yoga Center Shut Down Now or Later?

Scenario 1
The firm shuts down now, so revenues are zero, but the firm must pay fixed costs of $10,000.

$$\text{Total revenue} - (\text{fixed cost} + \text{variable cost}) = \text{profit}$$
$$0 - 10{,}000 = -10{,}000$$

Scenario 2
The firm keeps operating; variable costs are $15,000 and revenues are $10,000.

$$\text{Total revenue} - (\text{fixed cost} + \text{variable cost}) = \text{profit}$$
$$10{,}000 - (10{,}000 + 15{,}000) = -15{,}000$$

Conclusion: The firm should shut down now.

Scenario 3
The firm keeps operating; variable costs are $15,000 and revenues are $20,000.

$$\text{Total revenue} - (\text{fixed cost} + \text{variable cost}) = \text{profit}$$
$$20{,}000 - (10{,}000 + 15{,}000) = -5{,}000$$

Conclusion: The firm should shut down later.

This example suggests that the key factor for a firm deciding whether to shut down is whether the firm can at least cover its variable costs by remaining open. Exhibit 10-5 illustrates this lesson for the example of the Overdrive Production Shoppe, by adding the average variable cost curve to the marginal cost and average cost curves. At a price of $2.20 per flash drive, shown in Exhibit 10-5a, the firm produces at a level of 50. It is making losses of $56 (as explained earlier), but price is above average variable cost, and so the firm continues to operate. However, if the price declined to $1.80 per flash drive, as shown in Exhibit 10-5b, and if the firm applied its rule of producing where P = MR = MC, it would produce a quantity of 40. This price is below average variable cost for this level of output. At this price and output, total revenues would be $72 (quantity of 40 times price of $1.80) and total cost would be $144, for overall losses of $72. If the firm shuts down, it must only pay its fixed costs of $62, so shutting down is preferable to selling at a price of $1.80 per flash drive.

shutdown point: When the revenue a firm receives does not cover its average variable costs, the firm should shut down immediately; the point where the marginal cost curve crosses the average variable cost curve.

The intersection of the average variable cost curve and the marginal cost curve, which shows the price where the firm lacks enough revenue to cover its variable costs, is called the **shutdown point**. If the perfectly competitive firm can charge a price above the shut-

(a) Price is above the shutdown point.

Firm should not shut down because price is above shutdown point. The price is $2.20. Producing at the quantity where P = MC leads to a situation where price is below average cost but above average variable cost. Thus, the firm is suffering losses, but because it is covering its variable costs, it will continue to operate.

(b) Price is below the shutdown point.

Firm should shut down because price is below shutdown point. Price is $1.80, which leads to a quantity of output where price is less than average variable cost. Because the firm is now not even covering its variable costs, it should shut down immediately.

Quantity	Total Cost	Fixed Cost	Variable Cost	Marginal Cost	Average Cost	Average Variable Cost
0	$62	$62	—	—	—	—
10	$90	$62	$28	$2.80	$9.00	$2.80
20	$110	$62	$48	$2.00	$5.50	$2.40
30	$126	$62	$64	$1.60	$4.20	$2.13
40	$144	$62	$82	$1.80	$3.60	$2.05
50	$166	$62	$104	$2.20	$3.32	$2.08
60	$192	$62	$130	$2.60	$3.20	$2.16
70	$224	$62	$162	$3.20	$3.20	$2.31
80	$264	$62	$202	$4.00	$3.30	$2.52
90	$324	$62	$262	$6.00	$3.60	$2.91
100	$404	$62	$342	$8.00	$4.04	$3.42

EXHIBIT 10-5 The Shutdown Point for the Overdrive Production Shoppe

down point, then the firm is at least covering its average variable costs, and it should limp ahead even if it is making losses in the short run, since at least those losses will be smaller than if the firm shuts down immediately. However, if the firm is receiving a price below the price at the shutdown point, then the firm is not even covering its variable costs. In this case, staying open is making the firm's losses larger, and it should shut down immediately.

Short-Run Outcomes for Perfectly Competitive Firms

The average cost and average variable cost curves divide the marginal cost curve into three segments, as shown in Exhibit 10-6. At the market price, which the perfectly competitive firm accepts as given, the profit-maximizing firm chooses the output level where price or marginal revenue, which are the same thing for a perfectly competitive firm, is equal to marginal cost: P = MR = MC.

First consider the upper zone, where prices are above the level where marginal cost MC crosses AC at the zero-profit point. At any price above that level, the firm will earn profits in the short run. If the price falls exactly on the zero-profit point where the MC and AC curves cross, then the firm earns zero profits. Next consider a price that falls into the zone between the zero-profit point where MC crosses AC and the shutdown point where MC crosses AVC. In this case, the firm will be making losses in the short run—but since the firm is more than covering its variable costs, the losses are smaller than if the firm shut down immediately. Finally, consider a price below the shutdown point where MC crosses AVC. At any price like this one, the firm will shut down immediately because it cannot even cover its variable costs by operating.

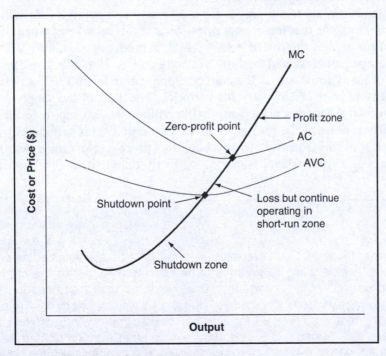

EXHIBIT 10-6 Profit, Loss, Shutdown

The marginal cost curve can be divided into three zones, based on where it is crossed by the average cost and average variable cost curves. The point where MC crosses AC is called the zero-profit point. If the market price is at a level higher than the price at the zero-profit point, then price will be above the average cost curve and the firm is earning profits. If the price is exactly at the zero-profit point, then the firm is making zero profits. If the price is below the price at the zero-profit point, then price will fall below the average cost curve and the firm will be making losses. If price falls in the zone between the shutdown point and the zero-profit point, then the firm is making losses but will continue to operate in the short run, since it is covering its variable costs. However, if price falls below the price at the shutdown point, then the firm will shut down immediately, since it is not even covering its variable costs.

Entry and Exit in the Long-Run Output

The line between the short run and the long run can't be defined precisely with a stopwatch or even with a calendar. It varies according to the specific business. But in the long run, the firm can adjust all factors of production.

In a competitive market, profits are a bugle call that incites businesses to charge. If a business is making a profit in the short run, it has an incentive to expand existing production facilities or to open new ones. New firms may start production, as well. **Entry** is the long-run process of expanding production in response to a sustained pattern of profit opportunities.

Losses are the black thunderclouds that cause businesses to flee. If a business is making losses in the short run, it will either keep limping along or just shut down, depending on whether its revenues are covering its variable costs. But in the long run, firms that are facing losses will shut down at least some of their output, and some firms will cease production altogether. **Exit** is the long-run process of reducing production in response to a sustained pattern of losses.

entry: The long-run process of firms beginning and expanding production when they see opportunity for profits.

exit: The long-run process of firms reducing production and shutting down because they expect losses.

How Entry and Exit Lead to Zero Profits

No perfectly competitive firm acting alone can affect the market price. However, the combination of many firms entering or exiting the market will affect overall supply in the market. In turn, a shift in supply for the market as a whole will affect the market price. Entry and exit are the driving forces behind a process that, in the long run, pushes the price in a perfectly competitive market to be at the zero-profit point, where the marginal cost curve crosses the average cost curve.

To understand how short-run profits for a perfectly competitive firm will evaporate in the long run, imagine that the market price starts at a level where, when the perfectly competitive firm applies the rule $P = MR = MC$, it produces a quantity where price is above the average cost curve and the firm is earning profits. However, these profits attract entry. Entry of many firms causes the market supply curve to shift to the right, so that a greater quantity is produced at every market price. The shift of the supply curve to the right pushes down the market price. Entry will continue to shift supply to the right until the price is driven down to the zero-profit level, where no firm is earning profits.

Short-run losses will fade away by reversing this process. Now imagine that the market price starts at a level where, when the perfectly competitive firm applies the rule

---

Business Failure

In the model of perfectly competitive firms, those that consistently can't make money will "exit," which is a nice bloodless word for a more painful process. When a business fails, after all, workers lose their jobs, investors lose their money, and owners and managers can lose their dreams, too. Many businesses fail. During the rough economic time period from 2009–2010, for example, 650,000 firms were born in the United States, but 720,000 firms died. About 80% of these business births and deaths involved small firms with fewer than 20 employees.

Sometimes a business fails because of poor management or workers, or because of tough domestic or foreign competition. Businesses also fail from a variety of causes that might best be summarized as bad luck. Conditions of demand and supply in the market shift in an unexpected way, so that the prices that can be charged for outputs fall or the prices that need to be paid for inputs rise. With millions of businesses in the U.S. economy, even a small fraction of them failing will affect many people—and business failures can be very hard on the workers and managers directly involved. But from the standpoint of the overall economic system, business deaths are sometimes a necessary evil if a market-oriented system is going to offer a flexible mechanism for satisfying customers, keeping costs low, and inventing new products.

P = MR = MC, it produces a quantity where price is below the average cost curve and the firm is experiencing losses. These losses lead some firms to exit. The process of exit by a number of firms causes the market supply curve to shift to the left, so that a lesser quantity is produced at every market price, and the market price rises. The process of exit will continue as long as firms are making losses, until the price rises to the zero-profit level, where firms are no longer suffering losses.

Thus, while a perfectly competitive firm can earn profits in the short run, in the long run, the process of entry will push down prices until they reach the zero-profit level. Conversely, while a perfectly competitive firm may suffer losses in the short run, firms will not continually lose money. In the long run, firms making losses are able to escape from their fixed costs, and their exit from the market will push the price back up to the zero-profit level. In the long run, this process of entry and exit will drive the price in perfectly competitive markets to the zero-profit point at the bottom of the AC curve, where marginal cost crosses average cost.

Economic Profit vs. Accounting Profit

This talk of "zero profit" in the long run must worry anyone who is thinking about starting a business—or making a financial investment in one. But the conclusion that perfectly competitive firms end up with zero profits in the long run is less dire than it may sound, because profit means something different to economists than it does to businesses. The difference arises because economists insist on considering all the opportunity costs of production, including both explicit and implicit costs.

To understand the difference between the economic view of profit and the business or accounting view of profit, think about a business where the owner plunks down $1 million to pay for fixed costs, and at the end of a year, after total revenues and total costs are tallied, the owner has a business that is still worth $1 million and in the meantime has earned a return of $50,000, or 5% of the original investment. How large a profit has the owner earned? To a business owner and the accountant, the answer is clear: the profit is the 5% or $50,000 that was earned. To put it another way, the **accounting profit** is total revenues minus the firm's expenditures on explicit costs.

accounting profit: Total revenues minus the firm's costs, without taking opportunity cost into account.

To an economist, the question is more difficult because the economist wants to take all opportunity costs, including both explicit and implicit costs, into account. Say that the business owner could have invested the money in another business, run by someone else, and it would have paid an 8% return. From the economic point of view, this implicit cost of how the financial capital could have been invested must be included as one of the firm's costs. Thus, **economic profit** is measured by total revenues minus all of the firm's opportunity costs, including both explicit expenditures and implicit costs of financial capital. From this perspective, the business owner has not experienced a gain of 5% for the year, but a loss of 3% (i.e., 5% accounting profit minus 8% in implicit costs).

economic profit: Total revenues minus all of the firm's costs, including opportunity costs.

For the economy as a whole, financial investors earn an average or "normal" level of profit. That normal level of profit determines the opportunity cost of financial investments. Thus, an economist who says that perfectly competitive firms will earn "zero profit" in the long run really means "zero profit after all opportunity costs, including implicit costs, have been taken into account," or to put it differently, that the firm will earn a normal level of profit. When an economist says that a firm will earn positive profits, the economist really means that the profits will be above the normal level. Conversely, losses to an economist include both returns that are negative in an accounting sense and also returns that are slightly positive in an accounting sense, but that do not cover the implicit cost of financial capital.

Although perfectly competitive firms will earn zero economic profits—or a normal rate of profit—in the long run, it's important to remember that not all industries are perfectly competitive, and the long run, by definition, takes some time to arrive. In the real world, businesses will often earn economic profits or losses in the short run.

The Economic Function of Profits

In popular discussions, the term "profit" is sometimes pronounced as if the speaker has been sucking on a lemon. But profits are not a dirty word, any more than "high prices" or "low prices" are dirty words. Profits have an economic rationale, which is built upon the incentives that they provide for entry and exit.

High profits are a messenger. They transmit the message that the willingness of people to pay for that good is higher than the average cost of production, and so society as a whole will benefit if more resources are allocated to production of that certain good or service. Losses are a messenger, too. They carry the message that fewer resources should be allocated to production of a certain good or service because the benefits people are receiving from that production—as measured by their willingness to pay for it—is below the cost of the resources used in the production process.

Profits also serve as a messenger to businesses to seek out the most cost-effective methods of production. As profits lead to entry or losses lead to exit, perfectly competitive firms are pressured to seek out the minimum point of the average cost curve, which is the point where economic profits are zero and also the point where output is being produced at the lowest possible average cost.

Factors of Production in Perfectly Competitive Markets

A firm in a perfectly competitive market must accept the market price for its output and must also pay the prevailing market price for its inputs like labor and physical capital. However, a perfectly competitive firm can decide what quantity of those inputs to use. The earlier discussion of how perfectly competitive firms make decisions about the quantity of output to produce was built on a distinction between short-run decisions, where certain input costs like physical capital investment were fixed, and long-run decisions, where all inputs to production could vary. In the same spirit, let's first consider how a perfectly competitive firm will determine the quantity that it uses of a variable input like labor in the short run, and then how it will determine its quantity of physical capital and its overall method of production in the long run.

The Derived Demand for Labor

When a profit-maximizing firm considers how much labor to hire in the short run, it may first calculate the profit-maximizing quantity of output, and then figure out the quantity of labor needed to produce that quantity of output. For this reason, the demand for labor (and other inputs) is sometimes called a "derived demand"; that is, the demand for labor is derived from the firm's decision about how much to produce.

For an example of how this decision process operates in the short run, consider the Cheep-Cheep Company in Exhibit 10-7, a firm in a perfectly competitive industry that

EXHIBIT 10-7 The Derived Demand for Labor: The Cheep-Cheep Birdhouse Company

Labor	Output	Fixed Cost	Variable Cost	Total Cost	Marginal Cost
0	0	$7,000	$0	$7,000	—
1	12	$7,000	$100	$7,100	$8.33
2	28	$7,000	$200	$7,200	$6.25
3	48	$7,000	$300	$7,300	$5.00
4	68	$7,000	$400	$7,400	$5.00
5	85	$7,000	$500	$7,500	$5.88
6	96	$7,000	$600	$7,600	$9.09
7	105	$7,000	$700	$7,700	$11.11

hires workers to assemble birdhouses. Assume that the cost of hiring a worker is $100 per day and that fixed costs of the birdhouse workshop are $7,000. The quantity of output for a profit-seeking perfectly competitive firm will be determined by applying the rule that production increases up to the point where P = MC. Thus, if the price for a birdhouse is $6, then the profit-maximizing level of output (from the choices in the table) is 85, and the derived demand for labor to produce that desired level of output is five workers. If a surge in demand for birdhouses drives the market price up to $10, then the optimal level of output would become 96, and the derived demand for labor rises to six workers.

Thus, one way to determine what quantity of a variable input to hire is first to determine the profit-maximizing quantity to produce, and then to work backwards and determine what quantity of the input is needed.

The Marginal Revenue Product of Labor

Instead of calculating the amount of labor to hire based on the profit-maximizing quantity, an alternative but equivalent approach is to compare the cost of hiring a worker to the value of what a worker produces.

The cost of hiring a worker is straightforward: it is the wage or compensation paid to the worker. To calculate the value of what a worker produces, find the quantity of production attributable to the marginal worker and multiply it by the price of that output. Exhibit 10-8 takes a different look at the basic cost information from Exhibit 10-7, focusing on the output of workers at the Cheep-Cheep Birdhouse Company. The first column repeats information from Exhibit 10-7, showing different numbers of workers and what they produce. The third column of the figure shows **marginal physical product**, which is the quantity of goods produced by the marginal worker. The fourth column shows the **marginal revenue product (MRP)**, which reveals how much revenue a firm could receive from hiring an additional worker and selling the output of that worker. The MRP is calculated by multiplying the marginal physical product by the market price of $6. A second calculation of marginal revenue product, this one based on a market price for birdhouses of $10, appears in the final column. The two different marginal revenue products, one based on a price for birdhouses of $6 and one based on a price of $10, are also shown in Exhibit 10-8. The marginal revenue product of hiring additional workers gradually declines because of diminishing marginal returns.

When a profit-seeking, price-taking, perfectly competitive firm is thinking about the quantity of labor to hire, it will compare the input price with the marginal revenue product for that input. For example, say that the cost for Cheep Cheep of hiring a birdhouse maker is $100. At a market price of $6, Cheep Cheep will notice that hiring a third worker and a fourth worker will have a marginal revenue product of $120, but only cost $100. So it will clearly make sense to hire these workers. In fact, it makes sense to hire the fifth worker as well, since the marginal revenue product of that worker is $102 and thus still exceeds the wage. But at a market price for birdhouses of $6, it won't make sense to hire the sixth or seventh worker, because the marginal revenue product of hiring those workers will be less than $100.

A higher market price for the output of birdhouses will encourage more hiring. If the market price for birdhouses increased to $10, then Cheep Cheep will wish to hire a sixth worker, with a marginal revenue product of $110, but not a seventh worker, since the marginal revenue product of that final worker would only be $90. The optimal quantity of labor to hire will be where the price of the input is equal to the marginal revenue product of that input.

The concept of the marginal revenue product of labor hired explains why the demand curve for labor slopes down. When the wage is lower, more workers will have a marginal revenue product above that wage, so that firms will be willing to hire them. Conversely, when the wage is higher, fewer workers will have a marginal revenue product above that wage, so firms will demand a lower quantity of workers.

The derived demand approach and the marginal revenue product approach to figuring out the quantity of labor to hire are just two different ways of using the same basic

marginal physical product: The quantity of goods produced by an additional input (like an additional worker).

marginal revenue product (MRP): Reveals how much revenue a firm could receive from hiring an additional worker and selling the output of that worker.

Labor	Output	Marginal Physical Product	Marginal Revenue Product (price $6)	Marginal Revenue Product (price $10)
0	0	—	—	—
1	12	12	$72	$120
2	28	16	$96	$160
3	48	20	$120	$200
4	68	20	$120	$200
5	85	17	$102	$170
6	96	11	$66	$110
7	105	9	$54	$90

EXHIBIT 10-8 Marginal Revenue Product: The Cheep-Cheep Example Continues

The wage is shown as a horizontal line, with a cost of $100 for hiring a worker, because it does not vary according to how many workers the firm hires. Marginal revenue product first slopes up because of the increasing marginal returns at low levels of output in this example, and then slopes down because of diminishing marginal returns at higher levels of output. If a worker brings in more than enough marginal revenue to cover the wage of that worker, it will make sense to hire the worker. If the price of the birdhouse is $6, then the firm will hire five workers because the marginal revenue product of the fifth worker is $102. If the price rises to $10 per birdhouse, then the value of what workers produce increases, and the firm will hire six workers. Finally, if the wage rises—in the diagram, imagine the horizontal line at a higher level—the firm will hire fewer workers because fewer workers will have a high enough marginal revenue product to justify paying the higher wage.

information on production functions, input costs, and output prices. The two approaches should always obtain the same answer; in fact, the two methods can be used to check on each other.

Are Workers Paid as Much as They Deserve?

Many workers strongly suspect that they are not being paid as much as they deserve. Is this complaint nothing more than self-interested people who desire some additional income? Or is there reason to believe that in a competitive labor market, workers are systematically paid too little? The argument here suggests that workers are paid what they deserve in the specific sense that they are paid according to their marginal revenue product—that is, according to the value of what the marginal worker produces.

In the real economy, calculating the marginal revenue product may be nearly impossible for many workers. Imagine a company making refrigerators where workers perform many jobs: some work on the assembly line, some maintain and repair equipment, some do paperwork for paying workers and suppliers, some plan future investment in physical capital, some do sales and marketing, and some work on the shipping dock. How could any accountant disentangle exactly what each of these very different workers contributes to making a refrigerator?

However, even when firms cannot calculate marginal revenue product directly, the pressures of competition in the labor market will push pay toward the marginal revenue product of labor. After all, if a foolish employer consistently paid its workers more than the marginal revenue product of what the workers produced, then that employer would make losses, and such pay could not be sustained. On the other hand, if an employer tried to pay workers less than what they produce as measured by their marginal revenue product, then other employers will see an opportunity to hire away some of the marginal workers by offering them a modest increase over their current pay. With these competitive pressures in the labor market, wages are pushed in the direction of marginal revenue product. Of course, just as a market price is not always exactly at equilibrium, but only tending toward equilibrium, it will also be true that wages are not always exactly at the marginal revenue product, although they tend toward that level. Studies of labor markets within countries over time, and between countries, show that differences in how much workers are paid are clearly linked to the market value of what workers produce.

If workers find it difficult or costly to switch between employers, and firms know that workers may be unable or unwilling to move to other jobs, then employers will be able to pay those workers somewhat less than their marginal revenue product. For example, a worker in a rural area may have relatively few employment options that do not involve high monetary and emotional costs of moving. A recent immigrant may lack the information and the social network that would provide information and connections to other jobs. A society with widespread discrimination on the basis of race or gender may block people in certain groups from taking certain jobs. In any of these cases, employers may be able to pay certain workers less than the marginal revenue product of their labor.

Physical Capital Investment and the Hurdle Rate

In the long term, a perfectly competitive firm can adjust all of its inputs, including its investments in physical capital like buildings and machinery. Such investments in physical capital, by their nature, involve thinking about a rate of return over time; that is, the firm purchases the inputs of physical capital in the present and then uses them for production over a period of time in the future.

Consider a firm making plans for investments in physical capital. Managers from all over the company submit proposals. Each proposal includes either an estimate of the marginal revenue product of this capital investment—that is, how much additional revenue will this investment generate, or alternatively, by how much will this investment reduce the costs of the current level of output. Higher-level managers collect these proposals and check them over, estimating the rate of return that can be realistically expected from each proposal. The rates of return for a hypothetical list of 25 projects, ranked from top to bottom, are illustrated by the bar graph in Exhibit 10-9. In deciding which project to carry out, the profit-seeking firm will obviously prefer projects with high rates of return rather than projects with low rates of return (as long as the risk of the projects is similar). But to determine how many investment projects the firm should undertake, the managers of the firm must compare the rates of return to the cost of financial capital.

EXHIBIT 10-9 Considering Investment Projects

When a firm makes plans for investments in physical capital, it compares the projected rates of return on these investments with the cost of financial capital to the firm. Often, this comparison will use a hurdle rate as the rate of return that must be exceeded to make the project worth undertaking. In this example, projects A to S do not exceed the hurdle rate. A lower cost of capital will result in more investment projects being undertaken (imagine the horizontal hurdle rate line moving down, so that more projects cross the hurdle). Conversely, a higher cost of financial capital will result in fewer physical capital investment projects being undertaken.

Financial capital always comes at a cost. Sometimes, the firm must pay this cost directly; for example, the firm may borrow financial capital from a bank and thus need to pay an interest rate. However, even if the firm can use funds that it has earned from past profits, spending this money on an investment in physical capital still has an opportunity cost. After all, the firm's financial capital could have been invested in some other way that would have paid a rate of return. Thus, the cost of financial capital to the firm can be conceived of either as a rate of return or interest rate paid to others, or as an opportunity cost of a rate of return that was not received. The specific ways in which firms can raise money for investment—including reinvesting the profits that they earn or using bank loans, bonds, and stocks—will be discussed in Chapter 19.

Firms must also remember that any physical capital investment has some degree of risk. The business world is full of horror stories of factories that were constructed months or years late and cost much more than expected. In other cases, the costs may be estimated accurately, but the returns turn out to be lower than expected. When a company drills for oil, or decides to make a major investment in upgrading its computer systems, it can't be certain of the results in advance.

Firms often take risk into account by using a "hurdle rate," which is an interest rate that is somewhat higher than the actual cost of financial capital to the firm. The intuitive meaning of the hurdle rate is the rate of return that proposed investment projects must cross before being approved. Estimates of typical hurdle rates, based on studies of the investment decisions that firms make, are often about 5–8 percentage points higher than the actual cost of financial capital, whether it is measured as the borrowing interest rate or the opportunity cost of capital. This higher hurdle interest rate can be thought of as a risk premium; that is, it's an adjustment for the risks involved, and it gives the firm a margin for errors of bad luck and overly optimistic forecasts.

If a firm chooses a 15% hurdle rate for its physical capital investment, then such projects must pay an expected return of at least 15% to be worthwhile. A 15% rate of return is represented by the dashed line across Exhibit 10-9. If the cost of financial capital for the firm is higher, then fewer investment projects will make economic sense. Conversely, if the cost of financial capital declines, then a larger number of investment projects will make sense. This logic explains why the demand for financial capital is a downward-sloping curve; the downward slope means that a higher interest rate leads to a lower demand for financial capital because fewer physical capital investments will have expected rates of return that exceed the hurdle rate.

Physical Capital Investment and Long-Run Average Cost

In a perfectly competitive market, firms seek out the combination of variable inputs like labor and fixed inputs like physical capital investment that will allow them to produce at the minimum of the long-run average cost curve. If a firm does not produce at the lowest possible average cost, then firms with a lower cost of production will be able to sell at a lower price. Thus, the pressure of competition between firms will shape both the specific kinds of machinery and equipment and the overall quantity of investment in physical capital.

Efficiency in Perfectly Competitive Markets

When profit-maximizing firms in perfectly competitive markets combine with utility-maximizing consumers, something remarkable happens: the resulting quantities of outputs of goods and services demonstrate both productive and allocative efficiency (terms that were first introduced back in Chapter 2).

Productive efficiency means producing without waste, so that the choice is on the production possibility frontier. In the long run in a perfectly competitive market, because of the process of entry and exit, the price in the market is equal to the minimum of the long-run average cost curve. In other words, goods are being produced and sold at the lowest possible average cost. When the average cost of production is as low as possible, the economy will be operating on the production possibility frontier.

Allocative efficiency means that among the points on the production possibility frontier, the point that is chosen is socially preferred—at least in a particular and specific sense. In a perfectly competitive market, price will be equal to the marginal cost of production. Think about the price that is paid for a good as a measure of the social benefit received for that good; after all, the willingness to pay conveys what the good was worth to a buyer. Then think about the marginal cost of producing the good as representing not just the cost for the firm, but more broadly as the social cost of producing that good. When perfectly competitive firms follow the rule that profits are maximized by producing at the quantity where price is equal to marginal cost, they are thus ensuring that the social benefits received from producing a good, as reflected in the demand curve for a good, are in line with the social costs of production, as reflected in the supply curve for a good.

To explore what is meant by allocative efficiency, it is useful to walk through an example of what allocative *inefficiency* would imply. Begin by assuming that the market for ordinary television sets is perfectly competitive, and so P = MC. Now consider what it would mean if firms produced a lesser quantity of television sets. At a lesser quantity, marginal costs will not yet have increased as much, so that price will exceed marginal cost; that is, P > MC. In that situation, the benefit to society as a whole of producing additional goods, as measured by the willingness of consumers to pay for marginal units of a good, would be higher than the cost of the inputs of labor and physical capital needed to produce the marginal good. In other words, the gains to society as a whole from producing additional marginal units will be greater than the costs. Conversely, consider what it would mean if, compared to the level of output at the allocatively efficient choice when P = MC, firms produced a greater quantity of television sets. At a greater quantity, marginal costs of production will have increased so that P < MC. In that case, the marginal costs of producing additional television sets are greater than the benefit to society as measured by what people are willing to pay. For society as a whole, since the costs are outstripping the benefits, it will make sense to produce a lower quantity of such goods.

When perfectly competitive firms maximize their profits by producing the quantity where P = MC, they also assure that the benefits to consumers of what they are buying, as measured by the price they are willing to pay, is equal to the costs to society of producing the marginal units, as measured by the marginal costs the firm must pay—and thus that allocative efficiency holds.

The statements that a perfectly competitive market in the long run will feature both productive and allocative efficiency do need to be taken with a few grains of salt. Remember, economists are using the concept of "efficiency" in a particular and specific sense, not as a synonym for "desirable in every way." Perfect competition in the long run is a hypothetical extreme. In other competitive situations discussed in the next two chapters, like monopoly, monopolistic competition, and oligopoly, firms will not always produce at the minimum of average cost, nor will they always set price equal to marginal cost. Thus, these other competitive situations will not lead to productive and allocative efficiency. Moreover, real-world markets include many issues that are assumed away in the model of perfect competition, including pollution, inventions of new technology, poverty that may make some people unable to pay for basic necessities of life, government programs like national defense or education, discrimination in labor markets, and buyers and sellers who must deal with imperfect and unclear information. These issues are explored in later chapters of this book. However, the theoretical efficiency of perfect competition does provide a useful benchmark for comparing what issues arise from these real-world problems.

Conclusion

Extreme assumptions often provide a useful starting point for analysis. In a physics class, it may be useful to analyze gravity by assuming that a ball that is dropped from a great height experiences zero friction as it falls through the air. This assumption of zero friction is not literally true. But if the amount of friction from the air is relatively small compared to the pull of gravity, then assuming zero friction may not make much difference to the results. If friction is significant, then calculations for the effects of friction can be added, once the basic no-friction example is understood.

The assumption of perfect competition—that firms are perfect price takers, unable to raise their price by so much as a penny without losing all of their sales—is not literally true. But in a market with many competitors that have highly similar products, the assumption of perfect competition may provide a reasonable start for the analysis. In a highly competitive market—even if it is not strictly speaking perfectly competitive—firms will not lose all of their sales if they raise prices by a penny, but they might lose a large enough proportion of their sales to cripple the firm if they raise prices by 5%. In a highly competitive real-world market, not all firms will be producing at the absolute bottom of the average cost curve at all times—but the firms will still face considerable pressure to keep average costs as low as possible. Firms in a highly competitive market may earn profits in the short run, but the entry of new firms or the expansion of existing firms means that such profits will not persist in the long run. Truly perfect competition is a hypothetical extreme, but many real-world producers face highly competitive markets every day.

Key Concepts and Summary

1. A **perfectly competitive** firm is a price taker, which means that it must accept the prices at which its sell goods and the prices at which it purchases inputs as determined in the market. If a perfectly competitive firm attempts to charge even a tiny amount more than the market price, it will be unable to make any sales.

2. As a perfectly competitive firm produces a greater quantity of output, its **total revenue** steadily increases at a constant rate determined by the given market price.

3. Profits will be highest (or losses will be smallest) at the quantity of output where total revenues exceed total costs by the greatest amount (or where total revenues fall short of total costs by the smallest amount). Alternatively, profits will be highest at the quantity of output where **marginal revenue**, which is price for a perfectly competitive firm, is equal to marginal cost.

4. If the market price faced by a perfectly competitive firm is above average cost at the profit-maximizing quantity of output, then the firm is making profits. If the market price is below average cost at the profit-maximizing quantity of output, then the firm is making losses. If the market price is at average cost, at the profit-maximizing level of output, then the firm is making zero profits. The point where the marginal cost curve crosses the average cost curve, at the minimum of the average cost curve, is called the "zero-profit point."

5. The point where the marginal cost curve crosses the average variable cost curve is called the **shutdown point**. If the market price faced by a perfectly competitive firm is below average variable cost at the profit-maximizing quantity of output, then the firm should shut down operations immediately. If the market price faced by a perfectly competitive firm is above average variable cost, but below average cost, then the firm

should continue producing in the short run, but exit in the long run.

6. In the long run, firms will respond to profits through a process of **entry**, where existing firms expand output and new firms enter the market. Conversely, firms will react to losses in the long run through a process of **exit**, in which existing firms reduce output or cease production altogether.

7. Through the process of entry in response to profits and exit in response to losses, the price level in a perfectly competitive market will move toward the zero-profit point, where the marginal cost curve crosses the AC curve, at the minimum of the average cost curve.

8. **Accounting profit** is measured by taking total revenues and subtracting expenditures. Economic profit is measured after taking total revenue, subtracting all expenditures, and also subtracting the opportunity cost of financial capital. Thus, zero **economic profit** actually means a normal accounting rate of profit.

9. A profit-maximizing firm will determine its optimal quantity of output and then hire the amount of the variable input, like labor, needed to produce that quantity of output.

10. The **marginal revenue product**, the value of what is produced by an additional worker, is calculated by taking the quantity of output produced by the marginal worker and multiplying it by the price of that output. A profit-maximizing firm will hire workers as long as the marginal revenue product of what they produce exceeds the wage, up to the point where the marginal revenue product is equal to the wage.

11. If an employer paid wages that were higher than marginal revenue product—that is, higher than the value of what workers produced—the employer would tend to make losses and such wages could not be continued. If one employer paid wages that were lower than

the marginal revenue product, then other employers would see a profit opportunity in hiring those workers and paying them more. If workers can move freely between comparable alternative jobs, the pressures of the labor market will tend to push wages toward marginal revenue product.

12. Firms will invest as long as the expected returns of the investment exceed the cost of capital, where the cost of capital typically includes a "hurdle rate" to take account of the risk involved.

13. When perfectly competitive firms produce at the minimum of the long-run average cost curve, the market will show productive efficiency, since they are producing at the lowest possible average cost. When perfectly competitive firms produce at the quantity where P = MC, the market will illustrate allocative efficiency, since each good is being produced up to the quantity where the amount that the good benefits society, as measured by the price people are willing to pay, is equal to the cost to society, as measured by the marginal cost of production.

Review Questions

1. How does a perfectly competitive firm decide what price to charge?
2. What prevents a perfectly competitive firm from seeking higher profits by increasing the price that it charges?
3. How does a perfectly competitive firm calculate total revenue?
4. Briefly explain the reason for the shape of a marginal revenue curve for a perfectly competitive firm.
5. What rule does a perfectly competitive firm apply to determine its profit-maximizing quantity of output?
6. How does the average cost curve help to show whether a firm is making profits or losses?
7. What two lines on a cost curve diagram intersect at the zero-profit point?
8. Should a firm shut down immediately if it is making losses?
9. How does the average variable cost curve help a firm know whether it should shut down immediately?
10. What two lines on a cost curve diagram intersect at the shutdown point?
11. Why does entry occur?

12. Why does exit occur?
13. Do entry and exit occur in the short run, the long run, both, or neither?
14. What price will a perfectly competitive firm end up charging in the long run? Why?
15. What's the difference between accounting profit and economic profit? Which one is higher?
16. Why is labor called a "derived demand"?
17. How can a perfectly competitive firm use derived demand to decide how much labor to hire?
18. How is the marginal revenue product of labor calculated?
19. How can a perfectly competitive firm use the marginal revenue product of labor to determine what quantity of labor to hire?
20. What is the "hurdle rate"?
21. How does a firm use the hurdle rate to decide which investments in physical capital to undertake?
22. Will a perfectly competitive industry display productive efficiency? Why or why not?
23. Will a perfectly competitive industry display allocative efficiency? Why or why not?

Monopoly

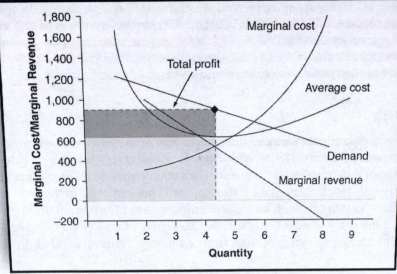

There is a widespread belief that top executives at firms are the strongest supporters of market competition, but this belief is far from the truth. Think about it this way: If you very much wanted to win an Olympic gold medal, would you rather be far better than everyone else, or locked in competition with many athletes just as good as you are—or even a little better? Similarly, if you'd like to attain a very high level of profits, would you rather manage a business with little or no competition, or struggle against many tough competitors who are trying to sell to your customers? Competition ⟨...⟩ as a whole because it encourages firms to try their hardest ⟨...⟩s. But for individual firms, a lesser degree of competition ⟨...⟩ active.

⟨...⟩ms of business managers rarely take place in a world of per⟨...⟩ with many firms selling identical products. Instead, top exec⟨...⟩er the idea of **imperfect competition**, which involves either a ⟨...⟩ of competing firms, or products that aren't identical, or both. ⟨...⟩tition comes in several flavors: monopoly, oligopoly, and ⟨...⟩mpetition. In the case of **monopoly**, one firm produces all or nearly all of the output in a market. In the case of **monopolistic competition**, a large number of firms compete, but their products differ meaningfully from each other. In the case of **oligopoly**, a small number of firms—perhaps just two or three or four—sell all or nearly all of the output in a market. This chapter focuses on monopoly; the next chapter addresses the intermediate cases of monopolistic competition and oligopoly.

One of the most-publicized U.S. monopolies in the last two decades is the Microsoft Corporation, which sells (among other products) the Windows operating system for personal computers—that is, the background software that organizes and enables all the other programs on the computer. In the early 2000s, the Windows system ran on 90% or more of the most commonly sold type of personal computers. But most people deal with monopolies

imperfect competition: Competition that does not fit the definition of perfect competition either because it involves a smaller number of firms or only one firm, or products that aren't identical.

monopoly: A firm that faces no competitors.

monopolistic competition: Many firms competing to sell similar but differentiated products.

oligopoly: When several large firms have all or most of the sales in an industry.

or near-monopolies every day. Google handles roughly 70% of all the Internet search requests in the United States. The U.S. Postal Service has a monopoly on the delivery of first-class mail. Most people have only one firm from which they can purchase electricity or garbage collection. Some new drugs are produced by only one pharmaceutical firm—and no close substitutes for that drug may exist.

This chapter begins with the ways in which monopolies may be protected from competition, including laws that prohibit competition, technological advantages, and certain configurations of demand and supply. The chapter then discusses how a monopoly will choose its profit-maximizing quantity to produce and what price to charge. While a monopoly must be concerned about whether consumers will purchase its products or spend their money on something altogether different, the monopolist need not worry about the actions of other competing firms. As a result, a monopoly is not a price-taker like a perfectly competitive firm, but instead exercises some power to choose its market price.

Barriers to Entry

barriers to entry: The legal, technological, or market forces that may discourage or prevent potential competitors from entering a market.

Barriers to entry are the legal, technological, or market forces that may discourage or prevent potential competitors from entering a market. In some cases, barriers to entry may lead to pure monopoly; in other cases, they may limit competition to a few oligopoly firms. Barriers to entry will block entry even if the firm or firms currently in the market are earning profits. Thus, in markets with barriers to entry, it is not true that abnormally high profits will attract the entry of new firms and that this entry of new firms will eventually cause the price to decline so that surviving firms earn only a normal level of profit in the long run.

Legal Restrictions

In some cases, the government erects barriers to entry by prohibiting or limiting competitors. Under U.S. law, no organization but the U.S. Post Office is legally allowed to deliver first-class mail. Many states or cities have laws or regulations that allow households a choice of only one electrical company, one water company, and one company to pick up the garbage.

deregulation: Removing government controls over setting prices and quantities in certain industries.

Government limitations on competition used to be even more common in the United States. For most of the twentieth century, only one phone company—AT&T—was legally allowed to provide local and long-distance service. From the 1930s up to the 1970s, federal regulations limited which destinations airlines could choose to fly to and what fares they could charge, another set of regulations limited the interest rates that banks could pay to depositors, and yet another set specified what trucking firms could charge customers. However, a wave of deregulation, starting in the late 1970s and running into the 1990s, eliminated or reduced U.S. government restrictions on the firms that could enter, the prices that could be charged, and the quantities that could be produced in many industries, including airlines, trucking, banking, telecommunications, electricity, and more. Around the world, from Europe to Latin America to Africa and Asia, many governments continue to control and limit competition in what those governments perceive to be key industries, including airlines, banks, steel companies, oil companies, telephone companies, and others.

Control of a Physical Resource

If a company can control a scarce physical resource, then other firms may find it difficult to compete. In the U.S. economy, one historical example of this pattern occurred when ALCOA—which stood for Aluminum Company of America—controlled most of the supply of bauxite, a key mineral used in making aluminum, back in the 1930s. Today, two well-known arrangements for controlling a physical resource involve oil and diamonds. The Organization for Petroleum Exporting Countries, commonly known as OPEC, includes many of the world's leading petroleum-exporting countries, including Saudi

Arabia and most of the Middle Eastern oil producers, along with Nigeria, Venezuela, and Indonesia. In one famous episode, from 1973–1975, OPEC more than doubled the price of oil, with dramatic effects on consumers of oil around the world. The majority of global diamond production is controlled by DeBeer's, a South African firm that controls over 10 prolific African diamond mines and also directs the Central Selling Organization, which controls a majority of the world's distribution and resale of rough diamonds.

Technological Superiority

Technological capabilities may also discourage competitors. The Windows operating system sold only by Microsoft is one example; it is technologically difficult, although not impossible, for other firms to produce an equivalent product. Attempts to gain a technological advantage are widespread. Pharmaceutical companies strive to invent new drugs that only they know how to make. Software companies strive to write distinctive new programs.

In some cases, technological superiority may combine with the law to create a barrier to entry. The Constitution of the United States specifies in Article I, Section 8: "The Congress shall have Power . . . To Promote the Progress of Science and Useful Arts, by securing for limited Times to Authors and Inventors the Exclusive Right to their Writings and Discoveries." Congress used this power to create the U.S. Patent and Trademark Office, as well as the U.S. Copyright Office. A **patent** gives the inventor the exclusive legal right to make, use, or sell the invention for a limited time; in the United States, exclusive patent rights last for 20 years.

A **trademark** is a word, name, symbol, or device that indicates the source of the goods, like the name Chiquita on bananas, the name Chevrolet on cars, or the Nike "swoosh" that appears on shoes and athletic gear. Roughly 800,000 trademarks are registered with the U.S. government. A firm can renew its trademarks over and over again, as long as it remains in active use.

A **copyright**, according the U.S. Copyright Office, "is a form of protection provided by the laws of the United States for 'original works of authorship' including literary, dramatic, musical, architectural, cartographic, choreographic, pantomimic, pictorial, graphic, sculptural, and audiovisual creations." No one can reproduce or display or perform a

patent: A government rule that gives the inventor the exclusive legal right to make, use, or sell the invention for a limited time.

trademark: A word, name, symbol, or device that indicates the source of the goods and can only be used by the firm that registered that trademark.

copyright: A form of legal protection to prevent copying for commercial purposes original works of authorship, including books and music.

Willy Wonka and Trade Secrets

Roald Dahl wrote a book in 1964 called *Charlie and the Chocolate Factory*, which has been made into a movie twice: the first time in a 1971 version starring Gene Wilder as the candy-maker Willy Wonka, and the second time in 2005 starring Johnny Depp. For economists, the story is about trying to steal candy industry trade secrets. Here's how Dahl tells it:

> "You see, Charlie, not so very long ago there used to be thousands of people working in Mr. Willy Wonka's factory. Then one day, all of a sudden, Mr. Wonka had to ask every single one of them to leave, to go home, never to come back."

> "But why?" asked Charlie.

> "Because of spies."

> "Spies?"

> "Yes. All the other chocolate makers, you see, had begun to grow jealous of the wonderful can-

dies that Mr. Wonka was making, and they started sending in spies to steal his secret recipes. The spies took jobs in the Wonka factory, pretending they were ordinary workers, and while they were there, each one of them found out exactly how a certain special thing was made."

Dahl's story was rooted in common business practices of the candy industry during his childhood. The two biggest candy makers of that time, Cadbury and Rowntree, were famous for the number of spies they attempted to infiltrate into other companies. Other candy firms were known to hire detectives to investigate their own workers and to require outside contractors to be blindfolded when they entered the factory. Dahl went to school not far from the Cadbury headquarters, where he and fellow students were sometimes brought in as taste testers for new kinds of chocolate bars in plain foil wrappings.

copyrighted work without permission of the author. Copyright protection ordinarily lasts for the life of the author plus 70 years.

Roughly speaking, patent law covers inventions and copyright protects books, songs, and art. But in certain areas, like the invention of new software, it has been unclear whether patent or copyright protection should apply. There is also a body of law known as **trade secrets**. Even if a company does not have a patent on an invention, competing firms are not allowed to break into their factories and files and steal their secrets. One famous trade secret is the formula for Coca Cola, which is not protected under copyright or patent law, but is simply kept secret by the company.

Taken together, this combination of patents, trademarks, copyrights, and trade secret law is called **intellectual property** because it implies ownership over an idea or concept or image, not a physical piece of property like house or a car. Countries around the world have enacted laws to protect intellectual property, although the time periods and exact provisions of such laws vary across countries. There are ongoing negotiations, both through the World Intellectual Property Organization (WIPO) and through international treaties, to bring greater harmony to the intellectual property laws of different countries and to determine the extent to which patents and copyrights in one country will be respected in other countries.

trade secrets: Methods of production kept secret by the producing firm.

intellectual property: The body of law including patents, trademarks, copyrights, and trade secret law that protects the right of inventors to produce and sell their inventions.

Natural Monopoly

Economies of scale can combine with the size of the market to limit competition. (This theme was introduced in Chapter 9.) Exhibit 11-1 presents a long-run average cost curve for the airplane manufacturing industry. The long-run average cost curve shows economies of scale up to an output of 8,000 planes per year and a price of p_0, then constant

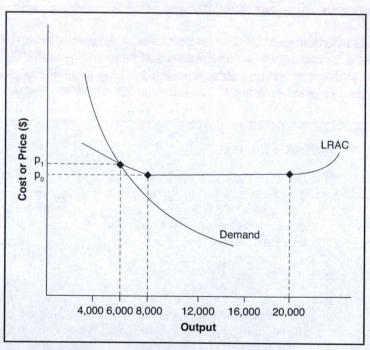

EXHIBIT 11-1 Economies of Scale and Natural Monopoly

In this market, the demand curve intersects the long-run average cost curve in the downward-sloping part of the LRAC curve. Imagine the situation where a monopoly is producing 6,000 units at a price of p_1. If a potential competitor tried to produce a smaller quantity, then its average costs would be too high to compete. If a potential competitor tried to produce a larger quantity, like 8,000 or 20,000, then it could produce at a lower average cost—but it could not sell the additional units because of a lack of demand in the market. Thus, a natural monopoly occurs when the quantity demanded is less than the minimum quantity it takes to be at the bottom of the long-run average cost curve.

returns to scale from 8,000 to 20,000 planes per year, and diseconomies of scale at a quantity of production greater than 20,000 planes per year. Now consider the market demand curve in the diagram, which intersects the long-run average cost curve at an output level of 6,000 planes per year and at a price p_1 which is higher than p_0. In this situation, the market has room for only one producer. If a second firm attempts to enter the market at a smaller size, say by producing a quantity of 4,000 planes, then its average costs will be higher than the existing firm, and it will be unable to compete. If the second firm attempts to enter the market at a larger size, like 8,000 planes per year, then it could produce at a lower average cost—but it couldn't sell all 8,000 planes that it produced because of insufficient demand in the market.

This situation, when economies of scale are large relative to the quantity demanded in the market, is called a **natural monopoly**. Natural monopolies often arise in industries where the marginal cost of adding an additional customer is very low, once the fixed costs of the overall system are in place. Once the main water pipes are laid through a neighborhood, the marginal cost of providing water service to another home is fairly low. Once electricity lines are installed through a neighborhood, the marginal cost of providing additional electrical service to one more home is very low. It would be costly and duplicative for a second water company to enter the market and invest in a whole second set of main water pipes, or for a second electricity company to enter the market and invest in a whole new set of electrical wires. These industries offer an example where, because of economies of scale, one producer could serve the entire market more efficiently than a number of smaller producers that would have needed to make duplicative physical capital investments. A natural monopoly can also arise in smaller local markets for products that are difficult to transport. For example, cement production exhibits economies of scale, and the quantity of cement demanded in a local area may not be much larger than what a single plant can produce. Moreover, the costs of transporting cement overland are high, and so a cement plant in an area without access to water transportation may be a natural monopoly.

natural monopoly: When the quantity demanded in the market is less than the quantity at the bottom of the long-run average cost curve.

Intimidating Potential Competition

Businesses have developed a number of schemes for creating barriers to entry by deterring potential competitors from entering the market. One method is known as **predatory pricing**, in which a firm uses the threat of sharp price cuts to discourage competition. Consider a large airline that provides most of the flights between two particular cities. A new, small start-up airline decides to offer service between these two cities. The large airline immediately slashes prices on this route to the bone, so that the new entrant can't make any money. After the new entrant has exited this market, the incumbent firm can raise prices again. After this pattern occurs once or twice, potential new entrants may decide that it isn't wise to try to compete. Small airlines often accuse larger airlines of predatory pricing: in the early 2000s, for example, ValuJet accused Delta of predatory pricing, Frontier accused United, and Reno Air accused Northwest. In late 2009, the American Booksellers Association, which represents independently owned and often smaller bookstores, accused Amazon, Wal-Mart, and Target of predatory pricing for selling new hardcover best-sellers at low prices.

predatory pricing: When an existing firm uses sharp but temporary price cuts to discourage new competition.

In some cases, large advertising budgets can also act as a way of discouraging the competition. If the only way to launch a successful new national cola drink is to spend more than the promotional budgets of Coca Cola and Pepsi Cola, not too many companies will try. A firmly established brand name can be difficult to dislodge.

Summing Up Barriers to Entry

The five categories of barriers to entry that have been discussed here are laws against entry and price changes, control of a physical resource, technological advantage, natural monopoly, and intimidating potential competitors. This list should not be viewed as exhaustive, since firms in many industries have proven to be highly creative in inventing business practices that discourage competition. When barriers to entry exist, perfect competition is no longer a reasonable description of how an industry works. When barriers to entry are high enough, monopoly can result.

How a Profit-Maximizing Monopoly Chooses Output and Price

Consider a monopoly firm, comfortably surrounded by barriers to entry so that it need not fear competition from other producers. How will this monopoly choose its profit-maximizing quantity of output, and what price will it charge? Profits for the monopolist, like any firm, will be equal to total revenues minus total costs. The pattern of costs for the monopoly can be analyzed within the same framework as the costs of a perfectly competitive firm—that is, by using total cost, fixed cost, variable cost, marginal cost, average cost, and average variable cost. However, because a monopoly faces no competition, its decision process will differ from that of a perfectly competitive firm.

Demand Curves Perceived by a Perfectly Competitive Firm and by a Monopoly

A perfectly competitive firm acts as a price taker, so its calculation of total revenue is made by taking the given market price and multiplying it by the quantity of output that the firm chooses. The demand curve *as it is perceived by a perfectly competitive firm* appears in Exhibit 11-2a. The flat perceived demand curve means that, from the price-taker viewpoint of a perfectly competitive firm, it could sell either a relatively low quantity like q_L or a relatively high quantity like q_H at the market price p^*.

No monopolist, even one who is thoroughly protected by high barriers to entry from other competing firms, can require consumers to purchase its product. The demand curve for the monopolist's products *as it is perceived by a monopolist* is exactly the same as the market demand curve—because the monopolist is the only firm in the market. Because demand for most products is neither completely elastic nor completely inelastic, an in-between case is drawn in Exhibit 11-2b. The monopolist can either choose a point like

(a) Perceived demand curve by perfect competitor

Perceived demand for a perfect competitor. A perfectly competitive firm is a price-taker and thus perceives the demand curve that it faces to be flat. The flat shape means that the firm can sell either a low quantity q_L or a high quantity q_H at exactly the same price p^*.

(b) Perceived demand curve by monopolist

Perceived demand for a monopolist. A monopolist is not a price-taker. It perceives the demand curve that it faces to be the same as the market demand curve, which for most goods is downward sloping. Thus, if the monopolist chooses a high level of output q_H, it can charge only a relatively low price p_L; conversely, if the monopolist chooses a low level of output q_L, it can then charge a higher price p_H. The monopolist can choose the combination of price and quantity that maximizes profits.

EXHIBIT 11-2 The Perceived Demand Curve for a Perfect Competitor and a Monopolist

R with a low price p_L and high quantity q_H, or a point like S with a high price p_H and a low quantity q_L, or some intermediate point. Setting the price too high will result in a low quantity sold and thus won't bring in much revenue. Conversely, setting the price too low may result in a high quantity sold, but because of the low price, it won't bring in much revenue either. The challenge of the monopolist is to strike a profit-maximizing balance between the price it charges and the quantity that it sells.

Total and Marginal Revenue for a Monopolist

Profits for a monopolist can be illustrated with a graph of total revenues and total costs, as shown with the example of the hypothetical HealthPill firm in Exhibit 11-3. The total cost curve has its typical shape; that is, total costs rise and grow steeper as output increases.

To calculate total revenue for a monopolist, start with the demand curve perceived by the monopolist. The table shows quantities along the demand curve, the price at each quantity demanded, and then calculates total revenue by multiplying price times quantity at each level of output. (In this example, the output is given as 1, 2, 3, 4, and the like, for the sake of simplicity. If you prefer a dash of greater realism, you can imagine that these output levels and the corresponding prices are measured per 1,000 or 10,000 pills.) As the exhibit illustrates, total revenue for a monopolist rises, flattens out, and then falls. In this example, total revenue is highest at a quantity of 6 or 7. Clearly, the total revenue for a monopolist is not a straight upward-sloping line, in the way that total revenue was for a perfectly competitive firm. The different total revenue pattern for a monopolist occurs because the quantity that a monopolist chooses to produce affects the market price, which was not true for a perfectly competitive firm. If the monopolist charges a very high price, then quantity demanded drops, and so total revenue is very low. If the monopolist charges a very low price, then even if quantity demanded is very high, total revenue won't add up to much. At some intermediate level, total revenue will be highest.

However, the monopolist is not seeking to maximize revenue, but instead to earn the highest possible profit. Profits are calculated in the final row of the table. In the HealthPill example in Exhibit 11-3, the highest profit will occur at the quantity where total revenue is the farthest above total cost. Of the choices given in the table, the highest profits occur at an output of 4, where profit is 900.

Quantity	Total Cost	Price	Total Revenue	Profit = Total Revenue − Total Cost
1	1,500	1,200	1,200	−300
2	1,800	1,100	2,200	400
3	2,200	1,000	3,000	800
4	2,700	900	3,600	900
5	3,300	800	4,000	700
6	4,200	700	4,200	0
7	5,400	600	4,200	−1,200
8	7,200	500	4,000	−3,200

EXHIBIT 11-3 Total Revenue and Total Cost for the HealthPill Monopoly

Total revenue for the monopoly firm called HealthPill first rises, then falls. Low levels of output bring in relatively little total revenue because the quantity is low. High levels of output bring in relatively less revenue because the high quantity pushes down the market price. The total cost curve is upward sloping. Profits will be highest at the quantity of output where total revenue is most above total cost; of the choices in the table, the highest profits happen at an output of 4. The profit-maximizing level of output is not the same as the revenue-maximizing level of output, which should make sense, because profits take costs into account and revenues don't.

What Is the Market?

A monopoly is a firm that sells all or nearly all of the goods and services in a given market. But what defines a "market"?

In a famous 1947 case, the federal government accused the DuPont company of having a monopoly in the cellophane market, pointing out that DuPont produced 75% of the cellophane in the United States. DuPont countered that even though it had 75% market share in cellophane, it produced less than 20% of the "flexible packaging materials," which includes all other moisture-proof papers, films, and foils. In 1956, after years of legal appeals, the U.S. Supreme Court held that the broader market definition was more appropriate, and the case against DuPont was dismissed.

Questions over how to define the market continue today. True, Microsoft in the 1990s had a dominant share of the software for computer operating systems, but in the total market for all computer software and services, including everything from games to scientific programs, the Microsoft share was only about 16% in 2000. The Greyhound bus company may have a near-monopoly on the market for intercity bus transportation, but it is only a small share of the market for intercity transportation if that market includes private cars, airplanes, and railroad service. DeBeer's has a monopoly in diamonds, but it is a much smaller share of the total market for precious gemstones and an even smaller share of the total market for jewelry. A small town in the country may have only one gas station: is this gas station a "monopoly" or does it compete with gas stations that might be five or ten or 50 miles away?

In general, if a firm produces a product without close substitutes, then the firm can be considered a monopoly producer in a single market, but if buyers have a range of similar—even if not identical—options available from other firms, then the firm is not a monopoly. But arguments over whether close substitutes are available can be controversial.

Perceived Demand and Market Demand

The demand curve as perceived by a perfectly competitive firm is not the overall market demand curve for that product. However, the firm's demand curve as perceived by a monopoly is the same as the market demand curve. The reason for the difference is that each perfectly competitive firm perceives the demand for its products in a market that includes many other firms; in effect, the demand curve perceived by a perfectly competitive firm is a tiny slice of the entire market demand curve. In contrast, a monopoly perceives demand for its product in a market where the monopoly is the only producer.

Marginal Revenue and Marginal Cost for a Monopolist

In the real world, a monopolist often does not have enough information to analyze its entire total revenues or total costs curves; after all, the firm doesn't know exactly what would happen if it was to alter production dramatically. But a monopoly often has fairly reliable information about how changing output by small or moderate amounts will affect its marginal revenues and marginal costs because it has had experience with such changes over time and because modest changes are easier to extrapolate from current experience. A monopolist can use information on marginal revenue and marginal cost to seek out the profit-maximizing combination of quantity and price.

The first four columns of Exhibit 11-4 use the numbers on total cost from the Health-Pill example in the previous exhibit and calculate marginal cost and average cost. This monopoly faces a typical U-shaped average cost curve and upward-sloping marginal cost curve. The second three columns use the total revenue information from the previous exhibit and calculate marginal revenue. Notice that marginal revenue is zero at a quantity of 7 and turns negative at quantities higher than 7. It may seem counterintuitive that marginal revenue could ever be zero or negative: after all, doesn't an increase in quantity sold always mean more revenue? For a perfect competitor, each additional unit sold brought a positive marginal revenue because marginal revenue was equal to the given market

	Cost Information				Revenue Information		
Quantity	Total Cost	Marginal Cost	Average Cost		Price	Total Revenue	Marginal Revenue
1	1,500	—	1,500		1,200	1,200	—
2	1,800	300	900		1,100	2,200	1,000
3	2,200	400	733		1,000	3,000	800
4	2,700	500	675		900	3,600	600
5	3,300	600	660		800	4,000	400
6	4,200	900	700		700	4,200	200
7	5,400	1,200	771		600	4,200	0
8	7,200	1,800	900		500	4,000	−200

EXHIBIT 11-4 Marginal Revenue and Marginal Cost for the HealthPill Monopoly

For a monopoly like HealthPill, marginal revenue decreases as additional units are sold. The reason is that each additional unit sold causes a decrease in the price for all units. Marginal revenue can even be zero, as at an output of 7, or negative, as at an output of 8. The marginal cost curve is upward sloping. The profit-maximizing choice for the monopoly will be to produce at the quantity where marginal revenue is equal to marginal cost: that is, MR = MC. If the monopoly produces a lower quantity, then MR > MC at those levels of output, and the firm can make higher profits by expanding output. If the firm produces at a greater quantity, then MC > MR, and the firm can make higher profits by reducing its quantity of output.

price. But a monopolist can sell a larger quantity and see a decline in total revenue. When a monopolist increases sales by one unit, it gains some marginal revenue from selling that extra unit but also loses some marginal revenue because every other unit must now be sold at a lower price. As the quantity sold becomes higher, the drop in price affects a greater quantity of sales, eventually causing a situation where more sales cause marginal revenue to be negative.

A monopolist can determine its profit-maximizing price and quantity by analyzing the marginal revenue and marginal costs of producing an extra unit. If the marginal revenue exceeds the marginal cost, then the firm should produce the extra unit. For example, at an output of 2 in the example, marginal revenue is 1,000 and marginal cost is 300, so producing this unit will clearly add to overall profits. At an output of 4, marginal revenue is 600 and marginal cost is 500, so producing this unit still adds to overall profits. However, expanding output from 4 to 5 would involve a marginal revenue of 400 and a marginal cost of 600, so that fifth unit would actually reduce profits. Thus, the monopoly can tell from the marginal revenue and marginal cost that of the choices given in the table, the profit-maximizing level of output is 4.

Indeed, the monopoly could seek out the profit-maximizing level of output by increasing quantity by a small amount, calculating marginal revenue and marginal cost, and then either increasing output if marginal revenue exceeds marginal cost or reducing output if marginal cost exceeds marginal revenue. This incremental process works without any need to calculate total revenue and total cost. Thus, a profit-maximizing monopoly should follow the rule of producing up to the quantity where marginal revenue is equal to marginal cost— that is, MR = MC. A perfectly competitive firm will also find its profit-maximizing level of output where MR = MC. The key difference with a perfectly competitive firm is that in the case of perfect competition, marginal revenue is equal to price (MR = P), while for a monopolist, marginal revenue is not equal to the price, because changes in monopoly quantity of output affect the price.

Illustrating Monopoly Profits

It is straightforward to calculate profits if given numbers for total revenue and total cost. However, the size of monopoly profits can also be illustrated graphically with Exhibit 11-5, which takes the marginal cost and marginal revenue curves from the previous exhibit and adds an average cost curve and the monopolist's perceived demand curve. This diagram can also illustrate the three-step process where a monopolist: (1) selects the profit-maximizing quantity to produce; (2) decides what price to charge; and (3) determines total revenue, total cost, and profit.

Step 1: The Monopolist Determines Its Profit-Maximizing Level of Output

The firm can use the price and quantity combinations on the demand curve to calculate total revenue, and then based on total revenue, it can calculate its marginal revenue curve. The profit-maximizing quantity will occur where MR = MC—or at the last possible point before marginal costs start exceeding marginal revenue. In this example, MR = MC at an output slightly above 4.

EXHIBIT 11-5 Illustrating Profits at the HealthPill Monopoly

This exhibit begins with the same marginal revenue and marginal cost curves from the HealthPill monopoly presented in Exhibit 11-4. It then adds an average cost curve and the demand curve faced by the monopolist. The HealthPill firm first chooses the quantity where MR = MC; in this example, 4 is the highest level of output before this occurs (although the intersection of MR and MC actually happens at a slightly higher level of output). The monopolist then decides what price to charge by looking at the demand curve it faces. The entire area of the shaded box (both dark and light shading), with quantity on the horizontal size and price on the vertical side, shows total revenue for the firm. Total costs for the firm are shown by the lighter-shaded area, which is quantity on the horizontal axis and average cost of production on the vertical axis. The large total revenue box minus the smaller total cost box leaves the darker-shaded area that shows total profits. Since the price charged is above average cost, the firm is earning positive profits.

Why Is a Monopolist's Marginal Revenue under the Demand Curve?

The marginal revenue curve for a monopolist always lies beneath the market demand curve. To understand why, think about increasing the quantity along the demand curve by one unit, so that you take one step down the demand curve to a slightly higher quantity but a slightly lower price. This step affects marginal revenue in two ways. First, it adds one additional unit sold at the new market price. Second, it means that all the previous units, which used to be sold at the higher price, now sell for less. Thus, the marginal revenue for a monopolist of selling an additional unit is equal to the price of that unit minus the reduction in price on all other units sold. For a monopolist, marginal revenue from expanding production is less than price—and the marginal revenue curve lies below the demand curve.

Step 2: The Monopolist Decides What Price to Charge

The monopolist will charge what the market is willing to pay. A dotted line drawn straight up from the profit-maximizing quantity to the demand curve shows the profit-maximizing price. This price is above the average cost curve, which shows that the firm is earning profits.

Step 3: Calculate Total Revenue, Total Cost, and Profit

Total revenue is the shaded box, including both lighter and darker shading, where the width of the box is the quantity being sold and the height is the price. The bottom part of the shaded box, which is shaded more lightly, shows total costs; that is, quantity on the horizontal axis multiplied by average cost on the vertical axis. The larger box of total revenues minus the smaller box of total costs will equal profits, which is shown by the darkly shaded box.

In a perfectly competitive market, the forces of entry would erode this profit in the long run. But a monopolist is protected by barriers to entry. In fact, one telltale sign of a possible monopoly is when a firm earns profits year after year, while doing more or less the same thing, without ever seeing those profits eroded by increased competition.

The Inefficiency of Monopoly

To understand why a monopoly is inefficient, it is useful to compare it with the benchmark model of perfect competition.

In perfect competition, the process of entry and exit means that eventually the market price is driven down to the price at the minimum of the average cost curve. Productive efficiency occurs when goods are being produced at the lowest possible average cost. However, a monopoly does not need to worry about entry, nor does it need to produce at the bottom of the average cost curve. As a result, a monopoly will not display productive efficiency.

The rule of profit maximization in a world of perfect competition was for each firm to produce the quantity of output where $P = MC$, where the price P is a measure of how much buyers value the good and the marginal cost MC is a measure of what marginal units cost society to produce. Following this rule assures allocative efficiency. If $P > MC$, then the benefit to society as measured by P is greater than the marginal cost to society MC of producing additional units, and a greater quantity should be produced. But in the case of monopoly, price is always greater than marginal cost at the profit-maximizing level of output, as can be seen by looking back at Exhibit 11-5. Thus, consumers will suffer from a monopoly because a lower quantity will be sold in the market, at a higher price, than would have been the case in a perfectly competitive market.

Productive and allocative efficiency in this discussion have referred to the quantity and price at a point in time. The problem of inefficiency for monopolies often runs even deeper than these issues and also involves incentives for efficiency over longer periods

Is a Diamond Monopoly Forever?

The DeBeer's diamond company is a South African firm that has organized a monopoly for selling diamonds around the world. The diamond monopoly works through a Central Selling Organization (CSO), which signs long-term exclusive contracts with diamond mines around the world to purchase all of their diamonds. It then groups the diamonds by size, brilliance, and other characteristics, and then sells them to diamond cutters and dealers. At its peak in the 1970s and 1980s, the CSO controlled about 85% of the world's diamonds. Thus, DeBeer's could control the quantity sold in the market and keep the price high.

But in the 1990s, a group of Australian diamond producers pulled out of the CSO. Diamonds were discovered in Canada at the Ekati mine. Diamond producers in Russia threatened to leave the CSO. Diamond production increased in Angola—organized in part by Russian and Australian firms. In the 2000s, the CSO controlled only about 40% of the world's diamond market.

What's next? DeBeer's will negotiate with other producers, pointing out that if the Central Selling Organization doesn't control the quantity produced, prices and profits will be lower for diamond producers as a group. However, the other producers may feel that they individually can earn higher profits by remaining outside the CSO. Instead of the "Diamonds are forever" ad campaign that DeBeer's started in the 1940s, which applied to all diamonds, different diamond producers will try to persuade consumers that there is something particularly special about the diamonds produced by their firm.

of time. There are counterbalancing incentives here. On one side, firms may strive for new inventions and new intellectual property because they want to become monopolies and earn high profits—at least for a few years until the competition catches up. In this way, monopolies may come to exist because of competitive pressures on firms. However, once a barrier to entry is in place, a monopoly that doesn't need to fear competition can just produce the same old products in the same old way—while still ringing up a healthy rate of profit. John Hicks, who won the Nobel Prize for economics in 1972, wrote back in 1935: "The best of all monopoly profits is a quiet life." He didn't mean the comment in a complimentary way. He meant that monopolies may bank their profits and slack off on trying to please their customers.

Until the early 1980s, for example, AT&T provided all of the local and long-distance phone service in the United States, along with manufacturing most of the phones. The old joke at the time was that you could have any color phone you wanted, as long as it was black. But in 1982, AT&T was split up by government litigation into a number of local phone companies, a long-distance phone company, and a phone equipment manufacturer. An explosion of innovation followed. Services like call waiting, caller ID, three-way calling, voicemail, mobile phones, and wireless connections to the Internet all became available. A wide range of payment plans was offered as well. It was no longer true that all phones were black; instead, phones came in a wild variety of shapes and colors. The end of the telephone monopoly helped to bring lower prices, a greater quantity of services, and also a wave of innovation aimed at attracting and pleasing customers.

Conclusion

A monopolist can analyze its costs with the same analytic tools as other firms: total cost, marginal cost, and average cost. Monopolists will often face the U-shaped average cost curve and upward-sloping marginal cost curve as shown in Exhibit 11-6. To maximize profits, Step 1 for the monopolist is to choose the quantity Q_1, where marginal costs and marginal revenues intersect. Step 2 is to sell that quantity at the price P_1, which is determined by point R on the demand curve. Step 3 is for the monopolist to determine its profits. As long as that monopoly price p_1 is above the average cost curve at the monopoly quantity Q_1, the monopoly is earning profits, shown by the shaded rectangle with its corners at P_1, R, S, and P_2. Moreover, if the monopolist is protected by sufficiently high barriers to entry, it can earn those profits forever, without fear of competitor firms that would be willing to sell at a lower price.

EXHIBIT 11-6 How a Profit-Maximizing Monopoly Decides

In Step 1, the monopoly chooses the profit-maximizing level of output Q_1, by choosing the quantity where MR = MC.

In Step 2, the monopoly decides how much to charge for output level Q_1 by drawing a line straight up from Q_1 to point R on its perceived demand curve. Thus, the monopoly will charge a price P_1.

In Step 3, the monopoly identifies its profit. Total revenue will be Q_1 multiplied by P_1. Total cost will be Q_1 multiplied by the average cost of producing Q_1, which is shown by point S on the average cost curve to be P_2. Profits will be the total revenue rectangle minus the total cost rectangle, shown by the shaded zone in the figure.

Chapter 13 will discuss how government policy may respond to monopolies that charge a higher price and produce a lower quantity than would a group of firms in a competitive industry. But before turning to the policy issues, Chapter 12 analyzes the profit-maximizing choices at two locations on the spectrum of competition between perfect competition and monopoly—that is, monopolistic competition and oligopoly.

Key Concepts and Summary

1. Perfect competition refers to an industry where many firms produce identical products. Conversely, **imperfect competition** refers to industries where either there are a small number of firms, or the firms don't sell an identical product, or both. There are three main varieties of imperfect competition: **monopoly**, which is the case of a single seller; **monopolistic competition**, where there are many sellers but their products are not identical; and **oligopoly**, which is the case of a small number of sellers.

2. **Barriers to entry** prevent or discourage competitors from entering the market. These barriers include legal restrictions on competition, control of a physical resource, technological superiority, economies of scale that lead to natural monopoly, and practices to intimidate the competition like **predatory pricing**.

3. **Intellectual property** refers to legally guaranteed ownership of an idea, rather than a physical item. The laws that protect intellectual property include **patents**, **trademarks**, **copyrights**, and **trade secrets**.

4. A **natural monopoly** arises when economies of scale persist over a large enough range of output that if one firm supplies the entire market, no second firm can enter without facing a cost disadvantage.

5. The demand curve perceived by a perfectly competitive firm is horizontal, which shows that such a firm is a price-taker, charging whatever price is determined in the market for the quantity that it sells. The demand curve perceived by a monopolist is the market demand curve, which is typically downward sloping. A monopolist is not a price-taker, because when it decides what quantity to produce, it also determines the market price.

6. For a monopolist, total revenue is relatively low at low quantities of output because not much is being sold if a very high price is charged. Total revenue is also relatively low at very high quantities of output because a very high quantity will sell only at a low price. Thus, as output of a monopolist rises, total revenue will start low, rise, and then decline.

7. The marginal revenue for a monopolist from selling additional units will decline. Each additional unit sold by a monopolist will push down the overall market price, and as more units are sold, this lower price applies to more and more units.

8. A monopolist can seek out the profit-maximizing quantity of output in two ways: it can choose the quantity where total revenue exceeds total cost by the highest amount, or it can choose the quantity where marginal revenue is equal to marginal cost.

9. The monopolist will select the profit-maximizing level of output where MR = MC and then charge the price for that quantity of output as determined by the market demand curve. If that price is above average cost, the monopolist earns positive profits.

10. Monopolists are not productively efficient, because they do not produce at the minimum of the average cost curve. Monopolists are not allocatively efficient, because they do not produce at the quantity where P = MC. As a result, monopolists produce less, at a higher average cost, and charge a higher price than would a combination of firms in a perfectly competitive industry. Monopolists also may lack incentives for innovation because they need not fear entry.

Review Questions

1. How is a monopoly industry different from an industry with perfect competition?
2. How is monopolistic competition different from perfect competition?
3. How is oligopoly different from perfect competition?
4. What is a barrier to entry? Give some examples.
5. What is predatory pricing?
6. How is intellectual property different from other property?
7. By what legal mechanisms is intellectual property protected?
8. In what sense is a natural monopoly "natural"?
9. How is the demand curve perceived by a perfectly competitive firm different from the demand curve perceived by a monopolist?
10. How does the demand curve perceived by a monopolist compare with the market demand curve?
11. Is a monopolist a price-taker? Explain briefly.
12. What is the usual shape of a total revenue curve for a monopolist? Why?
13. What is the usual shape of a marginal revenue curve for a monopolist? Why?
14. How can a monopolist identify the profit-maximizing level of output if it knows its total revenue and total cost curves?
15. How can a monopolist identify the profit-maximizing level of output if it knows its marginal revenue and marginal costs?
16. When a monopolist identifies its profit-maximizing quantity of output, how does it decide what price to charge?
17. Is a monopolist productively efficient? Why or why not?
18. Is a monopolist allocatively efficient? Why or why not?
19. How does the quantity produced and price charged by a monopolist compare to that of a perfectly competitive industry?

Monopolistic Competition and Oligopoly

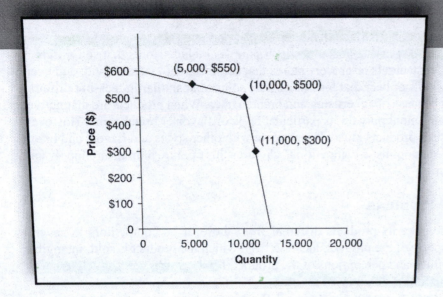

Chapter Outline

Monopolistic Competition

Oligopoly

Conclusion

Perfect competition and monopoly stand at opposite ends of the spectrum of competition. A perfectly competitive market involves many firms selling identical products, who must all act as price-takers in the face of the competition. Monopoly arises when a single firm sells a product for which there are no close substitutes. But what about the in-between cases?

Many markets feature a large number of competing firms, but the products that they sell are not identical. In 2016, the Mall of America in Minnesota, the largest shopping mall in the United States, had 29 stores that sold women's "ready-to-wear" clothing (like Ann Taylor and Coldwater Creek), another 60 stores that sold clothing for both men and women (like Banana Republic, J. Crew, and Nordstrom's), plus 19 more stores that sold women's specialty clothing (like Motherhood Maternity and Victoria's Secret). These many clothing stores, competing in the same shopping mall to sell similar but not identical products, engage in what economists call monopolistic competition. Other markets feature a small number of competing firms, which is called an oligopoly. One example of an oligopoly is Boeing and Airbus, the two major firms in the world that manufacture large passenger aircraft. Another example is the Coca-Cola Company and PepsiCo, Incorporated, the two firms that dominate sales in the U.S. soft drink market.

This chapter begins with a discussion of how monopolistic competition arises and how monopolistically competitive firms will choose their profit-maximizing level of quantity and output. As the name "monopolistic competition" implies, a firm's decisions in this setting will in certain ways resemble monopoly and in other ways resemble perfect competition. Because a monopolistically competitive firm is not selling an identical product to other firms, it has a sort of mini-monopoly; for example, clothing stores in the Mall of America have a mini-monopoly on some of the specific styles of clothing that they sell. However, monopolistic competitors must also expect a process of entry and exit, like perfectly competitive firms, so they cannot earn higher-than-normal profits in the long run. The chapter then turns to a discussion of oligopoly firms, which face two conflicting temptations. On one side, oligopoly firms will wish to cooperate as if they were a single monopoly, to make their decisions about the price to charge and quantity to produce accordingly, and then to divide up the monopoly profits. On the other side, each oligopoly firm acting individually may seek to gain profits by expanding its levels of output and cutting prices. Thus, the behavior of oligopoly firms can also take on elements both of monopoly and of perfect competition.

Monopolistic Competition

monopolistic competition:
Many firms competing to sell similar but differentiated products.

Monopolistic competition involves many firms competing against each other but selling products that are distinctive in some way. Examples include stores that sell different styles of clothing; restaurants or grocery stores that sell different kinds of food; and even products like golf balls or beer that may be at least somewhat similar in fact, but differ in public perception because of advertising and brand names. When products are distinctive, each firm has a mini-monopoly on its particular style or flavor or brand name. However, firms producing such products must also compete with other styles and flavors and brand names. The term "monopolistic competition" captures this mixture of mini-monopoly and tough competition.

Differentiated Products

differentiated products:
Products that are distinctive in a particular way.

A firm can try to make its products different from those of its competitors in several ways: physical aspects of the product, location from which the product is sold, intangible aspects of the product, and perceptions of the product. Products that are distinctive in one of these ways are called **differentiated products.**

Physical aspects of a product include all the phrases you hear in advertisements: unbreakable bottle, nonstick surface, freezer-to-microwave, non-shrink, extra spicy, newly redesigned for your comfort, and many others. The location of a firm can also create a difference between producers. For example, a gas station located at a heavily traveled intersection can probably sell more gas because more cars drive by that corner. A supplier to an automobile manufacturer may find that it is an advantage to locate close to the car factory. Intangible aspects can differentiate a product, too, including a guarantee of satisfaction or money back, a reputation for high quality, services like free delivery, or offering a loan to purchase the product.

Golf Balls and Product Differentiation

The U.S. Golf Association runs a laboratory that tests 20,000 golf balls a year. There are strict rules for what makes a golf ball legal. The weight of a golf ball cannot exceed 1.620 ounces and its diameter cannot be less than 1.680 inches (which is 45.93 grams and 42.67 millimeters, in case you were wondering). The balls are also tested by being hit at different speeds. For example, the distance test involves having a mechanical golfer hit the ball with a titanium driver and a swing speed of 120 miles per hour. As the testing center explains: "The USGA system then uses an array of sensors that accurately measure the flight of a golf ball during a short, indoor trajectory from a ball launcher. From this flight data, a computer calculates the lift and drag forces that are generated by the speed, spin, and dimple pattern of the ball. . . . The distance limit is 317 yards."

Over 1,800 golf balls made by more than 100 companies meet the USGA standards. The balls do differ in various ways, like the pattern of dimples on the ball, the types of plastic used on the cover and in the cores, and so on. But since all balls need to conform to the USGA tests, they are much more alike than different.

However, retail sales of golf balls are about $500 million per year, which means that a lot of large companies have a powerful incentive to persuade players that golf balls are highly differentiated and that it makes a huge difference which one you choose. Sure, Tiger Woods can tell the difference. But for the average duffer who plays a few times a summer—and who loses a lot of golf balls in the woods and the lake and needs to buy new ones—most golf balls are pretty much indistinguishable.

Finally, product differentiation may occur in the minds of buyers. For example, many people can't tell the difference in taste between common varieties of beer or cigarettes if they are blindfolded, but because of past habits and advertising, they have strong preferences for certain brands. Advertising can play a role in shaping these intangible preferences.

The concept of differentiated products is closely related to the degree of variety that is available. If everyone in the economy wore only blue jeans, ate only white bread, and drank only tap water, then the markets for clothing, food, and drink would be much closer to perfectly competitive. The variety of styles, flavors, locations, and characteristics creates product differentiation and monopolistic competition.

Perceived Demand for a Monopolistic Competitor

A monopolistically competitive firm perceives a demand for its goods that is an intermediate case between monopoly and competition. Exhibit 12-1 offers a reminder that the demand curve as perceived by a perfectly competitive firm is flat because the perfectly competitive firm can sell any quantity it wishes at the prevailing market price. In contrast, the demand curve as perceived by a monopolist is the market demand curve, since a monopolist is the only firm in the market.

The demand curve as *perceived by a monopolistic competitor* is not flat, but rather downward sloping, which means that the monopolistic competitor can raise its price without losing all of its customers. However, the demand curve as perceived by the monopolistic competitor is flatter than the demand curve perceived by a monopolist. If a monopolist raises its price, some consumers will choose not to purchase its product—but they will then need to buy a completely different product. However, when a monopolistic competitor raises its price, some consumers will choose not to purchase the product at all, but others will choose to buy a similar product from another firm. If a monopolistic competitor raises its price, it will not lose as many customers as would a perfectly competitive firm, but it will lose more customers than would a monopoly that raised its prices.

At a glance, the demand curves faced by a monopoly and by a monopolistic competitor look similar—that is, they both slope down. But the underlying economic meaning of these perceived demand curves is different because a monopolist faces the market demand curve and a monopolistic competitor does not.

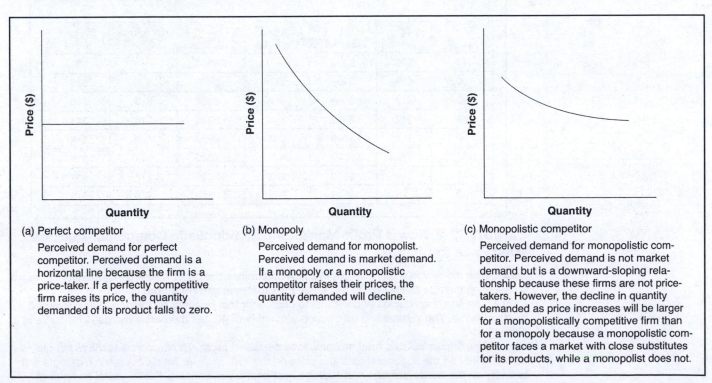

(a) Perfect competitor

Perceived demand for perfect competitor. Perceived demand is a horizontal line because the firm is a price-taker. If a perfectly competitive firm raises its price, the quantity demanded of its product falls to zero.

(b) Monopoly

Perceived demand for monopolist. Perceived demand is market demand. If a monopoly or a monopolistic competitor raises their prices, the quantity demanded will decline.

(c) Monopolistic competitor

Perceived demand for monopolistic competitor. Perceived demand is not market demand but is a downward-sloping relationship because these firms are not price-takers. However, the decline in quantity demanded as price increases will be larger for a monopolistically competitive firm than for a monopoly because a monopolistic competitor faces a market with close substitutes for its products, while a monopolist does not.

EXHIBIT 12-1 Perceived Demand for Firms in Different Competitive Settings

How a Monopolistic Competitor Chooses Price and Quantity

The monopolistically competitive firm decides on its profit-maximizing quantity and price in much the same way as a monopolist. A monopolistic competitor, like a monopolist, faces a downward-sloping demand curve, and so it will choose some combination of price and quantity along its perceived demand curve.

As an example of a profit-maximizing monopolistic competitor, consider the Authentic Chinese Pizza store, which serves pizza with cheese, sweet and sour sauce, and your choice of vegetables and meats. Although Authentic Chinese Pizza must compete against other pizza businesses and restaurants, it has a differentiated product. The firm's perceived demand curve is downward sloping, as shown in the first two columns of the table in Exhibit 12-2 and on the graph. The combinations of price and quantity at each point on the demand curve can be multiplied to calculate the total revenue that the firm would receive, which is shown in the third column. The fourth column, marginal revenue, is

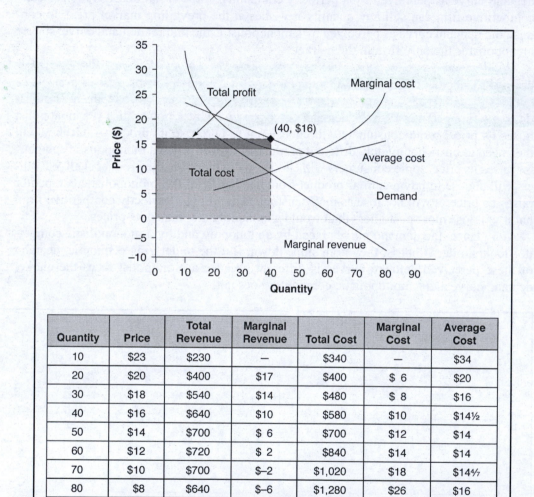

Quantity	Price	Total Revenue	Marginal Revenue	Total Cost	Marginal Cost	Average Cost
10	$23	$230	—	$340	—	$34
20	$20	$400	$17	$400	$ 6	$20
30	$18	$540	$14	$480	$ 8	$16
40	$16	$640	$10	$580	$10	$14½
50	$14	$700	$ 6	$700	$12	$14
60	$12	$720	$ 2	$840	$14	$14
70	$10	$700	$–2	$1,020	$18	$14⁴⁄₇
80	$8	$640	$–6	$1,280	$26	$16

EXHIBIT 12-2 How a Profit-Maximizing Monopolistic Competitor Decides What Price to Charge

Step 1: The monopolistically competitive firm determines the profit-maximizing quantity of output by applying the rule MR = MC. In this case, the profit-maximizing output is 40.

Step 2: The firm then decides how much to charge for this quantity by looking at its perceived demand curve. The vertical line up through a quantity of 40 hits the perceived demand curve at a price of $16.

Step 3: The firm calculates total revenue, total cost, and profit. Total revenue is the rectangle with quantity on the horizontal axis and price on the vertical axis. Total cost is the rectangle with quantity on the horizontal axis and average cost on the vertical axis. Profit is total revenue of $640 minus total cost of $580, or $60, which is the more darkly shaded area in the diagram.

calculated as the change in total revenue divided by the change in quantity. The final columns of the table show total cost, marginal cost, and average cost. As always, marginal cost is calculated by dividing the change in total cost by the change in quantity, while average cost is calculated by dividing total cost by quantity.

The process by which a monopolistic competitor chooses its profit-maximizing quantity and price resembles very closely how a monopoly makes these decisions, and can be summed up in the same three-step process in which the firm: (1) selects the profit-maximizing quantity to produce; (2) decides what price to charge; and (3) determines total revenue, total cost, and profit.

Step 1: The Monopolistic Competitor Determines Its Profit-Maximizing Level of Output

The Authentic Chinese Pizza company will determine the profit-maximizing quantity to produce by considering its marginal revenues and marginal costs. If the firm is producing at a quantity of output where marginal revenue exceeds marginal cost, then the firm should keep expanding production because each marginal unit is adding to profit by bringing in more revenue than its cost. In this way, the firm will produce up to the quantity where MR = MC. If the firm is producing at a quantity where marginal costs exceed marginal revenue, then each marginal unit is costing more than the revenue it brings in, and the firm will increase its profits by reducing the quantity of output. In this example, MR and MC intersect at a quantity of 40, which is the profit-maximizing level of output for the firm.

Step 2: The Monopolistic Competitor Decides What Price to Charge

When the firm has determined its profit-maximizing quantity of output, it can then look to its perceived demand curve to find out what it can charge for that quantity of output. In graphical terms, this process can be shown as a vertical line reaching up through the profit-maximizing quantity of 40 until it hits the firm's perceived demand curve. For Authentic Chinese Pizza, it should charge a price of $16 per pizza for a quantity of 40.

Step 3: Calculate Total Revenue, Total Cost, and Profit

At a quantity of 40, the price of $16 lies above the average cost curve, so the firm is making economic profits. From the table, at an output of 40, the firm's total revenue is $640 and its total cost are $580, so profits are $60. In Exhibit 12-2, the firm's total revenues are the rectangle with the quantity of 40 on the horizontal axis and the price of $16 on the vertical axis. The firm's total cost is the smaller rectangle with the same quantity of 40 on the horizontal axis but the average cost of $14.50 on the vertical axis. Profits are total revenues minus total costs, which is the shaded area above the average cost curve.

Although the process by which a monopolistic competitor makes decisions about quantity and price is similar to the way in which a monopolist makes such decisions, two differences are worth remembering. First, although both a monopolist and a monopolistic competitor face downward-sloping demand curves, the monopolist's perceived demand curve is the market demand curve, while the perceived demand curve for a monopolistic competitor is based on the extent of its product differentiation and how many competitors it faces. Second, a monopolist is surrounded by barriers to entry and need not fear entry, but a monopolistic competitor who earns profits must expect the entry of firms with similar, if differentiated, products.

Monopolistic Competitors and Entry

If one monopolistic competitor earns abnormally high profits, other firms will be tempted to enter the market. If one gas station is earning high profits, then it will be tempting for another gas station to open across the street or down the road—and perhaps the new gas station can also plan to sell coffee or have a carwash or some other attraction for potential customers. A successful restaurant with a unique barbecue sauce must be concerned that other restaurants will try to copy the sauce and offer their own unique recipes, too. A laundry detergent with a great reputation for quality must be concerned that competitors may seek to build their own reputations.

The entry of other firms into the same general market (like gas or restaurants or detergent) shifts the demand curve perceived by a monopolistically competitive firm. As more firms enter the market, the quantity demanded at a given price for any particular firm will decline, and the firm's perceived demand curve will shift to the left. As a firm's perceived demand curve shifts to the left, its marginal revenue curve will shift to the left, too. The shift in marginal revenue will change the profit-maximizing quantity that the firm chooses to produce, since marginal revenue will then equal marginal cost at a different point.

Exhibit 12-3a shows a situation where a monopolistic competitor was earning a profit with its original perceived demand curve D_0. The intersection of the marginal revenue curve MR_0 and marginal cost curve MC occurs at a quantity Q_0, which is associated on the demand curve at point T with price P_0. The combination of price P_0 and quantity Q_0 lies above the average cost curve, which shows that the firm is earning profits.

However, after entry occurred, the firm's perceived demand curve shifts to the left from D_0 to D_1, and the associated marginal revenue curve shifts from MR_0 to MR_1. The new quantity of profit-maximizing output is Q_1 because the intersection of the MR_1 and MC now occurs at point U. Moving vertically up from that quantity, the optimal price/quantity choice on the demand curve occurs at point V, where the firm's perceived demand curve touches the average cost curve. When price is equal to average cost, economic profits are zero. Thus, although a monopolistically competitive firm may earn abnormally high profits in the short term, the process of entry will drive those profits down to zero in the long run.

Exhibit 12-3b shows the reverse situation, where a monopolistically competitive firm is originally earning losses. The intersection of the original marginal revenue curve MR_0

The intersection of the original marginal revenue curve MR_0 and the marginal cost curve occurs at point S. Thus, the profit-maximizing quantity is Q_0, and the corresponding price on demand curve D_0 is P_0. The firm is earning a profit because price is above average cost. Profit encourages entry. As a result, the firm's perceived demand curve shifts from D_0 to D_1, and the marginal revenue curve shifts from MR_0 to MR_1. The new intersection of MR_1 and MC is at U. Now, the profit-maximizing quantity is Q_1, and the profit-maximizing price on demand curve D_1 is P_1. Point V sits right on the average cost curve, so because of entry, the firm is now earning zero profit.

(a) Profit induces entry; shift to zero profit

The intersection of the original marginal revenue curve MR_0 and the marginal cost curve occurs at point W. Thus, the profit-maximizing quantity is Q_0, and the corresponding price on demand curve D_0 is P_0. The firm is suffering a loss because price is below average cost. Loss leads to exit. As a result, the firm's perceived demand curve shifts from D_0 to D_1, and its marginal revenue curve shifts from MR_0 to MR_1. The new intersection of MR_1 and MC is at Y. Now, the profit-maximizing quantity is Q_1, and the profit-maximizing price on demand curve D_1 is P_1. Point Z sits right on the average cost curve, so because of exit, the firm is now earning zero profit.

(b) Loss induces exit; shift to zero profit

EXHIBIT 12-3 Monopolistic Competition, Entry, and Exit

Why Does a Shift in Perceived Demand Cause a Shift in Marginal Revenue?

The combinations of price and quantity at each point on a firm's perceived demand curve are used to calculate total revenue for each combination of price and quantity. This information on total revenue is then used to calculate marginal revenue, which is the change in total revenue divided by the change in quantity. A change in perceived demand will change total revenue at every quantity of output, and in turn, the change in total revenue will shift marginal revenue at each quantity of output. Thus, when entry occurs in a monopolistically competitive industry, the perceived demand curve for each firm will shift to the left because a smaller quantity will be demanded at any given price—and the marginal revenue curve will shift to the left as well. Conversely, exit causes the perceived demand curve for a monopolistically competitive firm to shift to the right, and the corresponding marginal revenue curve shifts right, too.

and the marginal cost curve MC occurs at point W, which represents a quantity of Q_0. The price associated with Q_0 at point X on the original demand curve D_0 is P_0. This price lies below the average cost curve, which shows that the firm is making losses. In the short run, firms may continue to produce, as long as the price covers their average variable costs (which for simplicity are not shown in this exhibit). But in the long run, some firms will exit. When exit occurs, the perceived demand curve for the remaining firms will shift to the right from D_0 to D_1 because at any given price, each of the remaining firms will be able to sell a larger quantity. The associated marginal revenue curve will shift from MR_0 to MR_1. The new intersection of MR_1 and MC occurs at point Y, which is at the quantity Q_1. The price P_1 associated with Q_1 on the firm's new perceived demand curve D_1 now sits right on the average cost curve at point Z. Through the process of exit, the monopolistically competitive firms remaining in the market are no longer earning losses, but instead are earning zero economic profits.

Monopolistic competitors can make a profit or loss in the short run, but in the long run, entry and exit will drive these firms toward a zero-profit outcome. However, the zero-profit outcome in monopolistic competition looks different from the zero-profit outcome in perfect competition in several ways relating both to efficiency and to variety in the market.

Monopolistic Competition and Efficiency

The long-term result of entry and exit in a perfectly competitive market is that all firms end up selling at the price level determined by the lowest point on the average cost curve. This outcome is why perfect competition displays productive efficiency; goods are being produced at the lowest possible average cost. However, in monopolistic competition, the end result of entry and exit is that firms end up with a price that lies on the downward-sloping portion of the average cost curve, not at the very bottom of the AC curve. Thus, monopolistic competition will not be productively efficient.

In a perfectly competitive market, each firm produces at a quantity where price is set equal to marginal cost, P = MC, both in the short run and in the long run. This outcome is why perfect competition displays allocative efficiency; the social benefits of additional production, as measured by the price that people are willing to pay, are in balance with the marginal costs to society of that production. But in a monopolistically competitive market, the rule for maximizing profit is to set MR = MC—and price is higher than marginal revenue, not equal to it. When P > MC, which is the outcome in a monopolistically competitive market, the benefits to society of providing additional quantity as measured by the price that people are willing to pay exceeds the marginal costs to society of producing those units. Thus, a monopolistically competitive industry will produce a lower quantity of a good and charge a higher price for it than would a perfectly competitive industry.

A monopolistically competitive industry does not display productive and allocative efficiency in either the short run, when firms are making profits and losses, or in the long run, when firms are earning zero profits.

Advertising and Monopolistic Competition

The U.S. economy was spending about $270 billion per year on advertising at the end of the first decade of the 2000s. Roughly one-seventh of this was newspaper advertising, one-quarter was television advertising, and one-fifth was direct mail. The rest was divided up between magazines, radio, telephone directory yellow pages, billboards, Internet ads, and some other miscellaneous sources. More than 400,000 workers held jobs in the advertising industry.

Advertising is all about explaining to people, or making people believe, that the products of one firm are differentiated from the products of another firm. In the framework of monopolistic competition, there are two ways to conceive of how advertising works: either advertising causes a firm's perceived demand curve to become more inelastic (i.e., it causes the perceived demand curve to become steeper), or advertising causes demand for the firm's product to increase (i.e., it causes

the firm's perceived demand curve to shift to the right). In either case, a successful advertising campaign may allow a firm to sell either a greater quantity or to charge a higher price, or both, and thus increase its profits.

However, economists and business owners have also long suspected that much of the advertising may only offset other advertising. Famous economist A. C. Pigou wrote all the way back in 1920:

It may happen that expenditures on advertisement made by competing monopolists [that is, what we now call monopolistic competitors] will simply neutralize one another, and leave the industrial position exactly as it would have been if neither had expended anything. For, clearly, if each of two rivals makes equal efforts to attract the favor of the public away from the other, the total result is the same as it would have been if neither had made any effort at all.

The Benefits of Variety and Product Differentiation

Even though monopolistic competition does not provide productive efficiency or allocative efficiency, it has benefits of its own. Product differentiation is based on variety and innovation. Many people would prefer to live in an economy with many kinds of clothes and foods and car styles, not a world of perfect competition where everyone will always wear blue jeans and white shirts, eat only spaghetti with plain red sauce, and drive an identical model of car. Many people would prefer to live in an economy where firms are struggling to figure out ways of attracting customers by methods like friendlier service, free delivery, guarantees of quality, variations on existing products, and a better shopping experience.

Economists have struggled, with only partial success, to address the question of whether a market-oriented economy produces the optimal amount of variety. Critics of market-oriented economies argue that society doesn't really need dozens of different athletic shoes or breakfast cereals or brands of deodorant. They argue that much of the cost of creating such a high degree of product differentiation, and then of advertising and marketing this differentiation, is socially wasteful—that is, most people would be just as happy with a smaller range of differentiated products produced and sold at a lower price. Defenders of a market-oriented economy respond that if people don't want to buy differentiated products or highly advertised brand names, no one is forcing them to do so. Moreover, they argue that consumers benefit substantially when firms seek short-term profits by providing differentiated products. This controversy may never be fully resolved, in part because deciding on the optimal amount of variety is very difficult, and in part because the two sides often place different values on what variety means for consumers.

Oligopoly

oligopoly: When a few large firms have all or most of the sales in an industry.

Oligopoly arises when a few large firms have all or most of the sales in an industry. Oligopolistic firms are like cats in a bag. They can either scratch each other to pieces or cuddle up and get comfortable with one another. If oligopolists compete hard against each other, the result may be that they end up acting very much like perfect competitors, driving down costs and leading to zero profits for all. But if oligopolists cooperate with each other, they may effectively act like a monopoly and succeed in pushing up prices and earning consistently high levels of profit. Analyzing the choices of oligopolistic firms about pricing and quantity produced involves thinking through these different choices.

Why Do Oligopolies Exist?

A combination of the barriers to entry that create monopolies and the product differentiation that characterizes monopolistic competition can create the setting for an oligopoly. For example, when a government grants a patent for an invention to one firm, it may create a monopoly. But when the government grants patents to, say, three different pharmaceutical companies that each has its own drug for reducing high blood pressure, those three firms may become an oligopoly.

Similarly, a natural monopoly will arise when the size of the firm that is needed to operate at the minimum of the long-run average cost curve is large compared to the quantity demanded in the market. In such a setting, the market only has room for one firm because no smaller firm can operate at a low enough average cost to compete, and no larger firm could sell what it produced, given the quantity demanded in the market. But quantity demanded in the market may also be, say, two or three times the quantity needed to produce at the minimum of the average cost curve—which means that the market would have room for only two or three oligopoly firms. Again, smaller firms would have higher average costs and be unable to compete, while larger firms would produce such a high quantity that they would not be able to sell it at a profitable price. This combination of economies of scale and market demand may explain the Boeing-Airbus oligopoly in making large passenger aircraft.

The product differentiation at the heart of monopolistic competition can also play a role in creating an oligopoly. For example, firms may reach at least a certain minimum size before they are able to spend enough on advertising and marketing to create a recognizable brand name. The problem in competing with, say, Coca-Cola or Pepsi is not that producing fizzy drinks is technologically difficult, but rather that creating a brand name and marketing effort to equal Coke or Pepsi is an enormous task.

Collusion or Competition?

When oligopoly firms in a certain market decide what quantity to produce and what price to charge, they face a temptation to act as if they were a monopoly. By acting together like a monopoly, oligopolistic firms could then hold down output, charge a higher price, and divide up the monopoly level of profit amongst themselves. When firms act together in this way to reduce output and keep prices high, it is called **collusion**. A group of firms that collude to produce the monopoly output and sell at the monopoly price is called a **cartel**. The desire of businesses to avoid competing with each other, so that they can instead raise the prices that they charge and earn higher profits, has been well-understood by economists for a long time. Adam Smith wrote in *The Wealth of Nations* way back in 1776: "People of the same trade seldom meet together, even for merriment and diversion, but the conversation ends in a conspiracy against the public, or in some contrivance to raise prices."

But even when oligopolists recognize that they would benefit as a group by acting like a monopoly, each individual oligopoly faces a private temptation to produce just a slightly higher quantity and earn slightly higher profit—while still counting on the other oligopolists to hold down their production and keep prices high. If at least some oligopolists give in to this temptation and start producing more, then the market price will fall. Indeed, a small handful of oligopoly firms may end up competing so fiercely that they all end up earning zero profits—as if they were perfect competitors.

The Prisoner's Dilemma

To gain a deeper understanding of how oligopoly firms may either act together like a monopolist or compete with each other, economists use **game theory**, a branch of mathematics that analyzes situations in which players must make decisions and then receive payoffs. Game theory has found widespread applications in the social sciences, as well

collusion: When firms act together to reduce output and keep prices high.

cartel: A group of firms that collude to produce the monopoly output and sell at the monopoly price.

game theory: A branch of mathematics often used by economists that analyzes situations in which players must make decisions and then receive payoffs.

	Prisoner B	
	Remain Silent (cooperate with other prisoner)	Confess (don't cooperate with other prisoner)
Prisoner A Remain Silent (cooperate with other prisoner)	A gets 2 years, B gets 2 years	B gets 1 year, A gets 8 years
Confess (don't cooperate with other prisoner)	A gets 1 year, B gets 8 years	A gets 5 years, B gets 5 years

EXHIBIT 12-4 The Prisoner's Dilemma Problem

as in business, law, and military strategy. The number of players, the range of choices available to them, the order in which they decide, the ways in which the players interact, the amount of the payoffs, and the amount of information available to the players can all differ from game to game.

The **prisoner's dilemma**, a game in which the gains from cooperation are larger than the rewards from pursing self-interest, can be used to illustrate the possibilities for acting together faced by oligopolistic firms. Many games are named for a story that offers an intuitive understanding of the situation, and the story behind the prisoner's dilemma runs like this. Two prisoners are arrested. When they are taken to the police station, they refuse to say anything and are put in separate interrogation rooms. Eventually, a police officer enters the room where Prisoner A is being held and says: "You know what? Your partner in the other room is confessing. So your partner is going to get a light prison sentence of just one year, and because you're remaining silent, the judge is going to stick you with eight years in prison. Why don't you get smart? If you confess, too, we'll cut your jail time down to five years." Over in the next room, another police officer is giving exactly the same speech to Prisoner B. What the police officers don't say is that if both prisoners remain silent, the evidence against them is not especially strong, and the prisoners will end up with only two years in jail each.

The game theory situation facing the two prisoners is illustrated in Exhibit 12-4. To understand the prisoner's dilemma, first consider the choices from Prisoner A's point of view. If A believes that his partner B will confess, then A ought to confess, too, so as to not get stuck with the eight years in prison. But if A believes that B will not confess, then A will be tempted to act selfishly and confess, so as to serve only one year. The key point is that A has an incentive to confess, regardless of what choice B makes! B faces the same set of choices and thus will have an incentive to confess regardless of what choice A makes. The result is that if the prisoners each pursue their own self-interest, both will confess, and they will end up doing a total of 10 years of jail time between them.

But if the two prisoners had cooperated by both remaining silent, they would only have had to serve a total of four years of jail time between them. If the two prisoners can work out some way of cooperating so that neither one will confess, they will both be better off than if they each follow their own individual self-interest, which in this case leads straight into longer jail terms for both.

The Oligopoly Version of the Prisoner's Dilemma

The members of an oligopoly can face a prisoner's dilemma, too. If each of the oligopolists cooperates in holding down output, then high monopoly profits are possible. But each oligopolist must worry that while it is holding down output, other firms are pursuing their own self-interest by raising output and earning higher profits. Exhibit 12-5 shows the prisoner's dilemma for a two-firm oligopoly—known as a **duopoly**. If Firms A and

prisoner's dilemma: A game in which if both players pursue their own self-interest, they both end up worse off than if they cooperate.

duopoly: An oligopoly with only two firms.

		Firm B	
		Holds Down Output (cooperates with other firm)	Increases Output (doesn't cooperate with other firm)
Firm A	Holds Down Output (cooperates with other firm)	A gets $1,000 B gets $1,000	B gets $200 A gets $1,500
	Increases Output (doesn't cooperate with other firm)	A gets $1,500 B gets $200	A gets $400 B gets $400

EXHIBIT 12-5 A Prisoner's Dilemma for Oligopolists

B both agree to hold down output, they are acting together as a monopoly and will each earn $1,000 in profits.

But can the two firms trust each other? Consider the situation of Firm A. If A thinks that B will cheat on their agreement and increase output, then A will increase output too, because for A the profit of $400 when both firms increase output (the bottom right-hand choice in the table) is better than a profit of only $200 if A keeps output low and B raises output (the upper right-hand choice in the table). But if A thinks that B will cooperate by holding down output, then A may seize the opportunity to earn higher profits by raising output. After all, if B is going to hold down output, then A can earn $1,500 in profits by expanding output (the bottom left-hand choice in the table) compared with only $1,000 by holding down output as well (the upper left-hand choice in the table). Thus, firm A

The Lysine Cartel: "Our Customers Are the Enemy"

Lysine, a $600-million-a-year industry, is an amino acid used by farmers as a feed additive to ensure the proper growth of swine and poultry. The primary U.S. producer of lysine is Archer Daniels Midland (ADM), but several other large European and Japanese firms are in this market. For a time in the first half of the 1990s, the world's major lysine producers met together in hotel conference rooms and decided together exactly how much each firm would sell and what it would charge. But the U.S. Federal Bureau of Investigation had learned of the cartel and bugged a number of their phone calls and meetings.

From FBI surveillance tapes, here's a comment that Terry Wilson, president of the corn processing division at ADM, made to the other lysine producers at a 1994 meeting in Mona, Hawaii:

I wanna go back and I wanna say something very simple. If we're going to trust each other, okay, and if I'm assured that I'm gonna get 67,000 tons by the year's end, we're gonna sell it at the prices we agreed to. . . . The only thing we need to talk about there because we are gonna get manipulated by these God damn buyers—they can be smarter

than us if we let them be smarter. . . . They [the customers] are not your friend. They are not my friend. And we gotta have 'em, but they are not my friends. You are my friend. I wanna be closer to you than I am to any customer. Cause you can make us . . . money. . . . And all I wanna to tell you again is let's—let's put the prices on the board. Let's all agree that's what we're gonna do and then walk out of here and do it.

The price of lysine doubled while the cartel was in effect. Confronted by the FBI tapes, Archer Daniels Midland pled guilty in 1996 and paid a fine of $100 million. A number of top executives, both at ADM and other firms, later paid fines of up to $350,000 and were sentenced to 24–30 months in prison.

In another one of the FBI recordings, the president of Archer Daniels Midland told an executive from another competing firm that ADM had a slogan that, in his words, had "penetrated the whole company." The company president stated the slogan this way: "Our competitors are our friends. Our customers are the enemy." That slogan could stand as the motto of cartels everywhere.

will reason that it makes sense to expand output if B holds down output and that it also makes sense to expand output if B raises output. Again, B faces a parallel set of decisions.

The result of this prisoner's dilemma is often that even though A and B could make the highest combined profits by cooperating in producing a lower level of output and acting like a monopolist, the two firms may well act in their own self-interest and end up in a situation where they both increase output and earn only $400 each in profits.

How to Enforce Cooperation

How can parties who find themselves in a prisoner's dilemma situation avoid the undesired outcome and cooperate with each other? The way out of a prisoner's dilemma is to find a way to penalize those who do not cooperate. For example, prisoners who confess to the police and cause others to be convicted may face verbal and physical abuse from other criminals. Given that one oligopoly can't physically beat up another oligopoly, firms that find themselves in a prisoner's dilemma may try to seek other alternatives to create pressure for members to keep output down and prices up.

Perhaps the easiest approach for colluding oligopolists, you might imagine, would be to sign a contract with each other that they will hold output low and keep prices high. But if a group of U.S. companies signed such a contract, it would be illegal. Certain international organizations, like the nations that are members of the Organization of Petroleum Exporting Countries (OPEC), have signed international agreements to act like a monopoly, hold down output, and keep prices high so that all of the countries can make high profits from oil exports. But such agreements are not legally enforceable. If Nigeria, for example, decides to start cutting prices and selling more oil, Saudi Arabia can't sue Nigeria in court and force it to stop.

kinked demand curve: A perceived demand curve that arises when competing oligopoly firms commit to match price cuts, but not price increases.

Because oligopolists cannot sign a legally enforceable contract to act like a monopoly, the firms may instead keep close tabs on what other firms are producing and charging. Alternatively, oligopolists may choose to act in a way that generates pressure on each firm to stick to its agreed quantity of output. For example, oligopolists may act in such a way that each firm perceives that it faces a **kinked demand curve**, as shown in Exhibit 12-6,

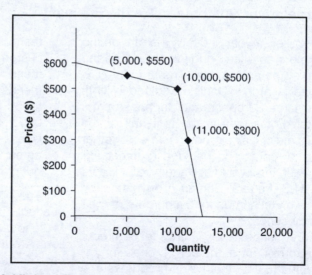

EXHIBIT 12-6 A Kinked Demand Curve

Consider a member firm in an oligopoly cartel that is supposed to produce a quantity of 10,000 and sell at a price of $500. The other members of the cartel can encourage this firm to honor its commitments by acting so that the firm perceives a kinked demand curve. If the oligopolist attempts to expand output and reduce price slightly, other firms also cut prices immediately—so if the firm expands output to 11,000, the price per unit falls dramatically, to $300. On the other side, if the oligopoly attempts to raise its price, other firms will not do so, so if the firm raises its price to $550, its sales decline sharply to 5,000. Thus, the members of a cartel can discipline each other to stick to the pre-agreed levels of quantity and price through a strategy of matching all price cuts but not matching any price increases.

which shows a perceived demand curve when competing oligopoly firms commit to match price cuts, but not price increases. Say that an oligopoly airline has agreed with the rest of a cartel to provide a quantity of 10,000 seats on the New York-to-Los Angeles route, at a price of $500. This choice is right at the kink in the firm's perceived demand curve. The reason that the firm perceives a kink in its demand curve is because of how the other oligopolists react to changes in prices. If the oligopoly decides to produce more and cut its price, other oligopolists will immediately match any price cuts—and therefore, a lower price brings very little increase in quantity sold. For example, if the firm cuts price to $300, it will only be able to sell 11,000 seats. However, if the airline seeks to raise prices, the other oligopolists will not raise their prices, and so the firm that raised prices will lose a considerable share of sales. For example, if the firm raises its price to $550, its sales drop to 5,000 seats sold. Thus, if oligopolists always match price cuts by other firms in the cartel, but don't match price increases, then none of the oligopolists will have any incentive to change prices. This strategy can work like a silent form of cooperation, in which the cartel successfully manages to hold down output, increase price, and share a monopoly level of profits even without any legally enforceable agreement.

Many real-world oligopolies, prodded by economic changes, legal and political pressures, and the egos of their top executives, go through episodes of cooperation and competition. If oligopolies could sustain cooperation with each other on output and pricing, they could earn profits as if they were a single monopoly. But each firm in an oligopoly has a self-interested incentive to produce more and grab a bigger share of the overall market, and when oligopoly firms start behaving in this way, the market outcome in terms of prices and quantity can be similar to that of a highly competitive market.

Conclusion

Competition has many faces. For example, perfect competition displays both productive and allocative efficiency; that is, products are produced at the lowest possible average cost, and the social benefits of products as measured by willingness to pay for them are balanced against the marginal cost of producing these products. But in the real world, perfect competition is rare. Firms in some industries are close to perfect competition, in the sense that they produce very similar products and must accept a market price as given. But very few markets for goods and services would meet the literal definition of perfect competition—that is, many firms selling near-identical products so that no firm can raise its price by even a penny.

Monopolistic competition among firms with differentiated products is probably the single most common form of competition in the U.S. economy. It provides useful incentives for innovation, as firms seek to earn profits in the short run, while entry assures that firms do not earn profits in the long run. However, monopolistically competitive firms do not produce at the lowest point on their average cost curves. In addition, the endless search to impress consumers through product differentiation provides greater variety, but it may also lead to excessive social expenses on advertising and marketing.

Oligopoly and monopoly are well-known, too. When oligopolies and monopolies result from patented innovations or from taking advantage of economies of scale to produce at low average cost, they may provide considerable benefit to consumers. But monopolies and oligopolies often try to earn sustained profits over long periods of time by holding down output and increasing price. They typically do not produce at the minimum of their average cost curves. Because they lack vibrant competition, even though oligopolies at least have some competitors, they may lack incentives to provide innovative products and high-quality service.

The task of public policy with regard to competition is to sort through these multiple realities, attempting to encourage firm behavior that is beneficial to the broader society and to discourage firm behavior that only adds to the profits of a few large companies with no corresponding benefit to consumers. The next chapter will discuss the delicate judgments that go into this task.

Key Concepts and Summary

1. **Monopolistic competition** refers to a market where many firms sell differentiated products. **Differentiated products** can arise from characteristics of the good or service, location from which the product is sold, intangible aspects of the product, and perceptions of the product.

2. The perceived demand curve for a monopolistically competitive firm is downward sloping, which shows that unlike a perfectly competitive firm with its flat perceived demand curve, a monopolistically competitive firm is not a price-taker, but rather chooses a combination of price and quantity. However, the perceived demand curve for a monopolistic competitor is flatter than the perceived demand curve for a monopolist because if a monopolistic competitor raises price, it will lose some customers to the competition, while a monopolist does not face any competition.

3. A profit-maximizing monopolistic competitor will seek out the quantity where marginal revenue is equal to marginal cost. The monopolistic competitor will produce that level of output and charge the price based on its perceived demand curve.

4. If the firms in a monopolistically competitive industry are earning economic profits, the industry will attract entry until profits are driven down to zero in the long run. If the firms in a monopolistically competitive industry are suffering losses, then the industry will experience exit until profits are driven up to zero in the long run.

5. A monopolistically competitive firm is not productively efficient, because it does not produce at the minimum of its average cost curve. A monopolistically competitive firm is not allocatively efficient, be-cause it does not produce where $P = MC$, but instead produces where $P > MC$. Thus, a monopolistically competitive firm will tend to produce a lower quantity at a higher cost and to charge a higher price than a perfectly competitive firm.

6. Monopolistically competitive industries do offer benefits to consumers in the form of greater variety and incentives for improved products and services. There is some controversy over whether a market-oriented economy generates "too much" variety.

7. An **oligopoly** is a situation where a few firms sell most or all of the goods in a market.

8. Oligopolists would earn their highest profits if they could band together as a **cartel** and act like a monopolist by reducing output and raising price. But since each member of the oligopoly can benefit individually from expanding output, such collusion often breaks down—especially since explicit collusion is illegal.

9. The **prisoner's dilemma** is an example of **game theory**. It shows how, in certain situations, all sides can benefit from cooperative behavior rather than self-interested behavior. However, the challenge for parties is to encourage cooperative behavior.

10. Competition has many faces. Perfect competition has powerful incentives for efficiency, flexibility, and responsiveness. But the profits to be derived from imperfect competition encourage variety and innovation, whether in the form of monopolistic competition, monopoly, or oligopoly. Moreover, there may be cases like natural monopoly where a monopolist or an oligopoly can produce at a lower price than competition.

Review Questions

1. What are some of the ways a product can be differentiated?

2. What is the relationship between product differentiation and monopolistic competition?

3. How is the perceived demand curve for a monopolistically competitive firm different from the perceived demand curve for a perfectly competitive firm?

4. How is the perceived demand curve for a monopolistically competitive firm different from the perceived demand curve for a monopoly?

5. How does a monopolistic competitor choose its profit-maximizing quantity of output?

6. When a monopolistic competitor has chosen its profit-maximizing quantity of output, how does it determine what price to charge?

7. How can a monopolistic competitor tell whether the price it is charging will cause the firm to earn profits or losses?

8. If the firms in a monopolistically competitive market are earning economic profits in the short run, would

you expect them to continue doing so in the long run? Why?

9. If the firms in a monopolistically competitive market are earning losses in the short run, would you expect them to continue doing so in the long run? Why?

10. Is a monopolistically competitive firm productively efficient? Why or why not?

11. Is a monopolistically competitive firm allocatively efficient? Why or why not?

12. Explain how a monopolistically competitive industry may offer benefits of variety.

13. Will the firms in an oligopoly act more like a monopoly or more like competitors? Briefly explain.

14. What is a cartel?

15. What is collusion?

16. Does each individual in a prisoner's dilemma benefit more from cooperation or from pursuing self-interest? Explain briefly.

17. What is game theory?

18. Compare the advantages of perfect competition with those of monopolistic competition and oligopoly.

Competition and Public Policy

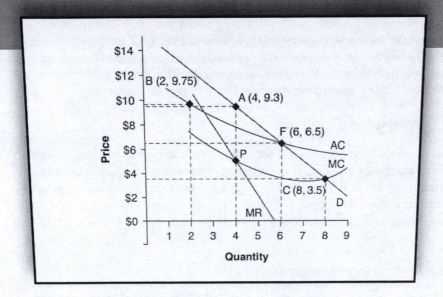

How much competition should society encourage? If an industry is perfectly competitive or monopolistically competitive, then the government has relatively little reason for concern about the extent of competition: after all, in these competitive settings, profits will lead firms to enter the market and losses will lead firms to exit, so the incentives for producing at low cost and coming up with new ways of pleasing customers are strong. But monopoly and oligopoly pose harder issues. On one side, the monopoly or oligopoly may have been created because a firm invented and patented a new product, or one or several large firms in an industry may be able to take advantage of economies of scale in a way that leads to lower production costs and potentially lower prices for consumers. On the other side, a monopoly or oligopoly may attempt to raise prices and reduce the quantity of output in a way that improves the firm's profits, but offers no corresponding benefits for consumers.

Government policy makers often must decide how to balance the potential benefits of corporate size against the potential benefits of competition. For example, in 2008, Delta Airlines merged with Northwest Airlines to create the largest airline in the world. Then in 2010, United Airlines purchased Continental Airlines, a transaction that (again) made United Airlines the largest airline in the world. In 2013, American Airlines merged with US Airways. Of course, the airlines argued that these mergers would benefit consumers, who would be able to purchase airline tickets at a lower price in a more coordinated and streamlined system of routes, because the newly created firm would be able to produce more efficiently, taking advantage of economies of scale and eliminating duplicative investments. However, a number of activist groups like the Consumer Travel Alliance expressed fears that the merger would reduce competition and lead to higher prices for consumers. Economists will spend years trying to determine whether these and other airline mergers helped consumers, hurt them, or didn't make much difference.

This chapter discusses public policy issues about competition. How can economists and governments analyze when mergers of companies like large airlines should be allowed and when they should be blocked? The government also plays a role in policing anticompetitive behavior other than mergers, like prohibiting certain kinds of contracts that might restrict competition. In the case of natural monopoly, however, trying to preserve competition probably won't work very well, and so government will often resort to regulation of price and/or quantity of output. In recent decades, there has been a global trend toward less government intervention in the price and output decisions of businesses. In the United States, for example, the government regulated the price and quantity in many industries during the twentieth century, but has removed many of those regulations since the late 1970s. Similarly, many governments around the world owned firms directly during much of the twentieth century. However, in recent decades, many countries have sold off many of those formerly government-owned firms to private ownership.

Corporate Mergers

merger: When two formerly separate firms combine to become a single firm; for practical purposes, often combined with acquisitions.

acquisition: When one firm purchases another; for practical purposes, often combined with mergers.

A corporate **merger** occurs when two formerly separate firms combine to become a single firm. When one firm purchases another, it is called an **acquisition**. An acquisition may appear different from a merger in that the newly purchased firm may continue to operate under its former company name. However, both mergers and acquisitions lead to two formerly separate firms being under common ownership, and so they are commonly grouped together.

Regulations for Approving Mergers

Since a merger combines two firms into one, it can reduce the extent of competition between firms. Therefore, when two U.S. firms announce a merger or acquisition where at least one of the firms is above a minimum size of sales (a set threshold that moves up gradually over time, and was at $78 million in 2016), or certain other conditions are met, they are required under law to notify the U.S. Federal Trade Commission (FTC). The left-hand panel of Exhibit 13-1 shows the number of mergers submitted for review to the FTC each year from 1999 to 2014. Mergers were very high in the late 1990s, diminished in the early 2000s, rebounded somewhat by around 2007, dipped during the grim economic times of 2008 and 2009, and then rebounded again. The right-hand panel of the exhibit shows the distribution of those mergers submitted for review in 2014 as measured by the size of the transaction. It's important to remember that this total leaves out many small mergers, which only need to be reported in certain limited circumstances. But about one-third of all reported merger and acquisition transactions in 2014 exceeded $500 million, while 14% exceeded $1 billion.

antitrust laws: Laws that give government the power to block certain mergers, and even in some cases to break up large firms into smaller ones.

The laws that give government the power to block certain mergers, and even in some cases to break up large firms into smaller ones, are called **antitrust laws**. Before a large merger happens, the antitrust regulators at the FTC and the U.S. Department of Justice can either allow the merger, prohibit it, or allow it if certain conditions are met. One common condition is that the merger will be allowed if the firm agrees to sell off certain parts. For example, in 2011, Google purchased ITA Software, which allowed people to search for airline flight schedules and fares. However, the government was concerned that a lack of competition in searching for airline prices might result. As a condition of making the purchase, Google was required to let other travel websites use the software in exchange for a licensing fee. In addition, Google was prohibited from entering into agreements with airlines that would limit airlines from sharing booking information with Google's competitors. Another requirement for the merger was that Google set up "firewall" restrictions to avoid unauthorized use of data gathered from customers. These additional conditions sought to preserve a greater degree of competition in the market for information about airline booking information—which in turn helps to encourage greater competition among airlines themselves.

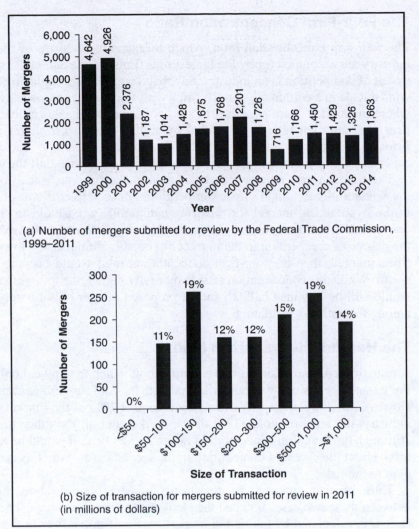

EXHIBIT 13-1 Mergers and Acquisitions: Number and Size

In the early 2000s, the number of mergers and acquisitions declined from the levels at the tail end of the 1990s, and has not yet recovered to those levels.

(a) Number of mergers submitted for review by the Federal Trade Commission, 1999–2011

(b) Size of transaction for mergers submitted for review in 2011 (in millions of dollars)

The government approves most proposed mergers. In a market-oriented economy, firms have the freedom to make their own choices. Private firms have the freedom to expand or reduce production; to set the price that they choose; to open new factories or sales facilities or to close them; to hire workers or to lay them off; and to start selling new products or to stop selling existing ones. If the owners want to acquire a firm or be acquired, or to merge with another firm, this decision is just one of many decisions that firms are free to make. Yes, the managers of private firms will make mistakes sometimes. They may close down a factory that, it later turns out, would have been profitable. They may start selling a product that loses money. A merger between two companies can sometimes lead to a clash of corporate personalities that makes both firms worse off. But the fundamental belief behind a market-oriented economy is that firms are in the best position to know if their actions will attract more customers or let them produce more efficiently.

Indeed, government regulators agree that most mergers are beneficial to consumers. As the Federal Trade Commission has noted on its website: "Most mergers actually benefit competition and consumers by allowing firms to operate more efficiently." But the FTC continues: "Some [mergers] are likely to lessen competition. That, in turn, can lead to higher prices, reduced availability of goods or services, lower quality of products, and less innovation. Indeed, some mergers create a concentrated market, while others enable a single firm to raise prices." Thus, the challenge for the antitrust regulators at the FTC and the U.S. Department of Justice is to figure out when a merger may hinder competition. This decision involves both numerical tools and some judgments that are more difficult to quantify.

The Four-Firm Concentration Ratio

four-firm concentration ratio: What percentage share of the total sales in the industry is accounted for by the largest four firms.

market share: The percentage share of total sales in the market.

The **four-firm concentration ratio**, which measures what share of the total sales in the industry are accounted for by the largest four firms, is one numerical way to measure the extent of competition in an industry. Say that the market for replacing broken automobile windshields in a certain city has 16 firms with the **market shares** shown in Exhibit 13-2, where the market share is each firm's proportion of total sales in that market. The four-firm concentration ratio is calculated by adding the market shares of the four largest firms: in this case, $16 + 10 + 8 + 6 = 40$. This concentration ratio would not be considered especially high, because the largest four firms have less than half the market.

The concentration ratio approach can help to clarify some of the fuzziness over deciding when a merger might affect competition. For example, if two of the smallest firms in the hypothetical market for repairing automobile windshields merged, the four-firm concentration ratio would not change—which implies that there isn't much worry that the degree of competition in the market has notably diminished. However, if the top two firms merged, then the four-firm concentration ratio would become 46 (i.e., $26 + 8 + 6 + 6$). While this concentration ratio is modestly higher, the four-firm concentration ratio would still be less than half, so such a proposed merger might barely raise an eyebrow among the antitrust regulators.

The Herfindahl-Hirschman Index

A four-firm concentration ratio is a simple tool, which may reveal only part of the story. For example, consider two industries that both have a four-firm concentration ratio of 80. However, in one industry five firms each control 20% of the market, while in the other industry, the top firm holds 77% of the market and all the other firms have 1% each. Although the four-firm concentration ratios are identical, it would be reasonable to worry more about the extent of competition in the second case—which is nearly a monopoly—than in the first.

Herfindahl-Hirschman Index (HHI): Take the market share of each firm in the industry, square each one, and add them.

Thus, another approach to measuring industry concentration that can distinguish between these two cases is called the **Herfindahl-Hirschman Index**. The HHI, as it is often called, is calculated by taking the market shares of every firm in the industry, squaring them, and adding them up to get a total. Exhibit 13-3 gives examples of an HHI calculation. For a monopoly with a market share of 100%, the HHI would reach a maximum value of 10,000. For an extremely competitive industry, with dozens or hundreds of extremely small competitors, the value of the HHI might drop as low as 100 or even less.

The HHI gives greater weight to large firms. Consider the example given a moment ago, comparing one industry where five firms each have 20% of the market with an industry where one firm has 77% and the other 23 firms have 1% each. The two industries have the same four-firm concentration ratio of 80. But the HHI for the first industry is $5(20^2) = 2,000$, while the HHI for the second industry is much higher at $77^2 + 23(1^2) = 5,952$. The near-monopolist in the second industry drives up the HHI measure of industrial concentration. Exhibit 13-4 gives some examples of the four-firm concentration ratio and the HHI in various U.S. industries in 2012.

EXHIBIT 13-2 Calculating Concentration Ratios from Market Shares

If the market shares in the market for replacing automobile windshields are:	
Smooth as Glass Repair Company	16% of the market
The Auto Glass Doctor Company	10% of the market
Your Car Shield Company	8% of the market
Seven firms that each have 6% of the market	42% of the market, combined
Eight firms that each have 3% of the market	24% of the market, combined
Then the four-firm concentration ratio is $16 + 10 + 8 + 6 = 40$.	

The Birth of Antitrust Law

In the closing decades of the nineteenth century, many industries in the U.S. economy were dominated by a single firm that had most of the sales for the entire country. The table lists some of the firms at this time that had more than 70% of sales for the entire United States in their industry. Supporters of these large firms argued that they could take advantage of economies of scale and careful planning to provide consumers with products at low prices. However, critics pointed out that when competition was reduced, these firms were free to charge more and make permanently higher profits, and that without the goad of competition, it wasn't clear that they were as efficient or innovative as they could be.

In many cases these large firms were organized in the legal form of a "trust," in which a group of formerly independent firms were consolidated together by mergers and purchases, and a group of "trustees" then ran the companies as if they were a single firm. Thus, when the U.S. government passed the Sherman Act in 1890 to limit the power of these trusts, it was called an "antitrust" law. In an early demonstration of the law's power, the U.S. Supreme Court in 1911 upheld the government's right to break up Standard Oil, which had controlled about 90% of the country's oil refining, into 34 independent firms. In 1914, the Federal Trade Commission (FTC) was created to define more specifically what competition was unfair. In the twenty-first century, the FTC continues to work with attorneys from the U.S. Department of Justice to enforce antitrust laws.

Single Companies That Had More Than 70% of the Total U.S. Market about 1900

- American Can
- American Fork and Hoe
- American Hide and Leather
- American Ice
- American Locomotive
- American School Furniture
- American Window Glass
- American Writing Paper
- Corn Products
- DuPont
- Eastman Kodak
- International Harvester
- International Paper
- National Asphalt
- Otis Elevator
- Union Box Board and Paper
- United Shoe Machinery
- United States Envelope

EXHIBIT 13-3 Some Herfindahl-Hirschman Index Calculations

HHI for a monopoly	$100^2 = 10,000$
HHI for an industry with 100 firms that each have 1% of the market	$100(1^2) = 100$
HHI for the industry market share in Exhibit 13-2	$16^2 + 10^2 + 8^2 + 7(6^2) + 8(3^2) = 744$

EXHIBIT 13-4 Some Examples of Concentration Ratios and HHIs in the U.S. Economy, 2015

U.S. Industry	Largest Five Firms by Market Share	Four-Firm Ratio	HHI
Banking	JP Morgan Chase, Wells Fargo, Bank of America, Citigroup, US Bancorp	74	1,446
Automobiles	Nissan, General Motors, Ford, Honda, Toyota	57	1,095
Information technology services	International Business Machines, Accenture, Xerox, Visa, Cognizant	57	1,190
Airlines	Southwest, Delta, United, American, US Airways	63	1,107
Property and casualty insurance	State Farm, Liberty Mutual, Allstate, Berkshire Hathaway, Travelers	25	300

In the 1980s, the FTC followed guidelines that if a merger would result in an HHI of less than 1,000 for the industry, the FTC would probably approve it. If a merger would result in an HHI of more than 1,800, the FTC would probably challenge it. If a merger would result in an HHI between 1,000 and 1,800, then the FTC would scrutinize the plan and make a case-by-case decision. However, in the last few decades the antitrust enforcement authorities have moved away from relying as heavily on measures of concentration ratios and HHIs to determine whether a merger will be allowed, and instead carried out more case-by-case analysis of the extent of competition in different industries.

New Directions for Antitrust

Both the four-firm concentration ratio and the Herfindahl-Hirschman index share some weaknesses. First, they begin from the assumption that the "market" under discussion is well defined, and the only question is measuring how sales are divided in that market. Second, they are based on an implicit assumption that competitive conditions across industries are similar enough that a broad measure of concentration in the market is enough information, all by itself, to make a decision about the effects of a merger. In response to these two problems, the antitrust regulators have been changing their approach in the last decade or two.

Defining a market is often controversial. For example, Microsoft in the early 2000s had a dominant share of the software for computer operating systems. However, in the total market for all computer software and services, including everything from games to scientific programs, the Microsoft share was only about 16% in 2000. A narrowly defined market will tend to make concentration appear higher, while a broadly defined market will tend to make it appear smaller.

There are two especially important shifts in how markets are defined in recent decades: one involves technology, and the other involves globalization. With the vast improvement in communications technologies, including the development of the Internet, a consumer can order books or pet supplies from all over the country or the world. As a result, the degree of competition faced by many local retail businesses has increased. The same effect may operate even more strongly in markets for business supplies, where so-called "business-to-business" websites can allow buyers and suppliers from anywhere in the world to find each other.

The effect of globalization has changed the boundaries of markets as well. As recently as the 1970s, it was common for measurements of concentration ratios and HHIs to stop at national borders. Now, many industries find that their competition comes from the global market. A few decades ago, three companies—General Motors, Ford, and Chrysler—dominated the U.S. auto market. Now, these three firms make less than half of U.S. auto sales and face competition from such well-known car manufacturers as Toyota, Honda, Nissan, Volkswagen, Mitsubishi, and Mazda. When HHIs are calculated on a global perspective, concentration in most major industries—including cars—is lower than it was several decades ago.

Because attempting to define a particular market can be difficult and controversial, the Federal Trade Commission has begun to look less at market share and more at the data on actual competition between businesses. For example, Whole Foods Market and Wild Oats Market announced that they wished to merge in 2007. These were the two largest companies in the market that the government defined as "premium natural and organic supermarket chains." However, one could also argue that they were two relatively small companies in the broader market for all stores that sell groceries or specialty food products. Thus, rather than relying on a market definition, the government antitrust regulators looked at detailed evidence on profits and prices for specific stores in different cities, both before and after other competitive stores entered or exited. Based on that evidence, the Federal Trade Commission decided to block the merger. After two years of legal battles, the merger was eventually allowed in 2009 under the conditions that Whole Foods sell off the Wild Oats brand name and a number of individual stores—to preserve competition in certain local markets.

This new approach to antitrust regulation involves detailed analysis of specific markets and companies, instead of just counting the sales of firms in a market. Modern antitrust regulators often use statistical tools and real-world evidence to estimate the demand and supply curves faced by the firms that are proposing the merger. Next, they specify how competition occurs in this specific industry: some possibilities include competing to cut prices, to raise output, to build a brand name, through advertising, and to build a reputation for good service or high quality. With these pieces of the puzzle in place, it's then possible to build a statistical model that estimates the likely outcome for consumers if the two firms are allowed to merge. Of course, these models do require some subjective judgment, and so they can become the subject of legal disputes between the antitrust authorities and the companies that wish to merge.

Regulating Anticompetitive Behavior

The U.S. antitrust laws reach beyond blocking mergers that would reduce competition to include a wide array of anticompetitive practices. For example, it is illegal for competitors to collude together and make pricing and output decisions, as if they were a monopoly firm. The Federal Trade Commission and the U.S. Department of Justice have guidelines that forbid firms from agreeing to fix prices or output, rig bids, or share or divide markets by allocating customers, suppliers, territories, or lines of commerce. In the late 1990s, for example, the antitrust regulators prosecuted an international cartel of vitamin manufacturers, including the Swiss firm Hoffman-La Roche, the German firm BASF, and the French firm Rhone-Poulenc. These firms reached agreements on how much to produce, how much to charge, and which firm would sell to which customers. The high-priced vitamins were then bought by firms like General Mills, Kellogg, Purina-Mills, and Proctor and Gamble, which pushed up the prices of products for people and animals. Hoffman-La Roche, for example, pleaded guilty in May 1999 and agreed both to pay a fine of $500 million and to have at least one top executive serve four months of jail time.

Under the U.S. antitrust laws, monopoly itself is not illegal. If a firm has a monopoly because of a newly patented invention, for example, the law explicitly allows a firm to earn higher-than-normal profits for a time as a reward for innovation. If a firm achieves a large share of the market by producing a better product at a lower price, such behavior is not prohibited by antitrust law.

Antitrust law includes rules against **restrictive practices**—practices that do not involve outright agreements to raise price or to reduce the quantity produced, but that might have the effect of reducing competition. Antitrust cases involving restrictive practices are often controversial because they delve into specific contracts or agreements between firms that are allowed in some cases but not in others.

restrictive practices: Practices that reduce competition but that do not involve outright agreements between firms to raise price.

For example, if a product manufacturer is selling to a group of dealers who then sell to the general public, it is illegal for the manufacturer to demand a **minimum resale price maintenance agreement**, which would require the dealers to sell for at least a certain minimum price. A minimum price contract is illegal because it would restrict competition among dealers. However, the manufacturer is legally allowed to "suggest" minimum prices and to stop selling to dealers who regularly undercut the suggested price. If you think this rule sounds like a fairly subtle distinction, you're right.

minimum resale price maintenance agreement: An agreement that requires a dealer who buys from a manufacturer to sell for at least a certain minimum price.

An **exclusive dealing** agreement between a manufacturer and a dealer, which requires that the dealer sell only products from one manufacturer, can be legal or illegal. It is legal if the purpose of the contract is to encourage competition between dealers; for example, it is legal for the Ford Motor Company to sell its cars only to Ford dealers, for General Motors to sell only to GM dealers, and so on. However, exclusive deals may also limit competition. For example, if one large retailer obtained the exclusive rights to be the sole distributor of televisions, computers, and audio equipment made by a number of companies, then this exclusive contract would have an anticompetitive effect on other retailers.

exclusive dealing: An agreement that a dealer will sell only products from one manufacturer.

Tie-in sales refer to a situation where a customer is allowed to buy one product only if the customer also buys a second product. Tie-in sales may sometimes be illegal: for example, suppose that in order to purchase a popular CD, the store required that you also

tie-in sales: A situation where a customer is allowed to buy one product only if the customer also buys another product; also called "bundling."

purchase two other CDs of your choice. However, in other cases, tie-in sales, or **bundling** as it is sometimes called because it wraps together several products, may be legal and even common. It is common for people to purchase season tickets to a sports team or a set of concerts so that they can be guaranteed tickets to the few contests or shows that are most popular and likely to sell out. Computer software may often bundle together a number of different programs, even when the buyer only actually wants a few of the programs.

Predatory pricing occurs when the existing firm (or firms) reacts to a new firm by dropping prices very low for a short time, until the new firm is driven out of the market, and then raising prices again. This pattern of pricing is aimed at deterring the entry of new firms into the market. But in practice, it can be hard to figure out when pricing should be considered predatory. Say that American Airlines is flying between two cities, and a new airline starts flying between the same two cities, at a lower price. If American Airlines cuts its price to match the new entrant, is this predatory pricing? Or is it just market competition at work? A commonly proposed rule is that if a firm is selling for less than its average variable cost—that is, at a price where it should be shutting down—then there is evidence for predatory pricing. But calculating in the real world what costs are variable and what costs are fixed is often not obvious, either.

The concept of restrictive practices is continually evolving, as firms seek out new ways to earn profits and government regulators define what is permissible and what is not. A situation where the law is evolving and changing is always somewhat troublesome, since laws are most useful and fair when firms know what they are in advance. In addition, since the law is open to interpretation, competitors who are losing out in the market can accuse successful firms of anticompetitive restrictive practices and try to win through government regulation what they have failed to accomplish in the market. Officials at the Federal Trade Commission and the Department of Justice are of course aware of these issues, but there is no easy way to address them.

When Breaking Up Is Hard to Do: Regulating Natural Monopolies

The case of natural monopoly poses a difficult challenge for competition policy because the structure of costs and demand seems to make competition unlikely or costly. A natural monopoly arises when average costs are declining over the range of production that satisfies market demand. As a result, one firm is able to supply the total quantity demanded in the market at lower cost than two or more firms—so splitting up the natural monopoly would raise the average cost of production and force customers to pay more.

Public utilities, the companies that have traditionally provided water and electrical service across much of the United States, are leading examples of natural monopoly. It would make little sense to argue that, say, a local water company should be broken up into several competing companies, each with its own separate set of pipes and water supplies. Installing four or five identical sets of pipes under a city, one for each water company, so that each household could choose its own provider of water, would be terribly costly. The same argument applies to the idea of having many competing companies for delivering electricity to homes, each with its own set of wires. Before the advent of wireless phones, the argument also applied to the idea of many different phone companies, each with its own set of phone wires running through the neighborhood.

The Choices in Regulating a Natural Monopoly

What is the appropriate competition policy for a natural monopoly? Exhibit 13-5 illustrates the case of natural monopoly, with a market demand curve that cuts through the downward-sloping portion of the average cost curve. Points A, B, C, and F illustrate four of the main choices for regulators.

The first possibility is to leave the natural monopoly alone. In this case, the monopoly will follow its usual approach to maximizing profits. It determines the quantity where

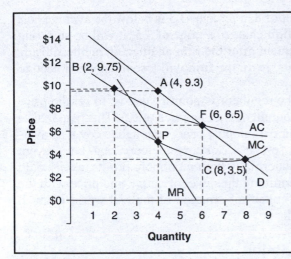

Quantity	Price	Total Revenue	Marginal Revenue	Total Cost	Marginal Cost	Average Cost
1	14.7	14.7	—	11	—	11
2	12.4	24.7	10	19.5	7.5	9.75
3	10.6	31.7	7	25.5	6	8.5
4	9.3	37.2	5.5	31	5.5	7.75
5	8	40	2.8	35	4	7
6	6.5	39	–1	39	4	6.5
7	5	35	–4	42	3	6
8	3.5	28	–7	45.5	3.5	5.7
9	2	18	–10	49.5	4	5.5

EXHIBIT 13-5 Regulatory Choices in Dealing with Natural Monopoly

A natural monopoly will maximize profits by producing at the quantity where MR = MC and by then looking to the market demand curve to see what price to charge for this quantity. This monopoly will produce at point A, with quantity of 4 and a price of 9.3. If antitrust regulators split this company exactly in half, then each half would produce at point B, with average costs of 9.75 and output of 2. Over time, these two firms might expand production, but with a downward-sloping AC curve, average costs for two smaller firms will always be higher than average costs for one large firm. The regulators might require the firm to produce where marginal cost crosses the market demand curve at point C. However, if the firm is required to produce at a quantity of 8 and sell at a price of 3.5, the firm will suffer losses because the price is below average cost for this quantity of output. The most likely choice is point F, where the firm is required to produce a quantity of 6 and charge a price of 6.5. Because price is equal to average cost, the firm is able to continue operating but does not make an abnormally high profit.

MR = MC, which happens at point P at a quantity of 4. The firm then looks to point A on the demand curve to find that it can charge a price of 9.3 for that profit-maximizing quantity. Since the price is above the average cost curve, the natural monopoly would earn economic profits.

A second outcome arises if antitrust authorities decide to divide the company, so that the new firms can compete with each other. As a simple example, imagine that the company is cut in half. Thus, instead of one large firm producing a quantity of 4, two half-size firms each produce a quantity of 2. Because of the declining average cost curve, the average cost of production for each of the half-size companies each producing 2, as shown at point B, would be 9.75, while the average cost of production for a larger firm producing 4 would only be 7.75. Thus, the economy would become less productively efficient, since the good is being produced at a higher average cost. In a situation with a downward-sloping average cost curve, two smaller firms will always have higher average costs of production than one larger firm for any quantity of total output. In addition, the antitrust authorities must worry that splitting the natural monopoly into pieces may be only the start of their problems. If one of the two firms grows larger than the other, it will have lower average costs and may be able to drive its competitor out of the market. Alternatively, two firms in a market may discover subtle ways of coordinating their behavior and keeping prices high. Either way, the result will not be the greater competition that was desired.

A third alternative is that regulators may decide to set prices and quantities produced for this industry. The regulators will try to choose a point along the market demand curve that benefits both consumers and the broader social interest. Point C illustrates one tempting choice: the regulator requires that the firm produce the quantity of output where marginal cost crosses the demand curve at an output of 8, and charge the price of 3.5, which is equal to marginal cost at that point. This rule is appealing because it requires price to be set equal to marginal cost, which is what would occur in a perfectly competitive market, and it would assure consumers a higher quantity and lower price than at the monopoly choice A. But attempting to bring about point C through force of regulation runs into a severe difficulty. At point C, with an output of 8, a price of 3.5 is below the average cost of production, which is 5.7, and so if the firm charges a price of 3.5, it will be suffering losses. Unless the regulators or the government offer the firm an ongoing public subsidy (which has obvious political problems of its own), the firm will lose money and need to go out of business.

Perhaps the most plausible option for the regulator is point F; that is, to set the price where AC crosses the demand curve at an output of 6 and a price of 6.5. This plan makes some sense at an intuitive level: let the natural monopoly charge enough to cover its average costs and earn a normal rate of profit, so that it can continue operating, but prevent the firm from raising prices and earning abnormally high monopoly profits, as it would at the monopoly choice A. Of course, determining this level of output and price with the political pressures, time constraints, and limited information of the real world is much harder than identifying the point on a graph.

Cost-Plus versus Price Cap Regulation

cost-plus regulation: When regulators permit a regulated firm to cover its costs and to make a normal level of profit.

Indeed, regulators of public utilities for many decades followed the general approach of attempting to choose a point like F in Exhibit 13-5. They calculated the average cost of production for the water or electricity companies, including an adjustment for the normal rate of profit the firm should expect to earn, and set the price for consumers accordingly. This method was known as **cost-plus regulation**. But cost-plus regulation raises difficulties of its own. If producers are reimbursed for their costs, plus a bit more, then at a minimum, producers have less reason to be concerned with high costs—because they can just pass those costs along in higher prices. Worse, firms under cost-plus regulation even have an incentive to generate high costs by building huge factories or employing lots of staff because what they can charge is linked to the costs they incur.

price cap regulation: When the regulator sets a price that a firm cannot exceed over the next few years.

Thus, in the 1980s and 1990s, some regulators of public utilities began to use **price cap regulation**, where regulators set a price that the firm can charge over the next few years. A common pattern was to require a price that declined slightly over time. If the firm can find ways of reducing its costs more quickly than the price caps, it can make a high level of profits. On the other hand, if the firm can't keep up with the price caps or suffers bad luck in the market, it may suffer losses. A few years down the road, the regulators will then set a new series of price caps based on the firm's recent performance.

Price cap regulation requires delicacy. It won't work well if the price regulators set the price cap unrealistically low. It may not work if the market changes dramatically so that the firm is doomed to incur losses no matter what it does—say, if energy prices rise dramatically on world markets, then a company selling natural gas or heating oil to homes may not be able to meet price caps that seemed reasonable a year or two ago. But if the regulators compare the prices with producers of the same good in other areas, they can in effect pressure a natural monopoly in one area to compete with the prices being charged in other areas. Moreover, the possibility of earning greater profits or experiencing losses—instead of having an average rate of profit locked in every year by cost-plus regulation—can provide the natural monopoly with incentives for efficiency and innovation.

Natural monopoly presents a situation where market competition is unlikely to take root, and so if consumers are not to suffer the high prices and restricted output of an unrestricted monopoly, government regulation will need to play a role. But in attempting to design a system of price cap regulation with flexibility and incentive, government regulators do not have an easy task, either.

The Great Deregulation Experiment

Governments have historically regulated the prices in a wide range of industries. In some cases, like water and electricity that have natural monopoly characteristics, there is some justification in economic theory for such regulation. But once politicians are given a basis to intervene in markets and to choose prices and quantities, it's hard to know where to stop.

Doubts about Regulation of Prices and Quantities

In the decades before wireless phones, when telephone technology required having a wire running to every home, it seemed plausible that telephone service had diminishing average costs and might need to be regulated like a natural monopoly. For most of the twentieth century, the national U.S. phone company was AT&T, and the company functioned as a regulated monopoly. A number of transportation-related industries may have declining marginal costs, in the sense that once a network of railroads or trucks or planes or buses was set up, the marginal cost of adding an extra passenger was low. Thus, for much of the twentieth century, the U.S. government had laws setting prices for the airline, railroad, bus, and trucking industries. Natural gas was shipped over pipelines, and since the fear of duplicate pipes could imply a natural monopoly, natural gas prices were regulated. In the United States until the late 1970s, banks were limited in the rate of interest they could pay to depositors. The argument was that if banks competed to pay higher rates of interest, they might also compete to make riskier loans, potentially imperiling the safety of the banking system.

However, by the 1970s, it became clear to policy makers of all political leanings that the widespread price regulation in all of these industries wasn't working especially well. The United States carried out a great policy experiment in **deregulation**, removing government controls over prices and quantities produced in airlines, railroads, trucking, intercity bus travel, natural gas, and bank interest rates.

One difficulty with government price regulation is what economists call **regulatory capture**, in which the firms supposedly being regulated end up playing a large role in setting the regulations that they will follow. When the airline industry was being regulated, for example, the airline industry would suggest appointees to the regulatory board, attend every meeting of the board, send lobbyists to argue with the board, provide most of the

deregulation: Removing government controls over setting prices and quantities in certain industries.

regulatory capture: When the firms supposedly being regulated end up playing a large role in setting the regulations that they will follow.

Airline Deregulation

In the early days of air travel, no airline could make a profit just by flying passengers. Airlines needed something else to carry. And so the first U.S. government regulation of the airline industry happened through the postal service, when in 1926 the postmaster general began giving airlines permission to fly certain routes based on the needs of mail delivery—and the airlines took some passengers along for the ride. In 1934, the postmaster general was charged by the antitrust authorities with colluding with the major airlines of that day to monopolize the nation's airways. In 1938, the Civil Aeronautics Board (CAB) was created to regulate airfares and routes instead. For 40 years, from 1938 to 1978, the CAB regulated the industry with a heavy hand. It approved all fares, controlled all entry and exit, and specified who could fly which routes. There was zero entry of new airlines on the main routes across the country for 40 years because the CAB didn't think it was necessary.

In 1978, the Airline Deregulation Act took the government out of the business of determining airfares and schedules. The new law shook up the industry. Famous old airlines like Pan American, Eastern, and Braniff went bankrupt and disappeared. Some new airlines like People Express were created—and then vanished.

But the greater competition from deregulation reduced airfares by about one-third over the next two decades, saving consumers billions of dollars a year. The average flight used to take off with just half its seats full; now it is two-thirds full, which is far more efficient. Airlines have also developed hub-and-spoke systems, where planes all fly into a central hub city at a certain time and then depart. As a result, one can fly between any of the spoke-cities with just one connection—and there is greater service to more cities than before deregulation. With lower fares and more service, the number of air passengers doubled from the late 1970s to the start of the 2000s—an increase that in turn doubled the number of jobs in the airline industry. Meanwhile, with the watchful oversight of government safety inspectors, commercial air travel has continued to get safer over time.

The U.S. airline industry is far from perfect: for example, a string of mergers in recent years has raised concerns over how competition might be affected. But it provides a better deal for consumers after deregulation than it did before.

information on which the board made decisions, and offer well-paid jobs to at least some of the people leaving the board. In comparison, consumers can easily end up not being very well represented by the regulators. The result of regulatory capture is that government price regulation can often become a way for existing competitors to act together to reduce output, keep prices high, and limit competition.

The Effects of Deregulation

Deregulation of airlines and other industries has been a mixed blessing. The greater pressure of competition led to entry and exit. When firms went bankrupt or contracted substantially in size, they laid off workers who had to find other jobs. Market competition is a full-contact sport.

But the bottom line is that after deregulation, firms in many industries found ways to make innovations in their management, operations, marketing, and technology. They offered more flexible arrangements to consumers and cut their costs substantially. For example, airline deregulation led to planes flying with two-thirds of the seats filled on average, compared to about half the seats filled before deregulation. In turn, fuller planes led to lower costs and to consumer prices that were one-third lower than they would otherwise have been. Since trucking prices were deregulated, trucks now drive many fewer empty miles, and the costs to shippers have fallen by 35%. When railroads were deregulated, they shut down a lot of track that was barely being used, and prices to shippers fell by 50%. Bottom line: by the start of the 2000s, the United States' great deregulation experiment of the 1970s and 1980s was saving consumers more than $50 billion per year in lower prices.

Frontiers of Deregulation

The overall success of the United States' great deregulation experiment in airlines, banking, trucking, and other industries has encouraged deregulators to push further and to think about injecting competition into industries where the arguments for deregulation are not as obvious. In the electricity and the telecommunications industry, for example, the challenge is to combine competition where possible with regulation where necessary.

Electricity had long been thought of as a natural monopoly. However, the argument that electricity is a natural monopoly focuses on the grid of wires that bring electricity to homes. It does not focus on how the electrical power is generated. Thus, a deregulation movement has grown up in which the electrical grid would continue to be publicly owned or regulated, but the business of producing electrical energy would become competitive. Since 1989, the United Kingdom has tried out various market arrangements for having electricity generators compete with each other. A number of U.S. states have also experimented with electricity deregulation, some with considerable success (Pennsylvania) and some with near-disastrous consequences (California). Many other states have been holding back on electricity deregulation, waiting to learn from the experience of the pioneers what methods work better or worse.

Another frontier for deregulation is the telecommunications industry. In 1982, the AT&T telephone monopoly that had served the United States for decades reached an agreement with the government antitrust lawyers to split itself up into several pieces: AT&T, which competed in the market for long-distance phone service; Bell Labs, the laboratory research arm and phone equipment maker, which later changed its name to Lucent Technologies; and seven local phone companies nicknamed the "Baby Bells" that each provided local phone service to a different geographic region of the United States. Since then, long-distance phone service has been a battleground for AT&T, Sprint, MCI, Worldcom, Internet firms that provide phone calls through a computer, and others. At least in theory, a variety of companies and technologies could provide local phone service, including existing regional "Baby Bell" phone companies, wireless phone companies, and cable TV companies that can use their cables to deliver phone service. In many areas, electricity or water companies own fiber optic cables that, at least in theory, could be used to provide phone service. In addition, the Internet is bringing a rising demand for high-speed computer connections, which can also carry telephone calls. As the degree of competition in telephone markets has risen, so has the level of innovation.

Deregulation does not eliminate all forms of government regulation. A deregulated airline industry, for example, still has government inspectors looking at airplane safety and counting the number of on-time departures. A deregulated banking system still has government bank inspectors seeking to make sure that banks are solvent and not taking crazy risks with depositor's money. A deregulated system of producing electricity still has government regulation of the electrical grid that delivers power. While deregulation expands the role of prices and incentives in production, market forces do rely on a foundation of laws and institutional arrangements to operate at their best.

Around the World: From Nationalization to Privatization

While the U.S. economy has had considerable experience with regulating the prices and output of various industries—airlines, water, electrical, telephones, trucking, and banking—**nationalization**, which is the outright ownership of firms by the government, has been relatively rare in the United States. However, other countries around the world have often had public ownership of a broad range of industries, including defense contracting, banking, airlines, energy production, and auto manufacturing. In many European countries in the 1990s, 8–10% of the economy consisted of government-owned production. In poorer countries of the world, including some nations in Latin America and Asia, the government-owned share of the economy was often larger, at perhaps 10–12%, and in Africa, the government-run share of the economy was often even higher.

nationalization: When government takes over ownership of firms.

Nationalization of an industry has many of the same problems as government regulation of prices charged and quantities produced. In theory, an industry is nationalized to serve the citizens of the country, but often it turns out that the nationalized industry can act as a monopoly, charging high prices and reducing the quantity of output. When nationalized industries suffer losses, they turn to taxpayers for a bailout. When a nationalized industry lacks competition, it also lacks incentives for productive efficiency and for innovation.

Thus, recent decades have seen a trend in which formerly government-owned firms are turned back into private companies. The early world leader in **privatization**, whereby a government-owned firm becomes privately owned, was the United Kingdom in the 1980s, under the leadership of Prime Minister Margaret Thatcher. Firms run by the British government constituted about 10% of Britain's economy in the mid-1970s, similar to the European average. But by the mid-1990s, after privatizing BritOil, British Steel, British Gas, British Telecom, British Aerospace, a national water company, a national electricity company, and others, government-run firms made up only about 2% of Britain's economy.

privatization: When a government-owned firm becomes privately owned.

After Britain led the way, a global wave of privatization followed in the 1990s and into the 2000s. More than 100 countries had privatization efforts in effect in the 2000s. Some of the most prominent cases have involved the shift of Russia and countries of Eastern Europe from communism to a more market-oriented society, but a great deal of privatization has also happened in Latin America and Western Europe. The main public argument for privatization often revolves around the amount of money it could raise for the government when the government sells off firms to private owners. But as economists are quick to point out, if Harriet the Homeowner sells her house, she doesn't get any richer. Instead of owning a house, which has a certain value, she now has money of that same value. Similarly, when the government sells a company, the government then has cash instead of a physical asset. The change in the form of the asset, from property to cash, doesn't make the government any richer. Instead, the deeper argument for privatization is that government regulators often aren't too good at quick reactions and innovation in an ever-changing marketplace, and that a private firm that can't rely on government bailouts will be exposed to incentives for efficiency and innovation.

Advocates of privatization often cite this motto: "Government should steer, not row." In other words, government should set the conditions and general direction of competition, but not try to micromanage the details of production. Although this motto is usually applied to privatization, it also conveys an appropriate government policy toward competition as a whole. All market-based economies operate against a background of laws and regulations, including laws about enforcing contracts, collecting taxes, and protecting health and the environment. The government competition policies discussed in this chapter—like blocking certain anticompetitive mergers, ending restrictive practices, imposing price cap regulation on natural monopolies, and deregulation—are not about eliminating government, but about shaping and reshaping the role of government to strengthen the incentives that come with a greater degree of competition.

Key Concepts and Summary

1. A corporate **merger** involves two private firms joining together. An **acquisition** refers to one firm buying another firm. In either case, two formerly independent firms become one firm.

2. **Antitrust laws** seek to ensure active competition in markets, sometimes by preventing large firms from forming through mergers and acquisitions, sometimes by regulating business practices that might restrict competition, and sometimes by breaking up large firms into smaller competitors.

3. A **four-firm concentration** ratio is one way of measuring the extent of competition in a market. It is calculated by adding the **market shares**—that is, the percentage of total sales—of the four largest firms in the market.

4. A **Herfindahl-Hirschman Index (HHI)** is another way of measuring the extent of competition in a market. It is calculated by taking the market shares of all firms in the market, squaring them, and then summing the total.

5. The forces of globalization and new communications and information technology have increased the level of competition faced by many firms by increasing the amount of competition from other regions and countries.

6. Because firms are blocked by antitrust authorities from openly colluding to form a cartel that will reduce output and raise prices, many antitrust cases involve **restrictive practices** that can reduce competition in certain circumstances, like **tie-in sales** (also called **bundling**) and **predatory pricing**.

7. In the case of a natural monopoly, market competition will not work well, and so rather than allowing an un-

regulated monopoly to raise price and reduce output, the government may wish to regulate price and/or output. Common examples of regulation are public utilities, the regulated firms that often provide electricity and water service.

8. **Cost-plus regulation** refers to government regulation of a firm that sets the price that a firm can charge over a period of time like a year by looking at the firm's accounting costs and then adding a normal rate of profit. **Price cap regulation** refers to government regulation of a firm where the government sets a price level several years in advance, and the firm can either make high profits by producing at lower costs or selling a higher quantity than expected, or suffer low profits or losses by producing at higher costs or selling a lower quantity than expected.

9. The U.S. economy experienced a wave of **deregulation** in the late 1970s and early 1980s, when a number of government regulations that had set prices and quantities produced in a number of industries were eliminated. There are current efforts to deregulate telecommunications and electricity—areas that were once thought to be natural monopolies.

10. **Regulatory capture** occurs when the industries being regulated end up having a strong influence over what regulations exist.

11. Privatization can increase the level of market competition and efficiency through the selling of previously **nationalized** assets to private owners. However, if privatization is to work well, it must provide incentives for a firm to be operated more efficiently, not just replace government ownership with an unregulated private monopoly.

1. What is a corporate merger? What is an acquisition?
2. What is the goal of antitrust policies?
3. How is a four-firm concentration ratio measured? What does a high measure mean about the extent of competition?
4. How is a Herfindahl-Hirschman Index measured? What does a low measure mean about the extent of competition?
5. Why can it be difficult to decide what a "market" is for purposes of measuring competition?
6. What is a minimum resale price maintenance agreement? How might it reduce competition, and when might it be acceptable?
7. What is exclusive dealing? How might it reduce competition, and when might it be acceptable?
8. What is a tie-in sale? How might it reduce competition, and when might it be acceptable?
9. What is predatory pricing? How might it reduce competition, and why might it be difficult to tell when it should be illegal?
10. If public utilities are a natural monopoly, what would be the danger in deregulating them?
11. If public utilities are a natural monopoly, what would be the danger in splitting them up into a number of separate competing firms?
12. What is cost-plus regulation?
13. What is price-cap regulation?
14. What is deregulation? Name some industries that have been deregulated in the United States.
15. What is regulatory capture?
16. Why does regulatory capture reduce the persuasiveness of the case for regulating industries for the benefit of consumers?
17. Who owns a nationalized firm?
18. Who owns a privatized firm?

Environmental Protection and Negative Externalities

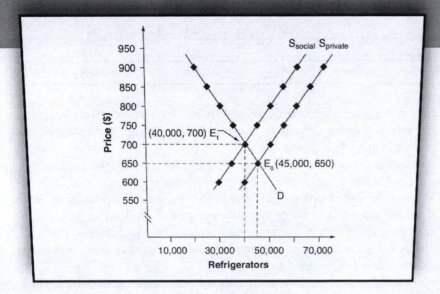

E conomic output can injure the environment. Any firm that has ever dumped waste into a river or puffed harmful gases into the air serves as an example. The problem of pollution arises for every economy in the world, whether high-income or low-income, and whether primarily market-oriented or command-oriented. Indeed, countries with low incomes and command economies have often been more willing to sacrifice their environmental quality for some additional economic output than high-income, market-oriented economies like the United States and the nations of the European Union.

In the United States, the overall quality of the air and water has been steadily improving for several decades. Many people don't realize how bad the quality of America's water and air was not all that long ago. In 1969, the Cuyahoga River in Ohio was so polluted that it spontaneously burst into flame. At that time, air pollution was so bad that Chattanooga, Tennessee, was a city where (as one news story put it) the "death rate from tuberculosis was double that of the rest of Tennessee and triple that of the rest of the U.S., a city in which the filth in the air was so bad it melted nylon stockings off women's legs, in which executives kept supplies of clean white shirts in their offices so they could change when a shirt became too gray to be presentable, in which headlights were turned on at high noon because the sun was eclipsed by the gunk in the sky."

Since then, the United States has made genuine progress against a number of pollutants. Exhibit 14-1 shows emissions of five key air pollutants in 1970 and 2014. During this time, the U.S. population increased by one-third and the size of the U.S. economy more than doubled. However, emissions of certain key air pollutants declined substantially. Data for water pollution is harder to gather, since gathering and comparing data from rivers, streams, lakes, marshes, and ocean coastlines is a huge task, but there is strong evidence that water quality has improved in many ways. The number of people served by advanced wastewater treatment plants doubled between 1968 and the mid-1990s, but because the treatment plants became so much more effective, the quantity of

EXHIBIT 14-1 U.S. Air Pollution: 1970 and 2014

Emissions of pollutants are measured in millions of tons.

	1970 Emissions	2014 Emissions	Percentage Change from 1970 to 2014
Anthropogenic particulates	12.2	2.6	–79%
Sulfur dioxide	31.2	5	–84%
Nitrogen oxides	26.9	12.4	–54%
Volatile organic compounds	34.7	17.1	–51%
Carbon monoxide	204.0	67.8	–67%

waste emitted into the water after treatment decreased by about one-third. Fish, beavers, and blue herons have returned to the Cuyahoga River in Ohio, although health warnings remain about the safety of eating fish caught there.

Of course, many important environmental issues remain. Along with the continuing levels of air and water pollution, a list of important environmental issues would include hazardous waste disposal, destruction of wetlands and other habitats, the possibility that rising emissions of carbon dioxide and other "greenhouse gases" are leading to climate change, concerns over extinction of species, and other issues as well. But these remaining problems don't alter the encouraging news that substantial progress toward a cleaner environment has been made in a number of areas.

The environmental record of high-income market-oriented economies like the United States and Europe looks greener than much of the rest of the world. In the former Soviet Union, before it split into Russia, Ukraine, and many other countries in the early 1990s, the communist government officially owned and managed all firms. The Soviet economic planners often sacrificed environmental protection in their quest for economic growth. For example, the Aral Sea in the southwestern part of the former Soviet Union, in what is now the country of Kazakhstan, was literally drained to provide irrigation water for growing cotton, leaving behind a desert of toxic salts. The meltdown of the Chernobyl nuclear reactor in 1986, in what is now the independent country of Ukraine, led to the evacuation of over 200,000 people from a region covering 4,000 square kilometers. Unfortunately, the evacuation was not in time to prevent a soaring rate of radiation-related childhood cancers. In the industrial town of Norilsk, in the western part of Russia north of the Arctic Circle, a news report stated: "The snow turns black, the air is yellow with sulfur and over 60% of the population have serious respiratory problems." The legacy of air and water pollution across the former Soviet Union is appalling; in fact, it did much to weaken popular support for the communist system.

Around the world, the cities with the dirtiest air and water typically are in low-income countries in Africa and Asia. The air quality in many of these cities is so bad that for children who live there, breathing the air has the negative health equivalent of smoking two packs of cigarettes a day. Each year, diseases from contaminated water kill about 2 million children in poor countries. In sub-Saharan Africa, about one-fifth of urban residents and half of the rural population lack access to safe water.

Every country—whether it is high-income or low-income and whether its economy is market-oriented or command-oriented—will need to strike some balance between economic output and environmental quality. This chapter begins by discussing how firms may fail to take certain social costs, like pollution, into their planning if they do not need to pay these costs. Traditionally, policies for environmental protection have focused on setting limits for how much of each pollutant could be emitted. While this approach has had some success, economists have suggested a range of more flexible and market-oriented pollution-control policies that offer mechanisms for greater reductions of pollution at lower cost. The chapter then discusses some of the costs, benefits, and challenges facing U.S. and international pollution-control efforts.

Externalities

The principle that voluntary exchange benefits both parties is a fundamental building block of the economic way of thinking. But what happens when a voluntary exchange affects a third party who is neither the buyer nor the seller?

As an example, consider a concert producer who wants to build an outdoor arena that will host country music concerts a half-mile from your neighborhood. You will be able to hear these outdoor concerts while sitting on your back porch—or perhaps even in your dining room. In this case, the sellers and buyers of concert tickets may both be quite satisfied with their voluntary exchange, but you have no voice in their market transaction. The effect of a market exchange on a third party who is outside or "external" to the exchange is called an **externality**. Because externalities that occur in market transactions affect other parties beyond those involved in the transaction, they are sometimes called **spillovers**.

Externalities can be negative or positive. If you hate country music, then having it waft over your house every night would be a **negative externality**, a situation where a third party suffers from a market transaction by others. If you love country music, then a series of free concerts would be a **positive externality**, a situation where a third party benefits from a market transaction by others. In either case, your like or dislike of country music is not a factor that the market takes into account. This chapter focuses on negative externalities, with a particular emphasis on the issue of pollution. For example, being forced to listen to concerts that you don't want to hear in your own home might reasonably be called "noise pollution." The next chapter then discusses positive externalities, with an emphasis on examples involving technology.

Pollution as a Negative Externality

People suffer from pollution even when they were neither a buyer nor a producer of the product that led to the pollution being produced. Nonetheless, the social costs of pollution can be illustrated with a demand and supply diagram. Exhibit 14-2 shows demand and supply for manufacturing refrigerators. The demand curve D shows the quantity demanded at each price. The supply curve $S_{private}$ shows the quantity of refrigerators supplied at each

externality: When a market exchange affects a third party who is outside or "external" to the exchange; sometimes called a "spillover."

spillover: When a market exchange affects a third party who is outside or "external" to the exchange; more formally called an externality.

negative externality: A situation where a third party, outside the transaction, suffers from a market transaction by others.

positive externality: A situation where a third party, outside the transaction, benefits from a market transaction by others.

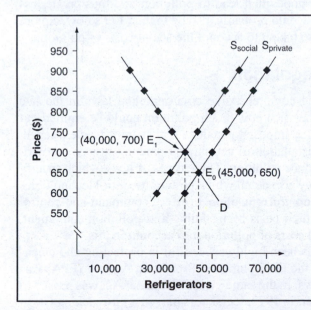

Price	Quantity Demanded	Quantity Supplied before Considering Pollution Cost	Quantity Supplied after Considering Pollution Cost
$600	50,000	40,000	30,000
$650	45,000	45,000	35,000
$700	40,000	50,000	40,000
$750	35,000	55,000	45,000
$800	30,000	60,000	50,000
$850	25,000	65,000	55,000
$900	20,000	70,000	60,000

EXHIBIT 14-2 Taking Social Costs into Account: A Supply Shift

If the firm takes only its private costs into account, then its supply curve will be $S_{private}$, and the market equilibrium will occur at E_0. Now imagine that the firm is required to take $100 of social costs of pollution into account each time it produces a refrigerator. Then the firm will need, for example, to receive $800 to produce the quantity of 50,000 that it used to be willing to produce for $700—and the firm's new supply curve will be S_{social}. The new equilibrium will occur at E_1. Taking the social costs of pollution into account results in a lower quantity of production and a lower quantity of pollution.

price if firms are is taking only their private costs into account and are allowed to emit pollution at zero cost. The market equilibrium E_0, where quantity supplied and quantity demanded are equal, is at a price of $650 and a quantity of 45,000.

However, as a by-product of the metals, plastics, chemicals, and energy that are used in manufacturing refrigerators, some pollution is created. Let's say that if these pollutants were emitted into the air and water, they would create costs of $100 per refrigerator produced. These costs might occur because of injuries to human health, property values, wildlife habitat, recreation possibilities, or in other ways. In a market with no anti-pollution restrictions, firms can receive one of their costs of production, the costs of disposing of certain wastes, absolutely free. But now imagine that firms that produce refrigerators must factor in these **social costs** of pollution—that is, the firms have to consider not only the costs of labor and materials making a refrigerator, but also the broader costs to society of injuries to health and other values caused by pollution.

Imagine that every time a firm produced a refrigerator, it had to pay an extra $100 to offset the social costs. As a result, the supply curve for producing refrigerators would shift back to the left to S_{social}. For example, if firms had been willing to produce 55,000 refrigerators at a price of $750 apiece, they would now need to receive $850 apiece before producing 55,000 refrigerators—to make up for the $100 charge for social costs. After this shift in the supply curve, the new equilibrium E_1 occurs at a price of $700 and a quantity of 40,000. As the quantity of refrigerators produced declines, so will the quantity of pollution.

Remember that the supply curve is based on choices about production that firms make while looking at their marginal costs, while the demand curve is based on the benefits that individuals perceive while maximizing utility. If no externalities existed, private costs would be the same as the costs to society as a whole, and private benefits would be the same as the benefits to society as a whole. Thus, if no externalities existed, the interaction of demand and supply would coordinate social costs and benefits. However, when the externality of pollution exists, the supply curve no longer represents all social costs. Because externalities represent a case where markets no longer consider all social costs, but only some of them, economists commonly refer to externalities as an example of **market failure**.

A general lesson holds here. If firms were required to pay the social costs of pollution, they would produce fewer of the goods that lead to pollution and thus create less pollution—although the price of goods would probably also be higher. Let's now explore how governments might require firms to take into account the social costs of pollution.

Command-and-Control Regulation

When the United States started passing comprehensive environmental laws in the late 1960s and early 1970s, a typical law specified how much pollution could be emitted out of a smokestack or a drainpipe, and then imposed penalties if that limit was exceeded. In other cases, the laws required the installation of certain equipment—say, on automobile tailpipes or on smokestacks—to reduce pollution. These types of laws, which specify allowable quantities of pollution and may also detail which pollution-control technologies must be used, are called **command-and-control regulation**. In effect, command-and-control regulation requires that firms increase their costs by installing anti-pollution equipment, and firms are required to take the social costs of pollution into account in this way.

Command-and-control regulation has been highly successful in protecting and cleaning up the U.S. environment. In 1970, the Environmental Protection Agency (EPA) was created to oversee all environmental laws. In the same year, a Clean Air Act was passed to address air pollution. Just two years later, in 1972, legislators passed a far-reaching Clean Water Act. These command-and-control environmental laws of the early 1970s and their amendments and updates over time can take considerable credit for improvements in the quality of America's air and water in recent decades.

However, economists have pointed out three difficulties with command-and-control environmental regulation.

social costs: Costs that include both the private costs incurred by firms and also costs incurred by third parties outside the production process, like costs of pollution.

market failure: A situation in which the market on its own fails to allocate resources efficiently in a way that balances social costs and benefits; externalities are one example of a market failure.

command-and-control regulation: Laws that specify allowable quantities of pollution and may also detail which pollution-control technologies must be used.

First, command-and-control regulation offers no incentive to improve the quality of the environment beyond the standard set by the law. Once the command-and-control regulation has been satisfied, zero incentive exists to do better.

Second, command-and-control regulation is inflexible. It usually requires the same standard for all potential polluters and often the same pollution-control technology as well. Thus, command-and-control regulation draws no distinctions between firms that would find it easy and inexpensive to meet the pollution standard—or to reduce pollution even further—and firms where it might be difficult and costly to meet the standard. When command-and-control regulation specifies that one particular pollution-control technology must be used, firms have no reason to rethink their production methods in fundamental ways that might reduce pollution by even greater amounts and at lower cost.

Third, command-and-control regulations are set by real-world legislators and bureaucrats, and so they are subject to compromises in the political process. For instance, existing firms often argue that stricter environmental standards should only apply to new firms that wish to start production, but not to existing firms. Real-world environmental laws are full of fine print, loopholes, and exceptions.

These arguments accept the goal of reducing pollution, but raise questions about whether command-and-control regulation is the best way to design policy tools for accomplishing that goal.

Market-Oriented Environmental Tools

Market-oriented environmental tools create incentives for firms to take the social costs of pollution into account, but then allow firms some flexibility in reacting to these incentives. The three main categories of market-oriented approaches to pollution control are pollution charges, marketable permits, and better-defined property rights. Each of these policy tools addresses the shortcomings of command-and-control regulation—albeit in different ways.

Market-Friendly Environmental Tool #1: Pollution Charges

A **pollution charge** is a tax imposed on the quantity of pollution that a firm emits. A pollution charge gives a profit-maximizing firm an incentive to figure out ways to reduce its emissions—as long as the marginal cost of reducing the emissions is less than the tax. For example, consider a small firm that emits 50 pounds per year of small particles, like soot, into the air. Particulate matter, as it is called, causes respiratory sickness and also raises cleaning bills for firms and individuals.

Exhibit 14-3 illustrates the marginal costs that a firm faces in reducing pollution. Reducing particulate emissions by the first 10 pounds costs the firm $300, a reduction of the second 10 pounds would cost $500, the third 10 pounds would cost $900, the fourth 10 pounds would cost $1,500, and the fifth 10 pounds would cost $2,500. This pattern for the costs of reducing pollution is common, since the initial reductions in pollution can use the cheapest and easiest method, but additional reductions in pollution become more expensive.

Imagine the firm now faces a pollution tax of $1,000 for every 10 pounds of particulates emitted. The firm will decide to reduce pollutants by 30 pounds because the marginal cost of reducing pollution by this much is less than the pollution tax. However, the firm will continue to emit the remaining 20 pounds, and pay a pollution tax of $2,000, because it is cheaper for the firm to pay the pollution tax than it would be to eliminate this remaining amount of pollution. A higher pollution tax leads a firm to reduce emissions by more, while a lower pollution tax leads a firm to reduce emissions by less.

A firm that pays a pollution tax will have an incentive to figure out the least expensive technologies for reducing pollution. The firm will also have an incentive to search for additional ways of reducing pollution, since it must pay the pollution charge on any remaining emissions. Firms that can reduce pollution cheaply and easily will do so to

pollution charge: A tax imposed on the quantity of pollution that a firm emits; also called a "pollution tax."

EXHIBIT 14-3 A Pollution Charge

If the pollution charge is set equal to $1,000, then the firm will have an incentive to reduce pollution by 30 pounds because the cost of these reductions would be less than the cost of paying the pollution charge. However, it would continue to emit pollution above this level. If the pollution charge is set higher, then the firm will have an incentive to reduce pollution further.

minimize their pollution taxes, while firms that have only a few costly ways of reducing pollution will end up paying the pollution tax instead. If the pollution tax applies to every source of pollution, then no special favoritism or loopholes are created for certain politically well-connected producers.

As an example of a pollution charge at the household level, consider two ways of charging for garbage collection. One method is to have a flat charge per household, no matter how much garbage a household produces. An alternative approach is to have several levels of charges, depending on how much garbage the household produces—and to offer lower or free charges for recyclable materials. Several thousand communities have implemented "pay as you throw" programs. When people have a financial incentive to put out less garbage and to increase recycling, they find ways of doing so.

A number of environmental policies resemble pollution charges, although they often don't travel under that name. For example, the federal government and many state governments impose taxes on gasoline, which can be viewed as a charge on the air pollution that is generated by cars. Indeed, petroleum taxes are far higher in most countries than in the United States, as shown in Exhibit 14-4. Similarly, the refundable charge of 5 or 10 cents that about a dozen states have for returning recyclable cans and bottles works like a pollution tax that provides an incentive to avoid littering or throwing bottles in the trash. Compared with command-and-control regulation, a pollution tax reduces pollution in a more flexible and cost-effective way.

EXHIBIT 14-4 Gasoline Prices and Taxes, 2016

	Before-Tax Price in U.S. Dollars per Gallon	After-Tax Consumer Price in U.S. Dollars per Gallon	Tax Rate (tax divided by before-tax price)
United States	$1.81	$2.26	25%
France	$1.96	$5.67	189%
Germany	$1.99	$5.69	186%
Italy	$1.99	$6.21	212%
United Kingdom	$1.79	$6.00	235%
Japan	$1.86	$4.12	121%
Canada	$2.00	$3.13	57%

Market-Friendly Environmental Tool #2: Marketable Permits

When a government establishes a **marketable permit** program, it must start by determining the overall quantity of a certain pollutant that will be allowed. Then, this quantity is divided up among the firms that emit that pollutant, with each firm receiving permits to emit a certain quantity of pollution. These permits to pollute could be auctioned to firms by the government, but in other cases, firms are simply given a permit, free of charge, that allows them in the current year to emit their current level of pollution. Now add two additional conditions. Imagine that these permits are designed to shrink the total emissions over time. For example, a permit may allow emitting 10 units of pollution one year, but only 9 units the next year, then 8 units the year after that, and so on down to some lower level. In addition, imagine that these are marketable permits, so that firms can buy and sell them.

To see how marketable permits can work to reduce pollution, consider the four firms listed in Exhibit 14-5. The current emissions of lead from each firm are shown, and at the start of the marketable permit program, each firm receives permits to allow this level of pollution. However, these permits are shrinkable, and next year the permits allow a firm to emit only half as much pollution. Let's say that in a year, Firm C finds it easy and cheap to reduce emissions from 600 tons of lead to 200 tons, which means that it has permits that it is not using to allow emitting 100 tons of lead. Firm B reduces its lead pollution from 400 tons to 200 tons, so it doesn't need to buy any permits, and it doesn't have any extra permits to sell. However, while Firm A can easily reduce pollution from 200 tons to 150 tons, it finds that it is cheaper to purchase permits from C rather than to reduce its own emissions to 100. Meanwhile, Firm D didn't even exist in the first period, so the only way it can start production is to purchase permits to emit 50 tons of lead. The total quantity of pollution will decline. But exactly which firms reduce pollution, and by how much, will be determined by the buying and selling of the marketable permits. With a system of marketable permits, the reduction in pollution will take place in the firms where it is least expensive to do so.

Marketable pollution permits have had several success stories in recent decades. In the early 1980s, the U.S. government decided to get the lead out of gasoline because medical studies showed that lead pollution in the air contributed to health problems like lower IQ and behavioral disorders in children and to high blood pressure in adults. In the 1970s, about three-quarters of all lead emissions came from burning leaded gasoline in car engines. In 1982, the EPA distributed tradable permits for lead at no cost to oil refineries. These permits were designed to phase down the permissible amount of lead over time until it was just 10% of its previous level. Oil refineries traded these permits with one another. By the end of the 1980s, lead emissions in the United States had fallen from about 50,000 tons a year in 1980 to less than 5,000 tons a year. Because of the flexibility of marketable permits in allowing the reduction in lead emissions to happen at the firms

marketable permit: A permit that allows a firm to emit a certain amount of pollution, where firms with more permits than pollution can sell the remaining permits to other firms.

EXHIBIT 14-5 How Marketable Permits Work

	Firm A	Firm B	Firm C	Firm D
Current emissions— permits distributed free for this amount	200 tons	400 tons	600 tons	0 tons
How much pollution will these permits allow in one year?	100 tons	200 tons	300 tons	0 tons
Actual emissions one year in the future	150 tons	200 tons	200 tons	50 tons
Buyer or seller of marketable permit?	Buys permits for 50 tons	Doesn't buy or sell permits	Sells permits for 100 tons	Buys permits for 50 tons

where it was cheapest to do so, the marketable permit program achieved the reduction in pollution at least 20% more cheaply than command-and-control regulation would have.

Another application of marketable permits occurred when the Clean Air Act was amended in 1990. The revised law sought to reduce sulfur dioxide emissions from electric power plants to half of the 1980 levels, out of concern that sulfur dioxide was causing "acid rain," which harms forests and buildings. In this case, the marketable permits were issued by the federal government free of charge to electricity-generating plants across the country, especially those that were burning coal (which produces sulfur dioxide). These permits were of the "shrinkable" type; that is, the amount of pollution allowed by a given permit declined with time. The plan went into effect in 1995. That year alone, emissions of sulfur dioxide fell from about 8 million tons in 1994 to just 5.3 million tons. Through the later 1990s, the cost of buying a permit to emit a ton of sulfur dioxide was about $100. Because of the flexibility of the marketable permit system, the reductions in sulfur emissions happened much faster than expected and cost millions of dollars a year less than a command-and-control approach.

Environmentalists have often tended to prefer marketable permits over pollution charges because the permits impose specific limits on the quantity of pollution—even if polluters are allowed to decide among themselves, through trading, which firms will actually emit that pollution. Also, some environmentalist groups have noticed that they can buy a marketable permit for pollution and then not use or re-sell it—thus directly reducing the amount of pollution that can be emitted. Marketable permits are a more efficient and flexible way than command-and-control regulation for society to allow a limited and declining amount of pollution to occur.

Market-Friendly Environmental Tool #3: Better-Defined Property Rights

A clarified and strengthened idea of property rights can also strike a balance between economic activity and pollution. Ronald Coase (1910–2013), who won the 1991 Nobel Prize in economics, once offered a vivid illustration of an externality: a railroad track running beside a farmer's field where the railroad locomotive sometimes gives off sparks and sets the field ablaze. Coase asked whose responsibility it was to address this spillover. Should the farmer be required to build a tall fence alongside the field to block the sparks? Should the railroad be required to put some gadget on the smokestack to reduce the number of sparks?

property rights: The legal rights of ownership on which others are not allowed to infringe without paying compensation.

Coase pointed out that this question could be viewed as one of **property rights**—that is, the legal rights of ownership on which others are not allowed to infringe without paying compensation. Does the farmer have a property right not to have a field burned? Does the railroad have a property right to run its own trains on its own tracks? From society's point of view, Coase observed, what matters is that that someone—either party!—should have a property right. If neither party has a property right, then the two sides may squabble endlessly, nothing will be done, and sparks will continue to set fields aflame. However, if either the farmer or the railroad has a well-defined legal responsibility, then that party will seek out and pay for the least costly method of reducing the risk that sparks will hit the fields. The property right determines whether the farmer or the railroad pays the bills.

The property rights approach to environmental issues often becomes highly relevant in cases involving endangered species. The U.S. government's endangered species list includes about 1,000 plants and animals, and about 90% of these species live on privately owned land. The protection of these endangered species requires careful thinking about incentives and property rights. The discovery of an endangered species on private land has often triggered an automatic reaction from the government to prohibit the landowner from using that land for any purpose that might disturb the imperiled creatures. Consider the incentives of that policy: If you admit to the government that you have an endangered species, the government effectively prohibits you from using your land! As a result, rumors abounded of landowners who followed a policy of "shoot, shovel, and shut up" when they found an endangered species on their land. Other landowners have deliberately cut trees or managed land in a way that they knew would discourage endangered species from locating there.

A more productive policy would consider how to provide private landowners with an incentive to protect the endangered species that they find and to provide a habitat for additional endangered species. For example, the government might pay landowners who provide and maintain suitable habitat for endangered species, or the government might pay when the use of private land is restricted to protect an endangered species. Again, an environmental law built on incentives and flexibility offers greater promise than a command-and-control approach, which tries to oversee millions of acres of private land ownership.

Applying Market-Oriented Environmental Tools

Market-oriented environmental policies are a tool kit, and specific tools will work better in some situations than in others. For example, marketable permits work best when there are a few dozen or a few hundred parties who are highly interested in trading, as in the cases of the oil refineries trading lead permits or the electrical utilities trading sulfur dioxide permits. However, for cases in which millions of users are emitting small amounts of pollution and have no strong interest in trading—like emissions from car engines or garbage from soda cans—pollution charges will typically offer a better choice. Market-oriented environmental tools can also be combined. Marketable permits can be viewed as a form of improved property rights. Or the government could combine marketable permits with a pollution tax that would be charged on any emissions not covered by a permit.

Market-oriented environmental tools, like all forms of government regulation, need to be applied with care, judgment, and even a dash of creativity.

The Benefits and Costs of U.S. Environmental Laws

Government economists have estimated that U.S. firms may pay more than $200 billion per year to comply with federal environmental laws. That's big bucks. Is the money well spent?

Benefits and Costs of Clean Air and Clean Water

The benefits of a cleaner environment can be divided into four areas: (1) people may stay healthier and live longer; (2) certain industries that rely on clean air and water may benefit, like farming or fishing or tourism; (3) property values may be higher and costs of cleaning and corrosion lower; and (4) people may simply enjoy a cleaner environment, in a way that does not need to involve a market transaction. Some of these benefits are relatively easy to value in economic terms, like gains to tourism or farming. Others are harder to assign a monetary value, such as the value of clean air for someone with asthma. Still others seem nearly impossible to put a clear-cut monetary value on, such as the satisfaction you might receive from knowing that the air is clear over the Grand Canyon, even if you have never visited the Grand Canyon.

Ecotourism: Making Environmentalism Pay

The definition of "ecotourism" is a little vague. Does it mean sleeping on the ground, eating roots, and being sniffed by wild animals? Does it mean flying in a helicopter to shoot anesthetic darts at African wildlife? A little of both? The definition may be fuzzy, but tourists who hope to appreciate the ecology of their destination—"ecotourists"—are a big and growing business. The International Ecotourism Society estimates that international tourists interested in seeing nature or wildlife spend roughly $500 billion per year. In comparison, the total amount of foreign aid from all the wealthy countries of the world to the poorest countries is about $130 billion per year.

Realizing the attraction of ecotourism, the residents of low-income countries may come to see that preserving wildlife habitats is more lucrative than, say, chopping down forests or grazing livestock. In South Africa, Namibia, and Zimbabwe, for example, a substantial expansion of both rhinoceros and elephant populations is broadly credited to ecotourism, which has given local communities an economic interest in protecting them. Some of the leading ecotourism destinations include: Costa Rica and Panama in Central America, the Caribbean, Malaysia and other South Pacific destinations, New Zealand, the Serengeti in Tanzania, the Amazon rain forests, and the Galapagos Islands. In many of these countries, governments have enacted policies where revenues from ecotourism are shared with local communities, to give people in those local communities a kind of property right that encourages them to conserve their local environment.

Ecotourism needs careful management, so that the combination of eager tourists and local entrepreneurs doesn't destroy what the visitors are coming to see. But whatever one's qualms about certain kinds of ecotourism—like the occasional practice of rich tourists shooting elderly lions with high-powered rifles—it is worth remembering that the alternative is often that low-income people in poor countries will damage their local environment in their effort to survive.

Although estimates of environmental benefits should not be treated as precise, they can still be revealing. For example, a study by the Environmental Protection Agency looked at the costs and benefits of the Clean Air Act from 1970 to 1990. It found that total costs over that time period were roughly $500 billion—a huge amount. However, it also found that a middle-range estimate of the health and other benefits from cleaner air was $22 trillion—about 44 times higher than the costs! A similar study examined costs and benefits of the Clean Water Act and reported that the benefits from 1990 to 1995 exceeded the costs by $6.3 trillion. Cost-benefit estimates like these are always fair ground for dispute. However, when the estimated benefits are a large multiple of costs, then it seems unlikely that performing the calculations in slightly different ways would reverse the results.

Saying that overall benefits of environmental regulation have exceeded costs in the past, however, is very different from saying that every environmental regulation makes sense. For example, detailed studies suggest that the benefits of reducing air pollution largely come from reducing particulates and lead—but the costs of reducing other air pollutants may be comparable to or greater than the benefits. Just because some environmental regulations have had benefits much higher than costs does not prove that every individual regulation is a sensible idea.

Marginal Benefits and Marginal Costs

The patterns of marginal costs and benefits of environmental regulation help to explain why market-oriented environmental tools were mostly ignored by lawmakers in the 1960s and 1970s, but are now becoming more popular. Exhibit 14-6 illustrates the common situation. When the quantity of environmental protection is low so that pollution is extensive, like at quantity Q_A, then there are usually a lot of relatively cheap and easy ways to reduce pollution and the marginal benefits of doing so are quite high. However, as the extent of environmental protection increases, the cheap and easy ways of reducing pollution begin to dwindle, and more costly and innovative methods must be used. The marginal cost curve rises. Also as environmental protection increases, the biggest marginal benefits are achieved first, to be followed by smaller marginal benefits. Thus, as the quantity of

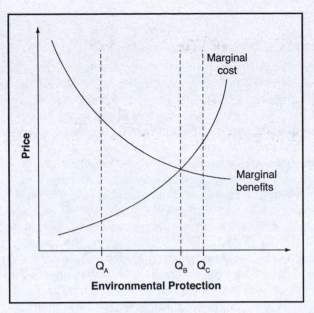

EXHIBIT 14-6 Marginal Costs and Marginal Benefits of Environmental Protection

The marginal costs of reducing pollution are generally rising because the least expensive and easiest reductions can be made first, leaving the more expensive steps for later. The marginal benefits of reducing pollution are generally declining because the steps that provide the greatest benefit can be taken first, and steps that provide less benefit can wait until later. When you are at a situation like the quantity of environmental protection Q_A, almost any step to reduce pollution will have marginal benefits greater than marginal costs. But as society draws closer to Q_B, it becomes more important to use market-oriented environment tools that hold down the costs of reducing pollution. After all, it's important to avoid environmental rules that would provide the quantity of environmental protection at Q_C, where marginal costs exceed marginal benefits.

environmental protection increases to, say, Q_B, the gap between marginal benefits and marginal costs narrows—and at some theoretical point shown as Q_C, the marginal costs will exceed the marginal benefits.

In the 1960s, before the pace of environmental protection picked up, U.S. environmental policy was probably at a choice like Q_A, where the air and water were so dirty that any policy tool, whether command-and-control or market-oriented, could accomplish a lot of good. But from our vantage point early in the twenty-first century, the United States has moved closer to a choice like Q_B, where the marginal benefits of environmental protection can often exceed the marginal costs, but the margin for error is smaller. It has become more important to target the specific kinds of pollution that are causing the greatest harms and to think about ways of using the market-oriented policy tools that offer the incentives and flexibility for firms to seek out ways of reducing pollution at the lowest possible cost.

The Unrealistic Goal of Zero Pollution

For some people, the economic way of looking at environmental problems makes sense in their heads, but not in their hearts. The head may appreciate the potential benefits of pollution charges, marketable permits, and better-defined property rights, but the heart keeps saying: "There's still too much pollution! None of these policy tools have reduced pollution to zero!"

The goal of reducing pollution to zero has a strong emotional appeal. Realistically, however, it doesn't make much sense. People exhale carbon dioxide and create bodily waste. The production of the foods we eat, the clothes we wear, and the cars we drive all cause pollution. Moreover, even if zero pollution serves as an important emotional goal,

What's a Life Worth?

In measuring the benefits of U.S. government environmental regulations (and other kinds of regulation, as well), a human life is often valued at approximately $9 million. Where does that number come from?

Economists value a human life based on studies of the value that people actually place on human lives in their own decisions. For example, some jobs have a higher probability of death than others, and these jobs typically pay more to compensate for the risk. Imagine that a certain job has an added risk of death of 1 in 10,000, but also pays an extra $900 per year. Thus, if 10,000 people take this job, then on average this group is being paid an extra $9 million (i.e., $900 multiplied by 10,000), even though one of them is expected to die on the job. A number of studies looking at jobs and wage levels have found an average cost per life roughly in the area of $9 million.

Government regulators use estimates like these when deciding what proposed rules are "reasonable," which inevitably means deciding which proposals have high enough benefits to justify their costs. The U.S. Department of Transportation, for example, when making decisions about what safety systems should be required in cars or airplanes, will only approve rules where the estimated cost per life saved is $9 million or less. The Environmental Protection Agency in some cases uses a similar rule for environmental regulations. Even resources spent on life-saving regulations create trade-offs. One study, by W. Kip Viscusi of Harvard University, estimated that when a regulation costs $50 million, it diverts enough spending in the rest of the economy from health care and safety expenditures that it costs a life. This finding suggests that any regulation that costs more than $50 million per life saved actually costs lives, rather than saving them.

it is certainly not going to happen in the next year or two. Protecting the environment is an ongoing task. Rather than arguing over whether the ultimate goal is zero pollution or a "reasonable" level of pollution, the immediate focus should be to tackle the environmental issues where the marginal benefits are greatest and the marginal costs are least.

International Environmental Issues

Many countries around the world have become more aware of the benefits of environmental protection. Yet even if most nations individually took steps to address their environmental issues, there are certain environmental problems that no nation acting alone can solve because the issues spill over national borders. One such issue is the risk that emissions of carbon dioxide and other gases are leading to a process of global warming. Another issue is the challenge of preserving **biodiversity**, which includes the full spectrum of animal and plant genetic material. No nation by itself can reduce emissions of carbon dioxide and other gases by enough to solve the problem of global warming, not without the cooperation of other nations. While a nation can protect biodiversity within its own borders, no nation acting alone can protect biodiversity around the world. Global warming and biodiversity are examples of international externalities or spillovers, where environmental effects arise across national borders.

Bringing the nations of the world to act together in addressing environmental issues that spill over national borders requires a difficult set of negotiations between countries with different income levels and different sets of priorities. If nations like China, India, Brazil, Mexico, and others develop their economies by burning vast amounts of fossil fuels or by stripping their forest and wildlife habitats, then the world's high-income countries acting alone will not be able to resolve the risks of greenhouse warming and reduced biodiversity. However, low- and middle-income countries, with some understandable exasperation, point out that high-income countries don't have much moral standing to lecture them on the necessities of putting environmental protection ahead of economic growth. After all, high-income countries have historically been the primary contributors to climate change and reduced biodiversity through their patterns of burning fossil fuels

biodiversity: The full spectrum of animal and plant genetic material.

and paving and draining their own ecosystems. It's hard to tell people who are living in a low-income country, where adequate diet, health care, and education are lacking, that they should sacrifice an improved quality of life to worrying about the cleanliness of their environment.

Can high-income and low-income countries come together to address global environmental spillovers? Every few years, it seems, there is a much-hyped global conference chock-full of impassioned speeches, but the follow-up has been only so-so. If high-income countries want low-income countries to reduce their projected emissions of greenhouse gases and to protect the biodiversity of their environments, then the high-income countries will need to pay some of the costs. Perhaps some of these payments will happen through private markets; for example, some tourists from rich countries will pay handsomely to vacation near the natural treasures of low-income countries. Perhaps some of the transfer of resources can happen through making modern pollution-control technology available to poorer countries. However, more and more, the conversation in environmental circles has come to focus on systems of pollution taxes and marketable permits. For example, perhaps oil refineries in high-income countries would be required to reduce their emissions of carbon dioxide—but as an alternative, they could buy a permit to emit carbon dioxide from governments or companies in low-income countries. One can imagine a number of deals in which a company in a high-income country would agree to provide pollution-control or energy-efficiency equipment to producers in a low-income country, thus limiting emissions in that country, and receive in turn the right to emit carbon dioxide elsewhere.

The practical details of what such a system might look like and how it would operate across international borders are forbiddingly complex. But it seems highly unlikely that some form of world government will impose a detailed system of environmental command-and-control regulation around the world. As a result, a decentralized and market-oriented approach may be the only practical way to address international issues like global warming and biodiversity.

The Trade-off between Economic Output and Environmental Protection

The trade-off between economic output and the environment can be analyzed with a production possibility frontier like Exhibit 14-7. At one extreme, at a choice like P, a country would be selecting a high level of economic output but very little environmental protection. At the other extreme, at a choice like T, a country would be selecting a high level of environmental protection but little economic output. Efficiency suggests that the choice should be on the production possibility frontier.

Economists might well disagree with one another, just like members of the general public, when considering the choice between P, Q, R, S, and T in Exhibit 14-7, which all lie along the production possibility frontier. Countries with very low income levels, like those across much of Africa, may place a greater emphasis on economic output—which in turn helps to produce nutrition, shelter, health, education, and desirable consumer goods. Countries with higher income levels, where a greater share of people have access to the basic necessities of life, may be willing to place a relatively greater emphasis on environmental protection.

However, economists are united in their belief that an inefficient choice like M is undesirable. Rather than choice M, it would be possible for a nation to achieve either greater economic output with the same environmental protection, as at point Q, or greater environmental protection with the same level of output, as at point S. The problem with command-and-control environmental laws is that they tend to lead to a choice like M. Market-oriented environmental tools offer a mechanism for providing either the same environmental protection at lower cost or providing a greater degree of environmental protection for the same cost.

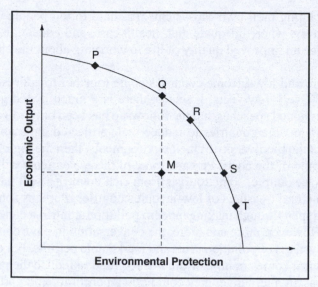

EXHIBIT 14-7 The Trade-off between Economic Output and Environmental Protection

Each society will have to weigh its own values and decide whether it prefers a choice like P with more economic output and less environmental protection, or a choice like T with more environmental protection and less economic output. But no matter what their preferences, all societies should wish to avoid choices like M, which are productively inefficient. A society at choice M could have either more economic output (like choice Q) or more environmental protection (like choice S) or more of both (like choice R). Market-oriented environmental policies help achieve environmental protection at lower cost and thus help to move from choices like M to choices on the production possibility frontier.

Key Concepts and Summary

1. Economic production can cause environmental damage. This trade-off arises for all countries, whether high-income or low-income, and whether their economies are market-oriented or command-oriented.

2. An **externality** occurs when an exchange between a buyer and seller has an impact on a third party who is not part of the exchange. An externality, which is sometimes also called a **spillover**, can have a negative or a positive impact on the third party.

3. If those parties imposing a **negative externality** on others had to take the broader social cost of their behavior into account, they would have an incentive to reduce the production of whatever is causing the negative externality.

4. **Command-and-control regulation** sets specific limits for pollution emissions and/or specific pollution-control technologies that must be used. Although such regulations have helped to protect the environment, they have three shortcomings: they provide no incentive to go beyond the limits they set, they offer limited flexibility in where and how pollution will be reduced, and they often have politically motivated loopholes.

5. Examples of market-oriented environmental policies include **pollution charges**, **marketable permits**, and better defined **property rights**. Market-oriented environmental policies use taxes, markets, and property

rights so that those who impose negative externalities must face the social cost.

6. A strong case can be made that, taken as a whole, the benefits of U.S. environmental regulation have outweighed the costs. However, in certain individual cases, the costs may have outweighed the benefits.

7. As the extent of environment regulation increases, additional expenditures on environmental protection will probably have increasing marginal costs and decreasing marginal benefits. This pattern suggests that the flexibility and cost savings of market-oriented environmental policies will become more important.

8. Certain global environmental issues, like global warming and **biodiversity**, spill over national borders and will need to be addressed with some form of international agreement.

9. Based on their different income levels and political preferences, countries are likely to make different choices about allocative efficiency—that is, the choice between economic output and environmental protection along the production possibility frontier. However, all countries should prefer to make a choice that shows productive efficiency—that is, the choice is somewhere on the production possibility frontier rather than inside it.

1. What is an externality?
2. Give an example of a positive externality and an example of a negative externality.
3. In a market without environmental regulations, will the supply curve for a firm take into account private costs, social costs, both, or neither? Explain.
4. What is command-and-control environmental regulation?
5. What are the three problems that economists have noted with regard to command-and-control regulation?
6. What is a pollution charge, and what incentive does it provide for a firm to take social costs into account?
7. What is a marketable permit, and what incentive does it provide for a firm to take social costs into account?
8. What are better-defined property rights, and what incentive do they provide to take social costs into account?
9. As the extent of environmental protection expands, would you expect marginal costs of environmental protection to rise or fall? Why?
10. As the extent of environmental protection expands, would you expect the marginal benefits of environmental protection to rise or fall? Why?
11. In the trade-off between economic output and environmental protection, how many choices will be both productively efficient and allocatively efficient? Explain.

Technology, Positive Externalities, and Public Goods

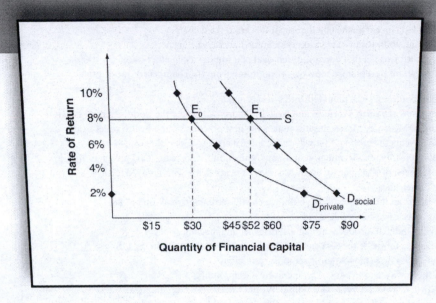

New technology changes how people live and work. Technology is the difference between horses and automobiles, between candles and electric lights, between fetching water in buckets and indoor plumbing, and between infection and antibiotics. The science fiction writer Arthur C. Clarke once said: "A sufficiently advanced technology is indistinguishable from magic." New technologies often appear magical—until we become accustomed to them and start taking them for granted.

A small sampling of the new technologies developed in the last two centuries are shown in the timeline in Exhibit 15-1. The variety of new inventions is remarkable. Some entries involve household products: the dishwasher, the coffee pot, roller skates, frozen food, video games. Some entries involve transportation: the steamboat, the gasoline-powered car, the airplane. Other entries are medical: spray medication, anesthesia, polio vaccine, antibiotics, and the artificial heart. Still other entries focus on communication: the telegraph, the telephone, radio, Internet communication.

Every invention has its own story of discovery and development, a story that often includes a parade of characters and firms over a period of years or decades. Consider the invention of the dishwasher by Josephine Cochrane in 1889. Cochrane was a wealthy woman living in Illinois who was concerned that her servants often chipped her family's fine china plates while washing them. She invented a machine where the plates sat in a wooden barrel while rollers turned them, and hot, soapy water could be pumped over them. Her invention won a grand prize at the 1893 Chicago World's Fair, but commercial success took longer. Cochrane's husband died, leaving her with few assets, and she started a company in the shed behind her house to make and sell her dishwashers. But at that time, soap for dishwashers was often expensive and of poor quality, so it often left a residue on the dishes. Moreover, a survey of women in the early twentieth century reported that they often found it enjoyable and relaxing to hand-wash dishes, so they weren't eager to purchase a

1794 Cotton Gin: Eli Whitney patents his machine to remove seeds from cotton.

1803 Medication Spray: Dr. Alan de Vilbiss of Toledo, Ohio, invents a device to spray medication into the mouth and nose.

1806 Coffee Pot: Benjamin Thompson, Count Rumford, invents a coffee pot with a metal sieve to strain away the grounds.

1807 Steamboat: The *Clermont*, invented by Robert Fulton, steams from New York City to Albany.

1809 Weaving Straw with Silk or Thread: Mary Dixon Kies becomes the first woman to receive a patent for her weaving process.

1831 Reaping Machine: The McCormick Reaper for cutting grain was not an economic success for several decades.

1833 Sewing Machine: Walter Hunt invents the sewing machine but does not patent his invention. Later, Isaac Singer becomes rich from a similar machine.

1834 Threshing Machine: John A. and Hiram Abial Pitts invent a machine that separates grain from chaff.

1840 Collapsible Metal Squeeze Tube for Artist's Paint: John Rand's invention is an immediate hit in Europe.

1842 Ether Anesthesia: Crawford Williamson Long performs the first operation (removal of a tumor) using ether-based anesthesia.

1844 Telegraph: Samuel Morse demonstrates his telegraph by sending a message to Baltimore from the chambers of the Supreme Court in Washington, DC.

1845 False Teeth: Claudius Ash's invention features porcelain teeth mounted with steel springs.

1859 Oil Well: Edwin Drake strikes oil at 69.5 feet below the earth's surface, and western Pennsylvania sees the world's first oil boom.

1863 Four-Wheeled Roller Skates: James Plimpton of Medford, Massachusetts, makes the first practical four-wheeled roller skate.

1867 Barbed Wire: Lucien B. Smith of Kent, Ohio, invents the product that will divide the American West.

1873 Typewriter: Christopher Latham Sholes sells a prototype to Remington and Sons, gunsmiths, who begin mass production.

1875 Electric Dental Drill: Be grateful to George F. Green of Kalamazoo, Michigan. Hey, it beats living with decayed teeth.

1876 Telephone: Alexander Graham Bell patents the telephone.

1879 Incandescent Light Bulb: Thomas Edison perfects an incandescent light bulb, which will see commercial use by 1881.

1882 Electric Fan: Dr. Schuyler Skaats Wheeler invents a two-bladed desk fan.

1889 Dishwasher: Josephine Cochrane of Shelbyville, Indiana, produces a practical dishwashing machine.

1892 Gasoline-Powered Car: Frank and Charles Duryea fabricate the first gasoline-powered automobile built in the U.S.

1901 Radio Over the Ocean: Guglielmo Marconi receives first trans-Atlantic radio transmission.

1902 Air Conditioning: Willis H. Carrier designs the first system to control temperature and humidity.

1903 Powered Airplane Flight: At Kitty Hawk, North Carolina, Orville and Wilbur Wright take a 12-second flight.

1908 Model T: Carmaker Henry Ford introduces his Model T automobile, which will be produced by an assembly line.

1920 First Commercial Radio Broadcast: AM station KDKA of Pittsburgh announces that Warren Harding has been elected president.

1926 Rocket Launch: Robert H. Goddard launches a liquid-fuel rocket to a height of 41 feet.

1929 Frozen Food: Clarence Birdseye offers his quick-frozen foods to the public.

1930 Scotch Tape: 3M introduces Scotch tape.

1932 Heart Defibrillator: Dr. William Bennett Kouwenhoven develops a device for jump-starting the heart with a burst of electricity.

1937 Chair Lift for Skiers: The Dollar Mountain ski resort in Sun Valley, Idaho, gets a chair lift.

1947 Transistor: William Shockley invents the transistor, the guts of the modern computer.

1948 Electric Guitar: Leo Fender debuts the first solid-bodied electric guitar.

1951 First Commercial Computer: Eckert and Mauchly Computer Co. of Philadelphia sells UNIVAC 1 to the U.S. Census Bureau.

1957 Polio Vaccine: Dr. Albert Sabin develops a polio vaccine.

1958 Satellite Space Exploration: The Soviet Union launches *Sputnik*. Three months later, the U.S. launches *Explorer I*.

1960 Laser: Theodore H. Maiman creates the first laser at Hughes Research Laboratories.

1960 Birth Control Pill: The Food and Drug Administration approves the birth control pill for sale.

1964 Operating System: IBM rolls out the OS/360, the first mass-produced computer operating system.

1970 Fiber Optics: Corning Glass announces a glass fiber that can transmit sound using pulses of light.

1972 Video Game: Nolan Bushnell invents Pong, one of the first mass-produced video games.

1974 Barcode: The first shipments of bar-coded products arrive in American stores.

1979 Cellular Phones: The first commercial cell phone system is started in Tokyo.

1981 Space Shuttle: NASA successfully launches—and lands—the first reusable space shuttle.

1982 Artificial Heart: Dr. Robert Jarvik implants a permanent artificial heart, which keeps Barney Clark alive for 112 days.

1982 First Genetically Engineered Product: Genentech gets permission to market human insulin produced through genetic engineering.

1984 The Mouse: Apple Computer introduces the mouse.

1990 Internet Programming Language Invented: Tim Berners-Lee invents HTTP and HTML.

1996 Cloning: "Dolly" is cloned from another sheep.

2000 Sequencing the Human Gene: The chemical bases of the human gene are listed in sequence.

2005 On-line Video Sharing: Steve Chen, Chad Hurley, and Jawed Karim invent YouTube.

2010 Driverless car: Google announces development of self-driving cars.

EXHIBIT 15-1 A Technology Timeline

dishwashing machine. Eventually, Cochrane's original company became the Kitchen Aid part of the Whirlpool Corporation in 1940. Today, about half of all U.S. households have a dishwasher.

Most inventions are motivated, at least in part, by a desire to earn a financial reward. This chapter begins by exploring the idea that an inventor typically receives only a fraction of the overall social benefit that an invention provides—with much of the benefit going to users of the invention or to other firms that can copy the idea behind the invention. Government has a variety of policies to increase the rate of return received by inventors, like granting patents and subsidizing research and development. However, the ultimate goal of such public policies is not to help inventors earn high returns, but to encourage a stream of inventions that will benefit society as a whole. The case of technology illustrates a broader problem that certain investments may be beneficial to society, but it may be difficult for private investors to earn a reasonable rate of return from these investments. The chapter concludes by discussing how a range of goods and services like police protection and highways share certain key characteristics with new technology, and that when these key characteristics exist, the government may need to encourage or coordinate production of the good or service, rather than leaving such investments up to incentives of the market.

The Incentives for Developing New Technology

Market competition and the invention of new technology, like quarreling relatives, have a complicated and unstable relationship. Market competition and technology sometimes support each other and sometimes oppose each other.

Market competition can provide an incentive for discovering new technology because a firm can earn higher profits by finding a way to produce existing products in cheaper ways or to create products with desirable characteristics. An innovative firm knows that it will usually have at least a temporary edge over its competitors and thus an ability to earn above-normal profits for a time before the competitors can catch up. Also, firms may innovate out of fear that if they aren't moving ahead, they will inevitably fall behind other competitors that are seeking out innovations.

However, in certain cases, market competition can also discourage new technology. Consider a pharmaceutical firm that is planning a research project to develop a new drug. On average, it can cost $800 million and take more than a decade to discover a new drug, to perform the necessary safety tests, and to bring the drug to market. If the research and development (R&D) effort fails—and every R&D project has some chance of failure—then the firm will suffer losses and could even be driven out of business. If the research and development project succeeds, then the firm's competitors may figure out ways of adapting and copying the underlying idea, but without having to pay the research and development costs themselves. As a result, the innovative company will bear the much higher costs of the R&D project and will enjoy at best only a small, temporary advantage over the competition—until the other firms copy its idea. Thus, a pharmaceutical firm might be willing to undertake certain research projects if the firm were guaranteed that if it succeeded, it could sell the new drug as a monopoly for at least a few years and earn sufficient profit to compensate for the costs of developing the new drug. But if that same firm must face market competition that can very quickly produce an identical product or a close substitute, the firm may decide against R&D projects of this sort.

Some Grumpy Inventors

Many inventors over the years have discovered that their inventions brought less of a return than they might have expected.

Eli Whitney (1765–1825) invented the cotton gin, a machine for separating seeds out of raw cotton. He received a patent on the cotton gin in 1794 and started a business to manufacture the machine. However, the machine was so wonderfully useful in the cotton-growing states of the American South that rather than paying for Whitney's gin, cotton planters built their own seed-separating devices with a few minor changes to Whitney's design. When Whitney sued in court for patent infringement, he found that the courts in southern states would not uphold his patent rights. Whitney never patented any of his other inventions and once wrote that "an invention can be so valuable as to be worthless to the inventor."

Thomas Edison (1847–1931) still holds the record for most patents granted to an individual. His first invention was an automatic vote counter, and despite the social benefits of such a machine in saving time, reducing error in vote counts, and preventing voter fraud, he could not find a government that wanted to buy it. After that experience, Edison vowed that he would work only on ideas for things that people would buy. Election controversies ever since then suggest that the market incentives have been inadequate to invent easy-to-use and accurate voting machines.

Gordon Gould (1920–2005) came up with the idea behind the laser in 1957; in fact, Gould had his research notebooks for November 1957 notarized so that he could prove when the idea had come to him. However, he put off applying for a patent, mistakenly believing that he needed to have a working laser before he could apply. By the time he did apply, other scientists had laser inventions of their own. A lengthy legal battle resulted, in which Gould had to spend $100,000 on lawyers before he eventually received a patent for the laser in 1977. But even though Gould received the patent, the laser seemed more like the work of a number of scientists working along intersecting and overlapping tracks, not the inspiration of a single person. The laser has had an enormous range of uses: manufacturing of compact discs, eye surgery tumor removal, precision measurement, navigational instruments, chemical research, printers, and as a cutting tool in textile and metalworking industries. Perhaps most of all, the laser has revolutionized telecommunications and computer networks by allowing so much more information to be carried over fiber-optic cable than could have been carried over old copper wires. Compared to the enormous social benefits of the laser, Gould received relatively little financial reward. Many of those other scientists who worked on the science leading up to lasers in the 1940s and 1950s, as well as the practical development of lasers since then, received no special benefit other than their usual salaries.

As these examples illustrate, inventors commonly receive only a portion of the total benefits of their inventions. A variety of studies done by economists have found that the original inventor often receives roughly one-third to one-half of the total economic benefits from innovations; other businesses and new-product users receive the rest of the benefits.

The Positive Externalities of New Technology

If a firm builds a factory or buys a piece of equipment, the firm will receive all of the economic benefits that result from such investments. However, when a firm invests in new technology, the private benefits that the firm receives are only a portion of the overall social benefits. In economic terms, positive externalities arise—a situation where a third party benefits from the spillover effects of a market transaction by others.

Consider the example of the Big Drug Company, which is planning its research and development budget for the next year. Economists working for Big Drug, together with scientists, have compiled a list of potential research and development projects and estimated the potential rates of return for each one. If the cost of financial capital is low, Big Drug will demand a large quantity of financial capital for research and development because many R&D projects are likely to exceed a low rate of return. However, as the cost of financial capital rises, the firm demands a lesser quantity of funding to invest in R&D, since fewer projects are likely to pay the higher rate of return. Big Drug's demand curve for financial capital to invest in R&D is shown by $D_{private}$ in Exhibit 15-2. For the sake of simplicity, say that Big Drug can borrow as much money as it wants at the prevailing market interest rate; thus, Big Drug perceives the supply curve S for financial capital as a horizontal line. At the equilibrium E_0, the quantity of financial capital that Big Drug will have invested in research and development is $30 million, and the interest rate prevailing in the market is 8%.

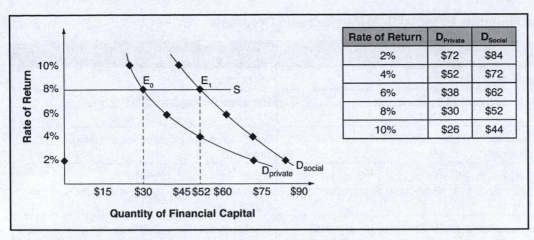

Rate of Return	D_Private	D_Social
2%	$72	$84
4%	$52	$72
6%	$38	$62
8%	$30	$52
10%	$26	$44

EXHIBIT 15-2 Positive Externalities and Technology

Big Drug faces a cost of financial capital of 8%. If the firm receives only the private benefits of investing in R&D, then its demand curve for financial capital is shown by D, and the equilibrium will occur at a quantity of $30. However, if the firm could also receive the social benefits of its investment in R&D, then its demand curve for financial capital would be D_{social}, and the equilibrium would be at a quantity of $52.

Big Drug's original demand for financial capital $D_{private}$ is based on the private rate of return received by the firm. However, every time Big Drug makes a new discovery, other pharmaceutical firms and health-care companies learn new lessons about how to treat certain medical conditions and become able to create their own improved (if not identical) products. Let's say that the economists at Big Drug calculated that the social rate of return on the investment would be twice as high—that is, a project that had a 4% private rate of return to Big Drug actually has an 8% social return. If Big Drug were able to gain this social return, its demand for financial capital would shift to the right to the new demand curve D_{social}. The new point of equilibrium E_1 will involve spending $52 million on research and development. Thus, if Big Drug could receive a greater share of the society's total benefits from its new pharmaceuticals, it would invest more in research and development. But if Big Drug is receiving only 50 cents of each dollar of social benefit that its innovations create, then the firm won't spend as much on creating new products as it would if it received a greater share of the total social benefit that it is creating.

Contrasting Positive Externalities and Negative Externalities

Exhibit 15-3 summarizes the parallels and contrasts between negative and positive externalities. For a negative externality, the private costs of an action are less than the costs imposed on society as a whole, and so private actors have an incentive to carry out activities, like emitting pollution, at a level that is greater than society as a whole desires. For a positive externality, the private benefits of an action are less than the social benefits, and so private actors lack an incentive to carry out activities, like innovation that leads to new technology, to the extent that society as a whole desires.

Although technology may be the most prominent example of a positive externality, it is far from the only one. For example, being vaccinated against disease is not only a protection for the individual, but it has the positive spillover of protecting those who might otherwise have been infected by that individual. Education clearly benefits the person who receives it, but a society where most people have a good level of education provides positive externalities for all. When a number of homes in a neighborhood are modernized, updated, and restored, not only does it increase the value of those homes, but the value of other properties in the neighborhood may increase as well. It's also possible, instead of talking about the connection between pollution and negative externalities, to flip-flop the terminology and instead talk about the connection from antipollution equipment to positive externalities. Just as too much pollution exists because firms do

EXHIBIT 15-3 Positive and Negative Externalities: Parallels and Contrasts

	Negative Externality	Positive Externality
A prominent example	Pollution	Technology
Market doesn't take into account . . .	Harms incurred by third parties	Benefits received by third parties
. . . so that as a result	Too much of the negative externality is provided	Too little of the positive externality is provided
General solution	Require those who produce the negative externality to take social costs into account	Assist those who provide the positive externality to receive a greater share of the social benefits
Specific solutions	Regulations, pollution taxes, marketable permits, better-defined property rights	Government R&D spending, tax incentives for private R&D spending, intellectual property protection, allowing business cooperation on R&D

not take negative externalities like pollution into account, one can argue that too little anti-pollution equipment is installed because firms do not take into account the positive externalities of doing so.

The last row of Exhibit 15-3 points out that the appropriate response of public policy to a negative externality like pollution is to find ways so that the social costs of the negative externality are taken into account in economic decisions. Conversely, the appropriate public policy response to a positive externality, like new technology, is to help the party creating the positive externality to receive a greater share of the social benefits. Practical proposals for reacting to the positive externalities of technology are discussed in the next section.

How to Raise the Rate of Return for Innovators

A number of different mechanisms can increase the rate of return earned by inventors of new technology: intellectual property rights, government assistance with the costs of research and development, even cooperative research ventures between companies. Let us explore these policies in turn.

Intellectual Property Rights

intellectual property: The body of law including patents, trademarks, copyrights, and trade secret law that protects the right of inventors to produce and sell their inventions.

Intellectual property rights include patents, which give the inventor the exclusive legal right to make, use, or sell the invention for a limited time, and copyright laws, which give the author an exclusive legal right over works of literature, music, movies, and pictures. These topics were introduced in Chapters 11–13 in the discussions of monopoly, oligopoly, and imperfect competition. For example, if a pharmaceutical firm has a patent on a new drug, then no other firm can manufacture or sell that drug unless the firm with the patent grants permission. Without a patent, the pharmaceutical firm would have to face entry and competition for any successful products, and thus it could earn no more than a normal rate of profit. But with a patent, a firm is able to earn monopoly profits on its product—which offers an incentive for research and development to take place. Exhibit 15-4 illustrates how the number of patent applications filed with the U.S. Patent and Trademark Office and the number of patents granted have changed since the 1980s. Intellectual property rights do provide a method for increasing the rate of return for inventors, but there are a number of reasons to doubt whether patents provide fully appropriate and sufficient incentives for innovation.

First, the economic studies that show that inventors receive only one-third to one-half of the total economic value of their inventions were all calculated in countries that already

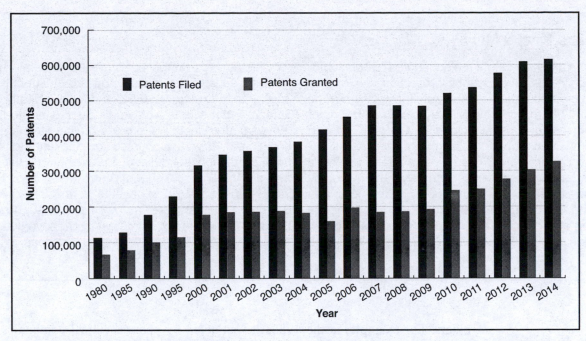

EXHIBIT 15-4 Patents Filed and Granted

The number of applications filed for patents increased substantially from the mid-1990s into the first half of the 2000s. The number of patents granted increased in the late 1990s, rose less quickly in the mid-2000s, and then seemed to increase again in the last few years.

had patents. Thus, even with patents in place, inventors of new technology are receiving only a slice of the social value of their inventions.

Second, in a fast-moving high-technology industry like biotechnology or semiconductor design, patents may be largely irrelevant. When technology is advancing so quickly, even a patent from, say, two years ago may be outdated because no firm is relying on that technology any longer. In these cases, the market forces firms to innovate as fast as they can just to keep up with others.

Third, not every new idea can be protected with a patent or a copyright. For example, a new way of organizing a factory, or a new way of training employees, or a new combination of product features may not be an "invention" in the sense that patent law uses the term. Moreover, a patent cannot cover the new ideas that it spurs others to create.

Fourth, patents and copyrights offer an incentive for research and development because they offer a temporary monopoly, which in turn allows charging a higher price for a reduced level of output. But if an alternative policy could encourage both invention and competition instead of invention and monopoly, consumers would benefit from the lower price and greater quantity sold.

Fifth, patents may sometimes cover too much or be granted too easily. In the early 1970s, Xerox had received over 1,700 patents on various elements of the photocopy machine. Every time Xerox improved the photocopier, it received a patent on the improvement. In the early 1970s, the U.S. government charged Xerox with abusing the patent process by using this potentially everlasting stream of patents to block the entry of other firms into the photocopier market. In 1975, while not admitting that it had done anything wrong, Xerox agreed to allow other companies to use its patents, to drop all of its lawsuits against other companies for violating its patents, and to provide competitors with access to certain future patents. A flood of new competition followed. Xerox's market share fell from about 95 percent of the U.S. photocopier market in the early 1970s to less than half by 1980.

Sixth, the 20-year time period for a patent is somewhat arbitrary. Ideally, a patent should cover a long enough period of time for the inventor to earn a hearty return, but not so long that it allows the inventor to charge a high monopoly price permanently. The 20-year time period for patents may be too long in some cases and not long enough in

Protecting Mickey Mouse

All patents and copyrights are scheduled to end someday, and in 2003, copyright protection for Mickey Mouse was scheduled to run out. In theory, anyone would be able to copy old Mickey Mouse cartoons or draw and sell new ones. But in 1998, Congress passed the Sonny Bono Copyright Term Extension Act. It extended copyright from 50 to 70 years after an author's death and, for works produced "for hire" and owned by firms, from 75 to 95 years after publication. Along with protecting Mickey for another 20 years, the copyright extension also affected about 400,000 books, movies, and songs, including books by Ernest Hemingway and songs by George Gershwin.

The act was not politically controversial; it passed the U.S. Senate with a unanimous vote. But copyright had already extended 50 years after the death of the author, and it seems highly unlikely that an additional 20 years after death will provide an incentive for additional creative work. Congress voted to lengthen copyright protection because of lobbying from the firms that are continuing to benefit from these copyrighted works—the way Disney benefits from Mickey Mouse. But copyrights (and patents) were never supposed to be forever, and the social interest might have been better served by allowing broad public access to these classic works.

others. For example, in the 1980s it was noted by pharmaceutical companies that for certain drugs, which are first patented and then need to go through years of testing before they can be broadly marketed, the typical term of a patent might result in only a few years of actual sales. Consequently, in 1984, Congress passed the Drug Price Competition and Patent Term Restoration Act to extend the patent life of brand-name drugs for five years, to make up for time lost between the original patent and the health and safety testing.

Patents serve a useful function in providing incentives for inventors. But patents are imperfect and blunt tools that usually protect only part of the value of an invention. Patents may also be granted or denied for unclear reasons; after all, many of the examiners who decide whether a patent will be granted are young lawyers who often leave the patent office after a few years for better-paying jobs in industry. Alternative methods of improving the rate of return for inventors of new technology are desirable as well.

Government Spending on Research and Development

If the private sector does not have sufficient incentive to carry out research and development, one possible response is for the government to fund such work directly. Government provides direct financial support for research and development, which is done at colleges and universities, nonprofit research entities, and sometimes private firms, as well as at government-run laboratories.

The first column of Exhibit 15-5 shows the sources of U.S. spending on research and development; about three-fifths of R&D is funded by industry and about one-third by the federal government. The second column shows where the R&D is actually performed; about two-thirds of R&D is done by industry and about one-eighth by universities and colleges. When the government pays directly for a share of an R&D project, it reduces the costs of innovation for firms.

basic research: Research on fundamental scientific breakthroughs that may offer commercial applications only in the distant future.

applied research: Research focused on a particular product that promises an economic payoff in the short or medium term.

Since the 1960s, R&D spending has grown at roughly the same rate as the overall U.S. economy. However, in the 1960s the federal government paid for about two-thirds of the nation's R&D. Thus, over time, the U.S. economy has come to rely much more heavily on industry-funded R&D. The federal government has tried to focus its direct R&D spending on areas where private firms are not as active. Of the more than $400 billion spent on R&D in 2011, $75 billion (roughly one-fifth) was classified as **basic research**. Basic research is defined as the search for fundamental scientific breakthroughs that may offer commercial applications only in the distant future. The remainder of R&D is **applied research**, which is often focused on a particular product that promises an economic payoff in the short term or the medium term. The federal government funds about half of the nation's basic R&D, much of it carried out at colleges and universities.

EXHIBIT 15-5 U.S. Research and Development Expenditures, 2011

Sources of R&D Funding		Where R&D Was Performed	
Federal government	$125 billion	Federal government	$49 billion
Industry	$267 billion	Industry	$294 billion
Universities/colleges	$12 billion	Universities/colleges	$62 billion
Nonprofits	$15 billion	Nonprofits	$17 billion
Nonfederal government	$3 billion		
Total	*$422 billion*	*Total*	*$422 billion*

Tax Breaks for Research and Development

One difficulty with direct government support of R&D is that it inevitably involves government decisions about which projects are worthy. In a political setting, the scientific question of whether research is worthwhile can easily become entangled with considerations like the location of the congressional district in which the research funding is being spent. A complementary approach to supporting R&D that does not involve the government's close scrutiny of particular R&D projects is to give firms a reduction in their taxes depending on how much research and development they do. Tax breaks to encourage R&D spending reduced the tax that would otherwise have been paid by corporations by about $10 billion in 2016, according to the U.S. Department of the Treasury.

Cooperative Research and Development

Another tool for increasing the returns to innovation was enacted by the National Cooperative Research and Production Act of 1993, which allowed companies to form jointly funded R&D institutions. When companies work together, they share the expenses of R&D and share any discoveries that result. Such joint agencies offer a way for firms to share the risks of R&D as well as the benefits, rather than facing the risk that one winner-take-all innovator will get the patent and lock up the market. Before this law passed, antitrust authorities might have challenged such joint research efforts, but the new 1993 law removed that threat.

A Balancing Act

Because new technology brings positive externalities, there is a case for some sort of government action to support the development of new technology. However, each of the policies discussed here involves some balancing of interests. Patents can serve a useful role in providing incentives for inventors, but they also create temporary monopolies, they may be granted too slowly in some cases and too easily in others, and even at their best, they allow the inventor to receive only a fraction of the social benefit of the invention. Government spending on research and development produces technology that is broadly available for firms to use, but it costs money to taxpayers and can sometimes be directed more for political than for scientific or economic reasons. Allowing firms to collaborate on research and development may help hold down costs, but it may also lead to a situation where firms strive less hard for new technology, since they know that any new technology will be shared anyway. Thus, while the general case for government action to support technology and innovation is a strong one, the enactment of such programs through the political system can be controversial.

Public Goods

Even though new technology creates positive externalities, so that perhaps one-third or one-half of the social benefit of new inventions spills over to others, the inventor still receives some private return from new technology. But what about a situation where the positive externalities are so extensive that the private firm producing a certain product could not expect to receive any of the social benefit at all? This kind of good is called a public good. Public goods include many items that are typically supplied to a considerable extent by government, like national defense and basic research. Let's begin by defining the characteristics of a public good. We'll then discuss why these characteristics make it difficult for private firms to supply public goods and how government may step in to address the issue.

The Definition of a Public Good

To understand the defining characteristics of a public good, first consider an ordinary private good, like a piece of pizza. A piece of pizza can be bought and sold fairly easily because it is a separate and identifiable item. However, public goods are not separate and identifiable in this way.

public good: A good that is nonexcludable and nonrivalrous and thus is difficult for market producers to sell to individual consumers.

nonexcludable: When it is costly or impossible to exclude someone from using the good, and thus it is hard to charge for it.

nonrivalrous: A good where, when one person uses the good, others can also use it.

Instead, **public goods** have two defining characteristics: they are nonexcludable and nonrivalrous. The first characteristic, that a public good is **nonexcludable**, means that it is costly or impossible to exclude someone from using the good. If Larry buys a private good like a piece of pizza, then he can exclude others like Lorna from eating that pizza. But if national defense is being provided, then it includes everyone. Even if you strongly disagree with America's defense policies or with the level of defense spending, the national defense still protects you. You can't choose to be unprotected, and national defense can't protect everyone else and exclude you.

The second main characteristic of a public good, that it is **nonrivalrous**, means that when one person uses the public good, another can also use it. With a private good like pizza, if Max is eating the pizza, then Michelle cannot also eat it; that is, the two people are rivals in consumption. But with a public good like national defense, Max's consumption of national defense doesn't reduce the amount left for Michelle, so they are nonrivalrous in this area.

Knowledge and information often display the two key characteristics of a public good. Thomas Jefferson expressed the notion that ideas are at least nonrivalrous, and perhaps nonexcludable as well, in elegant language: "If nature has made any one thing less susceptible than all others of exclusive property, it is the action of the thinking power called an idea. . . . No one possesses the less, because every other possess the whole of it. He, who receives an idea from me, receives instruction himself without lessening mine; as he who lights his taper [that is, his candle] at mine, receives light without darkening me."

Ideas discovered as a result of basic scientific research are certainly nonrivalrous; when Percival uses these ideas, it does not reduce Polly's use of them. Ideas stemming from basic research are also nonexcludable, at least to some extent, because once they are known, then understanding of the scientific situation is altered. A knowledge-based public good for which economists have a particularly warm spot in their hearts is the collection and publication of economic statistics. Again, this information is nonrivalrous: Quentin's knowing the rate at which the economy has grown doesn't prevent Quintessa from knowing the same information. Such knowledge is also nonexcludable in the sense that once the information is out there—perhaps in a news report about how the economy is growing—it would be very difficult to prevent that information from spreading.

A number of other government services are referred to as public goods even if they are not completely nonexcludable and nonrivalrous. For instance, fire and police protection are not easily excludable. It wouldn't be easy to provide fire and police service so that some people in a neighborhood would be protected from the burning and burglary of their property, while others would not be protected at all. Protecting some necessarily means protecting others, too. Police and fire protection are also in some ways nonrivalrous; Oliver's protection from crime or fire doesn't mean that Oleanna is less protected (except perhaps in the extreme case where all the fire or police personnel are busy in one area and can't respond anywhere else).

The Tragedy of the Commons

The historical meaning of a commons is a piece of pasture land that is open to anyone who wishes to graze cattle upon it. However, the term has come to apply to any area that is open to all, like a city park. In a famous 1968 article, a professor of ecology named Garrett Hardin (1915–2003) described a scenario called the tragedy of the commons, in which the utility-maximizing behavior of individuals ruins the commons for all.

Hardin imagined a pasture that is open to many herdsmen, each with their own herd of cattle. A herdsman benefits from adding cows, but too many cows will lead to overgrazing and even to ruining the commons. The problem is that when a herdsman adds a cow, the herdsman personally receives all of the gain, but when that cow contributes to overgrazing and injures the commons, the loss is suffered by all of the herdsmen as a group—so any individual herdsman suffers only a small fraction of the loss. Hardin wrote: "Therein is the tragedy. Each man is locked into a system that compels him to increase his herd without limit—in a world that is limited. Ruin is the destination toward which all men rush, each pursuing his own best interest in a society that believes in the freedom of the commons. Freedom in a commons brings ruin to all."

This tragedy of the commons can arise in any situation where benefits are primarily received by one party, while the costs are spread out over many parties. For example, clean air can be regarded as a commons, where firms that pollute air can gain higher profits, but firms that pay for anti-pollution equipment provide a benefit to others. A commons can be regarded as a public good, where it is difficult to exclude anyone from use (nonexcludability) and where many parties can use the resource simultaneously (nonrivalrous).

The historical commons was often protected, at least for a time, by social rules that limited how many cattle a herdsman could graze. Avoiding a tragedy of the commons with the environment will require its own set of rules that limit how the common resource can be used.

The Free Rider Problem

Competitive markets made up of a number of different firms and buyers may find it difficult to produce public goods. If a good or service is nonexcludable, like national defense, so that it is impossible or very costly to exclude people from using this good or service, then how can a firm charge people for it? If a good is nonrivalrous, then there is zero marginal cost to adding an additional user, a fact that seems to imply that if businesses compete against each other, the price will keep dropping all the way down to zero. But if businesses can't earn much or any revenue by selling a product, then they will lack an incentive to provide such a good.

When individuals make decisions about buying a public good, a **free rider** problem can arise, in which people have an incentive to let others pay for the public good and then to "free ride" on the purchases of others. The free rider problem can be expressed in terms of the prisoner's dilemma game, which we first discussed as a representation of oligopoly in Chapter 12.

free rider: Those who want others to pay for the public good and then plan to use the good themselves; if many people act as free riders, the public good may never be provided.

Say that two people are thinking about contributing to a public good: Rachel and Samuel. When either of them contributes to a public good such as a local fire department, their personal cost of doing so is 4, and the social benefit of that person's contribution is 6. Thus, the investment is a good idea for society as a whole. But the problem is that while Rachel and Samuel pay for the entire cost of their contribution to the public good, they receive only half of the benefit because the benefit of the public good is divided equally among the members of society. This sets up the prisoner's dilemma illustrated in Exhibit 15-6.

If neither Rachel nor Samuel contributes to the public good, then there are no costs and no benefits of the public good. If one person contributes and the other does not, then the contributor pays 4 but receives benefits of 3 (i.e., half of 6), while the noncontributing free rider also receives benefits of 3. Finally, if both parties contribute, then the total social contribution to the public good is 8 and the total payoff is 12, so each individual has a payoff of 2.

The difficulty with the prisoner's dilemma arises as each person thinks through his or her strategic choices. Rachel reasons in this way: If Samuel does not contribute, then I

		Samuel	
		Contribute	**Don't Contribute**
Rachel	**Contribute**	A pays 4, gets 6, +2 B pays 4, gets 6, +2	A pays 4, gets 3, −1 B pays 0, gets 3, +3
	Don't Contribute	A pays 0, gets 3, +3 B pays 4, gets 3, −1	A pays 0, gets 0 B pays 0, gets 0

EXHIBIT 15-6 Contributing to a Public Good as a Prisoner's Dilemma

would be a fool to contribute. However, if Samuel does contribute, then I can come out ahead by not contributing. Both ways, I should choose not to contribute, and instead hope that I can be a free rider who uses the public good paid for by Samuel. Samuel reasons the same way about Rachel. But when both people reason in that way, the public good never gets built, and there is no movement to the option where everyone cooperates that is actually best for all parties.

The free rider problem becomes greater if the concept of the prisoner's dilemma is expanded to include many people, not just two of them. For example, say that 10,000 people are asked to pay $100 in taxes apiece to finance a new road. Each person will reason as follows: This new road costs me personally $100, but the actual benefits from my $100 are divided by all 10,000 people, so my personal $100 only brings me 1 cent (i.e., $100 divided by 10,000) in benefits. If I act as a free rider and refuse to contribute to the road, the road will still be built, I can still drive on the road (because it is nonexcludable and nonrivalrous), and I can save my $100 for something I want to buy for myself. But if everyone reasons this way and acts as a free rider, then no money is collected and the road never gets built.

Why Are People Living Longer?

One of the most remarkable changes in the standard of living in the last several centuries is that people are living longer. Back in the Stone Age, thousands of years ago, human life expectancies are believed to have been in the range of 20–30 years. By 1900, average life expectancy in the United States at birth was 47 years. By the start of the twenty-first century, U.S. life expectancy was 77 years. Thus, most of the gains in life expectancy in the history of the human race happened in the twentieth century.

The rise in life expectancy stems from three primary factors. First, systems for providing clean water and disposing of human waste late in the nineteenth and into the twentieth century helped to prevent the transmission of many diseases. Second, changes in public behavior have advanced health. Early in the twentieth century, for example, people learned the importance of boiling bottles and milk, washing their hands, and protecting food from flies. More recent behavioral changes include reducing the number of people who smoke tobacco and precautions to limit sexually transmitted diseases. Third, medicine has played a role. Immuni-

zations for diphtheria, cholera, pertussis, tuberculosis, tetanus, and yellow fever were developed between 1890 and 1930. Penicillin, discovered in 1941, led to a series of other antibiotic drugs for bringing infectious diseases under control. In recent decades, drugs that reduce the risks of high blood pressure have had a dramatic effect in extending lives.

These advances in public health have all been closely linked to positive externalities and public goods. Public health officials taught hygienic practices to mothers in the early 1900s and encouraged less smoking in the late 1900s. Many medical discoveries came out of government- or university-funded research in the twentieth century. Patents and intellectual property rights provided an additional incentive for private inventors. The reason for requiring immunizations, phrased in economic terms, is that it prevents spillovers of illness to others—as well as helping the person immunized. Many of the public sanitation systems and storm sewers were funded by government because they have the key traits of public goods.

The Role of Government in Paying for Public Goods

The key insight in paying for public goods is to find a way of assuring that everyone will make a contribution. There must be a method for preventing too many free riders. For example, if people come together through the political process and agree to pay taxes and make group decisions about the quantity of public goods, they can defeat the free rider problem by requiring through the law that people contribute to public goods. Or some roads can become toll roads, which means that they can exclude users who do not pay to drive on them.

However, government purchases and charges are not the only way to provide public goods. Markets can in some cases produce public goods. For example, think about radio. It is nonexcludable because once the radio signal is being broadcast, it would be highly difficult to stop someone from receiving it. It is nonrivalrous, since one person listening to the signal does not prevent others from listening as well. Because of these features, it is practically impossible to charge listeners directly for listening to conventional radio broadcasts. However, radio found a way to collect revenue by selling advertising, which is an indirect way of "charging" listeners by taking up some of their time, and satellite radio manages to charge a regular subscription fee. Some public goods will also have a mixture of public provision at no charge along with fees for some purposes, like a public city park that is free to use, but where the government charges a fee for parking your car, for reserving certain picnic grounds, and for food sold at a refreshment stand.

In other cases, social pressures and personal appeals can be used, rather than the force of law, to reduce the number of free riders and to collect resources for the public good. For example, neighbors sometimes form an association to carry out beautification projects or to patrol their area after dark to discourage crime. In low-income countries, farmers in a region may come together to work on a large irrigation project that will benefit everyone and where social pressure strongly encourages all farmers to participate. Many fundraising efforts, including raising money for local charities and for the endowments of colleges and universities, also can be viewed as an attempt to use social pressure to discourage free riding and to serve the outcome that will produce a public benefit.

Positive Externalities and Public Goods

Positive externalities and public goods are closely related concepts. With regard to both positive externalities and public goods, private firms or individuals may fail to make an expenditure or investment that would produce broad social benefits because the private benefits of such expenditure will be substantially less than the social benefits. In such cases, the challenge for society is to assure that such socially beneficial expenditures are made, whether through direct government spending or by providing appropriate incentives for individuals and firms.

Key Concepts and Summary

1. The pressure of market competition can provide producers with incentives to develop and distribute new technologies. However, if new inventions can easily be copied by others, then the original inventor may not be able to earn a higher-than-usual rate of return, in which case innovators would have a reduced incentive to invest in new technologies.

2. New technology often has positive externalities; that is, there are often spillovers from the invention of new technology that benefit firms other than the inventor. The social benefit of an invention, once these spillovers are taken into account, typically exceeds the private benefit to the inventor. If inventors could receive a greater share of the broader social benefits for their behavior, they would have a greater incentive to seek out new inventions.

3. Government has a variety of policy tools for increasing the rate of return for new technology and encouraging

its development: direct government funding of R&D, tax incentives for R&D, protection of **intellectual property**, letting companies work jointly on R&D, and helping to finance the spread of available technology.

4. Public policy with regard to technology must often strike a balance. For example, patents provide an incentive for inventors, but they should be limited to genuinely new inventions and not extend forever. Government spending on R&D must be balanced against other government spending priorities.

5. A **public good** has two key characteristics: it is **nonexcludable** and **nonrivalrous**. Nonexcludable means that it is costly or impossible for one user to exclude others from using the good. Nonrivalrous means that when one person uses the good, it does not prevent others from using it.

6. Markets often have a difficult time producing public goods because **free riders** will attempt to use the public good without making a contribution to paying for it. The free rider problem can be overcome through measures to ensure that users of the public good pay for it. Such measures include government actions, social pressures, and specific situations where markets have discovered a way to collect payments.

Review Questions

1. Explain how competition in markets can often provide incentives for the invention of new technology.
2. Using the ideas of social benefit and private benefit, explain the concept of a positive externality.
3. Why does new technology have positive externalities?
4. Why might a competitive market tend to provide too few incentives for the development of new technology?
5. What can government do to encourage the development of new technology?
6. What are the two key characteristics of public goods?
7. Name two public goods, and explain why they are public goods.
8. What is the free rider problem?
9. How can the free rider problem be overcome?

Poverty and Economic Inequality

CHAPTER

16

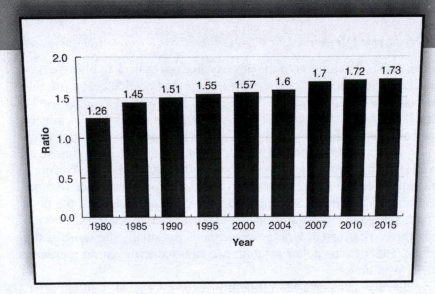

The labor markets that determine what workers are paid don't take into account how much income a family needs to afford necessities like food, shelter, clothing, and health care. Market forces don't worry about what happens to families when a major local employer goes out of business. Market forces don't contemplate whether those who are earning higher incomes should pay an even higher share of taxes.

However, labor markets do create considerable inequalities of income. In 2014, the median American family had income of $53,567 (the median is the level at which half of all families had more than that level and half had less). However, top executives at many companies earned much more. Also in 2014, for example, David Zaslav of Discovery Communications received total compensation of $156 million. The point here is not to pick on Zaslav or to pick on corporate executives—certain athletes, entertainers, and others have extremely high incomes, too. But the amounts are still amazing. Zaslov's $156 million was equal to the combined income of about 2,900 typical families.

At the other extreme, about 9.5 million U.S. families were classified by the federal government as being below the poverty line in 2014. Think about the practical aspects for a family of three—perhaps a single mother with two children—attempting to pay for the basics of life on perhaps $15,000 per year. After paying rent, health care, clothing, and transportation, such a family might have $6,000 to spend each year on food. Spread over 365 days per year, the food budget for the entire family would be about $17 per day. Most cities have upscale restaurants where $17 will buy you an appetizer for one.

Such comparisons of high and low incomes raise issues of economic inequality and poverty. While these two issues are often mentioned in the same breath, they are not the same.

Poverty is measured by the number of people who fall below a certain level of income—called the poverty line—that defines the income needed for a basic standard of living. Economic inequality compares the share of the total income

poverty: Falling below a certain level of income needed for a basic standard of living.

poverty line: The specific amount of income needed for a basic standard of living.

inequality: When one group receives a higher share of total income or wealth than others.

(or wealth) in society that is received by different groups; for example, comparing the share of income received by the top 10% to the share of income received by the bottom 10%. This chapter first explores the issues of poverty in detail: how the U.S. government defines poverty, the trade-offs between assisting the poor without discouraging work, and how U.S. antipoverty programs work. The chapter then moves to a discussion of inequality: how economists measure inequality, why inequality has changed in recent decades, the range of possible government policies to reduce inequality, and the danger of a trade-off that too great a reduction in inequality may reduce incentives for producing output.

Drawing the Poverty Line

In the United States, the official definition of the poverty line traces back to a single person: Mollie Orshansky. In 1963, Orshansky was working for the Social Security Administration, where she published an article called "Children of the Poor" in a highly useful and dry-as-dust publication called the *Social Security Bulletin*. Orshansky's idea was to define a poverty line based on the cost of a healthy diet. Her previous job had been at the U.S. Department of Agriculture, where she had worked in an agency called the Bureau of Home Economics and Human Nutrition, and one task of this bureau had been to calculate the cost of a nutritionally adequate diet for a family. Orshansky found evidence that the average family spent one-third of its income on food. Thus, she proposed that the poverty line be the amount needed to buy a nutritionally adequate diet, given the size of the family, multiplied by three. The current U.S. poverty line is essentially the same as the Orshansky poverty line, although the dollar amounts are adjusted each year to represent the same buying power over time.

The current U.S. poverty lines, based on family size, appear in Exhibit 16-1. Exhibit 16-2 shows the U.S. poverty rate over time; that is, the percentage of the population below the poverty rate in any given year. The poverty rate declined through the 1960s, rose in the early 1980s and early 1990s, dropped a bit in the mid-1990s, and then rose sharply. Exhibit 16-3 compares poverty rates for different groups in 2011. Poverty rates are relatively low for whites, for the elderly, for the well educated, and for male-headed households.

EXHIBIT 16-1 The U.S. Poverty Line in 2015

If a family, given its size, had less than the amount of income shown in the table, then it was considered officially "poor" or "in poverty."

Size of Family Unit	Poverty-Line Income Threshold
One person (unrelated individual)	$12,085
Under 65	$12,331
65 years and over	$11,367
Two people	$15,397
Householder under 65	$15,953
Householder 65 years and over	$14,343
Three people	$18,872
Four people	$24,259
Five people	$28,729
Six people	$32,512
Seven people	$36,971
Eight people	$41,017
Nine people or more	$49,079

EXHIBIT 16-2 The U.S. Poverty Rate since 1960

The poverty rate fell dramatically during the 1960s, but it has fluctuated within a fairly narrow band since the late 1970s.

EXHIBIT 16-3 Poverty Rates by Group, 2011

Poverty rates are lower for men than for women, lower for whites than for blacks or Hispanics, and lower for those of prime working age than for those earlier in life.

Group	Poverty Rate
Females	16.1%
Males	13.4%
White	12.7%
Black	26.2%
Hispanic	23.6%
Under age 18	21.1%
Ages 18–64	13.5%
Ages 65 and older	10.0%

The concept of a poverty line raises many tricky questions. In a vast country like the United States, should the same national poverty line apply in all states? After all, the median household income varies considerably across states, and prices of some basic goods like housing are quite different between states. The poverty line is based on cash income, which means it doesn't take into account government programs that provide assistance to the poor in a non-cash form, like Medicaid that provides health insurance to the poor or Supplemental Nutrition Assistance Program benefits that can be exchanged for food in grocery stores. Should the poverty line be adjusted to take the value of such programs into account? (These programs and other welfare programs will be discussed in detail later in this chapter.) Perhaps rather than just updating Molly Orshansky's poverty line from the early 1960s, the concept of what poverty means in the twenty-first century should be rethought from scratch?

Government statisticians at the U.S. Census Bureau have ongoing research programs to address questions like these. But any poverty line will be somewhat arbitrary, and it is useful to have a poverty line whose basic definition doesn't change much over time. If Congress voted every few years to redefine what poverty means, then it would be difficult to compare poverty rates over time. After all, would a lower poverty rate mean that the definition had been changed, or that people were actually better off?

Poverty in Low-Income Countries

The World Bank sets two poverty lines that it applies to low-income countries around the world. One poverty line is set at an income of $1.90/day per person; the other is at $3.10/day. By comparison, the U.S. poverty line of $18,872 annually for a family of three works out to $17.23 per person per day. Clearly, many people around the world are far poorer than Americans. China and India both have more than a billion people, and Nigeria is the most populous country in Africa. In all three of those countries, a substantial share of the population subsists in dire poverty on less than $3.10/day. Indeed, more than a third of the world lives on less than $3.10 a day, and about 80% of the world lives on less than $10/day.

Country	Share of Population below $1.90/Day	Share of Population below $3.10/Day
Brazil (2013)	4.9%	9.1%
China (2010)	11.2%	27.2%
India (2011)	21.3%	58.0%
Mexico (2012)	2.7%	10.3%
Nigeria (2009)	53.5%	76.5%

The Poverty Trap

A conflict lies at the heart of assisting the poor. When people are provided with food, shelter, health care, income, and other necessities, such assistance may reduce their incentives to work. For example, consider a program to fight poverty that works in this reasonable-sounding manner: the government provides assistance to the poor, but as the poor earn income to support themselves, the government reduces the level of assistance it provides. With such a program, every time a poor person earns $100, the person also loses $100 in government support. As a result of such a program, the person will experience no net gain to working. Economists call this problem the **poverty trap**.

For a concrete example of the poverty trap, consider the situation faced by a single mother with two children, as illustrated in Exhibit 16-4. First consider the labor-leisure budget constraint faced by this family in a situation without government assistance to

poverty trap: When antipoverty programs are set up so that government benefits decline substantially as people earn more income—and as a result, working provides little financial gain.

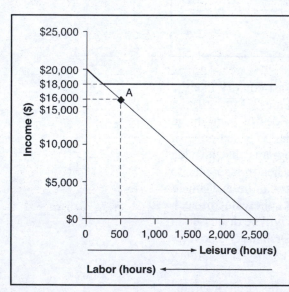

Amount Worked	Total Earnings	Government Support	Total Income
0	0	$18,000	$18,000
500 hours	$4,000	$14,000	$18,000
1,000 hours	$8,000	$10,000	$18,000
1,500 hours	$12,000	$6,000	$18,000
2,000 hours	$16,000	$2,000	$18,000
2,500 hours	$20,000	0	$20,000

EXHIBIT 16-4 The Poverty Trap in Action

The original choice is 500 hours of leisure, 2,000 hours of work at point A, and income of $16,000. With a guaranteed income of $18,000, this family would receive $18,000 whether it provides zero hours of work or 2,000 hours of work. Only if the family provides, say, 2,300 hours of work does its income rise above the guaranteed level of $18,000—and even then, the marginal gain to income from working many hours is small.

the poor. Assume that the mother can earn a wage of $8 per hour. By working 40 hours a week, 50 weeks a year, let's say that her utility-maximizing choice is to work a total of 2,000 hours per year and earn $16,000. Now suppose that a government antipoverty program is created that guarantees every family with a single mother and two children $18,000 in income. With this program, each time the mother earns $1,000, the government will deduct $1,000 of its support.

The new budget line, with the antipoverty program in place, is the heavy line that is flat at $18,000 and rising at the far left of the budget line. If the mother doesn't work at all, she receives $18,000, all from the government. If she works full time, giving up 40 hours per week with her children, she still ends up with $18,000 at the end of the year. Only if she works, say, 2,300 hours in the year—which is an average of 44 hours per week for 50 weeks a year—does household income rise to $18,400. But even in this case, all of her year's work means that household income rises by only $400 over the income she would receive if she did not work at all.

Clearly, this kind of government antipoverty program creates a powerful incentive not to work. Indeed, the poverty trap is even stronger than this simplified example shows because a working mother will have extra expenses like transportation and child care that a nonworking mother will not face—making the economic gains from working even smaller. Of course, those who don't work fail to build up job experience and contacts, which makes working in the future even less attractive.

The bite of the poverty trap can be reduced by designing the antipoverty program so that instead of reducing government payments by $1 for every $1 earned, payments are reduced by some smaller amount. Exhibit 16-5 illustrates a government program that guarantees $18,000 in income, even for those who do not work at all, but then reduces this amount by 50 cents for each $1 earned. The new, higher budget line in the figure shows that with this program in place, additional hours of work will bring some economic gain. However, this type of program raises some issues as well. First, even if it does not

Amount Worked	Total Earnings	Government Support	Total Income
0	0	$18,000	$18,000
500 hours	$4,000	$16,000	$20,000
1,000 hours	$8,000	$14,000	$22,000
1,500 hours	$12,000	$12,000	$24,000
2,000 hours	$16,000	$10,000	$26,000
2,500 hours	$20,000	$8,000	$28,000

EXHIBIT 16-5 Loosening the Poverty Trap: Reducing Government Assistance by 50 Cents for Every $1 Earned

On the original labor-leisure opportunity set, the lower budget set in the figure, the preferred choice P is 500 hours of leisure and $16,000 of income. Then the government created an antipoverty program that guarantees $18,000 in income even to those who work zero hours. In addition, every $1 earned leads to phasing out 50 cents of benefits. This program leads to the higher budget set shown in the diagram. The hope is that low-income workers will find that this program provides incentives to work the same or more hours, despite receiving income assistance. However, it is possible that the recipients will choose a point on the new budget set like S, with less work, more leisure, and greater income, or a point like R, with the same work and greater income.

eliminate the incentive to work by reducing government payments by $1 for every $1 earned, enacting such a program may still reduce the incentive to work. For example, at least some people who would be working 2,000 hours per year without this program might decide to work fewer hours but still end up with more income—that is, their choice on the new budget line would be like S, above and to the right of the original choice P. Of course, others may choose a point like R, which involves the same amount of work as P, or even a point to the left of R that involves more work. The second major issue is that when the government phases out its support payments more slowly, the antipoverty program costs the government more money. Still, it may be preferable in the long run to spend more money on a program that retains a greater incentive to work, rather than spending less money on a program that nearly eliminates any gains from working.

The next section will consider a variety of U.S. government support programs that are focused specifically on the poor, including welfare, Medicaid, the earned income tax credit, the Supplemental Nutrition Assistance Program, and more. Although these programs vary from state to state, it is generally a true statement that in many states from the 1960s into the 1990s, if poor people worked, their level of income barely rose—or did not rise at all—after the reduction in government support payments was factored in. One major issue with rethinking antipoverty programs in the last decade or two is to find ways to combine assistance for the poor with incentives to work—and to declaw the poverty trap.

The Safety Net

The U.S. government has implemented a number of programs to assist those below the poverty line and those who have incomes just above the poverty line, who are referred to as the **near-poor**. As a group, such programs are nicknamed the **safety net**, in recognition of the fact that they offer some protection for those who find themselves without jobs or income.

Temporary Assistance for Needy Families

From the Great Depression of the 1930s until 1996, the most visible U.S. antipoverty program was Aid to Families with Dependent Children (AFDC), which provided cash payments to mothers with children who were below the poverty line. This program was often just called "welfare." In 1996, Congress passed and President Bill Clinton signed into law the Personal Responsibility and Work Opportunity Reconciliation Act, more commonly called the welfare reform act. The new law replaced AFDC with Temporary Assistance for Needy Families (TANF).

TANF brought several dramatic changes in how welfare operated. Under the old AFDC program, states set the level of welfare benefits that they would pay to the poor, and the federal government guaranteed to chip in some money as well. Thus, the federal government's welfare spending would rise or fall depending on the number of poor people and on how each state set its own welfare contribution. Under TANF, however, the federal government gives a fixed amount of money to each state. The state can then use the money for almost any program with an antipoverty component: for example, the state might use the money to give cash to poor families, or to reduce teenage pregnancy, or even to raise the high school graduation rate. However, the federal government imposes two key requirements. First, if states are to keep receiving the TANF grants, they must impose work requirements so that most of those receiving TANF benefits are working (or attending school). Second, no one can receive TANF benefits with federal money for more than a total of five years over his or her lifetime. The old AFDC program had no such work requirements or time limits.

TANF attempts avoid the poverty trap by requiring that welfare recipients work and by limiting the length of time they can receive benefits. In its first few years, the program was quite successful. The number of families receiving payments in 1995, the last year of AFDC, was 4.8 million. By 2002, the number of families receiving payments under TANF was 2.0 million—a decline of more than half.

near-poor: Those who have incomes just above the poverty line.

safety net: Nickname for the group of government programs that provide assistance to the poor and the near-poor.

TANF benefits to poor families vary considerably across states; for example, in 2014 the highest monthly payment in California to a single mother with two children was $670, while in Mississippi the highest monthly payment to that family was $170. Total spending on TANF was $32 billion in 2014, split about evenly between the federal and state governments.

Earned Income Tax Credit (EITC)

The *earned income tax credit (EITC)* is a method of assisting the working poor through the tax system. For every $1 in earned income, a family with children receives a tax refund. The amount of the tax break increases with the amount of income earned, up to a point. In 2016, for example, a single parent with two children would have received a tax refund of 40 cents for every dollar earned up to an income level of $13,931—for a total tax refund of $5,572. The earned income credit has often been popular with both economists and the general public because of the way it effectively increases the payment received for work.

What about the danger of the poverty trap that every additional $1 earned will reduce government support payments by close to $1? To minimize this problem, the earned income credit is phased out slowly. For a single-parent family with two children in 2016, the credit is not reduced at all (but neither is it increased) as earnings rise from $13,931 to $18,190. Then, for every $1 earned above $18,190, the amount received from the credit is reduced by 21 cents, until the credit phases out completely at an income level of $44,648.

In recent years, the EITC has become the single most expensive government program for providing income assistance to the poor and near-poor, costing about $69 billion in 2015. In 2015, the EITC provided benefits to about 27 million families and individuals, and on average is worth about $2,400 per family with children. One reason that the welfare reform bill of 1996 worked as well as it did in the years just after its passage is that the EITC was greatly expanded in the late 1980s and again in the early 1990s, which increased the returns to work for low-income Americans.

Supplemental Nutrition Assistance Program

The Supplemental Nutrition Assistance Program (SNAP) is a federally funded program started in 1964 to assist poor people in buying food. Recipients used to receive this assistance in the form of coupons known as "food stamps." But now people receive SNAP benefits monthly through an Electronic Benefit Transfer card that can be used to buy food in grocery stores. The amount of benefits for which a household is eligible varies by income, number of children, and other factors, but in general, households are expected to spend about 30% of their own income on food, and if 30% of their income is not enough to purchase a nutritionally adequate diet, then those households are eligible for SNAP.

SNAP contributes to the poverty trap. For every $100 earned, the government assumes that a family can spend $30 more on food and thus reduces eligibility for SNAP by $30. This decreased benefit is not a complete disincentive to work, but combined with how other programs reduce benefits as income increases, it doesn't help. However, SNAP does try to address the poverty trap with its own set of work requirements and time limits for recipients.

Why provide assistance that must be spent on food, rather than just giving cash to SNAP recipients? Part of the political support for SNAP comes from a belief that since the benefits must be spent on food, they can't be "wasted" on other forms of consumption. But from an economic point of view, this belief seems wrong-headed. After all, say that a poor family is spending $2,500 per year on food, and then it starts receiving $1,000 per year in SNAP benefits. The family might react by spending $3,500 per year on food (own income plus government benefits), or it might react by continuing to spend $2,500 per year on food but use the $1,000 in SNAP benefits to free up $1,000 that can now be spent on other goods. Thus, it is reasonable to think of SNAP as an alternative method, along with TANF and the earned income tax credit, of transferring income to the working poor.

Indeed, anyone eligible for TANF is also eligible for SNAP, although states can expand eligibility for SNAP benefits if they wish to do so. In some states where TANF welfare spending is relatively low, a poor family may receive more in support from SNAP than from TANF. In 2015, about 46 million people received SNAP benefits at an annual cost of about $74 billion. The average monthly benefit was about $126 per person per month—thus, a qualifying mother with two children might receive $4,536 per year in SNAP benefits.

Medicaid

Medicaid is a federal-state joint program enacted in 1965 that provides medical insurance for certain (not all) low-income people, including the near-poor as well as those below the poverty line, and focusing on low-income families with children, the low-income elderly, and the disabled. About one-third of Medicaid spending is for low-income mothers with children; an increasing share of the program funding in recent years has gone to pay for nursing home costs for the elderly poor. States must provide a basic level of benefits under Medicaid, but they are free to provide higher levels if they wish.

In the past, a common problem has been that many low-paying jobs pay enough so that a family could lose its eligibility for Medicaid, yet the job doesn't offer health insurance benefits either. Thus, a poor parent considering such a job might choose not to work rather than to lose health insurance for his or her children. In this way, health insurance can become a part of the poverty trap. Many states recognized this problem in the 1980s and 1990s and expanded their Medicaid coverage to include not just the poor but also the near-poor earning up to 135% or even 185% of the poverty line. Some states also guaranteed that children would not lose coverage if their parents worked. These expanded guarantees cost money to the government, of course, but they also helped to encourage those on welfare to enter the labor force.

Medicaid spending totaled $496 billion in federal and state spending in 2014, which is roughly triple the total combined spending of TANF, the earned income tax credit, and SNAP benefits. About 70 million people were eligible for Medicaid in 2015.

Other Safety Net Programs

The safety net includes a number of other programs: government-subsidized school lunches and breakfasts for children from low-income families; the Special Supplemental Food Program for Women, Infants, and Children (WIC), which provides food assistance for pregnant women and newborns; the Low Income Home Energy Assistance Program, which provides help with home heating bills; housing assistance, which helps pay the rent; and Supplemental Security Income, which provides cash support for the elderly poor.

There is no straightforward answer to the problem of ensuring that the poor have a decent standard of living while also providing incentives to work. TANF tries to use work requirements and time limits. The earned income credit attempts to increase the incentives for work. Medicaid has been expanded to be widely available to the near-poor as well as the poor. But with all of these programs, and SNAP benefits as well, there comes a point where, as families earn more money, their government support payments are reduced, which inevitably reduces the incentives for the poor and near-poor to work. The poverty trap can be loosened, but it cannot be abolished.

Measuring Income Inequality

Economic inequality involves comparing those with high incomes, middle incomes, and low incomes—not just looking at those below or near the poverty line. In turn, measuring income inequality means dividing up the population into various groups and then comparing the groups, a task that can be carried out in several ways.

EXHIBIT 16-6 Share of Aggregate Income Received by Each Fifth and Top 5% of Households, 1967–2014

The share of income received by the top quintile has grown since the late 1970s. Much of this increase in the share of income going to the top fifth can be traced to an increase in the share of income going to those at the very top of the income distribution, as shown by the rising share going to the top 5% in the final column.

Year	Lowest Quintile	Second Quintile	Third Quintile	Fourth Quintile	Highest Quintile	Top 5%
1967	5.4	12.2	17.5	23.5	41.4	16.4
1970	5.4	12.2	17.6	23.8	40.9	15.6
1975	5.6	11.9	17.7	24.2	40.7	14.9
1980	5.3	11.6	17.6	24.4	41.1	14.6
1985	4.8	11.0	16.9	24.3	43.1	16.1
1990	4.6	10.8	16.6	23.8	44.3	17.4
1995	4.4	10.1	15.8	23.2	46.5	20.0
2000	4.3	9.8	15.4	22.7	47.7	21.1
2005	4.0	9.6	15.3	22.9	48.1	21.1
2010	3.8	9.4	15.4	23.5	47.9	20.0
2014	3.6	9.2	15.1	23.2	48.9	20.8

Income Distribution by Quintiles

One common way of measuring income inequality is to rank all households by income, from lowest to highest, and then to divide all households into five groups with equal numbers of people—known as quintiles. This calculation allows measuring inequality by comparing what share of the total income is earned by each quintile.

U.S. income distribution by quintile appears in Exhibit 16-6. In 2005, for example, the bottom quintile of the income distribution received 3.4% of income; the second quintile received 8.6%; the third quintile, 14.6%; and the fourth quintile, 23.0%; and the top quintile, 50.4%. The final column of the table shows what share of income went to households in the top 5% of the income distribution: specifically, 22.2% in 2005. Over time, from the late 1960s to the early 1980s, the top fifth of the income distribution typically received between 43–44% of all income. However, the share of income that the top fifth received then began to rise. Using the quintile measure, income inequality has increased in recent decades.

quintiles: Dividing a group into fifths, a method often used to look at distribution of income.

CLEARING IT UP

Separating Poverty and Income Inequality

Poverty can change even when inequality does not move at all. Imagine, for example, a situation in which income for everyone in the population declines by 10%. Poverty would rise, since a greater share of the population would now fall below the poverty line income level. However, inequality would be the same because everyone suffered the same proportional loss. Conversely, a general rise in income levels over time would keep inequality the same, but reduce poverty.

It's also possible for economic inequality to change without affecting the poverty rate. Imagine a situation in which a large number of people who already have high incomes increase their incomes by even more. Inequality would rise as a result—but the number of people below the poverty line would remain unchanged.

It can also be useful to divide the income distribution in ways other than quintiles— for example, into tenths or even into percentiles (i.e., hundredths). A more detailed breakdown can provide additional insights. For example, the last column of Exhibit 16-6 shows the income received by the top 5% of the income distribution. From 1980 to 2014 the share of income going to the top fifth increased by more than 7 percentage points (from 41.1% in 1980 to 48.9% in 2014). Over this same time, the share of income going to the top 5% increased by more than 6 percentage points (from 14.6% in 1980 to 20.8% in 2014). Thus, the increased share of income going to the top fifth is mostly accounted for by the increased share of income going to the top 5% of the income distribution.

Lorenz Curve

Lorenz curve: A graph that shows the share of population on the horizontal axis and the cumulative percentage of total income received on the vertical axis.

The data on income inequality can be presented in various ways. For example, you could draw a bar graph that showed the share of income going to each fifth of the income distribution. Exhibit 16-7 presents an alternative way of showing inequality data. The **Lorenz curve** shows the share of population on the horizontal axis and the *cumulative* percentage of total income received on the vertical axis.

Every Lorenz curve diagram begins with a line sloping up at a 45-degree angle, shown as a dashed line in Exhibit 16-7. The points along this line show what perfect equality of the income distribution looks like. It would mean, for example, that the bottom 20% of the income distribution has 20% of the total income, the bottom 40% has 40% of total income, and so on. The other lines in Exhibit 16-7 reflect actual U.S. data on inequality for 1980 and 2014. The trick in graphing a Lorenz curve is that you must transform the *shares* of income for each specific quintile, which are shown in the first column of numbers in the table, into *cumulative* income, shown in the second column of numbers. For example, the bottom 40% of the cumulative income distribution will be the sum of the first and second quintiles; the bottom 60% of the cumulative income distribution will be the sum of the first, second, and third quintiles, and so on. The final entry in the cumulative income column needs to be 100% because, by definition, 100% of the population receives 100% of the income.

In a Lorenz curve diagram, a more unequal distribution of income will loop further down and away from the 45-degree line, while a more equal distribution of income will cuddle closer to the 45-degree line. The greater inequality of the U.S. income distribution between 1980 and 2014 is illustrated in Exhibit 16-7 because the Lorenz curve for 2014 is farther from the 45-degree line than the Lorenz curve for 1980. The Lorenz curve is

Income Category	Share of Income in 1980	Cumulative Share of Income in 1980	Share of Income in 2014	Cumulative Share of Income in 2014
First quintile	5.3	5.3	3.6	3.6
Second quintile	11.6	16.9	9.2	12.8
Third quintile	17.6	34.5	15.1	27.9
Fourth quintile	24.4	58.9	23.2	51.1
Fifth quintile	41.1	100	48.9	100

EXHIBIT 16-7 Lorenz Curve

A Lorenz curve graphs the cumulative shares of income received by everyone up to a certain quintile. The income distribution in 1980 was closer to the perfect equality line than the income distribution in 2014—that is, the U.S. income distribution has become more unequal over time.

Economic Inequality around the World

The U.S. economy has a relatively high degree of income inequality by global standards. As the table shows, based on a variety of national surveys done for a selection of recent years (and adjusted to make the measures comparable), the U.S. economy has greater inequality than Germany (along with most western European countries). The region of the world with the highest level of income inequality is Latin America; this is illustrated in the numbers for Brazil and Mexico. The level of inequality in the United States is lower than in some of the low-income countries of the world, like Nigeria. However, not all poor countries have highly unequal income distributions; India provides a counterexample.

Country	Survey Year	First Quintile	Second Quintile	Third Quintile	Fourth Quintile	Fifth Quintile
United States	2014	3.6%	9.2%	15.1%	23.2%	48.9%
Germany	2011	8.4%	13.1%	17.2%	22.7%	38.6%
Brazil	2013	3.3%	7.6%	12.4%	19.3%	57.4%
Mexico	2012	4.9%	8.8%	12.8%	19.5%	54.1%
China	2010	4.7%	9.7%	15.3%	23.3%	47.1%
India	2011	8.2%	11.8%	15.2%	20.5%	44.2%
Russia	2012	5.9%	10.1%	14.5%	21.2%	48.3%
Nigeria	2010	4.4%	8.3%	13.0%	20.3%	54.0%

a useful way of presenting the quintile data that provides an image of all of the quintile data at once.

Causes of Growing Income Inequality

Why did inequality of household income increase in the United States in recent decades? Indeed, a trend toward greater income inequality has occurred in many countries around the world, although the effect has been more powerful in the U.S. economy. Economists have focused their explanations for the increasing inequality of income on two factors that changed more or less continually from the 1970s into the 2000s. One set of explanations focuses on the changing shape of American households; the other focuses on greater inequality of wages.

The Changing Composition of American Households

In 1970, 41% of married women were in the labor force, but by 2014, 58% of married women were in the labor force. One result of this trend is that more households have two people earning income. Moreover, it has become more common for one high earner to marry another high earner. A few decades ago, the common pattern featured a man with relatively high earnings, such as an executive or a doctor, marrying a woman who didn't earn as much, like a secretary or a nurse. Often, the woman would leave paid employment, at least for a few years, to raise a family. However, now doctors are marrying doctors and executives are marrying executives, and mothers with high-powered careers are often returning to work while their children are quite young. This pattern of households with two high-earners tends to increase the proportion of high-earning households.

Even as two-earner couples have increased, so have single-parent households. In 1970, 10.8% of all U.S. families were headed by single mothers; by 2014, about 19% of all families were headed by single mothers. The poverty rate among single-parent households tends to be relatively high.

These changes in family structure, including the growth of single-parent families who tend to be near the lower end of the income distribution and the growth of two-career high-earner couples near the top end of the income distribution, account for roughly half of the rise in income inequality across households in recent decades.

A Shift in the Distribution of Wages

Another factor behind the rise in U.S. income inequality is that earnings have become less equal since the late 1970s. In particular, the earnings received by high-skilled labor relative to low-skilled labor have increased. One way to measure this change is to take the earnings of workers with at least a four-year college bachelor's degree (including those who went on and completed an advanced degree) and divide them by the earnings of workers with only a high school degree. The result is illustrated in Exhibit 16-8, which shows that those in the 25–34 age bracket with college degrees earned about 1.2 times as much as high school graduates in 1980, but now earn about 1.7 times as much.

Economists use the demand and supply model to reason through the most likely causes of this shift. In recent decades, the supply of U.S. workers with college degrees has increased substantially; for example, 840,000 four-year bachelor's degrees were conferred on Americans in 1970; in the 2015–2016 academic year, 1.8 million such degrees were conferred—more than double. In Exhibit 16-9, this shift in supply to the right from S_0 to S_1 should result in a lower equilibrium wage for high-skilled labor. Thus, the increase in the price of high-skilled labor must be explained by a greater demand for high-skilled labor, like the movement from D_0 to D_1. Evidently, combining both the increase in supply and in demand has resulted in a shift from E_0 to E_1, and a resulting higher wage.

What factors would cause the demand for high-skilled labor to rise? One plausible explanation is that while the explosion in new information and communications technologies over the last several decades has helped many workers to become more productive, the benefits have been especially great for many high-skilled workers like top business managers, lawyers, consultants, design professionals, and others. The new communication and information technologies have also helped to encourage globalization, the remarkable increase in international trade over the last few decades, by making it more possible to learn about and coordinate economic interactions all around the world. In turn, the rise of globalization has opened up greater opportunities for high-skilled workers to sell their services around the world. Of course, a supply and demand analysis can also be applied to low- and medium-skilled labor. As U.S. education levels have risen in recent

EXHIBIT 16-8 Ratio of Median Earnings for Full-Time Workers, Ages 25–34, with a Bachelor's Degree or More to Those with Only a High School Diploma or Equivalent

The returns to skill have increased in the last few decades, in the sense that the additional wages gained from having a college degree, over having only a high school diploma, have increased.

EXHIBIT 16-9 Why Would Wages Rise for High-Skilled Labor?

The proportion of workers attending college has increased in recent decades, so the supply curve for high-skilled labor has shifted to the right from S_0 to S_1. If the demand for high-skilled labor had remained at D_0, then this shift in supply would have led to lower wages for high-skilled labor. But the relative wages for high-skilled labor have increased even with the shift in supply of such labor to the right. The explanation must lie in a shift to the right in demand for high-skilled labor from D_0 to D_1. The figure shows how a combination of the shift in supply from S_0 to S_1 and the shift in demand from D_0 to D_1 led to both an increase in the quantity of high-skilled labor hired and also to a rise in the wage for such labor from W_0 to W_1.

decades, the supply of low-skilled labor has fallen. But new technology has reduced the demand for certain types of low- and medium-skilled labor even faster. In some industries, automation or robots can replace low-skilled labor. Meanwhile, globalization has increased competitive pressures for medium- and lower-skilled U.S. workers, who may now find their employers competing with firms from lower-wage economies from Latin America to Asia and Africa. This shift in labor demand has been strong enough to reduce job prospects and hold down wages for many low- and medium-skill workers.

Government Policies to Reduce Income Inequality

No society should expect or desire complete equality of income at a given point in time, for a number of reasons. First, most workers receive relatively low earnings in their first few jobs, higher earnings as they reach middle age, and then lower earnings after retirement. Thus, a society with people of varying ages will have a certain amount of income inequality. Second, people's preferences and desires differ. Some are willing to work long hours to have income for large houses, fast cars and computers, luxury vacations, and the ability to support children and grandchildren. Others will work fewer hours and instead use their time for reading books, listening to music, and cooking meals to eat with their family. Third, people can be lucky or unlucky. Some people will take a job with a company that grows by leaps and bounds, or will be born with traits that help make it possible for them to be a professional athlete or model, or will win the lottery. Others may take a job with a company that goes broke, or their unique personal traits may not bring any special reward in the labor market. Finally, any economic system with incentives for acquiring skill, working hard, and inventing new goods and services will result in some inequality.

But even if some degree of economic inequality is expected at any point in time, how much inequality should there be? Some decades ago, an economist named Henry Simons (1889–1946) tried to find an objective, scientific way to determine how much inequality was appropriate. After a great deal of thought, he decided that the question had no answer

Wealth Inequality

Income is a flow of money received, often measured on a monthly or an annual basis; wealth is the total amount stored up. A retired person, for example, may have relatively little income in a given year, other than a pension or Social Security. However, if that person has saved and invested over time, the person's accumulated wealth can be substantial. Wealth is the sum of value of all assets, including money in bank accounts, financial investments, a pension fund, and value of a home. However, in calculating wealth, all debts must be subtracted, such as debt owed on a home mortgage and on credit cards.

The wealth distribution is more unequal than the income distribution, because differences in income can accumulate over time to make even larger differences in wealth. However, the degree of inequality in the wealth distribution can be measured with the same tools that we use to measure the inequality in the income distribution, like quintile measurements. Data on wealth in U.S. households is collected every three years in the Survey of Consumer Finance. A study based on this data found that in 2013, the top 3% of the wealth distribution had more wealth than the bottom 90% of the wealth distribution; that is, the top 1% held 54% of all wealth in the U.S. economy in 2013, while the bottom 90% of the wealth distribution held a total of 25% of all wealth.

and wrote that arguments against inequality ultimately depend on "the ethical or aesthetic judgment that the prevailing distribution of wealth and income reveals a degree (and/or kind) of inequality which is distinctly evil or unlovely."

But even if economics cannot answer the question of how much inequality is "evil or unlovely," economists can still play an important role in spelling out policy options and trade-offs. If a society decides to reduce the level of economic inequality, it has three main sets of tools that it might use: redistribution from those with high incomes to those with low incomes; trying to assure that a ladder of opportunity is widely available; and a tax on inheritances. Let's consider these in turn.

Redistribution

redistribution: Taking income from those with higher incomes and providing income to those with lower incomes.

Redistribution means taking income from those with higher incomes and providing income to those with lower incomes. Earlier in this chapter, we considered some of the key government policies that provide support for the poor: the welfare program TANF, the earned income tax credit, the Supplemental Nutrition Assistance Program, and Medicaid. If a reduction in inequality seemed socially desirable, these programs could receive additional funding.

These programs are paid for through the federal income tax, which is designed in such a way that the rich pay considerably more in income taxes than the poor. Exhibit 16-10 shows data from individual income tax returns in 2011. The top 1%, which had an average income of $1,413,100 per year in pre-tax income, paid 20.3% of their total income in income taxes, and 29% of their total income in all federal taxes combined. This top 1% paid 35.4% of all income taxes and 24% of total federal taxes. Meanwhile, the bottom two quintiles actually paid negative income taxes on average because of provisions like the earned income credit that provide income to many of these families. News stories occasionally report on a high-income person who has managed to pay very little in taxes, but while such individual cases exist, the typical pattern is that people with higher incomes pay a higher average share of their income to federal income taxes.

Of course, the fact that some degree of redistribution occurs now through the federal income tax and government antipoverty programs doesn't settle the questions of how much redistribution is appropriate and whether more redistribution should occur.

The Ladder of Opportunity

Economic inequality is perhaps most troubling when it is not the result of effort or talent, but instead is determined by the circumstances under which a child grows up. One child

EXHIBIT 16-10 Tax Rates and Share of Taxes Paid: 2011

Columns 2 and 3 show the average pre-tax and post-tax income for that quintile, or for the top 5% and 1% of the income distribution. The effective income tax rate in column 4 is the average share of income paid in federal income taxes. The effective tax rate for all federal taxes in column 5 includes non-income taxes like the payroll taxes that fund Social Security and Medicare, as well as federal alcohol and gasoline taxes. For example, the top 1% of the income distribution paid 20.3% of its income in individual income taxes and 29% of its income in total federal taxes. The share paid of income tax liabilities appears in column 6, while the share paid of total federal taxes is shown in column 7. For example, the top quintile paid 88% of all income taxes and 68.7% of all federal taxes in 2011.

Income category	Average Pre-tax Income	Average Post-tax Income	Effective Income Tax Rate	Effective Tax Rate All Federal Taxes	Share Paid of All Income Tax Liabilities	Share Paid of All Total Federal Taxes
Lowest quintile	$24,600	$24,100	–7.5%	1.9%	–4.7%	0.6%
Second quintile	$45,300	$42,100	n1.3%	7.0%	–1.5%	3.8%
Third quintile	$66,400	$59,000	2.4%	11.2%	4.0%	8.9%
Fourth quintile	$97,500	$82,600	5.8%	15.2%	14.2%	17.6%
Fifth quintile	$245,700	$188,200	14.2%	23.4%	88.0%	68.7%
Top 5%	$299,000	$226,400	15.6%	24.3%	23.6%	17.4%
Top 1%	$1,453,100	$1,031,900	20.3%	29.0%	35.4%	24.0%

attends a well-run grade school and high school and heads on to college, while parents help out by supporting education and other interests; paying for college, a first car, and a first house; and offering work connections that lead to internships and jobs. Another child attends a poorly run grade school, barely makes it through a low-quality high school, doesn't go to college, and lacks family and peer support. These two children may be similar in their underlying talents and in the effort they put forth, but their economic outcomes are likely to be quite different.

Public policy can attempt to build a ladder of opportunities so that, even though all children will never come from identical families and attend identical schools, each child has a reasonable opportunity to attain an economic niche in society based on his or her interests, desires, talents, and efforts. Opportunity-oriented policies begin with focus on children: for example, programs for improved day care; enrichment programs for pre-schoolers; improved public schools; after-school and community activities; and internships and apprenticeships to connect teenagers to the job market. At the college and university level, the ladder of opportunity might involve widespread loans and grants for those in financial need, along with public support for a range of institutions from two-year community colleges to large research universities. For adults, the ladder of opportunity might involve opportunities for retraining and acquiring new skills, as well as actively prohibiting discrimination in job markets and housing on the basis of race, gender, age, and disability.

The United States has often been called a land of opportunity. Although the general idea of a ladder of opportunity for all citizens continues to exert a powerful attraction, specifics are often controversial. One problem is that some of the policies to create more opportunity could be highly costly to taxpayers—for example, the costs would be very high if the government offered to pay for several years of preschool, to increase funding for all students from kindergarten through 12th grade, and also to help pay for college for every student. Moreover, the success of many of these proposals may depend less on the level of spending than on how the projects are managed and directed. For example, improving the quality of public schools is easy to say, but hard to achieve. Government training for adults seems to work well in some programs but not in others. Society can experiment with a wide variety of proposals for building a ladder of opportunity, especially for those who otherwise seem likely to start their lives in a disadvantaged position. But such policy experiments need to be carried out in a spirit of open-mindedness, because some will succeed while others will not show positive results or will cost too much to enact on a widespread basis.

Inheritance Taxes

If wealthy parents can give large gifts and inheritances to their children, then economic inequality may persist across generations. How much wealth should rich people be able to pass on to their children? On the one hand, it seems self-evident that people who have worked hard all their lives and saved up a substantial nest egg should be able to give their money and possessions to their children and grandchildren if they wish. In particular, it would seem un-American if children were unable to inherit a family business or a family home. On the other hand, many Americans are far more comfortable with inequality resulting from high-income people who earned their money by starting innovative new companies than they are with inequality resulting from high-income people who have inherited money from rich parents.

estate tax: A tax imposed on the value of an inheritance.

The United States does have an **estate tax**—that is, a tax imposed on the value of an inheritance—which suggests a willingness to limit how much wealth can be passed on as an inheritance. However, in 2016 the estate tax applied only to those leaving inheritances of more than $55.45million and thus applies to only a tiny percentage of the population who have very high levels of wealth. The estate tax collects less than 1% of federal tax revenues. Even for the small minority who are subject to the estate tax, a good tax lawyer or a savvy estate planner can often figure out ways to minimize what must be paid.

As a matter of practical politics, there seems to be relatively little support for a substantial increase in redistribution by taxing either the income or the inheritances of those with high incomes and wealth. In contrast, an opportunity agenda remains relatively popular. For example, the expansions of the earned income credit and of Medicaid to cover near-poor families can be viewed as attempts to strengthen the rungs on the ladder of opportunity, as can various proposals to improve education. The ultimate test will be whether detailed studies show that these policies are working reasonably well.

The Trade-off between Incentives and Income Equality

Government policies to reduce poverty or to encourage economic equality, if carried to extremes, can injure incentives for economic output. The poverty trap, for example, defines a situation where guaranteeing a certain level of income can eliminate or reduce the incentive to work at a low-paid job. Extremely high taxes on the rich would at some point be likely to discourage work and entrepreneurship. Thus, it is common to draw the trade-off between economic output and equality as shown in Exhibit 16-11a. In this formulation, if society wishes a high level of economic output like point A, it must also accept a high degree of inequality; conversely, if society wants a high level of equality like point B, it must accept a lower level of economic output because of reduced incentives for production.

But this view of the trade-off between economic output and equality may be too pessimistic, and Exhibit 16-11b presents an alternate vision. Here, the trade-off between economic output and equality first slopes up, in the vicinity of choice C, suggesting that certain programs might increase both output and economic equality. For example, the policy of providing free public education has an element of redistribution, since the value of the public schooling received by children of low-income families is clearly higher than what low-income families pay in taxes. But a well-educated population is also an enormously powerful factor in providing the skilled workers of tomorrow and helping the economy to grow and expand. In this case, equality and economic growth may complement each other. Moreover, policies to diminish inequality and soften the hardship of poverty may sustain political support for a market economy. After all, if society does not make at least some efforts toward reducing inequality and poverty, the alternative might

EXHIBIT 16-11 The Trade-off between Incentives and Economic Equality

(a) Greater equality always reduces output.

Society faces a trade-off where any attempt to move toward greater equality, like moving from choice A to B, involves a reduction in economic output.

(b) Equality and output rise together, but then face a trade-off.

Situations can arise like point C, where it is possible both to increase equality and also to increase economic output, to a choice like D. It may also be possible to increase equality with little impact on economic output, like the movement from choice D to E. However, at some point, too aggressive a push for equality will tend to reduce economic output, as in the shift from E to F.

be that fearful citizens would rebel against market forces. For example, citizens might seek economic security by demanding that their legislators pass laws that would forbid employers from ever laying off workers or reducing wages, or laws that would impose price floors and price ceilings and shut off international trade. From this viewpoint, policies to reduce inequality may help economic output by building social support for allowing markets to operate.

The trade-off in Exhibit 16-11*b* then flattens out in the area between points D and E, which reflects the pattern that there are a number of economies that provide roughly similar levels of income to their citizens—the United States, Canada, the nations of the European Union, Japan, Australia—but these countries have different levels of inequality. This pattern suggests that countries in this range could choose a greater or a lesser degree of inequality without much impact on economic output. Only if these countries push for a much higher level of equality, like at point F, will they experience the diminished incentives that lead to lower levels of economic output. In this view, while a danger always exists that an agenda to reduce poverty or inequality can be poorly designed or pushed too far, it is also possible to discover and design policies that improve equality and do not injure incentives for economic output by very much—or even improve such incentives.

Key Concepts and Summary

1. Labor markets will determine wages according to demand and supply, which can lead to very low incomes for some people and very high incomes for others.

2. **Poverty** and economic **inequality** are not the same thing. Poverty applies to the condition of people who cannot afford the necessities of life. Economic inequality refers to the disparity between those with higher and lower incomes.

3. The poverty rate is what percentage of the population lives below the **poverty line**, which is determined by

the amount of income that it takes to purchase the necessities of life. Choosing a poverty line will always be somewhat controversial. The near-poor are those with low incomes who are just above the poverty line.

4. A **poverty trap** occurs when government-support payments for the poor decline as the poor earn more income. As a result, the poor do not end up with much more income when they work because the loss of government support largely or completely offsets any income that is earned by working. The bite of the

poverty trap can be reduced by phasing out government benefits more slowly, as well as by imposing requirements for work as a condition of receiving benefits and a time limit on benefits.

5. The groups of government programs that assist the poor are called the **safety net**. In the United States, prominent safety net programs include Temporary Assistance to Needy Families (TANF), the earned income credit (EIC), Medicaid, and the Supplemental Nutrition Assistance Program.

6. Measuring inequality involves making comparisons across the entire distribution of income, not just the poor. One way of doing this is to divide the population into groups, like **quintiles**, and then calculate what share of income is received by each group. An alternative approach is to draw **Lorenz curves**, which compare the cumulative income actually received to a perfectly equal distribution of income.

7. Income inequality in the United States increased substantially from the late 1970s or early 1980s into the 2000s. The two most common explanation cited by economists are changes in the structure of households that have led to more two-earner couples and single-parent families, and the effect of new information and communications technology on wages.

8. There are a number of plausible reasons for a degree of income inequality: for example, differences in age, differences in preferences, a need for incentives, year-to-year fluctuations, and luck. However, inequality that is rising, or that is passed between generations, can create social and political tensions.

9. Policies that can affect the level of economic inequality include **redistribution** between rich and poor, making it easier for people to climb the ladder of opportunity, and **estate taxes**, which are taxes on inheritances.

10. Pushing too aggressively for economic equality can run the risk of decreasing economic incentives. However, a moderate push for economic equality can increase economic output, both through methods like improved education and by building a base of political support for market forces.

Review Questions

1. What is the difference between poverty and income inequality?
2. How is the poverty rate calculated?
3. What is the poverty line?
4. Who are the near-poor?
5. How does the poverty trap discourage people from working?
6. How can the effect of the poverty trap be reduced?
7. What is the safety net?
8. Briefly explain the differences between TANF, the earned income tax credit, the Supplemental Nutrition Assistance Program, and Medicaid.
9. Who is included in the top income quintile?
10. What is measured on the two axes of a Lorenz curve?
11. How has the inequality of income changed in the U.S. economy since the late 1970s?
12. What are some reasons why a certain degree of inequality of income would be expected in a market economy?
13. What are the main reasons economists give for the increase in inequality of incomes?
14. Name some public policies that can reduce the level of economic inequality.
15. Describe how a push for economic equality might reduce incentives to work and produce output. Then describe how a push for economic inequality might not have such effects.

Issues in Labor Markets: Unions, Discrimination, Immigration

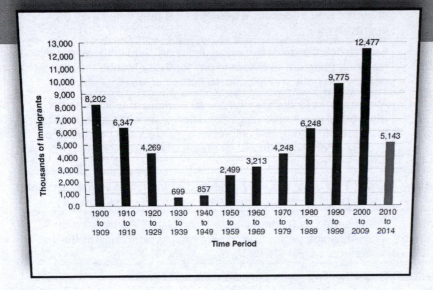

A worker without a job will feel considerable stress; after all, there are bills to pay and mouths to feed. But most employers have a number of employees. If a company fires a worker or delays hiring a worker, the company as a whole is unlikely to experience any noticeable rise or fall in profits. Thus, when a worker or job applicant is bargaining with an employer, the individual is often at a disadvantage because the worker needs the job more than the employer needs that particular worker. John Bates Clark (1847–1938), often named as the first great American economist, wrote in 1907: "In the making of the wage contract the individual laborer is always at a disadvantage. He has something which he is obliged to sell and which his employer is not obliged to take, since he [that is, the employer] can reject individual men with impunity."

A number of laws have been passed to create greater balance in negotiations between workers and employers. For example, there are laws setting minimum hourly wages, limiting the hours that employers can require (at least before they pay overtime rates), prohibiting child labor, regulating health and safety conditions in the workplace, and preventing discrimination on the basis of race, ethnicity, gender, and age. Laws have also been enacted to require that employers provide family leave, that employers give advance notice of layoffs, that workers have unemployment insurance, and to limit the number of immigrant workers from other countries. Exhibit 17-1 lists some prominent U.S. workplace protection laws. Many of the laws listed in the table were only the start of labor market regulations in these areas and have been followed over time by other related laws, regulations, and court rulings. Many of these laws are discussed at other places in this book: for example, Chapter 5 considered minimum wage laws as an example of a price floor.

This chapter will focus on three aspects of workplace protection. The first section discusses labor unions, in which workers join together and negotiate as a group for wages, benefits, and other conditions of employment with the firm.

EXHIBIT 17-1 Prominent U.S. Workplace Protection Laws

National Labor-Management Relations Act of 1935 (the "Wagner Act")	Establishes procedures for establishing a union that firms are obligated to follow, and sets up the National Labor Relations Board for deciding disputes
Social Security Act of 1935	Under Title III, establishes a state-run system of unemployment insurance, in which workers pay into a state fund when they are employed and receive benefits for a time when they are unemployed
Fair Labor Standards Act of 1938	Establishes the minimum wage, limits on child labor, and rules requiring payment of overtime pay for those in jobs that are paid by the hour and exceed 40 hours per week
Taft-Hartley Act of 1947	Allows states to decide whether all workers at a firm can be required to join a union as a condition of employment, and in the case of a disruptive union strike, permits the president to declare a "cooling-off period" during which workers have to return to work
Civil Rights Act of 1964	Under Title VII of the Act prohibits discrimination in employment on the basis of race, gender, national origin, or religion
Occupational Health and Safety Act of 1970	Creates the Occupational Safety and Health Administration (OSHA), which protects workers from physical harm in the workplace
Employee Retirement and Income Security Act of 1974	Regulates employee pension rules and benefits
Immigration Reform and Control Act of 1986	Prohibits hiring of illegal immigrants, requires employers to ask for proof of citizenship, protects rights of legal immigrants
Worker Adjustment and Retraining Notification Act of 1988	Requires employers with more than 100 employees to provide written notice 60 days before plant closings or large layoffs
Americans with Disabilities Act of 1990	Prohibits discrimination against those with disabilities and requires reasonable accommodations for them on the job
Family and Medical Leave Act of 1993	Allows employees to take up to 12 weeks of unpaid leave per year for family reasons, including birth or family illness
Pension Protection Act of 2006	Penalizes firms for underfunding their pension plans and gives employees more information about their pension accounts

The second section discusses the economics of discrimination against women or minority groups in the labor market. What effect has such discrimination had on wages and other work conditions? Finally, the chapter moves to a discussion of immigration, which in economic terms can be viewed as a situation where the supply of labor is extended to include workers who arrive from outside the country.

Labor Unions

labor union: An organization of workers that negotiates with employers as a group over wages and working conditions.

collective bargaining: Negotiations between unions and a firm or firms.

A **labor union** is an organization of workers that negotiates with employers as a group over wages and working conditions. A labor union seeks to change the balance of negotiations between employers and workers by forcing employers to deal with workers collectively, rather than as individuals. Thus, negotiations between unions and firms are sometimes called **collective bargaining**. Labor unions can be controversial. Supporters of labor unions view them as the workers' primary line of defense against efforts by profit-seeking firms to hold down wages. Critics of labor unions view them as having a tendency to grab as much as they can in the short term, even if it injures workers in

EXHIBIT 17-2 Which American Workers Belong to Unions in 2015?

- 11.5% of U.S. male workers belong to unions; 10.6% of female workers do.
- 10.8% of white workers, 13.6% of black workers, and 9.4% of Hispanic workers belong to unions.
- 12.2% of full-time workers and 5.9% of part-time workers are union members.
- 4.4% of workers ages 16–24 belong to unions, as do 9.7% of workers ages 25–34, 12.3% of workers ages 35–44, 13.6% of workers ages 45–54, 14.3% of workers ages 55–64, and 9.5% of workers ages 65 and older.
- Occupations in which relatively high percentages of workers belong to unions are government (35.2% belong to a union); transportation and utilities (19.3%); natural resources, construction, and maintenance (15%); and production, transportation, and material moving (14.2%).
- Occupations that have relatively low percentages of unionized workers are agricultural workers (1.2%), financial services (1.3%), professional and business services (2.5%), leisure and hospitality (3.1%), and wholesale and retail trade (4.6%).

EXHIBIT 17-3 The Five Largest American Unions in 2014

Union	Membership
National Education Association	2,963,000
Service Employees International Union	1,893,000
American Federation of State, County, and Municipal Employees	1,337,000
International Brotherhood of Teamsters	1,305,000
United Food and Commercial Workers International Union	1,274,000

the long run by driving firms into bankruptcy or by blocking the new technologies and production methods that lead to economic growth. Let's start here with some facts about union membership in the United States.

Facts about Union Membership and Pay

About 11% of all U.S. workers belong to unions. As Exhibit 17-2 shows, the percentage of workers belonging to a union is higher for men than women, higher for blacks than for whites or Hispanics, higher for people in the 45–64 age range, and higher among workers in government and manufacturing than workers in agriculture or service-oriented jobs. Exhibit 17-3 provides a list of the five largest U.S. labor unions and their membership.

In terms of pay and number of jobs, U.S. unions offer a good news/bad news story. The good news for unions is that their members earn about 20% more than nonunion members, even after adjusting for factors such as years of work experience and education level. The bad news for unions is that the share of U.S. workers who belong to a labor union has been steadily declining for 50 years, as shown in Exhibit 17-4. About one-quarter of all U.S. workers belonged to a union in the mid-1950s, but only 11% of U.S. workers are union members today. If you leave out workers employed by the government (which includes teachers in public schools), only 6.7% of the workers employed by private firms now belong to a union. The next section analyzes the higher pay for unions, and the following section analyzes declining union membership levels, two issues that will allow us to discuss many aspects of how unions work.

Higher Wages for Union Workers

Why might union workers receive higher pay? What are the limits on how much higher pay they can receive? To analyze these questions, let's consider a situation where, because

The share of wage and salary workers who belong to unions rose sharply in the 1930s and 1940s, but has tailed off since then to about 11% of all workers.

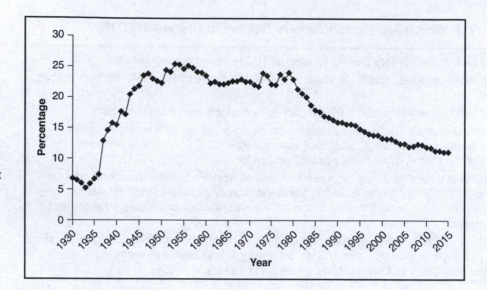

of some combination of laws that requires bargaining with unions and existing labor contracts, all firms in an industry must negotiate with a single union, and no firm is allowed to hire nonunion labor. If no labor union existed in this market, then equilibrium E in the labor market would occur at the intersection of the demand for labor D and the supply of labor S in Exhibit 17-5. But the union can threaten that unless firms agree to the wages they demand, the workers will strike. As a result, the labor union manages to achieve through negotiations with the firms a union wage of w_u for its members, above what the equilibrium wage would otherwise have been.

This labor market situation resembles what a monopoly firm does in selling a product, but in this case it is a union acting as a "monopoly" in selling labor to firms. At the higher union wage w_u, the firms in this industry will hire less labor than they would have hired in equilibrium. Moreover, an excess supply of workers will wish to take union jobs, but firms will not be hiring for such jobs.

From the union point of view, those workers who receive higher wages are better off. However, notice that the quantity of workers q_d hired at the union wage w_u is less than the quantity q_e that would have been hired at the original equilibrium wage. A sensible union must recognize that when it pushes up the wage, it also reduces the incentive of firms to hire. This situation doesn't necessarily mean that union workers are fired. Instead, it may be that when union workers move on to other jobs or retire, their jobs aren't always replaced. Or perhaps when a firm expands production, it expands employment somewhat less with a higher union wage than it would have done with the lower equilibrium wage.

EXHIBIT 17-5 Union Wage Negotiations

Without a union, the equilibrium at E would have involved the wage w_e and the quantity of labor q_e. However, the union is able to use its bargaining power to raise the wage to w_u. The result is an excess supply of labor for union jobs; that is, a quantity of workers q_s would like to work for a union firm at the wage w_u, but the firms will only demand a quantity of workers q_d at that wage.

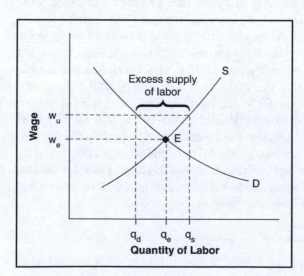

Or perhaps firms decide to purchase certain inputs from nonunion producers, rather than producing them with their own highly paid unionized workers.

From the firms' point of view, the key question is whether the higher wage of union workers is matched with higher productivity. If so, then the firm can afford to pay the higher union wages; if not, then the higher union wage will cause lower profits or losses for the firm. Union workers might have higher productivity than nonunion workers for a number of reasons. For example, union workers tend to stay longer at a given job, a trend that reduces the employer's costs for training and hiring and leads to workers with more years of experience. Many unions also offer job training, which can raise productivity.

In addition, firms that are confronted with union demands for higher wages may choose their production methods so that they use more physical capital and less labor. Exhibit 17-6 provides an example. Assume that a firm can produce a home exercise cycling machine with three different combinations of labor and machines. Say that labor is paid $16/hour and machines cost $200 each. Then the total cost of producing a home exercise cycle will be lowest if the firm adopts the technology of 50 hours of labor and one machine, as the table shows. Now suppose that a union negotiates a wage of $20/hour. In this case, the firm is indifferent between the total cost of the three technologies, but it might prefer to use more machines and to hire fewer union workers. (After all, machines never threaten to strike.) In the final column of the table, the wage has risen to $24/hour. In this case, the incentives of the firm are clearly to use the technology that involves hiring 30 workers and using three machines. If management responds to union demands for higher wages by investing more in machinery, then union workers can be more productive because they are working with more or better physical capital equipment than the typical nonunion worker.

The willingness of unions to adopt new technology has been questioned. In some cases, unions have discouraged the use of labor-saving physical capital equipment—out of the reasonable fear that new machinery would reduce the number of union jobs. For example, in 2002, the union representing longshoremen who unload ships and the firms that operate shipping companies and port facilities experienced a work stoppage that shut down the ports on the western coast of the United States. A key issue in the dispute was the desire of the shipping companies and port operators to use handheld scanners for record-keeping and computer-operated cabs for loading and unloading ships, while the union opposed these changes.

On the other side, unions have sometimes proved quite willing to adopt new technologies. In the 1950s and 1960s, to cite one prominent example, the United Mineworkers Union demanded that companies install labor-saving machinery in the mines. The mineworker's union realized that the new machines would reduce the number of jobs in the mines over time, but the union leaders also knew that jobs could only pay higher wages if the workers became more productive, and mechanization was a necessary step to that greater productivity. In fact, union workers may in some cases be more willing to accept new technology than nonunion workers because the union workers believe that the union will negotiate to protect their jobs and wages, while nonunion workers may have a greater fear that the new technology will replace their job. Overall, it is hard to make a definitive

EXHIBIT 17-6 Three Production Function Choices to Make a Home Exercise Cycling Machine

Hours of Labor	Number of Machines	Labor		
		$16/hour	$20/hour	$24/hr
30	3	480 + 600 = 1,080	600 + 600 = 1,200	720 + 600 = 1,320
40	2	640 + 400 = 1,040	800 + 400 = 1,200	960 + 400 = 1,360
50	1	800 + 200 = 1,000	1,000 + 200 = 1,200	1,200 + 200 = 1,400

When the Ports Closed

A dispute ignited in 2002 between the Pacific Maritime Association, which represents 80 shipping companies and operators of shipping terminals, and the International Longshore and Warehouse Union, which represents 10,500 workers at 29 ports from San Diego to Seattle on the West Coast of the United States.

The previous contract between management and the union had expired. In the new contract, the port operators and shipping companies wanted to introduce new technologies like optical scanners, so that less information would need to be entered by hand as cargo moved on and off ships. Management also wanted to use computerized crane cabs to speed up and cut the costs of loading and unloading of ships. Finally, management also wanted to hold down the costs of pensions and health care benefits. The union would only agree to accept the new technologies—which would have reduced the number of union jobs by several hundred—if certain other jobs at the ports became part of the union, like previously nonunion jobs that involved planning where shipping containers will be placed within ships. Moreover, the union wanted to maintain and increase wages and benefits.

The negotiations turned nasty. Port operators accused the longshoremen of deliberately working slowly and responded by shutting down the ports for 10 days. The port closings affected several hundred ships and by some estimates were costing the U.S. economy $1 billion per day.

On October 9, 2002, President George W. Bush invoked the Labor Management Relations Act of 1947—commonly known as the "Taft-Hartley law." One provision of the Act allows the president to ask a court to end a work stoppage and require firms and workers to get back to work for 80 days. This "cooling-off period," as it is called, both seeks to limit the economic damage that a work stoppage can cause to the rest of the economy, and also to create some time for labor negotiations to proceed without the work stoppage looming over the talks. Bush's action was the 36th time that Taft-Hartley had been invoked by a U.S. president to create a cooling-off period.

Federal mediators were called in, and the two sides agreed to a deal in November 2002. The ultimate agreement allowed the new technologies, but also kept wages, health, and pension benefits high for workers. In the past, presidential use of the Taft-Hartley law has sometimes made labor negotiations more bitter and argumentative, but in this case, it seems to have smoothed the road to an agreement.

case that union workers as a group are always either more or less welcoming to new technology than are nonunion workers.

Perhaps the strongest evidence that union workers are more productive is that in many markets where firms with union labor compete with firms that have nonunion labor, profits don't appear to be lower for the firms with union labor. At least in some cases, although not in all, the higher productivity of union workers does compensate for their higher wages.

The Decline in U.S. Union Membership

Economists have offered a number of possible explanations for why the proportion of U.S. workers belonging to unions has declined so dramatically since the early 1950s: (1) the shift from manufacturing to service industries; (2) the force of globalization and increased competition from foreign producers; (3) a reduced desire for unions because of the workplace protection laws now in place; and (4) a U.S. legal environment that makes it relatively more difficult for unions to organize workers and expand their membership. Let's consider these four explanations in turn.

A first possible explanation for the decline in the share of U.S. workers belonging to unions involves the patterns of job growth in the manufacturing and service sectors of the economy, shown in Exhibit 17-7. The U.S. economy had about 15 million manufacturing jobs in 1960. This total rose a bit to 19 million by the late 1970s and had declined to 12 million by 2015. Meanwhile, the number of jobs in service industries and in government combined rose from 35 million in 1960 to about 120 million by 2015. Because unions were historically stronger in manufacturing than in service industries, the growth in jobs wasn't happening where the unions were. Several of the biggest unions in the country are made up of government workers, including the American Federation of State,

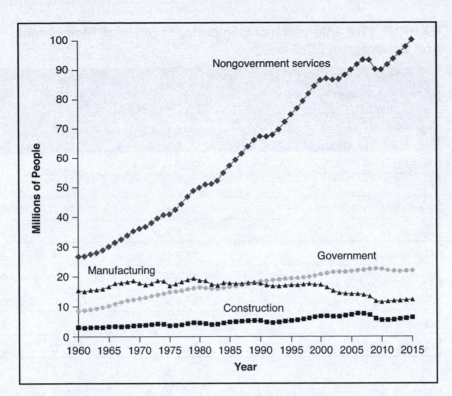

EXHIBIT 17-7 The Growth of Service Jobs

Jobs in services have increased dramatically in the last few decades. Jobs in government have increased modestly. Jobs in manufacturing have not changed much, although they have trended down in recent years.

County, and Municipal Employees (AFSCME); the Service Employees Union; and the National Education Association (whose memberships were listed earlier in Exhibit 17-3). But outside of government employees, unions have not had great success organizing the service sector.

A second explanation for the decline in the share of unionized workers focuses on patterns of international trade. Starting in the 1960s, U.S. carmakers and steelmakers faced increasing competition from Japanese and European manufacturers. As sales of imported cars, steel, and other products increased, union membership in these industries declined. For example, membership in the United Autoworkers union was 975,000 in 1985 but had fallen to 710,000 by 2000. In contrast, unions have performed relatively well at organizing public-sector workers, who are not threatened by import competition. By 2015, 35% of government workers belonged to unions. However, import competition can't be the entire story. Again, union membership has stayed very low in service industries, although many service industries like real estate or banking experience little import competition.

A third possible reason for the decline of unions focuses on how modern workers seek to address their problems. Instead of forming a union, workers often call upon their elected representatives to pass laws about work conditions, overtime, parental leave, regulation of pensions, and other issues like those addressed by the workplace protection laws in Exhibit 17-1. Unions offered political support for many of these laws aimed at protecting workers, but in an ironic twist, those laws then made many workers feel less need for unions.

These first three reasons for the decline of unions are all somewhat plausible, but they share a common problem. Most other developed economies have experienced similar economic and political trends, like the shift from manufacturing to services, globalization, and increasing government social benefits and regulation of the workplace. Yet in other countries, the share of the population belonging to unions is very high by U.S. standards. Exhibit 17-8 shows the proportion of workers in a number of the world's high-income economies who belong to unions. The share of American workers belonging to unions is near the bottom, along with France and Spain. However, in many countries, the wages of many workers who do not officially belong to a union are still determined by collective bargaining between unions and firms. The last column shows "union coverage," defined as those workers whose wages are largely determined by a union negotiation even if the

EXHIBIT 17-8 International Comparisons of Union Membership and Coverage in 2013

Country	Union Density: Percentage of Workers Belonging to a Union	Union Coverage: Percentage of Workers Whose Wages Are Determined by Union Bargaining
Austria	27.8%	98.0%
France	7.7%	98.0%
Germany	18.1%	57.6%
Japan	17.8%	17.1%
Netherlands	17.8%	84.8%
Spain	16.9%	77.6%
Sweden	67.7%	89.0%
United Kingdom	25.8%	29.5%
United States	10.8%	11.9%

workers don't officially belong to the union. In the United States, union membership is almost identical to union coverage. But in a number of other countries, unions effectively determine the wages of many workers who don't actually belong to the union.

These international differences in union membership suggest a fourth reason for the decline of union membership in the United States: perhaps U.S. laws are less friendly to the formation of unions than such laws in other countries. The close connection between union membership and a friendly legal environment is apparent in the history of U.S. unions. The great rise in union membership in the 1930s followed the passage of the National Labor-Management Relations Act of 1935, which specified that workers had a right to organize unions and that management had to give them a fair chance to do so. The U.S. government strongly encouraged unions to be formed in the early 1940s from a belief that unions would help to coordinate the all-out production efforts needed during World War II. However, after World War II came the passage of the Taft-Hartley Act of 1947, which gave states the power to allow workers to opt out of the union in their workplace if they so desired. This law made the legal climate less encouraging for unions, and union membership levels soon started declining.

The procedures for forming a union differ substantially from country to country. For example, in the United States, when a group of workers wish to form a union, they announce this fact and an election date is set when the employees at a firm will vote in a secret ballot on whether to form a union. Supporters of the union lobby for a "yes" vote, and the management of the firm often hires consultants to lobby for a "no" vote. In Canada, by contrast, a union is formed when a sufficient proportion of workers (usually about 60%) sign an official card saying that they want a union. There is no separate "election date." The management of Canadian firms is limited by law in its ability to lobby against the union. In short, forming unions is easier in Canada—and in many other countries—than in the United States. Thus, the declining share of workers belonging to unions may be because U.S. laws are less friendly to the formation of unions than laws of other countries.

Concluding Thoughts about the Economics of Unions

The economic analysis of unions, as is true of many issues, doesn't end up with blanket conclusions that they are automatically good or bad. Instead, economic insights are often phrased as "if . . . then. . . ." If unions push up wages, then employers will seek out ways of hiring fewer union workers. If unions block new technology, go on strike repeatedly, or negotiate so aggressively for higher wages that they injure the long-term health of firms, then they may be economically harmful. However, if unions help workers to feel more secure, be better trained and more flexible, and communicate better with management, then unions may be economically beneficial. There is little evidence that countries with high union membership tend to suffer economic damage as a result, nor that the reduction in U.S. union membership over time has brought broad benefits or costs for the U.S. economy as a whole. The study of unions and their economic effects needs to focus on specific situations, not on generalities. Economists are less interested in judging unions than they are in analyzing and understanding their patterns of pay and employment.

Employment Discrimination

Discrimination involves acting on the belief that members of a certain group have lesser ability solely because of a factor like their race, gender, or religion. Discrimination can arise in social circumstances, and also in goods, labor, and financial capital markets. Discrimination in goods markets would occur when a woman ends up paying a higher price at a car dealership than a man would have paid, or when a realtor steers a Hispanic family away from buying a home in a certain neighborhood. Discrimination in financial capital markets would arise if a bank is willing to make a loan to a white family with certain economic characteristics, but would deny the loan to a black family with those same economic characteristics. The focus here will be on race and gender discrimination in labor markets, which arises if workers with the same skill levels—say, as measured by education, experience, and expertise—receive different pay..

Earnings Gaps by Race and Gender

A possible signal of labor market discrimination is when one group is paid less than another. Exhibit 17-9 shows the average wages of black workers as a fraction of the average wage of white workers and the average wages of women workers as a fraction of the average wage of male workers. The gap between the earnings of women and men has declined since about 1980. Overall, the gap between the earnings of blacks and whites has overall declined a little since the late 1970s, but not by a large amount. In both gender and race, a substantial earnings gap remains.

But an earnings gap, in and of itself, does not prove that discrimination is occurring in the labor market. Instead, gender discrimination in the labor market means that women are paid less than men *given comparable levels of education, experience, and expertise.* Similarly, racial discrimination in the labor market exists when blacks are paid less than whites *with comparable levels of education, experience, and expertise.* Let's consider some evidence on such differences.

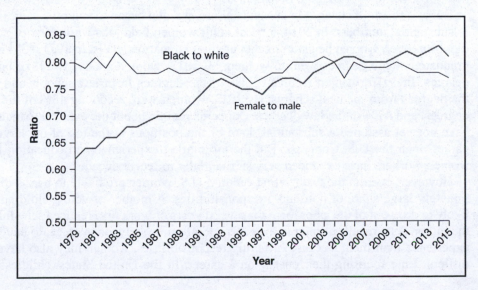

EXHIBIT 17-9 Wage Ratios by Sex and Race

Overall, the ratio of wages for black and white workers has declined a little since the late 1970s. The ratio of wages for female and male workers rose substantially since the 1980s and has continued to rise since then. In both cases, a gap remains between the average wages of black and white workers and between the average wages of female and male workers.

The U.S. Supreme Court Declares Women Workers Unequal

In 1903, the state of Oregon passed a law stating that no woman would be allowed to work more than ten hours in a day. In a 1905 case, the U.S. Supreme Court held that a law limiting male workers to a 10-hour day and a 60-hour week was unconstitutional because it was "an unreasonable, unnecessary, and arbitrary interference with the right and liberty of the individual" to make contracts with an employer. But in *Muller v. State of Oregon*, the U.S. Supreme Court ruled in 1908 that such a law was acceptable if it applied only to women. Using language that today would be laughable, the Supreme Court wrote:

> That woman's physical structure and the performance of maternal functions place her at a disadvantage in the struggle for subsistence is obvious. . . . [B]y abundant testimony of the medical fraternity continuance for a long time on her feet at work, repeating this from day to day, tends to injurious effects upon the body, and as healthy mothers are essential to vigorous offspring, the physical well-being of woman becomes an object of public interest and care in order to preserve the strength and vigor of the race.

> Still again, history discloses the fact that woman has always been dependent upon man. . . . Even

though all restrictions on political, personal and contractual rights were taken away, and she stood, so far as statutes are concerned, upon an absolutely equal plane with him, it would still be true that she is so constituted that she will rest upon and look to him for protection; that her physical structure and a proper discharge of her maternal functions—having in view not merely her own health, but the well-being of the race—justify legislation to protect her from the greed as well as the passion of man. The limitations which this statute places upon her contractual powers, upon her right to agree with her employer as to the time she shall labor, are not imposed solely for her benefit, but also largely for the benefit of all. Many words cannot make this plainer. The two sexes differ in structure of body, in the functions to be performed by each, in the amount of physical strength, in the capacity for long-continued labor, particularly when done standing, the influence of vigorous health upon the future well-being of the race, the self-reliance which enables one to assert full rights, and in the capacity to maintain the struggle for subsistence. This difference justifies a difference in legislation and upholds that which is designed to compensate for some of the burdens which rest upon her.

Investigating the Female/Male Earnings Gap

Labor market discrimination against women was open and legal for much of the twentieth century. For example, in the 1950s, newspaper help-wanted advertisements were often split into separate sections for men and for women. Social customs also discouraged women, especially married women, from working. Indeed, many firms and local school boards had explicit "marriage bar" rules until the 1950s that single women would be fired if they married and that married women would not be hired. In 1960, 35% of adult women held jobs, while 79% of adult men did.

But as a result of changes in law and culture, women began to enter the paid workforce in substantial numbers. In 2014, 57% of adult women held jobs while 69% of adult men did. Moreover, women began to ratchet up their education levels. In 1971, 43% of undergraduate college degrees went to women; by 2013, women received 62% of bachelor's degrees. In 1970, women received 5.4% of the degrees from law schools and 8.4% of the degrees from medical schools. By 2013, women were receiving 48% of the medical degrees, and 47% of the law degrees. Concerns remain about the extent to which women have not yet assumed a substantial share of the positions at the top of the largest companies or in the U.S. Congress. But the job market experience and education levels of women workers have expanded very substantially in recent decades.

However, even in the twenty-first century, U.S. women are likely to bear a disproportionately large share of household responsibilities. A mother of young children is more likely to drop out of the labor force for several years or work on a reduced schedule than is the father. As a result, women in their 30s and 40s are likely, on average, to have less job experience than men. Because of family responsibilities, women may also have a more difficult time focusing their energy on a career. In the United States, childless women with the same education and experience levels as men are typically paid comparably. However, women with families and children are typically paid about 10–15% less than other women of similar education and work experience. (Meanwhile, married men earn about 10–15% *more* than single men with comparable education and work experience.)

Thus, in the 1960s and 1970s, women who had not previously worked in the paid labor force started taking such jobs in large numbers, encouraged by changes in both social customs and law. At first, this trend led to large numbers of women in the labor market with relatively little job experience because they had just started recently, so the earnings gap between men and women barely budged. But by the 1980s, women workers had increased their educational levels and had built up their job experience, and the earnings gap began to close. The remaining gap in earnings seems to be largely explained by the fact that women continue to shoulder a larger share of family responsibilities, and thus have less work experience. The different patterns of family responsibilities might reasonably be called "discrimination," but it is primarily rooted in America's social patterns of discrimination that involve the roles that fathers and mothers play in child-rearing, rather than discrimination by employers in hiring and salary decisions.

Investigating the Black/White Earnings Gap

Blacks experienced open labor market discrimination during much of the twentieth century. Until the passage of the Civil Rights Act of 1964, it was legal in many states to refuse to hire a black worker, regardless of the credentials or experience of that worker. Moreover, blacks were often denied access to educational opportunities, which in turn meant that a disproportionate share of blacks had lower levels of qualifications for many jobs. A number of economic studies have shown that the 1964 Act is partially responsible for the narrowing of the gap in black/white earnings in the late 1960s and into the 1970s; for example, the ratio of total earnings of black male workers to white male workers rose dramatically from 0.62 in 1964 to 0.72 by 1975.

However, the earnings gap between black and white workers has moved up and down without changing dramatically since the 1980s. The remaining gap seems related both to continuing differences in education levels and to the presence of discrimination. Exhibit 17-10 shows that the percentage of blacks who complete a four-year college degree remains substantially lower than the percentage of whites. Both whites and blacks have higher levels of educational attainment than Hispanics but lower than those of Asians. The lower average levels of education for black workers surely explain part of the earnings gap. In fact, black women who have the same levels of education and experience as white women receive on average about the same level of pay. However, black men with the same levels of education and experience as white men are paid 12–15% less than white men, an outcome that suggests the possibility of continuing discrimination.

The lower levels of education for black workers can also be a result of discrimination—although it may be social discrimination, rather than direct discrimination by employers in the labor market. For example, if discrimination in housing markets causes low-income black families to live clustered together in certain neighborhoods, then the public schools that serve these neighborhoods may be overwhelmed with students who need additional help. When blacks were effectively barred from many high-paying jobs, getting additional education could have seemed somewhat pointless because the educational degrees were

EXHIBIT 17-10 Educational Attainment by Race and Ethnicity in 2015

Whites are more likely than blacks or Hispanics to complete college. However, Asians are more likely than whites to complete college.

	White	Hispanic	Black	Asian
Completed four years of high school or more	93.3	66.7	87.0	89.0
Completed four years of college or more	36.2	15.5	22.5	53.9

Audit Studies of Discrimination

Some of the most persuasive evidence that outright prejudicial discrimination continues in the U.S. economy comes from *audit studies*, in which pairs of people of different genders or races are assigned made-up characters with essentially identical economic characteristics, like income level and job experience. They receive training in how to respond to interview questions so that they will respond in the same ways. Then the pairs of individuals—perhaps one black and one white, or one male and one female—are sent out to apply for the same job, to buy a comparable house or car, or apply for a bank loan for the same amount of money. The results of these studies are disquieting.

A 1989 Housing Discrimination Study carried out audit studies over 20 metropolitan areas and found that blacks and Hispanics were often shown fewer places to buy and rent, were quoted higher prices, and were simply not shown certain available dwellings in mainly white neighborhoods. Similarly, in a 1997 audit study done in San Antonio, a Hispanic woman and a white woman who had been assigned very similar jobs and incomes applied for the same two-bedroom apartment. The Hispanic women was quoted a rent of $670/month with a $200 security deposit, while a white female was quoted a rent of $616/month and a $100 security deposit.

In a 2004 study, fictional resumes were sent to employers in Boston and Chicago, some with white-sounding names and some with black-sounding names. About 10% of the white-sounding names got a callback based on their resume, compared with 6% for the black-sounding names. The study also found that improved credentials, such as increased years of education and job experience, have less of an effect on callback rates for black-sounding names than for white-sounding names.

In the United States of the twenty-first century, nondiscrimination may be the ideal, but audit studies continue to demonstrate that it is not always the reality.

not likely to pay off. Even when labor market discrimination has been legally abolished, it can take some time to establish a tradition of valuing education highly. In these ways, a legacy of past discrimination may contribute to an attitude that blacks will have a difficult time succeeding in academic subjects. In any case, the impact of social discrimination in labor markets is more complicated than seeking to punish a few bigoted employers.

Competitive Markets and Discrimination

Gary Becker (1930–2014), who won the Nobel Prize in economics in 1992, was one of the first to analyze discrimination in economic terms. Becker pointed out that while competitive markets can allow some employers to practice discrimination, they can also provide profit-seeking firms with incentives not to discriminate. For example, if a business located in an area with a large minority population refuses to sell to minorities, it will cut into its own profits. If some businesses run by bigoted employers refuse to pay women and/or minorities a wage based on their productivity, then other profit-seeking employers can hire these workers, pay them a little more, and make a profit. Overall, if the owners of a business care more about the color of money than about the color of skin, they will have an incentive to make buying and selling and hiring and promotion decisions strictly based on economic factors.

The power of markets to offer at least a degree of freedom to oppressed groups should not be underestimated. In many countries, cohesive minority groups like Jews and emigrant Chinese have managed to carve out a space for themselves through their economic activities, despite legal and social discrimination against them. Many immigrants, including those who come to the United States, have taken advantage of economic freedom to make new lives for themselves. However, history teaches that market forces alone are unlikely to eliminate discrimination. After all, discrimination against African-Americans persisted in the market-oriented U.S. economy during the century between President Abraham Lincoln's Emancipation Proclamation that freed the slaves in 1863 and the passage of the Civil Rights Act of 1964—and has continued since then, too.

Gary Becker also sought to explain why market forces may not always reduce discrimination. Discriminatory impulses can emerge at a number of levels: among managers, among workers, and among customers. Consider the situation of a manager who is not personally prejudiced, but has many workers or customers who are prejudiced. If that manager treats minority groups or women fairly, the manager may find it hurts the morale of prejudiced co-workers or drives away prejudiced customers. In such a situation, a policy of nondiscrimination could reduce the firm's profits. After all, a business firm is part of society, and a firm that does not follow the social norms is likely to suffer. Market forces alone are unlikely to overwhelm strong social attitudes about discrimination.

Public Policies to Reduce Discrimination

A first public policy step against discrimination in the labor market is to make it illegal. For example, the Equal Pay Act of 1963 said that men and women who do equal work at a company must be paid the same. The Civil Rights Act of 1964 prohibits employment discrimination based on race, color, religion, sex, or national origin. The Age Discrimination in Employment Act of 1967 prohibits discrimination on the basis of age against individuals who are 40 years of age or older. The Civil Rights Act of 1991 provides monetary damages in cases of intentional employment discrimination. But passing a law is only part of the answer, since discrimination by prejudiced employers may be less important than broader social patterns.

In the case of the earnings gap between men and women, probably the single largest remaining cause is the differences in family responsibilities assumed by mothers and fathers. Sweden, for example, offers nearly a year of parental leave from work after the birth of a child, and child care is almost entirely paid for by tax dollars rather than by parents. By U.S. standards, these policies may seem extreme. However, without shifts in attitudes by men and women about home and child responsibilities, the U.S. labor market is likely to continue showing a wage gap between men and women.

In the case of the earnings gap between blacks and whites (and also between Hispanics and whites), probably the single largest step at this point in U.S. history would be to reduce the gap in educational achievement. Part of the answer involves finding ways to improve the performance of schools, which is a controversial topic in itself. But in addition, the education gap won't close unless black and Hispanic families and peer groups strengthen their culture of support for educational achievement.

Affirmative action is the name given to active efforts to improve the job opportunities or outcomes of minority groups or women. Affirmative action in its limited and not especially controversial form means making an effort to reach out to a broader range of minority candidates for jobs. In its more aggressive and controversial form, affirmative action might require businesses to set specific numerical targets or quotas for the percentages of minorities and women that the firms will hire and promote. Those who favor numerical goals argue that without hard results, the affirmative action will be more talk than action. Those opposed to numerical targets question how numerical goals are set. Surely, they say, it is not reasonable that every employer, for every job, in every area of the economy, should hire a statistical cross-section of the U.S. population. The critics also point out that numerical targets can cause resentment and backlash among other workers, who may be quick to assume that the successes of minorities and women are due to affirmative action policies rather than merit. The affirmative action controversy seems likely to continue simmering.

affirmative action: Active efforts to improve the job opportunities or outcomes of minority groups or women.

An Increasingly Diverse Workforce

Racial and ethnic diversity is on the rise in the U.S. population and work force. Exhibit 17-11 shows that while white Americans composed 69.4% of the population in 2000, the U.S. Bureau of the Census projects that whites will be less than half of the U.S. population by 2060. The proportion of U.S. citizens who are of Hispanic and Asian background will rise substantially. Moreover, the women who entered the workforce in the 1970s and 1980s and since then are moving up the promotion ladders within their organizations.

Fortune-telling isn't economics, but it still can be clarifying to speculate about the future. Optimists argue that the growing proportions of minority workers and highly

EXHIBIT 17-11 Projected Changes in Racial and Ethnic Diversity of U.S. Population

	2000	2014	2060
White alone (not Hispanic)	69.4%	62.2%	43.6%
Black alone	12.7%	13.2%	14.3%
Hispanic alone	12.6%	17.4%	28.6%
Asian alone	3.8%	5.4%	9.3%
All other races	2.5%	2.5%	3.1%

experienced and educated women will knock over remaining discriminatory barriers. The economy will benefit as an increasing proportion of workers from traditionally disadvantaged groups have a greater opportunity to fulfill their potential. Pessimists worry that the social tensions between men and women, and between ethnic groups, will rise and that workers will be less productive as a result. Anti-discrimination policy at its best seeks to help society move toward the more optimistic outcome.

Immigration

Most Americans would be outraged if a law prevented them from moving to another city or another state. But when the conversation turns to crossing national borders, and other people arriving in the United States, laws preventing such movement often seem more reasonable. Some of the tensions over immigration stem from worries over how it might affect a country's culture, including differences in language, and patterns of family, authority, or gender relationships. Economics doesn't have much to say about such cultural issues. But some of the worries about immigration have to do with its effects on wages and income levels, and how it affects government taxes and spending. On those topics, economists have insights and research to offer.

Historical Patterns of Immigration

Supporters and opponents of immigration look at the same data and see different patterns. Those who express concern about immigration levels to the United States point to Exhibit 17-12, which shows total inflows of immigrants decade by decade through the twentieth century. Clearly, the level of immigration has been high and rising in recent years, about as many as the towering levels of the early twentieth century. However, those who are less worried about immigration point out that the high immigration levels of the early twentieth century happened when total population was much lower. Because the U.S. population roughly tripled during the twentieth century, the seemingly high levels of immigration in the 1990s and 2000s would look relatively smaller if they were divided by the existing population at the time.

Where have the immigrants come from? Immigrants from Europe were more than 90% of the total in the first decade of the twentieth century, but less than 20% of the total by the end of the century. At the start of the 2000s, about half of U.S. immigration was coming from the rest of the Americas, especially Mexico, and about a quarter from various countries in Asia. By 2014, 42% of U.S. immigration was coming from Asia (including China and India) and 39% from the rest of North or South America.

Economic Effects of Immigration

A surge of immigration can affect the economy in a number of different ways. Here, we will consider how immigrants might benefit the rest of the economy, how they might affect wage levels, and how they might affect government spending at the federal and local level.

EXHIBIT 17-12 Immigration since 1900

The number of immigrants each decade declined in the middle of the twentieth century but has been at higher levels in recent decades.

To understand the economic consequences of immigration, consider the following scenario. Imagine that the immigrants entering the United States looked exactly like the existing U.S. population in terms of the range of ages, education, skill levels, family size, occupations, and so on. How would immigration of this type affect the rest of the U.S. economy? Immigrants themselves would be much better off because their standard of living would be higher in the United States. However, the pre-existing population would not be much benefited or harmed by this type of immigration. The reason is that the range of jobs performed, income earned, taxes paid, and public services needed would not be much affected by this kind of immigration. It would be as if the population was a little larger but had the same overall mix of characteristics.

Now consider the reality of recent immigration to the United States. Immigrants are *not* identical to the rest of the U.S. population. About one-third of immigrants over the age of 25 lack a high school degree. As a result, many of the recent immigrants end up in jobs like restaurant and hotel work, lawn care, and janitorial work. This kind of immigration represents a shift to the right in the supply of unskilled labor for a number of jobs, which will lead to lower wages for these jobs. The middle- and upper-income households that purchase the services of these unskilled workers will benefit from these lower wages. However, low-skilled U.S. workers who must compete with low-skilled immigrants for jobs will tend to suffer from immigration. A study commissioned some years ago by the prestigious and nonpartisan National Academy of Sciences estimated these gains and losses from immigration and found that, overall, immigration brings gains to the U.S. economy of $10 billion per year. In your checking account, that's a lot of money; in the context of the $15 trillion U.S. economy, $10 billion is less than one-tenth of 1%, which is barely noticeable.

The difficult policy questions about immigration are not so much about the overall gains to the rest of the economy, which seem to be real but small in the context of the U.S. economy, as they are about the disruptive effects of immigration in producing those gains. One disruptive effect, as just noted, is that immigration weighted toward low-skill workers tends to reduce wages for domestic low-skill workers. The effects on wages of low-skill workers are not large—perhaps in the range of decline of about 1%, and some studies find no effect at all—but any policy that provides gains to those with higher incomes and may impose costs on those with lower incomes deserves to be looked at twice, or even three times.

Another disruptive effect affects the budgets of state and local government. Many of the costs imposed by immigrants are costs that arise in state-run programs, like the cost of public schooling and of welfare benefits. However, many of the taxes that immigrants pay are federal taxes like income taxes and Social Security taxes. Many immigrants don't own property, so they don't pay property taxes, which are one of the main sources of state and local tax revenue. A number of studies have found that when all taxes paid and public services consumed are taken into account, the average immigrant brings an overall gain for the federal budget, but an overall cost for the state and local budget. In certain areas of the country where immigrants are highly concentrated, like some major cities in southern California, and parts of Texas along the Mexican border, these state and local costs can feel especially burdensome.

Proposals for Immigration Reform

In the 1990s, the U.S. Congress established a bipartisan U.S. Commission on Immigration Reform (CIR) to report to Congress on immigration policy. The commission was chaired by Barbara Jordan, a former member of the House of Representatives from Texas, and is often referred to as the "Jordan Commission." The commission issued several reports in the mid-1990s on a wide variety of immigration issues. Several of its recommendations were aimed at addressing the issues of the costs that immigration imposes on low-skill workers and on state and local governments.

For example, the Jordan Commission proposed reducing overall levels of immigration and refocusing U.S. immigration policy to give priority to immigrants with a higher level of skills. In the labor market, focusing on high-skilled immigrants would help prevent any negative effects on the wages of low-skilled workers. For government budgets, higher-skilled workers find jobs more quickly, earn higher wages, and pay more in taxes. Several other immigration-friendly countries, notably Canada and Australia, have immigration systems where those with high levels of education or job skills have a much better chance of obtaining permission to immigrate. Another proposal from the Jordan Commission was that the federal government could recognize that certain local governments are having their finances sorely tested by new immigrant arrivals, and that the national government could pick up some of the tab, too.

If the United States decided to reduce immigration substantially, the economic losses would be small relative to the overall economy. If the United States decided to increase immigration substantially, the U.S. economy certainly is large enough to afford some additional assistance to low-wage workers or to local governments that might be adversely affected by immigration. But whether immigration levels are increased, decreased, or left the same, the quality of the debate over immigration policy would be improved by an explicit recognition of who receives economic benefits from immigration and who bears its costs.

Conclusion

Many of the arguments about workplace protection are conducted in terms of claims about human rights and justice. The freedom of workers to organize into a union is often considered a basic human right, as is the right to be free of discrimination on the basis of race or sex. Arguments in favor of immigration often invoke the image of the Statue of Liberty welcoming newcomers to the United States.

Economic analysis steers away from these philosophical arguments and insists on digging down to specifics. The laws governing unions, and the unions themselves, can operate in many different ways. Addressing earnings gaps in the labor market may begin with laws against labor market discrimination, but must also consider patterns of social discrimination. Immigration is not a public policy question that can be addressed with a yes or a no, but instead requires arguments about how many and which people will be allowed to enter. Since the big philosophical questions are important, economic analysis will not provide a definitive answer to questions involved in workplace protection. But economic analysis can nonetheless illuminate the trade-offs involved in any specific policy choice.

Key Concepts and Summary

1. Employers have an advantage in bargaining with employees because it's usually easier for an employer to replace or do without a single employee than it is for an employee to find another job or be unemployed.
2. A **labor union** is an organization of workers that negotiates as a group with employers over compensation and work conditions.
3. Union workers in the United States are paid more on average than other workers with comparable education and experience. Thus, either union workers must be more productive to match this higher pay, or the higher pay will lead employers to find ways of hiring fewer union workers than they otherwise would.
4. American union membership has been falling for decades. Some possible reasons include the shift of jobs to service industries, greater competition from globalization, the passage of worker-friendly legislation, and U.S. laws that are less favorable to organizing unions.
5. Discrimination occurs in a labor market when workers with the same economic characteristics like education, experience, and skill are paid different amounts because of race, gender, religion, age, or disability status.
6. In the United States, female workers on average earn less than male workers, and black workers on aver-age earn less than white workers. There is controversy over the extent to which these earnings gaps can be explained by discrimination or by differences in factors like education and job experience.
7. Free markets can allow discrimination to occur, but the threat of a loss of sales or a loss of productive workers can also create incentives for a firm not to discriminate.
8. A range of public policies can be used to reduce earnings gaps between men and women or between white and other racial/ethnic groups: requiring equal pay for equal work, attaining more equal educational outcomes, providing greater support for mothers in the workforce, and **affirmative action**.
9. The recent level of U.S. immigration is at a historically high level if measured in absolute numbers, but appears somewhat lower if measured as a share of population.
10. The overall gains to the U.S. economy from immigration are real but relatively small. However, immigration also causes effects like slightly lower wages for low-skill workers and budget problems for certain state and local governments.

Review Questions

1. Why do employers have a natural advantage in bargaining with employees?
2. Why can't employers use their bargaining advantage over workers to push wages very close to zero?
3. What is a labor union?
4. How does the presence of a labor union change the negotiation that occurs between employers and workers?
5. Would you expect labor unions to lead to higher or lower pay for their workers? A higher or lower quantity of workers hired by those employers? Explain briefly.
6. What is the long-term trend in American union membership?
7. Describe how the earnings gap between men and women has evolved in recent decades.
8. Describe how the earnings gap between blacks and whites has evolved in recent decades.
9. Does a gap between the average earnings of men and women, or between whites and blacks, prove that employers are discriminating in the labor market? Explain briefly.
10. Will a free market tend to encourage or discourage discrimination? Explain briefly.
11. What policies, when used together with antidiscrimination laws, might help to reduce the earnings gap between men and women or between white and black workers?
12. What is affirmative action in the labor market?
13. Have levels of immigration to the United States been relatively high or low in recent years?
14. How would you expect immigration by primarily low-skill workers to affect American low-skilled workers?

Information, Risk, and Insurance

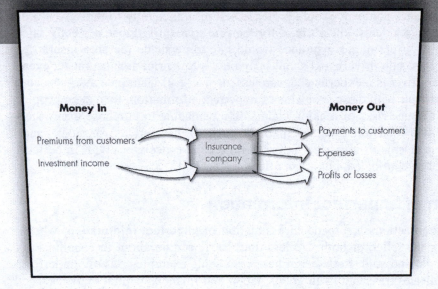

Every purchase is based on a belief about the satisfaction that will be provided by the good or service. In turn, these beliefs are based on the information that the buyer has available. But for many products, the information available to the buyer and the seller is imperfect or unclear, which can either make buyers regret past purchases or avoid making future ones.

Consider a purchase that many people make at important times in their lives: buying expensive jewelry. Most buyers face a situation of imperfect information when they buy gemstones.

The U.S. Federal Trade Commission warns on its website that many gemstones are treated or enhanced, for example: "heating can lighten, darken, or change the color of some gemstones, or improve a stone's clarity"; "irradiation can add color to colored diamonds, certain other gemstones, and pearls"; "Impregnating some gemstones with colorless oils, wax, or resins hides a variety of imperfections"; "fracture filling hides cracks in gemstones through an injection of colorless plastic or glass"; "diffusion treatment adds color to the surface . . . the center of the stone remains colorless"; "dying adds color and improves color uniformity in some gemstones and pearls"; "bleaching lightens and whitens some gemstones, including jade and pearls." Such treatments can sometimes alter the stone in undesirable ways. For example, emeralds often have internal flaws, and so they are often soaked in clear oil or an epoxy resin to hide the flaws and to deepen and clarify the color. But clear oil can leak out over time, and epoxy resin can discolor with age or heat. Many gemstones, such as rubies and sapphires, are heated in a furnace to improve their color and transparency, but one result is that the stones become more brittle, and thus the sharp edges of the stones can become scratched more easily. Diamond, topaz, and tourmaline are often irradiated to enhance their colors. The general rule is that all treatments to gemstones should be disclosed, along with the consequences of the treatments for the appearance and value of the stone—but either because the seller is dishonest or just doesn't know, such disclosure often doesn't happen.

This chapter discusses how imperfect information affects markets. The first major section of the chapter discusses how imperfect information affects markets for goods, labor, and financial capital. When buyers have imperfect information about a good, such as a gemstone, for example, sellers will be tempted to mislead buyers about quality. But if a buyer cannot have at least some confidence in the quality of what is being purchased, then buyers will be reluctant or unwilling to purchase such products. Thus, buyers and sellers will try to create mechanisms to bridge this information gap. The second part of the chapter discusses insurance markets, which also face problems of imperfect information. For example, a car insurance company would prefer to sell insurance only to those who are unlikely to have auto accidents, but it's hard for the firm to identify those perfectly safe drivers. Conversely, buyers of car insurance would like to persuade the auto insurance company that they are safe drivers and should pay only a low price for insurance, even when the particular driver is inexperienced, careless, or worse. If insurance markets cannot find ways to grapple with these problems of imperfect information, then even people who have low or average risks of making claims may be unable to purchase insurance. The next chapter will focus on financial markets, such as the markets for stocks and bonds, where the problems of imperfect information can be especially vivid. Imperfect information cannot be eliminated, but it can often be managed.

The Problem of Imperfect Information

imperfect information: A situation where the buyer or the seller, or both, are uncertain about the qualities of what is being bought and sold.

Many economic transactions are made in a situation of **imperfect information**, where either the buyer or the seller, or both, are less than 100% certain about the qualities of what is being bought and sold. Let's begin here with some examples of how imperfect information complicates transactions in goods, labor, and financial capital markets. The presence of imperfect information can easily cause a decline in prices or quantities of products sold. However, buyers and sellers also have incentives to create mechanisms that will allow them to make mutually beneficial transactions even in the face of imperfect information.

"Lemons" and Other Examples of Imperfect Information

Consider Marvin, who is trying to decide whether to buy a used car. Let's assume that Marvin is truly clueless about what happens inside a car's engine. He's willing to do some background research, like reading *Consumer Reports* or checking websites that offer information about makes and models of used cars and what they should cost. He might pay a mechanic to inspect the car. But even after devoting some money and time to collecting information, Marvin still can't be absolutely, positively sure that the car he is buying is a good value. He knows that he might buy the car, drive it home, and use it for a few weeks before discovering that the car is a "lemon," which is slang for an item (especially a car) that does not live up to expectations.

Imagine that Marvin, worried about getting stuck with a lemon, shops for used cars and finds two that appear very similar. One car costs just about what he expects this make and model to cost, while the other costs only half as much. Which car should Marvin buy? (Pause for a moment. If you were Marvin, which car would *you* buy?)

If Marvin were choosing in a world of perfect information, the answer would be simple. If he had perfect information to reveal that the two cars are equal in quality, he would buy the cheaper car. But Marvin is making a decision in a world of imperfect information, and so he must worry that the far-cheaper car is so much less expensive for a reason—that is, it is a lemon that the seller is trying to unload. With this concern in mind, Marvin's decision is no longer simple. Marvin might figure that the safer choice is to buy the used car that is selling for the expected price, even though it looks identical to him and costs more than the alternative, because he is fearful of getting stuck with a lemon and spending months in repair shops. Alternatively, Marvin might also decide that the half-price car has a low enough price to be worth the risk that it is a lemon. In either case, the presence of imperfect information complicates Marvin's decision and may even discourage him from buying at all.

Similar problems with imperfect information arise in labor and financial capital markets. Consider Greta, who is applying for a job. Her potential employer, like the used car buyer, is concerned about ending up with a lemon—in this case, a poor-quality employee rather than a car that breaks down frequently. The employer will collect information about Greta's academic and work history. In the end, however, a degree of uncertainty will inevitably remain with regard to Greta's abilities. Will she be a competent worker, or will she be a lemon? After all, resumes never tell the whole story. If the potential employer doesn't feel as if Greta has communicated enough information to show that she will be a good employee, then Greta may receive only an offer with a low salary—or no job offer may be extended at all.

Imagine a small business, Shorty's Trucking and Hauling, that wants to borrow some money from a local bank to buy a new truck and expand its business. The bank must worry over whether the loan will be a lemon—that is, whether the loan will be repaid on time. The bank will ask Shorty to fill out forms about his business: sales, profits, customers. The bank will also check Shorty's past record: has he repaid previous loans on time? But even if Shorty's Trucking and Hauling appears to be a profitable business that has repaid loans in the past, information about whether it will be able to repay in the future remains imperfect. Unless the bank is sufficiently persuaded, Shorty will not receive a loan.

How Imperfect Information Can Affect Equilibrium Price and Quantity

The presence of imperfect information can discourage both buyers and sellers from participating in the market. Buyers may become reluctant to participate because they can't be confident of purchasing a high-quality product. They will only pay a low price, if they are willing to buy at all. Sellers of high-quality or medium-quality goods may become reluctant to participate because they know that it will be difficult to demonstrate the quality of their goods to buyers—and because buyers can't perceive which goods have higher quality, they will be unwilling to pay a higher price for such goods.

A market with few buyers and few sellers is sometimes referred to as "thin"; by contrast, a market with many buyers and sellers is called a "thick" market. When imperfect information is severe and buyers and sellers are discouraged from participating, markets may become extremely thin as a relatively small number of buyers and sellers attempt to communicate enough information that they can agree on a price.

When Price Mixes with Imperfect Information about Quality

A buyer confronted with imperfect information will often believe that the price being charged reveals something about the quality of the product. For example, a buyer may assume that a gemstone or a used car that costs more must be of higher quality, even though the buyer is not expert enough to know why. Think of the expensive restaurant where the food *must* be good because it is so expensive, or the shop where the clothes *must* be stylish because they cost so much, or the gallery where the art *must* be great because it costs so much. If you are hiring a lawyer, you might assume that a lawyer who charges $400 per hour must be better than a lawyer who charges $150 per hour. If you have imperfect information, it's logical to make such connections between price and quantity: after all, you reason, even if I don't know much about used cars, some other buyers have more information, and the car dealer or the restaurant or the lawyer couldn't expect to charge more unless their goods and services were of higher quality.

But when buyers use the market price to draw inferences about the quality of products, then markets may have trouble reaching an equilibrium price and quantity. Imagine a situation where a used car dealer has a lot full of used cars that don't seem to be selling, and so the dealer decides to cut the prices of the cars to sell a greater quantity. In a market with imperfect information, many buyers may assume that the lower prices imply low-quality cars. As a result, the lower prices may not attract more customers. Conversely, a dealer who raises prices may find that customers assume that the higher prices mean that cars are of higher quality; as a result of raising prices, the dealer might sell more cars.

The idea that higher prices might cause a greater quantity demanded and that lower prices might cause a lower quantity demanded runs exactly counter to the basic model of demand and supply. These contrary effects will reach some natural limits. At some point, if the price is jacked up sky-high, the quantity demanded will surely decline. Conversely, if the price becomes dirt-cheap, at some point it will make sense for buyers to take a chance on low quality. In addition, information eventually becomes more widely known. An overpriced restaurant that charges more than the quality of its food is worth to many buyers won't last forever. But at least for a time, imperfect information can lead to a situation where, even if sellers are faced with a situation of excess supply, they will decide not to cut prices because they know that buyers reacting to imperfect information will not react by purchasing a higher quantity.

Mechanisms to Reduce the Risk of Imperfect Information

If you were selling a good like emeralds or used cars where imperfect information is likely to be a problem, how could you reassure possible buyers? (If you were buying a good where imperfect information is a problem, what would it take to reassure you?) Buyers and sellers in goods, labor, and financial capital markets have a long list of mechanisms to provide such reassurance: guarantees, warrantees, service contracts, and reputation in goods markets; occupational licenses and certification in labor markets; and cosigners and collateral in capital markets. Let's consider these in turn.

In the goods market, the seller of a good might offer a **money-back guarantee**, an agreement that functions as a promise of quality. This strategy may be especially important for a company that sells goods through mail-order catalogs or over the web, whose customers can't see the actual products, because it encourages people to buy something even if they aren't certain they want to keep it.

Sellers may offer a **warranty**, which is a promise to fix or replace the good, at least for a certain period of time. The seller may also offer a buyer a chance to buy a **service contract**, where the buyer pays an extra amount and the seller agrees to fix anything that goes wrong for a set time period. Service contracts often cover large purchases like cars and appliances, but they are also offered as part of buying a home—that is, if anything in the house breaks down in the first year, the seller will fix it at no additional charge.

Guarantees, warranties, and service contracts are examples of explicit reassurance that sellers provide. In many cases, firms also offer unstated guarantees. For example, some movie theaters might refund the cost of a ticket to a customer who walks out complaining

money-back guarantee: A promise that the buyer's money will be refunded under certain conditions, like if the product doesn't work or sometimes even if the buyer decides to return the product.

warranty: A promise to fix or replace the good, at least for a certain period of time.

service contract: The buyer pays an extra amount and the seller agrees to fix anything that goes wrong for a set time period.

Money-Back Guarantees and Imperfect Information

One way to reassure a buyer who is facing a situation of imperfect information is to offer a money-back guarantee. Many firms offer such guarantees for a few weeks or months. But L.L. Bean, a company based in Freeport, Maine, that sells outdoor wear and equipment, has offered a complete money-back guarantee since the firm was founded in 1912. Anything you have bought from L.L. Bean can always be returned, no matter how many years later or what condition the product is in, for a full money-back guarantee.

A story at the firm is that when the company's founder first decided to start a company in 1911, he stitched together some waterproof shoe rubbers to leather shoe tops, and sold them as hunting shoes. He guaranteed satisfaction. But the stitching came apart, and out of the first batch of 100 pairs that were sold, 90 pairs were returned. L.L. Bean took out a bank loan, repaired all of the shoes, and replaced them. The L.L. Bean reputation for customer satisfaction began to spread.

L.L. Bean has very few bricks-and-mortar stores. Instead, most of its sales are made by mail, telephone, or web-based orders. For this kind of firm, imperfect information may be an especially difficult problem because customers can't see and touch what they are buying. A combination of a money-back guarantee and a reputation for quality can help a mail-order firm to flourish.

---

about the show. Likewise, while many restaurants do not advertise a money-back guarantee or exchange policies, many restaurants allow customers to exchange one dish for another, or if a customer is dissatisfied with a meal, the restaurant will take the charge for the meal off of the customer's bill. (Helpful hint: If you devour a meal first and then complain about it afterward, it is less likely that you will receive a replacement or a refund.)

The reason behind these policies is that if a firm hopes to attract repeat customers, who in turn will recommend the business to others, it must be concerned about establishing a good reputation. When buyers know that a firm is concerned about its reputation, they are less likely to worry about receiving a poor-quality product. For example, a well-established grocery store with a good reputation can often charge a higher price than a temporary stand at a local farmer's market, where the buyer may never see the seller again.

Sellers in the labor market—that is, people looking for work—provide information through resumes, recommendations, school transcripts, and examples of their work. Another method of providing reassurance about quality in the labor market involves **occupational licenses**, which are licenses issued by government agencies, which mean that a worker has completed a certain type of education or passed a certain test. Some of the professionals who must hold a license are teachers, nurses, engineers, accountants, and lawyers. In addition, most states require a license to work as a barber, an embalmer, a dietitian, a massage therapist, a hearing aid dealer, a counselor, an insurance agent, and a real estate broker. Some other jobs require a license in only one state. Minnesota requires a state license to be a field archeologist; North Dakota has a state license for bait retailers. In Louisiana, a state license is needed to be a "stress analyst," and California requires a state license to be a furniture upholsterer. About one-fifth of U.S. workers have jobs that require occupational licenses.

occupational licenses: Licenses issued by government agencies that mean that a worker has completed a certain type of education or passed a certain test.

On the buyer's side of the labor market, a standard precaution against hiring a "lemon" of an employee is to specify that the first few months of employment are officially a trial period, and that the worker can be let go for any reason or no reason after that time. Sometimes workers also receive lower pay during this trial period.

Advertising and Imperfect Information

Many advertisements seem full of imperfect information—at least by what they imply. Driving a certain car, or drinking a particular soda, or wearing a certain shoe are all unlikely to bring fashionable friends and fun automatically, if at all. The government rules on advertising, enforced by the Federal Trade Commission, allow advertising to contain a certain amount of exaggeration about the general delight of using a product. But they also demand that if a claim is presented as a fact, it must be true.

A classic case of legally deceptive advertising from the 1950s occurred when Colgate-Palmolive created a television ad that claimed to show Rapid Shave shaving cream being spread on sandpaper, and then the sand was shaved off the sandpaper. But what the TV ad showed was sand sprinkled on Plexiglas—without glue—and then scraped aside by the razor.

In the 1960s, in magazine ads for Campbell's vegetable soup, the company was having problems getting an appetizing picture of the soup because the vegetables kept sinking. So they filled a bowl with marbles and poured the soup over the top, so that the bowl appeared to be crammed with vegetables.

In the late 1980s, the Volvo company filmed a TV ad that showed a monster truck driving over cars, crunching their roofs—all except for the Volvo, which did not crush. However, the FTC found in 1991 that the roof of the Volvo had been reinforced with an extra steel framework, while the roof supports on the other car brands had been cut.

The Wonder Bread company ran TV ads featuring "Professor Wonder," who said that because Wonder Bread contained extra calcium, it would help children's minds work better and improve their memory. The FTC objected, and in 2002 the company agreed to stop running the ads.

In short, factual claims about what products can do are checked to some extent by the Federal Trade Commission. But language and images that are exaggerated or ambiguous but not actually false are allowed in advertising. An old Latin saying applies when watching advertisements: *Caveat emptor*—that is, "let the buyer beware."

In the financial capital market, before a bank makes a loan, it tries to collect relevant information by having a prospective borrower fill out forms regarding the sources of income and by doing a credit check on the individual's past borrowing. Another approach is to require a **cosigner** on a loan—that is, another person or firm that legally pledges to repay some or all of the money if the original borrower does not do so. Yet another approach is to require **collateral**, which is something valuable—often property or equipment—that the bank would have a right to seize and sell if the loan is not repaid.

Buyers of goods and services cannot possibly become experts in evaluating the quality of gemstones, used cars, lawyers, and everything else they buy. Employers and lenders cannot be perfect fortune-tellers about whether possible workers will turn out well or potential borrowers will repay loans on time. But these mechanisms can reduce the risk associated with imperfect information by enough so that the buyer and seller are willing to proceed.

Insurance and Imperfect Information

An **insurance** system works like this: a group of people all make regular payments, called **premiums**, and then those members of the group who suffer a specified bad experience receive payments from this pool of money. Many people have several kinds of insurance: health insurance that pays when they receive medical care, car insurance that pays in the case of an auto accident, house or renter's insurance that pays if possessions are stolen or damaged by fire, and life insurance for their family if they die. Exhibit 18-1 lists a set of insurance markets.

All insurance involves imperfect information in both an obvious way and in a deeper way. At an obvious level, future events can't be predicted with certainty. For example, it cannot be known with certainty who will have a car accident, or become ill, or die, or have their home robbed in the next year. But imperfect information also applies to estimating the risk that something will happen to any individual. It's difficult for an insurance company to estimate the risk that, say, a particular 20-year-old male driver from New York City will have an accident, because even within that group, some drivers will drive more safely than others. Thus, adverse events occur out of a combination of people's characteristics and choices that make the risks higher or lower, and then the good or bad luck of what actually happens.

How Insurance Works

A simplified example of automobile insurance might work this way. Suppose that a group of 100 drivers can be divided into three groups. In a given year, 60 of those people have

cosigner: On a loan, another person or firm that legally pledges to repay some or all of the money if the original borrower does not do so.

collateral: Something valuable—often property or equipment—that a lender would have a right to seize and sell if the loan is not repaid.

insurance: A group of people who face a risk of a certain bad experience all make regular payments, and those members of the group who actually suffer a bad experience receive payments.

premiums: Payments made to an insurance company.

EXHIBIT 18-1 Some Insurance Markets

Type of Insurance	Who Pays for It?	It Pays Out When . . .
Health insurance	Employers and individuals	Medical expenses are incurred.
Life insurance	Employers and individuals	Policyholder dies.
Auto insurance	Individuals	Car is damaged or stolen, or causes damage to others.
Property and homeowner's insurance	Homeowners and renters	Dwelling is damaged or burglarized.
Liability insurance	Firms and individuals	An injury occurs for which you are partly responsible.
Malpractice insurance	Doctors, lawyers, and other professionals	A poor quality of service is provided that causes harm to others.

only a few door dings or chipped paint, which costs $100 each. Another 30 of the drivers have medium-sized accidents that cost an average of $1,000 in damages, and 10 of the drivers have large accidents that cost $15,000 in damages. For the moment, let's imagine that at the beginning of any year, there is no way of identifying which drivers are low risk, medium risk, or high risk. The total damage incurred by car accidents in this group of 100 drivers will be $186,000 (that is, [60 × $100] + [30 × $1,000] + [10 × $15,000]). If each of the 100 drivers pays a premium of $1,860 each year, the insurance company will collect the $186,000 that is needed to cover the costs of the accidents that occur.

   Insurance companies have one major source of income other than insurance premiums and one additional set of costs other than benefits payouts, as Exhibit 18-2 shows. The other additional source of income is investment income, which the insurance company receives from investing premiums that it has received in the past. Insurance companies need to plan ahead for the possibility of major disasters. The U.S. government's National Climatic Data Center found that from 2000 to 2015, the United States experienced 113 weather-related disasters that caused at least $1 billion in damages. For example, Hurricane Katrina caused $153 billion in damages and 1,833 deaths in Louisiana, Mississippi, and nearby states in 2005, while Superstorm Sandy caused $67 billion in damages and 159 deaths in 2012. Thus, insurance companies typically build up reserves, which are funds not paid out as insurance claims in the current year, so that they will have funds to pay off losses when costly disasters do occur. In the meantime, the insurance company receives a rate of return from making financial investments with these reserves.

EXHIBIT 18-2 An Insurance Company: What Comes In, What Goes Out

Government and Social Insurance

Federal and state governments run a number of insurance programs. Some of the programs look much like private insurance, in the sense that the members of a group make steady payments into a fund, and those in the group who suffer an adverse experience receive payments. Other programs protect against risk, but without an explicit fund being set up. Here are some examples.

- *Unemployment insurance:* Workers in every state have a small amount deducted from their paychecks for unemployment insurance, which goes into a fund that is used to pay benefits to workers for a period of time, usually six months, after they lose their jobs.
- *Pension insurance:* Employers that offer pensions to their retired employees are required by law to pay a small fraction of what they are setting aside for pensions to the Pension Benefit Guarantee Corporation, which is used to pay at least some pension benefits to workers if a company goes bankrupt and cannot pay the pensions it has promised.
- *Deposit insurance:* Banks are required by law to pay a small fraction of their deposits to the Federal Deposit Insurance Corporation, which goes into a fund that is used to pay depositors the value of their bank deposits up to $250,000 if the bank should go bankrupt.
- *Workman's compensation insurance:* Employers are required by law to pay a small percentage of the salaries that they pay into funds, typically run at the state level, that are used to compensate benefits to workers who suffer an injury on the job.
- *Retirement insurance:* All workers contribute a percentage of their income into Social Security and into Medicare, which then provides income and health-care benefits to the elderly. Social Security and Medicare are not literally "insurance" in the sense that those currently contributing to the fund are not eligible for benefits. But they function like insurance in the sense that regular payments are made into the programs today in exchange for benefits to be received in the case of a later event—either becoming old or becoming sick when old. Such programs are sometimes called "social insurance."

The major additional costs to insurance companies, other than the payment of claims, are the costs of running a business: the administrative costs of hiring workers, administering accounts, and processing insurance claims. For most insurance companies most of the time, the insurance premiums coming in and the claims payments going out are much larger than the amounts earned by investing money or the administrative costs.

Thus, while factors like investment income earned on reserves, administrative costs, and groups with different risks complicate the overall picture, a fundamental law of insurance must hold true: What the average person pays into insurance over time must be very similar to what the average person gets out, with relatively minor variations caused by the investment income of the insurance company and the costs of running the system.

Risk Groups and Actuarial Fairness

risk group: A group that shares roughly the same risks of an adverse event occurring.

Not all of those who purchase insurance face the same risks. Some people may be more likely, because of genetics or personal habits, to fall sick with certain diseases. Some people may live in an area where car theft or home robbery is more likely than others. Some drivers are safer than others. A **risk group** can be defined as a group that shares roughly the same risks of an adverse event occurring.

Insurance companies often classify people into risk groups and charge lower premiums to those with lower risks. If people are not separated into risk groups, then those with low risk must pay equal premiums as those with high risk. In the simple example of how car insurance works given earlier, 60 drivers had very low damage of $100 each, 30 drivers had medium-sized accidents that cost $1,000 each, and 10 of the drivers had large accidents that cost $15,000. If all 100 of these drivers pay the same $1,860, then those with low damages are in effect paying for those with high damages.

If it is possible to classify drivers according to risk group, then each group can be charged according to its expected losses. For example, the insurance company might charge the 60 drivers who seem safest of all $100 apiece, which is the average value of the damages they cause. Then the intermediate group could pay $1,000 apiece and the high-cost group $15,000 each. When the level of insurance premiums that someone pays is equal to the amount that an average person in that risk group would collect in insurance payments, the level of insurance is said to be "actuarially fair."

Classifying people into risk groups can be controversial. For example, if someone had a major auto accident last year, should that person be classified as a high-risk driver who is likely to have similar accidents in the future, or as a low-risk driver who was just extremely unlucky? The driver is likely to claim to be low risk, and thus someone who should be in a risk group with those who pay low insurance premiums in the future. The insurance company is likely to believe that, on average, having a major accident is a signal of being a high-risk driver, and thus try to charge this driver higher insurance premiums. The next two sections discuss the two major problems of imperfect information in insurance markets—called moral hazard and adverse selection. Both problems arise from attempts to categorize those purchasing insurance into risk groups.

The Moral Hazard Problem

moral hazard: When people have insurance against a certain event, they are less likely to guard against that event occurring.

The **moral hazard** problem arises because when people have insurance against a certain event, they are less likely to guard against that event occurring. For example, if you have health insurance that covers the cost of visiting the doctor, you are more likely to make a doctor's appointment every time you feel an ache or a sniffle. If you have car insurance, you will worry less about driving or parking your car in ways that make it more likely to get dented. In short, the presence of insurance against an event makes that event more likely to occur.

The word "moral" at the start of "moral hazard" may seem to imply that adjusting one's behavior to the presence of insurance is dishonest or wrong, but this conclusion is only sometimes true. The most extreme cases of moral hazard are those of outright insurance fraud; say, someone lies to the police that jewelry was stolen from their home and claims reimbursement from the insurance company, or someone puts a dent in their own car, claims that an accident occurred, and gets a new paint job when the car is repaired. But in other cases, the moral issue of moral hazard is more subtle. If you are applying for health insurance, and you know that your family has a rare genetic disorder that makes a certain disease more likely, are you morally required to tell the insurance company? Even though you know that the insurance company is likely to react by charging you a higher premium or refusing to sell you health insurance at all? In still other cases, moral hazard is about the level of protection that one takes against risk. A business without insurance might install absolute top-level security and fire sprinkler systems to guard against theft and fire. After buying insurance, that same business might only install a minimum level of security and fire sprinkler systems.

Moral hazard cannot be eliminated, but insurance companies have some ways of reducing its effect. Investigations to prevent insurance fraud are one way of reducing the extreme cases of moral hazard. Insurance companies can also monitor certain kinds of behavior; to return to the example of a moment ago, they might offer a business a lower rate on property insurance if the business installs a top-level security and fire sprinkler system and has those systems inspected once a year.

Another method to reduce moral hazard is to require the injured party to pay a share of the costs. For example, insurance policies often have **deductibles**, which is an amount that the insurance policyholders must pay out of their own pocket before the insurance coverage kicks in. For example, auto insurance might pay for all losses greater than $500. Health insurance policies often have a **copayment**, in which the policyholder must pay a small amount; for example, a person might have to pay $20 for each doctor visit, and the insurance company would cover the rest. Another method of cost-sharing is **coinsurance**, which means that the insurance company covers a certain percentage of the cost. For example, insurance might pay for 80% of the costs of repairing a home after a fire, but the homeowner would pay the other 20%.

All of these forms of cost-sharing discourage moral hazard because people know that that they will have to pay something out of their own pocket when they make an insurance claim. The effect can be powerful. One prominent study found that when people face moderate deductibles and copayments for their health insurance, they consume about one-third less medical care than people who have complete insurance and don't pay any-thing out of pocket—presumably because deductibles and copayments reduce the level of moral hazard. However, those who consumed less health care didn't seem to have any difference in health status.

A final way of reducing moral hazard, which is especially applicable to health care, is to focus on the incentives of providers of health care, rather than consumers. Tradi-tionally, most health care in the United States has been provided on a **fee-for-service** basis, which means that medical care providers are paid for the services they provide, and are paid more if they provide additional services. However, in the last decade or so, the structure of health-care provision has shifted to an emphasis on **health maintenance organizations (HMOs)**, in which health care is provided by an organization that receives a fixed amount per person enrolled in the plan—regardless of how many services are provided. In this case, a patient with insurance has an incentive to demand more care, but the health-care provider, which is receiving only a fixed payment, has an incentive to reduce the moral hazard problem by limiting the quantity of care provided— as long as it won't lead to worse health problems and higher costs later. Today, many doctors are paid with some combination of managed care and fee for service; that is, a flat amount per patient, but with additional payments for the treatment of certain health conditions.

Imperfect information is the cause of the moral hazard problem. If an insurance com-pany had perfect information on risk, it could simply raise its premiums every time an insured party engaged in riskier behavior. However, an insurance company cannot monitor all the risks that people take all the time, and so even with various checks and cost-sharing, moral hazard will remain a problem.

deductible: An amount that the insurance policyholders must pay out of their own pocket before the insurance coverage pays anything.

copayment: When an insurance policyholder must pay a small amount for each service, before insurance covers the rest.

coinsurance: When an insurance policyholder pays a percentage of a loss, and the insurance company pays the remaining cost.

fee-for-service: When medical care providers are paid according to the services they provide.

health maintenance organization (HMO): An organization that provides health care and is paid a fixed amount per person enrolled in the plan—regardless of how many services are provided.

The Adverse Selection Problem

adverse selection: The problem that arises when one party knows more about the quality of the good than the other, and as a result, the party with less knowledge must worry about ending up at a disadvantage.

Adverse selection arises when one party knows more about the quality of the good than the other, and as a result, the party with less knowledge must worry about ending up at a disadvantage. The problem of lemons in used car markets, discussed earlier in this chapter, is an adverse selection problem. In that case, a buyer of a used car typically has less information than the seller, and must be concerned about paying for a car of high or medium quality but ending up with a lemon. In the case of insurance, adverse selection arises because the buyers of insurance have more information about whether they are high risk or low risk than the insurance company does. For example, someone purchasing health insurance or life insurance probably knows more about their family's health history than an insurer can reasonably find out even with a costly investigation; someone purchasing car insurance may know that they are a high-risk driver who hasn't yet had a major accident—but it's hard for the insurance company to collect information about how people actually drive.

To understand how adverse selection can strangle an insurance market, return again to the situation of 100 drivers who are buying auto insurance, where 60 drivers have very low damages of $100 each, 30 drivers have medium-sized accidents that cost $1,000 each, and 10 of the drivers have large accidents that cost $15,000. Imagine that while the insurance company knows the overall size of the losses, it cannot identify the high-risk, medium-risk and low-risk drivers. However, the drivers themselves know their risk groups. Imagine that the insurance company sets the price of insurance at $1,860 per year, to cover the average loss. The result is that those with low risks of only $100 will decide not to buy insurance; after all, it makes no sense for them to pay $1,860 per year when they are only going to experience losses of $100. Those with medium risks of a $1,000 accident won't buy insurance either. So the insurance company ends up selling insurance for $1,860 to high risks who will average $15,000 in claims apiece—and losing a lot of money.

Thus, the problem of adverse selection in insurance markets is that if insurance companies cannot differentiate those with low and high risks, and tries to charge an insurance premium that averages together those with low risks and those with high risks, then those with low risks will avoid buying insurance and the company will be left with only the high risks—like those who are more likely to have health problems or car accidents. If the insurance company tries to raise its premiums to cover the losses of those with high risks, then those with low or medium risks will be even more discouraged from buying insurance. Rather than face such a situation of adverse selection, the insurance company may decide not to sell insurance in this market at all. If an insurance market is to exist, then one of two things must happen. First, the insurance company might find some way of separating insurance buyers into risk groups with some degree of accuracy and charging them accordingly, which in practice often means that the insurance company tries not to sell insurance to those who may pose high risks. Or second, those with low risks must be required to buy insurance, even if they have to pay more than the actuarially fair amount for their risk group. The notion that people can be required to purchase insurance raises the issue of government laws and regulations that influence the insurance industry.

Government Regulation of Insurance

The U.S. insurance industry has traditionally been regulated at the state level; indeed, since 1871 there has been a National Association of Insurance Commissioners that brings together these state regulators to exchange information and strategies. Since the passage of the Patient Protection and Affordable Care Act signed into law by President Barack Obama in 2010, health insurance has had a heavier dose of federal regulation. All insurance regulators typically attempt to accomplish two things: to keep the price of insurance low and to make sure that everyone has insurance. But these goals can conflict with each other and also can easily become entangled in politics.

U.S. Health Care in an International Context

The United States is the only high-income country in the world where most health insurance is paid for and provided by private firms. Greater government involvement in the provision of health insurance can be thought of as a way of addressing moral hazard and adverse selection problems.

The moral hazard problem with health insurance is that when people have insurance, they will demand higher quantities of health care. In the United States, private health-care insurance tends to encourage an ever-greater demand for health-care services that health-care providers are happy to fulfill. U.S. health expenditures were $3 trillion in 2014, or over 18% of the entire U.S. economy that year. The table shows that on a per-person basis, U.S. health-care spending towers above other countries.

The adverse selection problem in health insurance is that insurance companies fear that when they sell insurance, those with low risks will decide not to buy and the firm will end up selling insurance only to those with high risks. In the U.S. health insurance market, the main way of solving this adverse selection problem is that health insurance is often sold through groups based on place of employment. From an insurance company's point of view, selling insurance through an employer mixes together a group of people—some with high risks of future health problems and some with lower risks—and thus reduces the insurance firm's fear of attracting only those who have high risks. However, many small companies do not provide health insurance to their employees, and many lower-paying jobs do not include health insurance. Even after all U.S. government programs that provide health insurance for the elderly and the poor and the expanded health insurance coverage resulting from the Patient Protection and Affordable Care Act of 2010 are taken into account, roughly 30 million Americans lacked health insurance coverage in 2015. Despite the very high costs of the U.S. health-care system, the United States doesn't do better than other high-income countries on basic measures of health like longer life expectancies and lower rates of infant mortality, as shown in the table. The relatively modest U.S. health statistics shouldn't be blamed on the U.S. health-care industry. Many studies have shown that a country's health is not directly connected to its spending on medical care but is instead more closely related to diet, exercise, and genetic factors. But this fact only emphasizes further that the United States is spending very large amounts on medical care with little obvious health gain.

At its best, the largely private U.S. system of health insurance and health-care delivery provides an extraordinarily high quality of care, along with generating a seemingly endless parade of life-saving innovations. But the system also struggles to control its high costs and to provide basic medical care to all. Other countries have lower costs and more equal access, but they often struggle to provide rapid access to health care and to offer the near-miracles of the most up-to-date medical care. The challenge is a health-care system that strikes the right balance between quality, access, and cost.

Country	Health-Care Spending per Person (in 2013)	Life Expectancy at Birth in Years (in 2013)		Chance of Dying before Age 5, per 1,000 (in 2015)	
		Male	Female	Male	Female
United States	$9,146	77	81	7	6
Germany	$5,006	79	83	4	3
France	$4,864	79	85	4	4
Canada	$5,718	79	84	5	5
Japan	$3,966	80	87	3	3
United Kingdom	$3,598	79	83	4	4

If insurance premiums are set at actuarially fair levels, so that people end up paying an amount that accurately reflects their risk group, certain people will end up paying a lot. For example, if health insurance companies were trying to cover people who already have a chronic disease like AIDS, or who were elderly, they would charge these groups very high premiums for health insurance because their expected health-care costs are quite high. Women in the age bracket 18–44 consume, on average, about 65% more in health-care spending than men. Young male drivers have more car accidents than young female drivers; for example, among drivers aged 20 and younger, more than twice as many men as women are involved in fatal accidents. Thus, actuarially fair insurance would tend to charge young men much more for car insurance than young women. Because people in high-risk groups would find themselves charged so heavily for insurance, they might choose not to buy insurance at all.

Insurance regulators have sometimes reacted by passing rules that attempt to set low premiums for insurance. But over time, the fundamental law of insurance must hold: the average amount received by individuals must equal the average amount paid in premiums. When rules are passed to keep premiums low, insurance companies try to avoid insuring high-risk or even medium-risk parties or find ways to limit the amount of coverage provided by the insurance policies. If a legislature passes strict rules requiring insurance companies to sell to everyone at low prices, the insurance companies always have the option of withdrawing from doing business in that state. For example, the insurance regulators in New Jersey are well known for attempting to keep auto insurance premiums low, and more than 20 different insurance companies stopped doing business in the state in the late 1990s and early 2000s. Similarly, in 2009, State Farm announced that it was withdrawing from selling property insurance in Florida.

In short, government regulators can't force companies to charge low prices and provide high levels of insurance coverage—and thus take losses—for a sustained period of time. If insurance premiums are going to be set below the actuarially fair level for a certain group, some other group will have to pay to make up the difference. There are two other groups who can make up the difference: taxpayers or other buyers of insurance.

In some industries, the U.S. government has apparently decided free markets will not provide insurance at an affordable price, and so the government will pay for it directly. For example, private health insurance doesn't work well for the poor because their incomes are too low to afford it. Thus, the U.S. government together with the states runs the Medicaid program, which provides insurance to those with low incomes. Private health insurance also doesn't work well for the elderly because their average health-care costs can be very high. Thus, the U.S. government started the Medicare program, which finances health insurance for those over age 65. Other government-funded health-care programs are aimed at children in families with relatively low incomes and at military veterans.

Another common government intervention in insurance markets is to require that everyone buy certain kinds of insurance. For example, most states legally require car owners to buy auto insurance. Likewise, when a bank loans someone money to buy a home, the person is typically required to have homeowner's insurance, which protects against fire and other physical damage (like hailstorms) to the home. The Patient Protection and Affordable Care Act of 2010 contained an "individual mandate" requiring that people either obtain health insurance or pay a fine, but the provision was so controversial that it may be little enforced and thus have little effect. A legal requirement that everyone must buy insurance means that insurance companies don't need to worry that those with low risks will avoid buying insurance. Since insurance companies don't need to fear adverse selection, they can set their prices based on an average for the market, and those with lower risks will to some extent end up subsidizing those with higher risks. However, even when laws are passed requiring people to purchase insurance, insurance companies cannot be compelled to sell insurance to everyone who asks—at least not at low cost. Thus, insurance companies will still try to avoid selling insurance to those with high risks whenever possible.

Even the government cannot violate the fundamental law of insurance: that average payments going into an insurance fund must equal average payments coming out. Nor can government pass laws that make the problems of moral hazard and adverse selection disappear. But the government can make political decisions that certain groups should have insurance, even though the private market would not otherwise provide that insurance, and then the government can impose the costs of that decision on taxpayers or on other buyers of insurance.

Conclusion

The government has a wide variety of laws that seek to reduce the problem of imperfect information in markets. For example, the government requires that processed food products list their ingredients in order of importance on the outside of the package. Restaurants and workplaces are subject to government safety inspections, which reduce the imperfect information of diners about what is happening in the kitchen. Many states also have laws against fraud and deceptive or high-pressure sales tactics. These laws about providing information then combine with magazines like *Consumer Reports* or websites that discuss and compare products. Buyers and sellers have a number of ways of reducing the risks of imperfect information, too: for example, stores can offer warranties, money-back guarantees, and their reputation. Through the combined results of these factors, imperfect information can often be minimized enough that buyers and sellers can make mutually beneficial trades.

But in some markets for goods and services—like insurance markets—the problems of incomplete information are more difficult to resolve. The problems erupt into public view over issues of price and availability of insurance. For example, in 2015 auto insurance on average cost about $850 per year in Ohio and Iowa, but about $2,000 per year in Montana and Michigan—which makes auto insurance a political issue in those states. The medical-care costs of a severe accident or extensive illness can easily run into tens of thousands of dollars, which is more than most people can pay; yet tens of millions of Americans lack either private or government-provided health insurance. In these cases, economists can diagnose the problems of how moral hazard can drive up costs by encouraging those with insurance to demand more services, and how adverse selection can cause insurance companies to avoid offering insurance to many individuals. But addressing those problems will require political decisions about who receives how much insurance and who will pay the costs.

Key Concepts and Summary

1. Many economic transactions are made in a situation of **imperfect information**, where either the buyer or the seller or both are less than 100% certain about the qualities of what is being bought and sold. When information about the quality of products is highly imperfect, it may be difficult for a market to exist.

2. A "lemon" is the name given to a product that turns out, after the purchase, to have low quality. When the seller has more accurate information about the quality of the product than the buyer, the buyer will be hesitant to buy, out of fear of purchasing a lemon.

3. Markets have many ways to deal with imperfect information. In goods markets, buyers facing imperfect information about products may turn to guidebooks or product reviews, **money-back guarantees**, **warran-**ties, **service contracts**, and reputation. In labor markets, employers facing imperfect information about potential employees may turn to resumes, recommendations, **occupational licenses** for certain jobs, and employment for trial periods. In capital markets, lenders facing imperfect information about borrowers may require detailed loan applications and credit checks, **cosigners**, and **collateral**.

4. **Insurance** is a way of sharing risk. A group of people pay premiums for insurance against some unpleasant event, and those in the group who actually experience the unpleasant event then receive some compensation.

5. The fundamental law of insurance is that what the average person pays in over time must be very similar to what the average person gets out. In an actuarially

fair insurance policy, the premiums that a person pays to the insurance company are the same as the average amount of benefits for a person in that **risk group**.

6. **Moral hazard** arises in insurance markets because those who are insured against a risk will have less reason to take steps to avoid the costs from that risk.

7. Many insurance policies have **deductibles**, **copayments**, or **coinsurance**. A deductible is the maximum amount that the policyholder must pay out-of-pocket before the insurance company pays the rest of the bill. A copayment is a flat fee that an insurance policyholder must pay before receiving services. Coinsurance requires the policyholder to pay a certain percentage of costs. Deductibles, copayments, and coinsurance reduce moral hazard by requiring the insured party to bear some of the costs before collecting insurance benefits.

8. In a **fee-for-service** health financing system, medical care providers are reimbursed according to the cost of services they provide. An alternative method of organizing health care is through **health maintenance organizations (HMOs)**, where medical care providers are reimbursed according to the number of patients they handle, and it is up to the providers to allocate resources between patients who receive more or fewer health-care services.

9. **Adverse selection** arises in insurance markets when insurance buyers know more about the risks they face than does the insurance company. As a result, the insurance company runs the risk that low-risk parties will avoid its insurance because it is too costly for them, while high-risk parties will embrace it because it looks like a good deal to them.

Review Questions

1. Why might it be difficult for a buyer and seller to agree on a price when imperfect information exists?
2. What do economists (and used-car dealers) mean by a "lemon"?
3. What are some of the ways a seller of goods might reassure a possible buyer who is faced with imperfect information?
4. What are some of the ways a seller of labor (that is, someone looking for a job) might reassure a possible employer who is faced with imperfect information?
5. What are some of the ways that someone looking for a loan might reassure a bank that is faced with imperfect information about whether the loan will be repaid?
6. What is an insurance premium?
7. In an insurance system, would you expect each person to receive in benefits pretty much what they pay in premiums? Or is it just that the average benefits paid will equal the average premiums paid?

8. What is an actuarially fair insurance policy?
9. What is the problem of moral hazard?
10. How can moral hazard lead to insurance being more costly than was expected?
11. Define deductibles, copayments, and coinsurance.
12. How can deductibles, copayments, and coinsurance reduce moral hazard?
13. What is the key difference between a fee-for-service health-care system and a system based on health maintenance organizations?
14. What is adverse selection?
15. How might adverse selection make it difficult for an insurance market to operate?

Financial Markets

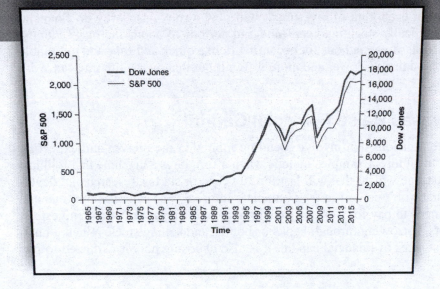

Chapter Outline

How Businesses Raise Financial Capital

How Households Supply Financial Capital

How to Become Rich

How Capital Markets Transform Financial Flows

F irms need financial capital to make real physical capital investments. For example, U.S. firms invested $2.3 trillion in new equipment and structures in 2016, hoping that these investments would bring higher profits in the years ahead. But many firms, from huge companies like General Motors to a start-up firm writing computer software, don't have the financial resources within the firm to make all of the desired investments. These firms need financial capital from outside investors, and the firms are willing to pay a rate of return for that financial capital. On the other side of the financial capital market, suppliers of financial capital, like households, wish to invest their savings in a way that will provide a rate of return. But individuals cannot take the few thousand dollars that they save in any given year, write a letter to General Motors or some other firm, and negotiate to invest their money with that firm. Financial capital markets bridge this gap: that is, they find ways to take the inflow of funds from many separate suppliers of financial capital and transform it into the funds desired by demanders of financial capital. Such financial markets discussed in this chapter include stocks, bonds, bank loans, and other financial investments.

Movements in financial markets have powerful consequences for both demanders and suppliers of capital. For example, consider the Dow Jones Industrial Average (DJIA), one widely reported measure of the stock market. In 2002 and 2003, the DJIA was at about 9,000. By July 2007, the DJIA had peaked at 13,900—an increase of more than 50%. In July 2009, the DJIA had fallen all the way to 8,100. The stocks that households held in mid-2007 had lost about $6 trillion in value by early 2009. By April 2016, the DJIA had risen to above 18,000, considerably above the peak in July 2007. This kind of roller coaster ride forces households that have financial investments in the stock market to rethink major life decisions like whether to retire, or whether to buy a house, or what sort of college or university is affordable.

This chapter describes and investigates financial markets. It begins on the demand side of financial capital markets, discussing how firms raise the money they need for investments through mechanisms like venture capital, reinvesting the firm's previously earned profits, bank loans, bonds, and stocks. The perspective then shifts to consider how these financial investments appear to suppliers of capital, such as the households that are saving money. Households have a range of financial investment options: bank accounts, certificates of deposit, bonds, stocks, mutual funds, housing, and even tangible assets like gold. In choosing among these alternatives, the expected rate of return, risk, and liquidity of each kind of investment will play a role. Also, why do financial markets—and specifically stock markets—undergo periods of boom and bust? Finally, the chapter investigates two methods for becoming rich: a quick and easy and unreliable method and a method that is slower and more difficult but that over a lifetime can work quite well.

How Businesses Raise Financial Capital

Firms often make decisions that involve spending money in the present and expecting to earn profits in the future. Examples include when a firm buys a machine that will last 10 years, or builds a new plant that will last for 30 years, or starts a research and development project that won't pay off in the immediate future. Firms can raise the financial capital that they need to pay for such projects in four main ways: early-stage investors, reinvesting profits, borrowing through banks or bonds, and selling stock. When a business chooses its sources of financial capital, it is also choosing how it will need to pay a rate of return.

Early-Stage Financial Capital

Firms that are just beginning often have an idea or a prototype for a product or service to sell, but they may have few customers, or even no customers at all, and thus are not earning profits. Such firms face a difficult problem when it comes to raising financial capital: that is, how can a firm that has not yet demonstrated any ability to earn profits pay a rate of return to financial investors?

Early-stage investors provide financial capital in exchange for part-ownership of the firm. For many small businesses, the original source of money is the owner of the business. For example, people who decide to start a restaurant or a gas station might cover the costs of starting the business by dipping into their own bank account or by borrowing money (perhaps using their homes as collateral). Alternatively, many cities have a network of well-to-do individuals known as "angel investors," who decide to put their own money into small new companies at an early stage of development, in exchange for owning some portion of the firm.

venture capital: Financial investments in new companies that are still relatively small in size but that have potential to grow substantially.

Venture capital firms make financial investments in new companies that are still relatively small in size but that have potential to grow substantially. These firms gather money from a variety of individual or institutional investors, including banks, institutions like college endowments, insurance companies that hold financial reserves, and corporate pension funds. Venture capital firms do more than just supply money to small start-up firms. They also provide advice to the firm on potential products, customers, and key employees. Typically, a venture capital fund invests in a number of firms, and then investors in that fund receive returns according to how the fund as a whole performs.

The amount of money invested in venture capital fluctuates substantially from year to year: as one example, venture capital firms invested $54 billion in 2015. All early-stage investors realize that the majority of small start-up businesses will never hit it big; indeed, many of them will go out of business within a few months or years. But they also know that getting in on the ground floor of a few huge successes like Google or Amazon can make up for a lot of failures.

Profits as a Source of Financial Capital

If firms are earning profits, then they can choose to reinvest some of these profits in equipment, structures, and research and development. In 2015, total corporate profits were about $2.0 trillion, although after firms paid taxes, the remaining profits were $1.5 trillion. For many established companies, reinvesting their own profits is one primary source of financial capital.

From a firm's point of view, profits have one big shortcoming as a source of financial capital: they may not provide financial capital when the firm needs it. For example, small companies and firms just getting started may find themselves in a situation where they have numerous attractive investment opportunities, but few current profits. Even large firms can experience a year or two of earning low profits or even suffering losses, but unless the firm can find a steady and reliable source of financial capital so that it can continue making real investments in its tough times, the firm may not survive until better times arrive. Thus, firms often find themselves in situations where they desire other methods, in addition to the profits they earn, to raise financial capital for real investment.

Borrowing: Banks and Bonds

When a firm has a record of at least earning significant revenues, and better still of earning profits, the firm can then make a credible promise to pay interest, and so it becomes possible for the firm to borrow money. Firms have two main methods of borrowing: banks and bonds.

A bank loan for a firm works in much the same way as a loan for an individual who is buying a car or a house. The firm borrows an amount of money and then promises to repay it, including some rate of interest, over a predetermined period of time. In some cases, for an especially big loan, several banks will join together to make the loan. If the firm fails to make its loan payments, the bank (or banks) can often take the firm to court and require the firm to sell buildings or equipment that the firm owns to make the loan payments.

A **bond** is a financial contract through which a borrower agrees to repay the amount that was borrowed and also a rate of interest over a period of time in the future. **Corporate bonds** are issued by firms, but bonds are also issued by various levels of government. For example, **municipal bonds** are issued by cities, state bonds by U.S. states, and **Treasury bonds** by the federal government through the U.S. Department of the Treasury. A bond specifies an amount that will be borrowed, the interest rate that will be paid, and the time until repayment. For example, a large company might issue bonds for $10 million, where the firm would promise to make interest payments at an annual rate of 8%, or $800,000 per year, and then after 10 years the firm would repay the $10 million that it originally borrowed. When a firm issues bonds, the total amount that is borrowed is divided up; for example, when a firm seeks to borrow $50 million by issuing bonds, it might actually issue 10,000 bonds that each involves borrowing $5,000. In this way, an individual financial investor could in effect loan the firm $5,000, or any multiple of that amount the investor desires. Those who own bonds and receive the interest payments are called **bondholders**. If a firm issues bonds and fails to make the promised interest payments, the bondholders can take the firm to court and require the firm to pay, even if the firm needs to raise the money by selling buildings or equipment that it owns.

Bank borrowing often works better for relatively small firms, where the bank can get to know the firm extremely well—often because the bank can monitor a firm's sales and expenses quite accurately by looking at the deposits and withdrawals that the firm makes. Relatively large and well-known firms often issue bonds instead. U.S. corporations issued $1.5 trillion in corporate bonds in 2015. Some of these bonds were to raise new financial capital that would pay for real investment; other bonds were used to raise financial capital to pay off old bonds or to buy other firms. However, the idea that banks are usually for relatively smaller loans and bonds are for larger loans is not an ironclad rule; sometimes,

bond: A financial contract through which a borrower like a corporation, a city or state, or the federal government agrees to repay the amount that was borrowed and also a rate of interest over a period of time in the future.

corporate bonds: Bonds issued by firms that wish to borrow.

municipal bonds: Bonds issued by cities that wish to borrow.

Treasury bonds: Bonds issued by the federal government through the U.S. Department of the Treasury.

bondholders: Those who own bonds and receive the interest payments.

groups of banks coordinate to make large loans, and sometimes, relatively small and lesser-known firms issue bonds.

Corporate Stock and Public Firms

stock: A claim on partial ownership of a firm.

shares: The stock of a firm is divided into individual shares.

shareholders: Those who own at least some stock in a firm.

Stock represents ownership of a firm; that is, a person who owns 100% of a company's stock by definition owns the entire company. The stock of a company is divided into **shares**. Corporate giants like IBM, AT&T, Ford, General Electric, Microsoft, Merck, and Exxon all have millions of shares of stock. Those who own some shares of stock in a company are called **shareholders**. In most large and well-known firms, no individual owns a majority of the shares of the stock. Instead, large numbers of shareholders—even those who hold thousands of shares—each have only a small slice of the overall ownership of the firm. When a company is owned by a large number of shareholders, there are three questions to answer: (1) How and when does the company get money from the sale of its stock? (2) What rate of return does the company promise to pay when it sells stock? (3) Who makes decisions in a company owned by a large number of shareholders? Let's consider these questions in turn.

initial public offering (IPO): When a firm first sells shares of stock to outside investors.

A firm receives money from the sale of its stock only when the company sells its own stock to the public. A firm's first sale of stock to the public is called an **initial public offering (IPO)**. The IPO is important for two reasons. First, the IPO or later stock offerings provide the funds to repay the early-stage investors, like the angel investors and the venture capital firms. For example, a venture capital firm may have provided funding in exchange for 40% ownership of the firm. When the firm sells stock, the venture capital firm sells its part-ownership of the firm to the public. A second reason for the importance of the IPO is that it provides a source of financial capital to the company for a substantial expansion of its operations.

But most of the time when corporate stock is bought or sold, the firm receives no financial capital at all. If you buy shares of stock in General Motors, you almost certainly buy them from the current owner of those shares, and General Motors doesn't receive any of your money. This pattern shouldn't seem particularly odd. After all, if you buy a house, the current owner gets your money, not the original owner of the land or the house. Similarly, when you buy shares of stock, you are buying a small slice of ownership of the firm from the existing owner—and the firm that originally issued the stock is not a part of this transaction.

dividend: A direct payment from a firm to its shareholders.

capital gain: A financial gain from buying an asset, like a share of stock or a house, and later selling it at a higher price.

When a firm decides to issue stock, it must recognize that investors will expect to receive a rate of return. That rate of return can come in two forms. A firm can make a direct payment to its shareholders, called a **dividend**. Alternatively, a financial investor might buy a share of stock in Wal-Mart for $45 and then later sell that share of stock to someone else for $60, for a gain of $15. The increase in the value of the stock (or of any asset) between when it is bought and when it is sold is called a **capital gain**. The factors that determine whether the price of a stock will rise and thus provide a capital gain to investors will be discussed later in this chapter. Here, focusing on the firm's point of view as it raises financial capital, notice that dividends are paid directly by the firm to the shareholder out of any profits the firm has earned; thus, dividends are usually paid by well-established firms that earn a steady stream of profits, while new and young firms often pay no dividend at all. When one financial investor sells shares of stock to another, it does not involve any direct payment to or from the firm; instead, it is only a payment between two financial investors.

Who makes the decisions about when a firm will issue stock, or pay dividends, or re-invest profits? To understand the answers to these questions, it's useful to separate firms into two groups: private and public.

private company: A firm owned by the people who run it on a day-to-day basis.

A **private company** is owned by the people who run it on a day-to-day basis. Private companies can either be run by individuals, in which case they are called *sole proprietorships*, or they can be run by a group, in which case they are *partnerships*. A small law firm run by one person, even if it employs some other lawyers, would be a sole proprietorship. However, a larger law firm may be owned jointly by its partners. In

2012, the U.S. economy had about 23 million sole proprietorships and 3.4 million partnerships. Most private companies are relatively small, but there are exceptions. Some large private companies, with tens of billions of dollars in annual sales, include the farm products dealer Cargill, the Mars candy company, and the Bechtel engineering and construction firm.

When a firm decides to sell stock, which in turn can be bought and sold by financial investors, it is then called a **public company.** Shareholders own a public company. Because the shareholders are a very broad group, often consisting of thousands or even millions of investors, they vote for a board of directors, who in turn hire top executives to run the firm on a day-to-day basis. The more shares of stock a shareholder owns, the more votes that shareholder is entitled to cast for the company's board of directors. In turn, this board of directors hires the top managers who run the company on a day-to-day basis, like the chief executive officer (CEO). In theory, the board of directors helps to make sure that the firm is run in the interests of the true owners—that is, the shareholders. However, conflicts often arise in which the top executives who run the firm have a strong voice in choosing the candidates who will be on their board of directors. After all, few shareholders are knowledgeable enough or have enough of a personal incentive to spend energy and money nominating alternative members of the board. Many corporate scandals raise the question of whether a firm was being run for the personal benefit of top executives or in the broader interests of shareholders as a group.

public company: A firm that has sold stock to the public, which in turn can be bought and sold by investors.

How Firms Choose between Sources of Financial Capital

There are clear patterns in how businesses raise financial capital. These patterns can be explained in terms of imperfect information, which as discussed in the previous chapter is a situation where buyers and sellers in a market do not both have full and equal information. Those who are actually running a firm day-to-day will almost always have more information about whether the firm is likely to earn profits in the future than outside investors who provide financial capital.

Any young start-up firm is a risk; indeed, some start-up firms are only a little more than an idea on paper. The firm's founders inevitably have better information about how hard they are willing to work, and whether the firm is likely to succeed, than anyone else does. When the founders of the firm put their own money into the firm, they demonstrate a belief in its prospects. At this early stage, angel investors and venture capitalists who support the firm try to overcome the imperfect information, at least in part, by knowing the managers and their business plan personally and by giving them advice.

As a firm becomes at least somewhat established and its strategy appears likely to lead to profits in the not-too-distant future, knowing the individual managers and their business plans on a personal basis becomes less important, because information has become more widely available regarding the company's products, revenues, costs, and profits. As a result, other outside investors who don't know the managers personally, like bondholders and shareholders, become willing to provide financial capital to the firm.

At this point, a firm must often choose between borrowing financial capital using banks or bonds, which means agreeing to pay a certain rate of interest, or instead raising financial capital by issuing share of stock, which only requires that the firm consider paying dividends to shareholders—although it is not required to do so.

If you owned a small firm that had become somewhat established, but you needed a surge of financial capital to carry out a major expansion, would you prefer to raise the funds through borrowing or by issuing stock? The great disadvantage of borrowing money rather than issuing stock is that when you have borrowed money, you need to make the scheduled interest payments, but when you have issued stock, you only need to think about whether to pay dividends. The great advantage of borrowing money rather than issuing stock is that stock involves selling off ownership of your company and becoming responsible to a board of directors, whereas if you borrow money and make the interest payments, you can still own and run your firm without outside control—and keep any profits it makes for yourself.

These trade-offs suggest that a firm will prefer to issue stock under two situations. One situation is that of a small and growing firm that would prefer to receive a large chunk of financial capital in the present, but not pay out any returns for a few years, until it becomes firmly established. In this situation, selling stock to the public can make sense for both the firm and for financial investors. The other situation where a firm prefers to issue stock is less cheerful; perhaps those running the firm aren't making profits *and aren't confident that they can make profits in the future, either*. Thus, they would rather receive financial capital by issuing stock because they don't believe that the firm will be able to make future interest payments.

Potential shareholders with imperfect information about the firm may have a hard time looking at a firm that is issuing stock and deciding whether the firm is issuing stock because its growth prospects are so good, or because its growth prospects are so poor. However, financial investors often follow this logic: if an established firm is trying to sell stock, a wary investor is likely to presume that the firm might have tried to get a loan for the project, but failed. Thus, financial investors often assume that if a well-established firm is trying to sell additional stock, it was already turned down for a loan by banks and

Corporate Governance and the Enron Story

On December 31, 2000, stock in Enron—a company that bought and sold natural gas and electricity, among other goods—was priced at $83. The stock price had risen 87% in 2000, following a 56% rise in 1999 and a 37% rise in 1998. Enron was rated the most innovative large company in America in *Fortune* magazine's survey of Most Admired Companies for its web-based markets and its strategies with long-term contracts. By December 2, 2001, less than one year later, Enron had filed for bankruptcy and several legal investigations had started into accusations that some of the firm's financial records were highly misleading or even fraudulent. How can a company go from being a role model to having its top executives threatened with jail in less than a year? What safeguards were supposed to be in place—but failed?

Corporate governance is the name that economists give to the institutions that are supposed to watch over top executives in companies owned by shareholders. In the case of Enron, corporate governance didn't perform well, misled by a toxic combination of wild over-optimism and shady management.

The board of directors, who are elected by the shareholders, are the first line of oversight for top executives. However, members of the board are often hand-picked by top executives, so their independence can be questioned. Also, board members may not have the time or information to provide close oversight. Being a board member is a part-time job that often consists of a few meetings a year, where information is provided by the top executives themselves.

A second institution of corporate governance is the auditing firm hired to go over the financial records of the company and certify that everything looks reasonable. The auditors for Enron were from the Arthur Andersen

company. In 2000, Andersen earned $52 million in fees from Enron, which may have created an incentive not to risk offending top management.

A third institution of corporate governance is outside investors, especially large shareholders like those who invest large mutual funds or pension funds. They should buy or sell stock based on their own views about the health of the company. Such large investors owned about 60% of the total Enron stock late in 2000. But they continued holding 60% of Enron stock right up to October 2001, many months after it had become clear that something was deeply wrong at the firm.

Other contributors to corporate governance include the stock market analysts who give advice to financial investors, government financial regulators, journalists who write for the business press, and even employees of the firm itself, who should speak up or seek employment elsewhere if they know that their employer is doing something illegal or unethical. But with a few exceptions (for example, *Fortune* magazine published a prominent story in March 2001 asking if Enron's stock price was headed for a fall), these watchdogs did not bark.

In response to the situation of Enron and other firms, Congress passed the Sarbanes-Oxley Act of 2002. The act imposed a number of new rules on the institutions of corporate governance, including boards of directors, auditors, and stock market analysts, along with a new government accounting oversight board. But the top executives of firms have strong incentives to report high profits, and others have strong incentives not to upset or anger top executives. Given these basic realities, it remains uncertain whether the new rules will provide substantial benefit.

bond investors—and so buying stock to finance the firm probably isn't such a good idea. Thus, because of the dynamics created by imperfect information, young companies often find it easier to sell stock, while established firms often raise financial capital by borrowing from banks and bond markets.

How Households Supply Financial Capital

The ways in which firms would prefer to raise funds are only half the story of financial markets. The other half is what those households who supply funds desire and how they perceive the available choices. Thus, the focus of the discussion now shifts from firms on the demand side of financial capital markets to households on the supply side of those markets. The mechanisms for saving available to households can be divided into several categories: deposits in bank accounts, bonds, stocks, mutual funds, and housing and other tangible assets like owning gold. For each of these investments, households will think about three factors: the expected rate of return it will pay, the risk that the return will be much lower or higher than expected, and the **liquidity** of the investment, which refers to how easy it is to sell a financial investment when desired.

liquidity: How easy it is to sell an asset when desired.

Bank Accounts

An "intermediary" is one who stands between two other parties; for example, a person who arranges a blind date between two other people is one kind of intermediary. In financial capital markets, banks are an example of a **financial intermediary**—that is, an institution that operates between a saver who deposits money in a bank and a borrower who receives a loan from that bank. But when a bank serves as a financial intermediary, unlike the situation with a couple on a blind date, the saver and the borrower never meet each other. In fact, it isn't even possible to make direct connections between those who deposit money in banks and those who borrow from banks, because all funds deposited end up in one big pool, which is then loaned out. Exhibit 19-1 illustrates the position of banks as a financial intermediary, with a pattern of deposits flowing into a bank and loans flowing out, and then repayment of the loans flowing back to the bank, with interest payments for the original savers.

financial intermediary: An institution, like a bank, that receives money from savers and provides funds to borrowers.

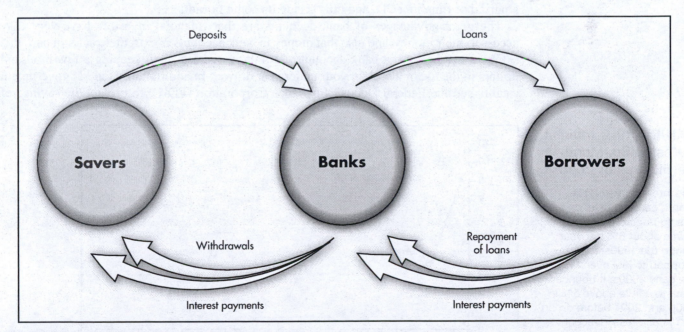

EXHIBIT 19-1 Banks as Financial Intermediaries

Banks are a financial intermediary because they stand between savers and borrowers. Savers place deposits with banks, and then receive interest payments and withdraw money. Borrowers receive loans from banks and repay the loans with interest.

Expected Rate of Return, Risk, and Actual Rate of Return

The expected rate of return refers to an average over a period of time usually measured in years or even decades. High risk refers to the fact that a wide range of actual outcomes are reasonably possible. Thus, a low-risk investment will have actual returns that are fairly close to its expected rate of return year after year. A high-risk investment will have actual returns that are much higher than the expected rate of return in some months or years and much lower than the expected rate of return in other months or years.

checking account: A bank account that typically pays little or no interest, but that gives easy access to your money, either by writing a check or by using a debit card.

debit card: A card that lets you make purchases, where the cost is immediately deducted from your checking account.

savings account: A bank account that pays an interest rate, but withdrawing the money typically requires you to make a trip to the bank or an automatic teller machine.

certificate of deposit (CD): A mechanism for a saver to deposit funds at a bank and promise to leave them at the bank for a time, in exchange for a higher rate of interest.

Banks offer a range of accounts to serve different needs. A **checking account** typically pays little or no interest, but it facilitates transactions by giving you easy access to your money, either by writing a check or by using a **debit card** (i.e., a card that works like a credit card, except that purchases are immediately deducted from your checking account rather than being billed separately through a credit card company). A **savings account** typically pays some interest rate, but withdrawing the money typically requires you to make a trip to the bank or an automatic teller machine. The lines between checking and savings accounts have blurred in the last few decades, as many banks offer checking accounts that will pay an interest rate similar to a savings account if you keep a certain minimum amount in the account, or conversely, offer savings accounts that allow you to write at least a few checks per month.

Another way to deposit savings at a bank is to use a **certificate of deposit (CD)**. With a CD, as it is commonly called, you agree to deposit a certain amount of money, often measured in hundreds or thousands of dollars, in the account for a stated period of time, typically ranging from a few months to several years. In exchange, the bank agrees to pay a higher interest rate than for a regular savings account. While you can withdraw the money before the allotted time, as the advertisements for CDs always warn, there is "a substantial penalty for early withdrawal." Exhibit 19-2 shows the annual rate of interest paid in a six-month CD since 1990. The interest rates paid by savings accounts are typically a little lower than the CD rate because financial investors need to receive a slightly higher rate of interest as compensation for promising to leave their deposits untouched for a period of time in a CD, and thus giving up some liquidity.

The great advantages of bank accounts are that financial investors have very easy access to their money, and also that money in bank accounts is extremely safe. In part, this safety arises because a bank account offers more security than keeping a few thousand dollars in the toe of a sock in your underwear drawer. In addition, the federal government established the Federal Deposit Insurance Corporation (FDIC) to protect the savings of

EXHIBIT 19-2 Interest Rates on Six-Month Certificates of Deposit

The interest rate on six-month certificates of deposit has fluctuated over time. It was about 6% per year during the 1990s, then dropped to just over 1% in the early 2000s. It bounced back to a little above 5% in 2006 and 2007 before diving to 1% and less in recent years.

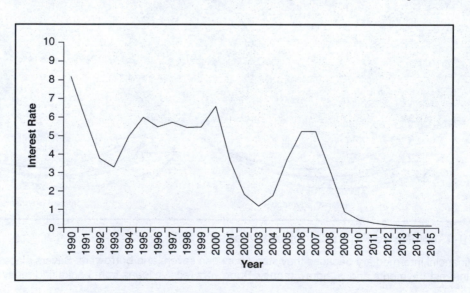

the average person. Every bank is required by law to pay a fee to the FDIC, based on the size of its deposits. Then, if a bank should happen to go bankrupt and not be able to repay depositors their money, the FDIC provides insurance, guaranteeing that all customers will receive their deposits back up to $250,000.

The bottom line on bank accounts looks like this: Rate of return—very low; Risk—very low; Liquidity—very high.

Bonds

An investor who buys a bond expects to receive a rate of return. However, bonds vary in the rates of return that they offer, according to the riskiness of the borrower. An interest rate can always be divided up into three components (as explained in Chapter 2): compensation for delaying consumption, an adjustment for an inflationary rise in the overall level of prices, and a risk premium that takes the borrower's riskiness into account. The U.S. government is considered to be an extremely safe borrower, so when the U.S. government issues Treasury bonds, it can pay a relatively low rate of interest. Firms that appear to be safe borrowers, perhaps because of their sheer size or because they have consistently earned profits over time, will still pay a higher interest rate than the U.S. government. Firms that appear to be riskier borrowers, perhaps because they are still growing or their businesses appear shaky, will pay the highest interest rates when they issue bonds. Bonds that offer high interest rates to compensate for their relatively high chance of default are sometimes called junk bonds. A number of today's well-known firms issued junk bonds back in the 1980s when they were starting to grow up, including Turner Broadcasting and Microsoft.

junk bonds: Bonds that offer relatively high interest rates to compensate for their relatively high chance of default.

A bond issued by the U.S. government or a large corporation may seem to be relatively low risk: after all, the issuer of the bond has promised to make certain payments over time, and except for rare cases of bankruptcy, these payments will be made. If the issuer of a corporate bond fails to make the payments that it owes to its bondholders, the bondholders can require that the company declare bankruptcy, sell off its assets, and pay them as much as it can. Even in the case of junk bonds, a wise investor can reduce the risk by purchasing bonds from a wide range of different companies, since even if a few firms go broke and don't pay, they aren't *all* likely to go bankrupt.

However, bonds present a different risk because even though the payments made by a typical bond do not change, interest rates in the economy do change. For example, imagine that you decide to buy a $1,000 bond that pays an annual interest rate of 8%. However, soon after you buy the bond, equilibrium interest rates rise in the financial capital market, so that now similar companies are paying an annual rate of 11% when they issue bonds. Thus, anyone who buys a bond in the present can receive annual payments of $110 per year, but since your bond was issued at an interest rate of 8%, you have tied up $1,000 and are receiving payments of only $80 per year. In the meaningful sense of opportunity cost, you are missing out on the higher payments that you could have received. (The Appendix to this chapter discusses specific calculations for how a change in interest rates will alter the value of a bond.)

The bond yield measures the rate of return that a bond is expected to pay at the time of purchase. Bonds are not only bought at the time they are issued, but they are also bought and sold during their lifetimes. When buying a bond that has been around for a few years, investors should know that the interest rate printed on a bond is often not the same as the bond yield. For example, consider a $1,000 bond that makes payments of $80 per year, based on an interest rate of 8%. However, the interest rates prevailing in the economy have now risen to 12%. What would you pay for this bond when it has one year left to run? The expected payments from the bond one year from now are $1080 because in the bond's last year, the issuer of the bond will make the final year of interest payments and then also repay the original $1000. Given that interest rates in this example are now 12%, you know that you could invest $964 in an alternative investment and receive $1080 a year from now; that is, $964[1 + 0.12] = $1080. Therefore, you will not pay more than $964 for the original $1,000 bond. Even though the annual payments of that bond were

bond yield: The rate of return that a bond is expected to pay at the time of purchase.

EXHIBIT 19-3 Interest Rates for Corporate Bonds and 10-Year U.S. Treasury Bonds

The interest rates for corporate bonds and U.S. Treasury bonds (officially "notes") rise and fall together, depending on conditions for borrowers and lenders in financial markets for borrowing. But the corporate bonds always must pay a higher interest rate, to make up for the higher risk that they have of defaulting compared with the U.S. government.

originally based on an 8% interest rate, the bond cannot be sold unless its payoff reflects the currently prevailing interest rate. When interest rates rise, bonds previously issued at lower interest rates will sell for less than face value. Conversely, when interest rates fall, bonds previously issued at higher interest rates will sell for more than face value.

Exhibit 19-3 shows bond yield for two kinds of bonds: 10-year Treasury bonds (which are officially called "notes") and corporate bonds issued by firms that have been given an Aaa rating as relatively safe borrowers by Moody's, an independent firm that publishes such ratings. Corporate bonds pay a higher interest rate because firms are riskier borrowers than the federal government. But the rates tend to rise and fall together. Treasury bonds typically pay more than bank accounts, and corporate bonds typically pay a higher interest rate than Treasury bonds.

The bottom line for bonds: Rate of return—low to moderate, depending on the risk of the borrower; Risk—low to moderate, depending on whether interest rates in the economy change substantially after the bond is issued; Liquidity—moderate, because the bond needs to be sold before the investor regains access to cash.

Stocks

The rate of return on a financial investment in a share of stock can come in two forms: as dividends paid by the firm and as a capital gain achieved by selling the stock for more than you paid. The range of possible returns from buying stock is mind-bending. Firms can decide to pay dividends or not. A stock price can rise to a multiple of its original price or sink all the way to zero. For example, Netflix, a company that specializes in on-demand video and streaming media, saw its stock price rise by 134% in 2015. Conversely, Chesapeake Energy, a company that specializes in oil and gas exploration and production, saw its stock price fall by 77% in 2015. The reasons why stock prices fall and rise so abruptly will be discussed in a moment.

But first, there are a number of different ways of measuring the overall performance of the stock market, based on averaging the stock prices of different subsets of companies. Perhaps the best-known measure of the stock markets is the Dow Jones Industrial Average, mentioned at the start of this chapter, which is based on the stock prices of 30 large U.S. companies. Another gauge of stock market performance, the Standard and Poor's 500, follows the stock prices of the 500 largest U.S. companies. The Wilshire 5000 tracks the stock prices of essentially all U.S. companies that have stock that the public can buy and sell. Other measures of stock markets focus on *where* stocks are traded. For example, the New York Stock Exchange monitors the performance of stocks that are traded on that exchange in New York City. The NASDAQ stock market includes about 3,100 stocks,

EXHIBIT 19-4 Some Measures of Stock Markets

Measure of the Stock Market	Comments
Dow Jones Industrial Average (DJIA) http://indexes.dowjones.com	Based on 30 large companies from a diverse set of representative industries, chosen by analysts at Dow Jones and Company, owners of the *Wall Street Journal*. Goes back to 1896.
Standard and Poor's 500 http://www.standardandpoors.com	Based on 500 large U.S. firms, chosen by analysts at Standard & Poor's to represent the economy as a whole.
Wilshire 5000 http://www.wilshire.com	Includes essentially all U.S. companies with stock ownership. Despite the name, this index includes about 7,000 firms.
New York Stock Exchange http://www.nyse.com	The oldest and largest U.S. stock market, dating back to 1792. It trades stocks for 2,800 companies of all sizes. It is located at 18 Broad St. in New York City.
NASDAQ http://www.nasdaq.com	Founded in 1971 as an electronic stock market, allowing people to buy or sell from many physical locations. It has about 3,100 companies.
Some Prominent Foreign Stock Exchanges	
FTSE http://www.ftse.com	Includes the 100 largest companies on the London Stock Exchange. Pronounced "footsie." Originally stood for Financial Time Stock Exchange.
Nikkei http://www.nni.nikkei.co.jp	*Nikkei* stands for *Nihon Keizai Shimbun*, which translates as the *Japan Economic Journal*, a major business newspaper in Japan. Index includes the 225 largest and most actively traded stocks on the Tokyo Stock Exchange.
DAX http://www.exchange.de	Tracks 30 of the largest companies on the Frankfurt, Germany stock exchange. DAX is an abbreviation for Deutscher Aktien Index.

with something of a concentration on technology stocks. Exhibit 19-4 lists some of the most commonly cited measures of U.S. and international stock markets.

The trend in the stock market is generally up over time, but with some large dips along the way. Exhibit 19-5 shows the path of the Standard & Poor's 500 index (which is measured on the left-hand vertical axis) and the Dow Jones Index (which is measured on the right-hand vertical axis). Broad measures of the stock market, like these two, tend to move together. When looking at graphs of the overall stock market like these, the numbers on the vertical axis are produced by formulas that don't have an easy intuitive explanation. However, when the Dow Jones average rises from 5,000 to 10,000, you know that the average price of the stocks in that index has (roughly) doubled. Thus, Exhibit 19-5 shows that stock prices didn't rise much in the 1970s, but then started a steady climb in the 1980s. From 2000 to 2012, stock prices bounced up and down but ended up at about the same level, preceding a sharp rise in 2013 and 2014.

Exhibit 19-6 shows the total annual rate of return that an investor would have received from buying the stocks in the S&P 500 index over recent decades. The total return here includes both dividends paid by these companies and also capital gains arising from increases in the value of the stock. (For technical reasons related to how the numbers are calculated, the dividends and capital gains don't add exactly to the total return.) From the 1950s up to the 1980s, the average firm paid annual dividends equal to about 4% of the value of its stock. But since the 1990s, dividends have dropped and now often provide

EXHIBIT 19-5 The Dow Jones Industrial Index and the Standard & Poor's 500, 1965–2015

Stock prices rose dramatically from the 1980s up to about 2000. From 2000 to 2012, stock prices bounced up and down but then rose in 2013 and 2014.

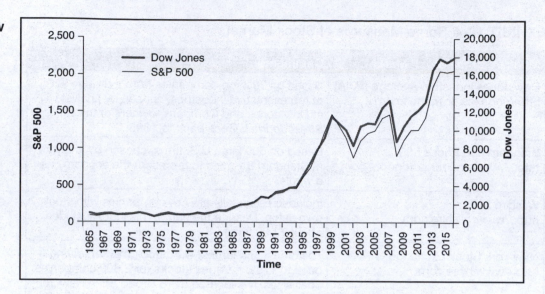

EXHIBIT 19-6 Annual Returns on Stocks: 1950–2015

Period	Total Annual Return (%)	Capital Gains (%)	Dividends (%)
1950–1959	19.25	14.26	4.99
1960–1969	7.78	4.53	3.25
1970–1979	5.88	1.68	4.20
1980–1989	17.55	13.15	4.40
1990–1999	18.21	15.70	2.51
2000	–9.10	–10.10	1.00
2001	–11.89	–13.21	1.32
2002	–22.10	–23.75	1.65
2003	28.68	26.86	1.82
2004	10.88	9.15	1.73
2005	4.91	3.06	1.85
2006	15.80	13.89	1.91
2007	5.49	3.60	1.89
2008	–37.00	–38.88	1.88
2009	23.45	21.47	1.98
2010	12.78	10.99	1.79
2011	0.00	–2.06	2.06
2012	13.41	11.30	2.11
2013	32.15	30.21	1.94
2014	13.52	11.60	1.92
2015	1.36	–0.75	2.11

a return closer to 1–2%. In the 1960s and 1970s, capital gains from owning stock were (very) roughly the same as dividends. But in the 1980s and 1990s, capital gains were far higher than dividends. In the 2000s, dividends remained low, and while stock prices fluctuated, they have remained low.

The overall pattern is that stocks as a group have provided a high rate of return over extended periods of time, but this return comes with risks. Individual companies can rise and fall substantially, both over short time periods and over the long run. During extended periods of time like the 1970s or the first decade of the 2000s, the overall return on the stock market can be quite modest. The stock market can sometimes fall sharply, as it did from 2000–2002 and in 2008. To understand why stocks are so risky, it's useful to consider the two basic motivations for buying and selling of stocks: fundamentals trading and momentum trading.

The value of the stock of a firm is ultimately determined by the future profits the firm is expected to earn. To understand why this statement must hold true, imagine that you purchase 100% of the shares of stock of a company, so that you become the sole owner. Being the sole owner means that, along with the power to run the firm, any profits the firm earns in the future belong to you. Thus, what you are willing to pay for all of the stock in the firm will depend on what it is worth to you to receive all of the future profits from the firm. The same lesson holds true, on a smaller scale, for investors who buy only a few shares of stock in a firm.

Fundamentals trading involves buying or selling stock based on estimates of the future expected profits of the firm. Say that you believe the future profits of the firm are currently worth $10 million, and the firm has 1 million shares of stock. Then you will believe that the fundamental value of the stock should be $10 a share. If the current market value of the stock is less than $10, you will want to purchase the stock. If the current market value of the stock is more than $10, you will want to sell the stock. Those who believe that the stock is overvalued, relative to the fundamental value of its future expected profits, will sell their shares to those who believe that the stock is undervalued. Of course, the firm's profits may turn out much higher or much lower than expected. If the firm's future profits turn out to be far above common expectations, then shareholders can recognize extremely large capital gains. If the firm's future profits turn out to be nonexistent, the price of the firm's stock can fall all the way to zero. Thus, one reason for the riskiness of stocks is because the future is uncertain, and shareholders are not guaranteed any dividends or other payments from the firm.

fundamentals trading: Buying or selling stock based on estimates of the future expected profits.

The risks of fundamentals trading are magnified by the second main motivation for stock market trading: Momentum trading refers to buying stock because the price seems to be rising, or selling stock because the price seems to be falling. In other words, momentum trading follows the trends, regardless of whether they match some notion of long-run fundamental value. The idea of momentum trading has been around a long time. The eighteenth century French author and philosopher Voltaire (1694–1778) once wrote: "If you see a Swiss banker jump out of a window, follow him—there is surely money to be made." The problem with momentum trading is that it creates unsustainable outcomes. When momentum traders expect a firm's stock price to rise, they buy that stock, but their own increased demand for stock also causes the stock's price to rise, thus encouraging other momentum traders to purchase still more stock, which drives the stock price still higher. Conversely, when momentum traders expect a firm's stock price to fall, they sell that stock, but as they sell their own stock, they also cause the stock's price to fall further, thus encouraging other momentum traders to sell still more stock. The result of momentum trading can be a stock market that soars or collapses based on the momentum of financial investors, without much change in the value of the fundamental value of the firm as determined by expected future profits. But momentum cannot last forever. Eventually, the future profits or losses start to occur. Stock prices gradually struggle back toward the fundamental levels that are justified by actual expectations of future profits.

momentum trading: Buying or selling stock by following the current trend; that is, buying when the price seems to be rising, or selling stock because the price seems to be falling.

One piece of evidence for the existence of a substantial number of momentum traders is that stock can move sharply in ways that are hard to explain as a result of fundamental factors. On October 19, 1987, for example, U.S. stock market prices fell 23% in a single day. From March 2000 to September 2001, the NASDAQ stock index, which includes many technology-oriented companies, dropped by 67%. In Japan stock prices sank by more than half from 1990 to 1992, and they have stayed roughly at that lower level ever since. In Thailand, stock prices toppled by more than half from February to September 1998. Over three weeks from September to October 2008, the U.S. stock market fell 26%. In these cases of market crashes, and many others like them, it seems implausible that fundamental factors about expectations of future profits shifted so dramatically that all the stocks in the market suddenly were worth so much less. Instead, it seems likelier that the self-fulfilling prophecy of momentum trading pushed the value of stocks above a price that could be justified by fundamental factors, but at some point as time passed and firms actually earned profits or made losses, stock prices dropped back toward their fundamental values. These episodes in which momentum trading pushes stock prices far above or below their fundamental values can last for years.

Bottom line on investing in individual stocks: Rate of return—High on average over lengthy periods of time; Risk—High, especially in the short run; Liquidity—Moderate, since stock does need to be sold to turn gains into spendable money.

Mutual Funds

diversification: Investing in a wide range of companies, to reduce the level of risk.

Buying stock or bonds issued by a single company is always somewhat risky. An individual firm may find itself buffeted by unfavorable supply and demand conditions or hurt by unlucky or unwise managerial decisions. Thus, a standard recommendation for financial investors, already hinted at in the earlier discussion, is **diversification**, which means buying stocks or bonds from a wide range of companies. A saver who diversifies is following the old proverb: "Don't put all your eggs in one basket." In any broad group of companies, some firms will do better than expected and some will do worse—but that random variation will have a tendency to cancel out, so the result will be the average for the group.

mutual funds: A fund that buys a range of stocks or bonds from different companies, thus allowing an investor an easy way to diversify.

To simplify the process of buying a diversified group of stocks, companies offer **mutual funds**, which are funds that buy a range of stocks or bonds from different companies. The financial investor buys shares of the mutual fund and then receives a return based on how the fund as a whole performs. Roughly half of U.S. households have a financial investment in a mutual fund—including many people who have their retirement savings or pension money invested in this way.

index fund: A mutual fund that seeks only to mimic the overall performance of the market.

Mutual funds can be focused in certain areas; for example, one mutual fund might invest only in stock of companies based in Indonesia, or only in bonds issued by large manufacturing companies, or only in stock of biotechnology companies. At the other end of the spectrum, a mutual fund might be quite broad; at the extreme, some mutual funds own a tiny share of every firm in the stock market, and thus the value of the mutual fund will fluctuate with the average of the overall stock market. A mutual fund that seeks only to mimic the overall performance of the market is called an **index fund**.

Diversification can offset some of the risks of individual stocks rising or falling. But even investors who buy an indexed mutual fund, designed to mimic some measure of the broad stock market like the Standard and Poor's 500, had better buckle their seatbelts against some ups and downs, like those the stock market experienced in the first decade of the 2000s.

Housing and Other Tangible Assets

equity: The monetary value a homeowner would have after selling the house and repaying any outstanding bank loans used to buy the house.

Households can also seek a rate of return by purchasing tangible assets, especially housing. About two-thirds of U.S. households own their own home. An owner's **equity** in a house is the monetary value the owner would have after selling the house and repaying any outstanding bank loans used to buy the house. For example, imagine that you buy a house for $200,000, paying 10% of the price as a down payment and taking out a bank loan for the remaining $180,000. Over time, you pay off some of your bank loan, so that only $100,000 remains, and the value of the house on the market rises to $250,000. At that point, your equity in the home is the value of the home minus the value of the loan outstanding, which is $150,000. For many middle-class Americans, their home equity is their single greatest financial asset. The total value of all home equity held by U.S. households was about $12 trillion in 2015.

Investment in a house is tangibly different from bank accounts, stocks, and bonds because a house offers both a financial and a non-financial return. If you buy a house to live in, part of the return on your investment occurs from your consumption of "housing services"—that is, having a place to live. (Of course, if you buy a home and rent it out, you receive rental payments for the housing services you provide, which would offer a financial return.) But buying a house to live in also offers the possibility of a capital gain from selling the house in the future for more than you paid for it.

In the second half of the twentieth century, housing prices averaged over the United States as a whole rose every year. However, the possible capital gains from rising housing prices are riskier than these national price averages reveal. Certain regions of the U.S. and certain metropolitan areas saw falls in housing prices. In the first decade of the 2000s, housing prices for the country as a whole first rose rapidly for several years, and then the median housing price for the United States as a whole fell almost 10% in 2008 and declined further in 2009 before rising again in the following years.

Investors can also put money into other tangible assets. For example, financial markets make it possible to invest in gold, silver, and other precious metals, or in duller commodities like sugar, cocoa, coffee, orange juice, oil, and natural gas. The return on these investments derives from the saver's hope of buying low, selling high, and receiving a capital gain. Investing in, say, gold or coffee offers relatively little in the way of nonfinancial benefits to the user (unless the investor likes to caress gold or gaze upon a warehouse full of coffee). Indeed, typically investors in these commodities never even see

Boom and Bust in the U.S. Housing Market

The price of an average U.S. home took off from 2003 to 2005, rising at more than 10% per year. No serious analyst believed that this rate of price growth rate was sustainable; after all, if housing prices grew at, say, 11% per year over time, the average price of a home would more than double every seven years. However, many serious analysts at the time saw no reason for deep concern. After all, housing prices often change in fits and starts, like all prices, and a price surge for a few years is often followed by prices that are flat or even declining a bit as local markets adjust.

The sharp rise in housing prices was driven by a high level of demand for housing. Interest rates were low, so people were encouraged to borrow money to buy a house. Banks became much more flexible in their lending, making what were called "subprime" loans. Banks loaned money with low or sometimes no down-payment. They sometimes offered loans with very low interest payments for the first two years but then much higher payments after that; the idea was that housing prices would keep rising, so the borrower would just refinance the mortgage two years in the future, and thus wouldn't ever have to make the higher payments. Some banks even offered so-called NINJA loans, which meant a loan given even though the borrower had No Income, No Job or Assets.

In retrospect, a number of these loans seem foolhardy. But many borrowers figured that as long as housing prices kept rising, it made sense to buy. Many lenders used a process called "securitizing," in which they sold their mortgages to financial companies that put all the mortgages into a big pool, creating large financial securities, and then re-sold these mortgage-backed securities to investors. In this way, the lenders felt that they had protected themselves against the risk of the mortgages not being repaid. Bank and financial regulators watched this process unfold, but saw no reason at the time to intervene.

When housing prices turned down, many households who had borrowed when prices were high found that what they owed the bank was more than their home was worth. Many banks believed that they had diversified by selling their individual loans and instead buying securities based on mortgage loans from all over the country. After all, back in 2005, banks knew that the average price of a house had not declined at any time since the Great Depression of the 1930s. But these securities based on mortgage loans turned out to be far riskier than expected. The bust in housing prices weakened the finances of both banks and households, and thus helped bring on the Great Recession of 2007–2009.

the physical goods; instead, they sign a contract that takes ownership of a certain quantity of these commodities, which are stored in a warehouse someplace, and later they sell the ownership to someone else. As one example, from 1981 to 2005, the price of gold generally fluctuated between about $300 and $500 per ounce, but then rose sharply to over $1,700 per ounce in late 2012, before falling back to $1,300 per ounce by mid-2016.

A final area of tangible assets are "collectibles" like paintings, fine wine, jewelry, antiques, or even baseball cards. Most collectibles provide returns both in the form of services or of a potentially higher selling price in the future. You can use paintings by hanging them on the wall, jewelry by wearing it, baseball cards by displaying them. You can also hope to sell them someday for more than you paid for them. However, the evidence on prices of collectibles, while scanty, is that while they may go through periods where prices skyrocket for a time, you should not expect to make a higher-than-average rate of return over a sustained period of time from investing in this way.

The bottom line on investing in tangible assets: Rate of return—Moderate, especially if you can receive nonfinancial benefits from, say, living in the house; Risk—Moderate for housing or high if you buy gold or baseball cards; Liquidity—Low, because it often takes considerable time and energy to sell a house or a piece of fine art and turn your capital gain into cash.

The Trade-offs between Return and Risk

The discussion of financial investments has emphasized the expected rate of return, the risk, and the liquidity of each investment. Exhibit 19-7 summarizes these characteristics.

The household investment choices listed here display a trade-off between the expected return and the degree of risk involved. Bank accounts have very low risk and very low returns; bonds have higher risk but higher returns; and stocks are riskiest of all but pay still higher returns. In effect, the higher average return compensates for the higher degree of risk. If risky assets like stocks did not also offer a higher average return, then few investors would desire them.

This trade-off between return and risk complicates the task of any financial investor: Is it better to invest safely for a low expected return, or to take a risk and go for the possibility of a higher return? Ultimately, investor choices about risk and return will be based on personal preferences. However, it is often useful to examine risk and return in the context of different time frames. The high returns of stock market investments refer to a high average return that can be expected over a period of several years or decades. The high risk of such investments refers to the fact that in shorter time frames, from months to a few years, the rate of return may fluctuate a great deal. Thus, a person near retirement age, who already owns a house, may prefer reduced risk and certainty about retirement income. For young workers, just starting to make a reasonable income, it may make sense

EXHIBIT 19-7 Key Characteristics for Financial Investors

Financial Investment	Return	Risk	Liquidity
Checking account	Very low	Very little	Very high
Savings account	Low	Very little	High
Certificate of deposit	Low to medium	Very little	Medium
Stocks	High	Medium to high	Medium
Bonds	Medium	Low to medium	Medium
Mutual funds	Medium to high	Medium to high	Medium-high
Housing	Medium	Medium	Low
Gold	Medium	High	Low
Collectibles	Low to medium	High	Low

to put most of their savings for retirement in stocks. Stocks are risky in the short term, to be sure, but when the worker can look forward to several decades during which bounces of the stock market up and down can even out, stocks will typically pay a substantially higher return over that extended period than will bonds or bank accounts. Thus, trade-offs between risk and return must be considered in the context of where the investor is in life.

How to Become Rich

Getting rich may seem straightforward enough. Figure out what companies are going to grow and earn high profits in the future, if you are a fundamental trader, or figure out what companies are going to become popular for everyone else to buy, if you are a momentum trader. Those companies are the ones that will pay high dividends or whose stock price will climb in the future. Then, buy stock in those companies. Presto! Multiply your money! Why isn't this path to riches as easy as it sounds? This section first discusses the problems with picking stocks and then discusses a more reliable but undeniably duller method of accumulating personal wealth.

Why It's Hard to Get Rich Quick: The Random Walk Theory

The chief problem with attempting to buy stock in companies that will have higher prices in the future is that many other financial investors are trying to do the same thing. Thus, in attempting to get rich in the stock market, it is no help to identify a company that is going to earn high profits if many other investors have already reached the same conclusion about the company, because the stock price will already be high, based on the commonly expected high level of future profits.

The idea that stock prices are based on expectations about the future has a powerful and unexpected implication. If expectations determine stock price, then *shifts* in expectations will determine *shifts* in the stock price. Thus, what matters for predicting whether the stock price of a company will do well in the future is not whether the company will actually earn profits in the future. Instead, one must find a company that is widely believed at present to have poor prospects, but that will actually turn out to be a shining star. Brigades of stock market analysts and individual investors are carrying out such research 24 hours a day.

The fundamental problem with predicting future stock winners is that by definition, no one can predict the future news that alters expectations about profits. Because stock prices will shift in response to unpredictable future news, these prices will tend to follow what mathematicians call a "random walk with a trend." The *random walk* part means that on any given day, stock prices are just as likely to rise as to fall. *With a trend* means that over time, the upward steps tend to be larger than the downward steps, so stocks do gradually climb.

If stocks follow a random walk, then not even financial professionals will be able to choose stocks that will beat the average consistently. While some investment advisers are better-than-average in any given year, and some even succeed for a number of years in a row, the majority of financial investors do not outguess the market. If one looks back over time, it is typically true that one-half or two-thirds of the mutual funds that attempted to pick stocks that would rise more than the market average actually ended up doing worse than the market average. For the average investor who reads the business pages of the newspaper over a cup of coffee in the morning, the odds of doing better than full-time professionals is not very good at all. Trying to pick the stocks that will gain a great deal in the future is a risky and unlikely way for the average investor to become rich.

Getting Rich the Slow, Boring Way

Many U.S. citizens can accumulate a large amount of wealth during their lifetime, if they make two key choices. The first choice is to complete additional education and training. In 2014, the median earnings for full-time workers age 25 and over who had only a high school degree were $40,930; for those with a two-year associate degree, median earnings were $51,110, and for those with a four-year bachelor's degree (but no further professional degrees), median annual earnings were $68,160. Learning is not only good for you, but it pays off financially, too.

The second key choice is to start saving money early in life and to give the power of compound interest a chance. Imagine that at age 25, you save $3,000 and sock that money into an account that you don't touch. In the long run, it's not unreasonable to assume a 5% real annual rate of return (i.e., 5% above the rate of inflation) on money invested in a well-diversified stock portfolio. After 40 years, using the formula for compound interest introduced in Chapter 2, the original $3,000 investment will have multiplied nearly fifteenfold:

$$\$3,000(1 + .05)^{40} = \$21,120$$

Of course, having $21,120 doesn't make you a millionaire. But notice that this tidy sum is the result of saving $3,000 exactly once. Saving that amount every year for several decades—and saving more as income rises—will multiply the total considerably. This type of wealth won't rival the riches of Microsoft chief executive officer Bill Gates or legendary investor Warren Buffett, but remember that only half of Americans have any money in mutual funds at all. Accumulating hundreds of thousands of dollars by retirement is a perfectly achievable goal for a well-educated person who starts saving early in life—and that amount of accumulated wealth will put you at or near the top 10% of all American households.

Getting additional education and saving money early in life obviously won't make you rich overnight. Additional education typically means putting off earning income and living like a student for more years. Saving money often require choices like driving an older or less fancy car, living in a smaller apartment or buying a smaller house, and making other day-to-day sacrifices. For most people, the trade-offs for achieving substantial personal wealth will require effort, patience, and sacrifice.

How Capital Markets Transform Financial Flows

Financial capital markets have the power to repackage money as it moves from those who supply financial capital to those who demand it. Banks accept checking account deposits, bundle them together, and turn them into long-term loans to companies. Individual firms sell shares of stock and issue bonds to raise capital. Firms make and sell an astonishing array of goods and services, but an investor can receive a return on the company's decisions by buying stock in a company. Stocks and bonds are sold and resold by financial investors to each other. Venture capitalists and angel investors search for promising small companies. Mutual funds combine the stocks and bonds—and thus, indirectly, the products and investments—of many different companies.

This chapter has discussed the basics mechanisms of financial markets, but a more advanced course in economics or finance will consider more sophisticated tools. For example, stocks and bonds come in many varieties. There is *nonvoting stock* where the holder can buy and sell the stock, but not vote for the board of directors. Some bonds make their payments based on interest rates that vary according to inflation or some other factor, rather than fixed interest rates. Other bonds make all of the interest payments in one lump sum when the bond comes due, not on a year-by-year basis. Some stocks give shareholders an option to convert them into bonds; some bonds give bondholders an option to convert them into stocks. In the "options market," a financial investor buys not the stock or bond itself but rather an option to buy the stock or bond at a predetermined price if the price rises in the future, or an option to sell the stock if the price falls.

But the fundamentals of financial capital markets remain the same. Firms are trying to raise financial capital, and households are looking for a desirable combination of rate of return, risk, and liquidity. Financial markets are society's mechanisms for bringing together these forces of demand and supply.

1. Companies can raise early-stage financial capital in several ways: from their managers' personal savings and from private investors like angel investors and **venture capital** firms.

2. For many firms, reinvesting their own previously earned profits is a substantial source of financial capital for investment. However, reinvesting profits will not work well for firms that have limited profits.

3. As companies become more established, with a record of earning profits, it becomes possible for them to borrow money, either from banks or by issuing bonds, because the lenders can have some confidence that they will be repaid.

4. A **bond** is a financial contract through which a borrower agrees to repay the amount that was borrowed A bond specifies an amount that will be borrowed, the amounts that will be repaid over time based on the interest rate when the bond is issued, and the time until repayment. **Corporate bonds** are issued by firms; **municipal bonds** are issued by cities, state bonds by U.S. states, and **Treasury bonds** by the federal government through the U.S. Department of the Treasury.

5. **Stock** represents ownership of a firm; that is, a person who owns 100% of a company's stock by definition owns the entire company. The stock of a company is divided into **shares**. A firm receives financial capital when it sells stock to the public. A company's first sale of stock to the public is called the **initial public offering (IPO)**. However, a firm does not receive any funds when one **shareholder** sells stock in the firm to another shareholder.

6. The rate of return on stock is received in two forms. Firms can make direct cash payments to shareholders called **dividends**. In addition, a shareholder might buy shares of stock at a lower price and sell them at a higher price, which is called a **capital gain**.

7. A **private company** is owned by the people who run it on a day-to-day basis. A private company owned and run by an individual is called a **sole proprietorship**, while a firm owned and run by a group is called a **partnership**. When a firm decides to sell stock that can be bought and sold by financial investors, then the firm is owned by its shareholders—who in turn elect a board of directors to hire top day-to-day management—and is called a **public company**.

8. All investments can be categorized according to three key characteristics: average expected return, degree of risk, and liquidity. To get a higher rate of return, an investor must typically accept either more risk or less liquidity.

9. Banks are an example of a **financial intermediary**, an institution that operates to coordinate supply and demand in the financial capital market. A bank, for example, receives money from suppliers of financial capital and provides loans to demanders of financial capital.

10. Banks offer a range of accounts, including **checking accounts**, **savings accounts**, and **certificates of deposit**. Under the federal program of **deposit insurance**, banks purchase insurance against the risk of a bank failure.

11. A typical bond promises the financial investor a series of payments over time, based on the interest rate at the time the bond is issued, and then repayment of what was borrowed. Bonds that offer a high rate of return but also a relatively high chance of defaulting on the payments are called junk bonds.

12. The **bond yield** is the rate of return that a bond promises to pay at the time of purchase. Even when bonds make payments based on a fixed rate of interest, they are somewhat risky, because if interest rates rise for the economy as a whole, an investor who owns bonds issued at lower interest rates is now locked into the low rate and suffers a loss.

13. The price of a company's stock will be determined by expectations of future profits. There are two main motivations for purchasing stock. **Fundamentals trading** involves buying or selling stock based on estimates of the future expected profits of the firm. **Momentum trading** involves buying stock because the price is rising or selling stock because the price is falling, without regard for long-term fundamental value. Momentum trading may lead to sharp rises and falls in stock prices.

14. Investing in any individual firm is somewhat risky, so investors are wise to practice **diversification**, which means investing in a range of companies.

15. A **mutual fund** purchases an array of stocks and/or bonds. An investor in the mutual fund then receives a return depending on the overall performance of the investments made by the fund as a whole. A mutual fund that seeks to imitate the overall behavior of the stock market is called an **index fund**.

16. Housing and other tangible assets can also be regarded as forms of financial investment, which pay a rate of return in the form of capital gains. Housing can also offer a nonfinancial return—specifically, you can live in it.

17. Changes in the price of a stock depend on changes in expectations about future profits. Because changes

in expectations are largely unpredictable, movements in stock prices will tend to be a "random walk." It is difficult, even for financial professionals, to predict changes in future expectations and thus to choose the stocks whose price is going to rise in the future.

18. Most Americans can accumulate considerable financial wealth if they follow two rules: complete significant additional education and training after graduating from high school, and start saving money early in life.

Review Questions

1. What are the most common ways for start-up firms to raise financial capital?
2. Why can't firms just use their own profits for financial capital, with no need for outside investors?
3. Why are banks more willing to lend to well-established firms?
4. What is a bond? What is a junk bond?
5. What does a share of stock represent?
6. When do firms receive money from the sale of stock in their firm, and when do they not receive money?
7. What is a dividend?
8. What is a capital gain?
9. What's the difference between a private company and a public company?
10. How do the shareholders who own a company choose the actual managers of the company?
11. What are the three main concerns of a financial investor?
12. Why are banks called "financial intermediaries"?
13. Name several different kinds of bank accounts. How are they different?
14. Why are bonds somewhat risky to buy, even though they make predetermined payments based on a fixed rate of interest?
15. What's the difference between fundamentals trading and momentum trading?
16. Why should a financial investor care about diversification?
17. What is a mutual fund?
18. What is an index fund?
19. How is buying a house to live in a type of financial investment?
20. Why is it hard to forecast future movements in stock prices?

Public Choice

Democratic governments are supposed to be, as President Abraham Lincoln famously said in his 1863 Gettysburg Address, "of the people, by the people, and for the people." But can democratic governments be relied on to enact sensible economic policies? After all, democratic government reacts to voters, not to analyses of demand and supply curves. The main focus of an economics course is, naturally enough, to analyze the characteristics of markets and purely economic institutions. But political institutions also play a role in allocating the scarce resources of society, and economists have played an active role along with other social scientists in analyzing how such political institutions work.

The previous nine chapters of this book have discussed situations in which market forces can sometimes lead to undesirable results: monopoly, imperfect competition, and antitrust policy (Chapters 11–13); negative externalities like pollution (Chapter 14); positive externalities and public goods like research and development (Chapter 15); poverty and inequality of incomes (Chapter 16); worker protection from employers, as in the case of discrimination (Chapter 17); failures to provide insurance and other issues related to imperfect information (Chapter 18); and financial markets that may go from boom to bust (Chapter 19). Many of these discussions suggested the possibility that government economic policies could be aimed at addressing these issues.

But just as markets can face issues and problems that lead to undesirable outcomes, a democratic system of government can also make mistakes, either by enacting policies that don't benefit society as a whole or by failing to enact policies that would have benefited society as a whole. This chapter discusses some practical difficulties of democracy from an economic point of view in which the actors in the political system are presumed to follow their own self-interest. For example, many voters don't vote, which obviously raises questions about whether a democratic system will reflect everyone's interests. Benefits or costs of government action are sometimes concentrated on small groups, who in some cases may organize together and have a disproportionately large effect on politics and in other cases may fail to organize and end up neglected. Legislators who worry about support from voters of their district may focus on local spending projects for their own district, without sufficient concern for whether this spending is in the interest of the nation as a whole. When more than two choices exist, the principle that the majority of voters should decide may not always make logical sense because situations can arise where it becomes literally impossible to decide what the "majority" prefers. Finally, government may be slower than private firms to correct its mistakes because government agencies do not face competition or a threat of new entry. Let's consider these factors in turn.

When Voters Don't Participate

In U.S. presidential elections over the last few decades, about 55–65% of voting-age citizens actually vote. In congressional elections when there is no presidential race, or in local elections, the turnout is typically lower, often less than half of the eligible voters. In other countries, the share of adults who vote is often higher than in the United States. For example, in national elections since the 1980s in Germany, Spain, and France, about 75–80% of those of voting age cast ballots. But even this total falls well short of 100%. Some countries have laws that require voting, among them Australia, Belgium, Italy, Greece, Turkey, Singapore, and most Latin American nations. At the time the United States was founded, voting was mandatory in Virginia, Maryland, Delaware, and Georgia. But even if the law can require people to vote, no law can require that each voter cast an informed or a thoughtful vote. Moreover, in the United States and in most countries around the world, the freedom to vote has typically meant the freedom *not* to vote, as well.

Why don't people vote? Perhaps they don't much care who wins, or they are uninformed about who is running, or they don't believe that their vote will matter. Indeed, these reasons are probably tied together, since people who don't believe their votes matter won't bother to become informed and won't much care who wins. Economists have suggested reasons why a utility-maximizing person might rationally decide not to vote or not to become informed about the election. While a few elections in very small towns may be decided by a single vote, in most elections of any size, the margin of victory is measured in hundreds, thousands, or even millions of votes. A rational voter will recognize that one vote is extremely unlikely to make a difference. This theory of **rational ignorance** holds that people won't bother incurring the costs of becoming informed and voting because they know that their vote won't be decisive in the election.

In a 1957 work, *An Economic Theory of Democracy*, the economist Anthony Downs stated the problem this way: "It seems probable that for a great many citizens in a democracy, rational behavior excludes any investment whatever in political information per se. No matter how significant a difference between parties is revealed to the rational citizen by his free information, or how uncertain he is about which party to support, he realizes that his vote has almost no chance of influencing the outcome. . . . He will not even utilize all the free information available, since assimilating it takes time." In his classic 1948 novel *Walden II*, the psychologist B. F. Skinner puts the issue even more succinctly via one of his characters, who states: "The chance that one man's vote will decide the issue in a national election . . . is less than the chance that he will be killed on his way to the polls."

While many Americans don't bother to vote in presidential elections, more than half do. What is the motivation of those who do vote? Research on voting behavior has shown that people who, on average, are more settled or more "connected" to society tend to vote more frequently. For example, married people vote more than single people. Those with a job vote more than the unemployed. Those who have lived longer in a neighborhood are more likely to vote than newcomers. Those who report that they know their neighbors and talk to them are more likely to vote than more socially isolated people. Those with a higher income and level of education are also more likely to vote. These factors suggest that political actions are likely to focus more on the interests of married, employed, well-educated people with at least a middle-class level of income than of other groups.

rational ignorance: The theory that rational people won't bother incurring the costs of becoming informed and voting because they know that their vote won't be decisive in the election.

Does the United States Spend Too Much Money on Elections?

In the 2012 elections for president, Congress, and a raft of state and local offices, a total of about $7 billion was spent on the election campaigns, including advertising, fundraising, travel, and staff. Many people worry that politicians spend too much of their time raising money and thus end up entangled with special interests. They would prefer a system that restricts what candidates can spend, perhaps in exchange for limited public campaign financing or TV advertising time that would be free to the candidates.

But how much spending on campaigns is too much? In the U.S. economy, which exceeded $15 trillion in 2012, the $7 billion spent on political campaigns is about 1/20 of 1% of the overall economy.

Total government spending in 2012, including federal and state government, totaled about $5.5 trillion, so the cost of choosing the people who would determine how this money would be spent cost about 1/8 of 1% of government spending.

In the context of the enormous U.S. economy, $7 billion isn't as much money as it sounds. For example, consumers in the U.S. economy spend about $2 billion per year on toothpaste. In 2012, Procter and Gamble spent $4.8 billion on advertising, and General Motors spent $3.1 billion. Americans spend about $22 billion per year on pet food—three times as much as was spent on the 2012 election.

Whatever we believe about whether candidates and their parties spend too much or too little on elections, the U.S. Supreme Court has placed limits on how government can limit campaign spending. In a 1976 decision, *Buckley vs. Valeo*, the Supreme Court emphasized that the first amendment to the U.S. Constitution specifies freedom of speech. The federal government and states can offer candidates a voluntary deal in which government makes some public financing available to candidates, but only if the candidates agree to abide by certain spending limits. Of course, candidates can also voluntarily agree to set certain spending limits if they wish to do so. But government cannot forbid people or organizations from raising and spending money that is above these limits if they choose to do so. There is an ongoing political and legal battle over what rules will govern campaign-related spending by groups that are not explicitly connected with a particular candidate.

For example, those who vote may tend to be more supportive of financial assistance for the two-year and four-year colleges that they expect their children to attend than they are of medical care or public school education aimed at families of the poor and unemployed.

A number of proposals have been offered to encourage greater voter turnout: making it easier to register to vote, keeping the polls open for more hours, or even moving election day to a weekend when more people don't need to worry about jobs or school commitments. In general, it has become easier to vote in the United States over recent decades. However, these changes do not seem to have caused a long-term upward trend in the number of people voting. After all, casting an informed vote will always impose some costs of time and energy. It's not clear how to strengthen people's feeling of connectedness to society in a way that will lead to a substantial increase in voter turnout. But otherwise, politicians elected by the votes of 60% or less of the population may not enact economic policy in the best interests of 100% of the population.

Special-Interest Politics

Many political issues are of intense interest to a relatively small group. For example, many Americans don't much care where the tires for their car were made. But in September 2009, President Obama enacted a tariff on tires imported from China, which would increase the import price of Chinese tires by 35 percent in its first year, 30 percent in the second year, and 25 percent in the third year. Interestingly, the U.S. companies that make tires did not favor this step because most of them also import tires from China and other countries. However, the United Steelworkers union, which had seen jobs making tires fall by 5,000 over the previous five years, lobbied fiercely for the tariffs to be enacted.

Special-interest groups are groups that are numerically small but quite well organized. A focused special-interest group can pressure legislators to enact public policies that do not benefit social surplus. For example, imagine an environmental rule to reduce air pollution

special-interest groups:
Groups that are numerically small but well organized and thus exert a disproportionate effect on political outcomes.

that will cost 10 large companies $8 million each, for a total cost of $80 million. The social benefits from enacting this rule provide an average of $10 for every person in the United States, so the benefits are about $3 trillion. But even though the benefits are far higher than the costs for society as a whole, the 10 companies are likely to lobby much more fiercely to avoid $8 million in costs than the average person is to argue for $10 worth of benefits.

As this example suggests, the problem of special interests in politics can be related to an issue raised back in Chapter 14 about economic policy with respect to negative externalities and pollution—the problem called "regulatory capture." In any government office where fine print is being written—laws and regulations about how much corporations will pay in taxes, or rules for safety in the workplace, or how to satisfy environmental regulations—you can bet that the specific industry affected has lobbyists who study every word and every comma. They talk with the legislators who are writing the legislation and suggest alternative wording. They contribute to the campaigns of legislators on the key committees—and may even offer those legislators high-paying jobs after they have left office. As a result, it often turns out that those who are being regulated can exercise considerable influence over the regulators. The idea of special interests takes this insight one step further and points out that when legislation is being considered and enacted, it can also be strongly affected by the groups that are most heavily involved in lobbying the politicians.

A democratic political system does offer some hope that neither an overemphasized and well-organized special-interest group nor an underemphasized and unorganized minority group will last forever. Special interests may develop a close relationship with one political party, and so their ability to influence legislation rises and falls as that party moves in or out of power. A special interest may even hurt a political party if it appears to a number of voters that the relationship is too cozy. In a close election, a small group that has been underemphasized in the past may find that it can tip the election one way or another—and so that group will suddenly receive considerable attention. Democratic institutions produce an ebb and flow of political parties and interests, and thus offer both opportunities for special interests and ways of counterbalancing those interests over time.

Identifiable Winners, Anonymous Losers

A number of economic policies involve gains where the beneficiaries are easily identifiable, but some or all of the costs are spread over those who are more anonymous. A democratic political system probably has a bias toward those who are identifiable.

For example, policies that impose price controls—like rent control—may look as if they benefit renters and only impose costs on landlords. But when landlords decide to contract or not to expand the number of rental units available, then a number of people who would have liked to rent an apartment end up living somewhere else because when they looked for rental apartments, none were available. These would-be renters have experienced a cost of rent control, but it's hard to identify who they are.

Similarly, policies that block imports will benefit the firms that would have competed with those imports—and workers at those firms—who are likely to be quite visible. On the other hand, consumers who would have preferred to purchase the imported products, and thus who bear some costs of the protectionist policy, are much less visible.

Specific tax breaks or spending programs can also fit this pattern of identifiable winners, with the costs of paying for these policies imposed on those who are hard to identify. Special interests are more likely to form from a group that is easily identifiable, rather than from a group where some of those who suffered may not even recognize that they are bearing costs.

Pork Barrels and Logrolling

pork-barrel spending:
Spending that benefits mainly a single political district.

Politicians have an incentive to assure that government money is spent in their home state or district, where it will benefit their constituents in a direct and obvious way. Thus, when legislators are negotiating over whether to support a piece of legislation, a common request is to include **pork-barrel spending**, which is defined as legislation that benefits mainly a single political district. Pork-barrel spending can be thought of as another case where democracy is challenged by concentrated benefits and widely dispersed costs: the benefits of pork-barrel spending are obvious and direct to local voters, while the costs are spread over the entire country.

U.S. Senator Robert C. Byrd of West Virginia, who was originally elected to the Senate in 1958 and had set the record for the longest-serving member by the time of his death in 2010, was widely regarded as one of the masters of pork-barrel politics, directing a steady stream of federal funds to his home state. A journalist once compiled a list of structures in West Virginia at least partly funded by the government and named after Byrd: "the Robert C. Byrd Highway, the Robert C. Byrd Locks and Dam, the Robert C. Byrd Institute, the Robert C. Byrd Life Long Learning Center, the Robert C. Byrd Honors Scholarship Program, the Robert C. Byrd Green Bank Telescope, the Robert C. Byrd Institute for Advanced Flexible Manufacturing, the Robert C. Byrd Federal Courthouse, the Robert C. Byrd Health Sciences Center, the Robert C. Byrd Academic and Technology Center, the Robert C. Byrd United Technical Center, the Robert C. Byrd Federal Building, the Robert C. Byrd Drive, the Robert C. Byrd Hilltop Office Complex, the Robert C. Byrd Library, the Robert C. Byrd Learning Resource Center, the Robert C. Byrd Rural Health Center." Moreover, this list doesn't include government-funded projects in West Virginia that were not named after Byrd. Of course, it would be necessary to analyze each of these expenditures in detail to figure out whether they should be treated as pork-barrel spending or whether they provide widespread benefits that reach beyond West Virginia. But at least some of them certainly smell like pork. The amount spent on individual pork-barrel projects is small, but many small projects can add up to a substantial total.

Pork-barrel spending can be encouraged by **logrolling** on the part of politicians, which refers to a situation where a group of legislators all agree to vote for a package of otherwise unrelated laws that they individually favor. For example, if one member of Congress suggests building a new bridge or hospital in that member's own congressional district, the other members might oppose it. But if 51% of the legislators come together, they can pass a bill that includes a bridge or hospital for every one of their districts. For example, the U.S. government has typically spread out its spending on military bases and weapons programs to congressional districts all across the country, in part to help create a situation where many members of Congress would be encouraged to vote in support of defense spending.

logrolling: When a group of legislators all agree to vote for a package of otherwise unrelated laws that they individually favor.

The Law and Economics Movement

A few decades ago, most lawyers and judges knew relatively little about economics. Conventional wisdom said that law was about legislation, rights and wrongs, and justice, while economics was an altogether different subject. But in the last few decades, the "law and economics movement" has tightened the connections between the two fields.

One place for close connections between law and economics lay in the area of antitrust law and enforcement. Issues of measuring the level of competition in a market and determining whether a firm is engaging in legal or illegal restrictive practices (as addressed in Chapter 12) are issues in which economists have many useful insights. In high-profile cases involving the conduct of large firms, economists have helped to analyze the issues.

But the law and economics movement goes much deeper. As one example, an economics framework can provide a ready interpretation in legal cases about lia-

bility, where one side is sued for causing harm to the other side. For example, scooters went through a wave of popularity about a decade ago, and the number of scooter-related injuries requiring an emergency room visit rose from 43,500 in 2000 to 99,800 in 2001—along with 10 deaths. Should society encourage lawsuits against those who make scooters in response to this data? Should laws be passed about scooter safety? Or should it just be accepted that some scooter-related accidents will occur? Moreover, economics can analyze how to address liability issues in terms of whether they provide the appropriate incentives to reduce injuries in the future.

Most legal rules don't just settle past disputes, but create incentives for future behavior that economics is well-suited to analyze. Most law schools now have at least a few faculty members who are both lawyers and Ph.D. economists, and require students to study at least basic economics.

Voting Cycles

Democracy is sometimes summed up (and oversimplified) in two words: "Majority rule." But when voters face three or more choices, then voting may not always be a useful way of determining what the majority prefers.

As one example, consider an election in a state where 60% of the population is liberal and 40% is conservative. If there are only two candidates, one from each side, and if similar proportions of liberals and conservatives vote, then the liberal will win. But what if the election includes two liberal candidates and only one conservative? It is possible that the liberal vote will split and victory will go to the minority party. In this case, the outcome does not reflect the majority's preference. In the French national elections of 2002, for example, the two leading candidates were expected to be Jacques Chirac and Lionel Jospin. But French elections happen in two rounds: a preliminary round that reduces the candidates to the top two and then a runoff round between those top two. In the preliminary round, the vote splintered: Chirac led with 19% of the vote, and Jospin received 16%. However, a candidate named Jean-Marie Le Pen received 17% of the vote and sneaked into the runoff ahead of Jospin. The other 48% of the vote was split between 13 other candidates. This outcome made international headlines because Le Pen had been frequently criticized for extreme nationalist views that sometimes seemed to cross the line into intolerance or racism. In the runoff, the supporters of other candidates united behind Chirac, who beat Le Pen by a majority of 82% to 18%. But Jospin might have beaten Chirac in a runoff, if voting had not been so splintered in the preliminary round.

In some cases with three or more options, it is not even clear how to define what the majority opinion might be. Step aside from politics for a moment and think about a choice facing three families—the Abbotts, the Burnses, and the Costellos—who are planning to celebrate New Year's Day together. They agree to vote on the menu, choosing from three entrees, and they agree that the majority vote wins. With three families, it seems reasonable that one choice of entree will get a 2–1 majority.

But what if their vote ends up looking like the choices in Exhibit 20-1? Clearly, the three families disagree on their first choice. But the problem goes even deeper. Instead of looking at all three choices at once, compare them two at a time. In a vote of turkey vs. beef, turkey wins by 2–1. In a vote of beef vs. lasagna, beef wins 2–1. If turkey beats beef, and beef beats lasagna, then it might seem only logical that turkey must also beat lasagna. However, with the preferences shown, lasagna is preferred to turkey by a 2–1 vote, as well. But if lasagna is preferred to turkey, and turkey beats beef, then surely it must be that lasagna also beats beef? Actually, no. Beef beats lasagna.

voting cycle: When a majority prefers A over B, B over C, and C over A.

The situation where Choice A is preferred by a majority over Choice B, Choice B is preferred by a majority over Choice C, and Choice C is preferred by a majority over Choice A is called a **voting cycle**. It's easy to imagine sets of government choices—say, perhaps the choice between increased defense spending, increased government spending on health care, and a tax cut—where a voting cycle could occur. When a voting cycle does occur, the result will be determined by the order in which choices are presented and voted on, not by majority rule, because every choice is both preferred to some alternative and also not preferred to another alternative.

Where Is Government's Self-Correcting Mechanism?

When a firm produces a product that no one wants to buy or produces at a higher cost than its competitors, the firm is likely to suffer losses, and if the firm cannot change its ways, it will go out of business altogether. This self-correcting mechanism of the private economy can have harsh effects in some cases on workers or on local economies, but it also puts pressure on firms for good performance.

Government agencies, on the other hand, do not sell their products in a market or face direct competitors. If the U.S. Department of Education or the U.S. Department of Defense is doing a poor job, citizens cannot purchase their services from another provider and drive the existing government agencies into bankruptcy. If you are upset that the

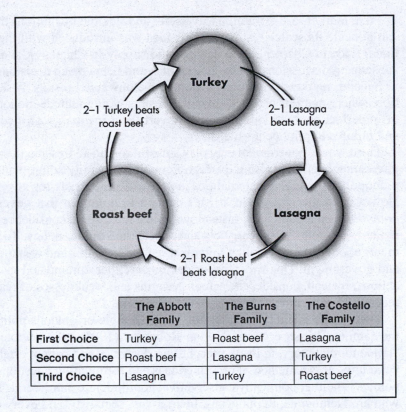

EXHIBIT 20-1 A Voting Cycle

Given these choices, voting will struggle to produce a majority outcome. Turkey is favored over roast beef by 2–1, and roast beef is favored over lasagna by 2–1. If turkey beats roast beef and roast beef beats lasagna, then it might seem that turkey must beat lasagna, too. But given these preferences, lasagna is favored over turkey by 2–1.

	The Abbott Family	The Burns Family	The Costello Family
First Choice	Turkey	Roast beef	Lasagna
Second Choice	Roast beef	Lasagna	Turkey
Third Choice	Lasagna	Turkey	Roast beef

Internal Revenue Service is slow in sending you a tax refund or seems unable to answer your questions, you can't decide to pay your income taxes through a different organization. Of course, elected politicians can assign new leaders to government agencies and instruct them to reorganize or to emphasize a different mission. But the pressure that government faces to make changes in its bureaucracy to seek greater efficiency and customer responsiveness is much milder than the threat of being put out of business altogether.

This insight suggests that when government provides goods or services directly, it might be expected to do so with less efficiency than private firms—except in certain cases where the government agency may compete directly with private firms. At the local level, for example, services like garbage collection can be provided by government directly, by private firms under contract to the government, or by a mix of government employees competing with private firms.

A Balanced View of Markets and Government

The British statesman Sir Winston Churchill (1874–1965) once wrote: "No one pretends that democracy is perfect or all-wise. Indeed, it has been said that democracy is the worst form of government except for all of the other forms which have been tried from time to time." In that spirit, the theme of this discussion is certainly not that democratic government should be abandoned. But a practical student of public policy needs to recognize that in some cases, like the case of well-organized special interests or pork-barrel legislation, a democratic government may seek to enact economically unwise projects or programs. In other cases, by placing a low priority on the problems of those who are not well organized or who are less likely to vote, the government may fail to act when it could do some good. In these and other cases, there is no automatic reason to believe that government will necessarily make economically sensible choices.

"The true test of a first-rate mind is the ability to hold two contradictory ideas at the same time," wrote the American author F. Scott Fitzgerald (1896–1940). At this point in your study of microeconomics, you should be able to go one better than Fitzgerald and to hold three somewhat contradictory ideas about the interrelationship between markets and government in your mind at the same time.

First, markets are extraordinarily useful and flexible institutions through which society can allocate its scarce resources. This idea was introduced with the subjects of international trade in Chapter 3, and demand and supply in Chapter 4, and reinforced in all the subsequent discussions of how households and firms make decisions.

Second, markets may sometimes produce unwanted results. A short list of the conditions where markets produce unwanted results would include monopoly and other issues of imperfect competition, pollution, poverty and inequality of incomes, discrimination, and failures to provide insurance.

Third, while government may play a useful role in addressing the problems of markets, government action is also imperfect. Economists readily admit that in those settings like monopoly or negative externalities, a *potential* role exists for government intervention. However, in the real world, it isn't enough to point out that government action might *potentially* be a good idea. Instead, you must have some confidence that the government is likely to identify and carry out the appropriate public policy. To make sensible judgments about economic policy, you must see the strengths and weaknesses of both markets and government. Don't idealize or demonize either unregulated markets or government actions. Instead, consider the actual strengths and weaknesses of real-world markets and real-world governments.

These three insights often do not lead to simple or obvious political conclusions. As the famous British economist, Joan Robinson (1903–1983), wrote some decades ago: "[E]conomic theory, in itself, preaches no doctrines and cannot establish any universally valid laws. It is a method of ordering ideas and formulating questions." The study of economics is neither politically conservative, nor moderate, nor liberal. There are economists who are Democrats, Republicans, libertarians, socialists, and every other political group you can name. Of course, conservatives may tend to emphasize the virtues of markets and the limitations of government, while liberals may tend to emphasize the shortcomings of markets and the need for government programs. But such differences only illustrate that the language and terminology of economics is not limited to one set of political beliefs, but can be used by all.

Key Concepts and Summary

1. The theory of **rational ignorance** holds that voters will recognize that their single vote is extremely unlikely to influence the outcome of an election, and they will thus choose to remain uninformed about issues and not to vote. This theory helps to explain why voter turnout is so low in the United States.
2. Special-interest politics arises when a relatively small group, called a **special-interest group**, each of whose members has a large interest in a political outcome, devotes a lot of time and energy to lobbying for the group's preferred choice. Meanwhile, the large majority, each of whose members has only a small interest in this issue, pays no attention.
3. **Pork-barrel spending** is defined as legislation where the benefits are concentrated on a single district while the costs are spread widely over the country. **Logrolling** refers to a situation where two or more legislators agree to vote for each other's legislation, which can then encourage pork-barrel spending in many districts.
4. Majority votes can run into difficulties when more than three choices exist. A **voting cycle** occurs when in a situation with at least three choices, choice A is preferred by a majority vote to choice B, choice B is preferred by a majority vote to choice C, and choice C is preferred by a majority vote to choice A. In such a situation, it is impossible even to define what the majority prefers. Another difficulty arises when the vote is so divided that a no choice receives a majority.
5. A practical approach to microeconomic policy will need to take a realistic view of the specific strengths and weaknesses of markets and the specific strengths and weaknesses of government, rather than making the easy, wrong assumption that either markets or government are always beneficial or always harmful.

Review Questions

1. How does rational ignorance discourage voting?
2. How can a small special-interest group win, since the benefits flow only to a small group, under a situation of majority voting?
3. How can pork-barrel spending occur, since it benefits only a small group, in a situation of majority voting?
4. Why does a voting cycle make it impossible to decide on a majority-approved choice?

Interpreting Graphs

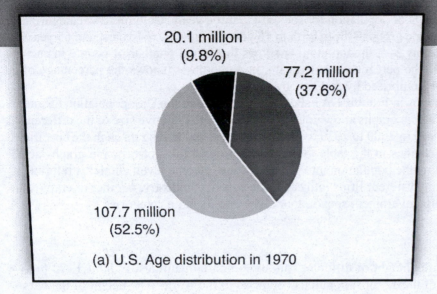

20.1 million
(9.8%)

77.2 million
(37.6%)

107.7 million
(52.5%)

(a) U.S. Age distribution in 1970

Numerical data can be presented in two ways: digital or analogue. Digital presentation uses numbers. For example, a digital clock might report the time as 3:46:11 P.M.—that is, as 46 minutes and 11 seconds after three o'clock in the afternoon. An analogue presentation uses a physical image to convey the information. An analogue clock, with an hour hand, a minute hand, and a second hand, would report the time of 3:46:11 P.M. by showing the hour hand a little before the four on the clock face, the minute hand just past the nine, and the second hand just past the two. Which presentation is best—digital or analogue? It depends on the purpose. If you are timing a runner who is training for a five-mile cross-country race, then a digital clock that clearly displays seconds is most useful. If you are on your way to 4:00 doctor's appointment and you want to know if you will make it on time, a glance at an analogue clock tells you what you need to know.

Graphs are an analogue method of presenting numerical patterns. They condense detailed numerical information into a visual form in which relationships and numerical patterns can be perceived more easily. For example, which countries have larger or smaller populations? A careful reader could examine a long list of numbers representing the populations of many countries, but with over 200 nations in the world, searching through such a list would take concentration and time. Putting these same numbers on a graph can quickly reveal population patterns. Economists use graphs both for a compact and readable presentation of groups of numbers and for building an intuitive grasp of relationships and connections.

This appendix discusses the three graphs used in this book: *pie graphs*, *bar graphs*, and *line graphs*. It also provides warnings about how graphs can be manipulated to alter viewers' perceptions of the relationships in the data.

Pie Graphs

Pie graphs (sometimes called pie charts) are used to show how an overall total is divided into parts. A circle represents a group as a whole. The slices of this circular "pie" show the relative sizes of subgroups.

Exhibit 1-A1 shows how the U.S. population is divided among children, working-age adults, and the elderly in 1970, 2000, and projected for 2030. The information is first conveyed with numbers in a table, and then in three pie charts. The first column of the table shows the total U.S. population for each of the three years. Columns 2–4 categorize the total in terms of age groups—from birth to 18 years, from 19 to 64 years, and 65 years and above. In columns 2–4, the top number shows the actual number of people in each age category, while the percentage underneath, in parentheses, shows the percentage of the total population comprised by that age group.

The three pie graphs in Exhibit 1-A1 show that the share of the U.S. population 65 and over is growing. The pie graphs allow you to get a feel for the relative size of the different age groups from 1970 to 2000 to 2030, without requiring you to slog through the specific numbers and percentages in the table. Some common examples of how pie graphs are used include dividing the population into groups by age, income level, ethnicity, religion, occupation; dividing different firms into categories by size, industry, number of employees; and dividing up government spending or taxes into its main categories.

Bar Graphs

A *bar graph* uses the height of different bars to compare quantities. Exhibit 1-A2 provides a bar graph of the 12 most populous countries in the world. The height of the bars corresponds to the population of each country. In 2014, the world population was about 7.2 billion (that is, 7,200 million) people. Although it is widely known that China and India are the most populous countries in the world, seeing how the bars on the graph tower over the other countries helps illustrate the magnitude of the difference between the sizes of national populations.

Year	Total Population	Divided into Age Groups		
		19 and Under	20–64 years	Over 65
1970	205.0	77.2 (37.6%)	107.7 (52.5%)	20.1 (9.8%)
2000	275.4	78.4 (28.5%)	162.2 (58.9%)	34.8 (12.6%)
2030	351.1	92.6 (26.4%)	188.2 (53.6%)	70.3 (20.0%)

- ■ 19 and under
- ■ 20–64 years
- ■ Over 65

(a) U.S. Age distribution in 1970   (b) U.S. age distribution in 2000   (c) U.S. age distribution in 2030

EXHIBIT 1-A1 Pie Graphs of the U.S. Age Distribution (numbers in millions)

The first column shows the total U.S. population in 1970, 2000, and projected for 2030. The next three columns divide up that total into three age groups. The three pie graphs illustrate the division of total population into these three age groups for the three years.

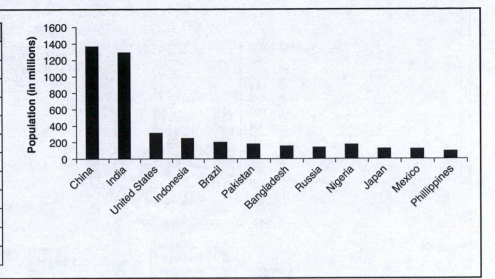

Country	Population (in millions)
China	1,369
India	1,295
United States	319
Indonesia	254
Brazil	206
Pakistan	185
Bangladesh	159
Russia	143
Nigeria	177
Japan	127
Mexico	125
Philippines	99

EXHIBIT 1-A2 Leading Countries of the World by Population, 2012 (in millions)

The table shows the 12 countries of the world with the largest population. The height of the bars in the bar graph shows the size of the population for each country.

Bar graphs can be subdivided in a way that reveals information similar to pie charts. Exhibit 1-A3 offers three bar graphs based on the information from Exhibit 1-A1 about the U.S. age distribution in 1970, 2000, and 2030. Exhibit 1-A3*a* shows three bars for each year, representing the total number of persons in each age bracket for each year. Exhibit 1-A3*b* shows just one bar for each year, but the different age groups are now shaded inside the bar. In Exhibit 1-A3*c*, still based on the same data, the vertical axis measures percentages rather than the number of persons. In this case, all three bar graphs are the same height, representing 100% of the population, with each bar divided according to the percentage of population in each age group. It is sometimes easier for the eyes of the reader to run across several bar graphs, comparing the shaded areas, rather than trying to compare several pie graphs.

Exhibits 1-A2 and 1-A3 show how the bars can represent countries or years, and how the vertical axis can represent a numerical or a percentage value. Bar graphs can also compare size, quantity, rates, distances, and other quantitative categories.

Line Graphs

To a mathematician or an economist, a "variable" is the name given to a quantity that may assume a range of values. Line graphs show a relationship between two variables: one measured on the horizontal axis and the other measured on the vertical axis.

Line Graphs with Two Variables

Exhibit 1-A4 shows the relationship between two variables: length and median weight for American baby boys and girls during the first three years of their life. (The "median" means that half of all babies weigh more than this and half weigh less.) The line graph measures length in inches on the horizontal axis and weight in pounds on the vertical axis. For example, point A on the figure shows that a boy who is 28 inches long will have a median weight of about 19 pounds. One line on the graph shows the length-weight relationship for boys and the other line shows the relationship for girls. This kind of graph is widely used by health care providers to check whether a child's physical development is roughly on track.

Exhibit 1-A5 presents another example of a line graph. In this case, the line graph shows how thin the air becomes when you climb a mountain. The horizontal axis of the

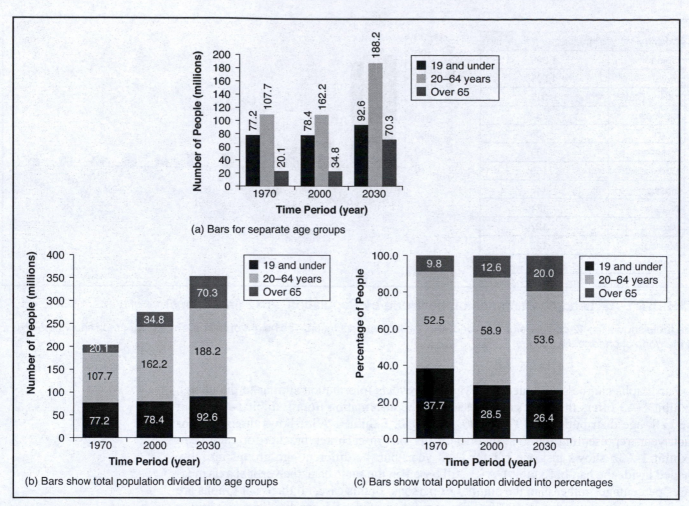

(a) Bars for separate age groups

(b) Bars show total population divided into age groups

(c) Bars show total population divided into percentages

EXHIBIT 1-A3 U.S. Population with Bar Graphs

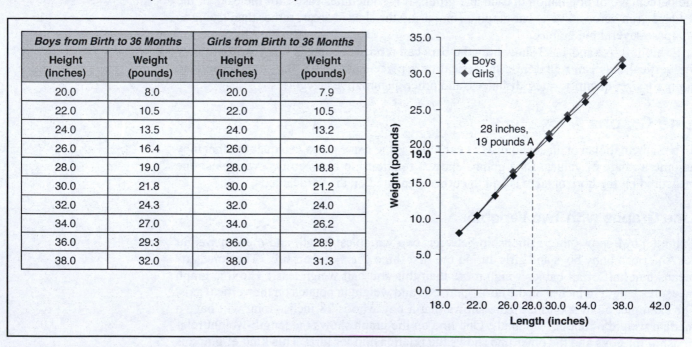

Boys from Birth to 36 Months		Girls from Birth to 36 Months	
Height (inches)	Weight (pounds)	Height (inches)	Weight (pounds)
20.0	8.0	20.0	7.9
22.0	10.5	22.0	10.5
24.0	13.5	24.0	13.2
26.0	16.4	26.0	16.0
28.0	19.0	28.0	18.8
30.0	21.8	30.0	21.2
32.0	24.3	32.0	24.0
34.0	27.0	34.0	26.2
36.0	29.3	36.0	28.9
38.0	32.0	38.0	31.3

EXHIBIT 1-A4 The Length-Weight Relationship for American Boys and Girls

The line graph shows the relationship between height and weight for boys and girls from birth to 36 months. Point A, for example, shows that a boy of 28 inches in height (measured on the horizontal axis) is typically 19 pounds in weight (measured on the vertical axis). These data apply only to children in the first three years of life.

Altitude (meters)	Air Density (kg/cubic meters)
0	1.200
500	1.093
1,000	0.831
1,500	0.678
2,000	0.569
2,500	0.484
3,000	0.415
3,500	0.357
4,000	0.307
4,500	0.231
5,000	0.182
5,500	0.142
6,000	0.100
6,500	0.085
7,000	0.066
7,500	0.051
8,000	0.041
8,500	0.025
9,000	0.022
9,500	0.019
10,000	0.014

Mount Everest (8,828 m, .023 kg/m3)

EXHIBIT 1-A5 Altitude-Air Density Relationship

This line graph shows the relationship between altitude, measured in meters above sea level, and air density, measured in kilograms of air per cubic meter. As altitude rises, air density declines. The point at the top of Mount Everest, shown in the diagram, has an altitude of approximately 8,828 meters above sea level (the horizontal axis) and air density of 0.23 kilograms per cubic meter (the vertical axis).

figure shows altitude, measured in meters above sea level. The vertical axis measures the density of the air at each altitude. Air density is measured by the weight of the air in a cubic meter of space (that is, a box measuring one meter in height, width, and depth). As the graph shows, air pressure is heaviest at ground level and becomes lighter as you climb. Exhibit 1-A5 shows that a cubic meter of air at an altitude of 500 meters weighs approximately 1 kilogram (about 2.2 pounds). However, as the altitude increases, air density decreases. A cubic meter of air at the top of Mount Everest, at about 8,828 meters, would weigh only .023 kilograms. The thin air at high altitudes explains why many mountain climbers need to breathe oxygen from tanks as they reach the top of a mountain.

The length-weight relationship and the altitude-air density relationships in these two exhibits represent averages. If you were to collect actual data on air pressure at different altitudes, the same altitude in different geographic locations will have slightly different air density, depending on factors like how far you are from the equator, the local weather conditions, and the humidity in the air. Similarly, in measuring the height and weight of children for the previous line graph, children of a particular height would have a range of different weights, some above average and some below. In the real world, this sort of variation in data is common. The task of a researcher is to organize that data in a way that helps to understand typical patterns. The study of statistics, especially when combined with computer statistics and spreadsheet programs, is a great help in organizing this kind of data, plotting line graphs, and looking for typical underlying relationships. For most economics and social science majors, a statistics course will be required at some point.

EXHIBIT 1-A6 U.S. Unemployment Rate, 1975–2015

Time Series

One common line graph is called a time series, in which the horizontal axis shows time and the vertical axis displays another variable. Thus, a time series graph shows how a variable changes over time. Exhibit 1-A6 shows the unemployment rate in the United States since 1975, where unemployment is defined as the percentage of adults who want jobs and are looking for a job, but cannot find one. The points for the unemployment rate in each year are plotted on the graph, and a line then connects the points, showing how the unemployment rate has moved up and down since 1975. The line graph makes it easy to see, for example, that the highest unemployment rate during this time period was slightly less than 10% in the early 1980s, while the unemployment rate declined from the early 1990s to the end of the 1990s, before rising and then falling back in the early 2000s, rising sharply during the recession from 2007–2009, and dropping after the end of the recession.

Slope

In discussing the shape of line graphs, the concept of slope is often helpful. Slope is defined as "rise over run." More specifically, if y is the variable on the vertical axis, x is the variable on the horizontal axis, and the Greek letter delta Δ means "the change in," then the definitions of slope is:

$$\text{Slope} = \frac{\Delta y \text{ (rise)}}{\Delta x \text{ (run)}}$$

A *positive slope* means that as a line on the line graph moves from left to right, the line rises. The length-weight relationship in Exhibit 1-A4 has a positive slope. A negative slope means that as the line on the line graph moves from left to right, the line falls. The altitude-air density relationship in Exhibit 1-A5 has a *negative slope*. A slope of zero means that the line is flat—that is, zero rise over the run. Exhibit 1-A6 of the unemployment rate illustrates a common pattern of many line graphs: some segments where the slope is positive, other segments where the slope is negative, and still other segments where the slope is close to zero.

The slope of a straight line between two points can be calculated in numerical terms. To calculate slope, begin by designating one point as the "starting point" and the other point as the "end point" and then calculating the rise over run between these two points.

As an example, consider the slope of the air density graph between the points representing an altitude of 4,000 meters and an altitude of 6,000 meters:

Rise: Change in variable on vertical axis (end point minus original point)
$$= .100 - .307 = -.207$$

Run: Change in variable on horizontal axis (end point minus original point)
$$= 6,000 - 4,000 = 2,000$$

Thus, the slope of a straight line between these two points would be that from the altitude of 4,000 meters up to 6,000 meters, the density of the air decreases by approximately .1 kilograms/cubic meter for each of the next 1,000 meters.

Many graphs of data are not perfectly straight lines, at least not in all places, so that trying to draw a single straight line will not accurately capture the relationship between the two variables. For example, the true relationship between altitude and air density in Exhibit 1-A5 is a curve, not a straight line. However, you can draw a close approximation of a curved line by using a series of many short straight lines with different slopes. Thus, it is common to calculate the slope of a part of a curved line by choosing a starting point and an ending point that are quite close together, in which case the slope of the straight line between those two close points will offer a good approximation of the slope of the curved line between those two points. A straight line will have the same slope, regardless of what starting point and end point you choose; in contrast, a curved line will have different slopes depending on what starting point and end point you choose.

A higher positive slope means a steeper upward tilt to the line, while a smaller positive slope means a flatter upward tilt to the line. A negative slope that is larger in absolute value (that is, more negative) means a steeper downward tilt to the line. A slope of zero is a horizontal flat line. A vertical line has an infinite slope.

Slope of Straight Lines in Algebraic Terms

Straight lines can also be expressed as an algebraic formula, and when they are, the slope is easily visible in the formula. The algebraic equation for a straight line is

$$y = a + bx$$

where x and y are the variables, with x on the horizontal axis and y on the vertical axis, and a and b representing factors that determine the shape of the line. To see how this equation works, consider a numerical example:

$$y = 9 + 3x$$

In this equation for a specific line, the a term has been set equal to 9 and the b term has been set equal to 3. Exhibit 1-A7 shows this equation with a table and a graph. To construct

x	y
0	9
1	12
2	15
3	18
4	21
5	24
6	27

EXHIBIT 1-A7 Slope and the Algebra of Straight Lines

This line graph has x on the horizontal axis and y on the vertical axis. The y-intercept—that is, the point where the line intersects the y-axis—is 9. The slope of the line is 3; that is, there is a rise of 3 on the vertical axis for every increase of 1 on the horizontal axis. The slope is the same all along a straight line.

the table, just plug in a series of different values for *x*, and then calculate what value of *y* results. In the figure, these points are plotted and a line is drawn through them.

This example illustrates how the *a* and *b* terms in an equation for a straight line determine the shape of the line. The *a* term is called the *y-intercept*. The reason for this name is that if *x* = 0, then the *a* term will reveal where the line intercepts, or crosses, the vertical or *y*-axis. In this example, the line hits the vertical axis at 9. The *b* term in the equation for the line is the slope. Remember that slope is defined as rise over run; more specifically, the change in the vertical axis divided by the change in the horizontal axis. In this example, each time the *x* term increases by 1 (the run), the *y* term rises by 3. Thus, the slope of this line is 3. Specifying a *y*-intercept and a slope—that is, specifying *a* and *b* in the equation for a line—will identify a specific line. Although it is rare for real-world data points to arrange themselves as an exact straight line, it often turns out that a straight line can offer a reasonable approximation of actual data.

Comparing Line Graphs with Pie Charts and Bar Graphs

Now that you are familiar with pie graphs, bar graphs, and line graphs, how do you know which graph to use for your data? Pie graphs are often better than line graphs at showing how an overall group is divided. However, if a pie graph has too many slices, it can become difficult to interpret.

Bar graphs are especially useful when comparing quantities. For example, if you are studying the populations of different countries, as in Exhibit 1-A2, bar graphs can show the relationships between the population sizes of multiple countries. Not only can it show these relationships, but it can also show breakdowns of different groups within the population.

A line graph is often the most effective format for illustrating a relationship between two variables that are both changing. For example, time series graphs can show patterns as time changes, like the unemployment rate over time. Line graphs are widely used in economics to present continuous data about prices, wages, quantities bought and sold, the size of the economy, and other economic variables.

How Graphs Can Mislead

Graphs not only reveal patterns; they can also alter how patterns are perceived. To see some of the ways this can be done, consider the line graphs of Exhibit 1-A8. These graphs all illustrate the unemployment rate—but from different perspectives.

Imagine that you wanted a graph which gives an impression that the rise in unemployment in 2009 wasn't all that large, or all that extraordinary by historical standards. You might choose to present your data as in Exhibit 1-A8*a*. Exhibit 1-A8*a* shows the exact data presented earlier in Exhibit 1-A6, but stretches the horizontal axis out longer relative to the vertical axis. By spreading the graph wide and flat, the visual appearance is that the rise in unemployment isn't so large, and similar to some past rises in unemployment.

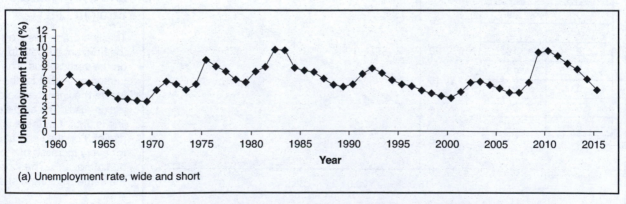

(a) Unemployment rate, wide and short

EXHIBIT 1-A8 Presenting Unemployment Rates in Different Ways, All of Them Accurate

Now imagine you wanted to emphasize how unemployment spiked substantially higher in 2009. In this case, using the same data, you can stretch the vertical axis out relative to the horizontal axis, as in Exhibit 1-A8*b*, which makes all rises and falls in unemployment appear sharper.

A similar effect can be accomplished without changing the length of the axes, but by changing the scale on the vertical axis. In Exhibit 1-A8*c*, the scale on the vertical axis runs from 0% to 30%, while in Exhibit 1-A8*d*, the vertical axis runs from 3% to 10%. Compared to Exhibit 1-A6, where the vertical scale runs from 0% to 12%, Exhibit 1-A8*c*

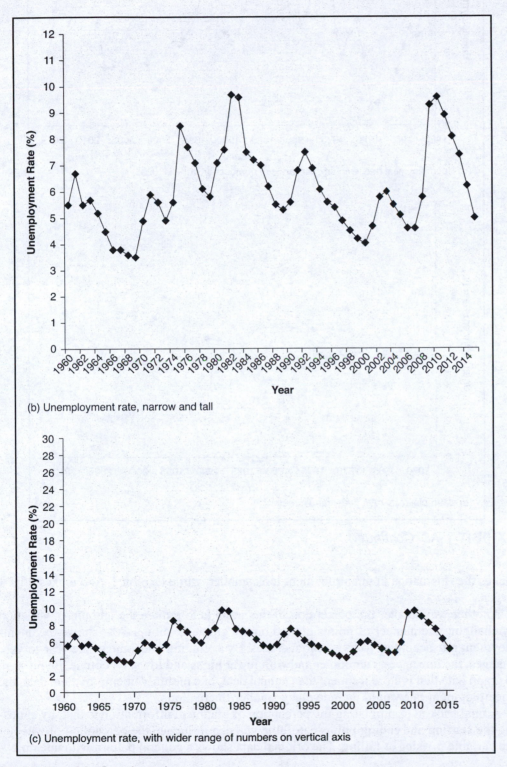

(b) Unemployment rate, narrow and tall

(c) Unemployment rate, with wider range of numbers on vertical axis

EXHIBIT 1-A8 *Continued*

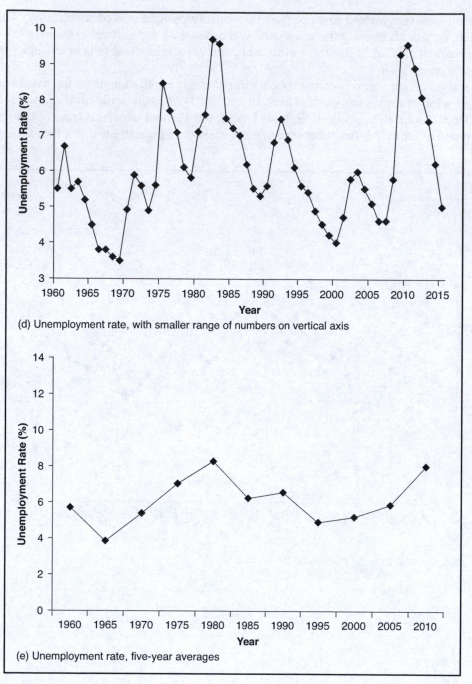

(d) Unemployment rate, with smaller range of numbers on vertical axis

(e) Unemployment rate, five-year averages

EXHIBIT 1-A8 *Continued*

makes the fluctuation in unemployment look smaller, while Exhibit 1-A8*d* makes it look larger.

Another way to alter the perception of the graph is to reduce the amount of variation by changing the number of points plotted on the graph. Exhibit 1-A8*e* shows the unemployment rate according to five-year averages. By averaging out some of the year-to-year changes, the line appears smoother and with fewer highs and lows. Of course, if you were to graph data that is more frequent than annual data, like monthly unemployment data, the unemployment rate would include many smaller fluctuations.

A final trick in manipulating the perception of graphical information is that, by choosing the starting and ending points carefully, you can influence the perception of whether the variable is rising or falling. The original data shows a general pattern with unemploy-

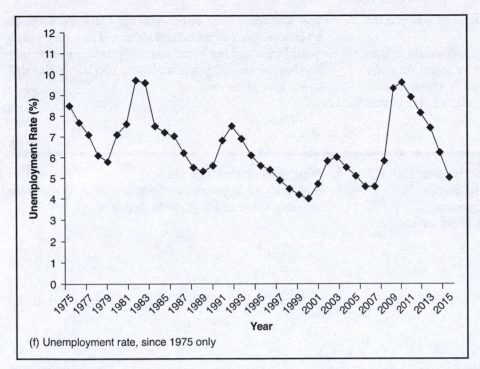

(f) Unemployment rate, since 1975 only

EXHIBIT 1-A8 *Continued*

ment low in the 1960s, but spiking up in the mid-1970s, early 1980s, early 1990s, early 2000s, and late 2000s. But Exhibit 1-A8*f* shows a graph that goes back only to 1975, which gives an impression that unemployment was more-or-less gradually falling over time until the 2009 recession pushed it back up to its "original" level—which is a plausible interpretation if one starts at the high point around 1975.

These kinds of tricks—or shall we just call them "choices about presentation"?— are not limited to line graphs. In a pie chart with many small slices and one large slice, someone must decide what categories should be used to produce these slices in the first place, thus making some slices appear bigger than others. If you are making a bar graph, you can make the vertical axis either taller or shorter, which will tend to make variations in the height of the bars appear more or less.

Being able to read graphs is an essential skill, both in economics and in life. But a graph is just one perspective or point of view, shaped by choices such as those discussed in this section. Don't always believe the first quick impression from a graph. View with caution.

Summary and Key Concepts

1. Graphs allow you to illustrate data graphically. They can illustrate patterns, comparisons, trends, and apportionment by condensing the numerical data and providing an intuitive sense of relationships in the data.

2. A *pie graph* shows how something is allotted, such as a sum of money or a group of people. The size of each slice of the pie is drawn to represent the corresponding percentage of the whole.

3. A *bar graph* uses the height of bars to show a relationship, where each bar represents a certain entity, like a country or a group of people. The bars on a bar graph can also be divided into segments to show subgroups.

4. A *line graph* shows the relationship between two variables: one is shown on the horizontal axis and one on the vertical axis.

5. Slope means "rise over run." The slope of the line on a line graph can be positive (upward-sloping), negative (downward-sloping), zero (flat), or infinite (vertical). The slope of a line on a graph may vary: for example, it may be positive in some segments, zero in other segments, and negative in other segments.

6. The algebraic equation for a line is $y = a + bx$, where x is the variable on the horizontal axis and y is the variable on the vertical axis, the *a* term is the *y-intercept*

and the *b* term is the slope. The slope of a line is the same at any point on the line.

7. Any graph is a single visual perspective on a subject. The impression it leaves will be based on many choices like what data or time frame is included, how data or groups are divided up, the relative size of vertical and horizontal axes, whether the scale used on a vertical starts at zero, and others. Thus, any graph should be regarded somewhat skeptically, remembering that the underlying relationship can be open to different interpretations.

Review Questions

1. Name three kinds of graphs and briefly state when it is most appropriate to use each type of graph.
2. What do the slices of a pie chart represent?
3. Why is a bar chart the best way to illustrate comparisons?
4. What is slope on a line graph?
5. How does the appearance of positive slope differ from negative slope and from zero slope?

Indifference Curves

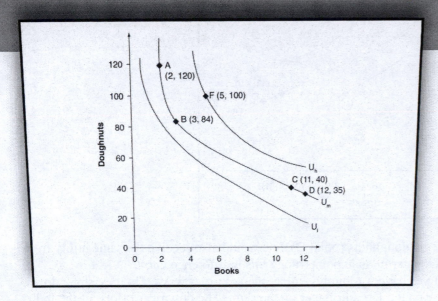

Economists use a vocabulary of maximizing utility to describe people's preferences. In Chapter 8, the level of utility that a person receives is described in numerical terms. This appendix presents an alternative approach to describing personal preferences, called indifference curves, which avoids any need for using numbers to measure utility. By setting aside the assumption of putting a numerical valuation on utility—an assumption that many students and economists find uncomfortably unrealistic—the indifference curve framework helps to clarify the logic of the underlying model.

What Is an Indifference Curve?

People can't place a numerical value on their level of satisfaction. However, they can and do identify what choices would give them more, or less, or the same amount of satisfaction. An indifference curve shows combinations of goods that provide an equal level of utility or satisfaction. For example, Exhibit 8-A1 presents three indifference curves that represent Lilly's preferences for the trade-offs that she faces in her two main relaxation activities: eating doughnuts and reading paperback books. Each indifference curve, U_L, U_M, and U_H, represents one level of utility. Let's first explore the meaning of one particular indifference curve, and then look at the indifference curves as a group.

The Shape of an Indifference Curve

The indifference curve U_M has four points labeled on it: A, B, C, and D. Since an indifference curve represents a set of choices that have the same level of utility, Lilly must receive an equal amount of utility, judged according to her personal preferences, from 2 books and 120 doughnuts (point A), from 3 books and 84 doughnuts (point B), from 11 books and 40 doughnuts (point C), or

EXHIBIT 8-A1 Lilly's Indifference Curves

Lilly would receive equal utility from all points on a given indifference curve. Any points on the highest indifference curve U_H, like F, provide greater utility than any points like A, B, C, and D on the middle indifference curve U_M. Similarly, any points on the middle indifference curve U_M provide greater utility than any points on the lowest indifference curve U_L.

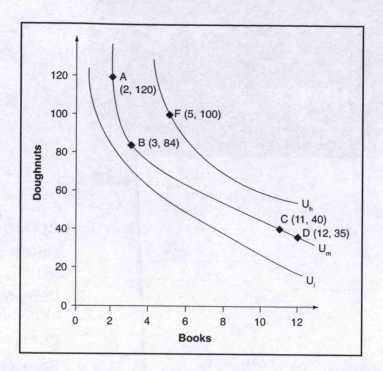

from 12 books and 35 doughnuts (point D). She would also receive the same utility from any of the unlabeled intermediate points along this indifference curve.

Indifference curves have a roughly similar shape in two ways: (1) they slope down; (2) they are steeper on the left and flatter on the right. The downward slope of the indifference curve means that as less of the good on the vertical axis (doughnuts) is consumed, if Lilly's utility is to remain the same, it will be necessary to have more consumption of the good on the vertical axis (in this case, books). For example, points A and B sit on the same indifference curve U_M, which means that they provide Lilly with the same level of utility. Thus, the marginal utility that Lilly would gain from, say, increasing her number of books from 2 to 3 must be equal to the marginal utility that she would lose if her number of doughnuts was cut from 120 to 84—so that her overall utility remains unchanged between points A and B. Indeed, the slope along an indifference curve is referred to as the *marginal rate of substitution*, which is the rate at which a person is willing to trade one good for another so that utility will remain the same.

Indifference curves like U_M are steeper on the left and flatter on the right. The reason behind this shape involves diminishing marginal utility—the notion that as a person consumes more of a good, the marginal utility from each additional unit becomes lower. Compare two different choices between points that all provide Lilly an equal amount of utility along the indifference curve U_M: the choice between A and B, and between C to D. In both choices, Lilly consumes one more book, but between A and B her consumption of doughnuts falls by 36 (from 120 to 84) and between C and D it falls by only 5 (from 40 to 35). The reason for this difference is that points A and C are different starting points, and thus have different implications for marginal utility. At point A, Lilly has few books and many doughnuts. Thus, her marginal utility from an extra book will be relatively high while the marginal utility of additional doughnuts is relatively low—so on the margin, it will take a relatively large number of doughnuts to offset the utility from the marginal book. At point C, however, Lilly has many books and few doughnuts. From this starting point, her marginal utility gained from extra books will be relatively low, while the marginal utility lost from additional doughnuts would be relatively high—so on the margin, it will take a relatively smaller number of doughnuts to offset the change of one marginal book. In short, the slope of the indifference curve changes because the marginal rate of substitution—that is, the quantity of one good that would be traded for the other good to keep utility constant—also changes, as a result of diminishing marginal utility of both goods.

The Field of Indifference Curves

Each indifference curve represents the choices that provide a single level of utility. Every level of utility will have its own indifference curve. Thus, Lilly's preferences will include an infinite number of indifference curves lying nestled together on the diagram—even though only three of the indifference curves representing three levels of utility appear on Exhibit 8-A1. In other words, an infinite number of indifference curves are not drawn on this diagram—but you should remember that they exist.

Higher indifference curves represent a greater level of utility than lower ones. In Exhibit 8-A1, indifference curve U_L can be thought of as a "low" level of utility, while U_M is a "medium" level of utility and U_H is a "high" level of utility. All of the choices on indifference curve U_H are preferred to all of the choices on indifference curve U_M, which in turn are preferred to all of the choices on U_L.

To understand why higher indifference curves are preferred to lower ones, compare point B on indifference curve U_M to point F on indifference curve U_H. Point F has greater consumption of both books (5 to 3) and doughnuts (100 to 84), so F is clearly preferable to point B. Given the definition of an indifference curve—that *all* the points on the curve have the same level of utility—if point F on indifference curve U_H is preferred to point B on indifference curve U_M, then it must be true that all points on indifference curve U_H have a higher level of utility than all points on U_M. More generally, for any point on a lower indifference curve, like U_L, you can identify a point on a higher indifference curve like U_M or U_H that has a higher consumption of both goods. Since one point on the higher indifference curve is preferred to one point on the lower curve, and since all the points on a given indifference curve have the same level of utility, it must be true that all points on higher indifference curves have greater utility than all points on lower indifference curves.

These arguments about the shapes of indifference curves and about higher or lower levels of utility do not require any numerical estimates of utility, either by the individual or by anyone else. They are only based on the assumptions that when people have less of one good, they need more of another good to make up for it if they are keeping the same level of utility, and that as people have more of a good, the marginal utility they receive from additional units of that good will diminish. Given these gentle assumptions, a field of indifference curves can be mapped out to describe the preferences of any individual.

The Individuality of Indifference Curves

Each person determines their own preferences and utility. Thus, while indifference curves have the same general shape—they slope down, and the slope is steeper on the left and flatter on the right—the specific shape of indifference curves can be different for every person. Exhibit 8-A1, for example, applies only to Lilly's preferences. Indifference curves for other people would travel through different points.

Utility-Maximizing with Indifference Curves

People seek the highest level of utility, which means that they wish to be on the highest possible indifference curve. However, people are limited by their budget constraints, which show what trade-offs are actually possible.

Maximizing Utility at the Highest Indifference Curve

Return to the situation of Lilly's choice between paperback books and doughnuts. Say that books cost $6, doughnuts are 50 cents apiece, and that Lilly has $60 to spend. This information provides the basis for the budget line shown in Exhibit 8-A2. Along with the budget line are shown the three indifference curves from Exhibit 8-A1. What is Lilly's utility-maximizing choice? Several possibilities are identified in the diagram.

The choice of F with 5 books and 100 doughnuts is highly desirable, since it is on the highest indifference curve U_H of those shown in the diagram. However, it isn't affordable

EXHIBIT 8-A2 Indifference Curves and a Budget Constraint

Lilly's preferences are shown by the indifference curves. Lilly's budget constraint, given the prices of books and doughnuts and her income, is shown by the straight line. Lilly's optimal choice will be point B, where the budget line is tangent to the indifference curve U_M. Lilly would have more utility at a point like F on the higher indifference curve U_H, but the budget line does not touch the higher indifference curve U_H at any point, so she cannot afford this choice. A choice like G is affordable to Lilly, but it lies on indifference curve U_L and thus provides less utility than choice B, which is on indifference curve U_M.

given Lilly's budget constraint. The choice of H with 3 books and 70 doughnuts on indifference curve U_L is a wasteful choice, since it is inside Lilly's budget set, and as a utility-maximizer, Lilly will always prefer a choice on the budget constraint itself. Choices B and G are both on the opportunity set. However, choice G of 6 books and 48 doughnuts is on lower indifference curve U_L than choice B of 3 books and 84 doughnuts, which is on the indifference curve U_M. If Lilly were to start at choice G, and then thought about whether the marginal utility she was deriving from doughnuts and books, she would decide that some additional doughnuts and fewer books would make her happier—which would cause her to move toward her preferred choice B. Given the combination of Lilly's personal preferences as identified by her indifference curves and Lilly's opportunity set, which is determined by prices and income, B will be her utility-maximizing choice.

The highest achievable indifference curve touches the opportunity set at a single point of tangency. Since an infinite number of indifference curves exist, even if only a few of them are drawn on any given diagram, there will always exist one indifference curve that touches the budget line at a single point of tangency. All higher indifference curves like U_H will be completely above the budget line, and although the choices on that indifference curve would provide higher utility, they aren't affordable given the budget set. All lower indifference curves, like U_L, will cross the budget line in two separate places. But when one indifference curve crosses the budget line in two places, there will be another, higher attainable indifference curve sitting above it that touches the budget line at only one point of tangency.

Changes in Income

A rise in income causes the budget constraint to shift to the right. In graphical terms, the new budget constraint will now be tangent to a higher indifference curve, representing

EXHIBIT 8-A3

Manuel and Natasha originally face the same budget constraints; that is, same prices and same income. However, the indifference curves that illustrate their preferences are not the same.

(a) Manuel's reaction to more income

Manuel's original choice at W involves more yogurt and more movies, and he reacts to the higher income by mainly increasing consumption of movies at X.

(b) Natasha's reaction to more income

Conversely, Natasha's original choice Y involves relatively more movies, but she reacts to the higher income by choosing relatively more yogurts. Even when budget constraints are the same, personal preferences lead to different original choices and to different reactions in response to a change in income.

a higher level of utility. A reduction in income will cause the budget constraint to shift to the left, which will cause it to be tangent to a lower indifference curve, representing a reduced level of utility. But if income rises by, say, 50%, exactly how much will a person alter consumption of books and doughnuts? Will consumption of both goods rise by 50%? Or the quantity of one good rises substantially, while the quantity of the other good rises only a little, or even declines?

Since personal preferences and the shape of indifference curves are different for each individual, the response to changes in income will be different, too. For example, consider the preferences of Manuel and Natasha in Exhibit 8-A3a and Exhibit 8-A3b. They each start with an identical income of $40, which they spend on yogurts that cost $1 and rental movies that cost $4. Thus, they face identical budget constraints. However, based on Manuel's preferences as revealed by his indifference curves, his utility-maximizing choice on the original budget set occurs where his opportunity set is tangent to the highest possible indifference curve at W, with 3 movies and 28 yogurts, while Natasha's utility-maximizing choice on the original budget set at Y will be 7 movies and 12 yogurts.

Now say that income rises to $60 for both Manuel and Natasha, so their budget constraints shift to the right. As shown in Exhibit 8-A3a, Manuel's new utility-maximizing choice at X will be 7 movies and 32 yogurts—that is, Manuel will choose to spend most of the extra income on movies. Natasha's new utility maximizing choice at Z will be 8 movies and 28 yogurts—that is, she will choose to spend most of the extra income on yogurt. In this way, the indifference curve approach allows for a range of possible responses. However, if both goods are normal goods, then the typical response to a higher level of income will be to purchase more of them—although exactly how much more is a matter of personal preference. If one of the goods is an inferior good, the response to a higher level of income will be to purchase less of it.

Responses to Price Changes: Substitution and Income Effects

A higher price for a good will cause the budget constraint to shift to the left, so that it is tangent to a lower indifference curve representing a reduced level of utility. Conversely, a lower price for a good will cause the opportunity set to shift to the right, so that it is tangent to a higher indifference curve representing an increased level of utility. Exactly how much a change in price will lead to the quantity demanded of each good will depend on personal preferences.

Anyone who faces a change in price will experience two interlinked motivations: a *substitution effect* and an *income effect*. The *substitution effect* is that when a good becomes more expensive, people seek out substitutes. If oranges become more expensive, fruit-lovers scale back on oranges and eat more apples or grapefruit or raisins. Conversely, when a good becomes cheaper, people substitute toward consuming more. If oranges get cheaper, people fire up their juicing machines and ease off on other fruits and foods. The *income effect* refers to how a change in the price of a good alters the effective buying power of one's income. If the price of a good that you have been buying falls, then in effect your buying power has risen—you are able to purchase more goods. Conversely, if the price of a good that you have been buying rises, then the buying power of a given amount of income is diminished. (One common confusion is that the "income effect" doesn't refer to a change in actual income. Instead, it refers to the situation in which the price of a good changes, and thus the quantities of goods that can be purchased with a fixed amount of income change. It might be more accurate to call the "income effect" a "buying power effect," but the "income effect" terminology has been used for decades, and it isn't going to change during this economics course.) Whenever a price changes, consumers feel the pull of both substitution and income effects at the same time.

Using indifference curves, you can illustrate the substitution and income effects on a graph. In Exhibit 8-A4, Ogden faces a choice between two goods: haircuts or personal pizzas. Haircuts cost $20, personal pizzas cost $6, and he has $120 to spend. The price of haircuts rises to $30. Ogden starts at choice A on the higher opportunity set and the

EXHIBIT 8-A4 Substitution and Income Effects

The original choice is A, the point of tangency between the original budget constraint and indifference curve. The new choice is B, the point of tangency between the new budget constraint and the lower indifference curve. Point C is the tangency between the dashed line, where the slope shows the new higher price of haircuts, and the original indifference curve. The substitution effect is the shift from A to C, which means getting fewer haircuts, which have become relatively more expensive, and more pizza, which is relatively less expensive. The income effect is the shift from C to B; that is, the reduction in buying power that causes a shift from the higher indifference curve to the lower indifference curve, with relative prices remaining unchanged. The income effect of lower buying power results in less consumed of both goods. Both substitution and income effects cause fewer haircuts to be consumed. For pizza, in this case, the substitution effect causing more pizza and income effect causing less pizza cancel out, leading to the same amount of pizza consumed.

higher indifference curve. After the price of pizza increases, he chooses B on the lower opportunity set and the lower indifference curve. Point B with 2 haircuts and 10 personal pizzas is immediately below point A with 3 haircuts and 10 personal pizzas, showing that Ogden reacted to a higher price of haircuts by cutting back only on haircuts, while leaving his consumption of pizza unchanged.

The dashed line in the diagram, and point C, are used to separate the substitution effect and the income effect. To understand their function, start by thinking about the substitution effect with this question: How would Ogden change his consumption if the relative prices of the two goods changed, but this change in relative prices did not affect his utility? The slope of the budget constraint is determined by the relative price of the two goods; thus, the slope of the original budget line is determined by the original relative prices, while the slope of the new budget line is determined by the new relative prices. With this thought in mind, the dashed line is a graphical tool inserted in a specific way: It is inserted so that it is parallel with the new budget constraint, so it reflects the new relative prices, but it is tangent to the original indifference curve, so it reflects the original level of utility or buying power.

Thus, the movement from the original choice A to point C is a substitution effect; it shows the choice that Ogden would make if relative prices shifted (as shown by the different slope between the original budget set and the dashed line) but if buying power did not shift (as shown by being tangent to the original indifference curve). The substitution effect will encourage people to shift away from the good that has become relatively more expensive—in Ogden's case, the haircuts on the vertical axis, and toward the good that has become relatively less expensive—in this case, the pizza on the vertical axis. The two arrows labeled with s for "substitution effect," one on each axis, show the direction of this movement.

The income effect is the movement from point C to B, which shows how Ogden reacts to a reduction in his buying power from the higher indifference curve to the lower indifference curve, but holding constant the relative prices (because the dashed line has the same slope as the new budget constraint). In this case where the price of one good increases, buying power is reduced, so the income effect means that consumption of both goods should fall (if they are both normal goods, which it is reasonable to assume unless there is reason to believe otherwise). The two arrows labeled with i for "income effect," one on each axis, show the direction of this income effect movement.

Now put the substitution and income effects together. When the price of pizza increased, Ogden consumed less of it, for two reasons shown in the exhibit: the substitution effect of the higher price led him to consume less, and the income effect of the higher price also led him to consume less. However, when the price of pizza increased, Ogden consumed the same quantity of haircuts. The substitution effect of a higher price for pizza meant that haircuts became relatively less expensive (compared to pizza), and this factor taken alone would have encouraged Ogden to consume more haircuts. However, the income effect of a higher price for pizza meant that he wished to consume less of both goods, and this factor taken alone would have encouraged Ogden to consume fewer haircuts. As shown in the exhibit, in this particular example the substitution effect and income effect on Ogden's consumption of haircuts are offsetting—so he ends up consuming the same quantity of haircuts after the price increase for pizza as before.

The size of these income and substitution effects will differ from person to person, depending on individual preferences. For example, if Ogden's substitution effect away from pizza and toward haircuts is especially strong, and outweighs the income effect, then a higher price for pizza might lead to increased consumption of haircuts. This case would be drawn on the graph so that the point of tangency between the new budget constraint and the relevant indifference curve occurred below point B and to the right. Conversely, if the substitution effect away from pizza and toward haircuts is not as strong, and the income effect on haircuts is relatively stronger, then Ogden will be more likely to react to the higher price of pizza by consuming less of both goods. In this case, his optimal choice after the price change will be above and to the left of choice B on the new budget constraint.

Although the substitution and income effects are often discussed as a sequence of events, it should be remembered that they are twin components of a single cause—a change in price. Although you can analyze them separately, the two effects are always proceeding hand in hand, happening at the same time.

Indifference Curves with Labor-Leisure and Intertemporal Choices

The concept of an indifference curve applies to trade-offs in any household choice, including the labor-leisure choice or the intertemporal choice between present and future consumption. In the labor-leisure choice, each indifference curve shows the combinations of leisure and income that provide a certain level of utility. In an intertemporal choice, each indifference curve shows the combinations of present and future consumption that provide a certain level of utility. The general shapes of the indifference curves—downward sloping, steeper on the left, and flatter on the right—also remain the same.

A Labor-Leisure Example

Petunia is working at a job that pays $12 per hour but she gets a raise to $20 per hour. After family responsibilities and sleep, she has 80 hours per week available for work or leisure. As shown in Exhibit 8-A5, the highest level of utility for Petunia on her original budget constraint is at choice A, where it is tangent to the lower indifference curve U_L. Point A has 30 hours of leisure and thus 50 hours per week of work, with income of $600 per week (that is, 50 hours of work times $12 per hour). Petunia then gets a raise to $20 per hour, which shifts her budget constraint to the right. Her new utility-maximizing choice occurs where the new budget constraint is tangent to the higher indifference curve U_L. At B, Petunia has 40 hours of leisure per week and works 40 hours, with income of $800 per week (that is, 40 hours of work times $20 per hour).

Substitution and income effects provide a vocabulary for discussing how Petunia reacts to a higher hourly wage. The dashed line serves as the tool for separating the two effects on the graph.

The substitution effect tells how Petunia would have changed her hours of work if her wage had risen, so that income was relatively cheaper to earn and leisure was relatively more expensive, but if she had remained at the same level of utility. The slope of the budget constraint in a labor-leisure diagram is determined by the wage rate. Thus, the dashed line is carefully inserted with the slope of the new opportunity set, reflecting the labor-leisure trade-off of the new wage rate, but tangent to the original indifference curve, showing the same level of utility or "buying power." The shift from original choice A to point C, which is the point of tangency between the original indifference curve and the dashed line, shows that because of the higher wage, Petunia will want to consume less leisure and more income. The s arrows on the horizontal and vertical axes of Exhibit 8-A5 show the substitution effect on leisure and on income.

The income effect is that the higher wage, by shifting the labor-leisure budget constraint to the right, makes it possible for Petunia to reach a higher level of utility. The income effect is the movement from point C to point B; that is, it shows how Petunia's behavior would change in response to a higher level of utility or "buying power," with the wage rate remaining the same (as shown by the dashed line being parallel to the new budget constraint). The income effect, encouraging Petunia to consume both more leisure and more income, is drawn with arrows on the horizontal and vertical axis of Exhibit 8-A5.

Putting these effects together, Petunia responds to the higher wage by moving from choice A to choice B. This movement involves choosing more income, both because the substitution effect of higher wages has made income relatively cheaper or easier to earn, and because the income effect of higher wages has made it possible to have more income and more leisure. Her movement from A to B also involves choosing more leisure because according to Petunia's preferences, the income effect that encourages choosing more leisure is stronger than the substitution effect that encourages choosing less leisure.

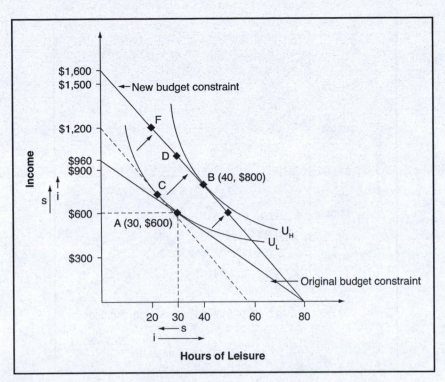

EXHIBIT 8-A5 Effects of a Change in Petunia's Wage

Petunia starts at choice A, the tangency between her original budget constraint and the lower indifference curve U_L. The wage increase shifts her budget constraint to the right, so that she can now choose B on indifference curve U_L. The substitution effect is the movement from A to C. It shows how Petunia would have changed her behavior if she had faced the new wage—which is represented by the dashed line having the same slope as the new budget line—but remained on the original indifference curve. In this case, the substitution effect would lead Petunia to choose less leisure, which is relatively more expensive, and more income, which is relatively cheaper to earn. The income effect is the movement from C to B. It shows how Petunia would change her behavior with the greater "buying power" of a higher wage, thus allowing a move to a higher indifference curve, but without a change in relative prices. The income effect in this example leads to greater consumption of both goods. Overall, in this example, income rises because of both substitution and income effects. However, leisure declines because of the substitution effect but increases because of the income effect—leading in Petunia's case to an overall increase in the quantity of leisure consumed.

But Exhibit 8-A5 represents only Petunia's preferences, and other people might make other choices. For example, a person whose substitution and income effects on leisure exactly counterbalanced each other would react to a higher wage with a choice like D, exactly above the original choice A, which means taking all of the benefit of the higher wages in the form of income while working the same number of hours. Yet another person, whose substitution effect on leisure outweighed the income effect, might react to a higher wage by making a choice like F, where the response to higher wages is to work more hours and earn much more income. To represent these different preferences, you could easily draw the indifference curve U_H to be tangent to the new budget constraint at D or F, rather than at B.

An Intertemporal Choice Example

Quentin has saved up $10,000. He is thinking about spending some or all of it on a vacation in the present, and then will save the rest for another big vacation five years from now. Over those five years, he expects to earn a total 80% rate of return. Exhibit 8-A6 shows Quentin's budget constraint and his indifference curves between present consumption and future consumption. The highest level of utility that Quentin can achieve at his original intertemporal budget constraint occurs at point A, where he is consuming $6,000,

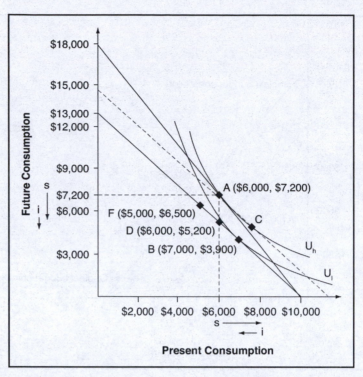

EXHIBIT 8-A6 Indifference Curve and an Intertemporal Budget Constraint

The original choice is A, at the tangency between the original budget constraint and the original indifference curve U_L. The dashed line is drawn parallel to the new budget set, so that its slope reflects the lower rate of return, but is tangent to the original indifference curve. The movement from A to C is the substitution effect: in this case, future consumption has become relatively more expensive, and present consumption has become relatively cheaper. The income effect is the shift from C to B; that is, the reduction in utility or "buying power" that causes a move to a lower indifference curve U_L, but with the relative price the same. It means less present and less future consumption. In the move from A to B, the substitution effect on present consumption is greater than the income effect, so the overall result is more present consumption. But notice that the lower indifference curve could have been drawn tangent to the lower budget constraint point D or point F, depending on personal preferences.

saving $4,000 for the future, and expecting with the accumulated interest to have $7,200 for future consumption (that is, $4,000 in current financial savings plus the 80% rate of return).

However, Quentin has just realized that his expected rate of return was unrealistically high. A more realistic expectation is that over five years he can earn a total return of 30%. In effect, his intertemporal budget constraint has pivoted to the left, so that his original utility-maximizing choice is no longer available. Will Quentin react to the lower rate of return by saving more, or less, or the same amount? Again, the language of substitution and income effects provides a framework for thinking about the motivations behind various choices. The dashed line, which is a graphical tool to separate the substitution and income effect, is carefully inserted with the same slope as the new opportunity set, so that it reflects the changed rate of return, but it is tangent to the original indifference curve, so that it shows no change in utility or "buying power."

The substitution effect tells how Quentin would have altered his consumption because the lower rate of return makes future consumption relatively more expensive and present consumption relatively cheaper. The movement from the original choice A to point C shows how Quentin substitutes toward more present consumption and less future consumption in response to the lower interest rate, with no change in utility. The substitution arrows on the horizontal and vertical axes of Exhibit 8-A6 show the direction of the substitution effect motivation. The substitution effect suggests that because of the lower interest rate, Quentin should consume more in the present and less in the future.

A Step-by-Step Guide to Sketching Substitution and Income Effects

If you are finding it a little tricky to sketch diagrams that show substitution and income effects so that the dashed line and the various points of tangency all come out correctly, it may be useful to follow this procedure.

Step 1: Begin with a budget constraint showing the choice between two goods, which this example will call "candy" and "movies." Choose a point A, which will be the optimal choice, where the indifference curve will be tangent—but it is often easier not to draw in the indifference curve just yet.

Draw the budget constraint. Insert optimal choice A.

Step 2: Now the price of movies changes: let's say that it rises. That shifts the budget set inward. You know that the higher price will push the decision-maker down to a lower level of utility, represented by a lower indifference curve. But at this stage, draw only the new budget set.

Draw the new budget constraint.

Step 3: The key tool in distinguishing between substitution and income effects is to insert a dashed line, parallel to the new budget line. This line is a graphical tool that allows you to distinguish between the two changes: (1) the effect on consumption of the two goods of the shift in prices—with the level of utility remaining unchanged—which is the substitution effect; and (2) the effect on consumption of the two goods of shifting from one indifference curve to the other—with relative prices staying unchanged—which is the income effect. The dashed line is inserted in this step. The trick is to have the dashed line travel close to the original choice A, but not directly through point A.

Draw in the dashed line, parallel to the new budget line, but crossing the original budget line near original choice A.

Step 4: Now draw the original indifference curve, so that it is tangent to both point A on the original budget line and to a point C on the dashed line. Many students find it easiest to first select the tangency point C where the original indifference curve touches the dashed line, and then to draw the original indifference curve through A and C. The substitution effect is illustrated by the movement along the original indifference curve as prices change but the level of utility holds constant, from A to C. As expected, the substitution effect leads to less consumed of the good that is relatively more expensive, as shown by the s-for-substitution arrow on the vertical axis, and more consumed of the good that is relatively less expensive, as shown by the s arrow on the horizontal axis.

A Step-by-Step Guide to Sketching Substitution and Income Effects *(Continued)*

Draw in the original indifference curve, tangent both to the original choice A and to a point C on the dashed line. Identify the substitution effect.

Identify new choice B on the new budget set, and draw the new indifference curve tangent to it. Think about whether B should be under A, or to the right or left of it, based on what the problem requires. The movement from C to B will be the income effect.

Step 5: With the substitution effect in place, now choose utility-maximizing point B on the new opportunity set. When you choose point B, think about whether you wish the substitution or the income effect to have a larger impact on the good on the horizontal axis. If you choose point B to be directly in a vertical line with point A (as is illustrated here), then the income effect will be exactly offsetting the substitution effect on the horizontal axis. If you insert point B so that it lies a little to the right of the original point A, then the substitution effect will exceed the income effect. If you insert point B so that it lies a little to the left of point A, then the income effect will exceed the substitution effect. The income effect is the movement from C to B, showing how choices shifted as a result of the decline in buying power and the movement between two levels of utility, with relative prices remaining the same. With normal goods, the negative income effect means less consumed of each good, as shown by the direction of the i-for-income-effect arrows on the vertical and horizontal axes.

In sketching substitution and income effect diagrams, you may wish to practice some of the following variations: (1) Price falls instead of rising; (2) The price change affects the good on either the vertical or the horizontal axis; (3) Sketch these diagrams so that the substitution effect exceeds the income effect; the income effect exceeds the substitution effect; and the two effects are equal.

One final note: The helpful dashed line can be drawn tangent to the new indifference curve, and parallel to the original budget line, rather than tangent to the original indifference curve and parallel to the new budget line. Some students find this approach more intuitively clear. But the answers you get about the direction and relative sizes of the substitution and income effects should be just the same.

Quentin also has an income effect motivation. The lower rate of return shifts the budget constraint to the left, which means that Quentin's utility or "buying power" is reduced. The income effect (assuming normal goods) encourages less of both present and future consumption. The impact of the income effect on reducing present and future consumption in this example is shown with i arrows on the horizontal and vertical axis of Exhibit 8-A6.

Taking both effects together, the substitution effect is encouraging Quentin toward more present and less future consumption because present consumption is relatively cheaper, while the income effect is encouraging him to less present and less future consumption because the lower interest rate is pushing him to a lower level of utility. For Quentin's personal preferences, the substitution effect is stronger so that overall, he reacts to the lower rate of return with more present consumption and less savings at choice B.

However, other people might have different preferences. They might react to a lower rate of return by choosing the same level of present consumption and savings at choice D, or by choosing less present consumption and more savings at a point like F. For these other sets of preferences, the income effect of a lower rate of return on present consumption would be relatively stronger, while the substitution effect would be relatively weaker.

Conclusion

Indifference curves provide an analytical tool for looking at all the choices that provide a single level of utility. They eliminate any need for placing numerical values on utility and help to illuminate the process of making utility-maximizing decisions. They also provide the basis for a more detailed investigation of the complementary motivations that arise in response to a change in a price, wage, or rate of return—namely, the substitution and income effects.

Key Concepts and Summary

1. An *indifference curve* is drawn on a budget constraint diagram that shows the tradeoffs between two goods. All points along a single indifference curve provide the same level of utility. Higher indifference curves represent higher levels of utility.

2. Indifference curves slope downward because, if utility is to remain the same at all points along the curve, a reduction in the quantity of the good on the vertical axis must be counterbalanced by an increase in the quantity of the good on the horizontal axis (or vice versa). Indifference curves are steeper on the far left and flatter on the far right, because of diminishing marginal utility.

3. The utility-maximizing choice along a budget constraint will be the point of tangency where the budget constraint touches an indifference curve at a single point.

4. A change in the price of any good has two effects: a *substitution effect* and an *income effect*. The substitution effect motivation encourages a utility-maximizer to buy less of what is relatively more expensive and more of what is relatively cheaper. The income effect motivation encourages a utility-maximizer to buy more of both goods if utility rises or less of both goods if utility falls (if they are both normal goods).

5. In a labor-leisure choice, every wage change has a substitution and an income effect. The substitution effect of a wage increase is to choose more income, since it is cheaper to earn, and less leisure, since its opportunity cost has increased. The income effect of a wage increase is to choose more of leisure and income, since they are both normal goods. The substitution and income effects of a wage decrease would reverse these directions.

6. In an intertemporal consumption choice, every interest rate change has a substitution and an income effect. The substitution effect of an interest rate increase is to choose more future consumption, since it is now cheaper to earn future consumption and less present consumption (more savings), since the opportunity cost of present consumption in terms of what is being given up in the future has increased. The income effect of an interest rate increase is to choose more of both present and future consumption, since they are both normal goods. The substitution and income effects of an interest rate decrease would reverse these directions.

Review Questions

1. What point is preferred along an indifference curve?
2. Why do indifference curves slope down?
3. Why are indifference curves steep on the left and flatter on the right?
4. How many indifference curves does a person have?
5. How can you tell which indifference curves represent higher or lower levels of utility?
6. What is a substitution effect?
7. What is an income effect?
8. Does the "income effect" involve a change in income? Explain.
9. Does a change in price have both an income effect and a substitution effect? Does a change in income have both an income effect and a substitution effect?
10. Would you expect in some cases to see only an income effect or only a substitution effect? Explain.
11. Which is larger, the income effect or the substitution effect?

Present Discounted Value

Calculating Present Discounted Value of a Stock

Payments from Firm	Present Value
15 in present	15
20 in one year	$20/(1 + .15)^1 = 17.4$
25 in two years	$25/(1 + .15)^2 = 18.9$
Total	**51.3**

The prices of stocks and bonds depend on future events. The price of a bond depends on the future payments that the bond is expected to make, including both payments of interest and the repayment of the face value of the bond. The price of a stock depends on the expected future profits earned by the firm. The concept of a present discounted value (PDV), which is defined as the amount you should be willing to pay in the present for a stream of expected future payments, can be used to calculate appropriate prices for stocks and bonds. To place a present discounted value on a future payment, think about what amount of money you would need to have in the present to equal a certain amount in the future. This calculation will require an interest rate. For example, if the interest rate is 10%, then a payment of $110 a year from now will have a present discounted value of $100—that is, you could take $100 in the present and have $110 in the future. This appendix first shows how to apply the idea of present discounted value to a stock and then to a bond.

Applying Present Discounted Value to a Stock

Consider the case of Babble, Inc., a company that offers speaking lessons. For the sake of simplicity, say that the founder of Babble is 63 years old and plans to retire in two years, at which point the company will be disbanded. The company is selling 200 shares of stock and profits are expected to be $15 million right away, in the present, $20 million one year from now, and $25 million two years from now. All profits will be paid out as dividends to shareholders as they occur. Given this information, what will an investor pay for a share of stock in this company?

A financial investor thinking about what future payments are worth in the present will need to choose an interest rate. This interest rate will reflect the rate of return on other available financial investment opportunities, which is the opportunity cost of investing financial capital, and also a risk premium

EXHIBIT 19–A1 Calculating Present Discounted Value of a Stock

Payments from Firm	Present Value
15 in present	15
20 in one year	$20/(1 + .15)^1 = 17.4$
25 in two years	$25/(1 + .15)^2 = 18.9$
Total	**51.3**

(that is, using a higher interest rate than the rates available elsewhere if this investment appears especially risky). In this example, say that the financial investor decides that appropriate interest rate to value these future payments is 15%.

Exhibit 19-A1 shows how to calculate the present discounted value of the future profits. For each time period when a benefit is going to be received, apply the formula:

$$\text{Present discounted value} = \frac{(\text{Future value received } t \text{ years in the future})}{(1 + \text{Interest rate})^{\text{number of years } t}}$$

Then add up all the present values for the different time periods to get a final answer. The present value calculations ask what the amount in the future is worth in the present, given the 15% interest rate. Notice that a different PDV calculation needs to be done separately for amounts received at different times. Then divide the PDV of total profits by the number of shares, 200 in this case, and the price per share should be 51.3/200 = .2565, or about 25 cents per share.

Of course, in the real world expected profits are a best guess, not a hard piece of data. Deciding which interest rate to apply for discounting to the present can be tricky. One needs to take into account both potential capital gains from the future sale of the stock and also dividends that might be paid. Differences of opinion on these issues are exactly why some financial investors want to buy a stock that other people want to sell: they are more optimistic about its future prospects. But conceptually, it all comes down to what you are willing to pay in the present for a stream of benefits to be received in the future.

Applying Present Discounted Value to a Bond

A similar calculation works in the case of bonds. The chapter explains that if the interest rate falls after a bond is issued, so that the investor has locked in a higher rate, then that bond will sell for more than its face value. Conversely, if the interest rate rises after a bond is issued, then the investor is locked into a lower rate, and the bond will sell for less than its face value. The present value calculation sharpens this intuition.

Think about a simple two-year bond. It was issued for $3,000, at an interest rate of 8%. Thus, after the first year the bond pays interest of $240 ($3,000 × 8%). At the end of the second year, the bond pays $240 in interest, plus repaying the $3,000 in principle. Calculate how much this bond is worth in the present if the discount rate is 8%. Then recalculate if interest rates rise and the applicable discount rate is 11%. To carry out these calculations, look at the stream of payments being received from the bond in the future and figure out what they are worth in present discounted value terms. The calculations applying the present value formula are shown in Exhibit 19-A2.

The first calculation shows that the present value of a $3,000 bond, issued at 8%, is just $3,000. After all, that's how much money the borrower is receiving. The calculation confirms that the present value is the same for the lender. The bond is moving money around in time, from those willing to save in the present to those who want to borrow in the present, but the present value of what is received by the borrower is identical to the present value of what will be repaid to the lender.

The second calculation shows what happens if the interest rate rises from 8% to 11%. The actual dollar payments in the first column, as determined by the 8% interest rate,

EXHIBIT 19–A2 Computing the Present Discounted Value of a Bond

For the 8% Interest Rate	
Stream of Payments	*Present Value*
$240 payment after one year	$240/(1 + .08)^1 = 222.2$
$3,240 payment after second year	$3,240/(1 + .08)^2 = 2,777.8$
Total	**$3,000**
For the 11% Interest Rate	
Stream of Payments	*Present Value*
$240 payment after one year	$240/(1 + .11)^1 = 216.2$
$3,240 payment after second year	$3,240/(1 + .11)^2 = 2,629.6$
Total	**$2,845.8**

don't change. However, the present value of those payments, now discounted at a higher interest rate, is lower. Even though the future dollar payments that the bond is receiving have not changed, a person who tries to sell the bond will find that the value of the investment has fallen.

Again, real-world calculations are often more complex, in part because not only the interest rate prevailing in the market but also the riskiness of whether the borrower will repay the loan will change. But in any case, the price of a bond is always the present value of a stream of future expected payments.

Other Applications

Present discounted value is a widely used analytical tool outside the world of finance. Every time a business thinks about making a physical capital investment, it must compare a set of present costs of making that investment to the present discounted value of future benefits. When government thinks about a proposal to, say, add safety features to a highway, it must compare costs incurred in the present to benefits received in the future. Some academic disputes over environmental policies, like how much to reduce carbon dioxide emissions because of the risk that they will lead to a warming of global temperatures several decades in the future, turn on how one compares present costs of pollution control with long-run future benefits. Someone who wins the lottery and is scheduled to receive a string of payments over 30 years might be interested in knowing what the present discounted value is of those payments. Whenever a string of costs and benefits stretches from the present into different times in the future, present discounted value becomes an indispensable tool of analysis.

Glossary

A

absolute advantage: When one nation can produce a product at lower cost relative to another nation.

accounting profit: Total revenues minus the firm's costs, without taking opportunity cost into account.

acquisition: When one firm purchases another; for practical purposes, often combined with mergers.

adverse selection: The problem that arises when one party knows more about the quality of the good than the other, and as a result, the party with less knowledge must worry about ending up at a disadvantage.

affirmative action: Active efforts to improve the job opportunities or outcomes of minority groups or women.

allocative efficiency: When the mix of goods being produced represents the allocation that society most desires.

anti-dumping laws: Laws that block imports sold below the cost of production and impose tariffs that would increase the price of these imports to reflect their cost of production.

antitrust laws: Laws that give government the power to block certain mergers, and even in some cases, to break up large firms into smaller ones.

applied research: Research focused on a particular product that promises an economic payoff in the short or medium term.

average cost: Total cost divided by the quantity of output.

average variable cost: Variable cost divided by the quantity of output.

B

backward-bending supply curve for labor: The situation when high-wage people can earn so much that they respond to a still-higher wage by working fewer hours.

barriers to entry: The legal, technological, or market forces that may discourage or prevent potential competitors from entering a market.

basic research: Research on fundamental scientific breakthroughs that may offer commercial applications only in the distant future.

biodiversity: The full spectrum of animal and plant genetic material.

black market: An illegal market that breaks government rules on prices or sales.

bond: A financial contract through which a borrower like a corporation, a city or state, or the federal government agrees to repay the amount that was borrowed and also a rate of interest over a period of time in the future.

bond yield: The rate of return that a bond is expected to pay at the time of purchase.

bondholders: Those who own bonds and receive the interest payments.

budget constraint: A diagram that shows the possible choices.

bundling: A situation where a customer is allowed to buy one product only if the customer also buys another product; also called "tie-in sales."

C

capital gain: A financial gain from buying an asset, like a share of stock or a house, and later selling it at a higher price.

cartel: A group of firms that collude to produce the monopoly output and sell at the monopoly price.

certificates of deposit (CD): A mechanism for a saver to deposit funds at a bank and promise to leave them at the bank for a time, in exchange for a higher rate of interest.

ceteris paribus: Other things being equal.

checking account: A bank account that typically pays little or no interest, but that gives easy access to your money, either by writing a check or by using a debit card.

circular flow diagram: A diagram that views the economy as consisting of households and firms interacting in a goods and services market, a labor market, and a financial capital market.

coinsurance: When an insurance policyholder pays a percentage of a loss, and the insurance company pays the remaining cost.

collateral: Something valuable—often property or equipment—that a lender would have a right to seize and sell if the loan is not repaid.

collective bargaining: Negotiations between unions and a firm or firms.

collusion: When firms act together to reduce output and keep prices high.

command economy: An economy in which the government either makes or strongly influences most economic decisions.

command-and-control regulation: Laws that specify allowable quantities of pollution and may also detail which pollution-control technologies must be used.

comparative advantage: The goods in which a nation has its greatest productivity advantage or its smallest productivity disadvantage; also, the goods that a nation can produce at a lower cost when measured in terms of opportunity cost.

complements: Goods that are often used together, so that a rise in the price of one good tends to decrease the quantity consumed of the other good, and vice versa.

compound interest: When interest payments in earlier periods are reinvested, so that in later time periods, the interest rate is paid on the total amount accumulated during previous years.

constant returns to scale: When expanding all inputs does not change the average cost of production.

consumer surplus: The benefit consumers receive from buying a good or service, measured by what the individuals would have been willing to pay minus the amount that they actually paid.

copayment: When an insurance policyholder must pay a small amount for each service, before insurance covers the rest.

copyright: A form of legal protection to prevent copying for commercial purposes original works of authorship, including books and music.

corporate bonds: Bonds issued by firms that wish to borrow.

cosigner: On a loan, another person or firm that legally pledges to repay some or all of the money if the original borrower does not do so.

cost-plus regulation: When regulators permit a regulated firm to cover its costs and to make a normal level of profit.

cross-price elasticity of demand: The percentage change in the quantity of good A that is demanded as a result of a percentage change in good B.

D

deadweight loss: The loss in social surplus that occurs when a market produces an inefficient quantity.

debit card: A card that lets you make purchases, where the cost is immediately deducted from your checking account.

decreasing returns to scale: A situation in which as the quantity of output rises, the average cost of production rises.

deductible: An amount that the insurance policyholders must pay out of their own pocket before the insurance coverage pays anything.

demand: A relationship between price and the quantity demanded of a certain good or service.

demand curve: A line that shows the relationship between price and quantity demanded of a certain good or service on a graph, with quantity on the horizontal axis and the price on the vertical axis.

demand schedule: A table that shows a range of prices for a certain good or service and the quantity demanded at each price.

deregulation: Removing government controls over setting prices and quantities in certain industries.

differentiated products: Products that are distinctive in a particular way.

diminishing marginal returns: When the marginal gain in output diminishes as each additional unit of input is added.

diminishing marginal utility: The common pattern that each marginal unit of a good consumed provides less of an addition to utility than the previous unit.

diseconomies of scale: Another term for decreasing returns to scale.

diversification: Investing in a wide range of companies, to reduce the level of risk.

dividend: A direct payment from a firm to its shareholders.

division of labor: Dividing the work required to produce a good or service into tasks performed by different workers.

dumping: Selling internationally traded goods below their cost of production.

duopoly: An oligopoly with only two firms.

E

economic profit: Total revenues minus all of the firm's costs, including opportunity costs.

economics: The study of the production, distribution, and consumption of goods and services.

economies of scale: When the average cost of producing each individual unit declines as total output increases.

economy: The social arrangements that determine what is produced, how it is produced, and for whom it is produced.

efficiency: When it is impossible to get more of something without experiencing a trade-off of less of something else.

elastic: The elasticity calculated from the appropriate formula has an absolute value greater than 1.

elasticity: How much a percentage change in quantity demanded or quantity supplied is affected by a percentage change in price.

elasticity of demand: The percentage change in quantity demanded divided by the percentage change in price.

elasticity of labor supply: The percentage change in hours worked divided by the percentage change in wages.

elasticity of savings: The percentage change in the quantity of savings divided by the percentage change in interest rates.

elasticity of supply: The percentage change in quantity supplied divided by the percentage change in price.

entry: The long-run process of firms beginning and expanding production when they see opportunity for profits.

equilibrium: The combination of price and quantity where there is no economic pressure from surpluses or shortages that would cause price or quantity to shift.

equilibrium price: The price where quantity demanded is equal to quantity supplied.

equilibrium quantity: The quantity at which quantity demanded and quantity supplied are equal at a certain price.

equity: The monetary value a homeowner would have after selling the house and repaying any outstanding bank loans used to buy the house.

estate tax: A tax imposed on the value of an inheritance.

excess demand: At the existing price, the quantity demanded exceeds the quantity supplied, also called "shortage."

excess supply: When at the existing price, quantity supplied exceeds the quantity demanded; also called a "surplus."

exclusive dealing: An agreement that a dealer will sell only products from one manufacturer.

exit: The long-run process of firms reducing production and shutting down because they expect losses.

exports: Goods and services that are produced domestically and sold in another country.

externality: When a market exchange affects a third party who is outside or "external" to the exchange; sometimes called a "spillover."

F

fee-for-service: When medical care providers are paid according to the services they provide.

final goods and services: Output used directly for consumption, investment, government, and trade purposes; contrast with "intermediate goods."

financial capital market: The market in which those who save money provide financial capital and receive a rate of return from those who wish to raise money and pay a rate of return.

financial intermediary: An institution that operates between a saver with financial assets to invest and an entity who will receive those assets and pay a rate of return.

fiscal policy: Economic policies that involve government spending and taxation.

fixed costs: Expenditures that must be made before production starts and that do not change regardless of the level of production.

four-firm concentration ratio: What percentage share of the total sales in the industry is accounted for by the largest four firms.

free rider: Those who want others to pay for the public good and then plan to use the good themselves; if many people act as free riders, the public good may never be provided.

fundamentals trading: Buying or selling stock based on estimates of the future expected profits.

G

game theory: A branch of mathematics often used by economists that analyzes situations in which players must make decisions and then receive payoffs.

Giffen good: The theoretical but unrealistic possibility that a higher price for a good could lead to a higher quantity demanded (or a lower price leads to a lesser quantity demanded).

globalization: The trend in which buying and selling in markets have increasingly crossed national borders.

goods and services market: A market in which firms are sellers of what they produce and households are buyers.

H

health maintenance organization (HMO): An organization that provides health care and is paid a fixed amount per person enrolled in the plan—regardless of how many services are provided.

Herfindahl-Hirschman Index (HHI): Take the market share of each firm in the industry, square each one, and add them.

I

imperfect competition: Competition that does not fit the definition of perfect competition either because it involves a smaller number of firms or only one firm, or products that aren't identical.

imperfect information: A situation where the buyer or the seller, or both, are uncertain about the qualities of what is being bought and sold.

import quotas: Numerical limitations on the quantity of products that can be imported.

imports: Goods and services produced abroad and then sold domestically.

income effect: A change in price affects the buying power of income, with a higher price meaning that the buying power of income has been reduced, so that there is usually (with normal goods) an incentive to buy less of both goods, and a lower price meaning that the buying power of income has been increased, so that there is usually an incentive to buy more of both goods; always happens simultaneously with a substitution effect.

increasing returns to scale: When a larger-scale firm can produce at a lower cost than a smaller-scale firm; also called economies of scale.

index fund: A mutual fund that seeks only to mimic the overall performance of the market.

inelastic: The elasticity calculated from the appropriate formula has an absolute value less than 1.

inequality: When one group receives a higher share of total income or wealth than others.

infant industry argument: An argument to block imports for a short time, to give the infant industry time to mature, before eventually it starts competing on equal terms in the global economy.

inferior goods: Goods where the quantity demanded falls as income rises.

infinite elasticity: The extremely elastic situation where quantity changes by an infinite amount in response to even a tiny change in price.

inflation: A general and ongoing rise in the level of prices in an economy.

initial public offering (IPO): When a firm first sells shares of stock to outside investors.

insurance: A group of people who face a risk of a certain bad experience all make regular payments, and those members of the group who actually suffer a bad experience receive payments.

intellectual property: The body of law including patents, trademarks, copyrights, and trade secret law that protects the right of inventors to produce and sell their inventions.

interest rate: A payment calculated as a percentage of the original amount saved or borrowed, and paid by the borrower to the saver.

intra-industry trade: International trade of goods within the same industry.

J

junk bonds: Bonds that offer relatively high interest rates to compensate for their relatively high chance of default.

K

kinked demand curve: A perceived demand curve that arises when competing oligopoly firms commit to match price cuts, but not price increases.

L

labor market: The market in which households sell their labor as workers to business firms or other employers.

labor union: An organization of workers that negotiates with employers as a group over wages and working conditions.

law of demand: The common relationship that a higher price leads to a lower quantity demanded of a certain good or service.

law of diminishing marginal utility: As a person receives more of a good, the marginal utility from each additional unit of the good is smaller than from the previous unit.

law of diminishing returns: As additional increments of resources are added to producing a good or service, the marginal benefit from those additional increments will decline.

law of supply: The common relationship that a higher price is associated with a greater quantity supplied.

life-cycle theory of savings: The common pattern that many people save little or borrow heavily early in life, save more in the middle of life, and then draw upon their accumulated savings later in life.

liquidity: How easy it is to sell an asset when desired.

logrolling: When a group of legislators all agree to vote for a package of otherwise unrelated laws that they individually favor.

Lorenz curve: A graph that shows the share of population on the horizontal axis and the cumulative percentage of total income received on the vertical axis.

M

macroeconomics: The branch of economics that focuses on the economy as a whole, including issues like growth, unemployment, inflation, and the balance of trade.

macroprudential policy: The bank and financial regulatory policies that are not aimed at a specific company, but instead at reducing the risk of financial instability for the macroeconomy as a whole.

marginal analysis: Comparing the benefits and costs of choosing a little more or a little less of a good.

marginal cost: The additional cost of producing one more unit.

marginal physical product: The quantity of goods produced by an additional input (like an additional worker).

marginal revenue: The additional revenue gained from selling one more unit.

marginal revenue product (MRP): Reveals how much revenue a firm could receive from hiring an additional worker and selling the output of that worker.

marginal utility: The additional utility provided by one additional unit of consumption.

market: An institution that brings together buyers and sellers of goods or services.

market failure: A situation in which the market on its own fails to allocate resources efficiently in a way that balances social costs and benefits; externalities are one example of a market failure.

market share: The percentage share of total sales in the market.

marketable permit: A permit that allows a firm to emit a certain amount of pollution, where firms with more permits than pollution can sell the remaining permits to other firms.

market-oriented economy: An economy in which most economic decisions are made by buyers and sellers, who may be individuals or firms.

merger: When two formerly separate firms combine to become a single firm; for practical purposes, often combined with acquisitions.

microeconomics: The branch of economics that focuses on actions of particular actors within the economy, like households, workers, and business firms.

minimum resale price maintenance agreement: An agreement that requires a dealer who buys from a manufacturer to sell for at least a certain minimum price.

minimum wage: A price floor that makes it illegal for an employer to pay employees less than a certain hourly rate.

model: A simplified representation of an object or situation that includes enough of the key features to be useful.

momentum trading: Buying or selling stock by following the current trend; that is, buying when the price seems to be rising, or selling stock because the price seems to be falling.

monetary policy: Policy that involves altering the quantity of money and thus affecting the level of interest rates and the extent of borrowing.

money-back guarantee: A promise that the buyer's money will be refunded under certain conditions, like if the product doesn't work or sometimes even if the buyer decides to return the product.

monopolistic competition: Many firms competing to sell similar but differentiated products.

monopoly: A firm that faces no competitors.

moral hazard: When people have insurance against a certain event, they are less likely to guard against that event occurring.

municipal bonds: Bonds issued by cities that wish to borrow.

mutual funds: A fund that buys a range of stocks or bonds from different companies, thus allowing an investor an easy way to diversify.

N

nationalization: When government takes over ownership of firms.

natural monopoly: When the quantity demanded in the market is less than the quantity at the bottom of the long-run average cost curve.

near-poor: Those who have incomes just above the poverty line.

negative externality: A situation where a third party, outside the transaction, suffers from a market transaction by others.

nonexcludable: When it is costly or impossible to exclude someone from using the good, and thus hard to charge for it.

nonrivalrous: A good where, when one person uses the good, others can also use it.

nontariff barriers: All the other ways a nation can draw up rules, regulations, inspections, and paperwork to make it more costly or difficult to import products.

normal goods: Goods where the quantity demanded rises when income rises.

normative statements: Statements that describe how the world should be.

O

occupational licenses: Licenses issued by government agencies that mean that a worker has completed a certain type of education or passed a certain test.

oligopoly: When a few firms have all or nearly all of the sales in an industry.

opportunity cost: Whatever must be given up to obtain something that is desired.

opportunity set: Another name for the budget constraint.

P

patent: A government rule that gives the inventor the exclusive legal right to make, use, or sell the invention for a limited time.

perfect competition: Each firm faces many competitors that sell identical products.

physical capital: The plant and equipment used by firms in production.

pollution charge: A tax imposed on the quantity of pollution that a firm emits; also called a "pollution tax."

pork-barrel spending: Spending that benefits mainly a single political district.

positive externality: A situation where a third party, outside the transaction, benefits from a market transaction by others.

positive statements: Statements that describe the world as it is.

poverty: Falling below a certain level of income needed for a basic standard of living.

poverty line: The specific amount of income needed for a basic standard of living.

poverty trap: When antipoverty programs are set up so that government benefits decline substantially as people earn more income—and as a result, working provides little financial gain.

predatory pricing: When an existing firm uses sharp but temporary price cuts to discourage new competition.

premiums: Payments made to an insurance company.

price cap regulation: When the regulator sets a price that a firm cannot exceed over the next few years.

price ceiling: A law that prevents a price from rising above a certain level.

price controls: Government laws to regulate prices.

price elasticity of demand: Same as elasticity of demand.

price elasticity of supply: Same as elasticity of supply.

price floor: A law that prevents a price from falling below a certain level.

price takers: A firm in a perfectly competitive market that must take the prevailing market price as given.

principal: The amount of an original financial investment, before any rate of return is paid.

prisoner's dilemma: A game in which if both players pursue their own self-interest, they both end up worse off than if they cooperate.

private company: A firm owned by the people who run it on a day-to-day basis.

privatization: When a government-owned firm becomes privately owned.

producer surplus: The benefit producers receive from selling a good or service, measured by the price the producer actually received minus the price the producer would have been willing to accept.

production function: The process of a firm turning economic inputs like labor, machinery, and raw materials into outputs like goods and services used by consumers.

production possibilities frontier: A diagram that shows the combinations of output that are possible for an economy to produce.

production technologies: Alternative methods of combining inputs to produce output.

productive efficiency: When it is impossible to produce more of one good without decreasing the quantity produced of another good.

productivity: What is produced per worker, or per hour worked.

property rights: The legal rights of ownership on which others are not allowed to infringe without paying compensation.

protectionism: Government policies to reduce or block imports.

public company: A firm that has sold stock to the public, which in turn can be bought and sold by investors.

public good: A good that is nonexcludable and nonrivalrous, and thus is difficult for market producers to sell to individual consumers.

Q

quantitative easing: A central bank policy of expanding the supply of lending and credit by direct large-scale purchase of government and private financial assets.

quantity demanded: The total number of units of a good or service purchased at a certain price.

quantity supplied: The total number of units of a good or service sold at a certain price.

quintiles: Dividing a group into fifths, a method often used to look at distribution of income.

R

race to the bottom: When production locates in countries with the lowest environmental (or other) standards, putting pressure on all countries to reduce their environmental standards.

rate of return: The payment in addition to the original investment from those who have received financial capital to those who provided it.

rational ignorance: The theory that rational people won't bother incurring the costs of becoming informed and voting because they know that their vote won't be decisive in the election.

redistribution: Taking income from those with higher incomes and providing income to those with lower incomes.

regulatory capture: When the firms supposedly being regulated end up playing a large role in setting the regulations that they will follow.

restrictive practices: Practices that reduce competition but that do not involve outright agreements between firms to raise price.

risk group: A group that shares roughly the same risks of an adverse event occurring.

risk premium: A payment to make up for the risk of not being repaid in full.

S

safety net: Nickname for the group of government programs that provide assistance to the poor and the near-poor.

savings account: A bank account that pays an interest rate, but withdrawing the money typically requires you to make a trip to the bank or an automatic teller machine.

service contract: The buyer pays an extra amount and the seller agrees to fix anything that goes wrong for a set time period.

shareholders: Those who own at least some stock in a firm.

shares: The stock of a firm is divided into individual shares.

shift in demand: When a change in some economic factor related to demand causes a different quantity to be demanded at every price.

shift in supply: When a change in some economic factor related to supply causes a different quantity to be supplied at every price.

shortage: At the existing price, the quantity demanded exceeds the quantity supplied; also called "excess demand."

shutdown point: When the revenue a firm receives does not cover its average variable costs, the firm should shut down immediately; the point where the marginal cost curve crosses the average variable cost curve.

social costs: Costs that include both the private costs incurred by firms and also costs incurred by third parties outside the production process, like costs of pollution.

social surplus: The sum of consumer surplus and producer surplus.

special-interest groups: Groups that are numerically small but well organized and thus exert a disproportionate effect on political outcomes.

specialization: When workers or firms focus on particular tasks in the overall production process for which they are well-suited.

spillover: When a market exchange affects a third party who is outside or "external" to the exchange; more formally called an externality.

splitting up the value chain: When many of the different stages of producing a good happen in different geographic locations.

stock: A claim on partial ownership of a firm.

substitutes: Goods that can replace each other to some extent, so that a rise in the price of one good leads to a greater quantity consumed of another good, and vice versa.

substitution effect: When a price changes, consumers have an incentive to consume less of the good with a relatively higher price and more of the good with a relatively lower price; always happens simultaneously with an income effect.

sunk cost: Costs that were incurred in the past and cannot be recovered, and thus should not affect current decisions.

supply: A relationship between price and the quantity supplied of a certain good or service.

supply curve: A line that shows the relationship between price and quantity supplied on a graph, with quantity supplied on the horizontal axis and price on the vertical axis.

supply schedule: A table that shows a range of prices for a good or service and the quantity supplied at each price.

surplus: When at the existing price, quantity supplied exceeds the quantity demanded; also called "excess supply."

T

tariffs: Taxes imposed on imported products.

technology: All the ways in which a certain level of capital investment can produce a greater quantity or higher quality, as well as different and altogether new products.

tie-in sales: A situation where a customer is allowed to buy one product only if the customer also buys another product; also called "bundling."

time value of money: The cost of having to wait for repayment.

total cost: All the costs that a firm must incur in the process of production.

total revenue: The quantity of goods and services sold by the firm multiplied by the selling price of these goods and services.

trade secrets: Methods of production kept secret by the producing firm.

trademark: A word, name, symbol, or device that indicates the source of the goods and can only be used by the firm that registered that trademark.

Treasury bonds: Bonds issued by the federal government through the U.S. Department of the Treasury.

U

usury laws: Laws that impose an upper limit on the interest rate that lenders can charge.

utility: The level of satisfaction or pleasure that people receive from their choices.

V

variable costs: Costs of production that increase with the quantity produced.

venture capital: Financial investments in new companies that are still relatively small in size but that have potential to grow substantially.

voting cycle: When a majority prefers A over B, B over C, and C over A.

W

warranty: A promise to fix or replace the good, at least for a certain period of time.

Z

zero elasticity: The highly inelastic case in which a percentage change in price, no matter how large, results in zero change in the quantity demanded or supplied.

Index

Note: Page numbers in *italics* refer to exhibits.